Contents

A NORTON CRITICAL EDITION

NEWTON

TEXTS

BACKGROUNDS

COMMENTARIES

Selected and Edited by

I. BERNARD COHEN
HARVARD UNIVERSITY

and

RICHARD S. WESTFALL
INDIANA UNIVERSITY

W • W • NORTON & COMPANY • *New York • London*

Printed in the United States of America

First Edition

The text of this book is composed in Electra
with the display set in Bernhard Modern
Composition and Manufacturing by Maple-Vail
Book design by A. Krass

Library of Congress Cataloging-in-Publication Data
Newton, Isaac, Sir, 1642–1727.
Newton : texts, backgrounds, commentaries / selected and edited by
I. Bernard Cohen and Richard S. Westfall.
p. cm.—(A Norton critical edition.)
1. Newton, Isaac, Sir, 1642–1727. 2. Science. I. Cohen,
I. Bernard, 1914– . II. Westfall, Richard S. III. Title.
QC16.N7N475 1995
500—dc20 92-21165

ISBN 0-393-95902-3

W. W. Norton & Company, Inc., 500 Fifth Avenue, New York, N.Y. 10110
W. W. Norton & Company Ltd., 10 Coptic Street, London WC1A 1PU

2 3 4 5 6 7 8 9 0

The Editors

I. BERNARD COHEN is Victor S. Thomas Professor (Emeritus) of the History of Science at Harvard University, where he taught from 1942 to 1984. He is the first American to receive the degree of Ph.D. in the History of Science. He is the author of many books, including *Science and the Founding Fathers: Science in the Political Thought of Thomas Jefferson, Benjamin Franklin, John Adams, and James Madison; The Science of Benjamin Franklin; Revolution in Science; The Newtonian Revolution; The Birth of a New Physics;* and, with Anne Whitman, *Isaac Newton's Principia: A New Translation of Newton's Mathematical Principles of Natural Philosophy.* He has edited several series of works including *Harvard Monographs in the History of Science, Three Centuries of Science in America,* and the ongoing *Studies & Texts in the History of Computing.* He is a Fellow of the American Academy of Arts and Sciences, the American Association for the Advancement of Science, the Royal Astronomical Society, the British Academy, and the Accademia Nazionale dei Lincei.

RICHARD S. WESTFALL is Distinguished Professor Emeritus of History and Philosophy of Science at Indiana University, where he taught from 1963 to 1989. His books include *Science and Religion in Seventeenth-Century England; The Construction of Modern Science; Force in Newton's Physics; Never at Rest: A Biography of Isaac Newton; Essays on the Trial of Galileo;* and *The Life of Isaac Newton.* He is a Fellow of the American Academy of Arts and Sciences and of the Royal Society of Literature.

Norton Critical Editions in the History of Ideas

AQUINAS *St. Thomas Aquinas on Politics and Ethics* translated and edited by Paul E. Sigmund
DARWIN *Darwin* selected and edited by Philip Appleman *Second Edition*
ERASMUS *The Praise of Folly and Other Writings* translated and edited by Robert M. Adams
HERODOTUS *The Histories* edited by Walter Blanco and Jennifer Tolbert Roberts; translated by Walter Blanco
MACHIAVELLI *The Prince* translated and edited by Robert M. Adams *Second Edition*
MALTHUS *An Essay on the Principle of Population* edited by Philip Appleman
MARX *The Communist Manifesto* edited by Frederic L. Bender
MILL *On Liberty* edited by David Spitz
MORE *Utopia* translated and edited by Robert M. Adams *Second Edition*
NEWMAN *Apologia pro Vita Sua* edited by David J. DeLaura *Second Edition*
NEWTON *Newton* selected and edited by I. Bernard Cohen and Richard S. Westfall
ROUSSEAU *Rousseau's Political Writings* edited by Alan Ritter and translated by Julia Conaway Bondanella
ST. PAUL *The Writings of St. Paul* edited by Wayne A. Meeks
THOREAU *Walden and Resistance to Civil Government* edited by William Rossi *Second Edition*
WATSON *The Double Helix: A Personal Account of the Discovery of the Structure of DNA* edited by Gunther S. Stent
WOLLSTONECRAFT *A Vindication of the Rights of Woman* edited by Carol H. Poston *Second Edition*

Preface

The purpose of this volume is to give the reader a collection of the writings of Isaac Newton, together with commentaries that extend over four centuries and display the continuing importance of his thought. In conformity with the goals of the series, this edition attempts to show why Newton has been almost universally hailed as one of the greatest scientists who ever lived, while at the same time illustrating why his achievements came to symbolize the rationality of the Enlightenment at its highest form, justifying the subsidiary title of the Age of Reason.

No attempt has been made here to include selections that would illustrate every aspect of Newton's life and career. For example, we have not included documents that relate to his activities as member of Parliament for Cambridge University, nor any documents relating to his activities as Warden and Master of the Mint, nor of his presidency of the Royal Society. Because the aim has been to make available the main lines of his thought, we have also omitted Newton's presentations of the scientific instruments he invented, notably, the reflecting telescope and the reflecting octant for use of navigators at sea. For some specialized subjects, especially those that we have not presented, a Selected Bibliography has been appended. Although many of the major Newton scholars are represented here, no attempt has been made to include writings from each and every contributor to the Newtonian corpus of scholarship—an almost impossible task considering the enormous magnitude of today's "Newton industry."

The seventeenth- and eighteenth-century texts presented here are given in what has been sometimes described as a "modern" but definitely not "modernized" form, that is, we have in no case altered the word order, sentence structure, or spelling of Newton's original documents, nor those of any contemporaries. We have, however, sometimes altered the punctuation for ease of readership, and we have generally spelled out the abbreviations, as eighteenth-century printers did: Where Newton would write a *thorn* (looking like a capital Y), we have replaced this with *th*, and we have similarly dropped all superscript letters. Thus, readers need not be puzzled by trying to interpret abbreviations with the superscript letters, nor need they be puzzled by such expressions (as are found in scholarly transcriptions of Newtonian documents) as *yt* ("that"), *yn* ("than" or "then"), or such almost unintelligible monstrosities as *matys* ("majesty's"). We have also spelled out the ampersand. The purpose of our edition is to make texts available and readable, not to pose puzzles for the reader.

The editors hope that this collection will prove of interest to scholars and students alike, as well as general readers interested in the history of thought, science and its history, philosophy, intellectual history, theology, and other disciplines.

I. Bernard Cohen
Richard S. Westfall

General Introduction

Scientists, philosophers, and historians agree that Newton's scientific achievements represent the peak of the Scientific Revolution that began in the late sixteenth century, the series of rapid changes in the knowledge of nature and the mode of studying natural phenomena that produced our modern science. Often, Newton's collective achievements are known as the Newtonian Revolution.

We get some measure of Isaac Newton's greatness when we learn that he was the author of not just one, but several revolutions. One was in mathematics, the others in the physical sciences. In fact, Newton made so many different kinds of fundamental contributions to science that even if we were to ignore most of them, we would still have to rank him as one of the ten or twelve most important scientists who ever lived.

In mathematics, Newton (along with Gottfried Wilhelm Leibniz) invented the calculus—the differential as well as the integral calculus—the language of the exact sciences and now increasingly of the social sciences. He pioneered the use of infinite series, and he introduced methods of calculation and approximation still in use today. This was his first revolution.

In optics, Newton established the heterogeneity of sunlight and reformulated understanding of the nature of color. His work revealed why the sky seems blue, and it led to a mathematical exposition of the formation of rainbows. His analysis of light and color has formed the basis of our continuing understanding of color vision.

One by-product of Newton's discoveries concerning light and color was his design of a new kind of telescope, a reflector, that eliminated chromatic aberration by forming the image by way of a mirror rather than an objective lens, a technique used in almost all large telescopes today. Newton's *Opticks*, first published in 1704, concluded with a general research program in experimental physical science that formed an agenda for research in the eighteenth century. The work in optics constitutes a second Newtonian Revolution.

A third revolution was Newton's codification of the science of mechanics, a subject that he dignified with the name *rational mechanics*. Anyone who has studied physics knows Newton's three laws of motion, which remain fundamental to that subject. It was Newton who defined the modern concept of mass, essential for the development of the study of matter. He recognized that there are two different measures of mass—one of which today we call gravitational and the other inertial. He appreciated that in classical mechanics only an experiment can prove their equivalence, and he designed and carried out such an experiment. This equivalence is a basic feature of Einsteinian relativity theory, but the recognition of the problem and of the need for a proof must rank as one of Newton's primary discoveries. The establishment of the science of rational mechanics on mathematical principles forms the core of Newton's third and possibly greatest revolution.

In Newton's day, however, and for at least a century or more afterward, when reference was made to the Newtonian Revolution, people had in mind a fourth revolution, symbolized by Newton's discovery of the principle of universal gravitation. Newton not only discovered the principle, but he also found the quantitative law of gravity. He used the law to elaborate the Newtonian "system of the world," to explain the phenomena of heaven and earth in a single mathematical system. He thus fulfilled the dream of Galileo Galilei, Johannes Kepler, and René Descartes.

Newton's gravitational cosmology accounted for the motions of planets, satellites, and comets—the constituent bodies of the universe in which we live—and also the motion of bodies on earth. He was able to explain such puzzling phenomena as Galileo's discovery that freely falling bodies on earth, whatever their weight, have the same acceleration or motion of fall. Newton's cosmology implied that comets are a kind of planet and that therefore most of them will move in elliptical orbits, returning to our part of the solar system from distant space at regular intervals. Newton also was able to explain how the phenomena of tides in the ocean are caused by the gravitational attraction of bodies of water by the sun and moon. Generally speaking, by the phrase "Newtonian Revolution," historians mean the codification and elaboration of rational mechanics and the development of the system of the world based on gravitational celestial mechanics.

Today's reader might find this partial catalogue to be impressive because of the differences among Newton's several areas of activity—pure mathematics, practical computation, experimental physics, optics, rational mechanics, astronomy. The student of Newton's life, however, might be even more impressed by the fact that all of this achievement in science and mathematics was the fruit of only a part of his creative activity. By profession he was a university teacher; later he served as a member of Parliament. During his mature years he was a public servant, directing the Mint during the recoinage in England in the last years of the seventeenth century and during the opening decades of the eighteenth.

Even during Newton's early creative years in science, while he was a university professor, his main concerns were not exclusively science as we would understand that term today, that is, physics or astronomy or mathematics. Rather, his intellectual activities embraced the interpretation of Scripture, biblical chronology, theology and prophecy, and alchemy. We stand in awe before his mighty scientific achievement, but all the more so when we recognize that it was the product of only a part of his creative energy. Even a modest portion of these achievements would have sufficed to earn him a place among the scientific immortals.

Isaac Newton was born on Christmas Day, 1642, in Woolsthorpe, England, the posthumous child of a father nearly three months dead. Descended from a family of yeomen, Newton seems to have been the first person in the line who could write his own name. His mother remarried when he was three, leaving him to be reared by his aged maternal grandparents. Thus deprived of any contact with his father and of a mother's loving care, Newton grew up an introvert. He never married and had few intimate friends. Suspicious of others, he was reluctant to give forth his discoveries. It has been said that every discovery of Newton had two aspects: Newton had to make the discovery and then others had to find out that he had done so. His life was punctuated by violent intellectual quarrels—with Robert Hooke, with John Flamsteed, and above all with Leibniz.

During most of his creative life, Newton was Lucasian Professor of Mathematics at Cambridge University, where he was a Fellow of Trinity College, which he had attended as an undergraduate. During these intense years, he produced the calculus and his other innovations in mathematics. These were also the years in which he developed his analysis of light and color and invented the reflecting telescope. It was the telescope that first brought him to the attention of the Royal Society, which promptly elected him a Fellow.

The crowning achievement of the years of Newton's professorship was his codification of the principles of rational mechanics and their elaboration in his classic *Mathematical Principles of Natural Philosophy (Philosophiae Naturalis Principia Mathematica;* often referred to as the *Principia)*, first published in Latin in 1687 and reissued in revised editions in 1713 and 1726. It was in the third "book" of this treatise that Newton set forth the principle and law of universal gravitation and elaborated his "system of the world."

In 1696, just nine years after publishing his *Principia*, Newton left university cloisters to become Warden and later Master of the Mint in London. He spent his remaining years supervising the coinage of English money and (curious to contemplate) the capture, interrogation, and prosecution of counterfeiters. During these years, as president of the Royal Society, he ruled British science with an iron hand. He died on March 20, 1727, at the age of 84 and was buried in Westminster Abbey.

In the eighteenth century and ever afterward, Newton has been esteemed not only for his technical achievements, but also as a formulator of the proper method of scientific investigation. Newton himself assumed this role by devoting the final "queries" of the *Opticks* to questions of methodology, the way to make experiments and to interpret experimental evidence, and by formulating a series of *regulae* ("rules") for proceeding in *natural philosophy*, or physical science. Furthermore, his own achievements in science stood as proofs of the validity of his method and rapidly became the paradigm of scientific investigation. Newton's great reputation—among scientists, philosophers, economists, political theorists, social thinkers, and even poets—derived from his *Opticks*, written in a simple and effective English style and dealing with a subject that captures the imagination. His *Principia*, on the other hand, was a difficult book, even for those initiated in the methods of mathematics. This book required of the reader a skill in such topics as conic sections and other technical aspects of mathematics and demanded an understanding of Newton's own new method of limits and the principles of *fluxions* (the name he gave to the calculus), with the result that the readership was necessarily small. Even the most accessible part of the *Principia*, the elaboration of the "system of the world," was purposely written by Newton in a difficult manner to prevent all but the hardiest readers from going through it.

In spite of the general inaccessibility of the *Principia*, Newtonian natural philosophy gained widespread currency because of the efforts of a dedicated group of interpreters who wrote about Newton's achievement in terms that the average well-educated person could understand. This group included Henry Pemberton, a medical doctor skilled in mathematics who had edited the third edition of the *Principia* under the author's direction, Colin Maclaurin, a mathematician whose fame today rests largely on the infinite series that bears his name, and Voltaire, who learned his Newtonian physics from the Marquise du Chastellet, the translator of the *Principia* into French, the best vernacular version of Newton's masterpiece for two centuries. The significance of Newton's achievement thus became generally recognized, even among people for whom the densely packed mathematical pages of the *Principia* remained forever a closed book.

In introducing Newton's *Opticks* in a modern reprint, Albert Einstein wrote of "fortunate Newton," living in the "happy childhood of science!" Einstein declared that to Newton, "nature . . . was an open book, whose letters he could read without effort." Above all, he saw Newton as "strong, certain, and alone," a scientist whose "joy in creation" and "minute precision" are evident in every word and in every figure. The confluence of Newton's creative genius and a state of science where, as Newton himself wrote, "great oceans of truth" lay undiscovered before him has been the envy of many of Newton's scientific successors. In different versions, both Joseph-Louis Lagrange and Pierre-Simon, Marquis de Laplace regretted that there was only one fundamental law of the universe, the law of universal gravitation, and that Newton had lived before them, foreclosing them from the glory of its discovery. Newton's position as the primary discoverer, the scientist who brought to a climax the researches initiated by his illustrious predecessors (scientists such as Nicolaus Copernicus, Galileo, Kepler, Descartes, Hooke, and Christiaan Huygens) became a common theme during the Enlightenment in the eighteenth century, when Newton was enthroned as the primary architect of the Age of Reason. Surely no one has ever captured this image of Newton better than the poet Alexander Pope, with his famous couplet:

> Nature and Nature's Laws lay hid in Night:
> God said, *Let Newton be!* and All was Light.

Part 1
NATURAL PHILOSOPHY

Introduction

Newton's introduction to natural philosophy was the Aristotelianism that continued to dominate the curriculum of European universities when he arrived at Cambridge in 1661. This philosophy, which had formed the core of higher education from the time the universities were created, remained the focus of the program that Newton's tutor set for him. Roughly halfway through his undergraduate years, however, apparently sometime during 1664, about the same time when he came upon mathematics, he discovered a new course of reading for himself, the writings of the men who were in the process of creating a new science of nature that was already displacing Aristotelian natural philosophy and would completely supplant it before the seventeenth century was over—the books of René Descartes, Pierre Gassendi, Robert Boyle, and others. The new course of reading determined the direction of Newton's life from that time, and his further advances down the paths the authors had pioneered determined his place in history.

Newton devoured the works he had discovered and effectively enlisted himself in the ranks of their authors. As the word *scientist* did not exist in the seventeenth century, Newton, if asked to define his new vocation, would probably have called himself a natural philosopher, one attempting to understand the nature of the world in which we live. A series of speculations on the nature of things extended from his student notebook, in which he recorded the fruits of his new reading, through the whole of his life, culminating in the final set of Queries that he added to his *Opticks* in 1717, his last important composition. These speculations formed the foundation of Newton's scientific achievements.

The initial set of speculations were the "Quaestiones quaedam philosophicae" ("Certain Philosophical Questions"), as he entitled the set of notes he began sometime during 1664. Above the title he entered the slogan "Amicus Plato amicus Aristoteles magis amica veritas," which can be translated freely as "Plato is my friend; Aristotle is my friend; but my best friend is truth." In the pages that followed, Plato and Aristotle did not appear again; Newton's best friend was the new natural philosophy, which Robert Boyle had recently dubbed the *mechanical philosophy*.

Newton set down forty-five headings under which to organize the material gained from his new reading. Under some headings, he never

In order not to encumber the reader with footnotes we have composed a Biographical Register, in which all the people mentioned in the text are identified, and a Glossary, in which technical terms are briefly explicated and such things as organizations, places, publications, and manuscript collections are identified. There is also a Glossary of Chemical Terms that will be useful for this part. The Biographical Register, Glossary, and Glossary of Chemical Terms are located near the end of the volume.

wrote anything; under others, he found so much that he had to continue the entries elsewhere. One crowded entry, the passage on colors, contained the germ of the central insight to which he devoted the whole of his work in optics, the heterogeneity of light. The title "Quaestiones" adequately describes Newton's tone of constant questioning. His questions, however, were posed within certain limits, probing details of the mechanical philosophy but accepting its general program. Newton had left the world of Aristotle for good.

The choice remaining for Newton lay between two different versions of mechanical philosophy. One version was represented by the philosophy of Descartes, who was most responsible for the new style of natural philosophy. Descartes equated matter with extension and insisted therefore that space cannot be empty, as it would be if it were a perfect vacuum, but is full of some kind of matter; that is, the universe is a *plenum*. He treated light as a pressure transmitted through the plenum. He also described the heavens as a set of huge whirlpools or vortices; our sun is at the center of one of these vortices, and the planets are carried around it like twigs floating in water. Although he explained all the phenomena of nature in terms of particles of matter in motion, he argued that no particle is indivisible. Opposed to the Cartesian philosophy was atomism, found especially in the works of another French philosopher, Gassendi. Although adhering to the same general program of explaining the phenomena of nature in terms of particles of matter in motion, Gassendi held that the ultimate particles are eternal and indivisible (which is the literal meaning of the Greek word *atom*). According to Gassendi, light consists not of pressure through a medium, but of atoms or corpuscles moving with immense velocity. They move, moreover, through a void, for one aspect of atomism was the denial of Descartes' plenum. In many ways, Newton's "Quaestiones" weighed the relative merits of Cartesian mechanical philosophy and atomism, an issue that would remain a central theme of his scientific career. From the beginning, however, Newton appears to have leaned toward atomism.

Through the whole series of Newton's speculations on the nature of things, a certain number of critical phenomena, keys to understanding the structure of reality, constantly reappeared. Chemical phenomena, above all those in which heat is generated and those that display elective affinities, held special importance for him. However, even though Boyle was one of the authors whom Newton read in detail at the time he composed the "Quaestiones," chemistry did not seriously appear in them. All of the other critical phenomena did—the cohesion of bodies, capillary action, surface tension in fluids, and the pressure and expansion of air. They would continue to appear in Newton's speculations, and shortly after the "Quaestiones" were composed the chemical phenomena joined them. Repeated appeal to the same phenomena did not mean that Newton's philosophy of nature remained fixed; on the contrary, the continued evolution of Newton's understanding of reality entailed the reinterpretation of the phenomena.

Part of Newton's reinterpretation of critical phenomena derived from his involvement in alchemy. In Part 7, Alchemy (below), we have included selections from an early chemical, or alchemical, manuscript, "Of natures obvious laws and processes in vegetation," written about 1669 or 1670. Although it does not invoke the critical phenomena mentioned above, the manuscript belongs also among his speculations on the nature of things.

About five years after "Of natures obvious laws and processes in vegetation," in early 1675, Newton composed the "An Hypothesis explaining the Properties of Light" to accompany a paper on colors that he was sending to the Royal Society. The "Hypothesis of Light" does eventually get around to optical phenomena, but only after it ranges over the whole of natural philosophy. By 1675 Newton's natural philosophy had already undergone sufficient development that other mechanical philosophers might have had difficulty in recognizing that he was one of them.

In 1675, Newton made the acquaintance of Robert Boyle, and in the correspondence that ensued Newton sent Boyle a long letter about the *aether*, the substance thought to fill all space, in 1678. The letter, which is well known and easily found, is not in this volume; rather, we have included a closely related piece, "De aere et aethere" ("Concerning the Air and the Aether"), which deals with much the same set of questions and embodies further development beyond the position of the "Hypothesis of Light" and toward the mature natural philosophy associated with the *Principia*, published in 1687.

With the *Principia*, the question of forces between bodies, and between particles of matter—a concept not present in his earlier speculations—became the central issue in Newton's natural philosophy. Forces were subject to precise mathematical treatment. The essence of the *Principia* lies in Newton's demonstration that celestial phenomena are the consequence of a universal force of attraction. As he composed the *Principia*, Newton considered the inclusion of a general statement about forces either as a preface or as a conclusion to the book. In the end, he did not include the essay at all, but nearly twenty years later, it appeared in an expanded version as one of the Queries appended to the 1706 Latin edition of the *Opticks*. When it was translated into English, it became Query 31, and it constitutes ones of Newton's most important mature speculations on the nature of things. We print with it Queries 1–8, which were published two years earlier with the first edition of the *Opticks*. In the second English edition of the *Opticks*, published in 1717, Newton added a further set of Queries (which were inserted into the middle of the earlier set and thus have numbers lower than some of the Queries published eleven years earlier) that returned again to the concept of a cosmic aether. We include Queries 18–22. They effectively concluded Newton's career as a natural philosopher, which extended over a period of more than sixty years.

From "Quaestiones quaedam philosophicae" †

Conjunction of Bodies

Whether the conjunction of bodies be from rest? No, for then sand by rest might be united sooner than by a furnace, etc.

Whether it be from the close crowding of all the matter in the world affirmed, for the air (though its pressure be but little in respect of that performed by the purer matter of the vortex, between the Sun and us, receding from the center) by its pressure to the center, and consequently crowding all things close together between which there is not air to keep them apart, it makes them stick together; as the two polished sides of two marbles, the parts of water, etc. But this juncture cannot be very firm by reason that the pressure of the air is not very strong, as appears by the experiments of Robert Boyle, Esquire.[1] But the pressure of all the matter between the Sun and us, made by reason of its endeavor from the Sun, being far greater (and it may be some other power by which matter is kept close together, etc.), when two or three or more little bodies once touch, so as to admit no other matter between them, they must be held very fast together; all the matter about them pressing them together but nothing striving to part them. And when two of the least particles meet whose sides, with which they touch one another, are pretty broad and fitted to touch close everywhere, those two may move together as one body and so may increase by having others joined to them in the same manner. But if the surrounding particles chance to be held off from pressing them together by some accident, as those about *a* or be variously pressed, as at *b* by the bodies *c* and *d*, they may be again

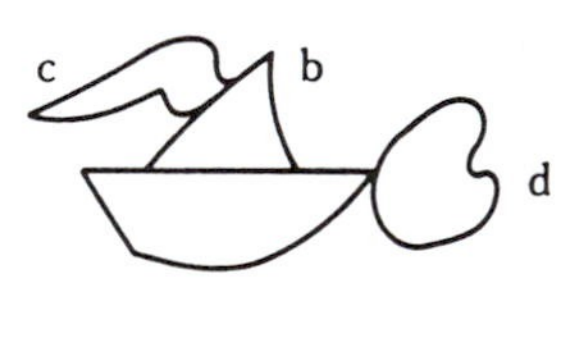

† J. E. McGuire and Martin Tamny, *Certain Philosophical Questions: Newton's Trinity Notebook* (Cambridge: Cambridge University Press, 1983), pp. 349–431. Reprinted with the permission of Cambridge University Press. The "Quaestiones quaedam philosophicae" ("Certain Philosophical Questions") are a set of notes and reflections on Newton's readings in the new natural philosophy, which he began to compile toward the end of his undergraduate years, about 1664. They constitute the first step in Newton's scientific career.

1. Boyle published a book of experiments with the first air pump in 1660.

severed. Yet in more compound bodies there is no danger, for the least particles are so wedged together that neither of these two chances could undo them; as for the first it cannot happen to a whole body but only in some little part of it, as some atom of a man's hand may chance not to be touched by the water into which he puts it, but this cannot happen to his whole hand. So that those particles which are pressed together may hold a particle wedged, as it were, among them, so that it cannot fall away from them, though it chance not to be pressed to them. The second can scarcely happen at all, for the neighboring matter can only press two touching particles toward the center, or it may be a little awry, but not from the body to which they adhere; but, let the worst happen that can, the particle may be wedged in among the rest. But it may be that the particles of compound matter were created bigger than those which serve for other offices.

Of the Celestial Matter and Orbs

Whether Descartes's first element can turn about the vortex and yet drive the matter of it continually from the Sun to produce light, and spend most of its motion in filling up the chinks between the globuli. Whether the least globuli can continue always next to the Sun and yet come always from it to cause light. Whether when the Sun is obscured, the motion of the first element must cease (and so whether by his hypothesis the Sun can be obscured). Whether upon the ceasing of the first element's motion the vortex must move slower. Whether some of the first element coming (as he confesses that he might find out a way to turn the globuli about their own axes to grate the third element into coils, like screws or cockle shells) immediately from the poles and other vortices into all the parts of our vortex would not impel the globuli so as to cause a light from the poles, and those places from whence they come.

Of the Sun, Stars, Planets, and Comets

Whether the Sun moves the vortex about (as Descartes's will) by his beams, page 54, *Principia Philosophiae*,[2] Part III. Whether the vortex can carry a comet toward the poles. How is it that the Sun is turned about upon his axis. Whether Descartes's notion of reflection will unriddle the mystery of the comet's tail.

* * *

Of Gravity and Levity

The matter causing gravity must pass through all of the pores of a body. It must ascend again, (1) for either the bowels of the Earth must

2. Published in 1644, this book presented the first complete philosophy of nature in rigorously mechanistic terms.

have had large cavities and inanities to contain it, (2) or else the matter must swell the Earth, or (3) the matter that has so forcibly borne down the Earth and all other bodies to the center (unless you will have it grown to as gross a consistence as the Earth is, and hardly then) cannot if added together be of a bulk so little as is the Earth. For it must descend very fast and swift as appears by the falling of bodies and by the great pressure toward the Earth. It must ascend in another form than it descends, or else it would have a like force to bear bodies up as it has to press them down, and so there would be no gravity. It must ascend in a grosser consistency than it descends, (1) because it may be slower and not strike bodies with so great a force as to impel them upward, (2) that it may only force the outside of a body and not sink into every pore, and then its denseness will little avail it, because it will yield from the superficies of a body with ease so as to run in an easier channel as though it never strove against them. If it should ascend thinner it can have only this advantage: that it would not hit bodies with so weighty a force, but then it would hit more parts of the body and would have more parts with which to hit with a smarter force, and so cause ascension with more force than the others could do descension. We know of no body that will not sink into the pores of bodies better than air, and it will sink into most if it be forcibly crowded in. The stream descending will lay some hold on the stream ascending, and so press it closer and make it denser. Therefore it will rise the slower. The stream descending will grow thicker as it comes nearer to the Earth; but it will not lose its swiftness until it finds as much opposition as it has help from the flood following behind it. But when the streams meet on all sides in the midst of the Earth, they must needs be compressed into a narrow room, closely pressed together, and thus very much opposing one another either turn back the same way that they came, or crowd through one another's streams with much difficulty and pressure, and so be compacted and the descending stream will keep them compacted, by continually pressing them to the Earth until they arise to the place from whence they came. There they will attain their former liberty.

The gravity of a body in diverse places as at the top and bottom of a hill, in different latitudes, etc., may be measured by an instrument of this form

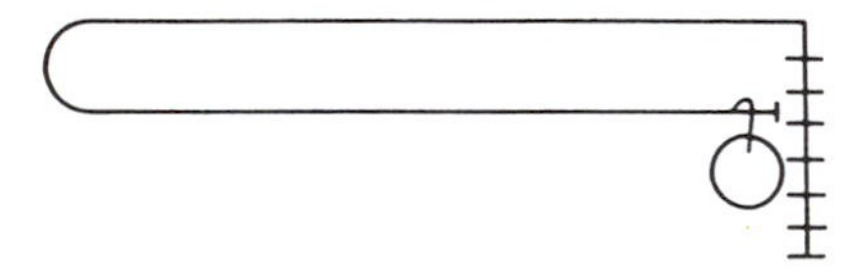

The weight of water is to the weight of quicksilver as 1 is to 14. Water is 400 (perhaps 2,000) times heavier than air and gold 19 times heavier than water.

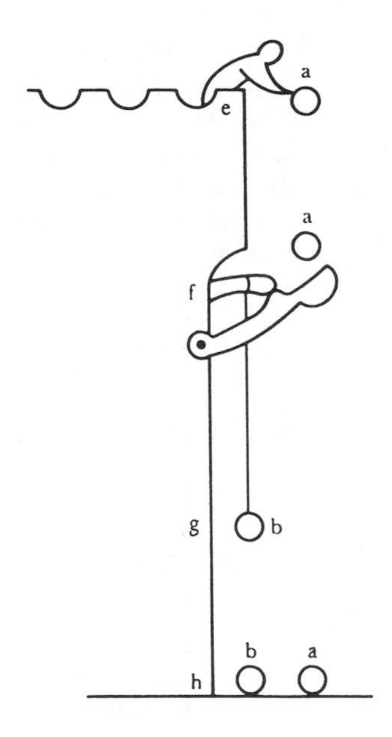

Question: what proportion the weights of two bodies, such as gold and silver, have in diverse mediums as in a vacuum, air, water, etc.: which, if known, the weight of the air or water in a vacuum, or the quantity of gold to silver, can be determined. For example: if in air the gold a is equiponderant to the silver z, their weight being called b, and in water the gold a is equiponderant to the silver $2z$ and c be the weight of so much water in the air as is equal to the gold a; then cz/a is the weight of so much water as is equal to the silver z. Since the gold and silver are weighed in water, their weights are diminished by the weight of the water whose place they contain. Therefore, $b-c$ is the weight of the gold a in the water, and $b-cz/a$ is the weight of the silver z in it. Since a is equiponderant to $2z$ in water, therefore $b-c=2b-(2cz)/(a)$, or $(ab+ac)/(2c)=z$. That is, $2c : b+c :: a : z$.Or, if c, the weight of water in the air is sought, then $(ab)/(2z-a)=c$. Thus might the absolute weights of bodies, i.e., their weights in a vacuum, be found. Similarly can the weight of air, bodies in a hot furnace minus flame, and fire be determined.

Try whether flame will descend in Torricelli's vacuum.[3]

In the descension of a body there is to be considered the force which it receives every moment from its gravity—which must be least in a swiftest body—and the opposition it receives from the air—which increases in proportion to its swiftness. To make an experiment concern-

3. Torricelli constructed the first barometer in 1644. Torricelli's vacuum refers to the space above the mercury in the barometer.

ing this increase of motion: when the globe *a* has fallen from *e* to *f* let the globe *b* begin to move at *g*, so that both globes fall together at *h*.

According to Galileo an iron ball of 100 lb. Florentine (that is 78 lb. at London avoirdupois weight) descends 100 Florentine braces or cubits (or 49.01 Ells, perhaps 66 yds.) in 5 seconds of an hour.

By this figure it may appear how to weigh without altering the weights, and to tell exactly the weight of bodies at the first trial. But it

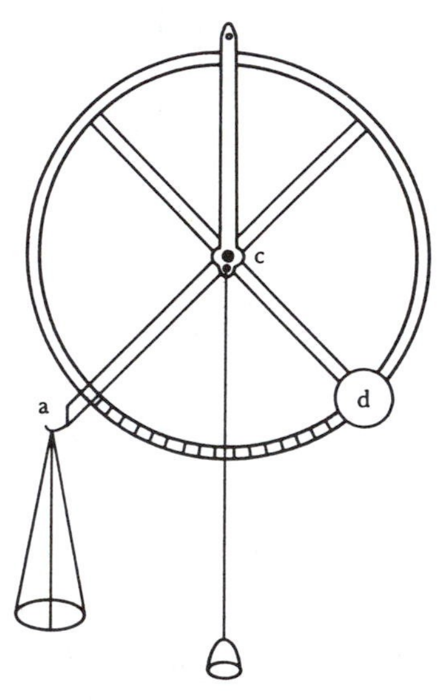

will be best to fix the wheel and make the arms *cd* and *ac* very long, especially *cd*. This balance may be of excellent use for finding the several weights of alloyed or mixed bodies by their weight in several mediums as in air and water (such as gold and copper), or to compare the quantity of any two bodies (such as gold and stone) by their difference of

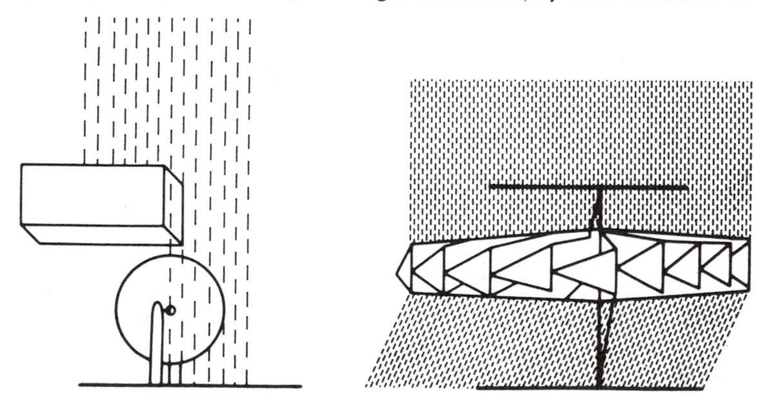

weight in diverse mediums, or to compare the weights of bodies, that is, to find what proportion the weights of those bodies would have were they equal.

Try whether the weight of a body may be altered by heat or cold, dilation or condensation, beating, powdering, transferring to several places or several heights, or placing a hot or heavy body over it or under it, or by magnetism. Whether lead or its dust spread abroad is heaviest. Whether a plate flat ways or edge ways is heaviest. Whether the rays of gravity may be stopped by reflecting or refracting them. If so a perpetual motion may be made in one of these two ways. The gravity of bodies is as their solidity, because all bodies descend equal spaces in equal times, consideration being had to the resistance of the air.

Of Light

Why light passes more easily through white than black paper and yet is more efficaciously reflected from it.

How light is conveyed from the Sun or a fire without stops.

Light is more easily admitted into black than reflected from it, for hold a paper between you and light with a black spot in it and it is blacker when toward you than when to the light.

Light cannot be by pression,[4] for then we should see in the night as well, or better, than in the day. We should see a bright light above us, because we are pressed downward. . . . There could be no refraction since the same matter cannot press two ways. The Sun could not be quite eclipsed. The Moon and planets would shine like suns. A man going or running would see in the night. When a fire or candle is extinguished we, looking another way, should see a light. The whole East would shine in the day time and the West in the night by reason of the flood which carries our vortex. A light would shine from the Earth, since the subtle matter tends from the center. A little body interposed could not hinder us from seeing. Pression could not render shapes so distinct. There is the greatest pression on that side of the Earth from the Sun, or else it would not move about *in equilibrio*, but from the Sun, therefore the nights should be lightest. Also the vortex is elliptical, therefore light cannot always come from the same direction, etc.

Whether the rays of light may not move a body as wind does a mill sail.

To know how swift light is: set a broad, well polished, looking-glass on a high steeple so that, with a telescope 1, 2, 3, 10, or 20 miles off, you may see yourself in it. Having by you a great candle, in the night, cover it and uncover it and observe how long it is before you see the candle in the glass appear and disappear.

4. Refers to Descartes' theory of light. See Glossary, *Cartesian natural philosophy*.

Of Sensation

The senses of diverse men are diversely affected by the same objects according to the diversity of their constitution.

To them of Java pepper is cold.

If the orifice of the stomach is wounded it sooner dispatches a man than if the head be wounded: the former having greater sympathy with the heart deads it and stops its motion, and so sense ceases. The latter though it take away sense, yet the heart's motion is not impeded thereby.

The common sensorium is either: (1) the whole body, (2) the orifice of the stomach, (3) the heart, (4) the brain, (5) the membranes, (6) the *septum lucidum*, (7) some very small and perfectly solid particle in the body, (8) the conarion, (9) the concourse of nerves about the 4th ventricle of the brain, or (10) the animal spirits in that 4th ventricle.

Of the Flux and Reflux of the Sea

To try whether the Moon pressing the atmosphere causes the flux and reflux of the sea.[5] Take a tube of above 30 inches filled with quicksilver, or else take a tube filled with water, which is so much longer than 30 inches as the quicksilver is weightier than water. The top being stopped, the liquor will sink three or four inches below it leaving a vacuum (perhaps). Then, as the air is more or less pressed without by the Moon, so will the water rise or fall as it does in a weatherglass by heat or cold. The same may be done by comparing the motions of the water of two weatherglasses, one whereof is within a vessel of water, the other not.

Observe if the sea water rises not in days and falls at nights by reason of the Earth pressing from the Sun upon the night water. Try also whether the water is higher in mornings or evenings, to know whether the Earth or its vortex press forward most in its annual motion.

Hypothesis of Light †

An Hypothesis explaining the Properties of Light discoursed of in my severall Papers.

Sir

In my Answer to Mr Hook you may remember I had occasion to say something of Hypotheses, where I gave a Reason, why all allowable

5. Refers to Descartes' explanation of tides. See Glossary, *Cartesian natural philosophy*.

† *The Correspondence of Isaac Newton*, eds. H. W. Turnbull, J. F. Scott, A. Rupert Hall, and Laura Tilling, 7 vols. (Cambridge: Cambridge University Press, 1959–77), vol. 1, pp. 362–83. Reprinted with the permission of The Royal Society. Newton sent the so-called "Hypothesis of Light" in the form of a letter to Henry Oldenburg, secretary of the Royal Society, on December 7, 1675, to accompany and explain his set of observations on the colored rings (Newton's rings) in a thin film of air between a lens and a sheet of glass.

Hypotheses in their genuine constitution should be conformable to my Theories, and said of Mr Hook's Hypothesis, that I took the most free and Naturall Application of it to Phænomena to be this: That the agitated parts of bodies according to their severall sizes, figure and motions, doe excite Vibrations in the Æther of various depths or bignesses, which being promiscuously propagated through that Medium to our Eyes, effect in us a Sensation of Light of a white colour, but if by any meanes those of unequall bignesses be seperated from one another, the largest beget a sensation of a Red colour, the least or shortest of a deep Violet, and the intermediate ones, of intermediate colours; much after the manner of bodies according to their severall sizes, shapes and motions excite Vibrations in the Air of various bignesses, which, according to those bignesses, make severall tones in sound etc. I was glad to understand, as I apprehended, from Mr Hooks discourse at my last being at one of your Assemblies, that he had changed his former notion of all colours being compounded of only two Originall ones, made by the two sides of an oblique pulse, and accomodated his Hypothesis to this my suggestion of colours, like sounds, being various according to the various bignesse of the Pulses. For this I take to be a more plausible Hypothesis than any other described by former Authors, because I see not, how the colours of thin transparent plates or skins can be hansomly explained, without haveing recourse to æthereall Pulses. But yet I like another Hypothesis better which I had occasion to hint something of in the same letter in these words:

'The Hypothesis of light's being a body, had I propounded it, has a much greater affinity with the Objectors owne Hypothesis, then he seems to be aware of; the vibrations of the æther being as usefull and necessary in this, as in his. For assumeing the Rayes of Light to be smal bodyes, emitted every way from shining substances, those when they impinge on any refracting or reflecting superficies, must as necessarily excite vibrations in the aether as stones doe in water when throwne into it. And supposeing these vibrations to be of several depths or thicknesses accordingly as they are excited by the said corpuscular rays of various sizes and velocities; of what use they will be for explicating the manner of reflexion and refraction, the production of heat by the Sunn beams, the emission of Light from burning, putrifying, or other substances whose parts are vehemently agitated, the Phænomena of thin transparent plates, and bubbles, and of all naturall bodyes, the manner of vision, and the difference of colours, as also their harmony and discord; I shall leave to their consideration, who may think it worth their endeavour to apply this Hypothesis to the Solution of Phænomena.'

Were I to assume an Hypothesis it should be this if propounded more generally, So as not to determin what Light is, farther then that it is something or other capable of exciting vibrations in the æther for thus it will become so generall and comprehensive of other Hypotheses as to leave little room for new ones to be invented. And therefore because I have observed the heads of some great virtuoso's to run much upon Hypotheses, as if my discourses wanted an Hypothesis to explain them by, and found, that some when I could not make them take my meaning, when I spake of the nature of light and colours abstractedly, have readily apprehended it when I illustrated my Discourse by an Hypothesis; for this reason I have here thought fitt to send you a description of the circumstances of this Hypothesis as much tending to the illustration of the papers I herewith send you. And though I shall not assume either this or any other Hypothesis, nor thinking it necessary to concerne my selfe whether the properties of Light, discovered by me, be explained by this or Mr Hook's or any other Hypothesis capable of explaining them; yet while I am describing this, I shall sometimes to avoyde Circumlocution and so represent it more conveniently speak of it as if I assumed it and propounded it to be beleived. This I thought fitt to Expresse, that no man may confound this with my other discourses, or measure the certainty of one by the other, or think me oblig'd to answer objections against this script. For I desire to decline being involved in such troublesome and insignificant Disputes.

But to proceed to the Hypothesis; first, it is to be supposed therein, that there is an æthereall Medium much of the same constitution with air, but far rarer, subtiler and more strongly Elastic. Of the existence of this Medium the motion of a Pendulum in a glasse exhausted of Air[1] almost as quickly as in the open Air, is no inconsiderable argument. But it is not to be supposed, that this Medium is one uniforme matter, but compounded partly of the maine flegmatic body of æther partly of other various æthereall Spirits, much after the manner that Air is compounded of the flegmatic body of Air intermixt with various vapours and exhalations. For the Electric and Magnetic effluvia and gravitating principle seem to argue such variety. Perhaps the whole frame of Nature may be nothing but various Contextures of some certaine æthereall Spirits or vapours condens'd as it were by præcipitation, much after the manner that vapours are condensed into water or exhalations into grosser Substances, though not so easily condensible; and after condensation wrought into various formes, at first by the immediate hand of the Creator, and ever since by the power of Nature, which by vertue of the command Increase and Multiply, became a complete Imitator of the copies sett her by the Protoplast. Thus perhaps may all things be originated from æther.

At least the electric effluvia seem to instruct us, that there is something of an æthereall Nature condens'd in bodies. I have sometimes laid upon a table a round peice of Glasse about 2 inches broad Sett in a brass ring, so that the glass might be about $\frac{1}{8}$ or $\frac{1}{6}$ of an inch from the table,

1. Refers to the receiver of an air pump.

and the Air between them inclosed on all sides by the ring, after the manner as if I had whelmed a little Sive upon the Table. And then rubbing a pretty while the Glass briskly with some ruff and rakeing stuffe, till some very little Fragments of very thin paper, laid on the Table under the glasse, began to be attracted and move nimbly to and fro: after I had done rubbing the Glass, the papers would continue a pretty while in various motions, sometimes leaping up to the Glass and resting there a while, then leaping downe and resting there, then leaping up and perhaps downe and up againe, and this sometimes in lines seeming perpendicular to the Table, Sometimes in oblique ones, Sometimes also they would leap up in one Arch and downe in another, divers times together, without Sensible resting between; Somtimes Skip in a bow from one part of the Glasse to another without touching the table, and Sometimes hang by a corner and turn often about very nimbly as if they had been carried about in the midst of a whirlwind, and be otherwise variously moved, every paper with a divers motion. And upon Sliding my finger on the upper Side of the Glasse, though neither the glass, nor inclosed Air below, were moved thereby, yet would the papers, as they hung under the glasse, receive some new motion, inclining this way or that way accordingly as I moved my finger. Now whence all these irregular motions should spring I cannot imagine, unless from some kind of subtill matter lyeing condens'd in the glass, and rarefied by rubbing as water is rarified into Vapour by heat, and in that rarefaction diffused through the Space round the glasse to a great distance, and made to move and circulate variously and accordingly to actuate the papers, till it returne into the glasse againe and be recondensed there. And as this condensed matter by rarefaction into an æthereall wind (for by its easy penetrating and circulating through Glass I esteeme it æthereall) may cause these odd motions, and by condensing againe may cause electricall attraction with its returning to the glass to succeed in the place of what is there continually recondensed; so may the gravitating attraction of the Earth be caused by the continuall condensation of some other such like æthereall Spirit, not of the maine body of flegmatic æther, but of something very thinly and subtily diffused through it, perhaps of an unctuous or Gummy, tenacious and Springy nature, and bearing much the same relation to æther, which the vitall æreall Spirit requisite for the conservation of flame and vitall motions[2] does to Air. For if such an æthereall Spirit may be condensed in fermenting or burning bodies, or otherwise coagulated, in the pores of the earth and water, into some kind of humid active matter for the continuall uses of nature, adhereing to the sides of those pores after the manner that vapours condense on the sides of a Vessell subtily set; the vast body of the Earth, which may be every where to the very center in perpetuall working, may continually

2. Experiments at about this time showed that there was something in air, called a variety of things, including "vital aerial spirit," that sustained both life and combustion.

condense so much of this Spirit as to cause it from above to descend with great celerity for a supply. In which descent it may beare downe with it the bodyes it pervades with force proportionall to the superficies of all their parts it acts upon; nature makeing a circulation by the slow ascent of as much matter out of the bowells of the Earth in an æreall forme which for a time constitutes the Atmosphere, but being continually boyed up by the new Air, Exhalations, and Vapours riseing underneath, at length, (Some part of the vapours which returne in rain excepted) vanishes againe into the æthereall Spaces, and there perhaps in time relents, and is attenuated into its first principle. For nature is a perpetuall circulatory worker, generating fluids out of solids, and solids out of fluids, fixed things out of volatile, and volatile out of fixed, subtile out of gross, and gross out of subtile, Some things to ascend and make the upper terrestriall juices, Rivers and the Atmosphere; and by consequence others to descend for a Requitall to the former. And as the Earth, so perhaps may the Sun imbibe this Spirit copiously to conserve his Shineing, and keep the Planets from recedeing further from him. And they that will, may also suppose, that this Spirit affords or carryes with it thither the solary fewell and materiall Principle of Light; And that the vast æthereall Spaces between us, and the stars are for a sufficient repository for this food of the Sunn and Planets. But this of the Constitution of æthereall Natures by the by.

In the second place, it is to be supposed, that the Æther is a vibrating Medium like Air; onely the vibrations far more swift and Minute; those of Aire, made by a mans ordinary voice succeeding one another at more than halfe a foot or a foot distance, but those of æther at a less distance then the hundred thousand part of an inch. And, as in Air the Vibrations are some larger then others, but yet all equally Swift (for in a ring of Bells the Sound of every tone is heard at two or three miles distance, in the Same Order that the bells are Stroke;) So I suppose the æthereall Vibrations differ in bignesse but not in Swiftnesse. Now these Vibrations, beside their use in reflexion and refraction, may be Supposed the cheif meanes, by which the parts of fermenting or putrifieing Substances, fluid Liquors, or melted burning or other hott bodyes continue in motion, are shaken asunder like a Ship by waves, and dissipated into vapours, exhalations, or Smoake, and Light loosed or excited in those bodyes, and consequently by which a Body becomes a burning coale, and Smoake, flame, and I suppose, flame is nothing but the particles of Smoake turned by the access of Light and heat to burning Coles little and innumerable.

Thirdly, as the Air can pervade the bores of Small Glasse pipes, but yet not so easily as if they were wider, and therefore stands at a greater degree of rarity then in the free æreall Spaces, and at so much a greater degree of rarity as the pipe is Smaller, as is knowne by the rising of water in such pipes to a much greater height then the Surface of the Stagnating water into which they are dipt; So I suppose æther, though it pervades the pores of chrystal, glass, water, and other Naturall bodyes, yet it stands at a greater degree of rarity in those pores then in the free æthereall Spaces, and at so much a greater degree of rarity as the pores of the body are Smaller. Whence it may be, that Spirit of Wine, for instance, though a Lighter body, yet haveing Subtiler parts and consequently Smaller pores then water, is the more Strongly refracting liquor. This also may be the principall cause of the cohæsion of the parts of Solids and Fluids, of the Springines of Glass and other bodyes whose parts Slide not one upon another in bending, and of the Standing of the Mercury in the Torricellian Experiment, sometimes to the top of the Glass, though a much greater height then 29 inches.[3] For the Denser æther, which Surrounds these Bodies, must croud and presse their parts together much after the manner that Air surrounding two Marbles presses them together if there be little or no Air between them. Yea and that puzleing Problem: By what means the Muscles are contracted and dilated to cause Animal motion, may receive greater Light from hence then from any other means men have hitherto been thinking on. For if there be any power in man to condense and dilate at will the æther that pervades the muscle; that condensation or dilatation must vary the compression of the Muscle, made by the Ambient æther, and cause it to Swell or Shrinck accordingly. For though common water will scarce Shrink by compression, and Swell by relaxation, yet (so far as my observation reaches) Spirit of Wine and Oyle will, and Mr Boyles Experimt of a Tadpole Shrinking very much by hard compressing the water in which it Swam, is an Argument that Animal juices doe the same. And as for their various pression by the Ambient æther, its plain, that that must be more or lesse accordingly as there is more or lesse æther within to Susteyne and Counterpoize the pressure of that without. If both æthers were equally dense, the muscle would be at liberty as if prest by neither. If there were no æther within, the Ambient would compresse it with the whole force of its Spring. If the æther within were twice as much dilated as that without, So as to have but halfe as much Springines, the Ambient would have half the force of its Springines counterpoized thereby, and exercise but the other half upon the muscle, And so in all other cases the Ambient Compresses the muscle by the excesse of the force of its Springines above that of the Springines of the include. To vary the compression of the muscle therefore and So to Swell and Shrink it, there needs nothing but to change the consistence of the included Æther, and a very little change may suffice, if the Spring of æther be supposed very strong, as I take it to be many degrees Stronger then that of Air.

Now for the changing the consistence of the æther, some may be

3. Huygens had discovered that, as long as the mercury remained in contact with the end of the tube, a column as high as seventy inches could be realized in a barometric tube.

ready to grant, that the soule may have an imediate power over the whole æther in any part of the body to Swell or Shrink it at will: but then how depends the Muscular motion on the nerves. Others therefore may be more apt to think it done by some certain æthereall Spirit included within the *Dura Mater*, which the soule may have power to contract or dilate at will in any Muscle and so cause it to flow thither through the Nerves, but still theres a difficulty why this force of the soule upon it does not take off the power of its Springines whereby it should susteyne more or less the force of the Outward Æther. A third supposition may be that the Soul has a power to inspire any muscle with this Spirit by impelling it thither through the Nerves, but this too has its difficulties; for it requires a forcible intending the Spring of the æther in the muscles by pressure exerted from the parts of the brain; and its hard to conceive, how so great force can be exercised amidst so tender matter as the braine is and besides, why does not this æthereall Spirit, being Subtile enough and urg'd with so great force go away through the *Dura Mater* and Skins of the muscle, or at least so much of the other æther go out to make way for this which is crouded in. To take away these difficulties is a digression, but seeing the Subject is a deserving one, I shall not Stick to tell you how I think it may be done.

First then, I suppose, there is such a Spirit, that is, that the Animall Spirits are neither like the liquor, vapour or Gas of Spirit of Wine, but of an æthereall Nature, Subtile enough to pervade the Animal juices as freely as the Electric or perhaps Magnetic effluvia do glass: And to know, how the Coats of the braine, Nerves and muscles may become a convenient vessell to hold so Subtile a Spirit, you may consider, how liquors and Spirits are disposed to pervade or not pervade things on other accounts then their Subtility; water and Oyle pervades Wood and Stone, which Quicksilver does not; and Quicksilver, Mettalls, which water and Oyle doe not. Water and Acids Spirits pervade Salts, which Oyle in Spirit of Wine do not, and oyle and Spirit of Wine pervade Sulphur which water Acid Spirits do not. So some fluids (as Oyle and water) though their pores are in freedome enough to mix with one another, yet by some secret principle of unsociablenes they keep asunder, and some that are Sociable may become unsociable by adding a third thing to one of them, as water to Spirit of Wine by dissolving Salt of Tartar in it. The like unsociablenes may be in æthereall Natures, as perhaps between the æthers in the vortices of the Sun and Planets; and the reason, why Air stands rarer in the boxes of Small Glass-pipes, and æther in the pores of bodies, then elsewhere may be, not want of Subtilty, but Sociablenes. And on this ground, if the æthereall vitall Spirit in a man be very Sociable to the marrow and Juices, and unsociable to the coats of the braine, Nerves and Muscles, or to any thing Lodged in the pores of those coats, it may be contained thereby notwithstanding its Subtilty; especially if we suppose no great violence done to it to Squeeze it out; and that it may not be altogether so Subtil as the main body of æther, though Subtil enough to pervade readily the Animall juices, and that, as any of it is Spent, it is continually supplyed by new Spirit from the heart.

In the next place for knowing how the Spirit may be used for Animal motion, you may consider, how some things unsociable are made Sociable by the Mediation of a Third. Water, which will not dissolve copper, will do it if the copper be melted with Sulphur: Aqua fortis, which will not pervade Gold will do it by addition of a little Sal Armoniac, or Spirit of Salt; Lead will not mix in melting with copper, but if a little Tin or Antimony be added, they mix readily, and part againe of their own accord, if the Antimony be wasted by throwing Saltpeter or otherwise. And so Lead melted with Silver quickly pervades and liquefies the Silver in a much less heat, then is requisite to melt the Silver alone; but if they be kept in the Test, till that little substance that reconciled them be wasted or altered, they part againe of their owne accord. And in like manner the æthereal Animal Spirit in a man may be a mediator between the common æther and the muscular juices to make them mix more freely; and so by sending a litle of this Spirit into any muscle, though so little as to cause no sensible tension of the muscle by its owne force, yet by rendering the juices more Sociable to the common external æther, it may cause that æther to pervade the muscle of its owne accord in a moment more freely and copiously then it would otherwise do and to recede againe as freely so soon as this Mediator of Sociablenes is retracted. Whence, according to what I said above, will proceed the Swelling or Shrinking of the Muscle and consequently the Animal motion depending thereon.

Thus may therefore the Soul by determining this æthereall Animal Spirit or Wind into this or that Nerve, perhaps with as much ease as Air is moved in open Spaces, cause all the motions wee see in Animals: for the making which motions Strong, it is not necessary, that we should suppose the æther within the muscle very much condenst or rarified by this means, but onely that it's Spring is so very great, that a little alteration of its density shall cause a great alteration in the pressure. And what is said of Muscular motion may be applyed to the motion of the heart, onely with this difference, that the Spirit is not sent thither as into other muscles, but continually generated there by the fermentation of the Juices, with which its flesh is replenished, and as it is generated, let out by starts into the braine through some convenient ductus to perform those motions in other muscles by inspiration which it did in the heart by its generation. For I see not, why the ferment in the heart may not raise as Subtile a Spirit out of it's juices to cause these motions, as rubbing does out of a glasse to cause electric attraction or burning out of fewel to penetrate glasse, as Mr Boyle has showne, and calcine by corrosion Mettalls melted therein.

Hitherto I have been contemplating the nature of Æther and Æthereall Substances by their effects and uses, and now I come to Joyne therewith the consideration of Light.

In the fourth place therefore I suppose Light is neither this Æther nor its vibrating motion, but something of a different kind propagated from lucid bodies. They that will may suppose it an aggregate of various peripatetic qualities. Others may suppose it multitudes of unimaginable small and swift Corpuscles of various sizes, springing from shining bodies at great distances one after another, but yet without any sensible interval of time, and continually urged forward by a Principle of motion, which in the beginning accelerates them till the resistance of the Æthereall Medium equal the force of that principle, much after the manner that bodies let fall in water are accelerated till the resistence of the water equalls the force of gravity. God who gave Animals self motion beyond our understanding is without doubt able to implant other principles of motion in bodies which we may understand as little. Some would readily grant this may be a Spiritual one; yet a mechanical one might be showne, did not I think it better to passe it by. But they that like not this, may suppose Light any other corporeal emanation or an Impulse or motion of any other Medium or æthereall Spirit diffused through the main body of Æther, or what else they can imagine proper for this purpose. To avoyde dispute and make this Hypothesis generall, let every man here take his fancy. Onely whatever Light be, I would suppose, it consists of Successive rayes differing from one another in contingent circumstances, as bignes, forme or vigour, like as the Sands on the Shore, the waves of the Sea, the faces of men, and all other naturall things of the same kind differ, it being almost impossible for any sort of things to be found without some contingent variety. And further I would suppose it divers from the vibrations of the æther, because (besides, that were it those vibrations, it ought alwayes to verge copiously in crooked lines into the dark or quiescent Medium, destroying all Shadowes, and to comply readily with any crooked pores or passages, as Sounds do,) I see not how any superficies, (as the side of a Glass Prism on which the rayes within are incident at an angle of above 40 degrees) can be totally opake. For the vibrations beating against the refracting confine of the rarer and denser aether must needs make that pliant Superficies undulate, and those undulations will Stir up and propagate vibrations on the other side. And further, how light incident on very thin Skins or plates of any transparent body, should for many successive thicknesses of the plate in Arithmeticall progression be alternately reflected and transmitted, as I find it is, puzels me as much. For though the Arithmeticall progression of those thicknesses, which reflect and transmit the rayes alternately, argues that it depends upon the number of vibrations between the two Superficies of the plate whether the ray shall be reflected or transmitted; yet I cannot see, how the number should vary the case, be it greater or lesse, whole or broken, unless Light be supposed something else then these vibrations. Something indeed I could fancy towards helping the two last difficulties, but nothing which I see not insufficient.

Fifthly, it is to be supposed, that Light and Æther mutually act upon one another, æther in refracting light, and Light in warming æther; and that the densest æther acts most strongly. When a ray therefore moves through æther of uneaven density, I suppose it most prest, urged or acted upon by the Medium on that side towards the Denser æther, and receivs a continuall impulse or ply from that side to recede towards the rarer, and so is accelerated if it move that way, or retarded if the contrary. On this ground, if a ray move obliquely through such an unevenly dense Medium (that is obliquely to those imaginary Superficies's which run through the equally Dense parts of the Medium and may be called the refracting Superficies) it must be incurved, as it is found to be by Observation in water, whose lower parts were made gradually more salt and so more dense then the upper. And this may be the ground of all refraction and reflexion. For as the rarer Air within a small glass pipe, and the denser without, are not distinguished by a meer Mathematicall Superficies, but have Air between them at the orifice of the Pipe running through all intermediate degrees of density: So I suppose the refracting Superficies of æther between unequally dense Mediums to be not a Mathematicall one; but of some breadth, the æther therein at the Orifices of the pores of the solid body being of all intermediate degrees of density between the rarer and denser æthereal Mediums, and the refraction I conceive to proceed from the continuall incurvation of the ray all the while it is passing the Physicall Superficies. Now if the motion of the ray be supposed in this passage to be increased or diminished in a certaine proportion according to the difference of the densities of the æthereall Mediums, and the addition or detraction of the motion be reckoned in the perpendicular from the refracting Superficies, as it ought to be, the Sines of incidence and refraction will be proportionall according to what Des Cartes has demonstrated.

The ray therefore in passing out of the rarer Medium into the denser, inclines continually more and more towards parallelism with the refracting Superficies, and if the differing densities of the Mediums be not so great, nor the incidence of the ray so oblique as to make it parallel to that Superficies before it gets through, then it goes through and is refracted; but if through the aforesaid causes the ray become parallel to that Superficies before it can get through, then it must turn back and be reflected. Thus for instance it may be observed in a triangular glass Prism *OEF*, that the rays *AN* that tend out of the glass into Air, do by inclining them more and more to the refracting Superficies, emerge more and more obliquely till they be infinitely oblique, that is in a manner parallel to the Superficies, which happens when the angle of incidence is about 40 degrees, and then if they be a little more inclind are all reflected, as at *Aνλ*, becoming I suppose parallel to the Superficies before they can gett through it. Let *ABDC* represent the rarer Medium; *EFHG* the Denser, *CDFE* the Space between them or refracting Physical Superficies in which the æther is of all intermediate degrees of density, from the rarest æther at *CD*, to the Densest at *EF*; *AMNL* a ray, *AM* its incident part, *MN* its incurvation by the refracting superficies, and *NL* its emergent part. Now if the ray *AM* be so much incurved as to become at its emergence *N*, as nearly as may be, parallel to *CD*, its plain, that if that ray had been incident a little more obliquely, it must have become parallel to *CD* before it had arrived at *EF* the further side of the refracting Superficies, and so could have gott no nearer to *EF* but must have turned back by further incurvation, and been reflected as it is represented at *Aμuλ*. And the like would have happened, if the density of the æther had further increased from *EF* to *PQ*, so that *PQHG* might be a denser Medium then *EFHG* was supposed; for then the ray in passing from *M* to *N*, being so much incurved as at *N* to become parallel to *CD* or *PQ*, its impossible it should ever gett nearer to *PQ*, but must at *N* begin by further incurvation to turn back and so be reflected. And because if a refracted ray (as *NL*) be made incident, the incident *(AM)* shall become the refracted, and therefore if the ray *Aμν*, after it is arived at *ν*, where I suppose it parallel to the refracting Superficies, should be reflected perpendicularly back, it would returne back in the line of incidence *νμA*. Therefore going forward, it must go forward in such another line *νπλ*, both cases being alike, and so be reflected at an angle equal to that of incidence.

This may be the cause and manner of reflexion when Light tends from the rarer towards the Denser æther: but to know, how it should be reflected when it stands from the denser towards the rarer, you are further to consider, how fluids near their Superficies are less pliant and yeelding then in their more inward parts, and if formed into thin plates or Shells, they become much more Stiff and tenacious then otherwise. Thus things which readily fall in water, if let fall upon a bubble of water,

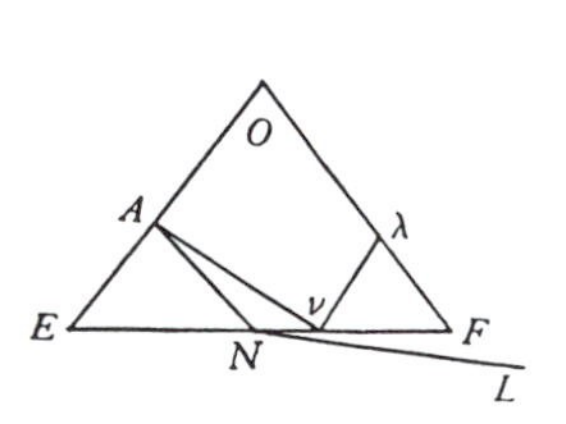

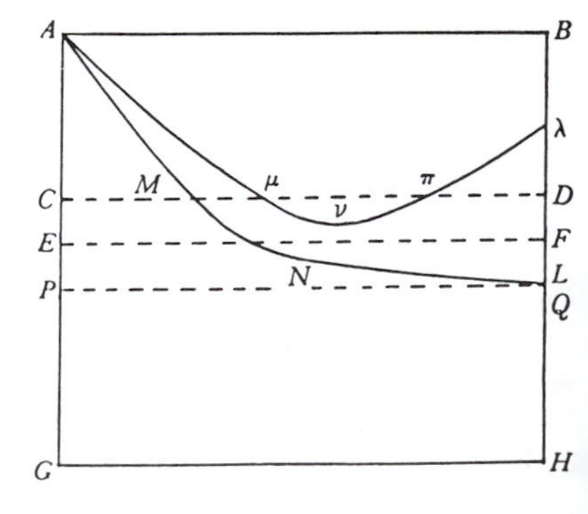

they do not easily break through it, but are apt to Slide downe by the sides of it, if they be not too big and heavy. So if two well-polished convex glasses, ground on very large spheres, be laid one upon another, the Air between them easily recedes, till they almost touch, but then begins to resist so much that the weight of the upper glass is too little to bring them together so as to make the black, mentioned in the other papers I send you, appear in the midst of the rings of colours. And if the glasses be plain, though no broader than a two-pence, a man with his whole strength is not able to press all the air out from between them, so as to make them fully touch. You may observe also, that insects will walk upon water without wetting their feet, and the water bearing them up; also motes falling upon water will often lie long upon it without being wetted: And so, I suppose, æther in the confine of two mediums is less pliant and yielding then in other places, and so much the less pliant by how much the mediums differ in density: so that in passing out of denser æther into rarer, when there remains but a very little of the denser æther to be past through, a ray finds more then ordinary difficulty to get through; and so great difficulty, where the mediums are of very differing density, as to be reflected by incurvation, after the manner described above; the parts of æther on that side, where they are less pliant and yielding, acting upon the ray much after the manner that they would do were they denser there then on the other side: for the resistence of the Medium ought to have the same effect on the ray, from what cause soever it arises. And this, I suppose, may be the cause of the reflexion of Quicksilver and other Metalline bodyes. It must also concurr to increase the reflective virtue of the Superficies when rayes tend out of the rarer Medium into the denser. And in that case therefore the reflexion haveing a double cause ought to be Stronger then in the æther, as it is apparently. But in refraction this rigid tenacity or unpliablenes of the Superficies need not be considered, because so much as the ray is thereby bent in passing to the most tenacious and rigid part of the Superficies, so much it is thereby unbent againe in passing on from thence through the next parts gradually less tenacious.

Thus may rayes be refracted by some Superficies and reflected by others, be the Medium, they tend into, denser or rarer. But it remains further to be explained how rays alike incident on the same Superficies, (suppose of Crystall, Glass or water) may be at the same time some refracted, others reflected. And for explaining this, I suppose, that the rays when they impinge on the rigid resisting æthereall Superficies, as they are acted upon by it, so they react upon it and cause vibrations in it, as stones throwne into water do in its Surface; and that these vibrations are propagated every way into both the rarer and denser Mediums, as the vibrations of Air which cause Sound are from a Stroke, but yet continue Strongest where they began, and alternately contract and dilate the æther in that Physicall Superficies. For its plaine by the heat which light produces in bodies, that it is able to put their parts in motion, and much more to heat and put in motion the more tender æther; and its more probable, that it communicates motion to the gross parts of bodies by the mediation of æther then immediately; as, for instance, in the inward parts of Quicksilver, Tin, Silver, and other very Opake bodyes, by generating vibrations that run through them, then by Striking the Outward parts onely without entring the body. The Shock of every Single ray may generate many thousand vibrations, and by sending them all over the body, move all the parts, and that perhaps with more motion then it could move one Single part by an Imediate Stroke: for the vibrations by Shaking each particle backward and forward may every time increase its motion, as a Ringer does a bells by often pulling it, and so at length move the particles to a very great degree of agitation which neither the Simple Shock of a ray nor any other motion in the æther, besides a vibrating one, could do. Thus in Air shut up in a vessell, the motion of its parts causd by heat, how violent soever, is unable to move the bodyes hung in it, with either a trembling or progressive motion; but if Air be put into a vibrating motion by beating a drum or two, it shakes Glass windowes, the whole body of a man and other massy things, especially those of a congruous tone: Yea I have observed it manifestly shake under my feet a cellar'd free stone floor of a large hall, so as I believe the immediate Stroke of five hundred Drum Sticks could not have done, unless perhaps quickly succeeding one another at equal intervals of time. Æthereal vibrations are therefore the best means by which such a Subtile Agent as Light can Shake the gross particles of Solid bodyes to heat them. And so supposeing that Light impingeing on a refracting or reflecting æthereal Superficies puts it into a vibrating motion; that Physical Superficies being by the perpetual appuls of rays alwayes kept in a vibrating motion, and the æther therein continually expanded and comprest by turnes; if a ray of Light impinge upon it while it is much comprest, I suppose it is then too dense and stiff to let the ray passe through, and so reflects it, but the rayes that impinge on it at other times when it is either expanded by the interval of two vibrations, or not too much comprest and condens'd, go through and are refracted.

These may be the causes of refractions and reflexions in all cases, but for understanding how they come to be so regular, its further to be considered, that as in a heap of Sand, although the Surface be rugged, yet if water be powred on it to fill its pores, that water so soone as its pores are filled, will eavenly overspread the Surface, and so much the more eavenly, as the Sand is finer. So although the Surface of all bodyes, even the most polished, be rugged, as I conceive, yet where that ruggednes is not too grosse and course, the refracting æthereall Superficies may eavenly overspread it. In polishing glasse or metall it is not to be imagined that Sand, Putty or other fretting pouders, should wear the surface so regularly as to make the front of every particle exactly plaine, and all those plaines look the same way, as they ought to do in well polished bodyes, were reflexion performed by their parts: but that those fretting pouders should wear the bodies first to a course ruggednes, such as is sensible, and then to a finer and finer ruggednes, till it be so fine that the Æthereall Superficies eavenly overspreads it, and so makes the body put on the appearance of a polish, is a very naturall and intelligible supposition. So in fluids it is not well to be conceived that the Surfaces of their parts should be all plaine, and the plains of the Superficiall parts always kept looking all the same way, notwithstanding that they are in perpetuall motion: and yet without these two Suppositions, the Superficies of fluids could not be so regularly reflexive as they are, were the reflexion done by the parts themselves and not by an Æthereall Superficies eavenly over Spreading the fluid.

Further concerning the regular motion of Light it might be suspected whether the various vibrations of the fluid through which it passes may not much disturb it; but that suspicion I suppose will vanish by considering that if at any time the foremost part of an oblique wave begin to turne it awry, the hindermost part by a contrary action must soon sett it streight againe.

Lastly because without doubt there are in every transparent body pores of various sizes, and I said, that æther stands at the greatest rarity in the smallest pores; hence the æther in every pore should be of a differing rarity, and so Light be refracted in its passage out of every pore into the next, which would cause a great confusion and spoile the bodyes transparency; but considering that the æther in all dense bodyes is agitated by continual vibrations and these vibrations cannot be performed without forceing the parts of æther forward and backward from one pore to another by a kind of tremor, so that the æther, which one moment is in a greater pore, is the next moment forced into a lesse; and on the contrary; this must eavenly spread the æther into all the pores not exceeding some certaine bigness, suppose the breadth of a vibration and so make it of an even density throughout the transparent body, agreeable to the midle sort of pore. But where the pores exceed a certaine bignesse, I suppose the æther suits its Density to the bignesse of the pore, or to the Medium within it and so being of a divers density from the æther that surrounds it, refracts or reflects light in its Superficies, and so makes the body, where many such interstices are, appeare opake.

Thus much of refraction, reflexion, transparency and opacity. And now to explain colours; I suppose, that as bodyes of various sizes, densities, or tensions, do by percussion or other action excite sounds of various tones and consequently vibrations in the Air of various bignesse so when the rayes of light, by impinging on the stif refracting Superficies excite vibrations in the æther, those rayes, what ever they be, as they happen to differ in magnitude, strength or vigour, excite vibrations of various bignesses; the biggest, strongest or most potent rayes, the largest vibrations and others shorter, according to their bignesse strength or power, And therefore the ends of the Capillamenta of the optique nerve, which pave or face the Retina, being such refracting Superficies, when the rayes impinge upon them, they must there excite these vibrations, which vibrations (like those of Sound in a trunk or trumpet,) will run along the aqueous pores or Crystalline pith of the Capillamenta through the optic Nerves into the sensorium (which Light itself cannot doe,) and there I suppose, affect the sense with various colours according to their bignesse and mixture; the biggest with the strongest colours, Reds and Yellows; the least with the weakest, blews and violets; the midle with green, and a confusion of all, with white, much after the manner, that in the sense of Hearing Nature makes use of aërial vibrations of severall bignesses to generate Sounds of divers tones, for the Analogy of Nature is to be observed. And further, as the harmony and discord of Sounds proceed from the proportions of the aereall vibrations; so may the harmony of some colours, as of a Golden and blew, and the discord of others, as of red and blew proceed from the proportions of the æthereall. And possibly colour may be distinguisht into its principall Degrees, Red, Orange, Yellow, Green, Blew, Indigo, and deep violett, on the same ground, that Sound within an eighth is graduated into tones. For, some years past, the prismatique colours being in a well darkened roome cast perpendicularly upon a paper about two and twenty foot distant from the Prism; I desired a friend to draw with a pencil lines crosse the Image or Pillar of colours where every one of the seven aforenamed colours was most full and brisk, and also where he judged the truest confines of them to be, whilst I held the paper so that the said Image might fall within a certaine compass marked on it. And this I did, partly because my owne eyes are not very criticall in distinguishing colours, partly because another, to whome I had not communicated my thoughts about this matter, could have nothing but his eyes to determin his fancy in makeing those marks. This observation we repeated divers times, both in the same and divers days to see how the marks on severall papers would agree, and comparing the Observations, though the just confines of the colours are hard to be Assigned, because they passe into one another by insensible gradation; yet the *differences* of the Observations were but little, especially towards the red end, and takeing meanes between those differences that were the length of the Image (reckoned not by the distance of the verges of the Semicircular ends but by the distance of the Centers of those Semicircles, or length of the Streight Sides as it ought to be) was divided in about the same proportion that a String is, between the end and the midle, to Sound the tones in an eight. You will understand me best by viewing the annexed figure, in which *AB* and *CD* represent the Streight Sides about tenn inches long, *APC* and *BTD* the Semicircular ends, x and y the Centers of those Semicircles, xz the length of a Musical String double to xy, and divided between *x* and *y*, so as to sound the tones exprest at the side, (that is *xH* the half, *xG* and *GI* the third part, *yK* the fift part, *yM* the eighth part, and *GE* the ninth part of *xy*;) and the intervals between these divisions express the spaces which the colours written there took up, every

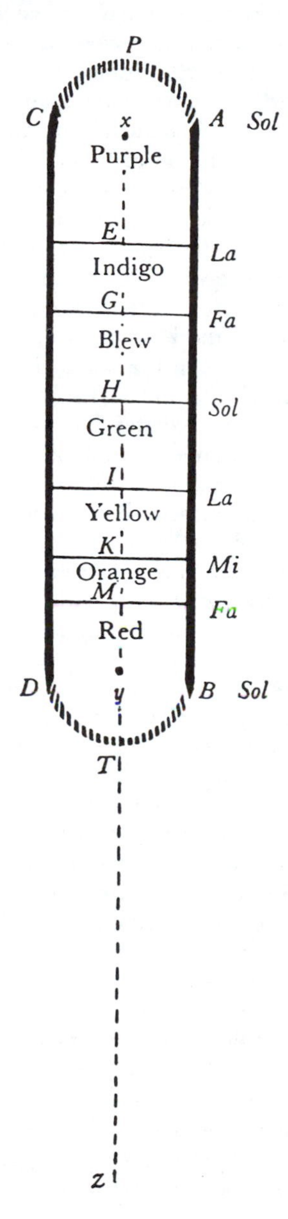

colour being most briskly specific in the midle of those spaces.

Now for the cause of these and such like colours made by refraction, the biggest or strongest rayes must penetrate the refracting superficies more freely and easily then the weaker, and so be less turned awry by it, that is, lesse refracted; which is as much as to say, the rays which make red, are least refrangible, those which make blew and violet most refrangible, and others otherwise refrangible according to their colour. Whence if the rayes which come promiscuously from the Sunn, be refracted by a Prism, as in the aforesaid experiment, those of *severall sorts* being variously refracted must go to severall places on an opposite paper or wall and so parted, exhibit every one their owne colours, which they could not do while blended together. And because refraction onely *severs* them, and *changes* not the bignesse or strength of the ray, thence it is, that after they are once well severed, refraction cannot make any further changes in their colour.

On this ground may all the Phænomena of *Refractions* be understood. But to explaine the colours, made by *Reflexions* I must further suppose, that, though light be unimaginably swift, yet the Æthereall Vibrations excited by a ray move faster then the ray it self, and so overtake and outrun it one after another. And this I suppose they will think an allowable supposition, who have been inclined to suspect that these vibrations themselves might be light. But to make it the more allowable, it's possible light it self may not be so swift as some are apt to think, for notwithstanding any argument that I know yet to the contrary it may be an houre or two, if not more in moveing from the sunn to us.[4] This celerity of the vibrations therefore supposed, if light be incident on a thin Skin or plate of any transparent body, the waves excited by its passage through the first Superficies, overtakeing it one after another, till it arrive at the second Superficies, will cause it to be there reflected or refracted accordingly as the condensed or expanded part of the wave overtakes it there to compres or relax that physical superficies and thereby augment or diminish its reflecting power. If the plate be of such a thicknesse, that the condensed part of the first wave overtake the ray at the second Superficies, it must be reflected there; if double that thicknesse that the following rarefied part of the wave, that is, the space between that and the next wave, overtake it, *there* it must be transmitted; if triple the thicknesse that the condensed part of the second wave overtake it, *there* it must be reflected, and so where the Plate is 5. 7. or 9 times that thickness it must be reflected by reason of the third fourth or fift wave overtakeing it at the second Superficies; but when it is 4. 6. or 8. times that thicknesse, so that the ray may be overtaken there by the dilated interval of those waves, it shall be *transmitted*, and so on; the second Superficies being made able or unable to reflect accordingly as it

4. A few years after Newton wrote this, the Danish astronomer Roemer made the first measurement of the velocity of light from astronomical phenomena.

is condensed or expanded by the waves. For instance, let *AH* represent the Superficies of a Spherically convex glass laid upon a plain Glass *AIR*, and *AIRQH* the thin plano-concave plate of Air between them, and *BC*, *DE*, *FG*, *HI* etc, thicknesses of that plate or distances of the Glasses in the Arithmetical Progression of the Numbers 1. 2. 3. 4 etc. whereof *BC* is the distance at which the ray is overtaken by the most condensed part of the first wave: I say, the rays incident at *B*, *F*, *K*, and *O* ought to be reflected at *C*, *G*, *L* and *P*, and those incident at *D*, *H*, *M*, and *Q* ought to be transmitted at *E*, *I*, *N* and *R*; and this, because the Ray *BC* arrives at the Superficies *AC* when it is condensed by the first wave that overtakes it; *DE*, when rarefied by the interval of the first and second; *FG*, when condensed by the second wave; *HI*, when rarified by the interval of the second and third, and so on for an indeterminate number of successions; and at A, the center or contact of the Glasses, the light must be transmitted, because there the æthereall Mediums in both glasses are continued as if but one uniforme Medium. Whence, if the Glasses in this posture be looked upon, there ought to appear at A, the contact of the Glasses, a black Spott, and about that many concentric circles of light and darknesse, the squares of whose semidiameters are to sense in arithmetical progression. Yet all the rayes without exception ought not to be thus reflected or transmitted: for sometimes a ray

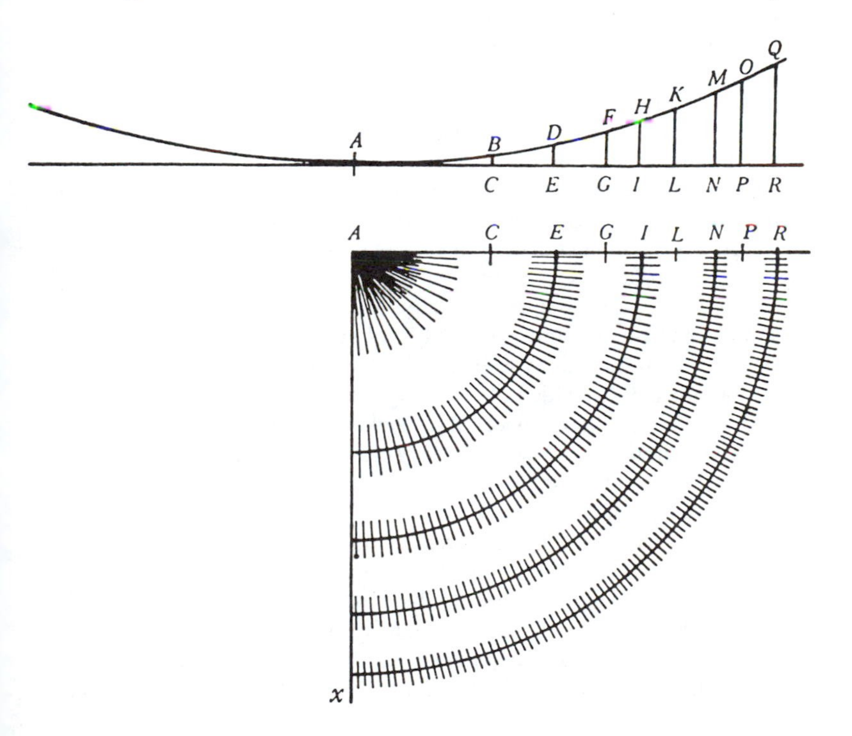

may be overtaken at the second superficies by the vibrations raised by another collaterall or imediately succeeding ray; which vibration, being as strong or stronger then its owne, may cause it to be reflected or transmitted when its owne vibration alone would do the contrary. And hence some little light will be reflected from the black rings which makes them rather black then totally dark; and some transmitted at the lucid Rings, which makes the black rings, appearing on the other side of the Glasses, not so black as they would otherwise be. And so at the Central black spot, where the glasses do not absolutely touch, a little light will be reflected, which makes the spot darkest in the midle and onely black at the verges. For thus I have observed it to be, by tyeing very hard together two Glasse Prisms which were accidentally (one of them at least) a very little convex, and viewing by divers lights this black spot at their contact. If a white paper was placed at a little distance behind a Candle and the Candle and paper viewed alternately by reflexion from the spot; the verges of the spot, which lookt by the light of the paper as black as the midle part, appeared by the stronger light of the candle lucid enough, so as to make the spot seem less then before; but the midle part continued as absolutely black in one case as in the other, some specks and streaks in it onely excepted, where I suppose the glasses through some uneveness in the polish did not fully touch. The same I have observed by viewing the spot by the like reflexion of the Sun and cloudes alternatly.

But to returne to the lucid and black Rings, those rings ought alwayes to appear after the manner described, were light uniforme. And after that manner, when the two contiguous glasses *AQ* and *AR* have been illustrated, in a dark room, by light of any uniforme colour made by a Prism. I have seen the lucid circles appear to about twenty in number with a many darke ones between them, the colour of the lucid ones being that of the light, with which the Glasses were illustrated. And if the glasses were held between the eye and the Prismatic colours, cast on a sheet of white paper, or if any Prismatic colour was directly trajected through the glasses to a sheet of paper placed a little way behind, there would appeare such other Rings of colour and darknesse (in the first case, between the glasses, in the second, on the paper,) oppositely corresponding to those which appeared by reflexion: I meane, that, whereas by *reflected* light there appeared a black spot in the midle, and then a coloured circle; on the contrary by *transmitted* light there appeared a coloured spot in the midle, and then a black circle; and so on; the diameters of the coloured Circles, made by transmission, equalling the diameters of the black ones made by reflexion.

Thus, I say, the rings do and ought to appeare when made by *uniforme* light, but in *compound* light it is otherwise. For the rayes, which exhibit red and yellow, exciting, as I said, larger pulses in the æther then those which make blew and violet, and consequently makeing bigger circles in a certaine proportion, as I have manifestly found they do, by illuminating the glasses successively by the aforesaid colours of Prism in a well darkened room, without changing the position of my eye or of the glasses; hence the circles, made by illustrating the Glasses with white Light, ought not to appeare black and white by turnes, as the Circles made by illustrating the Glasses, for instance, with red light, appeare red and black; but the colours which compound the white light must display themselves by being reflected, the blew and violet nearer to the center then the red and yellow, whereby every Lucid circle must become violet in the inward verge, red in the outward, and of intermediate colours in the intermediate parts, and be made broader then before, spreading its colours both wayes into those spaces which I call the black rings, and which would here appear black, were the red, yellow, blew and violet, which make the verge of the Rings, taken out of the incident white light which illustrates the glasses, and the green only left to make the lucid Rings. Suppose *CB*, *GD*, *LF*, *PM*, *RN*, *SX*, represent Quadrants of the Circles made in a dark room of the very deepest prismatic red alone; and $\eta\beta$, $\gamma\delta$, $\lambda\phi$, $\pi\mu$, $\rho\nu$, $\sigma\xi$, the Quadrants of like circles made also in a dark room by the very deepest prismatic violet alone; and then, if the glasses be illuminated by open day-light, in which all sorts of rayes are blended,

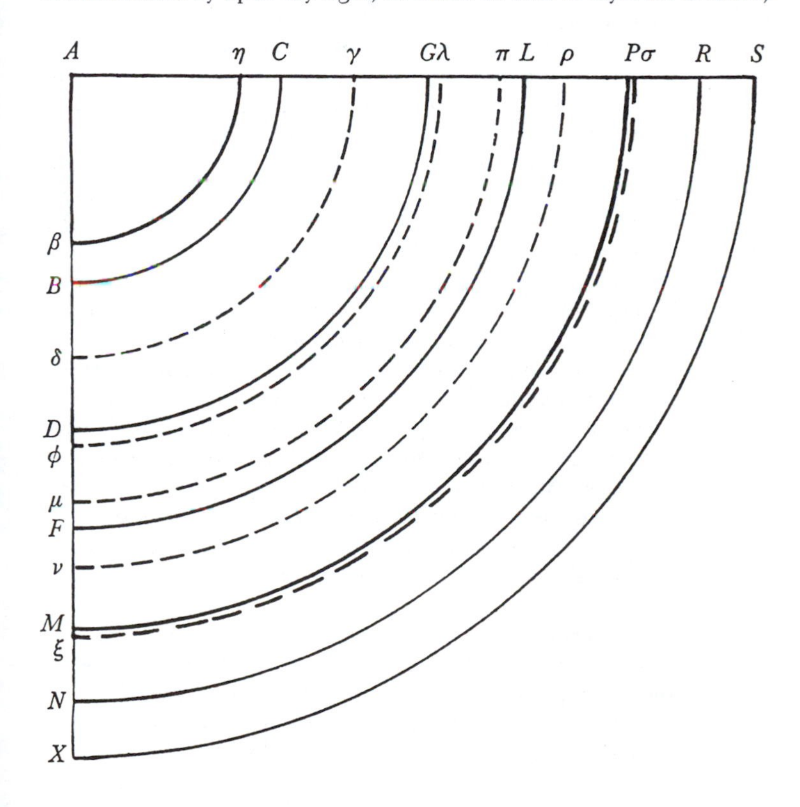

its manifest, that the first lucid ring will be $\eta\beta BC$; the second $\gamma\delta DG$, the third $\lambda\phi FL$, the fourth $\pi\mu MP$, the fift $\rho\nu$NR, the sixt $\sigma\xi XS$ etc: in all which the deepest violet must be reflected at the inward edges represented by the prickt lines, where it would be reflected were it alone, and the deepest red at the outward edges represented by the black lines where it would be reflected were it alone, and all intermediate colours at those places in order between these edges at which they would be reflected were they alone; each of them in a dark room parted from all other colours by the refraction of a Prism. And because the Squares of the Semidiameters of the Outward verges AC, AG, AL, etc. as also of Aη, Aγ, Aλ, etc. the Semidiameters of the inward are in arithmetical progression of the numbers 1, 3, 5, 7, 9, 11, etc and the squares of the inward are to the squares of the outward (Aη^q to AC^q, Aγ^q to AG^q, Aλ^q to AL^q, etc.) as 9 to 14 (as I have found by measuring them carefully and often, and compareing the Observations;) therefore the outward *red* verge of the Second Ring, and inward *violet* one of the third, shall border upon one another (as you may know by computation and see them represented on the figure) and the like edges of the third and fourth rings shall interfere, and those of the fourth and fifth interfere more, and so on. Yea the colours of every ring must spread themselves something more both wayes then is here represented, because the quadrantall arcs here described represent not the verges but the midle of the rings made in a darke room by the extreame violet and red; the *violet* falling on both sides the prickt arches, and red on both sides the black line arches. And hence it is, that these Rings or circuits of colours succeed one another continually without any intervening black, and that the colours are pure onely in the three or four first rings, and then interfereing and mixing more and more, dilute one another so much, that after 8 or 9 rings they are no more to be distinguisht, but seem to constitute an even whitenesse; whereas when they were made in a darke room by one of the Prismatic colours alone, I have, as I said, seen above twenty of them, and without doubt could have seen them to a greater Number, had I taken the paines to make the Prismatic colour more uncompounded. For by unfolding these rings from one another by certaine refractions exprest in the other papers I send you, I have even in day light, discovered them to above a hundred, and perhaps they would have appeared innumerable, had the light or colour illustrating the glasses been absolutely uncompounded, and the pupill of my eye but a Mathematical point, so that all the rayes, which come from the same point of the glasse might have gone into my eye at the same obliquity to the Glasse.

What has been hitherto said of these Rings, is to be understood of their appearance to an unmoved eye, but if you vary the position of the eye, the more obliquely you look on the glasse, the larger the rings appear. And of this the reason may be, *partly* that an oblique ray is longer in passing through the first Superficies and so there is more time between the waveing forward and backward of that Superficies and consequently a larger wave generated, and *partly* that the wave in creeping along between the two Superficies may be impeded and retarded by the rigidnesse of those Superficies bounding it at either end, and so not overtake the ray so soone as a wave that moves perpendicularly crosse.

The bignesse of the circles made by every colour, and at all obliquities of the eye to the glasses, and the thickness of the Air or intervalls of the glasses, where each circle is made, you will find exprest in the other papers I send you: where also I have more at large described, how much these Rings interfere or spread into one another; what colours appear in every ring; where they are most lively, where and how much diluted by mixing with the colours of other Rings; and how the contrary colours appear on the back side of the Glasses by the transmitted light, the glasses transmitting light of one colour at the same place where they reflect that of another. Nor need I add any thing further of the colours of other thinly plated Mediums, as of water between the aforesaid Glasses, or formed into bubles and so encompassed with Air; or of glass blowne into very thin bubles at a lamp furnace, etc, the case being the same in all these, excepting that, where the thicknesse of the plate is not regular, the rings will not be so, that in plates of denser transparent bodyes the rings are made at a lesse thicknesse of the plate, (the vibrations I suppose being shorter in rarer æther then in denser) and that in a denser plate, surrounded with a rarer body the colours are more vivid then in the rarer surrounded with the Denser; as, for instance, more vivid in a plate of glasse surrounded with Air, then in a plate of Air surrounded with Glass; of which the reason is that the reflexion of the second Superficies, which causes the colours, is, as was said above, stronger in the former case then in the latter: for which reason also the colours are most vivid, when the difference of the density of the Medium is greatest.

Of the colours of Naturall bodyes also I have said enough in those papers, shewing how the various sizes of the transparent particles, of which they consist, is sufficient to produce them all, those particles reflecting or transmitting this or that sort of rayes according to their thicknesse, like the aforesaid plates, as if they were fragments thereof. For, I suppose, if a plate of an eaven thicknesse, and consequently of an uniform colour were broaken into fragments of the same thicknesse with the plate, a heap of those fragments would be a powder much of the same colour with the plates. And so if the parts be of the thicknesse of the water in the black spott at the top of a buble described in the 17th of the Observations I send you, I suppose the body must be black. In the production of which blacknes I suppose, that the particles of that size being disposed to reflect almost no light outward, but to refract it continually in its passage from every part to the next, by this multitude of refractions the rays are kept so long stragling to and fro within the body, till at last almost all impinge on the solid parts of the body, and so are stop't and stifled: those parts haveing no sufficient elasticity or other disposition to returne nimbly enough the smart shock of the ray back upon it.

* * *

De Aere et Aethere †

Chapter 1. On Air

In writing about the nature of things, I begin with heavenly bodies and among them with the one most available to the senses, to wit, the air, in order that I may follow where the senses lead. Among the properties of air its great rarefaction and condensation are remarkable. Of these there are three chief causes: expansion, compression, heat and the proximity of bodies. The former accounts for the rest, and for the whole nature of air, and it may be demonstrated in several ways. As first that water ascends within a very narrow pipe whose lower end is immersed in stagnating water higher than the external level, and ascends the higher in proportion to the narrowness of the pipe, so that it will rise several inches in the narrowest pipes. This is a thing that does not happen when the water and the pipe are placed in an exhausted glass vessel.[1] And next, that when a glass jar filled with compressed ashes stands with its mouth immersed in stagnating water, it imbibes much of the water although no air escapes. And again, that water rises spontaneously in that paper or sheet of which filters are made. A rope, even when stretched by a heavy weight, is so swollen by the force of the absorption of water that the weight is lifted up. And those who philosophize rightly know that all of these effects occur because the air seeks to avoid the pores or intervals between the parts of these bodies; and so, since in these pores the air is more rare than in wider spaces, the water can penetrate into them, the air in the pores pressing the surface of the incoming water less than the external atmosphere presses the surface of the stagnant water, and thus not sustaining the pressure of the external air. For this reason standing water creeps little by little up the sides of vessels, the air withdrawing from their sides; and water commonly clings to the surface of all substances, or as we ordinarily say, wets everything. And lastly this rarefaction of air in the neighbourhood of bodies reveals itself by the refraction of light. For light being admitted into a very dark

† A. Rupert Hall and Marie Boas Hall, *Unpublished Scientific Papers of Isaac Newton* (Cambridge: Cambridge University Press, 1962), pp. 221–28. Reprinted with the permission of Cambridge University Press. "De aere et aethere" is the title drawn together from the titles of the two chapters of an undated manuscript that Newton composed around 1679. He left the essay unfinished, just as you find it here. The original is in Latin.

1. Compare the different treatment of this phenomenon in Query 31, written some twenty-five to thirty years later.

room through the hole A, and the image of the sun thrown to a great distance from the convex lens *B*, if you intercept all the light where the beam is the twentieth or thirtieth or fortieth part of an inch wide on the parallel sharp edges of two or more wedges *C*, *D*, placed there, you will see the image somewhat deflected from *E* towards *F* on account of the refraction which the light undergoes in passing through the rarefied medium close to the edges of the wedges.

Moreover air does not only seek to avoid bodies, but bodies also tend to fly from each other. For if you place upon a somewhat convex lens, very highly polished, such as the objective of a very long telescope, a second lens which is smaller, plane, and equally well polished, you will find that some effort is required to bring them into contact, and that when the pressure is removed they will spring apart spontaneously, the more so as the upper lens is less heavy; for you will see several coloured concentric circles appear as the pressure is applied, and finally a black spot at their centre which is the indication of complete contact at that spot, then begun; when the pressure is removed that spot and the colours then vanish in the reverse order from that of their appearance. When plane glasses are used, even though they are not more than half an inch wide, you can so compress them that the colours appear, but the whole strength of one man is scarcely or not quite sufficient to bring them into complete contact, so that the black spot appears. However, the intervening air because of the minuteness of the space becomes so rare that where the colours have appeared the glasses cannot be separated without the use of considerable force. The external air exerts a greater pressure than the internal air, with its elastic force weakened by rarefaction, is able to overcome. In the same way the parts of glass, steel or any broken body cannot even when pressed with the greatest force be reduced to their former contact so that they cohere as before, for were complete contact restored without doubt their cohesion would be restored also. Further, lead and tin when melted and poured into an iron vessel do

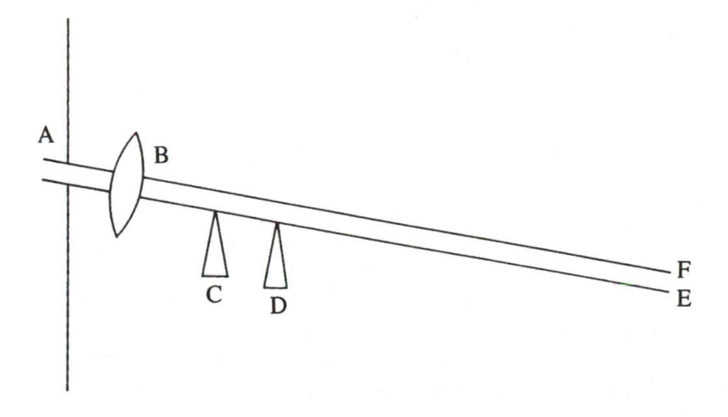

not attain contact in such a way that the casting adheres to the iron. Also powders floating on liquids avoid contact with the liquid and are submerged with difficulty even when they are fairly heavy, like filings of metal. Similarly, flies and other small creatures are wont to walk on the yielding surface of water without wetting their feet. Lastly, if the particles of any powder even though they seem to lie one upon another did fully touch they would cohere strongly, as they do when they are brought into contact by moistening with water and then drying.

Many opinions may be offered concerning the cause of this repulsion. The intervening medium may give way with difficulty or not suffer itself to be much compressed. Or God may have created a certain incorporeal nature which seeks to repel bodies and make them less packed together. Or it may be in the nature of bodies not only to have a hard and impenetrable nucleus but also to have a certain surrounding sphere of most fluid and tenuous matter which admits other bodies into it with difficulty. About these matters I do not dispute at all. But as it is equally true that air avoids bodies, and bodies repel each other mutually, I seem to gather rightly from this that air is composed of the particles of bodies torn away from contact, and repelling each other with a certain large force. Or lastly it may be that two or more of these causes sometimes operate together. About these matters I dispute not at all. Upon this foundation all the properties of air are easily understood.

In just the same remarkable manner air rarefies and is condensed according to the degree of pressure. The whole weight of the incumbent atmosphere by which the air here close to the Earth is compressed is known to philosophers from the Torricellian experiment, and Hooke proved by experiment that the double or treble weight compresses air into the half or third of its space, and conversely that under a half or a third or even a hundredth or a thousandth part of that normal weight the air is expanded to double or treble or even a hundred or a thousand times its normal space, which would hardly seem to be possible if the particles of air were in mutual contact; but if by some principle acting at a distance the particles tend to recede mutually from each other, reason persuades us that when the distance between their centres is doubled the force of recession will be halved, when trebled the force is reduced to a third and so on, and thus by an easy computation it is discovered that the expansion of the air is reciprocal to the compressive force.

Moreover we need not wonder that air is expanded by heat if we consider that its parts when agitated by heat must vibrate, and, by vibrating, propel hither and thither the neighbouring parts. Suppose A, *B*, *C*, three particles in a state of rest, and if *B* is set in motion by heat towards A, as far as the point *R*, it drives A away to a greater distance and, by the same action in reverse springing back towards S, drives away C and so on, *B* alternately repelling A and C with a vibrating motion and A and

A *B* *C*
R *S*

C similarly repelling their neighbouring particles so that all are scattered through a wider space proportionate to the quantity of motion. It is not necessary, however, that this vibration (of which I suppose heat to consist) should always be in a straight line, for the particles may revolve in curves. Nor need the rarefaction through heat arise only from this vibratory motion, for the motion . . .

On the same principle the undulatory motion by which sounds are propagated is easily explained. For suppose A the centre of the undulation, and that the particles A, *B*, *C*, *D*, *E*, *F*, vibrate along the lines *Aa*, *Bb*, *Cc*, *Dd*, etc. so that when A is at A, *B* is in the middle of *Bb*, *C* at c, *D* in the middle of *Dd* and *E* at *E*, and the greatest expansions of the air will be at the midpoints of *Bb* and *Ff*, and the greatest contractions at the midpoints but. . . .

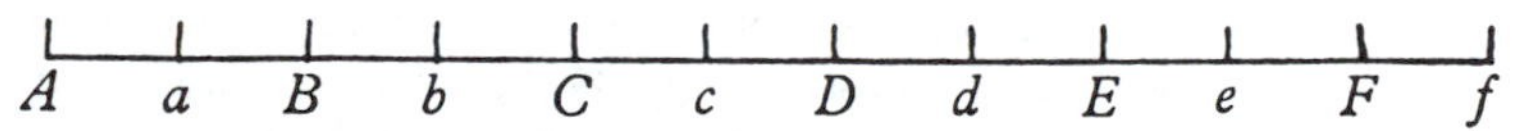

Furthermore, that air although fluid and subtle seems to creep through the pores of bodies with greater difficulty than water or oil, so that it may be contained in a bladder which a liquid easily pervades, results from the fact that its particles, keeping their distance from all others, are reluctant to approach the sides of the pores. They are indeed very small; but as to the faculty of permeating narrow places, their subtlety ought to be estimated from the whole sphere which each claims for itself. And thus it is that air is not at all inclined to any motion except the before-mentioned continuous vibration and that it is very difficult to force it out from the space between two smooth marble or glass surfaces, or when forced out to admit it again. For if a particle *a* situated in any imperceptible cavity *e* cannot move outwards unless by approaching nearer the sides of the cavity, and *b* cannot go out except by approaching

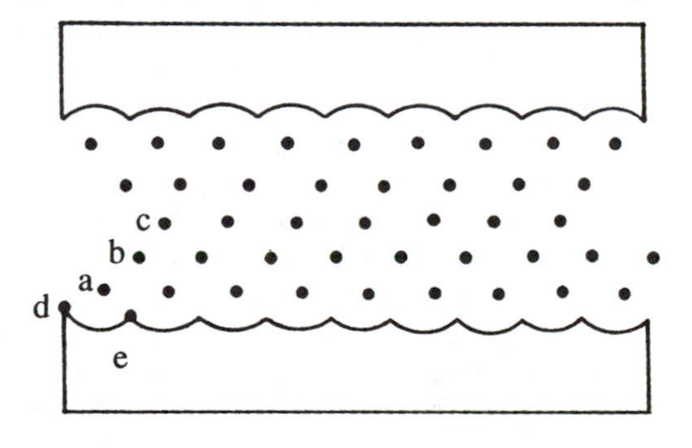

near *a*, nor *c* unless by approaching nearer *b* than their mutual force of repulsion permits; it is necessary that they adhere and that they keep all the remaining ones within enclosed, unless they are expelled as grindings by the sliding motion of the upper marble on the lower one. Whence it is that solid bodies are scarcely brought to full contact unless by fusion, and particles of powder scarcely except by infusion in water and evaporation; yet when at last brought into contact they cohere most strongly, compressed by the surrounding air, to say nothing now of the similar force of the aether.

Lastly, from these principles the generation of air is easily learned. For this nothing else is required save a certain action or motion which tears apart the small parts of bodies; since when separated they mutually flee from one another, like the other particles of air. And thus it is that every vehement agitation (like friction, fermentation, ignition and great heat) generates the aerial substance which reveals itself in liquids by ebullition; and the more vehement the action the more copiously that substance is generated. So filings of lead, brass, or iron dissolved in Aqua Fortis produce a great ebullition; these, however, dissolve without ebullition in vinegar or in the same Aqua Fortis sufficiently weakened by mixing with water. So nitre, melted and ignited by charcoal thrown upon it, emits much of the aerial substance, with much fixed salt remaining in the bottom; but if the action of the fire is hastened by the due admixture of sulphur and charcoal as is used in making gunpowder, almost all the substance of the mixt is changed by vehement agitation into an aerial form, the huge force of this powder arising from its sudden expansion, as is the nature of air. Moreover, aerial substances are very different according to the nature of the bodies from which they are generated. Metals by corrosion give true permanent air; vegetable and animal substances by corrosion, fermentation or burning give an air of short duration like an exhalation; and volatile substances rarefied by heat give an air least lasting of all, which we call a vapour. Among these there are great differences, the vapour of water condenses more quickly than the vapour of spirit of wine and the vapour of certain saline spirits, and more quickly than the vapour of water; as in the vapour of the sea where the spirit of salt condenses only when rising to the height of a few feet, and makes the air there thicker and less transparent and leaves behind the sweet vapour of water. There is a diversity in the weight of air, for air generated by the force of fire from vegetable and animal substances is so much lighter than the rest of the surrounding air that not only does it not descend itself but it also carries away the associated thicker fumes with it. So vapours of every kind seek to rise above the rest of the air—i.e., the atmosphere. And there is no doubt but that vapours and exhalations have various degrees of gravity; for there appear to be as many kinds of air as there are of substances on the Earth from which its origin comes. So the atmosphere is composed of many kinds of air, which nevertheless can be divided into three chief kinds: vapours, which arising from liquids seem to be the least permanent and the lightest; exhalations, which arise from thicker and more fixed substances, especially in the vegetable kingdom, are of a middle nature; and air properly so called whose permanence and gravity are indications that it is nothing else than a collection of metallic particles which subterranean corrosions daily disperse from each other. This is confirmed by the fact that this latter air serves (as the almost indestructible nature of metals demands) neither for the preservation of fire nor for the use of animals in breathing, as do serve some of the exhalations arising from the softer substances of vegetable matter or salts.

Chapter 2. On the Aether

And just as bodies of this Earth by breaking into small particles are converted into air, so these particles can be broken into lesser ones by some violent action and converted into yet more subtle air which, if it is subtle enough to penetrate the pores of glass, crystal and other terrestrial bodies, we may call the spirit of air, or the aether. That such spirits exist is shown by the experiments of Boyle in which metals, fused in a hermetically sealed glass for such a time that part is converted into calx, become heavier. It is clear that the increase is from a most subtle saline spirit which, coming through the pores of the glass, calcines the metal and turns it into calx. And that in a glass empty of air a pendulum preserves its oscillatory motion not much longer than in the open air, although that motion ought not to cease unless, when the air is exhausted, there remains in the glass something much more subtle which damps the motion of the bob. I believe everyone who sees iron filings arranged into curved lines like meridians by effluvia circulating from pole to pole of the [load-]stone will acknowledge that these magnetic effluvia are of this kind. So also the attraction of glass, amber, jet, wax and resin and similar substances seems to be caused in the same way by a most tenuous matter of this kind. . . .

Queries 1–7 and 31 †

Query 1. Do not Bodies act upon Light at a distance, and by their action bend its Rays; and is not this action *(cæteris paribus)* strongest at the least distance?

† Isaac Newton, *Opticks*, based on the 4th ed. (New York: Dover Publications, 1952), pp. 339–40, 375–406. Reprinted by permission of Dover Publications, Inc. Newton first published the *Opticks* in 1704, with sixteen Queries at the end. He used the word *query* to distinguish these speculations on the nature of things from the contents of the book, which he considered as firm demonstrations based on experiments. Two years later, a Latin edition added seven more Queries, including the one now numbered 31, although it did not have that number in 1706.

Qu. 2. Do not the Rays which differ in Refrangibility differ also in Flexibity; and are they not by their different Inflexions separated from one another, so as after separation to make the Colours in the three Fringes above described? And after what manner are they inflected to make those Fringes?

Qu. 3. Are not the Rays of Light in passing by the edges and sides of Bodies, bent several times backwards and forwards, with a motion like that of an Eel? And do not the three Fringes of colour'd Light above-mention'd arise from three such bendings?

Qu. 4. Do not the Rays of Light which fall upon Bodies, and are reflected or refracted, begin to bend before they arrive at the Bodies; and are they not reflected, refracted, and inflected, by one and the same Principle, acting variously in various Circumstances?

Qu. 5. Do not Bodies and Light act mutually upon one another; that is to say, Bodies upon Light in emitting, reflecting, refracting and inflecting it, and Light upon Bodies for heating them, and putting their parts into a vibrating motion wherein heat consists?

Qu. 6. Do not black Bodies conceive heat more easily from Light than those of other Colours do, by reason that the Light falling on them is not reflected outwards, but enters the Bodies, and is often reflected and refracted within them, until it be stifled and lost?

Qu. 7. Is not the strength and vigor of the action between Light and sulphureous Bodies observed above, one reason why sulphureous Bodies take fire more readily, and burn more vehemently than other Bodies do?

Quest. 31. Have not the small Particles of Bodies certain Powers, Virtues, or Forces, by which they act at a distance, not only upon the Rays of Light for reflecting, refracting, and inflecting them, but also upon one another for producing a great Part of the Phænomena of Nature? For it's well known, that Bodies act one upon another by the Attractions of Gravity, Magnetism, and Electricity; and these Instances shew the Tenor and Course of Nature, and make it not improbable but that there may be more attractive Powers than these. For Nature is very consonant and conformable to her self. How these Attractions may be perform'd, I do not here consider. What I call Attraction may be perform'd by impulse, or by some other means unknown to me. I use that Word here to signify only in general any Force by which Bodies tend towards one another, whatsoever be the Cause. For we must learn from the Phænomena of Nature what Bodies attract one another, and what are the Laws and Properties of the Attraction, before we enquire the Cause by which the Attraction is perform'd. The Attractions of Gravity, Magnetism, and Electricity, reach to very sensible distances, and so have been observed by vulgar Eyes, and there may be others which reach to so small distances as hitherto escape Observation; and perhaps electrical Attraction may reach to such small distances, even without being excited by Friction.

For when Salt of Tartar runs *per Deliquium*, is not this done by an Attraction between the Particles of the Salt of Tartar, and the Particles of the Water which float in the Air in the form of Vapours? And why does not common Salt, or Salt-petre, or Vitriol, run *per Deliquium*, but for want of such an Attraction? Or why does not Salt of Tartar draw more Water out of the Air than in a certain Proportion to its quantity, but for want of an attractive Force after it is satiated with Water? And whence is it but from this attractive Power that Water which alone distils with a gentle luke-warm Heat, will not distil from Salt of Tartar without a great Heat? And is it not from the like attractive Power between the Particles of Oil of Vitriol and the Particles of Water, that Oil of Vitriol draws to it a good quantity of Water out of the Air, and after it is satiated draws no more, and in Distillation lets go the Water very difficultly? And when Water and Oil of Vitriol poured successively into the same Vessel grow very hot in the mixing, does not this Heat argue a great Motion in the Parts of the Liquors? And does not this Motion argue, that the Parts of the two Liquors in mixing coalesce with Violence, and by consequence rush towards one another with an accelerated Motion? And when *Aqua fortis*, or Spirit of Vitriol poured upon Filings of Iron dissolves the Filings with a great Heat and Ebullition, is not this Heat and Ebullition effected by a violent Motion of the Parts, and does not that Motion argue that the acid Parts of the Liquor rush towards the Parts of the Metal with violence, and run forcibly into its Pores till they get between its outmost Particles, and the main Mass of the Metal, and surrounding those Particles loosen them from the main Mass, and set them at liberty to float off into the Water? And when the acid Particles, which alone would distil with an easy Heat, will not separate from the Particles of the Metal without a very violent Heat, does not this confirm the Attraction between them?

When Spirit of Vitriol poured upon common Salt or Salt-petre makes an Ebullition with the Salt, and unites with it, and in Distillation the Spirit of the common Salt or Salt-petre comes over much easier than it would do before, and the acid part of the Spirit of Vitriol stays behind; does not this argue that the fix'd Alcaly of the Salt attracts the acid Spirit of the Vitriol more strongly than its own Spirit, and not being able to hold them both, lets go its own? And when Oil of Vitriol is drawn off from its weight of Nitre, and from both the Ingredients a compound Spirit of Nitre is distilled, and two parts of this Spirit are poured on one part of Oil of Cloves or Carraway Seeds, or of any ponderous Oil of vegetable or animal Substances, or Oil of Turpentine thicken'd with a little Balsam of Sulphur, and the Liquors grow so very hot in mixing, as presently to send up a burning Flame; does not this very great and sudden Heat argue that the two Liquors mix with violence, and that their Parts in mixing run towards one another with an accelerated Motion, and clash with the greatest Force? And is it not for the same reason that well rectified Spirit of Wine poured on the same compound Spirit flashes; and that the *Pulvis fulminans*, composed of Sulphur, Nitre, and Salt of Tartar, goes off with a more sudden and violent Explosion than Gun-powder, the acid Spirits of the Sulphur and Nitre rushing towards one another, and towards the Salt of Tartar, with so great a violence, as by the shock to turn the whole at once into Vapour and Flame? Where the Dissolution is slow, it makes a slow Ebullition and a gentle Heat; and where it is quicker, it makes a greater Ebullition with more heat; and where it is done at once, the Ebullition is contracted into a sudden Blast or violent Explosion, with a heat equal to that of Fire and Flame. So when a Drachm of the above-mention'd compound Spirit of Nitre was poured upon half a Drachm of Oil of Carraway Seeds *in vacuo*, the Mixture immediately made a flash like Gun-powder, and burst the exhausted Receiver, which was a Glass six Inches wide, and eight Inches deep. And even the gross Body of Sulphur powder'd, and with an equal weight of Iron Filings and a little Water made into Paste, acts upon the Iron, and in five or six hours grows too hot to be touch'd, and emits a Flame. And by these Experiments compared with the great quantity of Sulphur with which the Earth abounds, and the warmth of the interior Parts of the Earth, and hot Springs, and burning Mountains, and with Damps, mineral Coruscations, Earthquakes, hot suffocating Exhalations, Hurricanes, and Spouts; we may learn that sulphureous Steams abound in the Bowels of the Earth and ferment with Minerals, and sometimes take fire with a sudden Coruscation and Explosion; and if pent up in subterraneous Caverns, burst the Caverns with a great shaking of the Earth, as in springing of a Mine.[1] And then the Vapour generated by the Explosion, expiring through the Pores of the Earth, feels hot and suffocates, and makes Tempests and Hurricanes, and sometimes causes the Land to slide, or the Sea to boil, and carries up the Water thereof in Drops, which by their weight fall down again in Spouts. Also some sulphureous Steams, at all times when the Earth is dry, ascending into the Air, ferment there with nitrous Acids, and sometimes taking fire cause Lightning and Thunder, and fiery Meteors. For the Air abounds with acid Vapours fit to promote Fermentations, as appears by the rusting of Iron and Copper in it, the kindling of Fire by blowing, and the beating of the Heart by means of Respiration. Now the above-mention'd Motions are so great and violent as to shew that in Fermentations the Particles of Bodies which almost rest, are put into new Motions by a very potent Principle, which acts upon them only when they approach one another, and causes them to meet and clash with great violence, and grow hot with the motion, and dash one another into pieces, and vanish into Air, and Vapour, and Flame.

1. A charge of explosive placed under enemy fortifications by tunneling. To "spring" a mine meant to explode it.

When Salt of Tartar *per deliquium*, being poured into the Solution of any Metal, precipitates the Metal and makes it fall down to the bottom of the Liquor in the form of Mud: Does not this argue that the acid Particles are attracted more strongly by the Salt of Tartar than by the Metal, and by the stronger Attraction go from the Metal to the Salt of Tartar? And so when a Solution of Iron in *Aqua fortis* dissolves the *Lapis Calaminaris*, and lets go the Iron, or a Solution of Copper dissolves Iron immersed in it and lets go the Copper, or a Solution of Silver dissolves Copper and lets go the Silver, or a Solution of Mercury in *Aqua fortis* being poured upon Iron, Copper, Tin, or Lead, dissolves the Metal and lets go the Mercury; does not this argue that the acid Particles of the *Aqua fortis* are attracted more strongly by the *Lapis Calaminaris* than by Iron, and more strongly by Iron than by Copper, and more strongly by Copper than by Silver, and more strongly by Iron, Copper, Tin, and Lead, than by Mercury? And is it not for the same reason that Iron requires more *Aqua fortis* to dissolve it than Copper, and Copper more than the other Metals; and that of all Metals, Iron is dissolved most easily, and is most apt to rust; and next after Iron, Copper?

When Oil of Vitriol is mix'd with a little Water, or is run *per deliquium*, and in Distillation the Water ascends difficultly, and brings over with it some part of the Oil of Vitriol in the form of Spirit of Vitriol, and this Spirit being poured upon Iron, Copper, or Salt of Tartar, unites with the Body and lets go the Water; doth not this shew that the acid Spirit is attracted by the Water, and more attracted by the fix'd Body than by the Water, and therefore lets go the Water to close with the fix'd Body? And is it not for the same reason that the Water and acid Spirits which are mix'd together in Vinegar, *Aqua fortis*, and Spirit of Salt, cohere and rise together in Distillation; but if the *Menstruum* be poured on Salt of Tartar, or on Lead, or Iron, or any fix'd Body which it can dissolve, the Acid by a stronger Attraction adheres to the Body, and lets go the Water? And is it not also from a mutual Attraction that the Spirits of Soot and Sea-Salt unite and compose the Particles of Sal-armoniac, which are less volatile than before, because grosser and freer from Water; and that the Particles of Sal-armoniac in Sublimation carry up the Particles of Antimony, which will not sublime alone; and that the Particles of Mercury uniting with the acid Particles of Spirit of Salt compose Mercury sublimate, and with the Particles of Sulphur, compose Cinnaber; and that the Particles of Spirit of Wine and Spirit of Urine well rectified unite, and letting go the Water which dissolved them, compose a consistent Body; and that in subliming Cinnaber from Salt of Tartar, or from quick Lime, the Sulphur by a stronger Attraction of the Salt or Lime lets go the Mercury, and stays with the fix'd Body; and that when Mercury sublimate is sublimed from Antimony, or from Regulus of Antimony, the Spirit of Salt lets go the Mercury, and unites with the antimonial metal which attracts it more strongly, and stays with it till the Heat be great enough to make them both ascend together, and then carries up the Metal with it in the form of a very fusible Salt, called Butter of Antimony, although the Spirit of Salt alone be almost as volatile as Water, and the Antimony alone as fix'd as Lead?

When *Aqua fortis* dissolves Silver and not Gold, and *Aqua regia* dissolves Gold and not Silver, may it not be said that *Aqua fortis* is subtil enough to penetrate Gold as well as Silver, but wants the attractive Force to give it Entrance; and that *Aqua regia* is subtil enough to penetrate Silver as well as Gold, but wants the attractive Force to give it Entrance? For *Aqua regia* is nothing else than *Aqua fortis* mix'd with some Spirit of Salt, or with Sal-armoniac; and even common Salt dissolved in *Aqua fortis*, enables the *Menstruum* to dissolve Gold, though the Salt be a gross Body. When therefore Spirit of Salt precipitates Silver out of *Aqua fortis*, is it not done by attracting and mixing with the *Aqua fortis*, and not attracting, or perhaps repelling Silver? And when Water precipitates Antimony out of the Sublimate of Antimony and Sal-armoniac, or out of Butter of Antimony, is it not done by its dissolving, mixing with, and weakening the Sal-armoniac or Spirit of Salt, and its not attracting, or perhaps repelling the Antimony? And is it not for want of an attractive virtue between the Parts of Water and Oil, of Quick-silver and Antimony, of Lead and Iron, that these Substances do not mix; and by a weak Attraction, that Quick-silver and Copper mix difficultly; and from a strong one, that Quick-silver and Tin, Antimony and Iron, Water and Salts, mix readily? And in general, is it not from the same Principle that Heat congregates homogeneal Bodies, and separates Heterogeneal ones?

When Arsenick with Soap gives a Regulus, and with Mercury sublimate a volatile fusible Salt, like Butter of Antimony, doth not this shew that Arsenick, which is a Substance totally volatile, is compounded of fix'd and volatile Parts, strongly cohering by a mutual Attraction, so that the volatile will not ascend without carrying up the fixed? And so, when an equal weight of Spirit of Wine and Oil of Vitriol are digested together, and in Distillation yield two fragrant and volatile Spirits which will not mix with one another, and a fix'd black Earth remains behind; doth not this shew that Oil of Vitriol is composed of volatile and fix'd Parts strongly united by Attraction, so as to ascend together in form of a volatile, acid, fluid Salt, until the Spirit of Wine attracts and separates the volatile Parts from the fixed? And therefore, since Oil of Sulphur *per Campanam* is of the same Nature with Oil of Vitriol, may it not be inferred, that Sulphur is also a mixture of volatile and fix'd Parts so strongly cohering by Attraction, as to ascend together in Sublimation. By dissolving Flowers of Sulphur in Oil of Turpentine, and distilling the Solution, it is found that Sulphur is composed of an inflamable thick Oil or fat Bitumen, an acid Salt, a very fix'd Earth, and a little Metal. The three first were found not much unequal to one another, the fourth in so small a quantity as scarce to be worth considering. The acid Salt dissolved in Water, is the same with Oil of Sulphur *per Campanam*, and abounding much in the Bowels of the Earth, and particularly in Markasites, unites it self to the other Ingredients of the Markasite, which are, Bitumen, Iron, Copper, and Earth, and with them compounds Allum, Vitriol, and Sulphur. With the Earth alone it compounds Allum; with the Metal alone, or Metal and Earth together, it compounds Vitriol; and with the Bitumen and Earth it compounds Sulphur. Whence it comes to pass that Markasites abound with those three Minerals. And is it not from the mutual Attraction of the Ingredients that they stick together for compounding these Minerals, and that the Bitumen carries up the other Ingredients of the Sulphur, which without it would not sublime? And the same Question may be put concerning all, or almost all the gross Bodies in Nature. For all the Parts of Animals and Vegetables are composed of Substances volatile and fix'd, fluid and solid, as appears by their Analysis; and so are Salts and Minerals, so far as Chymists have been hitherto able to examine their Composition.

When Mercury sublimate is re-sublimed with fresh Mercury, and becomes *Mercurius Dulcis*, which is a white tasteless Earth scarce dissolvable in Water, and *Mercurius Dulcis* re-sublimed with Spirit of Salt returns into Mercury sublimate; and when Metals corroded with a little acid turn into rust, which is an Earth tasteless and indissolvable in Water, and this Earth imbibed with more acid becomes a metallick Salt; and when some Stones, as Spar of Lead, dissolved in proper *Menstruums* become Salts; do not these things shew that Salts are dry Earth and watry Acid united by Attraction, and that the Earth will not become a Salt without so much acid as makes it dissolvable in Water? Do not the sharp and pungent Tastes of Acids arise from the strong Attraction whereby the acid Particles rush upon and agitate the Particles of the Tongue? And when Metals are dissolved in acid *Menstruums*, and the Acids in conjunction with the Metal act after a different manner, so that the Compound has a different Taste much milder than before, and sometimes a sweet one; is it not because the Acids adhere to the metallick Particles, and thereby lose much of their Activity? And if the Acid be in too small a Proportion to make the Compound dissolvable in Water, will it not by adhering strongly to the Metal become unactive and lose its Taste, and the Compound be a tasteless Earth? For such things as are not dissolvable by the Moisture of the Tongue, act not upon the Taste.

As Gravity makes the Sea flow round the denser and weightier Parts of the Globe of the Earth, so the Attraction may make the watry Acid flow round the denser and compacter Particles of Earth for composing the Particles of Salt. For otherwise the Acid would not do the Office of a Medium between the Earth and common Water, for making Salts dissolvable in the Water; nor would Salt of Tartar readily draw off the Acid from dissolved Metals, nor Metals the Acid from Mercury. Now, as in the great Globe of the Earth and Sea, the densest Bodies by their Gravity sink down in Water, and always endeavour to go towards the Center of the Globe; so in Particles of Salt, the densest Matter may always endeavour to approach the Center of the Particle: So that a Particle of Salt may be compared to a Chaos; being dense, hard, dry, and earthy in the Center; and rare, soft, moist, and watry in the Circumference. And hence it seems to be that Salts are of a lasting Nature, being scarce destroy'd, unless by drawing away their watry Parts by violence, or by letting them soak into the Pores of the central Earth by a gentle Heat in Putrefaction, until the Earth be dissolved by the Water, and separated into smaller Particles, which by reason of their Smallness make the rotten Compound appear of a black Colour. Hence also it may be, that the Parts of Animals and Vegetables preserve their several Forms, and assimilate their Nourishment; the soft and moist Nourishment easily changing its Texture by a gentle Heat and Motion, till it becomes like the dense, hard, dry, and durable Earth in the Center of each particle. But when the Nourishment grows unfit to be assimilated, or the central Earth grows too feeble to assimilate it, the Motion ends in Confusion, Putrefaction, and Death.

If a very small quantity of any Salt or Vitriol be dissolved in a great quantity of Water, the Particles of the Salt or Vitriol will not sink to the bottom, though they be heavier in Specie than the Water, but will evenly diffuse themselves into all the Water, so as to make it as saline at the top as at the bottom. And does not this imply that the Parts of the Salt or Vitriol recede from one another, and endeavour to expand themselves, and get as far asunder as the quantity of Water in which they float, will allow? And does not this Endeavour imply that they have a repulsive Force by which they fly from one another, or at least, that they attract the Water more strongly than they do one another? For as all things ascend in Water which are less attracted than Water, by the gravitating Power of the Earth; so all the Particles of Salt which float in Water, and are less attracted than Water by any one Particle of Salt, must recede from that Particle, and give way to the more attracted Water.

When any saline Liquor is evaporated to a Cuticle and let cool, the Salt concretes in regular Figures; which argues, that the Particles of the Salt before they concreted, floated in the Liquor at equal distances in rank and file, and by consequence that they acted upon one another by some Power which at equal distances is equal, at unequal distances unequal. For by such a Power they will range themselves uniformly, and without it they will float irregularly, and come together as irregularly. And since the Particles of Island-Crystal act all the same way upon the Rays of Light for causing the unusual Refraction, may it not be supposed that in the Formation of this Crystal, the Particles not only ranged themselves in rank and file for concreting in regular Figures, but also by some kind of polar Virtue turned their homogeneal Sides the same way.

The Parts of all homogeneal hard Bodies which fully touch one another, stick together very strongly. And for explaining how this may be, some have invented hooked Atoms, which is begging the Question; and others tell us that Bodies are glued together by rest, that is, by an occult Quality, or rather by nothing; and others, that they stick together by conspiring Motions, that is, by relative rest amongst themselves. I had rather infer from their Cohesion, that their Particles attract one another by some Force, which in immediate Contact is exceeding strong, at small distances performs the chymical Operations above-mention'd, and reaches not far from the Particles with any sensible Effect.

All Bodies seem to be composed of hard Particles: For otherwise Fluids would not congeal; as Water, Oils, Vinegar, and Spirit or Oil of Vitriol do by freezing; Mercury by Fumes of Lead; Spirit of Nitre and Mercury, by dissolving the Mercury and evaporating the Flegm; Spirit of Wine and Spirit of Urine, by deflegming and mixing them; and Spirit of Urine and Spirit of Salt, by subliming them together to make Sal-armoniac. Even the Rays of Light seem to be hard Bodies; for otherwise they would not retain different Properties in their different Sides. And therefore Hardness may be reckon'd the Property of all uncompounded Matter. At least, this seems to be as evident as the universal Impenetrability of Matter. For all Bodies, so far as Experience reaches, are either hard, or may be harden'd; and we have no other Evidence of universal Impenetrability, besides a large Experience without an experimental Exception. Now if compound Bodies are so very hard as we find some of them to be, and yet are very porous, and consist of Parts which are only laid together; the simple Particles which are void of Pores, and were never yet divided, must be much harder. For such hard Particles being heaped up together, can scarce touch one another in more than a few Points, and therefore must be separable by much less Force than is requisite to break a solid Particle, whose Parts touch in all the Space between them, without any Pores or Interstices to weaken their Cohesion. And how such very hard Particles which are only laid together and touch only in a few Points, can stick together, and that so firmly as they do, without the assistance of something which causes them to be attracted or press'd towards one another, is very difficult to conceive.

The same thing I infer also from the cohering of two polish'd Marbles *in vacuo*, and from the standing of Quick-silver in the Barometer at the height of 50, 60 or 70 Inches, or above, when ever it is well-purged of Air and carefully poured in, so that its Parts be every where contiguous both to one another and to the Glass. The Atmosphere by its weight presses the Quick-silver into the Glass, to the height of 29 or 30 Inches.

And some other Agent raises it higher, not by pressing it into the Glass, but by making its Parts stick to the Glass, and to one another. For upon any discontinuation of Parts, made either by Bubbles or by shaking the Glass, the whole Mercury falls down to the height of 29 or 30 Inches.

And of the same kind with these Experiments are those that follow. If two plane polish'd Plates of Glass (suppose two pieces of a polish'd Looking-glass) be laid together, so that their sides be parallel and at a very small distance from one another, and then their lower edges be dipped into Water, the Water will rise up between them. And the less the distance of the Glasses is, the greater will be the height to which the Water will rise. If the distance be about the hundredth part of an Inch, the Water will rise to the height of about an Inch; and if the distance be greater or less in any Proportion, the height will be reciprocally proportional to the distance very nearly. For the attractive Force of the Glasses is the same, whether the distance between them be greater or less; and the weight of the Water drawn up is the same, if the height of it be reciprocally proportional to the distance of the Glasses. And in like manner, Water ascends between two Marbles polish'd plane, when their polish'd sides are parallel, and at a very little distance from one another, And if slender Pipes of Glass be dipped at one end into stagnating Water, the Water will rise up within the Pipe, and the height to which it rises will be reciprocally proportional to the Diameter of the Cavity of the Pipe, and will equal the height to which it rises between two Planes of Glass, if the Semi-diameter of the Cavity of the Pipe be equal to the distance between the Planes, or thereabouts. And these Experiments succeed after the same manner *in vacuo* as in the open Air, (as hath been tried before the Royal Society,) and therefore are not influenced by the Weight or Pressure of the Atmosphere.[2]

And if a large Pipe of Glass be filled with sifted Ashes well pressed together in the Glass, and one end of the Pipe be dipped into stagnating Water, the Water will rise up slowly in the Ashes, so as in the space of a Week or Fortnight to reach up within the Glass, to the height of 30 or 40 Inches above the stagnating Water. And the Water rises up to this height by the Action only of those Particles of the Ashes which are upon the Surface of the elevated Water; the Particles which are within the Water, attracting or repelling it as much downwards as upwards. And therefore the Action of the Particles is very strong. But the Particles of the Ashes being not so dense and close together as those of Glass, their Action is not so strong as that of Glass, which keeps Quick-silver suspended to the height of 60 or 70 Inches, and therefore acts with a Force which would keep Water suspended to the height of above 60 Feet.

By the same Principle, a Sponge sucks in Water, and the Glands in

2. Compare the different treatment of these phenomena in "De aere et aethere," written some twenty-five or thirty years earlier.

the Bodies of Animals, according to their several Natures and Dispositions, suck in various Juices from the Blood.

If two plane polish'd Plates of Glass three or four Inches broad, and twenty or twenty five long, be laid one of them parallel to the Horizon, the other upon the first, so as at one of their ends to touch one another, and contain an Angle of about 10 or 15 Minutes, and the same be first moisten'd on their inward sides with a clean Cloth dipp'd into Oil of Oranges or Spirit of Turpentine, and a Drop or two of the Oil or Spirit be let fall upon the lower Glass at the other; so soon as the upper Glass is laid down upon the lower, so as to touch it at one end as above, and to touch the Drop at the other end, making with the lower Glass an Angle of about 10 or 15 Minutes; the Drop will begin to move towards the Concourse of the Glasses, and will continue to move with an accelerated Motion, till it arrives at that Concourse of the Glasses. For the two Glasses attract the Drop, and make it run that way towards which the Attractions Incline. And if when the Drop is in motion you lift up that end of the Glasses where they meet, and towards which the Drop moves, the Drop will ascend between the Glasses, and therefore is attracted. And as you lift up the Glasses more and more, the Drop will ascend slower and slower, and at length rest, being then carried downward by its Weight, as much as upwards by the Attraction. And by this means you may know the Force by which the Drop is attracted at all distances from the Concourse of the Glasses.

Now by some Experiments of this kind, (made by Mr. *Hauksbee*) it has been found that the Attraction is almost reciprocally in a duplicate Proportion of the distance of the middle of the Drop from the Concourse of the Glasses, *viz.* reciprocally in a simple Proportion, by reason of the spreading of the Drop, and its touching each Glass in a larger Surface; and again reciprocally in a simple Proportion, by reason of the Attractions growing stronger within the same quantity of attracting Surface. The Attraction therefore within the same quantity of attracting Surface, is reciprocally as the distance between the Glasses. And therefore where the distance is exceeding small, the Attraction must be exceeding great. By the Table in the second Part of the second Book, wherein the thicknesses of colour'd Plates of Water between two Glasses are set down, the thickness of the Plate where it appears very black, is three eighths of the ten hundred thousandth part of an Inch. And where the Oil of Oranges between the Glasses is of this thickness, the Attraction collected by the foregoing Rule, seems to be so strong, as within a Circle of an Inch in diameter, to suffice to hold up a Weight equal to that of a Cylinder of Water of an Inch in diameter, and two or three Furlongs in length. And where it is of a less thickness the Attraction may be proportionally greater, and continue to increase, until the thickness do not exceed that of a single Particle of the Oil. There are therefore Agents in Nature able to make the Particles of Bodies stick together by very strong Attractions.

And it is the Business of experimental Philosophy to find them out.

Now the smallest Particles of Matter may cohere by the strongest Attractions, and compose bigger Particles of weaker Virtue; and many of these may cohere and compose bigger Particles whose Virtue is still weaker, and so on for divers Successions, until the Progression end in the biggest Particles on which the Operations in Chymistry, and the Colours of natural Bodies depend, and which by cohering compose Bodies of a sensible Magnitude. If the Body is compact, and bends or yields inward to Pression without any sliding of its Parts, it is hard and elastick, returning to its Figure with a Force rising from the mutual Attraction of its Parts. If the Parts slide upon one another, the Body is malleable or soft. If they slip easily, and are of a fit Size to be agitated by Heat, and the Heat is big enough to keep them in Agitation, the Body is fluid; and if it be apt to stick to things, it is humid; and the Drops of every fluid affect a round Figure by the mutual Attraction of their Parts, as the Globe of the Earth and Sea affects a round Figure by the mutual Attraction of its Parts by Gravity.

Since Metals dissolved in Acids attract but a small quantity of the Acid, their attractive Force can reach but to a small distance from them. And as in Algebra, where affirmative Quantities vanish and cease, there negative ones begin; so in Mechanicks, where Attraction ceases, there a repulsive Virtue ought to succeed. And that there is such a Virtue, seems to follow from the Reflexions and Inflexions of the Rays of Light. For the Rays are repelled by Bodies in both these Cases, without the immediate Contact of the reflecting or inflecting Body. It seems also to follow from the Emission of Light; the Ray so soon as it is shaken off from a shining Body by the vibrating Motion of the Parts of the Body, and gets beyond the reach of Attraction, being driven away with exceeding great Velocity. For that Force which is sufficient to turn it back in Reflexion, may be sufficient to emit it. It seems also to follow from the Production of Air and Vapour. The Particles when they are shaken off from Bodies by Heat or Fermentation, so soon as they are beyond the reach of the Attraction of the Body, receding from it, and also from one another with great Strength, and keeping at a distance, so as sometimes to take up above a Million of Times more space than they did before in the form of a dense Body. Which vast Contraction and Expansion seems unintelligible, by feigning the Particles of Air to be springy and ramous, or rolled up like Hoops, or by any other means than a repulsive Power. The Particles of Fluids which do not cohere too strongly, and are of such a Smallness as renders them most susceptible of those Agitations which keep Liquors in a Fluor, are most easily separated and rarified into Vapour, and in the Language of the Chymists, they are volatile, rarifying with an easy Heat, and condensing with Cold. But those which are grosser, and so less susceptible of Agitation, or cohere by a stronger Attraction, are not separated without a stronger

Heat, or perhaps not without Fermentation. And these last are the Bodies which Chymists call fix'd, and being rarified by Fermentation, become true permanent Air; those Particles receding from one another with the greatest Force, and being most difficultly brought together, which upon Contact cohere most strongly. And because the Particles of permanent Air are grosser, and arise from denser Substances than those of Vapours, thence it is that true Air is more ponderous than Vapour, and that a moist Atmosphere is lighter than a dry one, quantity for quantity. From the same repelling Power it seems to be that Flies walk upon the Water without wetting their Feet; and that the Object-glasses of long Telescopes lie upon one another without touching; and that dry Powders are difficultly made to touch one another so as to stick together, unless by melting them, or wetting them with Water, which by exhaling may bring them together; and that two polish'd Marbles, which by immediate Contact stick together, are difficultly brought so close together as to stick.

And thus Nature will be very conformable to her self and very simple, performing all the great Motions of the heavenly Bodies by the Attraction of Gravity which intercedes those Bodies, and almost all the small ones of their Particles by some other attractive and repelling Powers which intercede the Particles. The *Vis inertiæ*[3] is a passive Principle by which Bodies persist in their Motion or Rest, receive Motion in proportion to the Force impressing it, and resist as much as they are resisted. By this Principle alone there never could have been any Motion in the World. Some other Principle was necessary for putting Bodies into Motion; and now they are in Motion, some other Principle is necessary for conserving the Motion. For from the various Composition of two Motions, 'tis very certain that there is not always the same quantity of Motion in the World.[4] For if two Globes joined by a slender Rod, revolve about their common Center of Gravity with an uniform Motion, while that Center moves on uniformly in a right Line drawn in the Plane of their circular Motion; the Sum of the Motions of the two Globes, as often as the Globes are in the right Line described by their common Center of Gravity, will be bigger than the Sum of their Motions, when they are in a Line perpendicular to that right Line. By this Instance it appears that Motion may be got or lost. But by reason of the Tenacity of Fluids, and Attrition of their Parts, and the Weakness of Elasticity in Solids, Motion is much more apt to be lost than got, and is always upon the Decay. For Bodies which are either absolutely hard, or so soft as to be void of Elasticity, will not rebound from one another. Impenetrability makes them only stop. If two equal Bodies meet directly *in vacuo*, they will by the Laws of Motion stop where they meet, and

3. See the Definitions from the *Principia* included in Part 5, Rational Mechanics (below).
4. Refers to a principle of Cartesian natural philosophy.

lose all their Motion, and remain in rest, unless they be elastick, and receive new Motion from their Spring. If they have so much Elasticity as suffices to make them re-bound with a quarter, or half, or three quarters of the Force with which they come together, they will lose three quarters, or half, or a quarter of their Motion. And this may be try'd, by letting two equal Pendulums fall against one another from equal heights. If the Pendulums be of Lead or soft Clay, they will lose all or almost all their Motions: If of elastick Bodies they will lose all but what they recover from their Elasticity. If it be said, that they can lose no Motion but what they communicate to other Bodies, the consequence is, that *in vacuo* they can lose no Motion, but when they meet they must go on and penetrate one another's Dimensions. If three equal round Vessels be filled, the one with Water, the other with Oil, the third with molten Pitch, and the Liquors be stirred about alike to give them a vortical Motion; the Pitch by its Tenacity will lose its Motion quickly, the Oil being less tenacious will keep it longer, and the Water being less tenacious will keep it longest, but yet will lose it in a short time. Whence it is easy to understand, that if many contiguous Vortices of molten Pitch were each of them as large as those which some suppose to revolve about the Sun and fix'd Stars, yet these and all their Parts would, by their Tenacity and Stiffness, communicate their Motion to one another till they all rested among themselves. Vortices of Oil or Water, or some fluider Matter, might continue longer in Motion; but unless the Matter were void of all Tenacity and Attrition of Parts, and Communication of Motion, (which is not to be supposed,) the Motion would constantly decay. Seeing therefore the variety of Motion which we find in the World is always decreasing, there is a necessity of conserving and recruiting it by active Principles, such as are the cause of Gravity, by which Planets and Comets keep their Motions in their Orbs, and Bodies acquire great Motion in falling; and the cause of Fermentation, by which the Heart and Blood of Animals are kept in perpetual Motion and Heat; the inward Parts of the Earth are constantly warm'd, and in some places grow very hot; Bodies burn and shine, Mountains take fire, the Caverns of the Earth are blown up, and the Sun continues violently hot and lucid, and warms all things by his Light. For we meet with very little Motion in the World, besides what is owing to these active Principles. And if it were not for these Principles, the Bodies of the Earth, Planets, Comets, Sun, and all things in them, would grow cold and freeze, and become inactive Masses; and all Putrefaction, Generation, Vegetation and Life would cease, and the Planets and Comets would not remain in their Orbs.

All these things being consider'd, it seems probable to me, that God in the Beginning form'd Matter in solid, massy, hard, impenetrable, moveable Particles, of such Sizes and Figures, and with such other Properties, and in such Proportion to Space, as most conduced to the

End for which he form'd them; and that these primitive Particles being Solids, are incomparably harder than any porous Bodies compounded of them; even so very hard, as never to wear or break in pieces; no ordinary Power being able to divide what God himself made one in the first Creation. While the Particles continue entire, they may compose Bodies of one and the same Nature and Texture in all Ages: But should they wear away, or break in pieces, the Nature of Things depending on them, would be changed. Water and Earth, composed of old worn Particles and Fragments of Particles, would not be of the same Nature and Texture now, with Water and Earth composed of entire Particles in the Beginning. And therefore, that Nature may be lasting, the Changes of corporeal Things are to be placed only in the various Separations and new Associations and Motions of these permanent Particles; compound Bodies being apt to break, not in the midst of solid Particles, but where those Particles are laid together, and only touch in a few Points.

It seems to me farther, that these Particles have not only a *Vis inertiæ*, accompanied with such passive Laws of Motion as naturally result from that Force, but also that they are moved by certain active Principles, such as is that of Gravity, and that which causes Fermentation, and the Cohesion of Bodies. These Principles I consider, not as occult Qualities, supposed to result from the specifick Forms of Things, but as general Laws of Nature, by which the Things themselves are form'd; their Truth appearing to us by Phænomena, though their Causes be not yet discover'd. For these are manifest Qualities, and their Causes only are occult. And the *Aristotelians* gave the Name of occult Qualities, not to manifest Qualities, but to such Qualities only as they supposed to lie hid in Bodies, and to be the unknown Causes of manifest Effects: Such as would be the Causes of Gravity, and of magnetick and electrick Attractions, and of Fermentations, if we should suppose that these Forces or Actions arose from Qualities unknown to us, and uncapable of being discovered and made manifest. Such occult Qualities put a stop to the Improvement of natural Philosophy, and therefore of late Years have been rejected. To tell us that every Species of Things is endow'd with an occult specifick Quality by which it acts and produces manifest Effects, is to tell us nothing: But to derive two or three general Principles of Motion from Phænomena, and afterwards to tell us how the Properties and Actions of all corporeal Things follow from those manifest Principles, would be a very great step in Philosophy, though the Causes of those Principles were not yet discover'd: And therefore I scruple not to propose the Principles of Motion above-mention'd, they being of very general Extent, and leave their Causes to be found out.

Now by the help of these Principles, all material Things seem to have been composed of the hard and solid Particles above-mention'd, variously associated in the first Creation by the Counsel of an intelligent Agent. For it became him who created them to set them in order. And if he did so, it's unphilosophical to seek for any other Origin of the World, or to pretend that it might arise out of a Chaos by the mere Laws of Nature; though being once form'd, it may continue by those Laws for many Ages. For while Comets move in very excentrick Orbs in all manner of Positions, blind Fate could never make all the Planets move one and the same way in Orbs concentrick, some inconsiderable Irregularities excepted, which may have risen from the mutual Actions of Comets and Planets upon one another, and which will be apt to increase, till this System wants a Reformation. Such a wonderful Uniformity in the Planetary System must be allowed the Effect of Choice. And so must the Uniformity in the Bodies of Animals, they having generally a right and a left side shaped alike, and on either side of their Bodies two Legs behind, and either two Arms, or two Legs, or two Wings before upon their Shoulders, and between their Shoulders a Neck running down into a Back-bone, and a Head upon it; and in the Head two Ears, two Eyes, a Nose, a Mouth, and a Tongue, alike situated. Also the first Contrivance of those very artificial Parts of Animals, the Eyes, Ears, Brain, Muscles, Heart, Lungs, Midriff, Glands, Larynx, Hands, Wings, swimming Bladders, natural Spectacles, and other Organs of Sense and Motion; and the Instinct of Brutes and Insects, can be the effect of nothing else than the Wisdom and Skill of a powerful ever-living Agent, who being in all Places, is more able by his Will to move the Bodies within his boundless uniform Sensorium, and thereby to form and reform the Parts of the Universe, than we are by our Will to move the Parts of our own Bodies. And yet we are not to consider the World as the Body of God, or the several Parts thereof, as the Parts of God. He is an uniform Being, void of Organs, Members or Parts, and they are his Creatures subordinate to him, and subservient to his Will; and he is no more the Soul of them, than the Soul of Man is the Soul of the Species of Things carried through the Organs of Sense into the place of its Sensation, where it perceives them by means of its immediate Presence, without the Intervention of any third thing. The Organs of Sense are not for enabling the Soul to perceive the Species of Things in its Sensorium, but only for conveying them thither; and God has no need of such Organs, he being every where present to the Things themselves. And since Space is divisible *in infinitum*, and Matter is not necessarily in all places, it may be also allow'd that God is able to create Particles of Matter of several Sizes and Figures, and in several Proportions to Space, and perhaps of different Densities and Forces, and thereby to vary the Laws of Nature, and make Worlds of several sorts in several Parts of the Universe. At least, I see nothing of Contradiction in all this.

As in Mathematicks, so in Natural Philosophy, the Investigation of difficult Things by the Method of Analysis, ought ever to precede the Method of Composition. This Analysis consists in making Experiments and Observations, and in drawing general Conclusions from them by

Induction, and admitting of no Objections against the Conclusions, but such as are taken from Experiments, or other certain Truths. For Hypotheses are not to be regarded in experimental Philosophy. And although the arguing from Experiments and Observations by Induction be no Demonstration of general Conclusions; yet it is the best way of arguing which the Nature of Things admits of, and may be looked upon as so much the stronger, by how much the Induction is more general. And if no Exception occur from Phænomena, the Conclusion may be pronounced generally. But if at any time afterwards any Exception shall occur from Experiments, it may then begin to be pronounced with such Exceptions as occur. By this way of Analysis we may proceed from Compounds to Ingredients, and from Motions to the Forces producing them; and in general, from Effects to their Causes, and from particular Causes to more general ones, till the Argument end in the most general. This is the Method of Analysis: And the Synthesis consists in assuming the Causes discover'd, and establish'd as Principles, and by them explaining the Phænomena proceeding from them, and proving the Explanations.

In the two first Books of these Opticks, I proceeded by this Analysis to discover and prove the original Differences of the Rays of Light in respect of Refrangibility, Reflexibility, and Colour, and their alternate Fits of easy Reflexion and easy Transmission,[5] and the Properties of Bodies, both opake and pellucid, on which their Reflexions and Colours depend. And these Discoveries being proved, may be assumed in the Method of Composition for explaining the Phænomena arising from them: An Instance of which Method I gave in the End of the first Book. In this third Book I have only begun the Analysis of what remains to be discover'd about Light and its Effects upon the Frame of Nature, hinting several things about it, and leaving the Hints to be examin'd and improv'd by the farther Experiments and Observations of such as are inquisitive. And if natural Philosophy in all its Parts, by pursuing this Method, shall at length be perfected, the Bounds of Moral Philosophy will be also enlarged. For so far as we can know by natural Philosophy what is the first Cause, what Power he has over us, and what Benefits we receive from him, so far our Duty towards him, as well as that towards one another, will appear to us by the Light of Nature. And no doubt, if the Worship of false Gods had not blinded the Heathen, their moral Philosophy would have gone farther than to the four Cardinal Virtues; and instead of teaching the Transmigration of Souls, and to worship the Sun and Moon, and dead Heroes, they would have taught us to worship our true Author and Benefactor, as their Ancestors did under the Government of *Noah* and his Sons before they corrupted themselves.

5. Refers to the phenomena of Newton's rings: see the paper on rings in Part 4, Optics (below).

Queries 18–22†

Qu. 18. If in two large tall cylindrical Vessels of Glass inverted, two little Thermometers be suspended so as not to touch the Vessels, and the Air be drawn out of one of these Vessels, and these Vessels thus prepared be carried out of a cold place into a warm one; the Thermometer *in vacuo* will grow warm as much, and almost as soon as the Thermometer which is not *in vacuo*. And when the Vessels are carried back into the cold place, the Thermometer *in vacuo* will grow cold almost as soon as the other Thermometer. Is not the Heat of the warm Room convey'd through the *Vacuum* by the Vibrations of a much subtiler Medium than Air, which after the Air was drawn out remained in the *Vacuum*? And is not this Medium the same with that Medium by which Light is refracted and reflected, and by whose Vibrations Light communicates Heat to Bodies, and is put into Fits of easy Reflexion and easy Transmission? And do not the Vibrations of this Medium in hot Bodies contribute to the intenseness and duration of their Heat? And do not hot Bodies communicate their Heat to contiguous cold ones, by the Vibrations of this Medium propagated from them into the cold ones? And is not this Medium exceedingly more rare and subtile than the Air, and exceedingly more elastick and active? And doth it not readily pervade all Bodies? And is it not (by its elastick force) expanded through all the Heavens?

Qu. 19. Doth not the Refraction of Light proceed from the different density of this Æthereal Medium in different places, the Light receding always from the denser parts of the Medium? And is not the density thereof greater in free and open Spaces void of Air and other grosser Bodies, than within the Pores of Water, Glass, Crystal, Gems, and other compact Bodies? For when Light passes through Glass or Crystal, and falling very obliquely upon the farther Surface thereof is totally reflected, the total Reflexion ought to proceed rather from the density and vigour of the Medium without and beyond the Glass, than from the rarity and weakness thereof.

Qu. 20. Doth not this Æthereal Medium in passing out of Water, Glass, Crystal, and other compact and dense Bodies into empty Spaces, grow denser and denser by degrees, and by that means refract the Rays of Light not in a point, but by bending them gradually in curve Lines? And doth not the gradual condensation of this Medium extend to some distance from the Bodies, and thereby cause the Inflexions of the Rays of Light, which pass by the edges of dense Bodies, at some distance from the Bodies?

† Isaac Newton, *Opticks*, based on the 4th ed. (New York: Dover Publications, 1952), pp. 348–53. Reprinted by permission of Dover Publications, Inc. In 1717, Newton published a second English edition of the *Opticks* with eight new Queries, which he placed immediately after the original group of sixteen and numbered 17–24. These final Queries constitute Newton's last significant contribution to natural philosophy.

Qu. 21. Is not this Medium much rarer within the dense Bodies of the Sun, Stars, Planets and Comets, than in the empty celestial Spaces between them? And in passing from them to great distances, doth it not grow denser and denser perpetually, and thereby cause the gravity of those great Bodies towards one another, and of their parts towards the Bodies; every Body endeavouring to go from the denser parts of the Medium towards the rarer? For if this Medium be rarer within the Sun's Body than at its Surface, and rarer there than at the hundredth part of an Inch from its Body, and rarer there than at the fiftieth part of an Inch from its Body, and rarer there than at the Orb of *Saturn*; I see no reason why the Increase of density should stop any where, and not rather be continued through all distances from the Sun to *Saturn*, and beyond. And though this Increase of density may at great distances be exceeding slow, yet if the elastick force of this Medium be exceeding great, it may suffice to impel Bodies from the denser parts of the Medium towards the rarer, with all that power which we call Gravity. And that the elastick force of this Medium is exceeding great, may be gather'd from the swiftness of its Vibrations. Sounds move about 1140 *English* Feet in a second Minute[1] of Time, and in seven or eight Minutes of Time they move about one hundred *English* Miles. Light moves from the Sun to us in about seven or eight Minutes of Time, which distance is about 70000000 *English* Miles, supposing the Horizontal Parallax of the Sun to be about 12″. And the Vibrations or Pulses of this Medium, that they may cause the alternate Fits of easy Transmission and easy Reflexion, must be swifter than Light, and by consequence above 700000 times swifter than Sounds. And therefore the elastick force of this Medium, in proportion to its density, must be above 700000 × 700000 (that is, above 490000000000) times greater than the elastick force of the Air is in proportion to its density. For the Velocities of the Pulses of elastick Mediums are in a subduplicate *Ratio* of the Elasticities and the Rarities of the Mediums taken together.

As Attraction is stronger in small Magnets than in great ones in proportion to their Bulk, and Gravity is greater in the Surfaces of small Planets than in those of great ones in proportion to their bulk, and small Bodies are agitated much more by electric attraction than great ones; so the smallness of the Rays of Light may contribute very much to the power of the Agent by which they are refracted. And so if any one should suppose that *Æther* (like our Air) may contain Particles which endeavour to recede from one another (for I do not know what this *Æther* is) and that its Particles are exceedingly smaller than those of Air, or even than those of Light: The exceeding smallness of its Particles may contribute to the greatness of the force by which those Particles may recede from one another, and thereby make that Medium exceedingly more rare and

1. That is, as we now say, a second.

elastick than Air, and by consequence exceedingly less able to resist the motions of Projectiles, and exceedingly more able to press upon gross Bodies, by endeavouring to expand it self.

Qu. 22. May not Planets and Comets, and all gross Bodies, perform their Motions more freely, and with less resistance in this Æthereal Medium than in any Fluid, which fills all Space adequately without leaving any Pores, and by consequence is much denser than Quick-silver or Gold?[2] And may not its resistance be so small, as to be inconsiderable? For instance; If this *Æther* (for so I will call it) should be supposed 700000 times more elastick than our Air, and above 700000 times more rare; its resistance would be above 600000000 times less than that of Water. And so small a resistance would scarce make any sensible alteration in the Motions of the Planets in ten thousand Years. If any one would ask how a Medium can be so rare, let him tell me how the Air, in the upper parts of the Atmosphere, can be above an hundred thousand thousand times rarer than Gold. Let him also tell me, how an electrick Body can by Friction emit an Exhalation so rare and subtile, and yet so potent, as by its Emission to cause no sensible Diminution of the weight of the electrick Body, and to be expanded through a Sphere, whose Diameter is above two Feet, and yet to be able to agitate and carry up Leaf Copper, or Leaf Gold, at the distance of above a Foot from the electrick Body? And how the Effluvia of a Magnet can be so rare and subtile, as to pass through a Plate of Glass without any Resistance or Diminution of their Force, and yet so potent as to turn a magnetick Needle beyond the Glass?

ALEXANDRE KOYRÉ

The Significance of the Newtonian Synthesis †

It is obviously utterly impossible to give in a brief space a detailed history of the birth, growth, and decay of the Newtonian world view. It is just as impossible even to give a reasonably complete account of the work performed by Newton himself. Thus, by necessity, I am obliged to restrict myself to the very essentials and to give the barest outline of the subject. Moreover, in doing so I will assume a certain amount of previous knowledge. It is, I believe, a legitimate assumption, because, as a matter of fact, we all know something about Newton, much more,

2. Refers to the Cartesian concept of nature as a plenum.

† Alexandre Koyré, *Newtonian Studies* (Cambridge, MA: Harvard University Press, 1965), pp. 3–24. Reprinted by permission of Harvard University Press. Koyré, a French scholar born in Russia, was a very influential historian of science in the middle of the twentieth century. He first delivered this paper as a lecture in 1948.

doubtless, than we know about any of the other great scientists and philosophers whose common effort fills the seventeenth century—the century of genius, as Whitehead has called it.

We know, for instance, that it is to Newton's insight and experimental genius—not *skill:* others, for instance, Robert Hooke, were just as skilled, or even more so than he—that we owe the idea of decomposition of light and the first scientific theory of spectral colors; that it is to his deep philosophical mind that we owe the formulation—though not the discovery—of the fundamental laws of motion and of action, together with the clear understanding of the method and meaning of scientific inquiry; that it was his invention of the calculus that enabled him to demonstrate the identity of terrestrial and celestial gravitation and to find out the fundamental law of attraction that binds—or at least until recently bound—together the smallest and the largest bodies—stars and atoms—of the infinite Universe. We know too, of course, that it is not to him, but to his great rival Leibniz, that we owe *de facto* the actual spread and development of the infinitesimal calculus, without which the gradual extension and perfection of the Newtonian *systema mundi* would be impossible.

Besides, all of us, or if not all still most of us, have been born and bred—or better and more exactly, not *born* (as this is impossible) but only *bred*—in the Newtonian or, at least, a semi-Newtonian world, and we have all, or nearly all, accepted the idea of the Newtonian world machine as the expression of the true picture of the universe and the embodiment of scientific truth—this because for more than two hundred years such has been the common creed, the *communis opinio*, of modern science and of enlightened mankind.

Thus it seems to me that I have the right to assume that when we are speaking about Newton and Newtonianism we know more or less what we are speaking of. More or less! Somehow this very expression used in connection with Newton strikes me as improper, because it is possible that the deepest meaning and aim of Newtonianism, or rather, of the whole scientific revolution of the seventeenth century, of which Newton is the heir and the highest expression, is just to abolish the world of the "more or less," the world of qualities and sense perception, the world of appreciation of our daily life, and to replace it by the (Archimedean) universe of precision, of exact measures, of strict determination.

Let us dwell for a moment upon this revolution, one of the deepest, if not the deepest, mutations and transformations accomplished—or suffered—by the human mind since the invention of the cosmos by the Greeks, two thousand years before. This revolution has been described and explained—much more explained than described—in quite a number of ways. Some people stress the role of experience and experiment in the new science, the fight against bookish learning, the new belief of modern man in himself, in his ability to discover truth by his own powers, by exercising his senses and his intelligence, so forcefully expressed by Bacon and by Descartes, in contradistinction to the formerly prevailing belief in the supreme and overwhelming value of tradition and consecrated authority.

Some others stress the practical attitude of modern man, who turns away from the *vita contemplativa*, in which the medieval and antique mind allegedly saw the very acme of human life, to the *vita activa*; who therefore is no longer able to content himself with pure speculation and theory; and who wants a knowledge that can be put to use: a *scientia activa, operativa*, as Bacon called it, or, as Descartes has said, a science that would make man master and possessor of nature.

The new science, we are told sometimes, is the science of the craftsman and the engineer, of the working, enterprising, and calculating tradesman, in fact, the science of the rising bourgeois classes of modern society.

There is certainly some truth in these descriptions and explanations: it is clear that the growth of modern science presupposes that of the cities, it is obvious that the development of firearms, especially of artillery, drew attention to problems of ballistics; that navigation, especially that to America and India, furthered the building of clocks, and so forth—yet I must confess that I am not satisfied with them. I do not see what the *scientia activa* has ever had to do with the development of the calculus, nor the rise of the bourgeoisie with that of the Copernican, or the Keplerian, astronomy. And as for experience and experiment—two things which we must not only distinguish but even oppose to each other—I am convinced that the rise and growth of experimental science is not the source but, on the contrary, the result of the new *theoretical*, that is, the new *metaphysical* approach to nature that forms the content of the scientific revolution of the seventeenth century, a content which we have to understand before we can attempt an explanation (whatever this may be) of its historical occurrence.

I shall therefore characterize this revolution by two closely connected and even complementary features: *(a)* the destruction of the cosmos, and therefore the disappearance from science—at least in principle, if not always in fact—of all considerations based on this concept, and *(b)* the geometrization of space, that is, the substitution of the homogeneous and abstract—however now considered as real—dimension space of the Euclidean geometry for the concrete and differentiated place-continuum of pre-Galilean physics and astronomy.

As a matter of fact, this characterization is very nearly equivalent to the mathematization (geometrization) of nature and therefore the mathematization (geometrization) of science.

The disappearance—or destruction—of the cosmos means that the world of science, the real world, is no more seen, or conceived, as a finite and hierarchically ordered, therefore qualitatively and ontologically differentiated, whole, but as an open, indefinite, and even infinite universe, united not by its immanent structure but only by the identity of its fundamental contents and laws; a universe in which, in contradistinction to the traditional conception with its separation and opposition of the two worlds of becoming and being, that is, of the heavens and the earth, all its components appear as placed on the same ontological level; a universe in which the *physica coelestis* and *physica terrestris*[1] are identified and unified, in which astronomy and physics become interdependent and united because of their common subjection to geometry.

This, in turn, implies the disappearance—or the violent expulsion—from scientific thought of all considerations based on value, perfection, harmony, meaning, and aim, because these concepts, from now on *merely subjective*, cannot have a place in the new ontology. Or, to put it in different words: all formal and final causes as modes of explanation disappear from—or are rejected by—the new science and are replaced by efficient and even material ones. Only these latter have right of way and are admitted to existence in the new universe of hypostatized geometry and it is only in this abstract-real (Archimedean) world, where abstract bodies move in an abstract space, that the laws of being and of motion of the new—the classical—science are valid and true.

It is easy now to understand why classical science—as has been said so often—has substituted a world of quantity for that of quality: just because, as Aristotle already knew quite well, there are no qualities in the world of numbers, or in that of geometrical figures. There is no place for them in the realm of mathematical ontology.

And even more. It is easy now to understand why classical science—as has been seen so seldom—has substituted a world of being for the world of becoming and change: just because, as Aristotle has said too, there is no change and no becoming in numbers and in figures. But, in doing so, it was obliged to reframe and to reformulate or rediscover its fundamental concepts, such as those of matter, motion, and so on.

If we take into account the tremendous scope and bearing of this so deep and so radical revolution, we shall have to admit that, on the whole, it has been surprisingly quick.

It was in 1543—one hundred years before the birth of Newton—that Copernicus wrested the earth from its foundations and hurled it into the skies. It was in the beginning of the century (1609 and 1619) that Kepler formulated his laws of celestial motions and thus destroyed the orbs and spheres that encompassed the world and held it together; and did it at the same time that Galileo, creating the first scientific instruments and showing to mankind things that no human eye had ever seen before, opened to scientific investigation the two connected worlds of the infinitely great and the infinitely small.

1. Science of the heavens and science of the earth. [Editor]

Moreover, it was by his "subjecting motion to number" that Galileo cleared the way for the formulation of the new concepts of matter and motion I have just mentioned, which formed the basis of the new science and cosmology; concepts with the aid of which—identifying matter and space—Descartes, in 1637, tried, and failed, to reconstruct the world; concepts that—redistinguishing between matter and space—Newton so brilliantly, and so successfully, used in his own reconstruction.

The new concept of motion which so victoriously asserts itself in the classical science is quite a simple one, so simple that, although very easy to use—once one is accustomed to it, as we all are—it is very difficult to grasp and fully to understand. Even for us, I cannot analyze it here, yet I would like to point out that, as Descartes quite clearly tells us, it substitutes a purely mathematical notion for a physical one and that, in opposition to the pre-Galilean and pre-Cartesian conception, which understood motion as a species of becoming, as a kind of process of change that affected the bodies subjected to it, in contradistinction to rest, which did not, the new—or classical—conception interprets motion as a kind of being, that is, not as a process, but as a *status*, a *status* that is just as permanent and indestructible as rest and that no more than this latter affects the bodies that are in motion. Being thus placed on the same ontological level, being deprived of their qualitative distinction, motion and rest become indistinguishable. Motion and rest are still—and even more than ever—opposed to each other, but their opposition becomes a pure correlation. Motion and rest no longer exist in the bodies themselves; bodies are only in rest or in motion in respect to each other, or to the space in which they exist, rest, and move; motion and rest are relations, though, at the same time, they are considered as *states*. It is this conception (of the inner difficulties of which Newton was doubtless quite aware) that carries—and perhaps undermines—the magnificent structure of classical science and it is about this motion that in his famous first law or axiom Newton tells us that *corpus omne perseverare in statu suo quiescendi vel movendi uniformiter in directum nisi quatenus a viribus impressis cogitur statum illum mutare.*[2]

The motion dealt with in this law is not the motion of the bodies of our experience; we do not encounter it in our daily lives. It is the motion of geometrical (Archimedean) bodies in abstract space. That is the reason why it has nothing to do with change. The "motion" of geometrical bodies in geometrical space changes nothing at all; the "places" in such a space are equivalent and even identical. It is a changeless change, if I may say so, a strange and paradoxical blending together of the same and the other that Plato tried—and failed—to effect in his *Parmenides*.

2. See the first law of motion, Part 5, Rational Mechanics (below). [Editor]

The transformation of the concept of motion by substituting for the empirical concept the hypostatized mathematical one is inevitable if we have to subject motion to number in order to deal with it mathematically, to build up a mathematical physics. But this is not enough. Conversely, mathematics itself has to be transformed (and to have achieved this transformation is the undying merit of Newton). Mathematical entities have to be, in some sense, brought nearer to physics, subjected to motion, and viewed not in their "being" but in their "becoming" or in their "flux."

The curves and figures of geometry have to be seen, and understood, not as built up of other geometrical elements, not as cut out in space by the intersection of geometrical bodies and planes, nor even as presenting a spatial image of the structural relations expressed in themselves by algebraic formulas, but as engendered or described by the motion of points and lines in space. It is a timeless motion, of course, that we are here dealing with, or, even stranger, a motion in a timeless time—a notion as paradoxical as that of changeless change. Yet it is only by making changeless change proceed in timeless time that we can deal—effectively as well as intellectually—with such realities as speed, acceleration, or direction of a moving body in any point of its trajectory, or, *vice versa*, at any moment of the motion describing that trajectory.

It is a thrilling story, the story of the successful and unsuccessful efforts of the human mind to formulate these new and strange ideas, to build up, or, as Spinoza so pregnantly has said, to *forge*, the new tools and patterns of thinking and of understanding. It fills the fifty years that separate the *Discours de la méthode*[3] from the *Philosophiae naturalis principia mathematica*. A series of great thinkers—to mention only Cavalieri and Fermat, Pascal and Wallis, Barrow and Huygens—had made their contributions to the final success, and without them the *Principia* would not have been written; the task would have been too arduous, even for Newton, *qui genus humanum ingenio superavit.*[4]

Thus, modifying somewhat the celebrated statement of Newton, made in his famous letter to Robert Hooke, we could, with truth, say that if Newton saw as far as he did, and so much farther than anybody had seen before him, it was because he was a giant standing on the shoulders of other giants.

The physicomathematical current I have just been sketching is certainly the most original and most important trend of seventeenth-century scientific thought. Yet, parallel to it there runs another one, less mathematical, less deductive, more empirical and experimental. Being less pretentious (or more diffident), it does not attempt the sweeping generalizations of the mathematicians. It views them with misgiving and

3. Descartes, *Discourse on Method* (1637). [Editor]
4. "Who in intellect excelled the human race," a line from Lucretius placed on the pedestal of the statue of Newton in Trinity College, Cambridge. [Editor]

even with hostility and it restricts itself to the discovery of new facts and to the building up of partial theories explaining them.

This current is inspired not by the Platonic idea of the mathematical structure and determination of being, but by the Lucretian, Epicurean, Democritean conception of its atomic composition (strange as it may seem, most modern ideas lead back to some old Greek fancy). Gassendi, Roberval, Boyle (the best representative of their group), Hooke—they all oppose the more timid, more cautious, and more secure *corpuscular philosophy* to the panmathematism of Galileo and Descartes.

Thus when Galileo tells us that the book of nature—that book in which the medieval mind perceived the *vestigia* and the *imagines Dei*[5] and read the glory of God expressed in sensible symbols of beauty and splendor revealing the hidden meaning and aim of the creation—was, in truth, written in geometrical characters, in circles, triangles, and squares, and only told us the intellectually marvelous story of rational connection and order, Boyle protests: the book of nature, said he, was certainly "a well-contrived romance" of which every part, "written in the stenography of God's omniscient hand," stood in relation to every other; but it was written not in geometrical but in *corpuscular* characters.

Not mathematical structure but corpuscular texture formed for him the inner reality of being. In the explanation of the universe we have to start with—or stop at—matter, not homogeneous Cartesian matter, but matter already formed by God into various, diversely determined corpuscles. These are the letters which motion forms into the words of the divine romance.

Looking at things from this perspective we see quite clearly that Newton presents us with a synthesis of both trends, of both views. For him, just as for Boyle, the book of nature is written in corpuscular characters and words. But, just as for Galileo and Descartes, it is a purely mathematical syntax that binds them together and gives its meaning to the text of the book.

Thus, in contradistinction to the world of Descartes, the world of Newton is conceived as composed not of two (extension and motion) but of three elements: (1) *matter*, that is, an infinite number of mutually separated and isolated, hard and unchangeable—but not identical—particles; (2) *motion*, that strange and paradoxical relation-state that does not affect the particles in their being, but only transports them hither and thither in the infinite, homogeneous void; and (3) *space*, that is, this very infinite and homogeneous void in which, unopposed, the corpuscles (and the bodies built of them) perform their motions.

There is, of course, a fourth component in that Newtonian world, namely, attraction which binds and holds it together. Yet this is not an *element* of its construction; it is either a hyperphysical power—God's

5. Footprints and reflections of God. [Editor]

action—or a mathematical stricture that lays down the rule of syntax in God's book of nature.

The introduction of the void—with its correlative, attraction—into the world view of Newton, in spite of the tremendous physical and metaphysical difficulties involved by this conception (action at a distance; existence of the nothing), was a stroke of genius and a step of decisive importance. It is this step that enabled Newton to oppose and unite at the same time—and to do it *really*, and not *seemingly*, like Descartes—the discontinuity of matter and the continuity of space. The corpuscular structure of matter, emphatically asserted, formed a firm basis for the application of mathematical dynamics to nature. It yielded the *fundamenta* for the relations expressed by space. The cautious corpuscular philosophy did not really know what it was doing. But, as a matter of fact, it had been only showing the way to the Newtonian synthesis of mathematics and experiment.

The void . . . action through the void . . . action at a distance (attraction)—it was against these features and implications of the Newtonian world view that the opposition of the great Continental contemporaries of Newton—Huygens, Leibniz, Bernoulli—well trained in the Cartesian rejection of unclear and unintelligible ideas, was directed.

In his famous, brilliant *Lettres anglaises*, or, to give them their official title, *Lettres philosophiques*—readable even today—Voltaire very wittily sums up the situation: a Frenchman who arrives in London finds himself in a completely changed world. He left the world *full*; he finds it *empty*. In Paris the universe is composed of vortices of subtle matter; in London there is nothing of that kind. In Paris everything is explained by pressure which nobody understands; in London by attraction which nobody understands either.

Voltaire is perfectly right: the Newtonian world is chiefly composed of void. It is an infinite void, and only a very small part of it—an infinitesimal part—is filled up, or occupied, by matter, by bodies which, indifferent and unattached, move freely and perfectly unhampered in—and through—that boundless and bottomless abyss. And yet it is a world and not a chaotic congeries of isolated and mutually alien particles. This, because all of these are bound together by a very simple mathematical law of connection and integration—the law of attraction—according to which *every one of them is related to and united with every other*. Thus each one takes its part and plays its role in the building of the *systema mundi*.[6]

The universal application of the law of attraction restores the physical unity of the Newtonian universe and, at the same time, gives it its intellectual unity. Identical relations hold together identical contents. In other words, it is the same set of laws which governs all the motions in

6. System of the world. [Editor]

the infinite universe: that of an apple which falls to the ground and that of the planets which move round the sun. Moreover, the very same laws explain not only the identical pattern (discovered by Kepler) of the celestial motions but even their individual differences, not only the regularities, but also the irregularities (inequalities). All the phenomena which for centuries baffled the sagacity of astronomers and physicists (such, for instance, as tides) appear as a result of the concatenation and combination of the same fundamental laws.

The Newtonian law of attraction according to which its force *diminishes* in proportion to the square of the distance is not only the only law of that kind that explains the facts but, besides, is the only one that can be uniformly and universally applied to large and small bodies, to apples and to the moon. It is the only one, therefore, that it was reasonable for God to have adopted as a law of creation.

Yet, in spite of all this, in spite of the rational plausibility and mathematical simplicity of the Newtonian law (the inverse-square law is simply the law of extension of spherical surfaces identical with that of the propagation of light), there was in it something that baffled the mind. Bodies attract each other, act upon each other (or, at least, behave as if they did). But how do they manage to perform this action, to overcome the chasm of the void that so radically separates and isolates them from each other? We must confess that nobody, not even Newton, could (or can) explain, or understand, this *how*.

Newton himself, as we well know, never admitted attraction as a "physical" force. Time and again he said, and repeated, that it was only a "mathematical force," that it was perfectly impossible—not only for matter but even for God—to act at a distance, that is, to exert action where the agent was not present; that the attractive force, therefore—and this gives us a singular insight into the limits of the so-called Newtonian empiricism—was not to be considered as one of the essential and fundamental properties of bodies (or matter), one of these properties such as extension, mobility, impenetrability, and mass, which could neither be diminished nor increased; that it was a property to be explained; that he could not do it, and that, as he did not want to give a fanciful explanation when lacking a good theory, and as science (mathematical philosophy of nature) could perfectly well proceed without one, he preferred to give none (this is one meaning of his celebrated *Hypotheses non fingo*[7]), and leave the question open. Yet, strange, or natural, as it may seem, nobody—with the single exception of Colin Maclaurin—followed him in that point. The very first generation of his pupils (Cotes, Keill, Pemberton) accepted the force of attraction as a real, physical, and even primary property of matter and it was their doctrine which swept over

7. "I do not feign hypotheses." Sometimes translated: "I do not frame hypotheses." See passage from the General Scholium to the *Principia*, Part 2, Scientific Method (below), and the entire General Scholium, Part 8, Theology (below). [Editor]

Europe and which was so strongly and persistently opposed by Newton's Continental contemporaries.

Newton did not admit action at a distance. Yet, as Maupertuis and Voltaire very reasonably pointed out, from the point of view of purely empirical knowledge (which seemed to be the point of view of Newton), the ontological distinction between the attraction and the other properties of bodies could not be justified. We do not, of course, understand attraction. But do we understand the other properties? Not understanding is not a reason to deny a fact. Now attraction is a fact. Thus we have to admit it just as we are admitting other facts or properties of bodies. Who knows, besides, what unknown properties we may discover as pertaining to them? Who knows with what sort of properties God has endowed matter?

The opposition to Newtonianism—understood as *physics*—was in the beginning deep and strong. But gradually it crumbled away. The system worked and proved its worth. And as for attraction, progressively it lost its strangeness. As Mach has very finely expressed it, "the uncommon incomprehensibility became a common incomprehensibility." Once used to it, people—with very few exceptions—did not speculate about it any more. Thus fifty years after the publication, in 1687, of the *Philosophiae naturalis principia mathematica*—a title just as daring and just as consciously challenging as the *Physica coelestis* of Kepler eighty years earlier or the *Evolution créatrice* of Bergson two hundred years later—the leading physicists and mathematicians of Europe—Maupertuis, Clairaut, D'Alembert, Euler, Lagrange, and Laplace—diligently began the work of perfecting the structure of the Newtonian world, of developing the tools and methods of mathematical and experimental investigation (Desaguliers, s'Gravesande, and Musschenbroek), and of leading it from success to success, till, by the end of the eighteenth century, in the *Mécanique analytique* of Lagrange and the *Mécanique céleste* of Laplace, the Newtonian science seemed to reach its final and definitive perfection—such a perfection that Laplace could proudly assert that his *System of the World* left no astronomical problem unsolved.

So much for the mathematicians and scientists. As for the others, for those who could not understand the difficult intricacies of geometrical and infinitesimal reasoning and who, like Locke (reassured by Huygens), took them for granted, there came forth a series of books—and very good ones—such as Pemberton's *View of Sir Isaac Newton's Philosophy* (London, 1728; French translation, Paris, 1755), Voltaire's *Lettres philosophiques* (1734) and *Éléments de la philosophie de Newton* (Amsterdam, 1738), Algarotti's *Il Newtonianismo per le dame* (Naples [Milan], 1737; 2nd ed., 1739; French translation, Paris, 1738), Colin Maclaurin's *Account of Sir Isaac Newton's Philosophical Discoveries* (London, 1746; French translation, Paris, 1749), Euler's *Lettres à une princesse d'Allemagne* (St. Petersburg, 1768–1772), and finally

Laplace's *Système du monde* (1796), which in a clear and accessible language preached to the *honnête homme*,[8] and even to the *honnête femme*, the Newtonian gospel of mathematicophysical and experimental science.

No wonder that (in a curious mingling with Locke's philosophy) Newtonianism became the scientific creed of the eighteenth century, and that already for his younger contemporaries, but especially for posterity, Newton appeared as a superhuman being who, once and for ever, solved the riddle of the universe.

Thus it was by no means in a spirit of flattery but in that of deep and honest conviction that Edmund Halley wrote, *nec fas est propius Mortali attingere Divos*.[9] Did not, a hundred years later, Laplace, somewhat regretfully, assign to the *Principia* the pre-eminence above all other productions of the human mind? Indeed, as Lagrange somewhat wistfully put it, there being only one universe to be explained, nobody could repeat the act of Newton, the luckiest of mortals.

Small wonder that, at the end of the eighteenth century, the century that witnessed the unfettered progress of Newtonian science, Pope could exclaim:

> Nature and Nature's Laws lay hid in Night:
> God said, *Let Newton be!* and All was Light.

Pope could not know indeed that

> It did not last: the Devil howling "Ho,
> Let Einstein be," restored the status quo.

But let us now come back to Newton. It has often been said that the unique greatness of Newton's mind and work consists in the combination of a supreme experimental with a supreme mathematical genius. It has often been said, too, that the distinctive feature of the Newtonian science consists precisely in the linking together of mathematics and experiment, in the mathematical treatment of the phenomena, that is, of the experimental or (as in astronomy, where we cannot perform experiments) observational data. Yet, though doubtless correct, this description does not seem to me to be a complete one: thus there is certainly much more in the mind of Newton than mathematics and experiment; there is, for instance—besides religion and mysticism—a deep intuition for the limits of the purely mechanical interpretation of nature. And as for Newtonian science, built, as I have already mentioned, on the firm basis of corpuscular philosophy, it follows, or, better, develops and brings to its utmost perfection, the very par-

8. Cultivated man. [Editor]
9. "Nearer the gods no mortal may approach." The final line of Edmond Halley's "Ode to Newton," published in the *Principia*. [Editor]

ticular logical pattern (by no means identical with mathematical treatment in general) of atomic analysis of global events and actions, that is, the pattern of reducing the given data to the sum total of the atomic, elementary components (into which they are in the first place dissolved).

The overwhelming success of Newtonian physics made it practically inevitable that its particular features became thought of as essential for the building of science—of any kind of science—as such, and that all the new sciences that emerged in the eighteenth century—sciences of man and of society—tried to conform to the Newtonian pattern of empirico-deductive knowledge, and to abide by the rules laid down by Newton in his famous *Regulae philosophandi,*[1] so often quoted and so often misunderstood. The results of this infatuation with Newtonian logic, that is, the results of the uncritical endeavor mechanically to apply Newtonian (or rather *pseudo* Newtonian) methods to fields quite different from that of their original application, have been by no means very happy, as we shall presently see. Yet, before turning our attention to these, in a certain sense illegitimate, offshoots of Newtonianism, we have to dwell for a moment upon the more general and more diffuse consequences of the universal adoption of the Newtonian synthesis, of which the most important seems to have been the tremendous reinforcement of the old dogmatic belief in the so-called "simplicity" of nature, and the reintroducing through science into this very nature of very important and very far-reaching elements of not only *factual* but even *structural* irrationality.

In other words, not only did Newton's physics use *de facto* such obscure ideas as power and attraction (ideas suggesting scholasticism and magic, protested the Continentals), not only did he give up the very idea of a rational deduction of the actual composition and formation of the choir of heaven and furniture of earth, but even its fundamental dynamic law (the inverse-square law), though plausible and reasonable, was by no means necessary, and, as Newton had carefully shown, could be quite different. Thus, the law of attraction itself was nothing more than a mere fact.

And yet the harmonious insertion of all these facts into the rational frame of spatiomathematical order, the marvelous *compages*[2] of the world, seemed clearly to exclude the subrationality of chance, but rather to imply the suprarationality of motive; it seemed perfectly clear that it had to be explained not by the necessity of cause, but by the freedom of choice.

The intricate and subtle machinery of the world seem obviously to require a purposeful action, as Newton did not fail to assert. Or, to

1. "Rules of Reasoning in Philosophy," which appear at the beginning of Book 3 of the *Principia*. See Part 2, Scientific Method (below). [Editor]
2. Composite whole. [Editor]

put it in Voltaire's words: the clockwork implies a clockmaker *(l'horloge implique l'horloger)*.

Thus the Newtonian science, though as *mathematical philosophy of nature* it expressedly[4] renounced the search for causes (both physical and metaphysical), appears in history as based on a dynamic conception of physical causality and as linked together with theistic or deistic metaphysics. This metaphysical system does not, of course, present itself as a constitutive or integrating part of the Newtonian science; it does not penetrate into its formal structure. Yet it is by no means an accident that not only for Newton himself, but also for all the Newtonians—with the exception only of Laplace—this science implied a reasonable belief in God.

Once more the book of nature seemed to reveal God, an engineering God this time, who not only had made the world clock, but who continuously had to supervise and tend it in order to mend its mechanism when needed (a rather bad clockmaker, this Newtonian God, objected Leibniz), thus manifesting his active presence and interest in his creation. Alas, the very development of the Newtonian science which gradually disclosed the consummate skill of the Divine Artifex and the infinite perfections of his work left less and less place for divine intervention. The world clock more and more appeared as needing neither rewinding nor repair. Once put in motion it ran for ever. The work of creation once executed, the God of Newton—like the Cartesian God after the first (and last) *chique-naude*[3] given to matter—could rest. Like the God of Descartes and of Leibniz—so bitterly opposed by the Newtonians—he had nothing more to do in the world.

Yet it was only at the end of the eighteenth century with Laplace's *Mécanique céleste* that the Newtonian God reached the exalted position of a *Dieu fainéant*[4] which practically banished him from the world ("I do not need that hypothesis," answered Laplace when Napoleon inquired about the place of God in his system), whereas for the first generation of Newtonians, as well as for Newton himself, God had been, quite on the contrary, an eminently active and present being, who not only supplied the dynamic power of the world machine but positively "ran" the universe according to his own, freely established, laws.

It was just this conception of God's presence and action in the world which forms the intellectual basis of the eighteenth century's world feeling and explains its particular emotional structure: its optimism, its divinization of nature, and so forth. Nature and nature's laws were known and felt to be the embodiment of God's will and reason. Could they, therefore, be anything but good? To follow nature and to accept as highest norm the law of nature, was just the same as to conform oneself to the will, and the law, of God.

3. Flick of the finger. [Editor]
4. Literally, a God who does nothing; that is, a God without a function in the universe after the act of creation. [Editor]

Now if order and harmony so obviously prevailed in the world of nature, why was it that, as obviously, they were lacking in the world of man? The answer seemed clear: disorder and disharmony were man-made, produced by man's stupid and ignorant attempt to tamper with the laws of nature or even to suppress them and to replace them by man-made rules. The remedy seemed clear too: let us go back to nature, to our own nature, and live and act according to its laws.

But what is human nature? How are we to determine it? Not, of course, by borrowing a definition from Greek or Scholastic philosophers. Not even from modern ones such as Descartes or Hobbes. We have to proceed according to pattern, and to apply the rules which Newton has given us. That is, we have to find out, by observation experience, and even experiment, the fundamental and permanent faculties, the properties of man's being and character that can be neither increased nor diminished; we have to find out the patterns of action or laws of behavior which relate to each other and link human atoms together. From these laws we have to deduce everything else.

A magnificent program! Alas, its application did not yield the expected result. To define "man" proved to be a much more difficult task than to define "matter," and human nature continued to be determined in a great number of different, and even conflicting, ways. Yet so strong was the belief in "nature," so overwhelming the prestige of the Newtonian (or pseudo-Newtonian) pattern of order arising automatically from interaction of isolated and self-contained atoms, that nobody dared to doubt that order and harmony would in some way be produced by human atoms acting according to their nature, whatever this might be—instinct for play and pleasure (Diderot) or pursuit of selfish gain (A. Smith). Thus return to nature could mean free passion as well as free competition. Needless to say, it was the last interpretation that prevailed.

The enthusiastic imitation (or pseudo-imitation) of the Newtonian (or pseudo-Newtonian) pattern of atomic analysis and reconstruction that up to our times proved to be so successful in physics, in chemistry, and even in biology, led elsewhere to rather bad results. Thus the unholy alliance of Newton and Locke produced an atomic psychology, which explained (or explained away) mind as a mosaic of "sensations" and "ideas" linked together by laws of association (attraction); we have had, too, atomic sociology, which reduced society to a cluster of human atoms, complete and self-contained each in itself and only mutually attracting and repelling each other.

Newton, of course, is by no means responsible for these, and other, *monstra* engendered by the overextension—or aping—of his method. Nor is he responsible for the more general, and not less disastrous, consequence of the widespread adoption of the atomic pattern of analysis of global events and actions according to which these latter appeared to be not *real*, but only *mathematical* results and summings up of the underlying elementary factors. This type of analysis led to the nominalistic misconception of the relation between a *totum* and its parts, a misconception which, as a matter of fact, amounted to a complete negation of *tota* (a *totum* reduced to a mere sum of its parts is not a *totum*) and which nineteenth- and twentieth-century thought has had such difficulty in overcoming. No man can ever be made responsible for the misuse of his work or the misinterpretation of his thought, even if such a misuse or misinterpretation appears to be—or to have been—historically inevitable.

Yet there is something for which Newton—or better to say not Newton alone, but modern science in general—can still be made responsible: it is the splitting of our world in two. I have been saying that modern science broke down the barriers that separated the heavens and the earth, and that it united and unified the universe. And that is true. But, as I have said, too, it did this by substituting for our world of quality and sense perception, the world in which we live, and love, and die, another world—the world of quantity, of reified geometry, a world in which, though there is place for everything, there is no place for man. Thus the world of science—the real world—became estranged and utterly divorced from the world of life, which science has been unable to explain—not even to explain away by calling it "subjective."

True, these worlds are every day—and even more and more—connected by the *praxis*. Yet for *theory* they are divided by an abyss.

Two worlds: this means two truths. Or no truth at all.

This is the tragedy of modern mind which "solved the riddle of the universe," but only to replace it by another riddle: the riddle of itself.

A. RUPERT HALL AND MARIE BOAS HALL

Newton and the Theory of Matter †

The analysis of Newton's theory of matter is a subject of perennial interest to everyone familiar with his writings, for Newton wrote virtually nothing, except in the field of pure mathematics, that did not either explicitly or tacitly reveal his commitment to some version or other of the seventeenth century's constant preoccupation, the mechanical philosophy. And whereas the mechanical philosophy in the hands of those predecessors who were in some sense Newton's masters (Descartes and Boyle especially) was relatively simple and clear cut, Newton's theory is

† Robert M. Palter, ed. *The "Annus Mirabilis" of Sir Isaac Newton, 1666–1966* (Cambridge, MA: MIT Press, 1970), pp. 54–67. Reprinted by permission of The MIT Press. Marie Boas Hall and A. Rupert Hall, historians of science, presented this paper originally at a conference on Newton's *annus mirabilis* held at the University of Texas in 1966.

both complex and unsettled, and his exact meaning has presented and continues to present a fascinating puzzle to scholars, a puzzle important for the understanding of both Newton and the Newtonians.

We ourselves have long been concerned with this aspect of Newton's achievement, and indeed our edition of *Unpublished Scientific Papers of Isaac Newton* was largely constructed out of extracts which we found of particular interest for Newton's theory of matter. We there stated our views of Newton's opinion of the structure of matter and his attitude towards aetherial and atomic explanations at some length. But for the benefit of those who have not been involved in this aspect of Newtonian scholarship, and as a general introduction to the more particular points we wish specifically to discuss in this paper, it seems desirable here to summarize very briefly the general position we have taken in the past.

It is, surely, fair to state that all Newtonian scholars now agree that a particulate theory of matter underlies all Newton's thinking about natural philosophy. Whether this is explicit, as in the 31st Query of *Opticks* ("it seems probable to me, that God in the Beginning form'd Matter in solid, massy, hard, impenetrable, moveable Particles," etc.) or relegated to prefatory hints, as in the *Principia*, it is nevertheless plain to be seen as a necessary mechanism, and as one which served Newton well in the interpretation and explanation of the laws of nature. Newton took particles virtually for granted; what for him deserved emphasis was the way in which these particles either possessed or were acted upon by the forces of attraction and repulsion. That the force of attraction existed between bodies, and by extension between particles was transparently evident from the one force which Newton could and did handle mathematically—gravity. Indeed the case of gravity showed explicitly that all forces acting between bodies could be reduced to forces acting between particles. Repulsion was a natural corollary to attraction: so he proclaimed in Query 31 "as in algebra, where affirmative quantities vanish and cease, there negative ones begin; so in mechanicks where attraction ceases, there a repulsive virtue ought to succeed." Of these things Newton had and could have no doubt, for it was to him obvious common sense; and he could and did insist that he spoke in the most ordinary way. As he said in the suppressed "Conclusio," the unpublished ending to the *Principia* which should have, but did not, explain publicly his deepest thoughts on problems of matter, "The force of whatever kind by which distant particles rush towards one another is usually, in popular speech, called an attraction. For I speak loosely when I call every force by which distant particles are impelled mutually towards one another, or come together by any means and cohere, an attraction."

This much was clear. There was a force of attraction, and its negative, a force of repulsion. But to say what this force was, this Newton regarded as quite a different matter. As he wrote agitatedly to Bentley in January 1692/3, "The Cause of Gravity is what I do not pretend to know, and therefore would take more Time to consider of it." As we have tried to show by printing the relevant documents, Newton had been considering the cause of gravity (or, more generally, attraction) from very early days as he was to continue to do until the end of his life; yet never to his own satisfaction. We have in connection with these documents shown how Newton constantly balanced an action-at-a-distance concept of pure attraction against a quasi-Cartesian impulse mechanism. This latter he developed in various forms, from an aerial to an aetherial mechanism of ever increasing sophistication. Over and over again he juggled with the experimental facts as he knew them (rather a small range of experimental evidence: capillary attraction, the lack of adhesion in dry powder, the difficulty of pressing two surfaces together, the walking of flies on water, the anomalous suspension of mercury, the refraction of light, chemical activity, electrical attraction, only the last three being unused in the earliest discussions). Over and over again Newton tried to persuade himself that there was enough experimental evidence to provide a firm basis for a definitive theory, and over and over again there patently was not. Only thus can one explain why he continually tried to write his considered judgment on the problem for publication, and each time until *Opticks* never ventured more than a hint.

Other problems were deeply enmeshed with the problem of the cause of the forces of attraction and repulsion: the interpretation of forces, the value of hypotheses, the immediate role of God in the mechanism of the universe. This last we have discussed at considerable length in our introduction to the documents. The others we propose to consider here.

Let us begin with the obvious point that any theory of matter entertained by Newton was necessarily hypothetical, and that concerning hypotheses he had certain reservations that are very well known. Thus the historian seems to find in Newton himself firm injunctions to heed only his positive achievements in science and to disregard any "hypotheses" of a secondary order upon which they might appear to depend; yet the same historian must be uncomfortably aware that such positive achievements of Newton remain incomplete and intellectually indigestible if they are taken in isolation, divorced from his deeper views about the structure of things and about the causes of those phenomena which are susceptible of positive discussion. Moreover, as the historian extends his knowledge of the Newtonian *oeuvre*, he finds that Newton himself was so far incapable of remaining on the plane of icy positivism to which he found it convenient to retreat from time to time, that he openly showed how there were multiple leads that might be pursued at the fascinating level of hypothesis. So we have not only the question, "Did Newton himself have ideas about the deeper infrastructure of Nature?"—a question which nowadays we can hardly fail to answer in the affirmative, since we know that he wrote altogether at least fifty thousand words on the subject; there is also the question, "Did Newton attach particular probability to one set of ideas in preference to others?" And this question is one which is, to the historian, neither trivial nor merely descriptive, for we would expect some relationship between the preferred hypothesis and the positive achievement. Indeed, such a correlation has often been assumed in the past without critical examination.

Hence, we cannot by any means separate a consideration of Newton's ideas about matter from his epistemology, though we can effect one simplification not open to him. We are not now any longer concerned with the problem of *living*, rather than historical, science; with the question "Is this positive theory correct or not?" Obviously, when treating both optics and celestial mechanics, it was highly important to Newton not to have the fate of what he called a "doctrine" hang upon his reader's reaction to what he called a "hypothesis." This he stresses again and again: I am telling you, he says, that these properties of light are true properties, and that these equations apply to the motions of physical bodies, and that they do so *whatever* we think about gravity, or whatever we think about the nature of light. So he writes of Pardies,

> I do not take it amiss that the reverend father calls my theory an hypothesis, since he had not yet grasped it. But I had proposed it from a different point of view, in which it seemed to embrace nothing but certain properties of light, which I think can easily be demonstrated once they have been discovered, and which if I did not know them to be true, I would rather repudiate them as empty and idle speculations than acknowledge them as my own hypotheses.

And, accordingly, Newton maintains more than once that the "properties" (same word again!) of light that he had discovered "were in some measure capable of being explicated not only by that [a corporeal hypothesis of light], but by many other mechanical hypotheses." Now if we followed Popperian analysis we would deduce from this the emptiness of such mechanical hypotheses, from each of which the same phenomena (the properties) may be predicted; and it may be that Newton too had some such idea in mind. More to the point, however, is his contention: you must not think this property is only comformable to *my* view of light, for I can show that it is also consonant with *yours*.

We are not now concerned to examine Newton's usage of such words as "hypothesis" or "doctrine," nor to discuss the failure of his attempts to make his contemporaries judge his newly discovered properties or newly advanced doctrine as things in themselves, independently of hypotheses. Here we need only point the obvious moral, that scientists do find it very difficult to judge new "doctrines" without, at the same time, reflecting upon the deeper level of hypothesis about the structure of things. Nor do we have to evaluate the rationality or otherwise of the feeling of Newton's contemporaries, that along with his "doctrine" itself he was trying to smuggle into their minds something of his own way of interpreting that "doctrine." It is, at the very least, easy enough to see that in his early optical days Newton found it very difficult not to write of light as "body," just as later, when writing of gravitation, the word "attraction" would come naturally to his pen.

Having recognized that Newton fell over backwards in his effort, in the face of criticism, to do what we would all try to do—to get his principal idea across by sacrificing all inessentials—we then arrive at our first real difficulty: must we discount *all* Newton's reservations about hypotheses because we have discredited *hypotheses non fingo?* Because we have ceased to describe Newton as a Comtian positivist, must we *now*, falling over on our own faces, have to allow that whenever Newton suggested a mechanism appropriate to explain certain phenomena, he necessarily believed it to be the true and only mechanism? Obviously not. For sometimes we perceive Newton saying something which is open to question as an hypothesis without seeming to recognize the fact, in which case we may assume that he was not viewing that hypothesis critically; sometimes he is distinguishing between "my hypothesis" (always guardedly so qualified, of course) and yours, or Hooke's, or Lucas'; sometimes he is discussing directly contradictory hypotheses.

In fact, we return, with circumspection, to the point from which we might have set out with careless confidence: we must in the last analysis evaluate each of Newton's discussions of structural hypotheses on its own merits; there are no general grounds for endorsing one more or less than another. To this there is perhaps one exception: for throughout his life Newton constantly drew essentially the same distinction between "doctrine" and "hypothesis," and this to quite a large extent corresponds to a distinction between "experimental and mathematical" on the one hand, and Cartesian or first-order "mechanical explanation" on the other. (By first-order mechanical explanation we mean to distinguish the Cartesian or more generally aetherist view which makes mechanical *impact* the prime phenomenon of Nature. It is easy to overlook the continued elaboration of such explanations during the early years of Newton's maturity, without as well as within the strict Cartesian tradition. As examples of the former one may cite William Neile's philosophy of motion, the Hooke-Mayow theory of combustion, and Leibniz' *Hypothesis physica nova*,[1] the first part of which was dedicated to the Royal Society. The aether was still the natural medium for all causal explanations. The term "second-order mechanical explanation" we apply to Newton's use of the concept of force which, unlike the former, proved in some special cases susceptible of a complete mathematical treatment.) It is perhaps hardly needful to add that Newton distinguished both mathematical and mechanical explanations from the qualitative explanations of the Peripatetics. In Newton's very first printed paper he wrote:

1. *New Physical Hypothesis* (1671). [Editor]

> to determine more absolutely, what Light is, after what manner refracted, and by what modes or actions it produceth in our minds the Phantasms of Colours, is not so easie. And I shall not mingle conjectures with certainties.

(Certain ideas, certain forms of words even, seem to have crystallized in his mind at an early age; we need not wonder that this passage so exactly parallels the more famous one in the General Scholium.) It is not surprising to find that others before Newton drew the distinction; the logical issue is indeed an obvious one, and must surely have been expressed many times.

Clearly any ideas that Newton held about the structure of matter and the mechanical causes of phenomena must lie in the realm of "hypotheses." Unless one is to classify such ideas as merely derivative (as borrowed from Boyle and Gassendi, etc.), which we would be loathe to do, they can only be regarded as the products of something we might loosely call Newton's metaphysics of Nature, guided by more precise but always indefinite inference from the phenomena of physics, chemistry, and biology as they were known to him. To take an interesting example, Newton relates his aether hypothesis of 1675 to

> that puzzling problem, "By what means the muscles are contracted and dilated to cause animal motion," [which] may receive greater light from hence than from any means men have hitherto been thinking on.

And he goes on to explain his thought in the following sentence:

> For if there be any power in man to condense and dilate at will the aether that pervades the muscle, that condensation or dilation must vary the compression of the muscle made by the ambient aether, and cause it to swell or shrink accordingly.

When Newton writes this, he is expressing his own modification of Cartesian nervous physiology—and incidentally providing in advance an explanation of a mysterious phrase in the *Scholium Generale* of forty years later. The problem, then, is to disentangle the various "hypotheses" that Newton entertained, and, further, even to allow for the various occasions when Newton appears to disdain hypotheses wholly. And we must first ask, was Newton always consistent?

Now palpably Newton's *utterances*—both those intended for public circulation and those not so intended—are inconsistent. This assertion is generally granted, and it may be easily confirmed by setting side by side such a well-known passage as this from the *Principia's* Preface:

> I wish we could derive the rest of the phaenomena of Nature by the same kind of reasoning [the reasoning of mathematical physics] from mechanical principles, for I am induced by many reasons to

> suspect that they may all depend upon certain forces by which the particles of bodies, by some causes hitherto unknown, are either mutually impelled towards one another, and cohere in regular figures, or are repelled and recede from one another . . .

with another passage, this from Book II (Section XI, Scholium)

> In mathematics we are to investigate the quantities of forces with their proportions consequent upon any conditions supposed; then, when we enter upon physics, we compare these proportions with the phenomena of Nature that we may know what conditions of those forces answer to the several kinds of attractive bodies.

Here we see Newton setting out in unmistakable language the structure of second-order mechanical explanation, which is mathematical and vacuist. To those, thirdly, we might add the already quoted proclamation of Newton's atomism in Query 31 of *Opticks*. And many other printed passages, not least the celebrated refutation of the Cartesian aether at the close of Book II of the *Principia*, could be combined with the evidence we collected from manuscripts to show that Newton was (in his mature years at least) an upholder of second-order mechanism and had rejected the aether required for first-order mechanism.

On the other side must be cited many long passages in which Newton did compose first-order mechanical explanations. Anti-Cartesian in his metaphysics though Newton seems to have been from his early years, the term "aether" yet ran easily from his pen. Again, his first published paper is unguarded in this respect: for example, the hypothesis or, as he called it, "plausible ground of suspition" that refracted rays of light are curved (which was refuted by measurements) rested on the possibility that "if the Rays of Light should possibly be globular bodies, and by their oblique passage out of one medium into another acquire a circulating motion, they ought to feel the greater resistance from the ambient Aether, on that side, where the motions conspire, and thence be continuously bowed to the other." Again, when Newton insists in his letter to Pardies of 10 June 1672 that it is the randomness of *whatever* mechanical effect be hypothetically identified with "light" that causes true whiteness, he exemplifies these effects as "inaequales pressiones, motiones aut mota corpuscula per aethera quaquaversum trajiciantur" (that is, "inequalities in pressure, inequalities in motion, or inequalities between moved particles, that travel through the aether"). It is clear that at this stage Newton was very far from supposing that an emission or corpuscular theory of light would liberate him from postulating an aether; hence his allusion to the aethero-emission theory (which was to become ultimately the theory of "Fits") in his reply to Hooke, and his development of it in the second optical paper, were quite in accord with his earliest view. As for the aether concepts in the "Letter to Boyle," and in the "Queries" in *Opticks*, these are too well known to require repetition.

Faced with two bodies of evidence, some historians have simply turned a blind eye to Newton's second-order mechanical explanations (perhaps on the ground that these are merely mathematical, or products of a deliberate but misleading positivist posture), and accordingly have declared that Newton was always at heart an aetherist, as it were a super-Cartesian. Thus Professor Rosenfeld writes that there could be (in the common metaphysic of More and Newton) no "direct interaction of God and gross matter," and, he suggests, "could not a finer kind of substance provide the missing link? An aetherial fluid filling all space could, as Descartes wanted it, transmit various forces between the bodies by appropriate cyclic motions. . . ." And although he further states that after writing the *Principia* Newton was forced to restrict considerably the scope of his aether hypothesis, so that his "experimental philosophy" was a "position of retreat," it is clear that in Rosenfeld's eyes aetherism is Newton's preferred and indeed only logical position. In his view what we have called second-order mechanical explanations were very much a *pis–aller*.[2]

Now we have mentioned Professor Rosenfeld in this context only because his is a recent statement of this position; and we shall have occasion later to borrow a good point he has made. However, it must be noted that his conception of what Newton's first-order mechanical explanation did for him is open to question; most recent writers, following Koyré, Professor Guerlac among them as well as we ourselves, have regarded Newton's views on the omnipresence of God as being antithetic to his aetherism. That issue is beside the point here, in any case; the main objection to wholehearted endorsement of the view that Newton was (at best) a discreet aetherist, is the obvious fact that it makes a nonsense of the *Principia* and of all that achievement in mechanics for which Newton has been venerated above all. For—if we may be forgiven here for reiterating an historical opinion we have often expressed before—*if* Newton meant what he said when he spoke of forces in physics (in the *Principia* texts as printed, and in so many manuscript passages), then he was indeed introducing a great new idea, analogous to and preparing the way for that of the field in nineteenth-century physics. This force concept introduced by Newton enabled him to transcend Cartesian, billiard-ball mechanism, the mechanism of impact. If particle A moves, it is not necessarily because it has been struck by particle B; it may be that a force (which is gravitational, magnetic, electrical, or chemical in nature) has acted upon it. It was this second-order mechanism that permitted Newton to extend the mathematization of physics so far, to construct celestial mechanics, and to reëstablish the void. In fact it enabled Newton to reëstablish atomism by returning to concepts closer to those of Epicuros than was the corpuscularian mechanism of

2. Last resort. [Editor]

the Cartesians; it was precisely the addition of the idea of force that made *mathematical* atomism feasible.

Here the Galileo-Descartes antithesis precisely parallels the Descartes-Newton antithesis. Descartes's criticism of Galileo's mathematical analysis of the fall of heavy bodies turned on Galileo's ignorance of the true cause of gravity, discovered by Descartes himself in the fabrication of the vortex. Descartes's hypothetical mechanism for gravity resisted mathematization; he could not devise the law $s = \frac{1}{2}gt^2$ The whole of Cartesian impact physics remained non-mathematical until after the appearance of the *Principia*—except, of course, insofar as Wren, Huygens, and Wallis stated the laws of impact themselves. Then Newton, following Galileo, again mathematized physics by ignoring impact mechanisms and adopting second-order mechanical explanations that depended on the concept of force; that is, by confessing a limitation to knowledge comparable to that made by Galileo when the latter declined to discuss the *cause* of natural acceleration. Comparable to, not identical with, since Galileo possessed no concept of force, whereas Newton had a definite, though not sharp, idea of what it is that causes motion. Impressed forces arise from percussion, from pressure, from centripetal force. Centripetal force is exemplified by gravity and magnetism; considered as absolute, it is proportional to the magnitude of the generative body; considered as accelerative it is proportional to the acceleration it produces; and considered as motive it is proportional to the motion generated in a given time. However, *force* is not the end of the chain; there is, Newton adds, a cause

> without which those motive forces would not be propagated through the spaces round about; whether that cause be of some central body (such as is the magnet in the center of the magnetic force, or the earth in the center of the gravitating force), or anything else that does not yet appear. For I here design only to give a mathematical notion of those forces, without considering their physical causes and seats.

There we have it—not quite fairly, perhaps, in that a mathematical notion of forces (simply expressing the quantity *ma* by the symbol *f*) would not permit us to speak of magnetism or gravity, and would not indeed allow us to see the special interest of centripetal forces—a working if not a fully philosophical justification for a new concept in mechanics. Or rather, since the notion of *vis* is old enough, a justification for refusing to go beyond second-order mechanism to find the cause of *vis*, before we have got what we can out of the idea itself.

No one will deny that there are difficulties in the analysis of Newtonian mechanics in terms of second-order mechanism alone. But by contrast (it seems to us) if one holds that, for Newton, all the forces were mere pseudo concepts and that the reality was always in corpuscular aetherial impact, then one is really saying that the *Principia* is about pseudo science. This is the question of *De revolutionibus* and Osiander's preface all over again. Does the *Principia* contain a view of reality or is it just a convenient mathematical model—a way of computing the effects of the aether without actually introducing the aetherial mechanism? Either Newton in introducing into the first of his *Principia* prefaces phrases like "mechanical principles" and "certain forces by which particles are impelled" and so forth, was being his own Osiander, or (for that time at least) he meant what he said; that is, that the concept of force was what one needed for mathematical physics, and mathematical physics gave a sufficient explanation of natural phenomena.

With this in mind, consider again Newton's notorious insistance on mathematical argument. We need hardly instance the *Principia*, though we might recall those passages in it where Newton discussed the transition from applied mathematics to the physics of nature. However, what we have particularly in mind is the sentence omitted for some reason from the printed version of the first optical letter (6 February 1672)[3]:

> I shall now proceed to acquaint you with another more notable difformity in its Rays, wherein the *Origin of Colours* is infolded. A naturalist would scarce expect to see the science of those become mathematicall, and yet I dare affirm that there is as much certainty in it as in any other part of Opticks.

To this Newton again referred in his reply to Hooke's observation (11 June 1672), in a passage similarly excised from the *Philosophical Transactions:*

> 12. That the Science of Colours is most properly a Mathematicall Science.
>
> In the last place I should take notice of a casuall expression which intimates a greater certainty in these things then I ever promised, viz: The certainty of *Mathematicall Demonstrations*. I said indeed that the *Science of Colours was Mathematicall and as certain as any other part of Optiques;* but who knows not that Optiques and many other Mathematicall Sciences depend as well on Physicall Principles as on Mathematicall Demonstrations: And the absolute certainty of a Science cannot exceed the certainty of its Principles.

No doubt both the original passage and the gloss upon it were struck out because Newton saw (from Hooke's criticism) that he had gone so far as to be liable to easy misunderstanding; nevertheless, in *Opticks* he was

3. See Part 4, Optics (below). [Editor]

to declare again that color is a mathematically identifiable property of light:

> by consequence . . . all the Productions and Appearances of Colours in the World are derived, not from any physical Change caused in Light by Refraction or Reflexion, but only from the various Mixtures or Separations of Rays, by virtue of their different Refrangibility or Reflexibility. And in this respect the Science of Colours becomes a speculation as truly mathematical as any other part of Opticks.

One cannot doubt that Newton was confident of the certainty of mathematical science and of its power to yield unique propositions—for if by the "mathematical way of reasoning" we derived multiple results—that a given planet could equally well move in any of three possible orbits for example—we should suspect our initial data or a mistake in the reasoning. Contrast this with Newton's attitude to first-order mechanical hypotheses: these are not unique, since it is possible to frame several, mutually equivalent, and they are uncertain because indemonstrable. On the other hand, second-order mechanical explanations in terms of forces are an integral part of the mathematization of physics; we cannot dispense with them, and by our very success in (for example) constructing celestial mechanics we find that our assumed force of gravitation is verified. There can be no doubt, then, that for Newton science moves to a new level of certainty when it moves from the nonmathematical state of multiple first-order hypotheses to the mathematical state of unique second-order explanations in terms of forces. Or, we need only employ the necessarily multiple and equivalent hypotheses of aether until such time as they are succeeded by a mathematical physics in terms of forces. If, now, having done this we were to step back and seek to explain forces once more in terms of first-order aetherial hypotheses we should gain nothing: for once more it is possible to feign any hypothesis.

It seems to us that it is impossible to account for Newton's scientific epistemology except in one way, if any attempt is made to reconcile his utterances with the actual texture of his science. One need not suppose—indeed for our part we have never supposed—that Newton's thought on these matters was fully mature from the start. We are now learning that his recollection of achievement in the *annus mirabilis*[4] of 1665–66 was by no means inflated, but we are also discovering more precisely how much he had to do in the next twenty years. We would not now ask why Newton did not write the *Principia* in 1666; we know he could not have written it then. In mathematics, optics, astronomy and mechanics Newton's thought slowly ripened, his technical expertise widened, and his knowledge deepened. Now Professor Rosenfeld has

4. Marvelous year. [Editor]

already remarked that Newton's late discovery of the true power of the law of gravitation—after 1680—was a blow to his aetherial hypotheses; for a Cartesian aether was not only needless after this as a last-resort fund of explanation for unresolved problems in celestial kinematics, it was positively difficult to see how it could agree with the unresisted motion of the planets. With the law came the interstellar vacuum. But this is by no means all that can be said. Remembering that "De motu corporum"[5] was long Newton's simple title for the growing work, one may well doubt whether he was cognizant (before it began to take shape) of the extent to which Natural Philosophy was founded on mathematical principles. He had gone far in that direction in optics already, yet by no means so far as he was to go in 1704. In other words, before the *Principia* Newton (still under the influence of Descartes) perforce was content to leave a large role for first-order mechanical hypotheses. What he discovered—not in his brilliant youth but in his mature development of mechanics—was the success of the concept of force in rendering mathematical science possible; this was something he could not learn fully until he had raised celestial mechanics on the foundation of the force of gravitation.

If this explains the dominance of second-order mechanical explanations during Newton's mature years we are still left with the question: Why did Newton make fresh, oracular pronouncements about the aether and mysterious spirits in 1706, 1713, and 1717? And in the later "Queries" and so forth, without withdrawing anything of what he had said before. It must first be said that this new aether of Newton's is strange indeed. It is emphatically distinguished from the crude, dense "first matter" of the Cartesians since

> to make way for the regular and lasting Motions of the Planets and Comets, it's necessary to empty the Heavens of all matter, except perhaps some very thin Vapours, Steams, or Effluvia, arising from the Atmospheres of the Earth, Planets, and Comets, and from such an exceedingly rare Aetherial Medium as we described above.

(The last twelve words were added in 1717 to the version of 1706. Newton was patching his text.) But to continue: the dense Cartesian aether "is of no use, and hinders the Operations of Nature . . . therefore it ought to be rejected." The new medium accordingly must be 49×10^{10} times more elastic than air in proportion to its density. In fact it is so utterly unphysical that it does not infringe the metaphysical interaction between God and his universe sketched directly by Newton in his letters to Bentley, and indirectly in those of Samuel Clarke to Leibniz. Consistent with this we still read in the text of Query 28 (lightly patched from the Latin of 1706) that it was a mistake on the part of natural philosophers to explain all things mechanically without recognition of a First

5. "Concerning the Motion of Bodies." [Editor]

Cause which is nonmechanical; and that these philosophers should seek "not only to unfold the mechanism of the world, but chiefly to resolve these and such like questions," which, when set out, turn on the Great Architect's eye to the harmony of Creation. There is here only the minimum alteration required by consistency in favor of aetherist interpretations.

The Queries remain enigmatic. Here are some new queries concerning them. Will any one explain how a particulate aether which is enormously less dense than air can have such force between its particles that it is more elastic than air? And whence does this force arise? Must it not be supposed that the divine intervention gives the aether these properties; and if so, why should God act thus deviously? How can the particles of aether press on material bodies to cause gravitation, yet not resist the motions of these bodies? How can the aether press on bodies not only to cause gravitation, but other forces also? And how can Newton, that great abstainer from hypotheses, not have seen how pressed with difficulties these hypotheses of his own are? Perhaps we must admit that Newton has, in the end, made the whole business of the relation between the universe, God, and mechanical hypotheses (or indeed, non-mechanical hypotheses) utterly incomprehensible.

This is perhaps a cry of despair. Some may continue to feel that the enigma of the Queries is adequately solved by simply stating that Newton abandoned forces in favor of his Mark II, God-powered aether. Professor Guerlac, for example, has lately drawn attention to the source of the fresh experimental evidence recited by Newton in the "Queries" and "Scholium Generale." He suggests that this fresh evidence revived the vigor of aetherial explanations in Newton's mind, to the extent that he resuscitated *in print* notions that he had carefully refused to publish during more than half a lifetime:

> Le revirement de Newton—sa nouvelle disposition en faveur d'un éther—date des experiences de [Francis] Hauksbee et de la collaboration scientifique toute particulière entre les deux hommes.

The point is well made. But it is still hard to understand why experiments on the electric fire should have invited Newton to revise his conception of the dynamics of Nature, and to recast his conceptions of light and gravitation, if this is really what happened. For note that Newton did not by any means revert to a simple, first-order aetherial theory, nor did he withdraw anything that he had written earlier in second-order terms, during the extensive revisions of the *Principia* and *Opticks*. Even in the latter work he did not reinstate the full aetherial explanation of the theory of "Fits" that he had provided in 1675; though it is hinted at in Query 18, the text remains unaltered. Yet these revised aetherial hypotheses are not wholly dependent on Hauksbee's new work; in Query 18, just mentioned, for example, Newton refers to the (erroneous) observation that a thermometer placed *in vacuo* shows external temperature changes as swiftly as another open to the atmosphere. "Is not the heat of the warm room," he asks, "conveyed through the vacuum by the vibrations of a much subtiler medium than Air, which after the Air was drawn out remained in the Vacuum?" So we find Newton in the Queries reverting once again to the familiar phenomena of first-order mechanism, and drawing the same antivacuist lessons that others had drawn before him.

It cannot be simply the case, then, that the aging Newton was compelled to change his mind by fresh evidence. Something deeper was occurring, or some other necessity pressed him. Now it seems impossible to believe that, at this stage of his life, Newton revolted against all he had learned from Henry More, and that he sought to return, via a revived aether, to the logically complete mechanism of Descartes for which, indeed, an aether was essential. We know that at just this same time Newton was conspiring with Clarke to defend the spiritual agency within the physical universe against the complete mechanism of Leibniz. It would be strange if Newton were developing a secret partiality toward his opponent's philosophy! Nor, it seems, can we believe the Newton had really changed his mind about the irrelevance and possible evils of mechanical hypotheses. However, we do know that Newton had employed such hypotheses before, in order to refute those who held that his "doctrines" were mechanically incomprehensible, or led to mechanically unacceptable consequences. It seems not impossible that he saw occasion enough in Hauksbee's new results for choosing yet again the same aetherial escape route. If mechanical hypotheses alone could make his "doctrines" acceptable, then mechanical hypotheses Newton would provide—in the form of Queries.

However, the extent to which these represent a genuine shift in Newton's opinion is debatable. Unfortunately we have no "Letters to Bentley" from the last years of Newton's life; on the other hand, we do have a consistent testimony from Newton's friends and associates. The second and all subsequent editions of the *Principia* contain a preface written by Roger Cotes, the editor whom Newton admired the most, which begins with a severe attack upon mechanical hypotheses, producing a "Fabulem quidem elegantem forte et venustam, Fabulam tamen";[6] and ends with scorn for those who would postulate a medium that is indistinguishable from vacuity:

> So that we must conclude that the celestial fluid has no inertia, because it has no resisting force; that it has no force to communicate motion with, because it has no inertia; that it has no force to produce any change in one or more bodies, because it has no force

6. Those who assume hypotheses as first principles "may indeed form an ingenious romance, but a romance it will still be." [Editor]

> wherewith to communicate motion; that it has no manner of efficacy, because it has no faculty wherewith to produce any change of any kind. Therefore certainly this hypothesis may be justly called ridiculous and unworthy a philosopher, since it is altogether without foundation and does not in the least serve to explain the nature of things.

This might almost be a critique of Query 21! And Cotes concludes (as one might expect) that those who deny the vacuum deny God for the sake of asserting Necessity.

Samuel Clarke, Newton's champion, translator and exponent, is no less clear, for he actually infers the vacuum from the fact of gravitation, in one of his notes to Rohault:

> But it is very evident from Gravity . . . that there must not only be a Vacuum in Nature, but that it is the far greatest Part . . . why should not the same quantity of matter, make the same Resistance, whether it be divided into a great many very small Parts [Clarke asks] or into a few large ones? . . . Since therefore the Essence of Matter does not consist in Extension, but in impenetrable solidity we must say that the whole world is made up of solid bodies which move in a vacuum. . .

Again, Henry Pemberton, last of Newton's editors, was equally emphatic that the phenomena of nature arise from the solid particles composing bodies, not from the interstices between them. He takes Newton as his authority for rejecting the plenitude of space:

> Sir Isaac Newton objects against the filling of space with such a subtle fluid, that all bodies in motion must be unmeasurably resisted by a fluid so dense, as absolutely to fill up all the space through which it is spread.

Like Clarke, Pemberton shows how (on Newtonian principles) resistance is proportional to density, unless the aether be supposed deprived of

> the same degree of inactivity as other matter. But if you deprive any substance of the property so universally belonging to all other matter, without impropriety of speech it can scarce be called by this name.

Indeed, Pemberton comes close to the offense of declaring that gravity is inherent in matter, for, he says, this

> power in the great bodies of the universe, is derived from the same power being lodged in every particle of the matter which composes them: and consequently, that this property is no less than universal to all matter whatever, though the power be too minute to produce any visible effects on small bodies.

These Newtonians all wrote in the last fifteen years of Newton's life; another, David Gregory, made a highly important record at a rather earlier date—21 December 1705—when Newton had told him of the additions he intended to make to the Latin edition of *Opticks*, obviously showing him the passage that was to appear at the end of Query 28 in the later English versions of the Queries. It begins, "What is there in places almost empty of Matter, and whence is it that the Sun and Planets gravitate towards one another, without dense Matter between them?" (The "almost" is an afterthought; Gregory calls it, "the space that is empty of body.") Gregory's comment is:

> The plain truth is, that he believes God to be omnipresent in the literal sense; And that we are sensible of Objects when their Images are brought home within the brain, so God must be sensible of every thing, being intimately present with every thing: for he supposes that as God is present in space where there is no body, he is present in space where a body is also present. But if this way of proposing this his notion be too bold, he thinks of doing it thus. *What cause did the Ancients assign of Gravity.* He believes that they reckoned God the Cause of it, nothing els, that is no body being the cause; since every body is heavy.

Notice again the consistent Newtonian dual linkage between inertia and matter, God and absence of matter. We find it difficult to believe that Newton ever gave up these principles, upon any evidence whatsoever. Certainly if he did, he was the only early Newtonian so to do.

ARNOLD THACKRAY

Matter in a Nut-Shell: Newton's *Opticks* and Eighteenth-Century Chemistry †

I

In 1777 Joseph Priestley wrote that

> The principles of the Newtonian philosophy were no sooner known, than it was seen how few, in comparison, of the phenomena of nature, were owing to *solid matter*, and how much to *powers*. . . . It has been asserted . . . that . . . all the solid matter in the solar system might be contained within a nut-shell. . . . Now

† *Ambix* 15 (1968), 29–37. Reprinted by permission of The Society for the History of Alchemy and Chemistry. Arnold Thackray remains today an active scholar of the history of science. We have excerpted his article, which can be seen entire in *Ambix*, and in a more expanded form in his book, *Atoms and Powers: An Essay on Newtonian Matter-Theory and the Development of Chemistry* (Cambridge, MA: Harvard University Press, 1970).

> when solidity had apparently so very little to do in the system, it is really a wonder that it did not occur to philosophers sooner . . . that there might be no such a thing in nature.

As so often, Priestley was carrying to their extreme but logical conclusion views widely accepted among his contemporaries. These contemporaries might reject the conclusion. Few should have quarrelled with the assertion that "all the solid matter in the solar system might be contained within a nut-shell." In the nineteenth century this characteristically Newtonian belief was over-shadowed, thanks to the triumph of the chemical atomic theory and the wave theory of light. As a result we have yet to appreciate the deep and pervasive influence that this Newtonian belief exercised on eighteenth-century scientific thought, especially thought about the nature and status of the chemical elements.

An inquiry into the development and influence of the "nut-shell" theory of matter is highly rewarding for other reasons too. It shows Newton at his most reluctant. It explains the so far overlooked inclusion of two pages of new material in the 1706 Latin *Opticks*. It reveals Newton's disciples vigorously developing a viewpoint to which their master hesitated to commit himself. It highlights previously neglected aspects of the Clarke-Leibniz controversy. And it illustrates the influence of theological and metaphysical beliefs on what we are still too prone to regard as the purely "scientific" discussions of the eighteenth century.

* * *

II

An important part of the mid-seventeenth-century establishment of a mechanical philosophy had been the agreement that science was concerned with the categories of matter and motion, not those of soul or "rational spirit." This agreement was subscribed to equally by Gassendian atomists, Cartesian plenum theorists, and Boyleian "corpuscularians." Recent research has shown how it is too simple to suppose that Newton drew inspiration only from such "correct" natural philosophers. He was also influenced by the rather different speculations of Henry More and the Cambridge Platonists. His adoption of a philosophy based on atoms and possibly immaterial forces was deeply rooted not only in the science, but also in the theology and metaphysics of the period. In this paper I have no wish to discuss the reasons that led Newton to formulate and first expound his ideas on the structure of matter. Instead I wish to focus on the later career of these ideas. I shall be concerned principally with the published *Opticks*, the debate with Leibniz, the emergence of a Newtonian "nut-shell" orthodoxy, and the great influence of this orthodoxy on many subsequent chemical theorists.

The ideas that were to be developed in the *Opticks*, and in later battles with Leibniz, are foreshadowed in Newton's papers on light and colours of the early 1670's. The 1687 first edition of the *Principia* in its turn makes plain Newton's commitment to a disseminate vacuum. Only with the vacuum's aid can his assumption of the uniform density of brute matter be reconciled with experience. Yet notwithstanding these earlier hints and clues, it was not until after Hooke's death and his own election as President of the Royal Society that Newton chose to make public more of his thoughts about the microstructure of matter. Even so the 1704 *Opticks* was less than forthcoming about the theological beliefs that lay behind Newton's ideas on this microstructure.

Thanks to the active research work of the past decade we now know much about those beliefs. The wealth of surviving manuscripts amply reveals just how far removed the Newton of the 1690's and early 1700's was from what he termed "the vulgar supposition that gravity is mechanical." To him this supposition could only offer a path to atheism. In contrast his own system of atoms, a vacuum, and gravity as an immaterial power, stood as the firm bulwark of true religion. The tone of Newton's physico-theology was well-caught by David Gregory in a 1705 note:

> 21 December, 1705. Sir Isaac Newton was with me and told me that he had put 7 pages of addenda to his book of light and colour in this new latin edition of it. . . . His doubt was whether he should put the last quaere thus. *What the space that is empty of body is filled with.* The plain truth is that he believes God to be omnipresent in the literal sense. . . . But if this way of proposing this his notion be too bold, he thinks of doing it thus. *What cause did the ancients assign of gravity.* He believes that they reckoned God the cause of it, nothing else, that is no body being the cause, since every body is heavy.

All this, by now, well known. What is not so often appreciated is the extreme length to which Newton developed a second belief associated with his non-mechanistic attitude toward gravity. This second belief was simply that the universe is an almost entirely vacuous entity—not merely in terms of the existence of a disseminate vacuum, but *also in terms of the interstitial vacuum*. The 1704 publication of the *Opticks* marked the beginning of the public development of the scientific aspects of this belief.

The main body of the *Opticks* repays closer study than it has often received. This is especially true of Book II, which deals with the colours of thin transparent bodies. The introduction is quite specific that knowledge of these colours "may conduce to further discoveries for completing the theory of light, especially as to the constitution of the parts of natural bodies." Parts I and II of the book consist of observation and comment. In part III Newton finally allows himself to discuss the theory "of the permanent colours of natural bodies, and the analogy between them and the colours of thin transparent plates." This discussion is crucial to our understanding of the later development of Newtonian matter theory, for it sketches a picture of that porous, structured and almost "matterless" matter by which later commentators set so much store.

To put it briefly, Newton believes all bodies to be highly porous, and the pores "for the most part spaces void of both air and water, but yet perhaps not wholly void of all substance." Reflection or refraction of light can only take place on passage to a medium of different density. The opacity of most known bodies is therefore a natural consequence of "the multitude of reflexions caused in their internal parts." The least particles of bodies are transparent, on account of their very small size. Larger "component parts" are not transparent. The theory of fits of easy reflection and easy transmission explains how only pores and parts of a certain minimum size give rise to reflection, the colours reflected and transmitted being a function of the size of the parts. Hence—and most important—"the bigness of the component parts of natural bodies may be conjectured by their colours." It is even possible "that microscopes may at length be improved to the discovery of the particles of bodies on which their colours depend." Newton is constrained to add that "if we shall at length attain to, I fear it will be the utmost improvement of this sense. For it seems impossible to see the more secret and noble works of nature within the corpuscles by reason of their transparency." Even so, something can be inferred about these "more secret and noble works."

The clue is that "the cause of reflexion is not the impinging of light on the solid or impervious parts of bodies, as is commonly believed." Indeed, "its probable that as many of its rays as impinge on the solid parts of bodies are not reflected but stifled and lost in the bodies." The implication that matter must be extremely tenuous, is plain. For whether light be a particle or a wave, if contact means loss, then light must be able to travel vast distances in right lines through substances such as water, without ever encountering a solid particle. Or, as Newton cautiously and modestly stated it in 1704:

> And hence we may understand that bodies are much more rare and porous than is commonly believed. Water is 19 times lighter, and by consequence 19 times rarer than gold, and gold . . . has more pores than solid parts. . . . And he that shall find out an hypothesis, by which water may be so rare, and yet not be capable of compression by force, may doubtless by the same hypothesis make gold and water, and all other bodies as much rarer as he pleases, so that light may find a ready passage through transparent substances.

* * *

When the second edition of the *Principia* finally appeared, it contained major alterations to the section on matter and the vacuum at the start of Book III. Among these changes was the addition of a sentence implying but not stating the "nut-shell" theory of matter. Revealingly, the added sentence is in the form of a query. It runs, "And if the quantity of matter in a given space can, by any rarefaction, be diminished, what should hinder a diminution to infinity?" This hint in query form was as far as Newton was prepared to go in public, at this stage.

* * *

The "nut-shell" view of matter was just as much part of the Newtonian position, as belief in a plenum was of the Leibnizian. That Newton took the whole exchange seriously enough to contemplate further revising the opening sections of Book III of the *Principia* in its light, is scarcely surprising. These revisions were never executed, perhaps because the eventual production of a *Principia* third edition was a work of Newton's extreme old-age. The *Opticks* fared better. The second English edition was published in 1717, but on the heels of the Leibniz-Clarke controversy.

In this new edition, the section of Book II part III that deal with bodies being "much more rare and porous than is commonly believed" is augmented with the two pages of further discussion that first appeared in the 1706 corrigenda. Now at last Newton permits himself to state publicly, as an unavoidable part of his text, the "nut-shell" theory that he had thought on for so long, and which his disciples had hinted at, developed and defended. He first notes that gravity and magnetism act through dense bodies "without any diminution." Also "the rays of light whether they be very small bodies projected, or only motion or force propagated, are . . . transmitted through pellucid solid bodies in right lines to very great distances." To explain these effects, he then expounds that same view of the internal structure of matter which David Gregory had so carefully noted down from his lips, twelve years before. To quote at length from the 1717 *Opticks* version:

> How bodies can have a sufficient quantity of pores for producing these effects is very difficult to conceive, but perhaps not altogether impossible. For the colours of bodies arise from the magnitudes of the particles which reflect them, as was explained above. Now if we conceive these particles of bodies to be so disposed amongst themselves, that the intervals or empty spaces between them may be equal in magnitude to them all; and that these particles may be composed of other particles much smaller, which have as much empty space between them as equals all the magnitudes of these smaller particles: And that in like manner these smaller particles are again composed of others much smaller, all which together are equal to all the pores or empty spaces between them; and so on perpetually till you come to solid particles, such as have no pores or empty spaces within them: And if in any gross body there be, for instance, three such degrees of particles, the least of which are

> solid; this body will have seven times more pores than solid parts. But if there be four such degrees of particles, the least of which are solid, the body will have fifteen times more pores than solid parts. If there be five degrees, the body will have one and thirty times more pores than solid parts. If six degrees, the body will have sixty and three times more pores than solid parts. And so on perpetually.

Having said all which, the passage enigmatically concludes, "And there are other ways of conceiving how bodies may be exceeding porous. But what is really their inward frame is not yet known to us."

There is no reason to doubt Newton's sincerity of intention in this last remark. His care in distinguishing between possible explanations and demonstrated truths was a major aspect of his unrivalled scientific ability. Yet his reiteration of this "conception" of the "inward frame" of bodies in other published passages, the tenor of a variety of his manuscripts, the 1708 and 1714 statements of John Keill, the course taken by the Leibniz–Clarke correspondence: all leave us with little room for doubt about the importance of the "nut-shell" idea in Newton's own thought. Certainly commentators had no such doubt. With Leibniz dead, and Newton himself at last plainly committed to an extended statement of the "nut-shell" theory, what need had they of further caution!

* * *

III

From what has been said so far, it should be apparent that the Newtonian vision of the universe as an almost matterless entity, sustained by God's will, regulated by his direct intervention, and operating through immaterial forces, received powerful experimental support from the phenomena of reflection, refraction and transmission set forth in the *Opticks*. The Newtonian belief that contact means loss, necessarily implied that transparent bodies transmit light only by virtue of their great porosity. The further assumption that "brute matter" is itself homogeneous and of one uniform density, inevitably led to the (to Newton very acceptable) position that all material objects are extremely porous. Leibniz had been at some pains to attack this position, for it offended his metaphysical and theological principles. The main practical result of these attacks was a further elaboration and defence of the "nut-shell" theory. The 1717 *Opticks* furnished the necessary "internal structure" model. This model showed how the apparently solid matter of everyday experience could be built up from almost literally nothing. The members of Newton's immediate circle were not slow for their part, in providing and propagating the geometrical 'theorems' that supported the nut-shell theory.

It is therefore not surprising that this powerfully-argued and widely-supported view of the internal structure of matter should have had a profound effect on eighteenth-century thought about the nature and status of the chemical elements. Earlier debate about these elements had been deeply influenced by rival Aristotelian, Paracelsian and corpuscularian cosmological schemes. In a similar fashion, this later discussion was greatly affected by the Newtonian *Weltanschauung*[1] in both its theological and its positivistic versions.

The net effect of Newton's work on white light, his views about the nature of transparent substances, and the "nut-shell" theory of matter, was to suggest to all Newtonian-inspired chemists that a deep gulf lay between chemical elements and ultimate physical atoms. Chemists might wish to learn of the latter, but they must of necessity be content with knowledge of the former. One of the earliest to make clear the distinction was, surprisingly, G. E. Stahl. How much, if anything, his discussion owed to Newton's work I am not in a position to say, nor do I wish to enter on a consideration of the complexities of Stahlian matter theory. Suffice it to state that Stahl was explicit how

> a difference, at present, prevails between the physical and chemical principles of mix'd bodies. Those are called physical principles whereof a mixt is really composed; but they are not hitherto settled. . . . And those are usually term'd chemical principles, into which all bodies are found reducible by the chemical operations hitherto known.

Such a distinction was more than welcome to Newtonian chemists. This is quickly evident from the work of such men as Shaw and Cullen.

* * *

The same distinction between physical atoms and chemical elements may be found in such French writers as P. J. Macquer and Guyton de Morveau. Their inspiration sprang from the same Newtonian sources, even if these sources were more positivistically interpreted, and shorn of the theological implications so important to Dutch and British authors. Again, it is instructive to turn to such a later and highly popular work as the *Chemical Essays* of Richard Watson, Cambridge professor, Bishop of Llandaff, and competent but unexciting chemist. Here we learn that

> by chemical elements, which are the last products of chemical analysis, we are to understand, not very minute indivisible particles of matter, but the simple homogeneal parts of bodies which are not capable, as far as our experience teaches us, of any farther resolution or division. . . .

1. Worldview. [Editor]

It thus comes not as a surprise, but rather an anticlimax, to read Lavoisier's famous declaration:

> that if, by the term elements, we mean to express those simple and indivisible atoms of which matter is composed, it is extremely probable we know nothing at all about them; but, if we apply the term elements, or principles of bodies, to express our idea of the last point which analysis is capable of reaching, we must admit, as elements, all the substances into which we are capable, by any means, to reduce bodies by decomposition.

While admirable for its lucidity, the statement was not notable for its originality. Indeed, it was entirely in accord with the then-prevailing assumptions of Newtonian matter theory.

The theological significance of these assumptions was by no means lost from sight in the later-eighteenth century. This much is apparent from the discussions of two influential but widely disparate figures, R. J. Boscovich and Joseph Priestley. It was the former's *Theoria Philosophiae Naturalis* that finally took the logical step, and emptied the Newtonian nut-shell of whatever "solid matter" it still contained. The step was taken with a lively concern for the theological implications of the resulting world-picture, as the *Theoria's* appendices reveal. Boscovich was at some pains to preserve a matter-spirit dualism in his new theory. This should not surprise us. Boscovich was after all a highly-placed Jesuit, and a devoted servant of his church. No more should it surprise us that his treatise met with little response in the hostile climate that France then provided, or that natural philosophers within the theologically-oriented British tradition greeted his ideas with enthusiasm.

Most enthusiastic of all was Joseph Priestley. His scientific writings amply testify to his Boscovichean sympathies. His *Disquisitions Relating to Matter and Spirit*, from which my opening quotation was taken, show how it was primarily for deeper theological reasons that he welcomed Boscovich's development of the Newtonian position. But unlike his mentor, the theologically advanced and rationalistically inclined Priestley took the opportunity to abolish matter-spirit dualism by calmly abandoning matter. Predictably, Boscovich was bitterly offended by the use made of his ideas. He voiced the sentiments of orthodox Churchmen everywhere when he rapidly objected to Priestley's "pure and unconcealed materialism" and to being made a "party to a doctrine that I detest and abhor as impiety in religion and senseless to sound philosophy." Yet this objection should not be allowed to obscure the far more significant fact that both were agreed on the relevance of matter-theory to theology. Neither should it obscure their agreement as to the hierarchical internal structure of matter, the complex nature of the known chemical elements, and the almost total vacuity of the universe.

V

The "nut-shell" aspects of the Newtonian natural philosophy had originally been articulated within a theologically-oriented debate. Thus it was natural that both Boscovich and Priestley should find reinforcement for their theological beliefs in further modifications to the "nut-shell" position. In this manner of thinking they were out of harmony with developing trends among late-eighteenth-century physical scientists. The continuing decay of religious enthusiasm among the educated classes, the increasing specialization and sophistication of the physical sciences, the growing realization that God was an unnecessary hypothesis *within* these sciences—all these factors militated against a too-straightforward linking of theology and matter-theory. When the "nut-shell" position was finally subjected to sustained scientific attack, no public defence was offered on grounds of theological principle, whatever may have been the private thoughts of some participants.

Nonetheless it is interesting to speculate as to how far the notoriety that attached to Priestley's views (especially after 1794) was a spur to British attempts to repudiate the "nut-shell" position. Newton had seen this position as part of a bulwark against atheism. But Priestley's ruthlessly logical development of it had led to a denial of that matter-spirit by which orthodox Christians set such store. The "pure and unconcealed materialism" of his matterless universe was cause enough for alarm at any time. How much more so in a country reacting deeply to the changing course of the French Revolution. It is thus not without interest that the scientific assault on the "nut-shell" theory was the work of two members of a [by then] conservative Christian sect. In their different ways, the Quakers Thomas Young and John Dalton were both concerned to re-emphasize the reality of material atoms.

In 1801 Thomas Young mounted a careful (and eventually successful) assault on the particle theory of light. A defeat for this theory meant a corresponding weakening in the "nut-shell" view of matter, since a major argument for this view derived from consideration of the transmission of light particles through transparent bodies. Young was fully aware of this. The way he put it was that

> if ten feet of the most transparent water transmits, without interruption, one half of the light that enters it . . . so much must the space or area occupied by the particles be smaller than the interstices between them . . . that the whole space occupied by the substance must be as little filled, as the whole of England would be filled by a hundred men. . . .

What to Newton had been one of the cardinal features of his system had by now become "this astonishing degree of porosity." To Young it was yet another virtue of the Huygenian wave-hypothesis that it

> does not require the disproportion to be by any means so great, since the general direction and even the intensity of an undulation should be very little affected by the interposition of the atoms of matter.

At the same time that Young was filling up the empty universe, John Dalton—by the boldest stroke of all—was denying the whole century-long tradition of thought about porosity and internal structure. Dalton's contribution was to equate physical atoms and chemical elements. That it should be another practising Quaker who thus recreated a materialist world, full of heterogeneous billiard-ball-like atoms, is at least worth remark. That both Dalton and Young met strenuous opposition from the many scientists still committed to a Newtonian world-view is not surprising. Indeed, Humphry Davy voiced the immediate reaction of most Newtonian-inspired chemists, when he dismissed Dalton's ideas as "rather more ingenious than important." Even in 1812 Davy still preferred the "sublime idea . . . sanctioned by the approbation of Newton . . . that there is only one species of matter." With it went the traditional conviction that the subject of light

> when fully understood, promises to connect together chemical and mechanical science, and to offer new and more comprehensive views of the corpuscular arrangements of matter.

Whatever Davy might think, it was to be Dalton's work that provided the fruitful new approach which would "connect together chemical and mechanical science." And so successful was the nineteenth-century career of Dalton's chemical atomic theory, that from it arose a new chemical historiography with little room for the nut-shell view of matter.

J. E. McGUIRE AND P. M. RATTANSI

Newton and the 'Pipes of Pan'†

> What is it, by means of which, bodies act on one another at a distance. And to what Agent did the Ancients attribute the gravity of their atoms and what did they mean by calling God an harmony and comparing him and matter (the corporeal part of the Universe) to the God Pan and his Pipe. Can any space be without something in it and what is that something in space void of matter (and what are its properties and operations on matter).
>
> —Draft of Query 27 of *Opticks*

† Excerpted from *Notes and Records of the Royal Society* 21 (1966): 108–26. Reprinted with the permission of The Royal Society.

Newtonian scholars have long been aware of a set of draft Scholia to Propositions IV to IX of Book III of the *Principia*. These were composed in the 1690's, as part of an unimplemented plan for a second edition of the work. Since they describe supposed anticipations of Newton's doctrines in the thought of Graeco-Roman antiquity, they have become known as the 'classical' Scholia. The analogies and parallels drawn in them are so strained, as judged by modern standards of scholarship, that it is tempting to consider them as merely literary embellishments of a scientific work.

However, the sheer bulk of the manuscripts, the number of copies and variants, their relation to Newton's other writings, and the testimony of Newton's associates together with their publication of some of the materials, all make it certain that he considered the arguments and conclusions of the Scholia an important part of his philosophy.

It would perhaps be possible to interpret the Scholia, with their discussions of legendary figures and their references to a 'mystical' philosophy, as the work of the 'magical' (and hence aberrant) Newton—as eccentric productions that possess little significance for the reconstruction of his genuinely scientific work, but merely throw light on his esoteric and occult interests. To us, however, this interpretation appears untenable. It is now amply clear that Newton's serious enquiries were not restricted to natural philosophy, investigated by an experimental-mathematical method. His studies of theology and ancient chronology were of equal importance to him and were pursued in as rigorous a fashion as his scientific work. There is sufficient evidence, even in his published writings, to show that he did not regard these different sorts of enquiry as unrelated exercises. Rather, he shared the belief, common in the seventeenth century, that natural and divine knowledge could be harmonized and shown to support each other.

We shall first describe the contents of these Scholia, and interpret them in the light of the statements of Newton's associates, and of other works by Newton. These materials will provide the basis for a re-examination of parts of the *General Scholium* and the *Opticks*. At that time, as is well known, Newton believed that he knew how God's agency operated in His created world, particularly in the cause of gravitation. Our analysis of the Scholia will show that Newton held (at least at the time of their composition) an equally firm belief about his own place among the *prisci theologi*[1] who had possessed such knowledge. He believed, in brief, that God had once revealed these and other truths, but they had soon been obscured and had been partially rediscovered by certain antique sages. In this respect, Newton's work has close similarities with that of the Cambridge Platonists. These similarities may be more significant than the well-known similarity between Newton's doc-

1. Antique (or venerable or original) theologians. [Editor]

trine of absolute space and that of Henry More. In reexamining Newton's relation to the Cambridge Platonists, we shall see that he did not merely borrow ideas from them, but was engaged in a private dialogue whose terms were set by a certain intellectual tradition.

The study of the 'classical' Scholia should therefore deepen our understanding of Newton's philosophical endeavour, and make it possible to relate his work to its contemporary English natural-philosophical and theological context with greater precision.

* * *

The Propositions of Book III, for which the Scholia were intended, exhibit a carefully developed structure. The Book starts with six solar Phaenomena, obtained through astronomical observation and calculation. Then the first three Propositions state that the circumjovial planets, the primary planets, and the moon, are all retained in their orbits by a force which is mathematically described by the inverse-square law. The proof of this is supplied by the first four Propositions of the First Book.

So far we are at the level of the mathematical description of the phenomena. But Proposition IV states that the forces mentioned in the first three Propositions are the force of gravity. Thus it is a statement about a real force in the physical world, embodying the famous proof that the gravitational force which pulls terrestrial objects to the Earth is the same as that which pulls the moon from its inertial path. By induction and by appeal to Rules 1 and 2, Propositions V and VI extend the reasoning to cover the primary planets and then all celestial bodies. Proposition VI also introduces the proportionality of gravity to the quantity of matter in a body, which leads to a discussion of the interstitial void in the corrollaries. But more importantly, Proposition VI not only asserts the generality of the action of gravity in affecting all sensible bodies, but it implies that sub-sensible particles gravitate as well. This latter doctrine is explicitly treated in Proposition VII. The inverse-square law of attraction is shown, in Proposition VIII, to apply not only to celestial bodies but also to their component particles. Finally, Proposition IX asserts the law of action of the real force of gravity *within* celestial bodies. Thus, by this series of extensions, gravity is concluded to be a completely universal force.

The central purpose of the 'classical' Scholia was to support the doctrine of universal gravitation as developed in these Propositions, and to enquire into its nature as a cosmic force. This doctrine is shown by Newton to be identifiable in the writings of the ancients. As will become clear, he is not using this historical evidence in a random fashion, or merely for literary ornamentation. Rather, the evidence is used in a serious and systematic fashion, as support for, and justification of, the components of Newton's theory of matter, space and gravitation. The evidence is used to establish four basic theses, which correspond to the matter of the Propositions IV to IX. These are, that there was an ancient knowledge of the truth of the following four principles: that matter is atomic in structure and moves by gravity through void space; that gravitational force acts universally; that gravity diminishes in the ratio of the inverse square of the distance between bodies; and that the true cause of gravity is the direct action of God. We shall analyse these in turn, using supporting texts from some associates of Newton, and from Newton's other writings.

It will be recalled that Propositions VI and VII are connected with gravity as a real physical force, moving both perceptible and imperceptible bodies in a non-resisting void. In the Scholium to Proposition VI, which includes 62 lines from Lucretius, Newton says:

> Even the ancients were aware that all bodies which are round about the Earth, air and fire as well as the rest, have gravity towards the Earth, and that their gravity is proportional to the quantity of the matter of which they consists. Lucretius thus argues in proof of the void.

Newton then quotes twelve lines from Book I of *De Rerum Natura* which state that void exists, and that of any bodies which are equal in magnitude, difference in weight is explained by more or less interstitial void. This doctrine is discussed in the Corollaries to Proposition VI. Newton's comment on this passage is important:

> Lucretius here relates gravity to the function of the body, or its nature by which it is distinguished from Void, which has no gravity, and from this concludes that weight is always proportional to body. In this argument he includes all bodies, both imperceptible and perceptible. For he attributes this gravity even to those atoms of which other things consist. For he affirms that fire, and other bodies which are designated weightless, rise upwards not of their own accord but by a force which drives from below, just as wood, which is a body with gravity, rises up in water, whereas all bodies are being borne downwards through void space.

Newton follows this with a passage of twenty-two lines from Book II of Lucretius, which shows his commentary to be, in part, a paraphrase. For the conclusion of this Lucretian passage states, after giving the same example of things which seem to rise upwards naturally:

> We do not doubt, but that all these things, as far as in them lies, are borne downwards through the empty void.

Thus it is clear from his commentary and from the passages quoted, that Newton regards Lucretius as holding in the manner of the *Principia* that all matter whatsoever gravitates in a non-resisting void. Another quotation of twenty-eight lines from Book II further supports this conclusion.

Newton then turns to the historical succession of the atomical hypothesis, which is implicit in the *Principia* and explicit in the Lucretian passages:

> This Lucretius taught from the mind of Epicurus, Epicurus from the mind of the more ancient Democritus. For certain persons, assuming the equality of the atoms, would have it that the gravity of bodies is in proportion to the number of the atoms of which they consist. Others, to whom the atoms were unequal, taught that gravity is proportional not to the number of the solids but to the quality of the solid.

This distinction is supported by a quotation from Aristotle on the atomists, and by a reference to Simplicius, who places Leucippus and Democritus in the second position. For them, the 'quality' of the body is measured by the ratio of solid parts to void interstices, which together make up the body:

> But by the levity of the void these philosophers did not understand any positive quality of the void, as Aristotle's opinion is, but merely absence of gravity.

Newton concludes by bringing the 'Italic' philosophers into the succession:

> Among the philosophers therefore who have held that bodies are composed of atoms, it was a received opinion that gravity accrues both to atoms and to composite bodies, and that in individual bodies it is proportional to the quantity of matter. That bodies are compound of atoms was the view of both Ionic and Italic philosophers. *The followers of Thales and Pythagoras,* Plutarch observes, *deny that the section of those bodies which are subject to movement proceeds to infinity but ceases at those things which are individual and are called atoms.*

In Proposition VII, Newton is explicitly concerned with the doctrine that the gravity of any composite body is the sum of its component parts which are held together by mutual gravitation. By analogy, he concludes that it follows that all celestial bodies mutually gravitate as the inverse square of the distance with respect to the components. Apart from the draft scholia in the Royal Society manuscript, there is another in the Portsmouth collection which is, in part, a summary of the longer set of scholia and which was probably intended as an alternative. Both documents are concerned with the absolute universality of gravitation. In the Royal Society manuscript there is a passage directly relevant to the main doctrine of Proposition VII, namely, that the quantity of matter of any body is a function of its parts:

> Therefore just as the attractive force of the whole Magnet is composed of the attractive forces of the individual particles of which the Magnet consists, even so the ancient opinion was that Gravity towards the whole Earth arises from the gravity towards its individual parts. For that reason, if the whole Earth were divided into several globes, gravity, by the mind of the ancients, would have to be extended towards each several globe, in the same way as magnetic attraction is extended towards individual fragments of the magnet. And the ratio of gravity is equally towards all bodies whatever.
>
> Hence Lucretius teaches that there exists no centre of the universe, and no lowest place, but that there are in infinite space worlds similar to this of ours, and in addition to this he argues for the infinity of things in these terms.

Following this is another passage from Lucretius, containing an argument for the infinity of the universe:

> . . . if all the space in the universe stood contained within fixed boundaries on all sides and were limited, by this time the store of matter would by its solid weight have run together from all sides to the bottom . . .

Newton's comments on this passage are similar in the two manuscripts. The Royal Society manuscript reads:

> The force of the argument is that if the nature of things were bounded in any direction, the remotest bodies, since they would have no bodies beyond them into which to have gravity, would not stand in equilibrium but would by their own gravity make their way towards the things inside, and by flowing together from all quarters since infinite time would long ago have settled down in the midst of the whole as it were in a lowest place. Therefore, to the mind of Lucretius, each several body has gravity towards the matter situated round about it, and by virtue of overpowering gravity is carried into the region where matter is more copious, and all worlds whatsoever have mutual gravity towards one another, and by their own gravity towards worlds which are in our direction are precluded from falling on to worlds which are in another direction.

An historical succession is added in the Portsmouth manuscript:

> This Lucretius records from Epicurus' philosophy, Book I line 983, and Book II lines 1064 and 1074. Now it is likely enough that Epicurus had learned all this from the mystical philosophers, seeing that Heraclides and the Pythagoreans and the followers of Orpheus said that all the stars were worlds in the infinite aether, as Plutarch has it in Book II, chapter 13, of the Beliefs of the Philosophers. This opinion also was held by Anaximander, who no doubt learned it from Thales, his teacher.

In the same document, Newton dates the atomic succession back to Moschus the Phoenician.

> That all matter consists of atoms was a very ancient opinion. This was the teaching of the multitude of philosophers who preceded Aristotle, namely Epicurus, Democritus, Ecphantus, Empedocles, Zenocrates, Heraclides, Asclepiades, Diodorus, Metrodorus of Chios, Pythagoras, and previous to these Moschus the Phoenician whom Strabo declares older than the Trojan war. For I think that same opinion obtained in that mystic philosophy which flowed down to the Greeks from Egypt and Phoenicia, since atoms are sometimes found to be designated by the mystics as monads. For the mysteries of numbers equally with the rest of hieroglyphics had regard to the mystical philosophy.

Newton goes on to say that such 'immutable seeds' account for the fact that 'the species of objects are conserved in perpetuity.'

It may be difficult for the modern reader to imagine Sir Isaac Newton being serious about such supposed 'anticipations' of his views. Indeed, were it not for the testimony of Fatio and Gregory, one would most naturally interpret them as adding a classical flourish to a scientific treatise. But the draft Scholium to Proposition VIII cannot be interpreted in such a fashion. For here Newton asserts unequivocally that Pythagoras discovered by experiment an inverse-square relation in the vibrations of strings (unison of two strings when tensions are reciprocally as the squares of lengths); that he extended such a relation to the weights and distances of the planets from the sun; and that this true knowledge, expressed esoterically, was lost through the misunderstanding of later generations. This is an instance of a fully developed *prisca sapientia*,[2] and as such merits extended quotation.

> By what proportion gravity decreases by receding from the Planets the ancients have not sufficiently explained. Yet they appear to have adumbrated it by the harmony of the celestial spheres, designating the Sun and the remaining six planets, Mercury, Venus, Earth, Mars, Jupiter, Saturn, by means of Apollo with the Lyre of seven strings, and measuring the intervals of the spheres by the intervals of the tones. Thus they alleged that seven tones are brought into being, which they called the harmony diapason, and that Saturn moved by the Dorian phthong, that is, the heavy one, and the rest of the Planets by sharper ones (as Pliny, bk. 1, ch. 22 relates, by the mind of Pythagoras) and that the Sun strikes the strings. Hence Macrobius, bk. 1, ch. 19, says: 'Apollo's Lyre of seven strings provides understanding of the motions of all the celestial spheres over which nature has set the Sun as moderator.' And Proclus on Plato's Timaeus, bk. 3, page 200, 'The number seven

2. Antique (or venerable or original) wisdom. [Editor]

they have dedicated to Apollo as to him who embraces all symphonies whatsoever, and therefore they used to call him the God the Hebdomagetes,' that is the Prince of the number Seven. Likewise in Eusebius' Preparation of the Gospel, bk. 5, ch. 14, the Sun is called by the oracle of Apollo the King of the seven sounding harmony. But by this symbol they indicated that the sun by his own force acts upon the planets in that harmonic ratio of distances by which the force of tension acts upon strings of different lengths, that is reciprocally in the duplicate ratio of the distances. For the force by which the same tension acts on the same string of different lengths is reciprocally as the square of the length of the string.

The same tension upon a string half as long acts four times as powerfully, for it generates the Octave, and the Octave is produced by a force four times as great. For if a string of given length stretched by a given weight produces a given tone, the same tension upon a string thrice as short acts nine times as much. For it produces the twelfth, and a string which stretched by a given weight produces a given tone needs to be stretched by nine times as much weight so as to produce the twelfth. And, in general terms, if two strings equal in thickness are stretched by weights appended, these strings will be in unison when the weights are reciprocally as the squares of the lengths of the strings. Now this argument is subtle, yet became known to the ancients. For Pythagoras, as Macrobius avows, stretched the intestines of sheep or the sinews of oxen by attaching various weights, and from this learned the ratio of the celestial harmony. Therefore, by means of such experiments he ascertained that the weights by which all tones on equal strings . . . were reciprocally as the squares of the lengths of the string by which the musical instrument emits the same tones. But the proportion discovered by these experiments, on the evidence of Macrobius, he applied to the heavens and consequently by comparing those weights with the weights of the Planets and the lengths of the strings with the distances of the Planets, he understood by means of the harmony of the heavens that the weights of the Planets towards the Sun were reciprocally as the squares of their distances from the Sun.

But the Philosophers loved so to mitigate their mystical discourses that in the presence of the vulgar they foolishly propounded vulgar matters for the sake of ridicule, and hid the truth beneath discourses of this kind. In this sense Pythagoras numbered his musical tones from the Earth, as though from here to the Moon were a tone, and thence to Mercury a semitone, and from thence to the rest of the Planets other musical intervals. But he taught that the sounds were emitted by the motion and attrition of the solid spheres, as though a greater sphere emitted a heavier tone as happens when iron hammers are smitten. And from this, it seems, was born the Ptolemaic system of solid orbs, when meanwhile Pythago-

> ras beneath parables of this sort was hiding his own system and the true harmony of the heavens.

There is a piece of personal testimony which confirms Newton's belief in the wisdom of Pythagoras: that of Conduitt.

> Sir I thought Pythagoras's music of the spheres was intended to typify gravity and as he makes the sounds and notes to depend on the size of the strings, so gravity depends on the density of matter.

* * *

The same theme was mentioned in a draft variant to Query 23 of the Latin edition of the *Opticks* of 1706:

> By what means do bodies act on one another at a distance? The ancient Philosophers who held Atoms and Vacuum attributed gravity to atoms without telling us the means unless in figures: as by calling God Harmony representing him and matter by the God Pan and his Pipe, or by calling the Sun the prison of Jupiter because he keeps the Planets in their Orbs. Whence it seems to have been an ancient opinion that matter depends upon a Deity for its laws of motion as well as for its existence.

This passage serves us as a bridge to the material of the Scholium intended for Proposition IX. We notice that at the end, Newton states the *cause* of gravity, for the ancients, was God. In this draft variant, Newton develops the idea further. After stating that matter is passive and non-active, he says:

> These are passive laws and to affirm that there are no others is to speak against experience. For we find in ourselves a power of moving our bodies by our thought. Life and will are active principles by which we move our bodies and thence arise other laws of motion unknown to us.
>
> And since all matter duly formed is attended with signes of life and all things are framed with perfect art and wisdom and nature does nothing in vain; if there be an universal life and all space be the sensorium of a thinking being who by immediate presence perceives all things in it, as that which thinks in us, perceives their pictures in the brain: those laws of motion arising from life or will may be of universal extent. To some such laws the ancient Philosophers seem to have alluded when they called God Harmony and signified his actuating matter harmonically by the God Pan's playing upon a Pipe and attributing musick to the spheres made the distances and motions of the heavenly bodies to be harmonical, and represented the Planets by the seven strings of Apollo's Harp.

The personal testimony of David Gregory confirms the importance of this set of ideas for Newton's philosophy. His memorandum of 21

December 1705 tells us that Newton would answer the question, 'What cause did the ancients assign to gravity?' (in the projected Latin edition of the *Opticks*) by saying that, 'they reckoned God the cause of it, nothing else, that is no body being the cause; since every body is heavy.' Thus we have in the intended Query, an expression of the Newtonian distinction between passive and active principles in an orderly universe, and the complete dependence of matter, for its existence and motion, on the will of God; and all of this expressed by the ancients through the idea of 'Harmony.'

The draft Scholium to Proposition IX develops the same theme in greater detail. It starts with Newton's customary abjuring of causal explanations, and concludes with an eloquent passage in which the ancient dieties are assimilated into the one true God.

> So far I have expounded the properties of gravity. Its cause I by no means recount. Yet I shall say what the ancients thought about this subject. Thales regarded all bodies as animate, deducing that from magnetic and electrical attractions. And by the same argument he ought to have referred the attraction of gravity to the soul of matter. Hence he taught that all things are full of Gods, understanding by Gods animate bodies. He held the sun and the Planets for Gods. And in the same sense Pythagoras, on account of its immense force of attraction, said that the sun was the prison of Zeus, that is, a body possessed of the greatest circuits. And to the mystical philosophers Pan was the supreme divinity inspiring this world with harmonic ratio like a musical instrument and handling it with modulation, according to that saying of Orpheus 'striking the harmony of the world in playful song.' Thence they named harmony God and soul of the world composed of harmonic numbers. But they said that the Planets move in their circuits by force of their own souls, that is, by force of the gravity which takes its origin from the action of the soul. From this, it seems, arose the opinion of the Peripatetics concerning Intelligences moving solid globes. But the souls of the sun and of all the Planets the more ancient philosophers held for one and the same divinity exercising its powers in all bodies whatsoever, according to that of Orpheus in the Bowl.
>
> Cylennius himself is the interpreter of divinity to all:
> The nymphs are water. Ceres corn, Vulcan is fire.
> Neptune is the sea striking the foaming shores
> Mars is war, kindly Venus is peace, the Bull-born
> Horned Bacchus frequenting gladsome feasts
> Is to mortals and to gods relief of mind from care.
> Golden Themis is guardian of Justice and right
> Next Apollo is the Sun, hurling his darts
> From afar, circling round, the Divines and the Soothsayers

> The Epidaurian God is the expeller of diseases: these things
> All are one thing, though there be many names.

For the material of this passage, Newton drew heavily on Macrobius, Cicero, Virgil, Porphyry, and the Orphic hymns. In it, he completes the view of nature which was developed in the earlier Scholia. In those, the universe was seen as comprising innumerable worlds, composed of immutable atoms, held together by gravity, moving in an absolute void. Now the immaterial, 'immechanical' cause of it, is seen to be God himself. Newton states this conception clearly in another manuscript intended for the same unimplemented edition of the 1690s:

> . . . those ancients who more rightly held unimpaired the mystical philosophy as Thales and the Stoics, taught that a certain infinite spirit pervades all space *into infinity*, and contains and vivifies the entire world. And this spirit was their supreme divinity, according to the Poet cited by the Apostle. In him we live and move and have our being.

Thus the more ancient philosophers, such as Orpheus, who were closer to the true philosophy, held that gravity was a direct result of the exercise of divine power. Later philosophers such as the Ionics, the Italics and Plato reveal themselves to have partial knowledge of this, if their utterances are properly interpreted. For instance, Newton says of Plato:

> Hence after Plato has, by succession from Pythagorean doctrine and by the divine profundity of his own genius, shown that apart from these ratios (i.e. musical ratios) there can be no possibility of conjunction: in his Timaeus, he constitutes the soul of the world by means of the composition of those ratios, by the ineffable providence of God the craftsman. Consequently the soul of the world, which propels into movement this body of the universe visible to us, being constructed of ratios which created from themselves a musical concord, must of necessity produce musical sounds from the movement which it provides by its proper impulse having found the origin of them in the craftsmanship of its own composition.

There is little doubt that Newton saw in analogy to musical harmony, the principles of law and order in the natural world. Such harmony was the profoundest expression of cosmos. But for Newton, nature operating according to these divine ratios, could scarcely be dependent on the guidance of an intermediate world soul. Rather (as we shall soon see) the exquisite structure of things immediately bespoke the providential governance of a Divine power actually present in the world.

* * *

In these principles, there is a direct link with Newton's immediate predecessors, the Cambridge Platonists. Newton's dialogue with the

Cambridge Platonists, and his concern with the theological implications of fundamental natural philosophy, were not a passing interest of his troubled middle years. A passage from *de Gravitatione et Aequipondio Fluidorum*,[3] written about 1670, confirms his continuing concern:

> . . . some may perhaps prefer to suppose that God imposes on the soul of the world, created by him, the task of endowing definite spaces with the properties of bodies, rather than to believe that this function is directly discharged by God. Therefore the world should not be called the creation of that soul but of God alone, who created it by constituting the soul of such a nature that the world necessarily emanates from it. But I do not see why God himself does not directly inform space with bodies; so long as we distinguish between the formal reason of bodies and the act of divine will.

Newton's Platonism was not entirely the Platonism of More and Cudworth, with their stress on such intermediaries as the Hylarchichal Principle; but it was also a Platonism in the spirit of the early Church Fathers. Still, as in More, Cudworth and the Fathers, the basic world picture of the 'classical' Scholia emerges from what Newton took to be an 'entire and genuine philosophy' which had been lost. Newton, and the Cambridge Platonists, saw as their task the unification and restoration of this philosophy. It will be one of the main tasks of the remainder of this paper to characterize further the origin and nature of this distinctively English tradition of natural philosophy.

The apparent contradiction between such a traditional Neo-Platonic philosophy, and the stern inductivism of the *Principia*, dissolves when we examine more closely how Newton modified the 'mechanical' philosophy of nature which was current earlier in the century. In one sense he expanded it, by allowing unexplained forces into his explanations of the phenomena; but in a deeper sense he restricted it, especially in its pretensions to knowledge of the natural world. A sign of this restrictive approach appeared in his early work in optics. There, he rejected the arbitrarily formulated hypotheses of such philosophers as Descartes and Hooke; for they could not from these deduce the phaenomena of nature, and their pictorial mechanisms were incompatible with the laws of such phaenomena. For Newton, the source of their error was that they did not sufficiently appreciate that the mechanical philosophy, rigorously conceived, was simply the estimation of forces in nature by geometrical calculation in terms of matter in motion. This conception was secured by the brilliant achievements of the *Principia*.

At times Newton certainly hoped that he could extend this approach to include the behaviour of the insensibly small particles of matter. But he realized that the most the 'analogy of nature' would allow was the

3. "Concerning the Gravity and Equilibrium of Fluids," a manuscript by Newton from about 1684. [Editor]

transference of his system of quantitative laws to the motions of such invisible particles. That is, they applied only to the *atomical* part of his system, to *vis inertiae:* 'a passive Principle by which Bodies persist in their Motion or Rest, receive Motion in proportion to the Force impressing it, and resist as much as they are resisted!' But the heart of Newton's philosophy of nature, the world of forces and active principles, lay categorically beyond the systems of the *Opticks* and the *Principia*. How these principles were to be explained was a great, though hidden, problem of Newton's work. There is evidence that he tried different approaches to it at different periods; and the material of the 'classical' Scholia comes from a time when he seems to have largely abandoned earlier attempts at a quasi-material explanation of forces, and of gravity in particular. However, even when in his later years he again entertained the possibility of an 'aetherial medium,' this did not obviate the 'necessity of conceiving and recruiting it (motion) by active principles, such as are the cause of Gravity. . . .' Newtonian forces were never such as to be explained away by aetherial mechanisms; by nature immaterial, they required a different category of existence for their explanation.

Thus the ontological problem of causation, conceived in the classical neoplatonic framework, was central to Newton's thought. His failure to solve it is less significant than his attempt to investigate it through a unique combination of methods: a rigorously inductive philosophy, using controlled experiment and elaborate mathematics; complemented by an historical approach, reconstructing the *prisca sapientia* of the laws of God's agency in the world.

In the light of this interpretation of Newton's programme for philosophy, we may re-examine the significance of the published *Queries*. It may well be that their hints and suggestions for further experimental and theoretical work were taken by Newton's successors to be guides to the complete achievement of the new natural philosophy within the mathematical framework of the *Principia*. But in his private thoughts, certainly in the period of the 'classical' Scholia and probably throughout his life, Newton knew that the programme was incomparably more vast. For he saw the task of natural philosophy as the restoration of the knowledge of the complete system of the cosmos, including God as the creator and as the ever-present agent.

The dream of a *science universelle* was not unique to Newton; it motivated the deepest philosophers of the seventeenth century, as Descartes and Leibniz. Where Newton stands out is in his choice of materials and methods for such a science, drawing partly on a neoplatonic tradition which flourished in England long after it had declined among leading philosophers on the Continent.

* * *

Part 2
SCIENTIFIC METHOD

Introduction

One important feature of the Scientific Revolution was an intense interest in method. The proper method for science was not just a concern of such philosophers as Bacon and Descartes but also attracted the attention of such practicing scientists as Galileo, Harvey, Hooke, Huygens, Leibniz, Boyle, and Newton. In each of Newton's major books, the *Principia* and the *Opticks*, there was a special section devoted to the method of science, the way to proceed if one wanted to make discoveries or to confirm or prove a theory or principle. Because Newton had made such great discoveries, his discussions of method attracted special attention.

Newton's most famous statement about method was the negative declaration: *hypotheses non fingo*. Written for the concluding General Scholium of the *Principia* in its second edition (1713), this slogan has been traditionally translated, "I frame no hypotheses." When this version appeared in 1729, in Andrew Motte's English translation of the *Principia*, readers were aware that the verb "to frame" had a pejorative sense. Alexandre Koyré found that Newton himself, on a number of occasions, used the English verb "to feign" (which is derived from the Latin *fingere*) rather than "to frame." Newton would thus appear to be saying that he would not follow the style of Descartes, who introduced the fiction of huge vortices of an invisible matter that swirled in space, carrying the planets around in their orbits. So adamant was Newton about not conflating such hypothetical imaginings with sound scientific explanations that he specified that no hypotheses or hypothetical explanations—whether they be "metaphysical or physical, whether of occult qualities or mechanical"—have a proper place in "experimental philosophy."

It was at this point that he explained to his readers, as he had done elsewhere in correspondence and publications, that in experimental philosophy, "particular propositions are inferred from the phenomena and afterwards rendered general by induction." The problem at hand was how to account for gravity, the universal force responsible for the tides in the ocean, the observed laws of falling bodies, the orbital motion of planets and comets, and much else besides. The law of universal gravity gave an explanation for all of these phenomena, but Newton admitted that he had not been able to assign a cause to this power. "It is enough *[Satis est]*," he wrote, that gravity "really exists" and that it acts "according to the laws we have explained and abundantly serves to

In order not to encumber the reader with footnotes we have composed a Biographical Register, in which all the people mentioned in the text are identified, and a Glossary, in which technical terms are briefly explicated and such things as organizations, places, publications, and manuscript collections are identified. Both the Biographical Register and the Glossary are located near the end of the volume.

account for all the motions of the celestial bodies and of our sea." This limited goal of science, the demise of the search for "first causes" or "ultimate causes," has been accepted by working scientists ever since Newton.

Method, for Newton, was not a single or simple path to scientific truth. A number of different and equally fundamental aspects of method appear in his science. One aspect concerned how to design and perform experiments and how to draw proper conclusions from them. Newton was an extremely gifted experimentalist at a time when the canons of experimental science were first being formulated. For example, unlike many of his contemporaries, Newton was concerned about eliminating secondary effects that would mask the way results were related to the fundamental questions being studied. Thus, in designing experiments with long pendulums, he made sure that any significant vibration in the support was eliminated. Again, in experiments in which heavy objects were let fall in St. Paul's Church, he took care with the release mechanisms to ensure that the results would not be influenced by problems of the apparatus.

Newton's first public appearance before the world of science was in relation to the reflecting telescope that he had designed and his presentation of his experiments and conclusions about color and dispersion—which, he said, had led him to the invention of the telescope.[1] The ensuing debate, published in epistolary exchanges in the *Philosophical Transactions* of the Royal Society, centered in part on whether Newton had actually drawn inferences correctly from his experiments and also on whether he had produced a theory or a hypothesis. Also at issue was the question of whether Newton had adopted the basic hypothesis of the corpuscularity of light.

During the course of this controversy, Newton stated his position as unambiguously as he could. His conclusions concerning "the *Origin of Colours*," he wrote (in a letter to Henry Oldenberg on February 6, 1672), are not "an Hypothesis but [a] most rigid consequence, not conjectured by barely inferring 'tis thus because not otherwise or because it satisfies all phænomena (the Philosophers universall Topick), but evinced by the mediation of experiments concluding directly and without any suspicion of doubt." In a manuscript version of his views concerning his procedure, he made it clear that "the inventing of . . . an

1. Newton published an account of the telescope he had invented in the *Philosophical Transactions*, the official journal of the Royal Society, in March 1672, a month after the publication of his new theory of light and colors. Previous telescopes had made use of glass lenses to produce the image of celestial objects. Newton's experiments on light and colors had shown that any wedge-shaped piece of glass (a prism or both halves of a lens) must necessarily break-up light into a spectrum of its component colors. Hence a glass lens must produce an image degraded by color fringes or be subject to what scientists call chromatic aberration. To avoid this problem, Newton devised a telescope making use of a magnifying mirror instead of a magnifying lens, a type we call a reflecting telescope. A century or so later, it was discovered that magnifying lenses could be made relatively free of chromatic aberration by cementing together lenses made of different kinds of glass.

Hypothesis is no part of my designe." He had undertaken, he said, "only to discover the properties of light so far as I could derive them from experiments and therefore content my self with having shewn these properties."

In correspondence with a French critic, Father Ignace Gaston Pardies, Newton took note that "the Rev. Father calls my theory an hypothesis." But Newton averred that his "design was quite different." He had been concerned with "certain properties of light." If he "had not considered them as true," he said, he "would rather have them rejected as vain and empty speculation, than acknowledged even as an hypothesis." In a subsequent letter, he made a distinction between properties of light derived from analysis of experimental phenomena and "hypotheses, by which those properties might be explained." He then suggested a way in which hypotheses might be useful—perhaps as a guide to further experiments or as sources of ideas for developing a theory—but not as parts of a theory. As he put it, the "best and safest way of philosophizing seems to be, first to inquire diligently into the properties of things, and establishing those properties by experiments, and then to proceed more slowly to hypotheses for the explanation of them." Hypotheses, he noted, may be useful in "so far as they may furnish experiments."

We should take note that during the controversy on light and colors, Newton objected to Hooke's having ascribed to him the "hypothesis" of the corporeity of light. It is true, Newton admitted, "that from my Theory I argue the *Corporeity* of Light; but I do it without any absolute positiveness, as the word *perhaps* intimates." This was, he insisted, "at most but a very plausible *consequence* of the Doctrine, and not a fundamental *supposition*." Had he "intended any such *Hypothesis*," he would "somewhere have explained it." In fact, later on he did write out and send to the Royal Society a general hypothesis about the nature of light (see Part 1, Natural Philosophy [above]).

Many years later, Newton restated his opinion on the possible usefulness of hypotheses at the end of the book review (which he published anonymously in the *Philosophical Transactions*) of the Royal Society's report on the priority controversy concerning the invention of the calculus. Declaring that the "Philosophy which Mr. *Newton* in his *Principles* and *Optiques* has pursued is Experimental," Newton (writing about himself in the third person) exclaimed in his customary manner that in this "Experimental Philosophy . . . Hypotheses have no place." And then he added that there was a legitimate way to use hypotheses, that is, "as Conjectures or Questions proposed to be examined by Experiments."

One of the most often quoted statements about method in Newton's first published scientific paper, on light and colors, was his discussion of the *experimentum crucis*, or "crucial experiment." This notion, and indeed its very name, was taken by Newton from the *Micrographia* of Robert Hooke. It refers to a method of deciding between two alternative theories, to a crossroad of thought (hence its name) where an experiment might decide which of two paths to follow. In the history of science, one of the most famous examples of such a crossroad of thought and a subsequent *experimentum crucis* was the nineteenth-century experimental test of whether to adopt the wave theory of light or to believe in the corpuscular theory. Measurements of the speed of light in different media seemed to decide for the wave theory. In a celebrated discussion of method, the historian and philosopher of science Pierre Duhem inveighed against such oversimplification of method, and after many decades the development of quantum physics showed him to have been right, proving that no decision based on an *experimentum crucis* can be considered final.

The *experimentum crucis* is related to the problem of verification, of the experimental basis of the choice between two theoretical alternatives. This was, for Newton, part of the general method of proof. A striking example of Newton's method of confirmation was the demonstration (in Proposition 4, Book 3, of the *Principia*) that the force of terrestrial gravity extends to the moon. If the force of gravity were to act on a body at a distance of 60 earth-radii from the earth's center, he argued, and if this force varied as the inverse square of the distance (as gravity does), then an object placed there would fall toward the earth with an acceleration 1/3600th of the acceleration of free fall on the surface of the earth. Simple direct calculation showed that the moon, which actually is at a distance of 60 earth-radii from the earth's center, does indeed move in orbit at such an observed speed that it falls away from the tangent toward the earth with an acceleration that is practically the predicted value of 1/3600th the acceleration of terrestrial free fall.

Some of Newton's statements on method present his views on the classic problem of resolution and composition or analysis and synthesis. This subject was expounded at some length in the methodological part of the *Opticks*, in the famous Queries that appear at the end of the book and were enlarged in each of the successive editions. Newton's *Opticks* is a veritable handbook of method, of the experimenter's art. He not only details certain fundamental experiments, but also discusses their theoretical implications and possible significance. Among these discussions of method, there is even a presentation of the problem of the cause of gravity in a way not introduced in the *Principia*. Newton's own procedures, as exhibited in the Queries of the *Opticks*, can with profit be compared and contrasted with his own description of his method that was published in his review of the documents relating to the dispute with Leibniz on the invention of the calculus.

In the *Principia*, Newton set forth a series of *regulae philosophandi*, or "rules for natural philosophy." In the first edition (1687), these were included among a set of preliminaries to Book 3, which concerned the system of the world, all of which were misleadingly lumped together in a section called "Hypotheses." In the second edition, however, Newton took care to remove any such ambiguity and separated out what he called "rules" and a series of statements about observations and observationally based laws (such as the laws of motion of Jupiter's satellites) that he called "phenomena." These rules (three at first, enlarged to four in the third edition, 1726) deal with problems of cause, analogy, the safeguarding of inductions against hypotheses, and the method of what has sometimes been called transduction. The latter is used to indicate a way to assign properties discernible in objects of an experiment to objects of the same or a similar kind beyond the reach of any experiment. For example, since mass is observed in every sample of matter on which we can perform direct experiments, and since the mass of any bit of matter is a constant under all physical conditions, Newton's third rule would justify the attribution of mass as a property of planets, comets, the sun, and stars.

Newton's method was displayed in two different manners. One was by direct precept, the other by example. It is of significance, therefore, to examine carefully how Newton actually proceeded in the *Principia* and not merely to read what he said about his procedure. For many centuries, Newton's *Principia* was considered the summit of exact science. Accordingly, his actual procedure, combining mathematical deductions with inductions from experimental and observational results, is a primary source for understanding the optimal method for exact science.

A Note by David Gregory †

The best way of overcoming a difficult Probleme is to solve it in some particular easy cases. This gives much light into the general solution. By this way Sir Isaac Newton says he overcame the most difficult things.

From Query 31 ‡

* * *

As in Mathematicks, so in Natural Philosophy, the Investigation of difficult Things by the Method of Analysis, ought ever to precede the Method of Composition. This Analysis consists in making Experiments and Observations, and in drawing general Conclusions from them by Induction, and admitting of no Objections against the Conclusions, but such as are taken from Experiments, or other certain Truths. For Hypotheses are not to be regarded in experimental Philosophy. And

† Walter George Hiscock, ed., *David Gregory, Isaac Newton, and Their Circle* (Oxford: printed for the editor, 1937), p. 25. David Gregory, a Scottish mathematician a generation younger than Newton, kept extensive notes of his conversations with the older man. This note appears to have come from 1705.

‡ Isaac Newton, *Opticks*, based on the 4th ed. (New York: Dover Publications, 1952), pp. 404–05. This passage from Query 31 on analysis and synthesis was published originally in Latin in 1706.

although the arguing from Experiments and Observations by Induction be no Demonstration of general Conclusions; yet it is the best way of arguing which the Nature of Things admits of, and may be looked upon as so much the stronger, by how much the Induction is more general. And if no Exception occur from Phænomena, the Conclusion may be pronounced generally. But if at any time afterwards any Exception shall occur from Experiments, it may then begin to be pronounced with such Exceptions as occur. By this way of Analysis we may proceed from Compounds to Ingredients, and from Motions to the Forces producing them; and in general, from Effects to their Causes, and from particular Causes to more general ones, till the Argument end in the most general. This is the Method of Analysis: And the Synthesis consists in assuming the Causes discover'd, and establish'd as Principles, and by them explaining the Phænomena proceeding from them, and proving the Explanations.

* * *

Rules of Reasoning in Philosophy †

Rule I

We are to admit no more causes of natural things than such as are both true and sufficient to explain their appearances.

To this purpose the philosophers say that Nature does nothing in vain, and more is in vain when less will serve; for Nature is pleased with simplicity, and affects not the pomp of superfluous causes.

Rule II

Therefore to the same natural effects we must, as far as possible, assign the same causes.

As to respiration in a man and in a beast; the descent of stones in *Europe* and in *America*; the light of our culinary fire and of the sun; the reflection of light in the earth, and in the planets.

Rule III

The qualities of bodies, which admit neither intension nor remission of degrees, and which are found to belong to all bodies within the reach of

† Isaac Newton, *Mathematical Principles of Natural Philosophy* and *System of the World*, translated by Andrew Motte, revised by Florian Cajori (Berkeley and Los Angeles: University of California Press, 1934 and later printings), pp. 398–400. Copyright © 1934 and 1962 Regents of the University of California. Newton's "Rules of Reasoning" appear at the beginning of Book 3 of the *Principia*. Rules 1 and 2 were in the first edition (but were not called "Rules" then); he added Rule 3 to the second edition in 1713 and Rule 4 to the third edition in 1726. This version, based on the translation by Andrew Motte (London, 1728), was "revised" in the 1930s by Florian Cajori. A whole new translation, by I. Bernard Cohen and Anne Whitman, is scheduled for publication by the University of California Press.

our experiments, are to be esteemed the universal qualities of all bodies whatsoever.

For since the qualities of bodies are only known to us by experiments, we are to hold for universal all such as universally agree with experiments; and such as are not liable to diminution can never be quite taken away. We are certainly not to relinquish the evidence of experiments for the sake of dreams and vain fictions of our own devising; nor are we to recede from the analogy of Nature, which is wont to be simple, and always consonant to itself. We no other way know the extension of bodies than by our senses, nor do these reach it in all bodies; but because we perceive extension in all that are sensible, therefore we ascribe it universally to all others also. That abundance of bodies are hard, we learn by experience; and because the hardness of the whole arises from the hardness of the parts, we therefore justly infer the hardness of the undivided particles not only of the bodies we feel but of all others. That all bodies are impenetrable, we gather not from reason, but from sensation. The bodies which we handle we find impenetrable, and thence conclude impenetrability to be an universal property of all bodies whatsoever. That all bodies are movable, and endowed with certain powers (which we call the inertia) of persevering in their motion, or in their rest, we only infer from the like properties observed in the bodies which we have seen. The extension, hardness, impenetrability, mobility, and inertia of the whole, result from the extension, hardness, impenetrability, mobility, and inertia of the parts; and hence we conclude the least particles of all bodies to be also all extended, and hard and impenetrable, and movable, and endowed with their proper inertia. And this is the foundation of all philosophy. Moreover, that the divided but contiguous particles of bodies may be separated from one another, is matter of observation; and, in the particles that remain undivided, our minds are able to distinguish yet lesser parts, as is mathematically demonstrated. But whether the parts so distinguished, and not yet divided, may, by the powers of Nature, be actually divided and separated from one another, we cannot certainly determine. Yet, had we the proof of but one experiment that any undivided particle, in breaking a hard and solid body, suffered a division, we might by virtue of this rule conclude that the undivided as well as the divided particles may be divided and actually separated to infinity.

Lastly, if it universally appears, by experiments and astronomical observations, that all bodies about the earth gravitate towards the earth, and that in proportion to the quantity of matter which they severally contain; that the moon likewise, according to the quantity of its matter, gravitates towards the earth; that, on the other hand, our sea gravitates towards the moon; and all the planets one towards another; and the comets in like manner towards the sun; we must, in consequence of this rule, universally allow that all bodies whatsoever are endowed with a principle of mutual gravitation. For the argument from the appearances concludes with more force for the universal gravitation of all bodies than for their impenetrability; of which, among those in the celestial regions, we have no experiments, nor any manner of observation. Not that I affirm gravity to be essential to bodies: by their inherent force I mean nothing but their force of inertia. This is immutable. Their gravity is diminished as they recede from the earth.

Rule IV

In experimental philosophy we are to look upon propositions inferred by general induction from phenomena as accurately or very nearly true, notwithstanding any contrary hypotheses that may be imagined, till such time as other phenomena occur, by which they may either be made more accurate, or liable to exceptions.

This rule we must follow, that the argument of induction may not be evaded by hypotheses.

From the General Scholium†

* * *

Hitherto we have explained the phenomena of the heavens and of our sea by the power of gravity, but have not yet assigned the cause of this power. This is certain, that it must proceed from a cause that penetrates to the very centres of the sun and planets, without suffering the least diminution of its force; that operates not according to the quantity of the surfaces of the particles upon which it acts (as mechanical cause used to do), but according to the quantity of the solid matter which they contain, and propagates its virtue on all sides to immense distances, decreasing always as the inverse square of the distances. Gravitation towards the sun is made up out of the gravitations towards the several particles of which the body of the sun is composed; and in receding from the sun decreases accurately as the inverse square of the distances as far as the orbit of Saturn, as evidently appears from the quiescence of the aphelion of the planets; nay, and even to the remotest aphelion of the comets, if those aphelions are also quiescent. But hitherto I have not been able to discover the cause of those properties of gravity from phenomena, and I frame no hypotheses; for whatever is not deduced from the phenomena is to be called an hypothesis; and hypotheses, whether metaphysical or physical, whether of occult qualities or mechanical, have no place in experimental philosophy. In this philosophy particular propositions are

† Isaac Newton, *Mathematical Principles of Natural Philosophy* and *System of the World*, translated by Andrew Motte, revised by Florian Cajori (Berkeley and Los Angeles: University of California Press, 1934 and later printings), pp. 546–47. This paragraph appears near the end of the General Scholium to the *Principia* that Newton added at the end of the second edition in 1713.

inferred from the phenomena, and afterwards rendered general by induction. Thus it was that the impenetrability, the mobility, and the impulsive force of bodies, and the laws of motion and of gravitation, were discovered. And to us it is enough that gravity does really exist, and act according to the laws which we have explained, and abundantly serves to account for all the motions of the celestial bodies, and of our sea.

* * *

From Newton to Cotes, March 28, 1713†

Sir

I had yours of Feb 18th, and the Difficulty you mention which lies in these words "Et cum Attractio omnis mutua sit" is removed by considering that as in Geometry the word Hypothesis is not taken in so large a sense as to include the Axiomes and Postulates, so in experimental Philosophy it is not to be taken in so large a sense as to include the first Principles or Axiomes which I call the laws of motion. These Principles are deduced from Phænomena, and made general by Induction: which is the highest evidence that a Proposition can have in this philosophy. And the word Hypothesis is here used by me to signify only such a Proposition as is not a Phænomenon nor deduced from any Phænomena but assumed or supposed without any experimental proof. Now the mutual and mutually equal attraction of bodies is a branch of the third Law of motion and how this branch is deduced from Phænomena you may see in the end of the Corollaries of the Laws of Motion, pag. 22. If a body attracts another body contiguous to it and is not mutually attracted by the other: the attracted body will drive the other before it and both will go away together with an accelerated motion in infinitum, as it were by a self moving principle, contrary to the first law of motion, whereas there is no such phænomenon in all nature.

* * *

From Newton to Oldenburg, February 6, 1672‡

* * *

A naturalist would scearce expect to see the science of those become mathematicall, and yet I dare affirm that there is as much certainty in it

† *The Correspondence of Isaac Newton*, eds. H. W. Turnbull, J. F. Scott, A. Rupert Hall, and Laura Tilling, 7 vols. (Cambridge: Cambridge University Press, 1959–77), vol. 5, pp. 396–97. Reprinted with the permission of Cambridge University Press. Roger Cotes edited the second edition of the *Principia*. During its preparation, he and Newton discussed many of its details in an extensive correspondence.

‡ *The Correspondence of Isaac Newton*, eds. H. W. Turnbull, J. F. Scott, A. Rupert Hall and Laura Tilling, 7 vols. (Cambridge: Cambridge University Press, 1959–77), vol. 1, pp. 96–97. Reprinted with the permission of Cambridge University Press.The passage comes from Newton's first publication, a paper on his theory of color, which appeared in the *Philosophical Transactions* of the Royal Society in the form of a letter to Henry Oldenburg, secretary of the society.

as in any other part of Opticks. For what I shall tell concerning them is not an Hypothesis but most rigid consequence, not conjectured by barely inferring 'tis thus because not otherwise or because it satisfies all phænomena (the Philosophers universall Topick,) but evinced by the mediation of experiments concluding directly and without any suspicion of doubt. To continue the historicall narration of these experiments would make a discourse too tedious and confused, and therefore I shall rather lay down the *Doctrine* first, and then, for its examination, give you an instance or two of the *Experiments*, as a specimen of the rest.

* * *

From Newton to Oldenburg, June 10, 1672†

* * *

For the best and safest method of philosophizing seems to be, first, to inquire diligently into the properties of things and to establish those properties by experiments, and to proceed later to hypotheses for the explanation of things themselves. For hypotheses ought to be applied only in the explanation of the properties of things, and not made use of in determining them; except in so far as they may furnish experiments. And if anyone offers conjectures about the truth of things from the mere possibility of hypotheses, I do not see by what stipulation anything certain can be determined in any science; since one or another set of hypotheses may always be devised which will appear to supply new difficulties. Hence I judged that one should abstain from contemplating hypotheses, as from improper argumentation.

* * *

From Newton to Oldenburg, July 6, 1672‡

* * *

In the meane while give me leave to insinuate that I cannot think it effectuall for determining truth to examin the severall ways by which Phænomena may be explained, unlesse where there can be a perfect

† *The Correspondence of Isaac Newton*, eds. H. W. Turnbull, J. F. Scott, A. Rupert Hall, and Laura Tilling, 7 vols. (Cambridge: Cambridge University Press, 1959–77), vol. 1, p. 169. Reprinted with the permission of Cambridge University Press. The discussion prompted by the publication of Newton's paper on colors in the *Philosophical Transactions* of the Royal Society was carried on in a correspondence that utilized Henry Oldenburg as intermediary. In this letter, Newton replies to an objection by the French Jesuit, Ignace Gaston Pardies, and here, as elsewhere, issues of methodology entered the discussion.

‡ *The Correspondence of Isaac Newton*, eds. H. W. Turnbull, J. F. Scott, A. Rupert Hall, and Laura Tilling, 7 vols. (Cambridge: Cambridge University Press, 1959–77), vol. 1, pp. 209–10. Reprinted with the permission of Cambridge University Press. This letter carries on the discussion of the published paper on colors and as part of it raises issues of methodology.

enumeration of all those ways. You know the proper Method for inquiring after the properties of things is to deduce them from Experiments. And I told you that the Theory which I propounded was evinced to me, *not by inferring tis thus because not otherwise*, that is not by deducing it onely from a confutation of contrary suppositions, but *by deriving it from Experiments concluding positively and directly*. The way therefore to examin it is by considering whether the experiments which I propound do prove those parts of the Theory to which they are applyed, or by prosecuting other experiments which the Theory may suggest for its examination. And this I would have done in a due Method; the Laws of Refraction being throughly inquired into and determined before the nature of colours be taken into consideration. It may not be amiss to proceed according to the series of these Queries: The decision of which I could wish to be stated, and the events declared by those that may have the curiosity to examin them.

1. Whether rays that are alike incident on the same Medium have unequall refractions, and how great are the inequalities of their refractions at any incidence?

2. What is the law according to which each ray is more or lesse refracted, whether it be that the same ray is ever refracted according to the same ratio of the sines of incidence and refraction; and divers rays, according to divers ratios; Or that the refraction of each ray is greater or lesse without any certain rule? That is, whether each ray have a certain degree of refrangibility according to which its refraction is performed, or is refracted without that regularity?

3. Whether rays which are indued with particular degrees of refrangibility, when they are by any meanes separated, have particular colours constantly belonging to them: viz, the least refrangible, scarlet; the most refrangible, deep violet; the middle, Sea-green; and others, other colours? And on the contrary?

4. Whether the colour of any sort of rays apart may be changed by refraction?

5. Whether colours by coalescing do really change one another to produce a new colour, or produce it by mixing onely?

6. Whether a due mixture of rays, indued with all variety of colours, produces light perfectly like that of the Sun, and which hath all the same properties and exhibits the same Phænomena?

8. Whether there be any other colours produced by refractions then such, as ought to result from the colours belonging to the diversly refrangible rays by their being separated or mixed by that refraction?

To determin by experiments these and such like Queries which involve the propounded Theory seemes the most proper and direct way to a conclusion. And therefore I could wish all objections were suspended, taken from Hypotheses or any other Heads then these two; Of showing the insufficiency of experiments to determin these Queries or prove any other parts of my Theory, by assigning the flaws and defects in my Conclusions drawn from them; Or of producing other Experiments which directly contradict me, if any such may seem to occur. For if the Experiments, which I urge be defective it cannot be difficult to show the defects, but if valid, then by proving the Theory they must render all other Objections invalid.

* * *

COLIN MACLAURIN

From *An Account of Sir Isaac Newton's Philosophical Discoveries*†

* * *

An entire liberty must be allowed in our enquiries, that natural philosophy may become subservient to the most valuable purposes, and acquire all the certainty and perfection of which it is capable: but we ought not to abuse this liberty by *supposing* instead of *enquiring*, and by imagining systems, instead of learning from observation and experience the true constitution of things. Speculative men, by the force of genius, may invent systems that will perhaps be greatly admired for a time; these however, are phantoms which the force of truth will sooner or later dispell: and while we are pleas'd with the deceit, true philosophy, with all the arts and improvements that depend upon it, suffers. The real state of things escapes our observation: or, if it presents itself to us, we are apt either to reject it wholly as fiction, or, by new efforts of a vain ingenuity, to interweave it with our own conceits, and labour to make it tally with our favourite schemes. Thus, by blending together parts so ill suited, the whole comes forth an absurd composition of truth and error.

Of the many difficulties that have stood in the way of philosophy, this vanity perhaps has had the worst effects. The love of the marvellous, and the prejudices of sense, obstructed the progress of natural knowledge; but experience and reflection soon taught men to examine and endeavour to correct these. Tho' philosophers met with great discouragements in the dark and superstitious ages, learning flourished, with liberty, in better times. The disputes amongst the sects, more fond of victory than of

† Colin Maclaurin, *An Account of Sir Isaac Newton's Philosophical Discoveries, in Four Books*, (London: printed for the author's children, 1748, rpt. 1970), ch. 1, pp. 6–12. Reprinted by permission of Georg Olms Verlag. During the first half of the eighteenth century, a number of books that attempted to explain Newton's work in language the general public could understand appeared. One of the best of these was by Maclaurin, a mathematician known for the infinite series that bears his name.

truth, produced a talkative sort of philosophy, and a vain ostentation of learning, that prevailed for a long time; but men could not be always diverted from pursuing after more real knowledge. These have not done near so much harm, as that pride and ambition, which has led philosophers to think it beneath them, to offer any thing less to the world than a compleat and finished system of nature; and, in order to obtain this at once, to take the liberty of inventing certain principles and hypotheses, from which they pretend to explain all her mysteries.

2. Sir *Isaac Newton* saw how extravagant such attempts were, and therefore did not set out with any favourite principle or supposition, never proposing to himself the invention of a system. He saw that it was necessary to consult nature herself, to attend carefully to her manifest operations, and to extort her secrets from her by well chosen and repeated experiments. He would admit no objections against plain experience from metaphysical considerations, which, he saw, had often misled philosophers, and had seldom been of real use in their enquiries. He avoided presumption, he had the necessary patience as well as genius; and having kept steadily to the right path, he therefore succeeded.

Experiments and observations, 'tis true, could not alone have carried him far in tracing the causes from their effects, and explaining the effects from their causes: a sublime geometry was his guide in this nice and difficult enquiry. This is the instrument, by which alone the machinery of a work, made with so much art, could be unfolded; and therefore he sought to carry it to the greatest height. Nor is it easy to discern, whether he has shewed greater skill, and been more successful, in improving and perfecting the instrument, or in applying it to use. He used to call his philosophy *experimental philosophy*, intimating, by the name, the essential difference there is betwixt it and those systems that are the product of genius and invention only. These could not long subsist; but his philosophy, being founded on experiment and demonstration, cannot fail till reason or the nature of things are changed.

In order to proceed with perfect security, and to put an end for ever to disputes, he proposed that, in our enquiries into nature, the methods of *analysis* and *synthesis* should be both employed in a proper order; that we should begin with the phænomena, or effects, and from them investigate the powers or causes that operate in nature; that, from particular causes, we should proceed to the more general ones, till the argument end in the most general: this is the method of *analysis*. Being once possest of these causes, we should then descend in a contrary order; and from them, as established principles, explain all the phænomena that are their consequences, and prove our explications: and this is the *synthesis*. It is evident that, as in mathematics, so in natural philosophy, the investigation of difficult things by the method of *analysis* ought ever to precede the method of composition, or the *synthesis*. For in any other way, we can never be sure that we assume the principles which really obtain in nature; and that our system, after we have composed it with great labour, is not mere dream and illusion.

By proceeding according to this method, he demonstrated from observations, analytically, that gravity is a general principle; from which he afterwards explained the system of the world. By *analysis* he discovered new and wonderful properties of light, and, from these, accounted for many curious phænomena in a *synthetic* way. But while he was thus demonstrating a great number of truths, he could not but meet with hints of many other things, that his sagacity and diligent observation suggested to him, which he was not able to establish with equal certainty: and as these were not to be neglected, but to be separated with care from the others, he therefore collected them together, and proposed them under the modest title of *queries*.

By distinguishing these so carefully from each other, he has done the greatest service to this part of learning, and has secured his philosophy against any hazard of being disproved or weakned by future discoveries. He has taken care to give nothing for demonstration but what must ever be found such; and having separated from this what he owns is not so certain, he has opened matter for the enquiries of future ages, which may confirm and enlarge his doctrines, but can never refute them. He knew where to stop when experiments were wanting, and when the subtilty of nature carried things out of his reach: nor would he abuse the great authority and reputation he had acquired, by delivering his opinion, concerning these, otherwise than as matter of question. It was long before he could be prevailed on to propose his opinion or conjectures concerning the cause of gravity; and what he has said of it, and of the other powers that act on the minute particles of matter, is delivered with a modesty and diffidence seldom to be met with amongst philosophers of a less name. Nor do they act in a conformity with the spirit of this philosophy who speak dogmatically on these subjects, till a clearer light from new observations and experiments brings them from the class of queries, and places them on the level of demonstration.

3. Such was the method of our incomparable philosopher, whose caution and modesty will ever do him the greatest honour in the opinion of the unprejudiced. But this strict method of proceeding was not relished by those who had been accustomed to treat philosophy in a very different way, and who saw that, by following it, they must give up their favourite systems. His observations and reasonings were unexceptionable; so, finding nothing to object to these, they endeavoured to lessen the character of his philosophy by general indirect insinuations, and sometimes, by unjust calumnies. They pretended to find a resemblance between his doctrines and the exploded tenets of the scholastick philosophy. They triumphed mightily in treating gravity as an occult quality, because he did not pretend to deduce this principle fully from its cause. His extending over all the system a power which is so well known to us

on the earth, and explaining by it the motions and influences of the celestial bodies, in the most satisfactory manner; and his determining the measures of the various motions that are consequences of this power, by so skilful an application of geometry to nature; all these had no merit with such philosophers, because he did not assign the mechanical cause of gravity. I know not that ever it was made an objection to the circulation of the blood that there is no small difficulty in accounting for it mechanically; they who first extended gravity to air, vapour, and to all bodies round the earth, had their praise, though the cause of gravity was as obscure as before; or rather appeared more mysterious, after they had shewn that there was no body found near the earth, exempt from gravity, that might be supposed to be its cause. Why then were his admirable discoveries, by which this principle was extended over the universe, so ill relished by some philosophers? The truth is, he had, with great evidence, overthrown the boasted schemes by which they pretended to unravel all the mysteries of nature; and the philosophy he introduced, in place of them, carrying with it a sincere confession of our being far from a complete and perfect knowledge of it, could not please those who had been accustom'd to imagine themselves possess'd of the eternal reasons and primary causes of all things.

But to all such as have just notions of the great author of the universe, and of his admirable workmanship, Sir *Isaac Newton*'s caution and modestly will recommend his philosophy; and even the avowed imperfection of some parts of it will, to them, rather appear a consequence of its conformity with nature. To such, all complete and finished systems must appear very suspicious: they will not be surprized that refined speculations, or even the labours of a few ages, are not sufficient to unfold the whole constitution of things, and trace every phænomenon through all the chain of causes to the first cause. Is the admirable progress which has been made in this arduous pursuit to be despised or neglected, because more remains behind undiscovered? Surely we ought rather to rejoice that so much is opened to us of the consummate art by which all things were made, and ought to be afraid to intermix with it our own extravagant conceits.

The processes of nature lie so deep, that, after all the pains we can take, much, perhaps, will remain undiscovered beyond the reach of human art or skill. But this is no reason why we should give ourselves up to the belief of fictions, be they ever so ingenious, instead of hearkening to the unerring voice of nature: for she alone can guide us in her own labyrinths; and it is a consequence of her real beauty, that the least part of true philosophy is incomparably more beautiful than the most complete systems which have been the product of invention. This is particularly true of Sir *Isaac Newton*'s philosophy; and we may compare it in this respect with those celebrated pieces of *Apelles*, which, though they never received his last hand, were in greater admiration amongst the antients, than the most finished pieces of other artists: and we wish posterity may not find cause to say of this philosophy what the antients said of those pieces,——*Ipsum defectum cessisse in gloriam artificis, nec qui succederet operi ad præscripta lineamenta inventum suisse.* ["The very lack of completeness contributed to the glory of the artist, nor could anyone be found to carry on the work in accordance with the design already sketched." (Adapted from Pliny's *Natural History*, book 35, ch. 36, pp. 91–92.)]

* * *

I. BERNARD COHEN

Newton's Method and Newton's Style†

The Newtonian Method

A feature of Newton's achievement was his attention to method. The attempts to codify method—by such diverse figures as Descartes, Bacon, and others—signify that discoveries were to be made by applying a new tool of inquiry (a *novum organum*, as Bacon put it) that would direct the mind unerringly to the uncovering of nature's secrets. The new method was largely experimental, and has been said to have been based on induction; it was also quantitative and not merely observational. Therefore it could lead to mathematical laws and principles. I believe that the seventeenth-century evaluation of the importance of method was directly related to the role of experience (experiment and observation) in the new science. For it seems to have been a tacit postulate that any reasonably skilled man or woman should be able to reproduce an experiment or observation, provided that the report of that experiment or observation was given honestly and in sufficient detail. A consequence of this postulate was that anyone who understood the true methods of scientific inquiry and had acquired the necessary skill to make experiments and observations could have made the discovery in the first instance—provided, of course, that he had been gifted with the wit and insight to ask the right questions.

Newton the physicist saw the primary importance of concepts and rules or laws that relate to (or arise directly from) experience. But Newton the mathematician could not help but be interested in other possibilities. Recognizing that certain relations are of physical significance (as

† Adapted from chapter 2 of Frank Durham and Robert D. Purrington, eds., *Some Truer Method: Reflections on the Heritage of Newton* (New York: Columbia University Press, 1990). Reprinted by permision of I. Bernard Cohen.

that "the periodic times are as the 3/2 power of the radii," or Kepler's third law), his mind leaped at once to the more universal condition (as that "the periodic time is as any power R^n of the radius R"). Though Newton was willing to explore the mathematical consequences of attractions of spheres according to any rational function of the distance, he concentrated on the powers of index 1 and -2 since they are the ones that occur in nature: the power of index 1 of the distance from the center applies to a particle within a solid sphere and the power of index -2 to a particle outside either a hollow or a solid sphere. It was his aim in the *Principia* to show that the abstract or "mathematical principles" of the first two books could be applied to the phenomenologically revealed world, an assignment which he undertook in the third book. To do so, after Galileo, Kepler, Descartes, and Huygens, was not in itself revolutionary, although the scope of the *Principia* and the degree of confirmed application could well be so designated and thus be integral to the Newtonian revolution in science.

From the point of view of the Newtonian revolution in science, there is one very significant aspect of the *Opticks:* the fact that Newton developed in it the most comprehensive public statement he ever made of his philosophy of science or of his conception of the experimental scientific method. This methodological declaration has, in fact, been a source of some confusion ever since, because it has been read as if it applies to all of Newton's work, including the *Principia*. The final paragraph of query 28 of the *Opticks* begins by discussing the rejection of any "dense Fluid" supposed to fill all space, and then castigates "Later Philosophers" (i.e., Cartesians and Leibnizians) for "feigning Hypotheses for explaining all things mechanically, and referring other Causes to Metaphysicks." Newton asserts, however, that "the main Business of natural Philosophy is to argue from Phaenomena without feigning Hypotheses, and to deduce Causes from Effects, till we come to the very first Cause, which certainly is not mechanical." Not only is the main assignment "to unfold the Mechanism of the World," but also to "resolve" such questions as: "What is there in places almost empty of Matter . . .?" "Whence is it that Nature doth nothing in vain; and whence arises all that Order and Beauty which we see in the World?" What "hinders the fix'd Stars from falling upon one another?" "Was the Eye contrived without Skill in Opticks, and the Ear without Knowledge of Sounds?" or "How do the Motions of the Body follow from the Will, and whence is the Instinct in Animals?" In query 31, Newton states his general principles of analysis and synthesis, or resolution and composition, and the method of induction:

> As in Mathematicks, so in Natural Philosophy, the Investigation of difficult things by the Method of Analysis, ought ever to precede the Method of Composition. This Analysis consists in making

> Experiments and Observations, and in drawing general Conclusions from them by Induction, and admitting of no Objections against the Conclusions, but such as are taken from Experiments, or other certain Truths. For Hypotheses are not to be regarded in experimental Philosophy. And although the arguing from Experiment and Observations by Induction be no Demonstration of general Conclusions; yet it is the best way of arguing which the Nature of Things admits of, and may be looked upon as so much the stronger, by how much the Induction is more general.

Analysis thus enables us to

> proceed from Compound to Ingredients, and from Motions to the Forces producing them; and in general, from Effects to their Causes, and from particular Causes to more general ones, till the Argument end in the most general.

This method of analysis is then compared to synthesis or composition:

> And the Synthesis consists in assuming the Causes discover'd, and establish'd as Principles, and by them explaining the Phaenomena proceeding from them, and proving the Explanations.

The lengthy paragraph embodying the foregoing three extracts is one of the most often quoted statements made by Newton, rivaled only by the concluding General Scholium of the *Principia*, with its noted expression: *Hypotheses non fingo*.

Newton would have us believe that he had himself followed this "scenario"; first to reveal by "analysis" some simple results that were generalized by induction, thus proceeding from effects to causes and from particular causes to general causes; then, on the basis of these causes considered as principles, to explain by "synthesis" the phenomena of observation and experiment that may be derived or deduced from them, "proving the Explanations."

The formal appearance of the *Opticks* might have suggested that it was a book of synthesis, rather than analysis, since it begins (Book One, part 1) with a set of eight "definitions" followed by eight "axioms." But the elucidation of the propositions that follow does not make explicit reference to these axioms, and many of the individual propositions are established by a method plainly labeled "The PROOF by Experiments." Newton himself states clearly at the end of the final Query 31 that in Books One and Two he has "proceeded by . . . Analysis" and that in Book Three (apart from the queries) he has "only begun the Analysis." The structure of the *Opticks* is superficially similar to that of the *Principia*, for the *Principia* also starts out with a set of definitions (again eight in number), followed by three axioms (three "axiomata sive leges motus"), upon which the propositions of the first two books are to be constructed (as in the model of Euclid's geometry). But then, in Book Three of the *Principia*, on the system of the world, an ancillary set of so-called "phenomena" mediate the application of the mathematical results of books one and two to the motions and properties of the physical universe. Unlike the *Opticks*, the *Principia* does make use of the axioms and definitions, although not in the systematic manner that one might have expected.

The confusing aspect of Newton's stated method of analysis and synthesis (or composition) in Query 31 of the *Opticks* is that it is introduced by the sentence "As in Mathematicks, so in Natural Philosophy," which was present when this query first appeared (as Query 23) in the Latin *Optice* in 1706, "Quaemadmodum in Mathematica, ita etiam in Physica." A careful study, however, shows that Newton's usage in experimental natural philosophy is just the reverse of the way "analysis" and "synthesis" (or "resolution" and "composition") have been traditionally used in relation to mathematics, and hence in the *Principia*—an aspect of Newton's philosophy of science that was fully understood by Dugald Stewart a century and a half ago but that has not been grasped by present-day commentators on Newton's scientific method, who would even see in the *Opticks* the same style that is to be found in the *Principia*.

In order to understand Newton's method, we must seek a middle ground between a study of physical or even metaphysical causes and the mathematical elucidation of their action and properties. The recognition of this hierarchy and the exploration of the properties of gravity as a cause of phenomena (without any overt commitment to the cause of gravity) was a great advance over the physics of Galileo.

Thus, in the exact sciences of the seventeenth century, we may observe a hierarchy of mathematical laws. First, there are those deduced from certain assumptions and definitions, and which lead to experimentally testable results. If, as in Galileo's case, the assumptions and definitions are consonant with nature, then the results should be verifiable by experience. When Galileo sets forth, as a postulate, that the speed acquired in naturally accelerated motion is the same along all planes of the same heights, whatever their inclination, he declares that the "absolute truth of this postulate will be later established for us by our seeing that other conclusions, built on this hypothesis, do indeed correspond with and exactly conform to experiment." This reads like a classic statement of the hypothetico-deductive method; but it is to be observed that it is devoid of any reference to the physical nature of the cause of the acceleration. Such a level of discourse is not essentially different in its results from another seventeenth-century way of finding mathematical laws of nature without going into causes: by the direct analysis of the data of experiment and observation. This was in all probability Kepler's procedure in finding his third (or "harmonic") law of planetary motion. Other examples are Boyle's law of gases and Snel's law of refraction.

The second level of the hierarchy is to go beyond the mathematical description to some sort of causes. Boyle's law, for example, is a mathematical statement of proportionality between two variables, each of which is a physical entity related to an observable or measurable quantity. Thus the volume (V) of the confined gas is measured by the mercury level according to some volumetric scale, and the pressure of the confined gas is determined by the difference between two mercury levels (h) plus the height of the mercury column in a barometer (h_1). Boyle's experiments showed that the product of V and $h+h_1$ is a constant. But nothing is said concerning the cause of pressure in a confined gas, nor of the reason why this pressure should increase as the gas is confined into a smaller volume, a phenomenon known to Boyle before he undertook the experiments and which he called the "spring" of the air. Now the second level of hierarchy is to explore the cause of this "spring." Boyle suggested two physical models that might serve to explain this phenomenon. One is to think of each particle being itself compressible, in the manner of a coiled spring or a piece of wood, so that the air would be "a heap of little bodies, lying one upon another, as may be resembled to a fleece of wool." Another is to conceive that the particles are in constant agitation, in which case "their elastic power is not made to depend upon their shape or structure, but upon the vehement agitation." Boyle himself, on this occasion, did not choose to decide between these explanations or to propose any other. But the example does show that in the exact or quantitative sciences of the seventeenth century, there was a carefully observed distinction between a purely mathematical statement of a law and a causal mechanism for explaining such a law, that is, between such a law as a mathematical description of phenomena and the mathematical and physical exploration of its cause.

In some cases, the exploration of the cause did not require such a mechanical model, or explanation of cause, as the two mentioned by Boyle. For example, the parabolic path of projectiles is a mathematical statement of a phenomenon, with the qualifications arising from air resistance. But the mathematical conditions of a parabola are themselves suggestive of causes: for—again with the qualifications arising from air resistance—they state that there is uniform motion in the horizontal component and accelerated motion in the downward component. Since gravity acts downward and has no influence in the horizontal component, the very mathematics of the situation may lead an inquirer toward the physical causes of uniform and accelerated motion in the parabolic path of projectiles. Similarly, Newton's exploration of the physical nature and cause of universal gravity was guided by the mathematical properties of this force: that it varies inversely as the square of the distance, is proportional to the masses of the gravitating bodies and not their surfaces, extends to vast distances, is null within a uniform spherical shell, acts on a particle outside of a uniform spherical shell (or a body made up of a series of uniform spherical shells) as if the mass of that shell (or body made up of shells) were concentrated at its geometric center, has a value proportional to the distance from the center within a uniform sphere, and so on.

Such mathematical specifications of causes are different from physical explanations of the origin and mode of action of causes. This leads us to a recognition of the hierarchy of causes which it is important to keep in mind in understanding the specific qualities of the Newtonian revolution in science. For instance, Kepler found that planets move in ellipses with the sun at one focus, and that a line drawn from the sun to a planet sweeps out equal areas in equal times. Both of these laws encompass actual observations within a mathematical framework. The area law enabled Kepler to account for (or to explain) the nonuniformity of the oribital motion of planets, the speed being least at aphelion and greatest at perihelion. This is on the level of a mathematical explanation of the nonuniform motion of planets. Kepler, however, had gone well beyond such a mathematical explanation, since he had assigned a physical cause for this variation by supposing a celestial magnetic force; but he was never successful in linking this particular force mathematically to the elliptical orbits and the area law, or in finding an independent phenomenological or empirical demonstration that the sun does exert this kind of magnetic force on the planets.

Newton proceeded in a different manner. In the *Principia*, he did not begin with a discussion of what kind of force might act on planets. Rather he asked what are the mathematical properties of a force—whatever might be its causes or its mode of action, or whatever kind of force it might be—that can produce the law of areas. He showed that, for a body with an initial component of inertial motion, a necessary and sufficient condition for the area law is that the said force be centripetal, directed continually toward the point about which the areas are reckoned. Thus a mathematically descriptive law of motion was shown by mathematics to be equivalent to a set of causal conditions of forces and motions. Parenthetically it may be observed that the situation of a necessary and sufficient condition is rather unusual; most frequently it is the case that a force or other "cause" is but a sufficient condition for a given effect, and in fact only one of a number of such possible sufficient conditions. In the *Principia* the conditions of central forces and equal areas in equal times lead to considerations of elliptical orbits, which were shown by Newton to be a consequence of the central force varying inversely as the square of the distance.

Newton's mathematical argument does not, of course, show that in the orbital motion of planets or of planetary satellites these bodies are acted on by physical force; Newton shows only that within the conceptual framework of forces and the law of inertia, the forces acting on planets and satellites must be directed toward a center and must as well vary inversely as the square of the distance. But in the hierarchy of causal explanation, Newton's result does finally direct us to seek out the possible physical properties and mode of action of such a centrally directed inverse-square force. What is important in the Newtonian mode of analysis is that there is no need to specify at this first state of analysis what kind of force this is, nor how it acts. Yet Newton's aim was ultimately to go on by a different mode of analysis from the mathematical to the physical properties of causes (or forces) and so he was primarily concerned with "verae causae," causes—as he said—that are "both true and sufficient to explain the phenomena."

There is a great and wide gulf between the supposition of a set of mathematical conditions from which Newton derives Boyle's law and the assertion that this is a physical description of the reality of nature. As will be explained below, it is precisely Newton's ability to separate problems into their mathematical and physical aspects that enabled Newton to achieve such spectacular results in the *Principia*. And it is the possibility of working out the mathematical consequences of assumptions that are related to possible physical conditions, without having to discuss the physical reality of these conditions at the earliest stages, that marks the Newtonian style.

The Newtonian Style

The Newtonian revolution in the sciences did not consist merely of his use of deductive reasoning, or of an external form of argument presented as a series of demonstrations from first principles or axioms. Newton's outstanding achievement was to show how to introduce mathematical analysis into the study of nature in a particularly fruitful way, so as to disclose *Mathematical Principles of Natural Philosophy*, as the *Principia* was titled in full: *Philosophiae naturalis principia mathematica*. Newton not only exhibited a powerful means of applying mathematics to nature but also made use of a new mathematics which he himself had been forging and which may be hidden from a superficial observer by the external mask of what appears to be an example of geometry in the traditional Greek style.

In the *Principia* the science of motion is developed in a way that I have characterized as the Newtonian style. It shall be seen that this style consists of an interplay between the simplification and idealization of situations occurring in nature and their analogues in the mathematical domain. In this manner Newton was able to produce a mathematical system and mathematical principles that could then be applied to natural philosophy, that is, to the system of the world and its rules and data as determined by experience. This style permitted Newton to treat problems in the exact sciences as if they were exercises in pure mathematics and to link experiment and observation to mathematics in a notably fruitful manner. The Newtonian style also made it possible to put to one side, and to treat as an independent question, the problem of the cause of universal gravity and the manner of its action and transmission. Of course, this style does not imply that Newton did fully believe in attraction as a "real" physical entity, only that he could lay aside any such considerations while elaborating the mathematical consequences of such a force.

An outstanding feature of Newton's scientific thought is the close interplay of mathematics and physical science. It is, no doubt, a mark of his extraordinary genius that he could exercise such skill in imagining and designing experiments, in performing such experiments, and in drawing from them their theoretical significance. He also displayed a fertile imagination in speculating about the nature of matter (including its structure, the forces that might hold it together, and the causes of the interactions between varieties of matter) and in his investigations of alchemy. In the present context, my primary concern is with mathematics in relation to the physical sciences of dynamics and celestial mechanics, and not with these other aspects of Newton's scientific endeavors.

The "principles of natural philosophy" that Isaac Newton displayed and elaborated in his *Principia* are "mathematical principles." His exploration of the properties of various motions under given conditions of force is based on mathematics and not on experiment and induction. What is not so well known is that his essays in pure mathematics (analytic geometry and calculus) often tend to be couched in the language and principles of the physics of motion. This interweaving of dynamics and pure mathematics is also a characteristic feature of the science of the *Principia*. We shall see that Newton shows himself to be a mathematical empiricist to the extent that he believed that both basic postulates and the final results of mathematical analysis based on those postulates could be consonant with the real or external world as revealed by experiment and critical or precise observation. But his goal was attained by a kind of elaboration that he declared explicitly to be on the plane of mathematical rather than physical discourse and that corresponds to what we would call today the exploration of the consequences of a mathematical construct or a mathematical system abstracted from, yet analogous to, nature.

Newton's achievement in the *Principia* was, in my opinion, due to his extraordinary ability to mathematicize empirical or physical science. Mathematics at once served to discipline his creative imagination and thereby to sharpen or focus its productivity and to endow that creative imagination with singular new powers. For example, it was the extension of Newton's intellectual powers by mathematics and not merely some kind of physical or philosophical insight that enabled him to find the meaning of each of Kepler's laws and to show the relationship between the area law and the law of inertia. The power of mathematics may also be seen in Newton's analysis of the attraction of a homogeneous sphere. Newton proves that if the force varies either as the distance directly or as the square of the distance inversely, then the gravitational action of the sphere will be the same as if the whole mass of the sphere were to be concentrated at the geometric center. The two conditions (as Newton points out in the scholium to proposition 78, book one) are the two principal cases in nature. The inverse-square law applies to the gravitational action on the surface or at a point outside the sphere (the force inside having been proved to be null). The direct-distance law applies to the action on a particle within a solid sphere. It might have been supposed that in any solid body, the centripetal force (as Newton says) of the whole body would "observe the same law of increase or decrease in the recess from the center as the forces of the particles themselves do," but for Newton this is a result that must be attained by mathematics. Mathematics shows this to be the case for the above two conditions, a fact which Newton observes "is very remarkable."

The main thrust of the present discussion is the way in which Newton's mathematical thought was especially suitable for the analysis of physical problems and the construction and alteration of models and imaginative constructs and systems. Yet it must be kept in mind that some of Newton's basic mathematical concepts were themselves derived from physical situations. Since Newton tended to think in terms of curves that are drawn or traced out by moving points, his primary independent variable was time. In fact, his discussion of time in his purely mathematical treatises so closely resembles the presentation of time in the *Principia* (under the heading "absolute, true, and mathematical time") that it would be difficult to tell them apart, out of context.

There is an obvious pitfall in making too much of the language (images as well as metaphors) of physics in Newton's mathematics. For, when in his October 1666 tract on fluxions (or calculus), he writes "To resolve Problems by Motion," he is actually concerned with pure mathematics, even though the language may suggest physics; but this would have been true of all writers on "locus" problems since Greek times, who would trace out a curve or a line by a moving point or construct a solid by revolving a plane figure about an axis. Newton's success in analyzing the physics of motion depended to a large degree on his ability to reduce complex physical situations to a mathematical simplicity, in effect by studying the mathematical properties of an analogue of the reality that he eventually wished to understand. Thus we shall see him exploring by mathematics the motion of a mass point in a central force field as a first step toward understanding the significance of Kepler's area law as a general rule and not in relation to any specific oribital system. Newton was quite aware of the difference between the mathematical properties of such simplified analogous constructs and the physical properties expressed in mathematical relations or rules or principles of the physical world as revealed by experiments and observations; but later readers and some scholars today have tended to blur Newton's usually clear distinctions. In formalizing and developing his mathematical principles of natural philosophy, Newton made use of his own new mathematics, although this fact is apt to be masked from the reader by the general absence of a formal algorithm for the calculus in the *Principia*. This new mathematics appears in his early papers both in a purely algebraic or symbolic presentation much as in a present-day treatise on analysis (although with different symbols), and in a discussion of motion from a mathematical point of view. The latter is of interest to us here, because what is at issue is not merely a vague kinematical tracing-out of the conditions of a locus, but rather the elaboration for the purposes of pure mathematics of the geometry of curves based on principles of motion that are also used in physical kinematics. What is perhaps even more significant than the close conceptual fit of Newton's pure mathematics to solutions of physical problems is that, while there is a mode of thought common to both his mathematics and physics, there is in the *Principia* a continual awareness of the fundamental difference between mathematical principles and natural philosophy expressed through mathematical principles.

By this I mean that for purely mathematical purposes—that is, in a mathematical context and not with the aim of elucidating problems of physics—Newton uses principles of motion that read just as if they were physical principles being applied to physical local motion (locomotion), including the resolution and composition of vector speeds and the concept of inertial or uniform motion. Care must be exercised, according to D. T. Whiteside's warning, lest we assume too hastily that Newton was using physical principles in pure mathematics. Rather he was constructing a mathematical system that was analogous to (but not identical with) a physical system. That is, his mathematical "time" is not the physical time of experience; and it is the same with respect to mathematical "speed," and so on. Nevertheless, he did use the same language in both his writings on the physics of motion and his development of mathematics by a mathematics of motion. I believe, although of course there can be no proof, that there is a close bond between Newton's tendency to think about pure mathematics in terms that are the same as those arising in the physics of motion and his insight and skill in using pure mathematics to solve problems in physical motion. Yet one should not make too much of such a linkage, which would have been operative only on the subconscious level, since Isaac Barrow (for one) had also written pure mathematics in the language of motion, which may been Newton's direct source of inspiration.

The reader who has never studied Newton's mathematical writings can have no idea of the quasi-physical imagery of motion in his presentation of the method of fluxions. For example, in his *Treatise of the Method of Fluxions and Infinite Series,* he observed that "all the difficulties" may be "reduced to these two Problems only, which I shall propose, concerning a space described by local Motion, any how accelerated or retarded":

> I. The length of the Space described being continually (that is, at all times) given; to find the velocity of the motion at any time proposed.
> II. The velocity of the motion being continually given; to find the length of the Space described at any time proposed.

If Newton thus conceived of fluxions and limits in terms of a mathematical local motion, it may not be surprising that he should have developed a powerful tool for analyzing local motion in a physical sense by means of mathematics that used the method of limits, as in the *Principia*. Many years later, in about 1714, in a draft of his anonymous book review of the *Commercium Epistolicum,* in which the Newtonian priority in the discovery of the calculus is asserted, Newton made it clear once again that mathematical concepts similar to those used in the physics of motion were basic to his own version of the calculus. "I consider time," he wrote, "as flowing or increasing by continual flux and other quantities as increasing continually in time, and from the fluxion of time I give the name of fluxions to the velocities with which all other quantities increase." His method was to "expose time by any quantity flowing uniformly" and, in a manner reminiscent of Galileo, he said that his "Method is derived immediately from Nature her self."

This intimate connection between pure mathematics and the physics of motion is, I believe, a characteristic feature of Newton's *Principia* wherein certain aspects of natural philosophy are reduced to mathematical principles, then developed as mathematical exercises, and finally reapplied to physical problems. The main subject of the *Principia* is terrestrial and celestial dynamics: the physics of motion, or the motion of bodies under the action of various kinds of forces and different conditions of restraint and resistance, and the mathematical method is fluxional and uses vanishing infinitesimals; it is a characteristic feature to apply the limit process to geometric conditions and to proportions (or equations) arising from or representing those conditions. Hence the quasi-physical nature of Newton's mathematics was eminently suited to the solution of the problems to which he addressed himself in his *Principia*. But while this intermingling of a pure mathematics derived from or related to motion and the physical problems of motion may have led Newton to achieve unheard-of results of astonishing fecundity, this very aspect of his work has caused great confusion among his commentators and interpreters ever since. In particular, they have not always known when Newton was speaking on the level of mathematics and when on the level of physics. Or, they have perhaps assumed this to be a distinction without a difference and have not bothered to ascertain whether Newton as a mathematician was—in the *Principia*—everywhere intending to be understood as a physicist. It will be seen below that a major aspect of Newton's method in the *Principia* (and possibly in other aspects of his work in the exact sciences) was his intuitive separation of these two levels of discourse and then, on the proper occasion, using his mathematical results to illuminate the physical problem. The blurring of Newton's distinctions, which has led to continual misunderstandings concerning Newton's method and his intentions, probably derives from a reading of certain scholia and introductory sections of the *Principia* out of the context of the mathematical physics in which they are embedded and which they were intended to illuminate.

One of the clearest statements Newton ever made of his own position was in reply to a criticism made by Leibniz. The details of this criticism would take us far afield, and we need only take notice here that Newton held that what his critic "saith about Philosophy is foreign to the Question and therefor I shall be very short upon it." Newton's grounds for this statement of disagreement with Leibniz concerning the foundation of "Philosophy" (i.e., natural philosophy) were threefold. First, "Leibniz denies conclusions without telling the fault of the premises." Second, "His arguments against me are founded upon metaphysical and precarious hypotheses and therefore do not affect me: for I meddle only with experimental Philosophy." Third, "He changes the signification of the words Miracles and Occult qualities that he may use them in railing at universal gravity . . ." In writing the last sentence, he had at first used the words "railing at me," which shows the degree to which in his own mind he had equated himself with the conceptual fruit of his intellect.

As Newton said again and again, there was a fundamental difference in philosophy between himself and Leibniz. To deny universal gravitation could be legitimate in Newton's philosophy only by going back to the arguments given by Newton, and to the premises of those arguments: a combination of empirical finding, mathematical development, and sound logic. It was not enough merely to say that a concept of universal gravitation is not acceptable in philosophy. And so to understand the foundations of Newtonian exact science (i.e., the exact science of the *Principia*), it is necessary to see what in fact were the stages by which Newton got to universal gravitation. In so doing, we shall see why Newton held that there is a profound difference between "metaphysical and precarious hypotheses" and "experimental Philosophy." Finally, Newton was particularly concerned about "Miracles and Occult qualities." He stoutly denied the relevance of "Miracles" to his natural philosophy in the sense of a suspension of the ordinary laws of nature, and he equally denied that he had reintroduced into science the "Occult qualities" of late Aristotelian-scholastic philosophy. Gravitation itself was not

"Occult," but its cause was, to the degree that it was still hidden from us.

Newton's spectacular achievement in producing a unified explanation of the events in the heavens and on our earth, and in showing how such diverse phenomena as the ebb and flow of the tides and the irregularities in the moon's motion might be derived from a single principle of universal gravity, draw attention to his mode of procedure—a special blend of imaginative reasoning plus the use of mathematical techniques applied to empirical data—which I have called the Newtonian style. Its essential feature is to start out (phase one) with a set of assumed physical entities and physical conditions that are simpler than those of nature, and which can be transferred from the world of physical nature to the domain of mathematics. An example would be to reduce the problems of planetary motion to a one-body system, a single body moving in a central force field; then to consider a mass point rather than a physical body, and to suppose it to move in a mathematical space in mathematical time. In this construct Newton has not only simplified and idealized a system found in nature, but he has also imaginatively conceived a system in mathematics that is the parallel or analogue of the natural system. To the degree that the physical conditions of the system become mathematical rules or propositions, their consequences may be deduced by the application of mathematical techniques.

Because the mathematical system (to use an expression of Newton's in another context) duplicates the idealized physical system, the rules or proportions derived mathematically in one may be transferred back to the other and then compared and contrasted with the data of experiment and observation (and with experiential laws, rules, and proportions drawn from those data). This is phase two. For instance, the condition of a mass point moving with an initial component of inertial motion in a central force field is shown (*Principia*, propositions 1 and 2, Book One) to be a necessary and sufficient condition for the law of areas, which had been found to be a phenomenologically verifiable relation in the external astronomical world.

The comparison and contrast with the reality of experiential nature (that is, with the laws, rules, and systems based upon observations and experiments) usually require a modification of the original phase one. This leads to further deductions and yet a new comparison and contrast with nature, a new phase two. In this way, there is an alternation of phases one and two leading to systems of greater and greater complexity and to an increased *vraisemblance* of nature. That is, Newton successively adds further entities, concepts, or conditions to the imaginatively constructed system, so as to make either its mathematically deduced consequences or the set conditions become more closely an analogue of the world of experience. In the example under discussion, the first of these additional steps is to introduce Kepler's third law.

In the next stage of complexity or generality, Newton adds to the system a second body or mass point, since (as Newton says at the start of section 11, Book One, of the *Principia*) attractions are not made toward a spatial point, but rather "toward bodies," in which case the actions of each of the bodies on the other are always equal in magnitude though oppositely directed. Yet additional conditions include the introduction of bodies with finite sizes and defined shapes, and of a system of more than two interacting bodies. (There is also the question of whether bodies move through mediums according to some specified law of resistance.)

For Newton there is a final stage in this process: when the system and its conditions no longer merely represent nature simplified and idealized or an imaginative mathematical construct, but seem to conform to (or at least to duplicate) all the major conditions of the external world. Then it becomes possible, as in Book Three of the *Principia*, to apply the aggregate of mathematical principles to natural philosophy, to elaborate the Newtonian system of the world. This is the final phase three of the Newtonian style, the crown of all, to display the variety of natural phenomena that can be attributed to the action of universal gravity. It is not until after this stage that Newton himself would have to yield to the demand for investigation into the nature, cause, or mode of operation of such forces as he had used in accounting for the motions of terrestrial bodies, the planets, their moons, our moon, the comets, the tides, and various other phenomena. This additional inquiry, a kind of sequel to phase three, went beyond the requirements of the Newtonian style, however, at least insofar as the *Principia* is concerned. Even in the General Scholium, with which the later editions of the *Principia* conclude, Newton insisted that his gravitational dynamics and his system of the world could be accepted even though he had said nothing about the cause of gravity. But he did then express his personal conviction that gravity "really exists."

All of the evidence of Newton's writing, correspondence, and reported conversations indicates that he firmly believed in the reality of universal gravity and its action in the solar system. The adoption of the Newtonian style had, therefore, nothing to do with Newton's own personal beliefs. But for Newton, as for his contemporaries, there were fundamental problems about how forces could act over great distances of empty space. How could the gravitational force of the sun act on Saturn, extending in some unknown manner over thousands of millions of miles? How could the sun's gravitational force act over even greater distances from the sun to the aphelions of comets? As Newton said in the General Scholium, gravity "really exists," but how is one to "assign a cause"?

The Newtonian style enabled Newton to explore the properties of such forces as universal gravity from the point of view of mathematics rather than physics. Without being inhibited by philosophical considerations, he was able to develop the laws of the action of a gravity-like force in a mathematical analogue of the world of nature. In this procedure, he could lay aside (for the time being) any deeply felt concerns about how such forces can possibly act. In private documents, however, and in his many attempts to explain how gravity can act, he would resort to all the interrelated realms of his belief, giving due weight to the larger questions of a philosophical kind. In book three of the *Principia*, he shifted from mathematical constructs to physical concepts and offered evidence for the existence of a universal force of gravity that acts according to the laws he had found. The mathematical construct of the Newtonian style thus proved to be a close analogue of the physical universe. The problem then was how to account for the action of such a force.

Because of the Newtonian style, Newton was not, in the first stages—that is, in books one and two of the *Principia*—inhibited by the philosophical problems associated with such forces. He hoped that his readers would go along with him and would not reject the physics of the *Principia* on philosophical grounds without going through the mathematical development he had presented and then seeing how the physical universe would prove to be an analogue of the mathematical system he had developed. Many readers, however, and many scholars from that day to ours, have seen his form of presentation only as a subterfuge and have not been willing to accept Newton's presentation at its face value. Critics such as Huygens and Leibniz were more concerned with arguments about first principles than with the mathematical elaboration of the properties of forces. Unlike Newton, they could not postpone such inhibiting questions until after the demonstration that just such a universal force can produce the many phenomena observed on earth and in the solar system.

It is a feature of the Newtonian style that mathematics and not a series of experiments leads to a profound knowledge of the universe and its workings. Of course, the data of experiment and observation are used in determining the initial conditions of the inquiry, the features that yield the mathematical principles that are applied to natural philosophy. Newton was also aware that the success of the eventual natural philosophy (or of the system of the world) must rest ultimately on the accuracy or validity of the empirical data of which it was constructed. Furthermore, the test of the end result was necessarily the degree and extent of the ability to predict and to retrodict observed phenomena or phenomenologically determined "rules" (such as Kepler's laws). Even so, on some significant occasions Newton seems to have given priority to the exactness of mathematical system rather than the coarseness of empirical law. In the case of Kepler's laws, the reason is that they prove in Newton's analysis to be exact only in a very limited situation and to be no more than phenomenologically "true" (that is, "true" only within certain conventionally acceptable limits of observational accuracy) of the real world as revealed by experience. Hence, even the Newtonian system of the world, when said by Newton (in the final edition of the *Principia*) to be based on "phenomena," is in fact based also, to some degree, on truths of mathematical systems or idealizations of nature that are seen to be approximate to but not identical equivalents of the conditions of the external world.

The simplified physical system (and its mathematical analogue that Newton develops at the beginning of the *Principia*) exhibits all three of Kepler's laws and in fact serves to explain these laws by showing the physical significance of each one separately. In short, this system or construct is not a figment of the free imagination, or a purely arbitrary or hypothetical fiction created by the mind, but is rather closely related to the real Copernico-Keplerian world that is made known to us by phenomena and by laws that are phenomenologically based. In his first flush of victory, just before writing the *Principia*, when he had completed his analysis of this system, Newton himself thought that it was more than an imagined construct. Indeed, in a first version he expressed his belief that he had now explained exactly and fully how nature works in the operation of the solar system. But not for long. It was almost at once plain that the construct he had been studying did not accord with the real world. And so, bit by bit, it was endowed with more and more features that would bring it into closer harmony with the world of reality. In the course of these transformations of his construct, Newton was led by degrees to the concept of a mutual gravitating force, a concept all the more conspicuous by its absence from the first considerations. As a result, it is possible to assign a precise limiting date to the first step toward that great concept: no earlier than December 1684.

The advantage of the Newtonian approach, as I have outlined it, are manifold. First of all, by making the construct simple at the start, Newton escapes the complexities of studying nature herself. He starts out with an idealized version of nature, in which certain descriptive laws of observed position and speeds—Kepler's planetary laws—hold exactly. Then, on the basis of the laws and principles that underlie these descriptive laws, Newton proceeds to new constructs and to more general underlying laws and principles, and eventually gets to the law of universal gravity in a new system in which the original three planetary laws as stated by Kepler are—strictly speaking—false.

Is Newton's ultimate system still only an imagined construct? Or is it now so congruent with reality that its laws and principles are the laws and principles of the universe? Newton does not tell us what he believes on this score, but we may guess at his position. His first construct, for which Kepler's laws are valid, proved to be a one-body system: essentially a single mass-particle moving under the action of a force directed toward a fixed center. Next he extended and modified the results found true of the one-body system so that they would apply to a two-body system, in which each of the two bodies acts mutually on the other with the same inverse-square force that acts on the single body in the first one. Then there are many bodies, each acting on all the other mutually with an inverse-square force; and, finally, the bodies have physical dimensions and determinate shapes, and are no longer mere mass points or particles. The force is shown to duplicate gravity and to be mutually acting, and is then found to be a universal force proportional to the product of the masses. In this way, Newton extended his construct from one to two mass points and then to many, and from particles or mass points to physical bodies. Since there are no more bodies to be added, I believe he would have argued that the system was complete. Further physical complexities or mathematical conditions might be imagined and put in: for instance, gross bodies with negative masses; or bodies that would interact with other bodies, but that might have negative gravitational forces (repulsions) as well as positive ones (attractions), just as in electrical and magnetic phenomena. But in terms of accumulated observations over many centuries, any such condition would then have been ruled out as highly improbable, if not downright impossible. Of course, since Newton was unable to give a general solution to the problem of three mutually gravitating bodies, there might have been unforeseen complications in a many-body system. But we may guess that these speculative conditions would not have carried much weight with him. He had found the system of the world.

Furthermore, the final system would certainly have seemed to have transcended the status of being merely an imagined construct in the degree to which its results agreed with many different kinds of observations. The Newtonian theory could explain not only why all bodies fall with the same acceleration at a given place on earth, but also the observed fact that the acceleration varies in a certain definite manner with latitude (as shown by the concomitant variation in the period of a freely swinging simple pendulum) and other factors. The theory of gravity could also explain the tides and many features of the motion of the moon, and could even predict the oblate shape of the earth from the known facts of precession. The variety and exactness of the verifiable predictions and retrodictions of experience gave every reason to believe that the Newtonian system of the world, displayed in book three of his *Principia*, and developed and extended by others, was indeed the true system of the world. And so it was conceived for over two hundred years—until Einstein developed his theory of relativity.

Because the final system achieved by Newton was found to work so well, it no longer had to be treated as an imagined construct. As Newton himself put it in the General Scholium, there are three conditions for gravity that are enough, that suffice in natural (or experimental) philosophy. It is enough ("Satis est"), first of all, "that gravity really exists";

second, that gravity "acts according to the laws that we have set forth"; third, that gravity "is sufficient to explain all the motions of the heavenly bodies and of our sea." For Newton there then arose two wholly different sets of questions. The first were technical: to work out, as he saw, the "details" of gravitational celestial mechanics and thus to get better results for such problems as the motion of the moon. This range of activity can be described as completing the *Principia* on the "operative" level. The second set of questions was of another type altogether: to explain gravity and its mode of action or to assign "a cause of gravity." His critics however, proceeded in just the opposite manner, starting out with the vexing problem of how such a force as the proposed Newtonian universal gravity can possibly exist and act according to the Newtonian laws, and not accepting the formal results of the *Principia* so long as they did not find its conceptual basis to be satisfactory. These critics, in other words, were not willing to go along with the procedural mode of the Newtonian style.

Part 3
EXPERIMENTAL PROCEDURE

Introduction

Newton was a scientist of many different dimensions. He was a superb mathematician who saw as well how mathematics could be effectively applied to physics, and he was a theoretician whose imagination ranged boldly beyond the limits of prevailing orthodoxies. He was also one of the early masters of experimental procedure, and his example helped to install experimentation as the distinctive method of modern science.

The age of the Scientific Revolution did not invent experimentation. We can find valid experiments in the writings of natural philosophers and physicians of earlier times. Nevertheless, when the seventeenth century dawned, experimentation had not been accepted as the principal method of science. Aristotle, the source of the natural philosophy that prevailed in the universities, had certainly insisted on the observational foundation of knowledge. As he put it, there is nothing in the mind that was not first in the senses. Observation is not identical to experimentation, however. Observation tends to be passive, accepting the data that nature offers. Experimentation actively interrogates nature, asking questions that nature may not answer spontaneously and defining conditions under which the questions can be put, ideally in such a way that the answers will be unambiguous.

Galileo was one of the early masters of experimentation. The set of questions concerning pumps and syphons that led to the barometer, the air pump, and Boyle's law provided one of the early demonstrations of the power of experimental procedure. The mercury barometer itself was initially an experiment. The questions about pumps had led to the construction of a water barometer in Rome. Opinions differed as to what sustained the column of water inside the closed tube. Evangelista Torricelli belonged to those who thought there was nothing more than a simple equilibrium of weights between the water in the tube and the air, which bore down on the surface of water in the vessel in which the tube stood. If that were the case, he reasoned, then a column of mercury, a fluid fourteen times as dense as water, ought to stand only one-fourteenth as high. The barometer was born when Torricelli queried nature in this way. A few years later, in the most famous experiment performed during the seventeenth century, Blaise Pascal extended the line of questioning by having a barometer carried to the top of a mountain. When it was high on the mountain, above part of the atmosphere so that less air bore down on the surface of mercury, the height of the column in the tube that the air could sustain likewise decreased. With the air pump, Boyle was able to pose a further set of questions that had

In order not to encumber the reader with footnotes we have composed a Biographical Register, in which all the people mentioned in the text are identified, and a Glossary, in which technical terms are briefly explicated and such things as organizations, places, publications, and manuscript collections are identified. Both the Biographical Register and the Glossary are located near the end of the volume.

been impossible to scientists equipped only with barometers and mountains.

Experimentation pervaded the literature of the new science that Newton discovered in 1664. The "Quaestiones" (see Part 1, Natural Philosophy [above]) make it clear that Newton seized on the procedure as though by instinct. Look back again at the passages on Descartes's theory of light and his explanation of the tides. There is no evidence that Newton actually performed any experiment in connection with these passages, but the tone of active questioning that informs those and other passages is the tone of experimentation.

The "Quaestiones" contain the first hesitant statement of Newton's central insight in optics, that light is heterogeneous. They contain also, immediately following the statement, an experiment with a colored thread designed to test the new idea. Not too long after that, stimulated apparently by the effort to grind hyperbolic lenses and the realization that the new property of light he had apparently discovered would make them useless for obtaining a perfect focus, Newton launched into an investigation of the heterogeneity of light. From the beginning, it was an experimental investigation—the preeminent experimental investigation of the seventeenth century. In Part 4, Optics (below), we have included some of the experiments. We are able to include here only a few of the many others that Newton imagined in order to test various conclusions that had to follow if the central idea of the heterogeneity of light were true. Some of them come from the paper, "Of Colours," that he composed about 1666 and some of them from a letter to the Royal Society of June 11, 1672, which elaborates on the letter of February and draws on experiments performed in 1669 in connection with his initial lectures as the Lucasian Professor of Mathematics at Cambridge. Readers who want to pursue these matters further can find the whole of Newton's endeavor in optics in the excellent edition of the *Optical Papers* edited by Alan E. Shapiro (see Selected Bibliography).

Newton's experimentation was not limited to optics. The *Principia*, a book on theoretical physics, was filled with experiments. In an age that did not possess many of the instruments of measurement that science can call on today, he recognized the potential of the pendulum, in which the addition of small increments on successive swings could make minute quantities manifest, to carry part of the burden of a quantitative physics. We include two experiments with the pendulum from the *Principia*. In one of them, Newton tests the idea, fundamental to his conception of universal gravitation, that quantity of matter (or mass) is proportional to weight. In the other, he uses the same pendulum, which was eleven feet long, possibly hanging in a stairwell in Trinity College, to test his own idea, expressed in his early speculations, that a cosmic aether pervades all space and influences the motion of bodies.

Experimentation became a principle as well as method with Newton, who came to see the experimental foundation of his philosophy as the feature that set it apart from other natural philosophies and made it superior to them. As he asserted, not without belligerence, in the opening line of his *Opticks*, "My Design in this Book is not to explain the Properties of Light by Hypotheses, but to propose and prove them by Reason and Experiments." The dichotomy between explanatory hypotheses and experimental demonstrations that Newton asserted went back to the reception of his initial paper on colors in 1672. In Part 2, Scientific Method (above), we have included a passage from a letter to Henry Oldenburg of July 6, 1672, replying to the critique of the paper by the French scientist Pardies, and Newton's "Rules of Reasoning in Philosophy," which speak to this point. In this part, we include a statement of philosophic principle from the end of "An Account of the Book entituled *Commercium Epistolicum*," which Newton published anonymously in the *Philosophical Transactions* at the height of the controversy with Leibniz over priority in the discovery of the calculus. For Newton, the difference with Leibniz had come to embrace not only the issue of priority in discovery, but also the fundamental natures of two philosophies, with Leibniz standing in this case as the representative of the continental philosophers, the very school that introduced Newton to the new science in 1664, who rejected Newton's conception of gravitational attraction.

From "Of Colours" †

Experiments with the Prisme

On a black peice of paper I drew a line *opq*, whereof one half *op* was a good blew, the other *pq* a good deepe red (chosen by Prob of Colours). And looking on it through the Prisme *adf*, it appeared broken in two betwixt the colours, as at *rst*, the blew parte *rs* being nearer the vertex

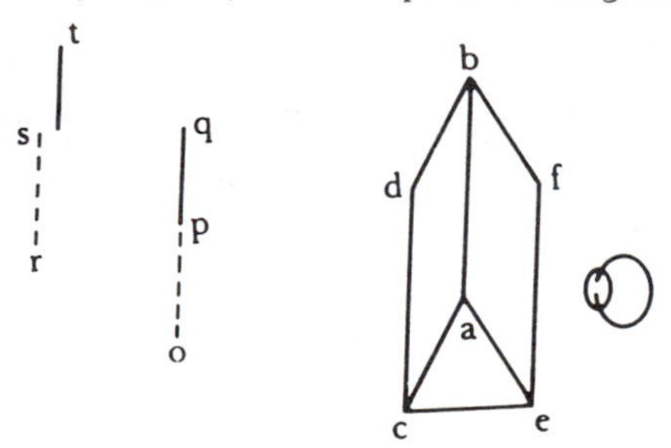

† J. E. McGuire and Martin Tammy, *Certain Philosophical Questions: Newton's Trinity Notebook* (Cambridge: Cambridge University Press 1983), pp. 466–80. Reprinted with the permission of Cambridge University Press. The undated essay, "Of Colours," probably composed in early 1666, contains the first sustained elaboration of Newton's developing theory of color.

ab of the Prisme than the red parts *st*. Soe that blew rays suffer a greater refraction than red ones. Note: I call those blew or red rays etc, which make the Phantome of such colours.

The same Experiment may bee tryed with a thred of two colours held against the darke.

Taking a Prisme, (whose angle *fbd* was about 60° into a darke roome into which the sun shone only at one little round hole *k*. And laying it close to the hole *k* in such manner that the rays, being equally refracted at (*n* and *h*) their going in and out of it, cast colours *rstv* on the opposite wall. The colours should have beene in a round circle were all the rays alike refracted, but their forme was oblong terminated at theire sides *r* and *s* with streight lines; theire bredth *rs* being 2⅓ inches, theire length to about 7 or eight inches, and the centers of the red and blew, (*q* and *p*) being distant, about 2¾ or 3 inches. The distance of the wall *trsv* from the Prisme being 260 inches.

Setting the Prisme in the midst twixt the hole *k* and the opposite wall, in the same posture, and laying a boarde *xy* betwixt the hole *k* and the Prisme close to the Prisme, in which board there was a small hole as big as the hole *k* (viz: ⅛ of an inch in Diameter) soe that the rays passing through both those holes to the Prisme might all bee almost parallell (wanting lesse than 7 minutes, whereas in the former experiment some rays were inclined 31 minutes). Then was the length and breadth of the colours on the wall every way lesse than halfe the former by about 2 inches viz *rs* = ⅜ inch, *tv* = 2¾ inch. And *pq* = 1¼ inch. Soe that the Red and blew rays which were parallel before refraction may bee esteemed to be generally inclined one to another after refraction (some more some lesse than) 34 minutes. And yet some of them are inclined more than a degree, in this case. And therefore if theire sines of incidence (out of glass into air) be the same, theire sines of refraction will generally bee in the proportion of 285 to 286 and for the most

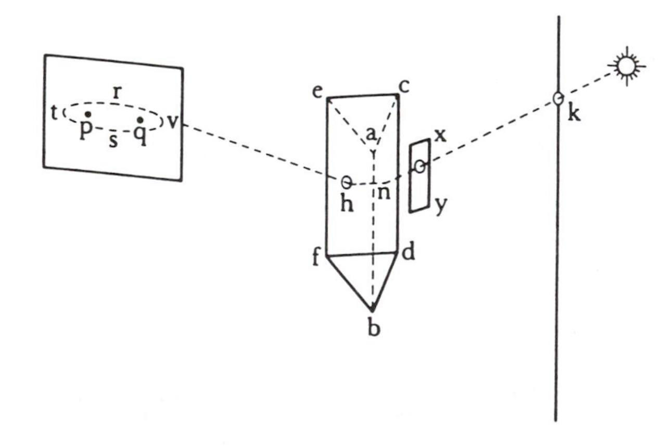

extreamely red and blew rays, they will bee as 130 to 131+, For by the experiment if their angle of incidence out of the glasse into the aire bee 30°, The angle refraction of the red rays being 48° 35′: the angle refraction of the blew rays will bee 48°, 52′. generally: but if the rays bee extreamly red and blew the angle of refraction of the blew rays may bee more than 49°, 5′.

* * *

If the sun S shine upon the Prisme *def*, some of his rays being transmitted through the base *ef* will make colours on the wall *cb* at *b*, others will bee reflected to the wall at *c* making only a white without colours; Now if the Prisme bee soe inclined as that the rays *ab* bee refracted more and more obliquly, the blew colour will at last vanish from *b*; soe that the red alone being refracted to *b*, the blew will bee reflected to *c* and make the white coloure there to appeare a little blewish. But if the Prisme bee yet more inclined, the red colour at *b* will vanish too and being reflected to *c* will will make the blewish colour turne white againe.

If in the open aire you looke at the Image of the sky reflected from the bases of the Prism *ef*, holding your eye O almost perpendicular to the basis you will see one part of the sky *ep* (being as it were shaded with a thin curtaine) to appeare darker than the other *qf*. [For all the rays

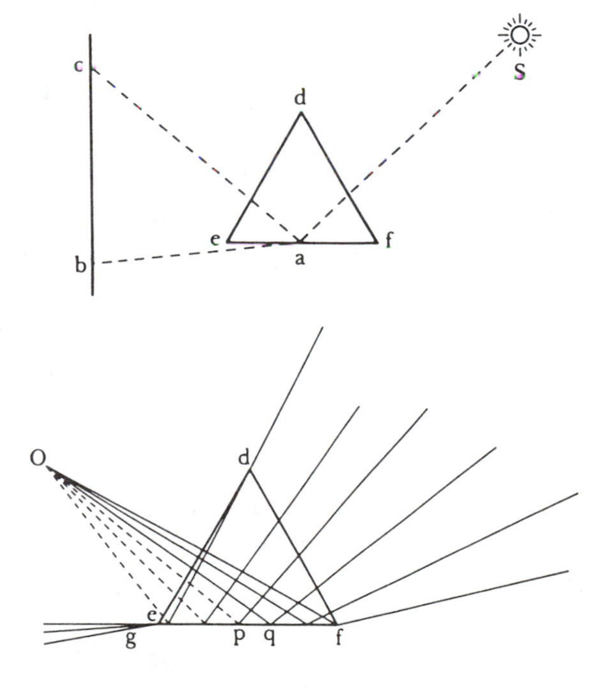

within can come to the eye from *qf*, fall soe obliquly on the basis as to bee all reflected to the eye. Whereas those which can come to the eye from *ep* are so direct to the basis as to bee most of them transmitted to *g*]: and the partition of those two parts of the sky, *pq*, appeares blew; [For the rays which can come to the eye from *pq*, are so inclined to the basis that all the blew rays are reflected to the eye whilst most of the red rays are transmitted through to *g*, as in experiment 22].

Tying two Prismes basis to basis *def* & *bef* together: I so held them in the sun beames, transmitted through a hole into a darke roome, that they falling pretty directly upon the base *ef* (in fig 1) were most of them transmitted to *B* on the paper *CB*; though some of them were reflected to *c* by the filme of aire *ef* betwixt the Prismes. But both *C* & *B* were white. Then I inclined the Basis *(ef)* of the Prismes more and more to the rays untill *B* changed from white to Red, and the white at *C* became blewish; and inclining the Prisme a little more the Red at *B* vanished, and the blewish colour at *c* became white againe. As in the 22th Experiment.

If I held the said Prismes in the open air as in the 23d experiment, holding my eye at O (in the 2d fig) to see the reflected sky the Phænomena were the same as in that 23d experiment; *ep* appearing darker than *qf*, and *pq* being blew. But if I held my eye at N to see the sky through the base of the Prismes *ef* (or rather through the plate of aire betwixt those bases) there appeared the contrary Phænomena but much more faint; *ep* being very light, *qf* very darke, and *pq* very red. [The reason was given in the 23d Experiment.]

Note, That the 22th and 24th (and all such like experiments that require that the rays coming from a luminous body be all wholly or almost parallell) would bee more conspicuous were the suns Diameter lesse, & therefore for such like experiments his rays may bee straitned through two small holes at a good distance assunder, as was done in the 8th Experiment.

Also the 23th and 25t Experiment (most other such like in which

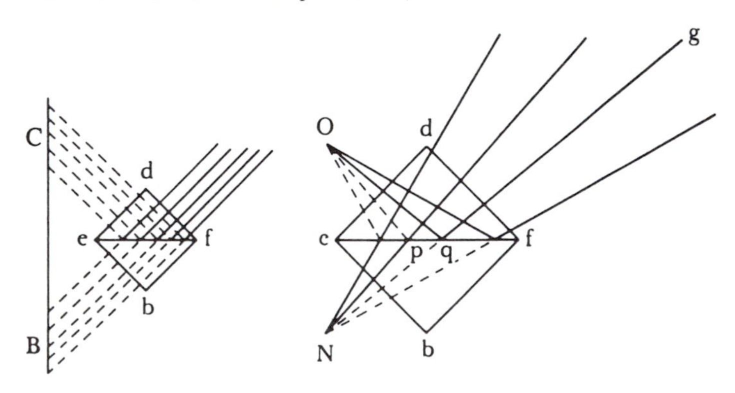

the rays passe immediatly from the prisme to the eye) would bee more conspicuous were the Pupill lesse than it is, And therefore it would bee convenient to look through a small hole at the Prisme.

* * *

If three or more Prismes A, *B*, *C*, bee held in the sun soe that the Red colour of the Prisme *B* falls upon the Greene or yellow colour of Prisme

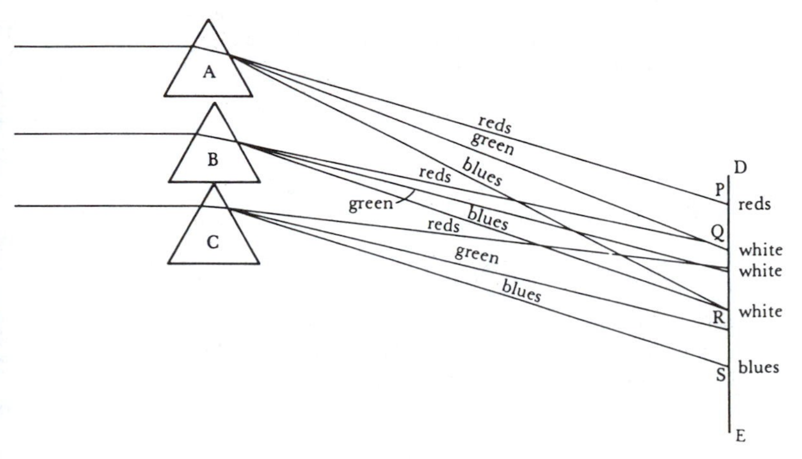

A and the Red colour of the Prisme C falls on the Greene or yellow colour of the Prisme *B*; the Said colours falling upon the Paper *DE* at *P*, *Q*, *R*, *S*. There will appeare a Red colour at *P* and a blew one at *S* but betwixt *Q* and *R* where the Reds, yellows, Greenes, blews, and Purples

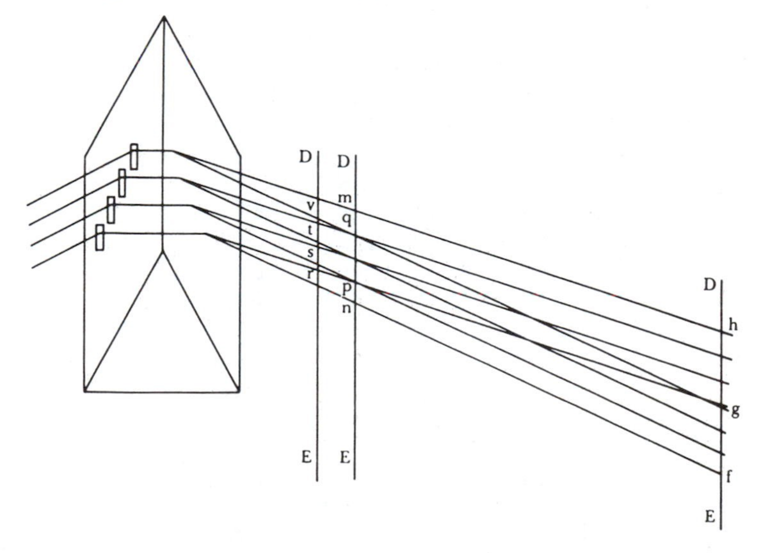

of the severall Prismes are blended together there appeares a white.

Of if you cleane a peice of Paper on one side of the Prisme with severall slits *a*, *b*, *c*, *d*, in it parallel to the edges of the Prisme soe that the light passing through those slits make colours on the Paper *DE*; If the said paper be held neare to the Prisme there will appeare for each slit *a*, *b*, *c*, *d*, a coloured line *r*, *s*, *t*, *v*. The paper being held farther of untill the said coloured lines bee blended together, there will appeare white twixt *p* & *q* where those colours are blended; at *m* there appeares Reds & at *n* blews. But if the paper bee still held farther of the white colour *(pq)* will appeare narrower and narrower untill it vanish. and then *gh* on one side appeares Red and *gf* on the other side is blew.

* * *

From Newton to Oldenburg, June 11, 1672†

7. That the Ray Is Not Split or Any Otherwise Dilated.

[Whether the unequall refractions made without respect to any inequality of incidence, be caused by the different refrangibility of severall rays, or by the splitting breaking or dissipating the same ray into diverging parts]

The first of these Queries you may find already determined by an experiment in my former Letter, the designe of which was to show that the length of the coloured Image proceeded not from any unevennesse in the glasse, or any other *contingent irregularity* in the refractions. Amongst other irregularities I know not what is more obvious to suspect then a fortuitous dilating and spreading of light after some such manner as Des-Cartes hath described in his æthereall refractions for explicating the Tayle of a Comet, or as Mr Hook now supposeth to be effected by the splitting and rarefying of his æthereall pulses. And to prevent the suspicion of any such irregularities, I told you that I refracted the light contrary ways with two Prisms successively, to destroy thereby the regular effects of the first Prism by the second, and to discover the irregular effects by augmenting them with iterated refractions. Now amongst other irregularities, if the first Prism had spread and dissipated every ray into an indefinite number of diverging parts, the second should in like manner have spread and dissipated every one of those parts into a further indefinite number, whereby the Image would have been still more dilated; contrary to the event. And this ought to have happened because

† *The Correspondence of Isaac Newton*, eds. H. W. Turnbull, J. F. Scott, A Rupert Hall, and Laura Tilling, 7 vols. (Cambridge: Cambridge University Press, 1959–77), vol. 1, pp. 178–85. Reprinted with the permission of Cambridge University Press. The most detailed critique of Newton's first paper on colors came from Robert Hooke. In his long letter of June 11, 1672, to Oldenburg, Newton replied to Hooke by drawing on material cited in lectures on color theory that he had delivered in 1670 and 1671 as the lucasian Professor of Mathematics at Cambridge.

those linear diverging parts depend not on one another for the manner of their refraction, but are every one of them as truly and completely rays as the whole was before its incidence; as may appeare by intercepting them severally.

The reasonablenesse of this proceeding will perhaps better appear by acquainting you with this further circumstance. I sometimes placed the second Prism in a position transverse to the first, on designe to try if it would make the long Image become four-square by refractions crossing those which had drawn the round Image into a long one. For if amongst other irregularities the refraction of the first Prism did by splitting dilate a linear ray into a superficiall, the crosse refractions of that second Prism ought by further splitting to dilate and draw that superficiall ray into a pyramidall Solid. But upon tryall I found it otherwise, the image being as regularly oblong as before, and inclined to both the Prisms at an angle of 45 degrees.

I tryed also all other positions of the second Prism by turning the ends about its middle part, and in no case could observe any such irregularity. The Image was ever alike inclined to both Prisms, its breadth answering to the Suns diameter, and its length being greater or lesse accordingly as the refractions more or less agreed or contradicted one another.

And by these observations since the breadth of the Image was not augmented by the crosse refraction of the second Prism, that refraction must have been performed without any splitting or dilating of the ray, and therefore at least the light incident on that Prism must be granted an aggregate of rays *unequally refrangible* in my sense. And since the Image was equally inclined to both Prisms, and consequently the refractions alike in both, it argues that they were performed according to some constant *law* without any irregularity.

* * *

9. *That Whitenesse is a Mixture of All Colours.*

There remaines now the third Query to be considered, and that is, whether *whitenesse* be an uniform colour or a dissimilar mixture of all colours. The *experiment* which I brought to decide it Mr Hook thinks may be otherwise explaned, and so concludes nothing. But he might easily have satisfied himselfe by trying what would be the result of a mixture of all colours. And that very Experiment might have satisfied him if he had examined it by the various circumstances. One circumstance I there declared of which I see no notice taken: and it is that if any colour at the Lens be intercepted, the whitenesse will be changed into the other colours. If all the colours but red be intercepted, that red alone in the concourse or crossing of the rays will not constitute whitenesse, but continues as much red as before; and so of the other colours. So that the businesse is not onely to shew how rays which before the concours exhibit colours, doe in the concours exhibit white: But to show how in the same place where the severall sorts of rays apart exhibit severall colours, a confusion of all together make white. For instance if Red alone be first transmitted to the paper at the place of concourse, and then the other colours be let fall on that Red, the question will be whether they convert it into white by mixing with it onely, as Blew falling on Yellow light is supposed to compound Green; or whether there be some further change wrought in the colours by their mutuall acting on one another, untill, like contrary Peripatetic Qualities, they become assimilated. And he that shall explicate this last case *Mechanically* must conquer a double impossibility. He must first show that many unlike motions in a fluid can by clashing so act on one another and change each other as to become one uniform motion; and then that an uniform motion can of it selfe without any new unequall impressions, depart into a great variety of motions regularly unequall. And after this he must further tell me why all objects appeare not of the same colour, that is why their colours in the Air where the rays that convey them every way are confusedly mixed, doe not assimilate one another and become uniforme before they arrive at the Spectators eye.

But if there be yet any doubting, tis better to put the event on further *circumstances* of the *experiment*, then to acquiesce in the possibility of any Hypotheticall Explication. As for instance by trying what will be the apparition of these colours in a very quick consecution of one another. And this may be easily performed by the rapid gyration of a *wheel* with many spoakes or coggs in its perimeter, whose interstices and thicknesses may be equall and of such a largenesse that if the wheel be interposed between the Prism and the white concourse of the colours, one half of the colours may be intercepted by a spoak or cogg and the other halfe passe through an interstice. The wheel being in this posture you may first turne it slowly about to see all the colours fall successively on the same place of the paper held at their afforesaid concours, and if you then accelerate its gyration untill the consecution of those colours be so quick that you cannot distinguish them severally, the resulting colour will be a whitenesse perfectly like that which an unrefracted beam of light exhibiteth when in like manner successively interrupted by the spoakes or Coggs of that circulating Wheel. And that this whitenesse is produced onely by a successive intermixture of the colours without their being assimilated or reduced to any uniformity, is certainly beyond all possibility of doubting, unlesse things that exist not at the same time may notwithstanding act on one another.

There are yet other circumstances by which the truth might have been decided, as by viewing the white concourse of the colours through another Prism placed close to the eye, by whose refraction that whitenesse may appeare again transformed into colours. And then to examin their origin, if an Assistant intercept any of the colours at the Lens before their arrivall at the whitenesse, the same colours will vanish from amongst those into which that whitenesse is converted by the second Prism. Now if the rays which disappeare be the same with those that are intercepted, then it must be acknowledged that the second Prism makes no new colours in any rays which were not in them before their concours at the paper. Which is a plane indication that the rays of severall colours remain distinct from one another in the whitenesse, and that from their previous dispositions are derived the colours of the second Prism. And by the way what is said of their colours may be applyed to their refrangibility.

The afforesaid *wheel* may be also here made use of; And if its gyration be neither too quick nor too slow, the succession of the colours may be discerned through the Prism, whilst to the naked eye of a By-stander they exhibit whitenesse.

There is something still remaining to be said of this Experiment. But this I conceive is enough to enforce it, and so to decide the controversy. However I shall now proceed to show some other ways of producing *whitenesse by mixtures*, since I perswade my selfe that this assertion above the rest appeares *Paradoxicall*, and is with most difficulty admitted. And because Mr Hook desires an instance of it in bodies of divers colours, I shall begin with that. But in order thereto it must be considered that such coloured bodies reflect but some part of the light incident on them, as is evident by the 13th Proposition; and therefore the light reflected from an aggregate of them will be much weakened by the losse of many rays. Whence a perfect and intense whitenesse is not to be expected, but rather a colour between those of light and shaddow, or such a grey or dirty colour as may be made by mixing white and black together.

And that such a colour will result may be collected from the colour of *dust* found in every corner of a house, which hath been observed to consist of many coloured particles. There may be also produced the like dirty colour by mixing severall *Painters colours* together. And the same may be effected by painting a *Top* (such as Boys play with) of divers colours, for when it is made to circulate by whipping it will appear of such a dirty colour.

Now the compounding of these colours is proper to my purpose because they differ not from whitenesse in the species of colour but onely in degree of luminousnesse. Which (did not Mr Hook concede it) I might thus evince. A beam of the suns light being transmitted into a darkened Room if you illuminate a sheet of white paper by that light reflected from a body of any colour the paper will always appeare of the colour of that body by whose reflected light it is illuminated. If it be a red body, the paper will be red; if a green body, it will be green; and so of the other colours. And the reason is that the fibers or threds of which the paper consists are all transparent and specular, and such substances are known to reflect colours without changing them. To know therefore to what species of colour a *Grey* belongeth, place any Grey body, (suppose a mixture of Painters colours) in the said light, and the Paper being illuminated by its reflexion shall appear *white*. And the same thing will happen if it be illuminated by reflexion from a *black* substance.

These therefore are all of one species, but yet they seem to be distinguished not onely by degrees of luminousnesse, but also by some other inequalities whereby they become more harsh or pleasant. And the distinction seems to be that Greys and perhaps Black are made by an uneven defect of light, consisting as it were of many little veines or streames which differ either in luminousnesse or in the unequall distribution of diversly coloured rays; such as ought to be caused by reflexion from a mixture of white and black or of diversly coloured corpuscles. But when such imperfectly mixed light is by a second reflexion from the paper more evenly and uniformely blended, it becomes more pleasant, and exhibits a faint or shaddowed whitenesse. And that such little irregularities as these may cause these differences is not improbable if wee consider how much variety may be caused in sounds of the same tone by irregular and uneven jarrings. And besides, these differences are so little that I have sometimes doubted whether they be any at all, when I have considered that a black and white body being placed together, the one in a strong light and the other in a very faint light so proportioned that they might appear equally luminous; it hath been difficult to distinguish them when viewed at distance, unlesse when the Black seemed more blewish; and the white body in a light still fainter hath in comparison of the black body it selfe appeared black.

This leads me to another way of compounding whitenesse; which is, that if four or five Bodies of the more eminent colours, or a paper painted all over in severall parts of it with those severall colours in a due proportion, be placed in the said beam of light, the light reflected from those colours to another white paper held at a convenient distance shall make that paper appeare white. If it be held too neare the colours, its parts will seem of those colours which are nearest them, but by removing it further that all its parts may be equally illuminated by all the colours, they will be more and more diluted untill they become perfectly white. And you may further observe that if any of the colours be intercepted, the paper will no longer appeare white, but of the other colours which are not intercepted. Now that this whitenesse is a mixture of the severally coloured rays falling confusedly on the Paper, I see no reason to doubt of, because if the light became uniforme and similar before it fell on the paper, it must much more be uniforme when at a greater distance it falls on the spectators eye; and so the rays which come from severall colours would in no qualities differ from one another, but all of them exhibit the same colour to the Spectator, contrary to what he sees.

* * *

From Proposition 6, Book 3 of the *Principia* †

* * *

It has been, now for a long time, observed by others, that all sorts of heavy bodies (allowance being made for the inequality of retardation which they suffer from a small power of resistance in the air) descend to the earth *from equal heights* in equal times; and that equality of times we may distinguish to a great accuracy, by the help of pendulums. I tried experiments with gold, silver, lead, glass, sand, common salt, wood, water, and wheat. I provided two wooden boxes, round and equal: I filled the one with wood, and suspended an equal weight of gold (as exactly as I could) in the centre of oscillation of the other. The boxes, hanging by equal threads of 11 feet, made a couple of pendulums perfectly equal in weight and figure, and equally receiving the resistance of the air. And, placing the one by the other, I observed them to play together forwards and backwards, for a long time, with equal vibrations. And therefore the quantity of matter in the gold (by Cor. 1 and 6, Prop. 24, Book 2) was to the quantity of matter in the wood as the action of the motive force (or *vis motrix*) upon all the gold to the action of the same upon all the wood; that is, as the weight of the one to the weight of the other: and the like happened in the other bodies. By these experiments, in bodies of the same weight, I could manifestly have discovered a difference of matter less than the thousandth part of the whole, had any such been.

* * *

From the General Scholium to Section 6, Book 2 of the *Principia* ‡

* * *

Lastly, since it is the opinion of some that there is a certain ethereal medium extremely rare and subtile, which freely pervades the pores of

† Isaac Newton, *Mathematical Principles of Natural Philosophy* and *System of the World*, translated by Andrew Motte, revised by Florian Cajori (Berkeley and Los Angeles: University of California Press, 1934 and latter printings), p. 411. Copyright © 1934 and 1962 Regents of the University of California. Reprinted by permission. This experiment, which established the proportionality of weight to mass, was one of Newton's most important steps toward the concept of universal gravitation. He first recorded it in early 1685 in a paper of definitions of concepts fundamental to the science of mechanics.

‡ Isaac Newton, *Mathemetical Principles of Natural Philosophy* and *System of the World*, translated by Andrew Motte, revised by Florian Cajori (Berkeley and Los Angeles: University of California Press, 1934 and later printings), pp. 325–26. Copyright © 1934 and 1962 Regents of the University of California. Reprinted by permission. This experiment helped to shatter Newton's belief in the existence of a cosmic aether, such as that set forth in his "Hypothesis of Light." Some evidence suggests that he performed the experiment about 1679 or 1680.

all bodies; and from such a medium, so pervading the pores of bodies, some resistance must needs arise; in order to try whether the resistance, which we experience in bodies in motion, be made upon their outward surfaces only, or whether their internal parts meet with any considerable resistance upon their surfaces, I thought of the following experiment. I suspended a round deal box by a thread 11 feet long, on a steel hook, by means of a ring of the same metal, so as to make a pendulum of the aforesaid length. The hook had a sharp hollow edge on its upper part, so that the upper arc of the ring pressing on the edge might move the more freely; and the thread was fastened to the lower arc of the ring. The pendulum being thus prepared, I drew it aside from the perpendicular to the distance of about 6 feet, and that in a plane perpendicular to the edge of the hook, lest the ring, while the pendulum oscillated, should slide to and fro on the edge of the hook; for the point of suspension, in which the ring touches the hook, ought to remain immovable. I therefore accurately noted the place to which the pendulum was brought, and letting it go, I marked three other places, to which it returned at the end of the 1st, 2d, and 3d oscillation. This I often repeated, that I might find those places as accurately as possible. Then I filled the box with lead and other heavy metals that were near at hand. But, first, I weighed the box when empty, and that part of the thread that went round it, and half the remaining part, extended between the hook and the suspended box; for the thread so extended always acts upon the pendulum, when drawn aside from the perpendicular, with half its weight. To this weight I added the weight of the air contained in the box. And this whole weight was about 1/78 of the weight of the box when filled with the metals. Then because the box when full of the metals, by extending the thread with its weight, increased the length of the pendulum, I shortened the thread so as to make the length of the pendulum, when oscillating, the same as before. Then drawing aside the pendulum to the place first marked, and letting it go, I reckoned about 77 oscillations before the box returned to the second mark, and as many afterwards before it came to the third mark, and as many after that before it came to the fourth mark. From this I conclude that the whole resistance of the box, when full, had not a greater proportion to the resistance of the box, when empty, than 78 to 77. For if their resistances were equal, the box, when full, by reason of its inertia, which was 78 times greater than the inertia of the same when empty, ought to have continued its oscillating motion so much the longer, and therefore to have returned to those marks at the end of 78 oscillations. But it returned to them at the end of 77 oscillations.

Let, therefore, A represent the resistance of the box upon its external surface, and B the resistance of the empty box on its internal surface, and if the resistances to the internal parts of bodies equally swift be as the matter, or the number of particles that are resisted, then 78B will be the resistance made to the internal parts of the box, when full; and therefore the whole resistance A + B of the empty box will be to the whole resistance A + 78B of the full box as 77 to 78, and, by subtraction, A + B to 77B as 77 to 1; and thence A + B to B as 77·77 to 1, and, by subtraction, again, A to B as 5928 to 1. Therefore the resistance of the empty box in its internal parts will be above 5000 times less than the resistance on its external surface. This reasoning depends upon the supposition that the greater resistance of the full box arises not from any other latent cause, but only from the action of some subtile fluid upon the included metal.

This experiment is related by memory, the paper being lost in which I had described it; so that I have been obliged to omit some fractional parts, which are slipped out of my memory; and I have no leisure to try it again. The first time I made it, the hook being weak, the full box was retarded sooner. The cause I found to be, that the hook was not strong enough to bear the weight of the box; so that, as it oscillated to and fro, the hook was bent sometimes this and sometimes that way. I therefore procured a hook of sufficient strength, so that the point of suspension might remain unmoved, and then all things happened as is above described.

* * *

From "An Account of the Book entituled *Commercium Epistolicum*" †

* * *

The Philosophy which Mr. *Newton* in his *Principles* and *Optiques* has pursued is Experimental; and it is not the Business of Experimental Philosophy to teach the Causes of things any further than they can be proved by Experiments. We are not to fill this Philosophy with Opinions which cannot be proved by Phænomena. In this Philosophy Hypotheses have no place, unless as Conjectures or Questions proposed to be examined by Experiments. For this Reason Mr. *Newton* in his Optiques distinguished those things which were made certain by Experiments from those things which remained uncertain, and which he therefore proposed in the End of his Optiques in the Form of Queries. For this

† *Philosophical Transactions* 29 (1714–15): 222–24. Reprinted with the permission of The Royal Society. Newton's bitter controversy with Leibniz over priority in invention of the calculus reached a climax with the publication, by the Royal Society, of a volume entitled *Commercium Epistolicum*, purporting to demonstrate that Newton was the first inventor and that Leibniz had plagiarized from him. As president of the Royal Society, Newton had in fact covertly written the book himself. Two years later he composed a long review of the book, which stated his case again, and published it anonymously in the society's *Philosophical Transactions*. The "Account" closed with a statement of the philosophical and methodological differences that distinguished Newton from Leibniz. In this selection, we have replaced the original quotations (in Latin) from the *Principia* with the equivalent English versions.

Reason, in the Preface to his *Principles*, when he had mentioned the Motions of the Planets, Comets, Moon and Sea as deduced in this Book from Gravity, he added:
"I wish we could derive the rest of the phenomena of Nature by the same kind of reasoning from mechanical principles, for I am induced by many reasons to suspect that they may all depend upon certain forces by which the particles of bodies, by some causes hitherto unknown, are either mutually impelled towards one another, and cohere in regular figures, or are repelled and recede from one another. These forces being unknown, philosophers have hitherto attempted the search of Nature in vain." And in the End of this Book in the second Edition, he said that for want of a sufficient Number of Experiments, he forbore to describe the Laws of the Actions of the Spirit or Agent by which this Attraction is performed. And for the same Reason he is silent about the Cause of Gravity, there occurring no Experiments or Phænomena by which he might prove what was the Cause thereof. And this he hath abundantly declared in his *Principles*, near the Beginning thereof, in these Words; "For I here design only to give a mathematical notion of those forces, without considering their physical causes and seats." And a little after: "I use the words attraction, impulse, or propensity of any sort towards a center, promiscuously, and indifferently, one for another; considering those forces not physically, but mathematically: wherefore the reader is not to imagine that by those words I anywhere take upon me to define the kind, or the manner of any action, the causes or the physical reason thereof, or that I attribute forces, in a true and physical sense, to certain centers (which are only mathematical points); when at any time I happen to speak of centers as attracting, or as endued with attractive powers." And in the End of his Opticks: "How these Attractions may be performed, I do not here consider. What I call Attraction may be performed by impulse, or by some other means unknown to me. I use that Word here to signify only in general any Force by which Bodies tend towards one another, whatsoever be the Cause. For we must learn from the Phenomena of Nature what Bodies attract one another, and what are the Laws and Properties of the Attraction, before we enquire the Cause by which the Attraction is performed." And a little after he mentions the same Attractions as Forces which by Phænomena appear to have a Being in Nature, tho' their Causes be not yet known; and distinguishes them from occult Qualities which are supposed to flow from the specifick Forms of things. And in the Scholium at the End of his *Principles*, after he had mentioned the Properties of Gravity, he added: "But hitherto I have not been able to discover the cause of those properties of gravity from phenomena, and I feign no hypotheses; for whatever is not deduced from the phenomena is to be called an hypothesis; and hypotheses, whether metaphysical or physical, whether of occult qualities or mechanical, have no place in experimental philosophy. . . . And

to us it is enough that gravity does really exist, and act according to the laws which we have explained, and abundantly serves to account for all the motions of the celestial bodies, and of our sea." And after all this, one would wonder that Mr. *Newton* should be reflected upon for not explaining the Causes of Gravity and other Attractions by Hypotheses; as if it were a Crime to content himself with Certainties and let Uncertainties alone. And yet the Editors of the *Acta Eruditorum*, have told the World that Mr. *Newton* denies that the cause of Gravity is Mechanical, and that if the Spirit or Agent by which Electrical Attraction is performed, be not the Ether or *subtile Matter* of *Cartes*, it is less valuable than an Hypothesis and perhaps may be the Hylarchic Principle of Dr. *Henry Moor*: and Mr. *Leibnitz* hath accused him of making Gravity a natural or essential Property of Bodies, and an occult Quality and Miracle. And by this sort of Railery they are perswading the *Germans* that Mr. *Newton* wants Judgment, and was not able to invent the Infinitesimal Method.

It must be allowed that these two Gentlemen differ very much in Philosophy. The one proceeds upon the Evidence arising from Experiments and Phænomena, and stops where such Evidence is wanting; the other is taken up with Hypotheses, and propounds them, not to be examined by Experiments, but to be believed without Examination. The one for want of Experiments to decide the Question, doth not affirm whether the Cause of Gravity be Mechanical or not Mechanical: the other that it is a perpetual Miracle if it be not Mechanical. The one (by way of Enquiry) attributes it to the Power of the Creator that the least Particles of Matter are hard: the other attributes the Hardness of Matter to conspiring Motions, and calls it a perpetual Miracle if the Cause of this Hardness be other than Mechanical. The one doth not affirm that animal Motion in Man is purely mechanical: the other teaches that it is purely mechanical, the Soul or Mind (according to the Hypothesis of an *Harmonia Præstabilita*) never acting upon the Body so as to alter or influence its Motions. The one teaches that God (the God in whom we live and move and have our Being) is Omnipresent; but not as a Soul of the World: the other that he is not the Soul of the World, but *INTELLIGENTIA SUPRAMUNDANA*, an Intelligence above the Bounds of the World; whence it seems to follow that he cannot do any thing within the Bounds of the World, unless by an incredible Miracle. The one teaches that Philosophers are to argue from Phænomena and *Experiments* to the Causes thereof, and thence to the Causes of those Causes, and so on till we come to the first Cause: the other that all the Actions of the first Cause are Miracles, and all the Laws imprest on Nature by the Will of God are perpetual Miracles and occult Qualities, and therefore not to be considered in Philosophy. But must the constant and universal Laws of Nature, if derived from the Power of God or the Action of a Cause not yet known to us, be called

Miracles and occult Qualities, that is to say, *Wonders* and *Absurdities?* Must all the Arguments for a God taken from the Phænomena of Nature be exploded by *new hard Names?* And must Experimental Philosophy be exploded as *miraculous* and *absurd*, because it asserts nothing more than can be proved by Experiments, and we cannot yet prove by Experiments that all the Phænomena in Nature can be solved by meer Mechanical Causes? Certainly these things deserve to be better considered.

Part 4
OPTICS

Introduction

The program of study in mathematics and the new natural philosophy that Newton undertook toward the end of his undergraduate career produced such notable achievements that his early biographers attached the phrase *annus mirabilis* (or "marvelous year") to a period, not precisely defined, from the years 1665–1666. The definition of the period hardly matters; the achievements do. About fifty years later, in connection with the controversy with Leibniz over the discovery of the calculus, Newton himself recalled the time.

> In the beginning of the year 1665 I found the method of approximating series and the rule for reducing any dignity [or power] of any binomial into such a series. The same year in May I found the method of tangents of Gregory and Slusius, and in November had the direct method of fluxions and the next year in January had the theory of colours and in May following I had entrance into the inverse method of fluxions. And the same year I began to think of gravity extending to the orb of the Moon and (having found out how to estimate the force with which a globe revolving within a sphere presses the surface of the sphere) from Kepler's rule of the periodical times of the planets being in sesquialterate proportion of their distances from the center of their orbs, I deduced that the forces which keep the planets in their orbs must be reciprocally as the squares of their distances from the centers about which they revolve; and thereby compared the force requisite to keep the Moon in her orb with the force of gravity at the surface of the earth, and found them answer pretty nearly. All this was in the two plague years of 1665–1666. For in those days I was in the prime of my age for invention and minded mathematics and philosophy more than at any time since.

The heart of Newton's study of optics, his "theory of colours," the discovery of which he placed in January 1666, was prominent among his initial interests in natural philosophy. We can find an earlier reference to colors among the "Quaestiones quaedam philosophicae." One of the first entries there was a series of probing questions about current theories of colors, and somewhat later, as he continued the "Quaestiones," he returned to the topic again to reason about the fringes of colors seen around bodies viewed through a prism. It was in this context that he first began to entertain ideas that would lead to his central insight in optics.

In order not to encumber the reader with footnotes we have composed a Biographical Register, in which all the people mentioned in the text are identified, and a Glossary, in which technical terms are briefly explicated and such things as organizations, places, publications, and manuscript collections are identified. Both the Biographical Register and the Glossary are located near the end of the volume.

According to the theories that Newton found in his reading, colors arise from the modification of light. In its pristine form, for example, as it comes from the sun, light appears, and perhaps even is, white. In passing through transparent media, such as a glass prism, or in reflecting from the colored surfaces of bodies, light is modified by the admixture of darkness, according to the usual view, and comes to appear colored. Newton, however, began to wonder whether light might not be heterogeneous rather than homogeneous and whether phenomena of colors might not be associated in some manner with the differences between light's component parts. The passage in his notebook contains a diagram of an eye observing a fringe of colors through a prism; rays from the two sides of the boundary, where the fringe appears, are refracted at different angles so that they enter the eye along the same line. He thought of an experiment to test the idea. Red and blue were universally considered the two extremes in the scale of colors. He could color one end of a thread red and the other blue; if his ideas were correct, the thread should appear disjoined when observed through a prism, which was in fact the case.

At the time, Newton took the thought no further. Later, however, he was trying to grind lenses of a hyperbolic crosssection, which Descartes had demonstrated would bring parallel rays of light, for example, from a star, to a perfect focus, as spherical lenses do not. Descartes' demonstration had assumed that light is homogeneous. Thinking back to the implication of his experiment with the colored thread, Newton realized that eliminating the aberration caused by spherical lenses could not lead to a perfect focus; the heterogeneity of light produces another aberration.

At this point, according to Newton's own testimony, he began a systematic investigation of his idea. Probably this investigation is what he had in mind when he said that he "had the theory of colours" in January 1666. It is also probably what he set down in another notebook under the title "Of Colours," where his theory of colors emerged in a form recognizably close to its final one—the heterogeneity of light, the different refrangibility of the different rays, the capacity of individual rays to excite unique sensations of color, and hence the production of phenomena of colors, not by the modification of homogeneous light, but by the analysis or separation of the heterogeneous mixture into its component parts. The theory leans heavily on the basic concept of atomism, that all of the phenomena of nature arise from the rearrangement of particles that themselves remain unaltered.

In the fall of 1669, Newton was appointed Lucasian Professor of Mathematics at Cambridge, and he faced the need to deliver an annual series of lectures. For his first three series, treated really as one continuous series, he turned to the theory of colors. In the process of thinking it through again for presentation, Newton polished the theory into its virtually mature and completed form.

It was about this time that he first performed his experiments involving what are known as Newton's rings, the phenomena of colored rings in the film of air between a lens and a sheet of glass. Because he knew the radius of curvature of the lens, he could compute the thickness of the film where each ring appeared from the measured diameter of the ring. These measurements and computations were the first empirical demonstration of the periodicity of an optical phenomenon.

We treat the rings today as a product of interference between the light reflected from the two surfaces of the film of air, and more than a century after Newton's original experiments, their periodicity helped to establish the wave theory of light. To Newton, however, the wave theory was anathema, and the periodicity he demonstrated largely an embarrassment. He ended up referring to the periodic repetitions of dark rings, where the light is transmitted through the film, and colored rings, where it is reflected to the observer's eye, as fits of easy transmission and fits of easy reflection. What mattered to him was the contribution of the experiments to his theory of color. The experiments with prisms had shown that refractions can analyse sunlight into its component rays. The theory would not be complete, however, until he could explain the colors of solid bodies in analogous terms. The experiments with the film of air showed that each color is reflected from a thickness specific to it (a thickness that repeats periodically with the addition of the same increment), and those thicknesses, computed from empirical measurements of the diameters of rings, he applied to the particles that he hypothesized make up solid bodies. Thus, processes of analysis that occur both in refraction and reflection, by which the heterogeneous mixture we call sunlight is separated into its components, account for all the phenomena of colors in nature.

The theory of colors also led Newton to the invention of a new instrument. The heterogeneity of light appeared to mean that refracting telescopes, that is, ordinary telescopes with lenses, could never be perfected; whatever the shape of the lens, a halo of colors would always surround every image the telescope formed. Mirrors did not separate different rays from each other, however, and about the same time that he prepared his first Lucasian lectures, Newton built a reflecting telescope. It was about six-inches long, and it magnified about forty times in diameter, which was more than a six-foot refracting telescope could do. Newton was proud of the work of his hands and not reluctant to show it off. His first surviving letter, from February 1669, discussed it. In 1671, the Royal Society in London heard about the telescope and wrote late in the year asking to see it. When it arrived, it created a sensation. The society sent a description of the instrument abroad to protect Newton's priority, and they elected him to membership on January 11, 1672. Newton had kept his discoveries in mathematics, made near the end of his undergraduate years, largely to himself, but the warm reception of the telescope by the Royal Society encouraged him to prepare a summary statement of the theory of colors that had led to the instrument.

Even though it says nothing about the experiments with rings, Newton's letter to Henry Oldenburg of February 6, 1672 presents the essence of his achievement in optics. Nearly four years later, at the end of 1675, he sent the Royal Society another paper, describing his experiments with the rings formed in the film of air between a lens and a flat surface of glass. By the time he wrote the papers to the Royal Society, however, he had already ceased actively to work on the topic, and he presented the work done in the earlier period. After the triumph of the *Principia*, Newton began to prepare his optics for publication in the early 1690s, but he lost interest again before he was done. Then in 1703 he was elected president of the Royal Society, and a few months later he presented the society with a copy of the *Opticks*, more than thirty years after he had performed the experiments and elaborated the theory about the heterogeneity of light that the book contained.

Two years later, in the Latin edition of the work, Newton added a group of seven new queries (the ones numbered 25 through 31 in the second English edition, and ever since) to the sixteen that had concluded the first edition. Among them were Queries 28 and 29 (to use their final numbers), on the nature of light. Back in 1672, on the publication of the letter to Oldenburg, Robert Hooke criticized Newton's theory of color by criticizing the corpuscular conception of light, which he found implicit in it. Newton objected vigorously. The theory of colors, he argued, proved the heterogeneity of light, which was its central assertion, from experiments, and he took heterogeneity to be demonstrated fact. Any theory of light would have to adjust to heterogeneity, which was as compatible with the wave theory as with the corpuscular one. In this contention, Newton surely had logic on his side, and the subsequent history of optics has borne him out. Nevertheless, it is clear that he never ceased to believe that wave conceptions of light went hand in hand with modification theories of color, while the immutable properties of rays, such as their degree of refrangibility and their capacity to excite specific sensations of color, which he was convinced that he had demonstrated experimentally, were in his mind expressions of the immutability of atoms. Queries 28 and 29 make clear the connection, in Newton's mind, between his theory of colors and his conception of light.

Newton to Oldenburg, February 6, 1672 †

Sir,

To perform my late promise to you, I shall without further ceremony acquaint you, that in the beginning of the Year 1666 (at which time I applyed my self to the grinding of Optick glasses of other figures than *Spherical*,) I procured me a Triangular glass-Prisme, to try therewith the celebrated *Phænomena* of *Colours*. And in order thereto having darkened my chamber, and made a small hole in my window-shuts, to let in a convenient quantity of the Suns light, I placed my Prisme at its entrance, that it might be thereby refracted to the opposite wall. It was at first a very pleasing divertisement, to view the vivid and intense colours produced thereby; but after a while applying my self to consider them more circumspectly, I became surprised to see them in an *oblong* form; which, according to the received laws of Refraction, I expected should have been *circular*.

They were terminated at the sides with streight lines, but at the ends, the decay of light was so gradual, that it was difficult to determine justly, what was their figure; yet they seemed *semicircular*.

Comparing the length of this coloured *Spectrum* with its breadth, I found it about five times greater; a disproportion so extravagant, that it excited me to a more then ordinary curiosity of examining, from whence it might proceed. I could scarce think, that the various *Thickness* of the glass, or the termination with shadow or darkness, could have any Influence on light to produce such an effect; yet I thought it not amiss to examine first these circumstances, and so tryed, what would happen by transmitting light through parts of the glass of divers thicknesses, or through holes in the window of divers bignesses, or by setting the Prisme without, so that the light might pass through it, and be refracted before it was terminated by the hole: But I found none of those circumstances material. The fashion of the colours was in all these cases the same.

Then I suspected, whether by any *unevenness* in the glass, or other contingent irregularity, these colours might be thus dilated. And to try this, I took another Prisme like the former, and so placed it, that the light, passing through them both, might be refracted contrary ways, and so by the latter returned into that course, from which the former had diverted it. For, by this means I thought, the *regular* effects of the first Prisme would be destroyed by the second Prisme, but the *irregular* ones more augmented, by the multiplicity of refractions. The event was, that

† *The Correspondence of Isaac Newton*, eds. H. W. Turnbull, J. F. Scott, A. Rupert Hall, and Laura Tilling, 7 vols. (Cambridge: Cambridge University Press, 1959–77), vol. 1, pp. 92–102. Reprinted with the permission of the Royal Society. Newton first expounded his theory of colors in his initial series of lectures as Lucasian Professor of Mathematics at Cambridge. His first publication of the theory was a paper sent to the Royal Society, in the form of a letter to Henry Oldenburg, the society's secretary.

the light, which by the first Prisme was diffused into an *oblong* form, was by the second reduced into an *orbicular* one with as much regularity, as when it did not at all pass through them. So that, what ever was the cause of that length, 'twas not any contingent irregularity.

I then proceeded to examine more critically, what might be effected by the difference of the incidence of Rays coming from divers parts of the Sun; and to that end, measured the several lines and angles, belonging to the Image. Its distance from the hole or Prisme was 22 foot; its utmost length 13¼ inches; its breadth 2⅝ inches; the diameter of the hole ¼ of an inch; the angle, which the Rays, tending towards the middle of the image, made with those lines, in which they would have proceeded without refraction, 44 deg. 56′. And the vertical Angle of the Prisme, 63 deg. 12′. Also the Refractions on both sides the Prisme, that is, of the Incident, and Emergent Rays, were as near, as I could make them, equal, and consequently about 54 deg. 4′. And the Rays fell perpendicularly upon the wall. Now subducting the diameter of the hole from the length and breadth of the Image, there remains 13 Inches the length, and 2⅜ the breadth, comprehended by those Rays, which passed through the center of the said hole, and consequently the angle at the hole, which that breadth subtended, was about 31′, answerable to the Suns Diameter; but the angle, which its length subtended, was more than five such diameters, namely 2 deg. 49′.

Having made these observations, I first computed from them the refractive power of that glass, and found it measured by the *ratio* of the sines, 20 to 31. And then, by that *ratio*, I computed the Refractions of two Rays flowing from opposite parts of the Sun's *discus*, so as to differ 31′ in their its obliquity of Incidence, and found, that the emergent Rays should have comprehended an angle of 31′, as they did, before they were incident.

But because this computation was founded on the Hypothesis of the proportionality of the *sines* of Incidence, and Refraction, which though by my own and others Experience I could not imagine to be so erroneous, as to make that Angle but 31′, which in reality was 2 deg. 49′; yet my curiosity caused me again to take my Prisme. And having placed it at my window, as before, I observed, that by turning it a little about its *axis* to and fro, so as to vary its obliquity to the light, more then by an angle of 4 or 5 degrees, the Colours were not thereby sensibly translated from their place on the wall, and consequently by that variation of Incidence, the quantity of Refraction was not sensibly varied. By this Experiment therefore, as well as by the former computation, it was evident, that the difference of the Incidence of Rays, flowing from divers parts of the Sun, could not make them after decussation diverge at a sensibly greater angle, than that at which they before converged; which being, at most, but about 31 or 32 minutes, there still remained some other cause to be found out, from whence it could be 2 deg. 49′.

Then I began to suspect, whether the Rays, after their trajection through the Prisme, did not move in curve lines, and according to their more or less curvity tend to divers parts of the wall. And it increased my suspition, when I remembered that I had often seen a Tennis-ball, struck with an oblique Racket, describe such a curve line. For, a circular as well as a progressive motion being communicated to it by that stroak, its parts on that side, where the motions conspire, must press and beat the contiguous Air more violently than on the other, and there excite a reluctancy and reaction of the Air proportionably greater. And for the same reason, if the Rays of light should possibly be globular bodies, and by their oblique passage out of one medium into another acquire a circulating motion, they ought to feel the greater resistance from the ambient Æther, on that side, where the motions conspire, and thence be continually bowed to the other. But notwithstanding this plausible ground of suspition, when I came to examine it, I could observe no such curvity in them. And besides (which was enough for my purpose) I observed, that the difference betwixt the length of the Image, and diameter of the hole, through which the light was transmitted, was proportionable to their distance.

The gradual removal of these suspitions at length led me to the *Experimentum Crucis*, which was this: I took two boards, and placed one of them close behind the Prisme at the window, so that the light might pass through a small hole, made in it for that purpose, and fall on the other board, which I placed at about 12 foot distance, having first made a small hole in it also, for some of that Incident light to pass through. Then I placed another Prisme behind this second board, so that the light, trajected through both the boards, might pass through that also, and be again refracted before it arrived at the wall. This done, I took the first Prisme in my hand, and turned it to and fro slowly about its *Axis*, so much as to make the several parts of the Image, cast on the second board, successively pass through the hole in it, that I might observe to what places on the wall the second Prisme would refract them. And I saw by the variation of those places, that the light, tending to that end of the Image, towards which the refraction of the first Prisme was made, did in the second Prisme suffer a Refraction considerably greater than the light tending to the other end. And so the true cause of the length of that Image was detected to be no other, then that *Light* consists of *Rays differently refrangible*, which, without any respect to a difference in their incidence, were, according to their degrees of refrangibility, transmitted towards divers parts of the wall.

When I understood this, I left off my aforesaid Glass-works; for I saw, that the perfection of Telescopes was hitherto limited, not so much for want of glasses truly figured according to the prescriptions of Optick Authors, (which all men have hitherto imagined,) as because that Light it self is a *Heterogeneous mixture of differently refrangible Rays*. So that, were a glass so exactly figured, as to collect any one sort of rays into one point, it could not collect those also into the same point, which having the same Incidence upon the same Medium are apt to suffer a different refraction. Nay, I wondered, that seeing the difference of refrangibility was so great, as I found it, Telescopes should arrive to that perfection they are now at. For, measuring the refractions in one of my Prismes, I found, that supposing the common *sine* of Incidence upon one of its planes was 44 parts, the *sine* of refraction of the utmost Rays on the red end of the Colours, made out of the glass into the Air, would be 68 parts, and the *sine* of refraction of the utmost rays on the other end, 69 parts: So that the difference is about a 24th or 25th part of the whole refraction. And consequently, the object-glass of any Telescope cannot collect all the rays, which come from one point of an object so as to make them convene at its *focus* in less room then in a circular space, whose diameter is the 50th part of the Diameter of its Aperture; which is an irregularity, some hundreds of times greater, then a circularly figured *Lens*, of so small a section as the Object glasses of long Telescopes are, would cause by the unfitness of its figure, were Light *uniform*.

This made me take *Reflections* into consideration, and finding them regular, so that the Angle of Reflection of all sorts of Rays was equal to their Angle of Incidence; I understood, that by their mediation Optick instruments might be brought to any degree of perfection imaginable, provided a *Reflecting* substance could be found, which would polish as finely as Glass, and *reflect* as much light, as glass *transmits*, and the art of communicating to it a *Parabolick* figure be also attained. But these seemed very great difficulties, and I almost thought them insuperable, when I further considered, that every irregularity in a reflecting superficies makes the rays stray 5 or 6 times more out of their due course, than the like irregularities in a refracting one. So that a much greater curiosity would be here requisite, than in figuring glasses for Refraction.

Amidst these thoughts I was forced from *Cambridge* by the Intervening Plague, and it was more than two years, before I proceeded further. But then having thought on a tender way of polishing, proper for metall, whereby, as I imagined, the figure also would be corrected to the last; I began to try, what might be effected in this kind, and by degrees so far perfected an Instrument (in the essential parts of it like that I sent to *London*), by which I could discern Jupiters 4 Concomitants, and shewed them divers times to two others of my acquaintance. I could also discern the Moon-like phase of *Venus*, but not very distinctly, nor without some niceness in disposing the Instrument.

From that time I was interrupted till this last Autumn, when I made the other. And as that was sensibly better then the first (especially for Day-Objects,) so I doubt not, but they will be still brought to a much greater perfection by their endeavours, who, as you inform me, are taking care about it at *London*.

I have sometimes thought to make a Microscope, which in like manner should have, instead of an Object-glass, a Reflecting piece of metall. And this I hope they will also take into consideration. For those Instruments seem as capable of improvement as *Telescopes*, and perhaps more, because but one reflective piece of metall is requisite in them, as you may perceive by the annexed diagram, where A *B* representeth the object metall, *C D* the eye glass, *F* their common Focus, and *O* the other focus of the metall, in which the object is placed.

But to return from this digression, I told you, that Light is not similar, or homogeneal, but consists of *difform* Rays, some of which are more refrangible than others: So that of those, which are alike incident on the same medium, some shall be more refracted than others, and that not by any virtue of the glass, or other external cause, but from a predisposition, which every particular Ray hath to suffer a particular degree of Refraction.

I shall now proceed to acquaint you with another more notable difformity in its Rays, wherein the *Origin of Colours* is infolded. A naturalist would scearce expect to see the science of those become mathematicall, and yet I dare affirm that there is as much certainty in it as in any other part of Opticks. For what I shall tell concerning them is not an Hypothesis but most rigid consequence, not conjectured by barely inferring 'tis thus because not otherwise or because it satisfied all phænomena (the Philosophers universall Topick,) but evinced by the mediation of experiments concluding directly and without any suspicion of doubt. To continue the historicall narration of these experiments would make a discourse too tedious and confused, and therefore I shall rather lay down the *Doctrine* first, and then, for its examination, give you an instance or two of the *Experiments*, as a specimen of the rest.

The Doctrine you will find comprehended and illustrated in the following propositions.

1. As the Rays of light differ in degrees of Refrangibility, so they also differ in their disposition to exhibit this or that particular colour. Colours are not *Qualifications of Light*, derived from Refractions, or Reflections of natural Bodies (as 'tis generally believed,) but *Original* and *connate properties*, which in divers Rays are divers. Some Rays are disposed to exhibit a red colour and no other; some a yellow and no other, some a green and no other, and so of the rest. Nor are there only

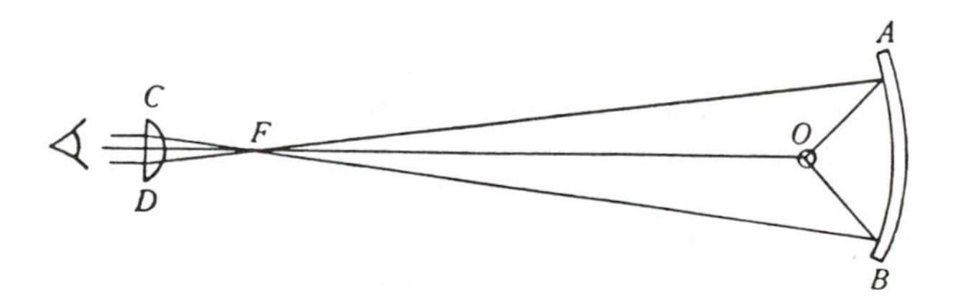

Rays proper and particular to the more eminent colours, but even to all their intermediate gradations.

2. To the same degree of Refrangibility ever belongs the same colour, and to the same colour ever belongs the same degree of refrangibility. The *least Refrangible* Rays are all disposed to exhibit a *Red* colour, and contrarily those Rays, which are disposed to exhibit a *Red* colour, are all the least refrangible: So the most *refrangible* Rays are all disposed to exhibit a deep *Violet* colour, and contrarily those which are apt to exhibit such a violet colour, are all the most Refrangible. And so to all the intermediate colours in a continued series belong intermediate degrees of refrangibility. And this Analogy 'twixt colours, and refrangibility, is very precise and strict: The Rays always either exactly agreeing in both, or proportionally disagreeing in both.

3. The species of colour, and degree of Refrangibility proper to any particular sort of Rays, is not mutable by Refraction, nor by Reflection from natural bodies, nor by any other cause, that I could yet observe. When any one sort of Rays hath been well parted from those of other kinds, it hath afterwards obstinately retained its colour, notwithstanding my utmost endeavours to change it. I have refracted it with Prismes and reflected it with Bodies, which in Day-light were of other colours; I have intercepted it with the coloured film of Air interceding two compressed plates of glass; transmitted it through coloured Mediums, and through Mediums irradiated with other sort of Rays, and diversly terminated it, and yet could never produce any new colour out of it. It would by contracting or dilating become more brisk, or faint, and by the loss of many Rays, in some cases very obscure and dark; but I could never see it changed *in specie*.

4. Yet seeming transmutations of Colours may be made where there is any mixture of divers sorts of Rays. For in such mixtures, the component colours appear not, but, by their mutual allaying each other, constitute a midling colour. And therefore, if by refraction, or any other of the aforesaid causes, the difform Rays, latent in such a mixture, be separated, there shall emerge colours different from the colour of the composition. Which colours are not New generated, but only made Apparent by being parted; for if they be again intirely mix't and blended together, they will again compose that colour, which they did before separation. And for the same reason, Transmutations made by the convening of divers colours are not real; for when the difform Rays are again severed, they will exhibit the very same colours, which they did before they entered the composition; as you see, *Blew* and *Yellow* powders, when finely mixed, appear to the naked eye *Green*, and yet the colours of the Component corpuscles are not thereby really transmuted, but only blended. For, when viewed with a good Microscope, they still appear *Blew and Yellow* interspersedly.

5. There are therefore two sorts of colours. The one original and

simple, the other compounded of these. The Original or primary colours are, *Red, Yellow, Green, Blew*, and a *Violet-purple*, together with Orange, Indico, and an indefinite variety of Intermediate gradations.

6. The same colours in *Specie* with these Primary ones may be also produced by composition: For, a mixture of *Yellow* and *Blew* makes *Green;* of *Red* and *Yellow* makes *Orange;* of *Orange* and *Yellowish green* makes *yellow*. And in general, if any two Colours be mixed, which in the series of those, generated by the Prisme, are not too far distant one from another, they by their mutual alloy compound that colour, which in the said series appeareth in the mid-way between them. But those, which are situated at too great a distance, do not so. *Orange* and *Indico* produce not the intermediate Green, nor Scarlet and Green the intermediate yellow.

7. But the most surprising and wonderful composition was that of *Whiteness*. There is no one sort of Rays which alone can exhibit this. 'Tis ever compounded, and to its composition are requisite all the aforesaid primary Colours, mixed in a due proportion. I have often with Admiration beheld, that all the Colours of the Prisme being made to converge, and thereby to be again mixed as they were in the light before it was Incident upon the Prisme, reproduced light, intirely and perfectly white, and not at all sensibly differing from the *direct* Light of the Sun, unless when the glasses, I used, were not sufficiently clear; for then they would a little incline it to *their* colour.

8. Hence therefore it comes to pass, that *Whiteness* is the usual colour of *Light;* for, Light is a confused aggregate of Rays indued with all sorts of Colors, as they are promiscuously darted from the various parts of luminous bodies. And of such a confused aggregate, as I said, is generated Whiteness, if there be a due proportion of the Ingredients; but if any one predominate, the Light must incline to that colour; as it happens in the Blew flame of Brimstone; the yellow flame of a Candle; and the various colours of the Fixed stars.

9. These things considered, the *manner*, how colours are produced by the Prisme, is evident. For, of the Rays, constituting the incident light, since those which differ in Colour proportionally differ in refrangibility, *they* by their unequal refractions must be severed and dispersed into an oblong form in an orderly succession from the least refracted Scarlet to the most refracted Violet. And for the same reason it is, that objects, when looked upon through a Prisme, appear coloured. For, the difform Rays, by their unequal Refractions, are made to diverge towards several parts of the *Retina*, and there express the Images of things coloured, as in the former case they did the Suns Image upon a wall. And by this inequality of refractions they become not only coloured, but also very confused and indistinct.

10. Why the Colours of the *Rainbow* appear in falling drops of Rain, is also from hence evident. For, those drops, which refract the Rays,

disposed to appear purple, in greatest quantity to the Spectators eye, refract the Rays of other sorts so much less, as to make them pass beside it; and such are the drops in the inside of the *Primary* bow, and on the outside of the *Second* or Exteriour one. So those drops, which refract in greatest plenty the Rays, apt to appear red, toward the Spectators eye, refract those of other sorts so much more, as to make them pass beside it; and such are the drops on the exterior part of the *Primary*, and interior part of the *Secondary* Bow.

11. The odd Phænomena of an infusion of *Lignum Nephriticum*, *Leaf gold*, *Fragments of coloured glass*, and some other transparently coloured bodies, appearing in one position of one colour, and of another in another, are on these grounds no longer riddles. For, those are substances apt to reflect one sort of light and transmit another; as may be seen in a dark room, by illuminating them with similar or uncompounded light. For then they appear of that colour only, with which they are illuminated, but yet in one position more vivid and luminous than in another, accordingly as they are disposed more or less to reflect or transmit the incident colour.

12. From hence also is manifest the reason of an unexpected Experiment, which Mr. *Hook* somewhere in his *Micrographia* relates to have made with two wedg-like transparent vessels, fill'd the one with a red, the other with a blew liquor: namely, that though they were severally transparent enough, yet both together became opake; For, if one transmitted only red, and the other only blew, no rays could pass through both.

13. I might add more instances of this nature, but I shall conclude with this general one, that the Colours of all natural Bodies have no other origin than this, that they are variously qualified to reflect one sort of light in greater plenty then another. And this I have experimented in a dark Room by illuminating those bodies with uncompounded light of divers colours. For by that means any body may be made to appear of any colour. They have there no appropriate colour, but ever appear of the colour of the light cast upon them, but yet with this difference, that they are most brisk and vivid in the light of their own day-light colour. *Minium* appeareth there of any colour indifferently, with which 'tis illustrated, but yet most luminous in red, and so *Bise* appeareth indifferently of any colour with which 'tis illustrated, but yet most luminous in blew. And therefore *Minium* reflecteth Rays of any colour, but most copiously those indued with red; and consequently when illustrated with day-light, that is, with all sorts of Rays promiscuously blended, those qualified with red shall abound most in the reflected light, and by their prevalence cause it to appear of that colour. And for the same reason *Bise*, reflecting blew most copiously, shall appear blew by the excess of those Rays in its reflected light; and the like of other bodies. And that this is the intire and adequate cause of their colours, is manifest, because

they have no power to change or alter the colour of any sort of Rays incident apart, but put on all colours indifferently, with which they are enlightened.

These things being so, it can be no longer disputed, whether there be colours in the dark, nor whether they be the qualities of the objects we see, no nor perhaps, whether Light be a Body. For, since Colours are the *qualities* of Light, having its Rays for their intire and immediate subject, how can we think those Rays *qualities* also, unless one quality may be the subject of and sustain another; which in effect is to call it *substance*. We should not know Bodies for substances, were it not for their sensible qualities, and the Principal of those being now found due to something else, we have as good reason to believe that to be a substance also.

Besides, who ever thought any quality to be a *heterogeneous* aggregate, such as Light is discovered to be. But, to determine more absolutely, what Light is, after what manner refracted, and by what modes or actions it produceth in our minds the Phantasms of Colours, is not so easie. And I shall not mingle conjectures with certainties.

Reviewing what I have written, I see the discourse it self will lead to divers Experiments sufficient for its examination: And therefore I shall not trouble you further, than to describe one of those, which I have already insinuated.

In a darkened Room make a hole in the shut of a window, whose diameter may conveniently be about a third part of an inch, to admit a convenient quantity of the Sun's light: And there place a clear and colourless Prisme, to refract the entring light towards the further part of the Room, which, as I said, will thereby be diffused into an oblong coloured Image. Then place a *Lens* of about three foot radius (suppose a broad Object-glass of a three foot Telescope,) at the distance of about four or five foot from thence, through which all those colours may at once be transmitted, and made by its Refraction to convene at a further distance of about ten or twelve foot. If at that distance you intercept this light with a sheet of white paper, you will see the colours converted into whiteness again by being mingled. But it is requisite, that the *Prisme*

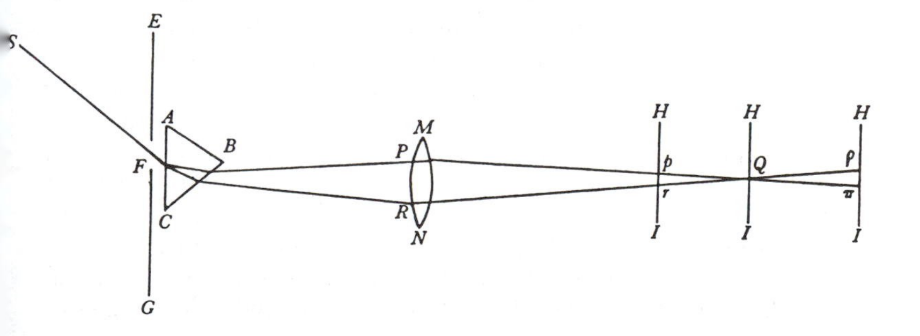

and *Lens* be placed steddy, and that the paper, on which the colours are cast, be moved to and fro; for, by such motion, you will not only find, at what distance the whiteness is most perfect, but also see, how the colours gradually convene, and vanish into whiteness, and afterwards having crossed one another in that place where they compound Whiteness, are again dissipated, and severed, and in an inverted order retain the same colours, which they had before they entered the composition. You may also see, that, if any of the Colours at the *Lens* be intercepted, the Whiteness will be changed into the other colours. And therefore, that the composition of whiteness be perfect, care must be taken, that none of the colours fall beside the *Lens*.

In the annexed design of this Experiment, *A B C* representeth the Prism set endwise to sight, close by the hole *F* of the window *E G*. Its vertical Angle *A C B* may conveniently be about 60 degrees: *M N* designes the *Lens*. Its breadth 2½ or 3 inches. *S F* one of the streight lines, in which difform Rays may be conceived to flow successively from the Sun. *F P* and *F R* two of those Rays unequally refracted, which the *Lens* makes to converge towards *Q*, and after decussation to diverge again. And *H I* the paper, at divers distances, on which the colours are projected: which in *Q* constitute *Whiteness*, but are *Red* and *Yellow* in *R*, *r*, and ρ, and *Blew* and *Purple* in *P*, *p*, and π.

If you proceed further to try the impossibility of changing any uncompounded colour (which I have asserted in the third and thirteenth Propositions,) 'tis requisite that the Room be made very dark, least any scattering light, mixing with the colour, disturb and allay it, and render it compound, contrary to the design of the Experiment. 'Tis also requisite, that there be a perfecter separation of the Colours, than, after the manner above described, can be made by the Refraction of one single Prisme, and how to make such further separations, will scarce be difficult to them, that consider the discovered laws of Refractions. But if tryal shall be made with colours not throughly separated, there must be allowed changes proportionable to the mixture. Thus if compound Yellow light fall upon Blew *Bise*, the Bise will not appear perfectly yellow, but rather green, because there are in the yellow mixture many rays indued with green, and Green being less remote from the usual blew colour of Bise than yellow, is the more copiously reflected by it.

In like manner, if any one of the Prismatick colours, suppose Red, be intercepted, on design to try the asserted impossibility of reproducing that Colour out of the others, which are pretermitted; 'tis necessary, either that the colours be very well parted before the red be intercepted, or that together with the red the neighbouring colours, into which any red is secretly dispersed, (that is, the yellow, and perhaps green too) be intercepted, or else, that allowance be made for the emerging of so much red out of the yellow and green, as may possibly have been diffused, and scatteringly blended in those colours. And if these things be observed, the new Production of Red, or any intercepted colour will be found impossible.

This, I conceive, is enough for an Introduction to Experiments of this kind; which if any of the *R. Society* shall be so curious as to prosecute, I should be very glad to be informed with what success: That, if any thing seem to be defective, or to thwart this relation, I may have an opportunity of giving further direction about it, or of acknowledging my errors, if I have committed any.

Your humble Servant
Isaac Newton

From a Paper on Rings †

* * *

Obs. 4. To observe more nicely the order of the colours, which arose out of the white circles, as the rays became less and less inclined to the plate of air; I took two object-glasses, the one a plane-convex for a fourteen foot telescope, and the other a large double convex for one of fifty foot; and upon this laying the other with its plane side downwards, I pressed them slowly together, to make the colours successively emerge in the middle of the circles, and then slowly lifted the upper glass from the lower, to make them successively vanish again in the same place, where being of a considerable breadth, I could more easily discern them. And by this means I observed their succession and quantity to be as followeth.

Next to the pellucid central spot made by the contact of the glasses, succeeded violet, blue, white, yellow, and red. The violet and blue were so very little in quantity, that I could not discern them in the circles made by the prisms; but the yellow and red were pretty copious, and seemed about as much in extent as the white, and four or five times more than the blue and violet. The next circuit or order of colours immediately encompassing these was violet, blue, green, yellow, and red. And these were all of them copious and vivid, excepting the green, which was very little in quantity, and seemed much more faint and dilute than the other colours. Of the other four the violet was least, and the blue less than the yellow or red. The third circuit or order was also purple, blue, green, yellow, and red, in which the purple seemed more reddish than the violet in the former circuit, and the green was much more conspicuous, being as brisk and copious as any of the other colours except the yellow; but the red began to be a little faded, inclining very

† I. Bernard Cohen, ed., *Isaac Newton's Papers and Letters on Natural Philosophy* (Cambridge, MA: Harvard University Press, 1958), pp. 204–08. Reprinted by permission of Harvard University Press. Newton's first paper on colors in 1672 concerned phenomena of color produced by refraction. In late 1675 he sent a second paper to the Royal Society describing experiments in which light is reflected from a thin film of air confined between a lens and a flat sheet of glass. The resultant phenomena are known as "Newton's rings."

much to purple. After these succeeded green and red; the green was very copious and lively, inclining on the one side to blue, and the other to yellow. But in this fourth circuit there was neither violet, blue, nor yellow, and the red was very imperfect and dirty. Also the succeeding colours became more and more imperfect and dilute, till after three or four more revolutions they ended in perfect whiteness.

Obs. 5. To determine the interval of the glasses, or thickness of the interjacent air, by which each colour was produced; I measured the diameter of the first six rings at the most lucid part of their orbits, and squaring them I found their squares to be in arithmetical progression of the odd numbers, 1. 3. 5. 7. 9. 11. And since one of the glasses was plane and the other spherical, their intervals at those rings must be in the same progression. I measured also the diameters of the dark or faint rings between the more lucid colours, and found their squares to be in arithmetical progression, of the even numbers 2, 4, 6, 8, 10, 12; and it being very nice and difficult to take these measures exactly, I repeated them divers times, at divers parts of the glasses, that by their agreement I might be confirmed in them; and the same method I used in determining some others of the following observations.

Obs. 6. The diameter of the first ring, at the most lucid part of its orbit, was $^{58}/_{100}$ parts of an inch, and the diameter of the sphere, on which the double convex object-glass was ground, was an hundred and two foot, as I found by measuring it; and consequently the thickness of the air, or aereal interval of the glasses at that ring, was $^{1}/_{14554}$ of an inch. For as the diameter of the said sphere (an hundred and two foot, or twelve hundred and twenty-four inches) is to the semidiameter of the ring $^{29}/_{160}$, so very nearly is that semidiameter to $^{1}/_{14554}$, the said distance of the glasses. Now, by the precedent observations, the eleventh part of this distance ($^{1}/_{160094}$) is the thickness of the air at that part of the first ring, where the yellow would be most vivid, were it not mixed with other colours in the white; and this doubled gives the difference of its thickness at the yellow in all the other rings, viz. $^{1}/_{80047}$, or, to use a round number, the eighty thousand part of an inch.

* * *

Obs. 9. By looking through the two contiguous object-glasses, I found, that the interjacent air exhibited rings of colours, as well by transmitting light as by reflecting it. The central spot was now white, and from it the order of the colours were yellowish, red, black, violet, blue, white, yellow, red; violet, blue, green, yellow, red, etc. but these colours were very faint and dilute, unless when the light was trajected very obliquely through the glasses; for by that means they became pretty vivid, only the first yellowish red, like the blue in the fourth observation, was so little and faint as scarcely to be discerned. Comparing the coloured rings made by reflection with these made by transmission of the light, I found, that white was opposite to black, red to blue, yellow to violet, and green to a compound of red and violet; that is, those parts of the glass were black when, looked through, which when looked upon appeared white, and on the contrary; and so those, which in one case exhibited blue, did in the other case exhibit red; and the like of the other colours.

Obs. 10. Wetting the object-glass a little at their edges, the water crept in slowly between them, and the circles thereby became less, and the colours more faint; insomuch that, as the water crept along, one half of them, at which it first arrived, would appear broken off from the other half, and contracted into a less room. By measuring them I found the proportion of their diameters to the diameters of the like circles made by air, to be about seven to eight; and consequently the intervals of the glasses at like circles, caused by these two mediums, water and air, are as about three to four. Perhaps it may be a general rule, that if any other medium, more or less dense than water, be compressed between the glasses, their interval at the rings, caused thereby, will be to their interval, caused by interjacent air, as the sines are, which measure the refraction made out of that medium into air.

Obs. 11. When the water was between the glasses, if I pressed the upper glass variously at its edges to make the rings move nimbly from one place to another, a little bright spot would immediately follow the center of them, which, upon creeping in of the ambient water into that place, would presently vanish. Its appearance was such, as interjacent air would have caused, and it exhibited the same colours; but it was not air, for where any aereal bubbles were in the water they would not vanish. The reflection must rather have been caused by a subtiler medium, which could recede through the glass at the creeping in of the water.

Obs. 12. These observations were made in the open air. But further, to examine the effects of coloured light falling on the glasses, I darkened the room, and viewed them by reflection of the colours of a prism cast on a sheet of white paper; and by this means the rings became distincter, and visible to a far greater number than in the open air.

I have seen more than twenty of them, whereas in the open air I could not discern above eight or nine.

Obs. 13. Appointing an assistant to move the prism to and fro about its axis, that all its colours might successively fall on the same place of the paper, and be reflected from the circles to my eye whilst I held it immoveable; I found the circles, which the red light made, to be manifestly bigger than those, which were made by the blue and violet; and it was very pleasant to see them gradually swell or contract, accordingly as the colour of the light was changed. The interval of the glass at any of the rings, when they were made by the utmost red light, was to their interval at the same ring, when made by the utmost violet, greater than three to two, and less than thirteen to eight. By the most of my observations it was as nine to fourteen. And this proportion seemed very nearly the same in all obliquities of my eye, unless when two prisms were made use of instead of the object-glasses: for then, at a certain great obliquity, the rings made by the several colours seemed equal; and, at a greater obliquity, those made by the violet would be greater than the same rings made by the red.

Obs. 14. While the prism was turned about uniformly, the contraction or dilatation of a ring made by all the several colours of the prism successively reflected from the object-glasses, was swiftest in the red, slowest in the violet, and in intermediate colours it had intermediate degrees of celerity. Comparing the extent, which each colour obtained by this contraction or dilation, I found, that the blue was sensibly more extended than the violet, the yellow than the blue, and the red than the yellow. And, to make a juster estimation of their proportions, I observed, that the extent of the red was almost double to that of the violet, and that the light was of a middle colour between yellow and green at that interval of the glasses, which was an arithmetical mean between the two extremes; contrary to what happens in the colours made by the refraction of a prism, where the red is most contracted, the violet most expanded, and in the midst of them is the confine of green and blue.

Obs. 15. These rings were not of various colours, like those in the open air, but appeared all over of that prismatic colour only, with which they were illuminated: and, by projecting the prismatic colours immediately upon the glasses, I found, that the light, which fell on the dark spaces, which were between the coloured rings, was transmitted through the glasses without any variation of colour. For, on a white paper placed behind, it would paint rings of the same colour with those, which were reflected, and of the bigness of their intermediate spaces. And from hence the origin of these rings is manifest, namely, that the aereal interval of the glasses, according to its various thickness, is disposed in some places to reflect, and in others to transmit, the light of any colour; and, in the same place to reflect one colour, where it transmits another.

* * *

Queries 28 and 29†

Qu. 28. Are not all Hypotheses erroneous, in which Light is supposed to consist in Pression or Motion, propagated through a fluid Medium? For in all these Hypotheses the Phænomena of Light have been hitherto explain'd by supposing that they arise from new Modifications of the Rays; which is an erroneous Supposition.

† Isaac Newton, *Opticks*, based on the 4th ed. (New York: Dover Publications, 1952), pp. 362–74. Reprinted by permission of Dover Publications, Inc. In these Queries, part of the group of seven added to the Latin edition of 1706, Newton expresses his conception of the nature of light.

If Light consisted only in Pression propagated without actual Motion, it would not be able to agitate and heat the Bodies which refract and reflect it. If it consisted in Motion propagated to all distances in an instant, it would require an infinite force every moment, in every shining Particle, to generate that Motion. And if it consisted in Pression or Motion, propagated either in an instant or in time, it would bend into the Shadow. For Pression or Motion cannot be propagated in a Fluid in right Lines, beyond an Obstacle which stops part of the Motion, but will bend and spread every way into the quiescent Medium which lies beyond the Obstacle. Gravity tends downwards, but the Pressure of Water arising from Gravity tends every way with equal Force, and is propagated as readily, and with as much force sideways as downwards, and through crooked passages as through strait ones. The Waves on the Surface of stagnating Water, passing by the sides of a broad Obstacle which stops part of them, bend afterwards and dilate themselves gradually into the quiet Water behind the Obstacle. The Waves, Pulses or Vibrations of the Air, wherein Sounds consist, bend manifestly, though not so much as the Waves of Water. For a Bell or a Cannon may be heard beyond a Hill which intercepts the sight of the sounding Body, and Sounds are propagated as readily through crooked Pipes as through streight ones. But Light is never known to follow crooked Passages nor to bend into the Shadow. For the fix'd Stars by the Interposition of any of the Planets cease to be seen. And so do the Parts of the Sun by the Interposition of the Moon, *Mercury* or *Venus*. The Rays which pass very near to the edges of any Body, are bent a little by the action of the Body, as we shew'd above; but this bending is not towards but from the Shadow, and is perform'd only in the passage of the Ray by the Body, and at a very small distance from it. So soon as the Ray is past the Body, it goes right on.

To explain the unusual Refraction of Island Crystal by Pression or Motion propagated, has not hitherto been attempted (to my knowledge) except by *Huygens*, who for that end supposed two several vibrating Mediums within that Crystal. But when he tried the Refractions in two successive pieces of that Crystal, and found them such as is mention'd above; he confessed himself at a loss for explaining them. For Pressions or Motions, propagated from a shining Body through an uniform Medium, must be on all sides alike; whereas by those Experiments it appears, that the Rays of Light have different Properties in their different Sides. He suspected that the Pulses of *Æther* in passing through the first Crystal might receive certain new Modifications, which might determine them to be propagated in this or that Medium within the second Crystal, according to the Position of that Crystal. But what Modifications those might be he could not say, nor think of any thing satisfactory in that Point. And if he had known that the unusual Refraction depends not on new Modifications, but on the original and unchangeable Dispositions of the Rays, he would have found it as difficult to explain how those Dispositions which he supposed to be impress'd on the Rays by the first Crystal, could be in them before their Incidence on that Crystal, and in general, how all Rays emitted by shining Bodies, can have those Dispositions in them from the beginning. To me, at least, this seems inexplicable, if Light be nothing else than Pression or Motion propagated through *Æther*.

And it is as difficult to explain by these Hypotheses, how Rays can be alternately in Fits of easy Reflexion and easy Transmission; unless perhaps one might suppose that there are in all Space two Æthereal vibrating Mediums, and that the Vibrations of one of them constitute Light, and the Vibrations of the other are swifter, and as often as they overtake the Vibrations of the first, put them into those Fits. But how two *Æthers* can be diffused through all Space, one of which acts upon the other, and by consequence is re-acted upon, without retarding, shattering, dispersing and confounding one anothers Motions, is inconceivable. And against filling the Heavens with fluid Mediums, unless they be exceeding rare, a great Objection arises from the regular and very lasting Motions of the Planets and Comets in all manner of Courses through the Heavens. For thence it is manifest, that the Heavens are void of all sensible Resistance, and by consequence of all sensible Matter.

For the resisting Power of fluid Mediums arises partly from the Attrition of the Parts of the Medium, and partly from the *Vis inertiae* of the Matter. That part of the Resistance of a spherical Body which arises from the Attrition of the Parts of the Medium is very nearly as the Diameter, or, at the most, as the *Factum* of the Diameter, and the Velocity of the spherical Body together. And that part of the Resistance which arises from the *Vis inertiae* of the Matter, is as the Square of that *Factum*. And by this difference the two sorts of Resistance may be distinguish'd from one another in any Medium; and these being distinguish'd, it will be found that almost all the Resistance of Bodies of a competent Magnitude moving in Air, Water, Quick-silver, and such like Fluids with a competent Velocity, arises from the *Vis inertiae* of the Parts of the Fluid.

Now that part of the resisting Power of any Medium which arises from the Tenacity, Friction or Attrition of the Parts of the Medium, may be diminish'd by dividing the Matter into smaller Parts, and making the Parts more smooth and slippery: But that part of the Resistance which arises from the *Vis inertiae*, is proportional to the Density of the Matter, and cannot be diminish'd by dividing the Matter into smaller Parts, nor by any other means than by decreasing the Density of the Medium. And for these Reasons the Density of fluid Mediums is very nearly proportional to their Resistance. Liquors which differ not much in Density, as Water, Spirit of Wine, Spirit of Turpentine, hot Oil, differ not much in Resistance. Water is thirteen or fourteen times lighter than Quick-silver and by consequence thirteen or fourteen times rarer, and its Resistance is less than that of Quick-silver in the same Proportion, or thereabouts, as I have found by Experiments made with Pendulums. The open Air in which we breathe is eight or nine hundred times lighter than Water, and by consequence eight or nine hundred times rarer, and accordingly its Resistance is less than that of Water in the same Proportion, or thereabouts; as I have also found by Experiments made with Pendulums. And in thinner Air the Resistance is still less, and at length, by rarifying the Air, becomes insensible. For small Feathers falling in the open Air meet with great Resistance, but in a tall Glass well emptied of Air, they fall as fast as Lead or Gold, as I have seen tried several times. Whence the Resistance seems still to decrease in proportion to the Density of the Fluid. For I do not find by any Experiments, that Bodies moving in Quick-silver, Water or Air, meet with any other sensible Resistance than what arises from the Density and Tenacity of those sensible Fluids, as they would do if the Pores of those Fluids, and all other Spaces, were filled with a dense and subtile Fluid. Now if the Resistance in a Vessel well emptied of Air, was but an hundred times less than in the open Air, it would be about a million of times less than in Quick-silver. But it seems to be much less in such a Vessel, and still much less in the Heavens, at the height of three or four hundred Miles from the Earth, or above. For Mr. *Boyle* has shew'd that Air may be rarified above ten thousand times in Vessels of Glass; and the Heavens are much emptier of Air than any *Vacuum* we can make below. For since the Air is compress'd by the Weight of the incumbent Atmosphere, and the Density of Air is proportional to the Force compressing it, it follows by Computation, that at the height of about seven and a half *English* Miles from the Earth, the Air is four times rarer than at the Surface of the Earth; and at the height of 15 Miles it is sixteen times rarer than at the Surface of the Earth; and at the height of 22½, 30, or 38 Miles, it is respectively 64, 256, or 1024 times rarer, or thereabouts; and at the height of 76, 152, 228 Miles, it is about 1000000, 1000000000000, or 1000000000000000000 times rarer; and so on.

Heat promotes Fluidity very much by diminishing the Tenacity of Bodies. It makes many Bodies fluid which are not fluid in cold, and increases the Fluidity of tenacious Liquids, as of Oil, Balsam, and Honey, and thereby decreases their Resistance. But it decreases not the Resistance of Water considerably, as it would do if any considerable part of the Resistance of Water arose from the Attrition or Tenacity of its Parts. And therefore the Resistance of Water arises principally and almost entirely from the *Vis inertiae* of its Matter; and by consequence, if the Heavens were as dense as Water, they would not have much less Resistance than Water; if as dense as Quick-silver, they would not have much less Resistance than Quick-silver; if absolutely dense, or full of

Matter without any *Vacuum*, let the Matter be never so subtil and fluid, they would have a greater Resistance than Quick-silver. A solid Globe in such a Medium would lose above half its Motion in moving three times the length of its Diameter, and a Globe not solid (such as are the Planets,) would be retarded sooner. And therefore to make way for the regular and lasting Motions of the Planets and Comets, it's necessary to empty the Heavens of all Matter, except perhaps some very thin Vapours, Steams, or Effluvia, arising from the Atmospheres of the Earth, Planets, and Comets, and from such an exceedingly rare Æthereal Medium as we described above. A dense Fluid can be of no use for explaining the Phænomena of Nature, the Motions of the Planets and Comets being better explain'd without it. It serves only to disturb and retard the Motions of those great Bodies, and make the Frame of Nature languish: And in the Pores of Bodies, it serves only to stop the vibrating Motions of their Parts, wherein their Heat and Activity consists. And as it is of no use, and hinders the Operations of Nature, and makes her languish, so there is no evidence for its Existence, and therefore it ought to be rejected. And if it be rejected, the Hypotheses that Light consists in Pression or Motion, propagated through such a Medium, are rejected with it.

And for rejecting such a Medium, we have the Authority of those the oldest and most celebrated Philosophers of *Greece* and *Phœnicia*, who made a *Vacuum*, and Atoms, and the Gravity of Atoms, the first Principles of their Philosophy; tacitly attributing Gravity to some other Cause than dense Matter. Later Philosophers banish the Consideration of such a Cause out of natural Philosophy, feigning Hypotheses for explaining all things mechanically, and referring other Causes to Metaphysicks: Whereas the main Business of natural Philosophy is to argue from Phænomena without feigning Hypotheses, and to deduce Causes from Effects, till we come to the very first Cause, which certainly is not mechanical; and not only to unfold the Mechanism of the World, but chiefly to resolve these and such like Questions. What is there in places almost empty of Matter, and whence is it that the Sun and Planets gravitate towards one another, without dense Matter between them? Whence is it that Nature doth nothing in vain; and whence arises all that Order and Beauty which we see in the World? To what end are Comets, and whence is it that Planets move all one and the same way in Orbs concentrick, while Comets move all manner of ways in Orbs very excentrick; and what hinders the fix'd Stars from falling upon one another? How came the Bodies of Animals to be contrived with so much Art, and for what ends were their several Parts? Was the Eye contrived without Skill in Opticks, and the Ear without Knowledge of Sounds? How do the Motions of the Body follow from the Will, and whence is the Instinct in Animals? Is not the Sensory of Animals that place to which the sensitive Substance is present, and into which the sensible Species of Things are carried through the Nerves and Brain, that there they may be perceived by their immediate presence to that Substance? And these things being rightly dispatch'd, does it not appear from Phænomena that there is a Being incorporeal, living, intelligent, omnipresent, who in infinite Space, as it were in his Sensory, sees the things themselves intimately, and throughly perceives them, and comprehends them wholly by their immediate presence to himself: Of which things the Images only carried through the Organs of Sense into our little Sensoriums, are there seen and beheld by that which in us perceives and thinks. And though every true Step made in this Philosophy brings us not immediately to the Knowledge of the first Cause, yet it brings us nearer to it, and on that account is to be highly valued.

Qu. 29. Are not the Rays of Light very small Bodies emitted from shining Substances? For such Bodies will pass through uniform Mediums in right Lines without bending into the Shadow, which is the Nature of the Rays of Light. They will also be capable of several Properties, and be able to conserve their Properties unchanged in passing through several Mediums, which is another Condition of the Rays of Light. Pellucid Substances act upon the Rays of Light at a distance in refracting, reflecting, and inflecting them, and the Rays mutually agitate the Parts of those Substances at a distance for heating them; and this Action and Re-action at a distance very much resembles an attractive Force between Bodies. If Refraction be perform'd by Attraction of the Rays, the Sines of Incidence must be to the Sines of Refraction in a given Proportion, as we shew'd in our Principles of Philosophy: And this Rule is true by Experience. The Rays of Light in going out of Glass into a *Vacuum*, are bent towards the Glass; and if they fall too obliquely on the *Vacuum*, they are bent backwards into the Glass, and totally reflected; and this Reflexion cannot be ascribed to the Resistance of an absolute *Vacuum*, but must be caused by the Power of the Glass attracting the Rays at their going out of it into the *Vacuum*, and bringing them back. For if the farther Surface of the Glass be moisten'd with Water or clear Oil, or liquid and clear Honey, the Rays which would otherwise be reflected will go into the Water, Oil, or Honey; and therefore are not reflected before they arrive at the farther Surface of the Glass, and begin to go out of it. If they go out of it into the Water, Oil, or Honey, they go on, because the Attraction of the Glass is almost balanced and rendered ineffectual by the contrary Attraction of the Liquor. But if they go out of it into a *Vacuum* which has no Attraction to balance that of the Glass, the Attraction of the Glass either bends and refracts them, or brings them back and reflects them. And this is still more evident by laying together two Prisms of Glass, or two Object-glasses of very long Telescopes, the one plane, the other a little convex, and so compressing them that they do not fully touch, nor are too far asunder. For the Light which falls upon the farther Surface of the first

Glass where the Interval between the Glasses is not above the ten hundred thousandth Part of an Inch, will go through that Surface, and through the Air or *Vacuum* between the Glasses, and enter into the second Glass, as was explain'd in the first, fourth, and eighth Observations of the first Part of the second Book. But, if the second Glass be taken away, the Light which goes out of the second Surface of the first Glass into the Air or *Vacuum*, will not go on forwards, but turns back into the first Glass, and is reflected; and therefore it is drawn back by the Power of the first Glass, there being nothing else to turn it back. Nothing more is requisite for producing all the variety of Colours, and degrees of Refrangibility, than that the Rays of Light be Bodies of different Sizes, the least of which may take violet the weakest and darkest of the Colours, and be more easily diverted by refracting Surfaces from the right Course; and the rest as they are bigger and bigger, may make the stronger and more lucid Colours, blue, green, yellow, and red, and be more and more difficultly diverted. Nothing more is requisite for putting the Rays of Light into Fits of easy Reflexion and easy Transmission, than that they be small Bodies which by their attractive Powers, or some other Force, stir up Vibrations in what they act upon, which Vibrations being swifter than the Rays, overtake them successively, and agitate them so as by turns to increase and decrease their Velocities, and thereby put them into those Fits. And lastly, the unusual Refraction of Island-Crystal looks very much as if it were perform'd by some kind of attractive virtue lodged in certain Sides both of the Rays, and of the Particles of the Crystal. For were it not for some kind of Disposition or Virtue lodged in some Sides of the Particles of the Crystal, and not in their other Sides, and which inclines and bends the Rays towards the Coast of unusual Refraction, the Rays which fall perpendicularly on the Crystal, would not be refracted towards that Coast rather than towards any other Coast, both at their Incidence and at their Emergence, so as to emerge perpendicularly by a contrary Situation of the Coast of unusual Refraction at the second Surface; the Crystal acting upon the Rays after they have pass'd through it, and are emerging into the Air; or, if you please, into a *Vacuum*. And since the Crystal by this Disposition or Virtue does not act upon the Rays, unless when one of their Sides of unusual Refraction looks towards that Coast, this argues a Virtue or Disposition in those Sides of the Rays, which answers to, and sympathizes with that Virtue or Disposition of the Crystal, as the Poles of two Magnets answer to one another. And as Magnetism may be intended and remitted, and is found only in the Magnet and in Iron: So this Virtue of refracting the perpendicular Rays is greater in Island-Crystal, less in Crystal of the Rock, and is not yet found in other Bodies. I do not say that this Virtue is magnetical: It seems to be of another kind. I only say, that whatever it be, it's difficult to conceive how the Rays of Light, unless they be Bodies, can have a permanent Virtue in two of their Sides which is not in their other Sides, and this without any regard to their Position to the Space or Medium through which they pass.

* * *

ALAN E. SHAPIRO

Experiment and Mathematics in Newton's Theory of Color†

On 18 January 1672 Isaac Newton wrote Henry Oldenburg, Secretary of the Royal Society, that he would send him a paper that he modestly described as "being in my Judgment the oddest if not the most considerable detection which hath hitherto beene made in the operations of Nature." Newton was not referring to his theory of gravitation—that was still more than a dozen years away—but rather to his new theory of the nature of white light and color. He had discovered that rays of different color have different degrees of refrangibility—or, as we would put it, that the index of refraction varies with wavelength—and that white light and, in particular, sunlight consist of a mixture of innumerable colors. Less than three weeks later, as Newton promised, he sent to the Royal Society his famous paper, "A New theory about light and colors," which was published at once in the *Philosophical Transactions*. In the "New theory" he boldly proclaims:

> A naturalist would scearce expect to see the science of [colours] become mathematicall, and yet I dare affirm that there is as much certainty in it as in any other part of Opticks. For what I shall tell concerning them is not an Hypothesis but most rigid consequence, not conjectured by barely inferring 'tis thus because not otherwise or because it satisfies all phænomena (the Philosophers universall Topick), but evinced by the mediation of experiments concluding directly and without any suspicion of doubt.

These are pretty strong claims, and my first aim in this article is to consider Newton's quest for certainty, his attempt in his *Optical Lectures* to create a mathematical science of color, and the role of experiment in this endeavor. Then I will describe how he came to abandon his new mathematical science and acknowledge the contingency of an experimental theory. To caricature my own argument, I will show how Newton initially intended his *Optical Lectures* to be, as it were, his

† *Physics Today* (Sept. 1984): 34–42. Reprinted by permission of the American Institute of Physics. Alan E. Shapiro is the editor of Newton's *Optical Papers*, an edition planned in three volumes of which the first has appeared at this time (see Selected Bibliography).

Principia, or a mathematical treatise, and then how it became his *Opticks*, an experimental treatise. In fact, I will show that the mathematical theory of his *Lectures* is of a very different sort from that of the *Principia*.

Lectiones Opticae

Most physicists know Newton's theory of color from his *Opticks*, which he composed in the early 1690s and published in 1704, about thirty to forty years after he had made his optical discoveries. Some also know the "New theory," but that is just a brief outline of his theory of color. Newton's principal early work on the subject is his little-known (even by historians of science) *Lectiones opticae* or *Optical Lectures*. When Newton, who was not yet 27 years old, was appointed Lucasian Professor of Mathematics at the University of Cambridge in the fall of 1669, he chose to deliver his inaugural series of lectures from 1670 to 1672 on the theory of color and refraction that he had developed in the preceding half decade. This was Newton's first physical treatise and the most comprehensive account of his theory of color that he would ever present, serving as the immediate source for his "New theory" and, twenty years later, the foundation for Book I of his *Opticks*.

There are two versions of his *Optical Lectures*, with the second one being a substantially enlarged and reorganized version of the first. Both are in Latin. In early 1672 Newton had intended to publish the revised version, but he soon decided against it. However, in accordance with university statutes, in October 1674 he deposited a copy in the university library, from which a number of copies were made.

Newton begins the *Optical Lectures*, as he does the "New theory," with a demonstration of the central idea of his theory, that sunlight consists of rays of unequal refrangibility. The fundamental experiment in demonstrating that discovery is that of passing light through a prism and projecting its image or spectrum onto a screen. Experiments with prismatic spectra were quite common in the seventeenth century, but Newton's arrangement of passing a narrow circular beam of light through a prism at minimum deviation was an original, and by no means obvious, one. He deduced that in this situation if all rays were equally refrangible, as was then universally held, then the image should be nearly circular. He then measured the spectrum and found that it was greatly elongated, about five times longer than broad. This was the key—measurement and calculation. He had to eliminate other possible causes for the elongation, of course, but once he had established that there could be no other cause than that the Sun's direct light consists of rays of unequal refrangibility, he had, or so it seemed, a mathematical measure for color: the degree of refrangibility. On the one hand, this allowed the possibility of developing a mathematical theory of color. On the other hand, this experiment provided Newton with the fundamental experimental and conceptual tool of his theory of color. It gave him his method of analysis or decomposition: separating rays of different colors from one another by their unequal refrangibility.

Argument for mathematics. At this point in the enlarged and reorganized *Optical Lectures*, after Newton had demonstrated unequal refrangibility, we encounter the most striking change from the earlier version, for Newton interchanged the mathematical part on refraction and the experimental part on color, putting the mathematical part first. However, in both versions, immediately after he introduces the propositions of his experimental theory, he makes a pronouncement on his method for demonstrating them that provides us with an early, revealing insight into his conception of a scientific theory. To justify his mathematical treatment of colors, Newton makes the following argument, which characterizes well the outlook that guides him throughout his *Optical Lectures*. (Here we can read Newton's terms "geometry" and "philosophy" as "mathematics" and "physics," respectively):

> . . . the generation of colors includes so much geometry, and the understanding of colors is supported by so much evidence, that for their sake I can thus attempt to extend the bounds of mathematics somewhat, just as astronomy, geography, navigation, optics, and mechanics are truly considered mathematical sciences even if they deal with physical things. . . . Thus although colors may belong to physics, the science of them must nevertheless be considered mathematical, insofar as they are treated by mathematical reasoning. Indeed . . . I hope to show—as it were, by my example—how valuable mathematics is in natural philosophy. I therefore urge geometers to investigate nature more rigorously, and those devoted to natural science to learn geometry first. Hence the former shall not entirely spend their time in speculations of no value to human life, nor shall the latter, while working assiduously with an absurd method, fail to reach their goal. But truly with the help of philosophical geometers and geometrical philosophers, instead of the conjectures and probabilities that are being blazoned about everywhere, we shall finally achieve a natural science supported by the greatest evidence.

Thus, from the beginning of his career, Newton was as concerned with reforming the methods of natural science as with the science itself. While in the heading to this passage Newton avows that "these propositions are to be treated not hypothetically and probably, but by experiments or demonstratively," in the passage itself he speaks only about mathematics and not experiment, except for a vague reference to "evidence." In his desire to establish a new, more certain science, Newton does not clearly separate two distinct aspects of this reform, the introduction of mathematics and the elimination of the "hypothetical physics" that René Descartes and other mechanical philosophers had introduced earlier in the Scientific Revolution. The mechanical philosophers claimed that we could not truly know the inner workings of nature, as the Aristotelians had believed, and that the best we could do was to construct a likely account—an hypothesis—that could explain the phenomena. The "hypothetical physics" had indeed gotten out of hand with the construction of arbitrary models, based on conjectured invisible mechanisms. Newton's aim was to replace these qualitative, probable explanations, and to establish a new sort of certainty and truth in which the description of nature is mathematical and based directly on the phenomenon, or on experiment and observation.

Experimental Theory of Color

Besides the intrinsic problem that in Newton's day the study of color was simply not ready for a unified mathematical treatment, perhaps the major weakness of his attempted mathematical theory of color was that it was only loosely related to his experimental theory or, for that matter, to any experiment or observation. The two theories had few principles in common, and to appreciate their relation, I will briefly sketch them, beginning with the experimental theory. Because that theory is rather well known, I will present only Newton's most important conclusions and simply allude to the extensive series of experiments that he uses to justify them. My sketch will synthesize his three early accounts—the two versions of the *Optical Lectures* and the "New theory"—while noting significant differences between them.

Newton fully accepted the fundamental assumption of the mechanical philosophy that light rays are not colored but rather cause sensations of different colors depending on their physical constitution. For convenience's sake, however, I will speak of red rays, yellow rays, and so on—as Newton himself often did—instead of using his more precise, though cumbersome, terms, red-making rays, yellow-making rays, and so on.

- Sunlight consists of rays of unequal refrangibility. I already indicated the essence of Newton's proof of this principle, which is the foundation of both theories.
- There is a one-to-one correspondence between refrangibility and color. Newton implicitly assumes that this correspondence is independent of the refracting material. This proposition allows the possibility of constructing a mathematical theory of color, for it in principle assigns a metric to color. However, because it is proved and applied only qualitatively, namely, by observing that red rays are always refracted the least, violet the most, and so on, it could not be strictly established or mathematically formulated.

Nonetheless, in the "New theory" Newton (erroneously) asserts that the correspondence "is very precise and strict."

- Color is immutable by refraction, reflection, transmission or any other means. This proposition should be restricted to simple or monochromatic colors, and the fact that it is not reflects Newton's initial problem with properly defining simple and compound colors. He first made this a proposition in the second version of the *Optical Lectures*, when he recognized that it could be used to prove that colors are innate to white light.
- There are two sorts of color, "simple" and "compound." Orange, for example, can be a simple spectral orange or a compound orange made up of red and yellow rays. These two sorts of color are sensibly identical but physically distinguishable, because compound colors, but not simple ones, are decomposed by a prism. Newton gradually clarified these concepts. In the first version of the *Optical Lectures* they were not even defined, but in a reformulation of his theory for Christiaan Huygens in 1673, he rigorously defined them in terms of refrangibility and solved this problem.
- Colors similar in sensible appearance to the simple spectral colors can be made by a mixture of the colors on each side of them. Again, this is a proposition that was added in the revision of the *Optical Lectures*, and it shows Newton's growing concern with the composition of colors.
- "But the most surprising and wonderful composition," Newton explained in the "New theory," "was that of *Whiteness* . . . 'Tis ever compounded. . . ." That is, white light, particularly sunlight, is a mixture of rays of every color. Newton recognized that one could not directly prove experimentally that colors are innate to sunlight, and most of his experiments in support of this principle depend on a similarity argument: By various, often ingenious, means he composes white from a mixture of the innumerable spectral colors and shows that in all its properties it is similar to direct sunlight. In his *Opticks*, Newton concedes that white could also be composed from a smaller number of colors, perhaps as few as three.

While there are certainly problems with Newton's experiment-based theory—imprecise and circular definitions and unjustified idealizations and generalizations, for example—there can be no doubt that it is firmly grounded on experiment and observation. It was proved by experiment, and its fundamental concepts, such as unequal refrangibility and simple and compound colors, are operational ones derived from experiment. In contrast, the mathematical theory, as we will now see, makes a virtue of the fact that it has little need for experiment and observation.

Mathematical Theory of Color

Almost as soon as Newton discovered in 1666 that rays of unequal refrangibility are innate to the Sun's light, he set out to apply mathematics to this new phenomenon: He calculated the chromatic aberration of a plano-convex lens; and he developed a mathematical-physical model of refraction and dispersion to calculate the refractions of various simple colors at the interfaces between various substances, for instance, air and water, or air and glass. I will call the former sort of application of mathematics simply quantitative to distinguish it from a mathematical theory: In the quantitative approach, one determines particular effects by applying traditional geometrical optics with the additional assumption of a varying index of refraction. As a masterful mathematical physicist, Newton was quite successful at this endeavor. The calculation of the table of refractions represents, at least in principle, what I will call a *mathematical theory*, and the sort of theory to which Newton aspired: From a few fundamental mathematical-physical laws, one may deduce a large variety of phenomena.

Newton's plan to develop a mathematical science of color was never more than a program, and it must be reconstructed from his *Optical Lectures*. Its foundation was to be refrangibility, or index of refraction, which Newton found corresponded to color directly. He assumed in the first place that the sine law of refraction, or Snel's law, was valid for each color apart, and though he proposed an experimental verification, he rejected it as unnecessary. Then, to describe the variation of the degree of refrangibility with color, that is, the dispersion, Newton constructed a refraction model that we now know is based on Descartes's earlier model of corpuscles that receive an impulse as they cross a refractive surface. In his *Optical Lectures*, however, Newton carefully eliminated all traces of its mechanical underpinnings and presented it solely as a mathematical law. The model assumes that at grazing incidence in any given medium, rays (or corpuscles) of all colors receive the same increment of velocity normal to the refracting surface. This model yields what I call Newton's quadratic dispersion law:

$$\frac{\Delta n}{\Delta n'} = \frac{(1/n)(n^2 - 1)}{(1/n')(n'^2 - 1)}$$

In this proportion, Δn is the dispersion or the difference in the indices of refraction for extreme red rays and extreme violet rays in a given medium, n is the mean index of refraction, and the prime indicates a second medium. While the exact form of the law need not concern us, we should note that implicit in it is the simple but erroneous assumption that dispersion is independent of the nature of the refracting substance and is solely a property of light. For, once the parameters of this model are determined—and only three measurements in one substance are necessary—then knowledge of just a single value of the index of refraction in some substance allows one to determine all refractions in it. Newton was quite proud of this feature and even boasted that with this law one need not "bother anew with experiments."

Three principles of refraction. Newton's goal evidently was to develop a rational science of color:

- The sine law defines the refraction of every ray at any angle of incidence in a given medium.
- The dispersion law defines the index of refraction of rays of every color given that of any one color.
- The law of relative indices of refraction, which was already known, but which Newton extended to rays of different refrangibility, gives the index of refraction for any two media with no additional measurements whatever, provided their refraction is known with respect to some common medium, such as air.

Thus, Newton developed a theory in which the barest minimum of measurements are needed to describe the refractions of any color in every medium. When he set forth his refraction model in his *Optical Lectures*, he freely admitted that

> Although I have not yet derived the certainty of this proposition from experiments, nevertheless I do not doubt that it will satisfy all of them which it is possible to do with respect to it . . . meanwhile [I am] content to assume it gratuitously.

The three principles of refraction given above, as Newton later explained in a draft of a letter for Robert Hooke, were to serve as the foundation for his mathematical science of color. Although Newton considered a different dispersion law in that letter, it is important to note that the actual dispersion law adopted is irrelevant for this program, only the existence of such a law is essential.

We can at this point already discern that the goal of Newton's mathematical science of color was to describe the behavior of colored light, and not to explain its causes. His approach was to be more like that of traditional geometrical optics or kinematics than that of physical optics or dynamics. It is as if Newton had later attempted to derive a celestial mechanics from Kepler's laws rather than Newton's laws and central forces.

Newton devotes most of the remainder of the mathematical part of the *Optical Lectures* to what proved to be a futile attempt to deduce from the three principles of refraction, especially his dispersion law, the propositions that were to form his mathematical science of color. (In the following, I will perforce pass over Newton's most notable optical achievements, which are in traditional geometrical optics with monochromatic radiation.) He first devotes a number of propositions to the relative order and inclination of rays of different colors refracted at a plane surface under different initial conditions, which is as physically uninteresting as it sounds. Then, in two complex pairs of lectures containing some sophisticated mathematics, he turns to an investigation of the variation of dispersion with respect to variation of the index of refraction. He demonstrates, for instance, that the dispersion increases at a faster rate than the index of refraction. This proposition is wrong, as are all but one in these lectures, because all but one are based on his quadratic dispersion law. Newton, however, could have readily tested this proposition, for example, by comparing common glass and turpentine, where it does not hold. On only one occasion, though, in these two long lectures does he suggest an experimental test, and then only to reject it as insufficiently sensitive.

Likewise, in the brief concluding lecture of the first version, which is on refraction in prisms—the fundamental experimental technique of his entire theory—two of the eight propositions are erroneous. It is particularly notable that one of these establishes incorrectly that the minimum of angular dispersion (that is, the angle contained by the extreme red and violet refracted rays) occurs when the rays pass through the prism symmetrically. Not only is the position of the minimum mistaken, but with the large-angled prisms Newton used there is no minimum at all. Although it is somewhat difficult to distinguish variations of the deviation and those of the angular dispersion, Newton was an acute observer and performed this experiment many times; in an observation in the *Opticks* he did correct this error. Newton seems almost oblivious to relating his mathematical constructions to the real world by experimental tests.

Newton Revises Optical Lectures

When Newton revised his *Optical Lectures*, he interchanged the two parts so that the mathematical part on refraction would precede that on color. This new order apparently reflected his growing commitment to develop a mathematical theory of color founded upon refraction, but, insofar as I can determine, it had no significant influence on the structure of either the mathematical or experimental theories or on their relation to one another. The dispersion law, by Newton's own admission, was still untested, and while he revised and rearranged his mathematical theory of color a bit, it remained essentially the same. Although he did not—or could not—advance the fundamental mathematical theory, he did add a brilliant section on refraction at spherical surfaces. This section contains two important calculations that treat polychromatic radiation: the chromatic aberration of a lens and the breadth of a rainbow.

For my immediate purpose, Newton's most significant, if not felicitous, addition was his musical division of the spectrum. He divided the spectrum into seven "more prominent" colors from red to violet and found that this division of the spectrum was

> . . . proportional to a string so divided that it would cause the individual degrees of the octave to sound. . . . I could not, however, so precisely observe and define this without being compelled to admit that it could perhaps be constituted somewhat differently.

Nonetheless, he chose the musical division because of his belief in an analogy between the harmonies of sounds and colors. Thus far, Newton was simply adding a new twist to an ancient quest for harmonies, but he then explained that by an approximation one can find the index of refraction for each color by dividing the indices of refraction between the two extreme colors in the same proportion as the spectrum. This musical division readily yields another (erroneous) dispersion law, which I call Newton's linear dispersion law,

$$\Delta n/\Delta n' = (n-1)/(n'-1)$$

As in Newton's earlier quadratic dispersion law, the dispersion here is independent of the nature of the refracting substance, for any two media with the same mean index of refraction will have the same dispersion. Although Newton did not deduce this new law in the *Optical Lectures*, he did briefly adopt it in his draft reply to Hooke just a few months later.

Contradictory Laws of Dispersion

For the very limited range of substances and indices of refraction examined by Newton, this law does not quantitatively differ much from the earlier quadratic law. However, it has fundamentally different physical implications and is incompatible with that law. Newton based his quadratic law on a dynamical theory of refraction, which he later further developed in the *Principia* using forces. He based his linear law directly on principles of his color theory—the immutability of color and degree of refrangibility—for the linear law implies that the proportion of the spectrum occupied by each color is identical in all spectra. Thus, Newton derived both laws from fundamental theoretical principles whose truth he never doubted. Choosing between them was therefore not in the first place an empirical issue for Newton, and this probably explains, at least in part, why he never subjected them to systematic experimental tests. In the reply that Newton finally sent to Hooke, he suppressed any reference to his dispersion laws, and for the next thirty years he remained publicly silent on this issue. When he finally chose the linear dispersion law in the *Opticks*, he supported it with fabricated experimental evidence, but that is a difficult issue that I will not treat here.

In this same letter to Hooke, Newton was already backing down from the strong claim of certainty that he had made in the "New theory," as he came to distinguish more clearly between his mathematical and experimental theories and to acknowledge the contingency of his experimental theory. To Hooke's charge that his theory was "not soe certain as mathematical Demonstrations," Newton replied:

> I should take notice of a casuall expression which intimates a greater certainty in these things then I ever promised, viz: The certainty of *Mathematicall Demonstrations*. I said indeed that the *Science of Colours was Mathematicall and as certain as any other part of Optiques*; but who knows not that Optiques and many other Mathematicall Sciences depend as well on Physicall Principles as on Mathematicall Demonstrations: And the absolute certainty of a Science cannot exceed the certainty of its Principles. Now the evidence by which I asserted the Propositions of colours is in the next words expressed to be from *Experments* and so but *Physicall*: Whence the Propositions themselves can be esteemed no more then *Physicall Principles* of a Science. And if those Principles be such that on them a Mathematician may determine all the Phaenomena of colours that can be caused by refractions . . . I suppose the *Science of Colours* will be granted *Mathematicall* and as certain as any part of *Optiques*.

Even this concession, however, is somewhat misleading in its description of Newton's new science, for Newton's mathematical theory was founded upon his three principles of refraction, as he explained in the draft of his reply to Hooke, and not upon the "physicall principles" of his experimental theory. His experimental and mathematical theories in fact had only one and a half principles in common, namely, that sunlight consists of unequally refrangible rays, and that there is a correspondence between refrangibility and color, which, however, is only qualitatively exploited—hence the half.

Why did Newton moderate his claims as to the certainty of his experimental theory and differentiate it from the mathematical theory? The immediate cause, of course, was Hooke's objection, which compelled him to ponder more carefully the nature of scientific theories, and in particular, the methodology and formal structure of his own. But at the same time, I suspect that Newton wanted to sever the two theories, for his goal of developing a mathematical science of color had become stymied. I say this for three reasons:

- First, Newton lacked a dispersion law—or rather he had two—and an exact science must have a certain foundation.
- Second, I find it difficult to believe that after two attempts in his *Optical Lectures* Newton himself did not recognize that he had not actually progressed very far in developing a fundamental the-

ory that modeled reality. His mathematical theory was, rather, nearly a free construction of his intellect. While this approach may have failed Newton here, we should not fail to recognize that his willingness and ability to formulate general mathematical-physical laws and pursue them in all their ramifications shows the boldness of scientific approach and breadth of intellectual grasp that otherwise served him so well.

- Third, I think that with his growing concern for the composition of colors, Newton had come to recognize that he had fashioned only one part of a theory of color, a theory of unequal refrangibility that could account for the spatial distribution or separation of colors but not for their sensible appearance—that is, their color. I think this would have troubled Newton even if his mathematical theory had been more successful.

Abandons Mathematical Theory

Whatever the precise reasons, Newton did abandon his mathematical theory and suppress the mathematical part of the *Optical Lectures*. Less than four months after he sent off the "New theory," he decided to suspend publication of his *Optical Lectures* because the apperance of the "New theory" and the ensuing controversies had so disturbed his tranquility. By the time he recovered his equanimity in late 1675 and once again judged the world receptive to his optical theories, much of the *Optical Lectures* was already outdated. Newton was now planning a new work that was very much like the later *Opticks*. For this projected work, he intended to redo the experimental part of the *Optical Lectures* on color as a "discourse about the colours of the Prism," to omit altogether the mathematical part of the *Lectures*, and to add his recent papers on the colors of thin films. When Newton finally published the *Opticks* in 1704, he included only some specific quantitative results from the *Optical Lectures*, and he even considered it necessary to disavow his *Lectures* in its preface.

In 1672 Newton's experimental theory had also encountered a serious snag that threatened its certainty. In revising his *Optical Lectures*, he had discovered a new, logically rigorous proof that colors are innate to sunlight. The proof depends on the principle of color immutability, and in essence runs as follows: Because colors are absolutely immutable, and sunlight exhibits colors after it is refracted, then it necessarily follows that those colors are innate to sunlight prior to refraction, even though they are not yet apparent.

Newton soon perceived a difficulty in experimentally establishing this proof as formulated, and in 1673 he developed an alternative version. He continued to try to establish the certainty of this proof, returning to it in the early 1690s and again in 1703, but he eventually came to accept that no matter how he formulated it, it was impossible experimentally to prove color immutability for the Sun's immediate light, and thus that the colors are innate to it. The problem is that before refraction sunlight appears white, and afterwards it displays all the spectral colors; and if the two are compared, the colors do *appear* to have changed. The careful reader of the *Opticks* will note that Newton has all but given up his attempt to prove that sunlight *is* composed of all colors; he devotes just nine rather weak lines of text to it, whereas he spends sixteen pages showing that white light, similar to the Sun's light, *may* be compounded of all colors. This is indeed a long way from the "most rigid consequence" of the "New theory."

We can now view the *Opticks* from Newton's perspective and his early hopes for a certain and mathematical science of color, and appreciate what must have been his disappointment when he penned the modest opening lines of the *Opticks* that are just a faint echo of his earlier confident assertions: "My Design in this Book is not to explain the properties of Light by Hypotheses, but to propose and prove them by reason and experiments." To be sure, because we do not put such severe restrictions on the certainty of a scientific theory, we rightly judge the *Opticks* to be one of the great experimental works of the Scientific Revolution. However, if we are properly to appreciate Newton's *Opticks*, then we must understand it within its own historical context and especially in its relation to his brilliant, but flawed, *Optical Lectures*.

SIMON SCHAFFER

Glass works †

* * *

Newton Transforms the Uses of the 'Glass-prism' (1666–72)

In his 1664 notes, Newton sought to emulate some of Boyle's colourmixing trials with prisms but his experiments did not involve any prismatic projection, that is, they did not yet involve the casting of an iris upon a screen or wall. Instead, he examined coloured bands and threads by looking at these objects through a prism. These experiments, particularly that with a bicoloured thread examined through a prism, prompted the thought that blue-making rays were refracted more than red-making ones. Such an examination made the blue and red parts of the thread seem to separate from each other. Newton attributed this

† David Gooding, Trevor Pinch, and Simon Schaffer, eds., *The Uses of Experiment: Studies in the Natural Sciences* (Cambridge: Cambridge University Press, 1989), pp. 67–104. Reprinted with the permission of Cambridge University Press. Simon Schaffer is a scholar very active in the exploration of seventeenth-century science.

phenomenon to differing refrangibility. He did not record a projection until his manuscript 'Of colours', written in 1666 after his reading of Hooke's *Micrographia* and the beginning of his 'glass works'.

In contrast with the strategies of Boyle and Hooke, Newton's manuscript of 1666 marked an important change in prism techniques. He used at least three different prisms separately and in combination. He also noted the use of a prism made of a 'four square vessell' of polished glass filled with water and a device constructed of two prisms tied together 'basis to basis'. Newton began changing the commercial 'triangular glass prism' into a complex experimental instrument. He recorded a long series of 'Experiments with ye Prisme', two of which are particularly important. The seventh experiment involved a prismatic projection of an image across a space of at least 21 feet in a darkened room. This was designed to show that even when the prism was set so that light passed through it symmetrically, the prismatic image was oblong rather than circular, for from this Newton would argue that the shape of the image was due to the different refrangibility of different rays. This experiment appeared, carefully rewritten, as the first trial presented both in 1670 at Cambridge and in 1672 in his letter to Oldenburg, the 'celebrated phaenomena of colours'. The forty-fourth trial involved the use of a second prism to refract light rays again after their emergence from the first one. This experiment was designed to show that each ray had a specific refrangibility and made a specific colour. It was later to be substantially reworked as the celebrated *experimentum crucis*.

Both experiments fulfilled their role because of a set of claims about the way in which prisms worked. In order to understand these transformations in presentation and meaning and the persuasive role which Newton designed them to serve, it is necessary to consider the role and use of the prisms deployed in these trials.

The claims about prisms which Newton made in these early notes remained tacit in the initial publication of his experiments. The dramatic innovation in the tactics of prism trials and the challenges to the utility of common prisms were not made visible. But controversy prompts protagonists to expose such tacit knowledge. During his trials of the 1660s and the controversies of the 1670s, Newton specified more details of how prisms should properly be prepared and used. He gave experimenters instructions about the *differences* between prisms which were commonly available and those which could best display the phenomena he reported. This implies that the provenance of Newton's own instruments is an important factor. However, none of the extant prisms associated with Newton seems to correspond to any of those whose use he describes. It is reported that Newton bought a prism at Stourbridge Fair in Cambridge in August 1665. Since 'he could not demonstrate' his hypothesis of colours against Descartes without a second one, he bought another there in 1666. But Newton left Cambridge before the

1665 Stourbridge fair and none was held in 1666. It has been suggested that Newton was recalling the fairs held at midsummer in those two years. A notebook also records the purchase of three prisms and collections of 'glasses' in London and Cambridge during 1668. As we have seen, the essay 'Of colours' suggests that Newton already had three prisms available to him during 1666. Further manuscripts of the period from 1668 record the purchase of optical machinery and work on lens grinding.

Two implications of these stories are of interest. First, prisms were evidently the sort of objects purchased at commercial fairs and in the City. They were correspondingly priced; prisms were relatively cheap tools for Newton's expanding programme of practical natural philosophy. Second, while it would rapidly become clear to Newton that it was necessary to prepare prisms carefully for his optical trials, to concentrate attention on glass quality and prism design, nevertheless he gave no details of these protocols in his first communications with the London experimenters. As he put it bluntly in February 1672, 'I shall without further ceremony acquaint you that in the beginning of the year 1666 . . . I procured me a Triangular glass-Prisme'. Later in the letter he gave the dimensions of the prism and the refractive power of its glass (a value which indicates that this prism was unusual in containing some lead). Rather few indications were added in the body of the paper, which itself contained but four trials, save the instruction that the prism should be 'clear and colourless.'. A second prism was invoked without any specification of its quality or geometry.

Newton's instructions proved insufficiently detailed for his audience. In experiments designed to show the important and controversial fact that 'uncompounded' rays could not be changed, Newton did not provide a recipe for making these 'primitive' or 'uncompounded' rays. Instead, he said that 'there should be perfecter separation of the Colours, than, after the manner above described, can be made by the Refraction of one single Prisme'. Evidently the perfect separation of an 'uncompounded' ray relied on special techniques in handling prisms. The separation of such rays was a novel feature of experimental optics. The existence of such rays was a novel feature of optical theory. Yet Newton relied on the familiarity of the common prism, and merely added that 'how to make such further separations will scarce be difficult to them, that consider the discovered laws of Refractions'. But these laws were precisely the matter of dispute. The subsequent career of Newton's *experimentum crucis* and the detailed interpretations of its author and critics show how vulnerable was the 'obviousness' of Newton's account and how important were the 'difficulties' of his instruments.

Newton's Prisms and His Audiences (1670–72)

When he chose to give his first published account of his new doctrine of light and colours in early 1672, Newton helped himself to the rich resource of prism experiments which he had described in his Lucasian lectures at Cambridge. The contrast between these lectures and the version Newton released to his audience helps reveal how he sought to persuade that audience. In the lectures Newton described experiments using several prisms to show that light rays were differently refrangible and that differently refrangible rays displayed different colours. Each refracted colour-making ray was sent successively through a second prism onto a screen. In his sixth lecture, he drew the same conclusions from set-ups where the refracted rays were made to undergo total internal reflection in the second prism. Very few of these trials were then summarised for the Royal Society during the 1670s. In the lectures, no one trial appeared to be especially significant and most experiments seemed to need special equipment and technique. But in his communications with his fellow experimenters Newton made one trial 'crucial' and also suppressed most of the details of the procedures he had used.

Nowhere in the earlier version of his lectures did Newton provide a clear demonstration of his doctrine of the immutability of the colour displayed by 'primitive' rays. There was no 'crucial' experiment. Instead, he rehearsed variations in the placing of screens, the illumination of the chamber in which the experiments were to be performed and the movement, position and quality of the prisms themselves. He proposed moving the first prism from its original place behind the first screen to a position between the sun and the screen. This was designed to remove the suspicion that the different angles of refraction of different rays might be due to different angles of incidence of sunlight at the first prism. He tried covering the leading side of the second prism with black paper pierced with a single hole, in order to admit only a few rays to the second refraction. In his sixth lecture he also changed the orientation of the two prisms so that sometimes they were crossed, and at others parallel.

While enriching the possible tactics of prismatic trials, Newton also addressed the problem of prism quality and design. He was making prisms into experimental instruments. These instruments were supposed to demonstrate a novel and complex doctrine of the origin of colour. Colours were not generated by modifications of light inside prisms. Refractions analysed light into its constituent rays. This doctrine would not stand if it could be shown that irregularities in Newton's prisms were the cause of dispersion. Furthermore, his prisms had to be capable of separating 'primitive' colour-making rays. He identified three troubles with common prisms: their small angles, their refractive powers and most importantly, the fact that common prisms were often tinged with colour and vitiated with bubbles and veins. He lectured that

> instead of the glass prisms commonly sold (which are too slender) you must use broader ones, such as those you can make from glass plates highly polished on both sides and joined together in the form of a small prism-shaped vessel; the vessel should be filled with very clear water and sealed all around with cement . . . Those prisms, moreover, that are made wholly of glass are often tinged with some colour, such as green or yellow.

He repeated this advice in the sixth lecture when discussing total internal reflection and later recommended that the best glass was that 'used to make mirrors.'. Therefore, much of Newton's work centred on ways of telling whether prisms were working 'properly'. Only properly working prisms could show that his doctrine was right. To persuade his audience of this doctrine, he would have to persuade them to change the way they used prisms and to change the prisms they used.

This task proved troublesome during the 1670s. There was an ambiguity about the lessons Newton claimed his experiments taught. In the forty-fourth experiment of his notebook of 1666, Newton had derived two important consequences: first, blue-making rays were refracted more than red; second, these rays could not be split into further colours. But during the 1670s these two consequences were often separated from each other. The second lesson raised more trouble, because it was not easy to make 'uncompounded colours' with common prisms. Special instruments and protocols were needed. All colours 'proper to bodys' were mixed, as Newton noted in 1666. Furthermore, even in his lectures Newton had trouble demonstrating immutability. In his sixth lecture he briefly commented that he would 'show afterward' that 'no light of any simple colour can be changed in its colour . . . in refractions. But he did not honour this promise in the original lectures. He did so only in the revised version he completed in October 1674. Writing in the midst of his disputes with critics, he conceded that the two prism trial 'is not yet perfect in all respects'. In this trial, a red-making ray from the first prism did not display further colours when refracted through a second prism placed transverse to the first. However, if the second prism was placed parallel to the first, then the red-making ray also displayed yellow colours after the second refraction. This seemed to challenge the fundamental doctrine of immutability. To ward off this possible challenge, made all too obvious in the responses he was receiving from his correspondents in London and elsewhere, Newton changed the experimental protocol. He now stipulated that the holes through which the light was transmitted should be made as small as possible, while he also claimed that the best way to perform the experiment was to subject each ray to *many successive refractions*, not just two. He held that immutability would be proven if 'the apparent changes [in colour] would become smaller by repeated refractions, because simpler colours would arise at every step'. As Alan Shapiro has pointed out, this was just the strategy Newton used much later in his published *Opticks*. But he did not make these details clear to any of his colleagues during the seventeenth century.

The differences in presentation fomented dispute between Newton and his audiences. In the letter to Oldenburg of February 1672, Newton selected some of his earlier trials, rewrote his autobiography, omitted many important details, notably those on prism quality and design, and revised some of the lessons these experiments were supposed to teach. The *experimentum crucis* was a simplified and revised form of large numbers of experiments given in the third and sixth Cambridge lectures. The first prism was placed between the Sun and the first screen and then turned slowly by hand. The lesson Newton derived here was the existence of differing refrangibility, not any consequence about the specificity or immutability of colour. But elsewhere in the letter Newton did discuss his commitment to immutability of colour. He claimed boldly that 'when any one sort of Rays hath been well parted from those of other kinds, it hath afterwards obstinately retained its colour, notwithstanding my utmost endeavours to change it'. He mentioned efforts involving prisms, coloured reflectors and thin films, but gave no 'history' of these attempts.

The technique for making a 'well parted ray' was not spelt out. The criterion for a 'well parted ray' seemed tautological to some of Newton's audience. 'Well parted rays' were only recognisable as just those which did not display further colours after a refraction, yet the doctrine in question was whether the colours displayed by such rays could be changed. In May 1673, for example, Newton told the Dutch natural philosopher Christiaan Huygens that he had given sufficient details for 'them who know how to examin whether a colour be simple or compounded', while in June he wrote again that the proposition of immutability 'might be further proved apart by experiments, too long to be here described'. This reticence was important, for several reasons. Ronald Laymon has suggested that Newton's *experimentum crucis* only works if 'idealized descriptions of the experiments are used'. Newton's 'idealization' of his group of trials demanded that his prisms be seen as commonplace and the lay-out of his trials be treated in a highly abstracted form. This was part of his effort to win assent to his new doctrine. Furthermore, many of his readers assumed that the experiments reported by Newton to Oldenburg from 1672, particularly the *experimentum crucis*, were designed to demonstrate immutability *of colour*. Thus if the experimenters could show immutability was false, they held that Newton's doctrine would fall. Since Newton held that the demonstration of immutability, or of specific refrangibility, demanded prisms handled in special ways, the details of experimental tactics and of instruments were fundamental items in this dispute.

Experimenters Debate 'Mr. Newton's Directions' (1672–78)

The response to Newton's first paper showed that the techniques for handling prisms were an important part of the dispute about his claims. This response varied a great deal. Many found Newton's work dramatic and compelling. For them, Newton became 'our happy wonder of ingenuity and best broacher of *new light*'. But not all were persuaded. These differences evince contrasting experimental technologies and philosophies. In London, Hooke replicated trials with two prisms but denied their decisive role. Newton was also countered by a group of English Jesuits at Liège, including the mathematics professor Francis Line, his student John Gascoines and the theology professor Anthony Lucas. The Jesuits initially proffered challenges to the presuppositions of Newton's trials and series of experiments of their own. When told by Newton that the *experimentum crucis* was the only trial to be examined, they reported a failure to replicate his alleged result. There was here no agreement on proper use and design of prisms. Nor was there agreement on the meaning and authority of the *experimentum crucis*.

Critics often contested Newton's implied claim that the *experimentum crucis* rendered the performance of long series of trials unnecessary. For example, Newton criticised Lucas for his effort to perform large numbers of optical trials. 'Instead of a multitude of things', Lucas should 'try only the *Experimentum Crucis*. For it is not number of Experiments, but weight to be regarded; and where one will do, what need many?' Yet this was not always the view which Newton and his interlocutors expressed. Newton himself denied in 1677 that 'I brought ye *Experimentum Crucis* to prove all'. Hooke denied that this so-called 'crucial experiment' proved anything decisive: 'it is not that, which he soe calls, will doe the turne, for the same phaenomenon will be salved by my hypothesis as well as by his'. Indeed, Hooke implied that one of Newton's principal failings was the small number of trials the Cambridge professor reported, in contrast with the 'many hundreds of tryalls' which Hooke himself had performed and described. Hooke said he had not erected an hypothesis 'without first trying some hundreds of expts'.

Hooke was writing a week after reading Newton's first paper on colours. Hooke, Boyle and the mathematician and divine Seth Ward were appointed by the Society to report on Newton's letter when it was read in London on February 8, 1672. Hooke also recalled his 'crucial experiment' of 1665, one which did not use a prism. While he attributed great weight to the simple 'Experiment or Observation of Crystal', which, he held, decisively proved his own hypothesis of colour, he did not privilege the prism in the way Newton sought to achieve. His favoured experiments, used tellingly against Descartes in 1665, involved mica, thin plates and glasses filled with variously coloured liquids. He did not pay attention to the detailed flaws and corrections of commercial prisms which Newton charted in his Cambridge lectures. Newton sought to minimise what he saw as the defects of these objects: but bubbles, veins and tints provided Hooke with opportunities for further mechanical ingenuity. Hooke and Newton had different experimental technologies in their treatment of these devices and they drew very different conclusions from their trials.

In April and May 1672, Hooke showed the Society a series of trials with two prisms, including one which demonstrated that 'rays of light being separated by one prism into distinct colours, the reflection [sic] made by another prism does not alter those colours'. By June, he had also replicated the *experimentum crucis*: yet he still insisted that 'I think it not an *Experimentum crucis*, as I may possibly shew hereafter'. He told the Royal Society's President that this trial might prove that 'colourd Radiations' maintain fixed refrangibilities: it did *not* prove what Hooke claimed Newton wanted to prove, that there was a 'colourd ray in the light before refraction'. Indeed, Newton did not seem consistent in his account of what this trial showed. In February, he said that it demonstrated that there were differently refrangible rays in light without reference to colour; in June, when publicly answering Hooke, he said that it demonstrated that 'rays of divers colours considered apart do at equall incidences suffer unequall refractions', so raising the issue of specific colour.

Throughout their subsequent exchanges on prismatic colours, which continued to 1678, Hooke accepted what he took to be matters of fact in Newton's trials, and freely acknowledged that his replications had worked. But Hooke read Newton as arguing for specific refrangibility and for immutability in the 'crucial' experiment, and he denied that this trial was persuasive. Thus when Newton was at a meeting of the Society in March 1675, he apparently heard Hooke confirm that the trials reported three years earlier had been replicated. However, at the same meetings, Hooke developed his own vibration theory of light and colour, citing new experiments on diffraction to show that 'colours may be made without refraction' and that his own doctrine could successfully save all the phenomena of colour. By the end of 1675, Newton was prepared to claim that Hooke had 'accommodated his Hypothesis to this my suggestion' of the origin of colours. Hooke, in his turn, was reported as believing Newton had plagiarised his 'suggestion' from the *Micrographia*. Despite attempts at reconciliation between the protagonists, it appeared that Newton's 'crucial' experiment had not acquired authority, nor a fixed meaning. As late as 1690, Hooke told the Royal Society that he was aware of no 'Better' theory of colour than his own, thus writing Newton out of the history of optics.

Newton and his Jesuit critics also discussed rival prism techniques and the meaning of the *experimentum crucis*. In spring 1672, Newton already found himself compelled to give fuller details of his trials than those presented in his initial paper. Newton sent Oldenburg a diagram of the experiment and conceded that 'I am apt to beleive [sic] that some of the experiments may seem obscure by reason of the brevity wherewith I writ them which should have been described more largely and explained with schemes if they had been then intended for the publick'. The reaction of Line and the colleagues who continued his work from autumn 1674 showed how hard it was for Newton to achieve authority over his 'publick'. It demonstrated the problems of achieving agreed replication. During 1675, Newton appealed to the Royal Society in order to authorise his claim that the 'crucial' experiment had been replicated in London and was, allegedly, easy to perform anywhere: 'it may be tryed (though not so perfectly) even without darkning a room, or the expence of any more time then a qter of an hower'.

As the argument with the Liège experimenters became angrier, during 1676, Newton was told that they had often done their own optical experiments before witnesses at Line's house: 'we think it probable he hath tried his experiment thrice for Mr. Newton's once'. Gascoines suggested that only some unreported difference in the arrangement or type of prism could explain this conflicting result. In January and February 1676, Newton responded to this challenge with many more details of his own trials. He gave the dimension of the holes used to admit light. He re-emphasised the placing of the prism at minimum deviation and said the trial worked best when the sky was clear. He advised on the best way of darkening the room. Importantly, he said Gascoines should 'get a prism with an angle about 60 or 65 degrees . . . If his prism be pretty nearly equilateral, such as I suppose are usually sold in other places as well as in *England*, he may make use of the biggest angle'.

These specifications were designed to elicit a replication of the experiment in Liège. 'Ye business being about matter of fact was not proper to be decided by writing but by trying it before competent witnesses'. Newton implied that if the Jesuits could not make these experiments work, then it must be due to their wilful incompetence rather than to subtle differences in technique. Newton wanted pictures, because 'a scheme or two . . . will make the business plainer'. The trial was demonstrated at the Society in April 1676 and Oldenburg told Gascoines and his colleagues of this allegedly decisive success. However, the immediate response of the Liège natural philosophers showed that this result was not compelling. On the contrary: Lucas immediately answered Oldenburg's letter with the comment that 'I was much rejoyced to see the tryalls of that Illustrious Company, agree soe exactly with ours here, tho in somewhat ours disagree from Mr. Newton'. Lucas and his colleagues interpreted the Royal Society's experiment as reconcilable with their own. They continued to produce evidence which they held refuted Newton's doctrine. Newton was astonished: the Royal Society 'found them succeed as I affirmed'. Exchanges with Lucas continued until 1678 when Newton violently withdrew from all such dispute.

In this correspondence the status of the *experimentum crucis* was challenged at once. Lucas reported a set of new experiments designed to show that different colour-making rays did not differ in refrangibility. Newton told Lucas to try only the *experimentum crucis*. Lucas did so in October 1676, but without conceding its privileged role or the lesson which Newton claimed it taught. Lucas appealed to the precedent of Boyle's pneumatics, which had been supported by 'a vast number of new experiments'. He asked why he should accept Newton's stricture that the controversy must hinge on the outcome of one trial. Lucas also argued that the experiment, if successful, would not show intrinsically different refrangibilities in different colour-making rays. Lucas read Newton as seeking to prove a doctrine about colour with his 'crucial' trial, not merely a simpler result about unequal refraction; and he read Newton as illegitimately basing his authority on a single trial, rather than a mass of evidence. Newton, once again, was furious with what he saw as a failure to grasp the sense, or the authority, of his key experiment. He contemplated a publication of a major treatise on his optical work. The alternative was silence.

Newton was drawn into a final exchange with Lucas. For when Lucas did try the *experimentum crucis* in autumn 1676, he reported a result different from that attributed to Newton. He reported that even though he had worked 'exactly according to Mr. Newtons directions' he found as 'a result of many trialls' that violet rays displayed a 'considerable quantity of red ones' after the second refraction. Newton's delayed reply re-emphasised the meaning he wished to give this trial: 'you think I brought it to prove that rays of different colours are differently refrangible'. Newton held that this thought was mistaken. Yet there were grounds for Lucas's reading. Recall Newton's public statement of June 1672 that the 'crucial' experiment proved that 'rays of divers colours considered apart do at equall incidences suffer unequall refractions'. But Newton told Lucas that 'I bring it to prove (without respect to colours) that light consists in rays differently refrangible'. Here Newton insisted that the crucial experiment taught nothing about colours. He did so because he had to discredit Lucas's version of this experiment. Lucas's report suggested that Newton was wrong about the constant colour displayed by truly uncompounded rays. So Newton replied that the experiment was not designed to prove the homogeneity of 'uncompounded' rays. This answer was directly linked with the problem of the quality and design of prisms. Newton's other tactic in his attack on Lucas was to challenge the Jesuit's instruments. Newton alleged that they were incapable of producing 'uncompounded' colours.

The controversy demonstrates a central trouble of replication and instrumentation. Further work was necessary to establish whether the two men were discussing the 'same' experiment. Newton said that since Lucas's experiment was different from the 'crucial' experiment, its different result did not discredit that experiment. Lucas insisted that he had 'but follow'd the way which [Newton] himselfe had track'd out for me'. At several points in this exchange, Newton drew attention to the need for proper prisms. In August 1676, he reported trials which compared changing prism angles with changes in the length of the spectrum produced. He then advised that the *experimentum crucis* must be made with 'Prisms which refract so much as to make the length of the Image five times its breadth, and rather more than less; for, otherwise Experiments will not succeed so plainly with others as they have done with me'. He also pointed out the need for prisms with plane or convex sides when making spectra: Newton suspected that Lucas was using a concave instrument. Lucas confirmed that this was so in October; later, he also considered 'the difference of glasse the prismes are made of'.

These details affected the debate on changes of colour displayed by refracted rays, since Newton claimed that the ability to make a wide spectrum affected the ability to separate genuinely 'uncompounded' rays. He instructed Lucas on the character of 'compound' rays. Lucas was wrong 'to take your ordinary colours of the Prism to be my [un]compounded ones'. So Newton emphasised that Lucas had not obtained properly 'uncompounded' rays because he had the wrong prisms and used them badly. Lucas believed that none of these differences in *prisms* could explain why he had managed to change the colour of light rays by refraction. He told Newton that 'if all rayes differently coloured had an unequall refrangibility', as Newton apparently believed, then 'the variety of prismes could no more refract different colours *equally*, that it can change the nature of rayes'. To reach closure here, Newton would have had to persuade Lucas to change his prisms and then, as Newton himself did, to interpret these changes as the correction of important defects. In March 1678 Lucas did report difficulty in getting prisms with good glass. But closure was not accomplished: instead, as we have seen, from summer 1678 Newton broke off any further debate on the issue.

Newton's arguments with Hooke and Lucas show that the *status of the experimentum crucis* was hard to fix. There was no agreed criterion for a competent prism experiment or for a good prism. Only when the status of the experiment was fixed did this criterion become available. Replicability and meaning both hinged on the establishment of this emblem. Some of Newton's audience read the experiment as a claim about colour immutability. Newton sometimes provided them with grounds for this reading. By the 1720s, in fact, he seemed to have come to agree with this reading. That is, the experiment which Newton now counted as his decisive one had a new and fixed meaning: 'refracted light does not change its colour'. This slogan appeared on a technically defective but important emblem of Newton's programme, the vignette of the *experimentum crucis* which Newton designed for the 1722 French edition of his magisterial *Opticks*. 'Cherubs and spectators' were excised from this design so as to give pride of place to the prisms, which testified to the truth of this incontrovertible fact of immutability of colour. Once this fact was established and firmly wedded to the instruments, a means then existed for discriminating good prisms and competent experimental arrangements. The process by which this criterion acquired self-evidence will be examined in the final sections of this chapter.

'An Unhappy Choice of Prisms'; The Achievement of 'Transparency' (1704–22)

Those who eventually accepted the emblematic status of the *experimentum crucis* and Newton's prisms produced a story which explained why the experiment and the instruments had not swayed critics in the 1670s. In popular texts such as Voltaire's *Elements of Sir Isaac Newton's Philosophy* (1738) and Algarotti's *Newtonianism for Ladies* (1737) it was claimed that those who had not succeeded in replicating Newton's trials 'had not been happy enough in the Choice of . . . Prisms'. They were recording a rather common view. Experimenters who had reported trials which differed from those of Newton were now dismissed from consideration because their instruments must have been defective. This claim depended on a prior consensus on the status of Newton's trials and his instruments. After assuming the Presidency of the Royal Society in 1703, producing the *Opticks* and working closely with the experimental philosopher J. T. Desaguliers, Newton was in a position to claim that any optical experiment, if performed with the right prisms, would guarantee the truth of his doctrine. In London, the prism had become a 'transparent' instrument. This was an accomplishment of Newton and his allies. It demanded a reconstruction of the record of the optical controversies. This reconstruction involved both the public exposition of new prism techniques and a reinterpretation of previous failures to replicate Newton's claims. As Newton took power over the key resources of experimental philosophy, Newtonian optics acquired a disciplinary history and a standardised technology.

The appearance of Newton's *Opticks* was a key event in this process. Consideration of its opening sections shows how Newton reconstructed his trials to make his authority inside the experimental community. Initial passages described ways of separating 'uncompounded' rays. This had been a key trouble of the 1670s. Then, Newton had faced a dilemma: he could, apparently, only sway his colleagues with prisms they were used to employing. Yet he reckoned that with these, an 'uncompounded' ray could not easily be made. So it was hard to spell out a decisive experiment to prove that such rays could be made and did not display further new colours when passed through a second prism. The work of Lucas or of the French experimenter Edmé Mariotte made this problem only too clear. Like Lucas, Mariotte had performed trials in the 1670s which purported to challenge the *experimentum crucis* and demonstrate that the doctrine of colour immutability was false. He had considerable expertise in experimental optics. Within a year of Newton's first paper on light and colour, he had conducted trials in Paris on the mutability of colours which challenged Newton's claims about the hues of 'uncompounded' rays.

In his book, Mariotte developed an anti-Cartesian version of the modification hypothesis, supposing that the colour of a light ray could be changed in refraction. In his version of Newton's experiment with two prisms, he did not place the first prism at minimum deviation, nor did he place a screen immediately after this prism to collimate the rays produced. He used a white card to separate out a single ray after the first refraction and then examined what happened to this ray when it was refracted a second time. Mariotte was confident that this arrangement allowed him to make well separated rays. His card was at least 30 feet from the first prism, displaying a spectrum of a similar width to that Newton reported. He also ensured that 'the room is very dark and no sensible light passes through the slit in the card apart from that which is coloured'. Yet he reported that a purely violet ray displayed red and yellow tinges after the second refraction. Assuming that Newton's whole theory was supposed to stand or fall by this experiment, Mariotte concluded that 'the ingenious hypothesis of Mr. Newton must not at all be accepted'. This single report of a single refutation of a view Newton had not quite expressed in print was an important resource in European responses to Newton's optical doctrine. Mariotte was often cited, notably by Leibniz, as providing an important challenge to Newton's theory. Leibniz, Mariotte's 'old friend', repeatedly reminded correspondents of the challenge to the matter of fact of colour immutability which the trials of the 1670s suggested.

Newton's *Opticks*, painstakingly assembled during the 1690s, provided new resources with which to respond to these worries. Neither Lucas nor Mariotte was mentioned in the new book. Hooke, recently deceased, received only a cursory reference. Nor did Newton use the name *experimentum crucis* to sanctify the sixth experiment of the book, which used two prisms to prove constant refrangibility. Constancy of colour became at least as important a feature of his scheme. Thus Newton shifted the weight of his argument. The whole of the fourth proposition was devoted to a description of the way to make 'uncompounded' rays. At last, Newton gave a relatively full public account of the instruments 'sufficient for trying all the experiments in this book about simple light'. Notable techniques included the positioning of a lens before the first prism to diminish the incident image. He also detailed the kinds of glass to be used: recalling remarks made in the Cambridge lectures, he specified 'Glass free from Bubbles and Veins'. The prisms must have 'truly plane' sides, not convex as he had suggested to Lucas. The polish should be 'elaborate', not 'wrought with Putty' which produced 'little convex polite Risings like waves'. The edges of prisms and lenses should be covered in black paper. Yet he conceded that 'it's difficult to get Glass prisms fit for this Purpose', referring to his own practice of using vessels made of 'broken Looking-Glasses' filled with rain water and a lead salt to increase the refraction. Elsewhere, he discussed ways these water-filled vessels should be used and reported the failings of a prism 'made of a dark coloured Glass inclining to green'. When he replaced this with a prism of 'clear white Glass' he still found 'two or three little Bubbles' and covered the defective parts of the Prism with black paper. After 1704, Newton annotated his own copy of the book with further changes in specified prism angles and in details of liquids with which to fill prismatic vessels. Once again, these remarks changed the way prisms were to be handled and then assessed. The stage was set for the claim that unsuccessful replicators were using bad prisms. The book provided a range of such resources and Newton set out to get the Royal Society's experimenters to use them.

Newton used his power over the Society against his critics, notably what he perceived as a conspiracy headed by Leibniz and the writers of the Leipzig journal *Acta eruditorum*. This strategy exploited the resources of the Presidency and the expertise of the experimenters, Hauksbee and Desaguliers, in a campaign in which the allegedly superior quality of English prisms soon became important. As Steven Shapin has argued, this was a campaign with very important political resonances. One of its most dramatic aspects was the assertion of the authority of the experimenters of Augustan London. In late 1707, Leibniz heard about French interest in the *Opticks* and urged experimenters there to replicate the troubled Mariotte report. At the same moment, Newton ordered Hauksbee to begin trying the *Opticks* experiments before the Royal Society. These trials were then reported in the *Acta eruditorum*. As the war with Newton began to consume his attention, Leibniz decided to publish his views on Mariotte in the Leipzig journal. So from the summer of 1714, Newton directed Desaguliers, Hauksbee's successor, to show that uncompounded colours could be made, that Mariotte's instruments were defective and that Leibniz was wrong.

Desaguliers had to address the problem of *replicability*. To destroy Mariotte's credit, he had to show experiments which resembled those of the 1670s. If he used too many of the new protocols outlined in the *Opticks* it would appear that Mariotte had been reading Newton's initial reports correctly. If he did not use these new protocols, then he would fail to produce 'uncompounded' colours. Desaguliers turned to Newton for aid: the President helped draft the paper which appeared under Desaguliers's name in the *Philosophical Transactions*. The two men emphasised that previously printed reports were sufficient to allow replication. 'Some Gentlemen abroad' had 'complained that they had not found the Experiments answer, for want of sufficient Directions in *Sir Isaac Newton's Opticks;* tho' I had no other Directions than what I found there'. But Desaguliers also accepted that much new information was necessary to allow these trials to be successfully repeated. He allowed that Newton's original papers of the 1670s were inadequately detailed. A technique for separating monochromatic rays 'was not published before Sir Is. Newton's *Opticks* came abroad' in 1704. This explained why Lucas and Mariotte had 'reported that the [crucial] Experiment did not succeed'. Furthermore, Desaguliers added many significant details even to the fuller descriptions of the *Opticks*, including the lenses and prisms to be used in the optical trials. Prisms should be made of the green glass used for the object glasses of telescopes. 'The best white prisms', it emerged, were inadequate for the purpose, being 'commonly full of veins'. Desaguliers' tactic, following Newton's advice, was to marry the techniques for making uncompounded colours described in the fourth proposition of the *Opticks*, including the careful treatment of clear glass prisms and the use of a collimating lens, with the lay-out of experiment six, that which most closely resembled the original *experimentum crucis* of 1672. Desaguliers now did what Newton had not done. He revived the name *experimentum crucis* for this completely reconstructed trial. Part of this reconstruction involved the claim that the 'crucial' experiment demonstrated colour homogeneity rather than specific refrangibility. Desaguliers tailored his experiments for effective witnessing. Spectators were each given a hand-held prism through which to view the spectrum cast on the final screen. Desaguliers made all these important changes and conceded that 'several have confessed to me that they at first used to fail in this experiment'. But it was essential that he stipulate that he had followed Newton's text to the letter, with no other resource at his disposal. Hence his insinuation that he had relied only on Newton's *publicly available* accounts.

These experiments now had to be deployed in public. After a dry run at his house in Westminster, Desaguliers showed them to the Society. In early 1715, they were displayed to visiting natural philosophers from Holland, Italy and France. The repertoire of reformulated experiments soon became the prize exemplar of Newtonian optics. The visit of the French in 1715 was swiftly followed by successful replications in Paris and elsewhere. Two aspects of this work are of importance for the career of the optical instruments: first, Newton and Desaguliers worked hard to make Mariotte's result depend on his bad glassware. Desaguliers announced in the *Philosophical Transactions* that he had proven this in 1714 and 'still shews it to those who desire to see it', presumably during his courses of experimental philosophy in the capital. News of these lectures, together with the view about the insufficiency of Mariotte's experiment, were then reproduced in Desaguliers's publications and by his colleague Pierre Coste in a French version of the *Opticks* in 1720. Second, they also asserted that any experimenter must use the prisms which were available to the London natural philosophers. Personal visits to London were significant means by which natural philosophers could be won to this new practice. Once local agreement had been accomplished at the Society and among its audience in France, Italy and Holland on the doctrine of colour immutability, it was possible to define good prisms as those which displayed this result. The local and tenuous nature of this agreement was demonstrated by subsequent exchanges with European experimenters.

* * *

Part 5
RATIONAL MECHANICS

Introduction

Rational mechanics, or to put it in more familiar language, the science of dynamics, was the very heart of Newtonian science. It was also the heart of the restructuring of natural philosophy in the seventeenth century that historians have come to call the Scientific Revolution. Newton's role was to bring the Scientific Revolution to its culmination, largely by completing and perfecting rational mechanics.

In the first decades of the seventeenth century, Galileo created a new science of motion, that is, a new science of mechanics. It contained two central aspects—on the one hand, a conception of motion radically different from the prevailing one; on the other hand, an ideal of what the science of motion, and by implication all science, should be, again different from the prevailing one. The new conception of motion was substantially identical to what we know today as the principle of inertia. Where the old conception held that a body will move only as long as some agent moves it, Galileo insisted that motion perseveres and requires no agent. A body set in motion on a perfectly smooth horizontal plane will continue to move forever if the plane has no limit, and on the less than perfectly smooth planes with which we are familiar, it takes some time, contrary to what the earlier philosophy asserted, for friction to bring a moving body to rest.

Galileo fitted this conception of motion into the ideal that a proper science of motion should be mathematical. In his hands, this ideal was concerned mainly with motion in a vertical line near the surface of the earth: free fall. He often referred to this as a natural motion. Everywhere on the earth, heavy bodies fall in the same way. Denying that some bodies have positive levity, as the prevailing philosophy maintained, Galileo contended that all bodies are heavy, though some are less dense than others so that bodies less dense than water or air do not descend in those media. He was convinced that the free fall common to all heavy bodies had to be described mathematically if it were to be described adequately, and for this purpose he defined the concept of uniformly accelerated motion, a motion in which equal increments of velocity are added in equal periods of time (equivalent to the formula still taught at the beginning of introductory courses in physics, $v = at$). He proceeded then to deduce mathematically the consequences of such a motion. Distances covered in a uniformly accelerated motion from rest increase in proportion to the time squared; that is, in our formula, $s = 1/2(at^2)$. Velocities acquired in fall from different heights are proportional to the square root of the heights (or, $v^2 = 2as$). He applied his formulae to

In order not to encumber the reader with footnotes we have composed a Biographical Register, in which all the people mentioned in the text are identified, and a Glossary, in which technical terms are briefly explicated and such things as organizations, places, publications, and manuscript collections are identified. Both the Biographical Register and the Glossary are located near the end of the volume.

inclined planes, which have a vertical component, and devised experiments using inclined planes to support the validity of the definition of uniformly accelerated motion by testing whether the consequences do in fact appear. He demonstrated that compound motions, such as those of projectiles, can also be described in similar mathematical terms; it was Galileo who discovered that the trajectory of a projectile, again under ideal conditions of no resistance, is a parabola.

Galileo's science of mechanics was part of the new natural philosophy that Newton discovered as an undergraduate in Cambridge. Newton embraced the new ideal wholeheartedly; his entire rational mechanics expressed the same ideal and carried it to a higher level of generality. What he did not find in Galileo, or in any of the students of mechanics who had followed him, was a science of dynamics that would describe consistently not only motions, but also the forces that produce them. Such a science would be universal, because it would be applicable to all motions; it would not be confined to the accelerated motions of heavy bodies at the surface of the earth. In August 1684, a visit from Edmond Halley led Newton to compose a short tract on orbital motion that is known as *De motu*, the first draft of what grew to be the *Principia* during the following two and a half years. In some respects *De motu* is surprising. In it, Newton succeeded in demonstrating an orbital dynamics that produced Kepler's three laws as necessary consequences, but it did not contain an explicit enunciation of a single one of the three laws of motion that we associate with Newton. Most of what we reproduce in this section was created by Newton during the early months of 1685 as he worked at revising and expanding *De motu*.

One concept central to the *Principia* was present in *De motu*, the concept of centripetal force, which expressed the perception that circular or orbital motion is an accelerated motion and that a body will continue to move in a closed orbit only so long as a force toward the center (centripetal means "seeking the center") holds it in that path. Newton coined the name "centripetal force" *(vis centripeta)* to replace the then-current and confusing notion of "centrifugal force" ("fleeing the center"). He had not yet arrived, however, at the generalized conception of force that finally found expression in the second law. During the early months of 1685, he defined nearly twenty different concepts before he discarded most of them and settled on the ones included in the *Principia*. A major discovery at this time was his realization that a consistent dynamics demanded a rigorous idea of what is meant by quantity of matter, and the classical idea of mass, defined and given its name by Newton, was one of the products of his investigation.

Most crucial of all was the conception of motion. In 1684, Newton had not yet embraced the principle of inertia. *De motu* worked with the idea that a body in uniform motion is carried by a force internal to it. Echoes of that conception can still be heard in the language of Proposition 1 of the *Principia*, in Newton's demonstration of Kepler's law of areas. As he worked in the early months of 1685 at defining a general science of dynamics that would describe equally well all motions, not just free fall at the surface of the earth, but also (and most important) orbital motion in the heavens, he found the principle of inertia indispensable. Thus he arrived at Definition 3, in which he converted the innate force that sustained uniform motion in *De motu* into a new form, which effectively installed the word *inertia* in the language of science, and the first law, which remains today the definitive statement of the principle of inertia.

The principle of inertia implies a relativity, the impossibility of determining that any inertial frame of reference is at rest. Newton found relativity, which he encountered in the philosophy of Descartes, dangerously close to atheism. As he embraced the principle of inertia, he inserted the concepts of absolute space and time, which he intended as bulwarks against atheism. See also in this regard his statements in the General Scholium to the *Principia*, which we have included in Part 8, Theology (below).

Along with the basic principles of Newtonian dynamics, the definitions, and the laws of motion, we have included in this part a skeletal outline of the *Principia*'s argument, in which Newton worked out the necessary consequences of his dynamics. For the most part, we include only his statements of propositions; we do cite three crucial demonstrations as indications of his procedure. In the early propositions, he demonstrated that his system entails Kepler's laws of planetary motion as well as Galileo's kinematics of terrestrial motion. The three demonstrations we reproduce are of Proposition 1 (the area law, or Kepler's second law), Proposition 6, (the general expression for the centripetal force to hold a body in any curved motion), and Proposition 11 (that an elliptical orbit entails an inverse-square force toward one focus, that is, Kepler's first law). Propositions 57, 63, and 66 explore the consequences of mutual attractions. Proposition 66 has twenty-two corollaries, which became the foundation of Newton's treatment of the moon (as its orbit around the earth is perturbed by the attraction of the sun), the tides, and a conical motion of the earth's axis (the results of the attractions of both the moon and the sun on an earth that is not perfectly spherical). Propositions 70 and 71 derive the law of attraction of a large body, such as the earth, that is composed of particles, all of which attract other particles of matter. In both the introduction and the scholium to Section 11, Newton insisted on the mathematical nature of his science of dynamics, which produces valid demonstrations regardless of the physical cause of what we call attractions.

In Book 2 of the *Principia* Newton examined motion through physical (and therefore resisting) media and the motions of such media. The climax of the book lay in Section 9 in which Newton explored the dynamic conditions of vortical motion. The explication of the heavens that was accepted at the time Newton wrote was Descartes's theory of vortices. The Scholium to Section 9, which was also the conclusion of Book 2, sums up Newton's argument of why the theory of vortices cannot be true.

There have been few episodes in the intellectual history of humanity more fraught with significance than those months near the beginning of 1685 when Newton formulated his science of dynamics. The whole of modern science and the whole of the modern world, which is unthinkable without science, hung then in the balance.

Newton's "Author's Preface to the Reader" of the *Principia* †

Since the ancients (as we are told by *Pappus*) esteemed the science of mechanics of greatest importance in the investigation of natural things, and the moderns, rejecting substantial forms and occult qualities, have endeavored to subject the phenomena of nature to the laws of mathematics, I have in this treatise cultivated mathematics as far as it relates to philosophy. The ancients considered mechanics in a twofold respect; as rational, which proceeds accurately by demonstration, and practical. To practical mechanics all the manual arts belong, from which mechanics took its name. But as artificers do not work with perfect accuracy, it comes to pass that mechanics is so distinguished from geometry that what is perfectly accurate is called geometrical; what is less so, is called mechanical. However, the errors are not in the art, but in the artificers. He that works with less accuracy is an imperfect mechanic; and if any could work with perfect accuracy, he would be the most perfect mechanic of all, for the description of right lines and circles, upon which geometry is founded, belongs to mechanics. Geometry does not teach us to draw these lines, but requires them to be drawn, for it requires that the learner should first be taught to describe these accurately before he enters upon geometry, then it shows how by these operations problems may be solved. To describe right lines and circles are problems, but not geometrical problems. The solution of these problems is required from mechanics, and by geometry the use of them, when so solved, is shown; and it is the glory of geometry that from those few principles, brought from without, it is able to produce so many things. Therefore geometry is founded in mechanical practice, and is nothing but that part of universal mechanics which accurately proposes and demonstrates the art of measuring. But since the manual arts are chiefly

† Isaac Newton, *Mathematical Principles of Natural Philosophy* and *System of the World*, translated by Andrew Motte, revised by Florian Cajori (Berkeley and Los Angeles: University of California Press, 1934 and later printings), pp. xvii–xviii. This preface, dated May 8, 1686, appeared at the head of the first edition of the *Principia* (London, 1687). See note on the Cajori translation on p. 116.

employed in the moving of bodies, it happens that geometry is commonly referred to their magnitude, and mechanics to their motion. In this sense rational mechanics will be the science of motions resulting from any forces whatsoever, and of the forces required to produce any motions, accurately proposed and demonstrated. This part of mechanics, as far as it extended to the five powers which relate to manual arts, was cultivated by the ancients, who considered gravity (it not being a manual power) no otherwise than in moving weights by those powers. But I consider philosophy rather than arts and write not concerning manual but natural powers, and consider chiefly those things which relate to gravity, levity, elastic force, the resistance of fluids, and the like forces, whether attractive or impulsive; and therefore I offer this work as the mathematical principles of philosophy, for the whole burden of philosophy seems to consist in this—from the phenomena of motions to investigate the forces of nature, and then from these forces to demonstrate the other phenomena; and to this end the general propositions in the first and second Books are directed. In the third Book I give an example of this in the explication of the System of the World; for by the propositions mathematically demonstrated in the former Books, in the third I derive from the celestial phenomena the forces of gravity with which bodies tend to the sun and the several planets. Then from these forces, by other propositions which are also mathematical, I deduce the motions of the planets, the comets, the moon, and the sea. I wish we could derive the rest of the phenomena of Nature by the same kind of reasoning from mechanical principles, for I am induced by many reasons to suspect that they may all depend upon certain forces by which the particles of bodies, by some causes hitherto unknown, are either mutually impelled towards one another, and cohere in regular figures, or are repelled and recede from one another. These forces being unknown, philosophers have hitherto attempted the search of Nature in vain; but I hope the principles here laid down will afford some light either to this or some truer method of philosophy.

In the publication of this work the most acute and universally learned Mr. *Edmund Halley* not only assisted me in correcting the errors of the press and preparing the geometrical figures, but it was through his solicitations that it came to be published; for when he had obtained of me my demonstrations of the figure of the celestial orbits, he continually pressed me to communicate the same to the *Royal Society*, who afterwards, by their kind encouragement and entreaties, engaged me to think of publishing them. But after I had begun to consider the inequalities of the lunar motions, and had entered upon some other things relating to the laws and measures of gravity and other forces; and the figures that would be described by bodies attracted according to given laws; and the motion of several bodies moving among themselves; the motion of bodies in resisting mediums; the forces, densities, and motions, of mediums;

the orbits of the comets, and such like, I deferred that publication till I had made a search into those matters, and could put forth the whole together. What relates to the lunar motions (being imperfect), I have put all together in the corollaries of Prop. LXVI, to avoid being obliged to propose and distinctly demonstrate the several things there contained in a method more prolix than the subject deserved and interrupt the series of the other propositions. Some things, found out after the rest, I chose to insert in places less suitable, rather than change the number of the propositions and the citations. I heartily beg that what I have here done may be read with forbearance; and that my labors in a subject so difficult may be examined, not so much with the view to censure, as to remedy their defects.

Paper of Directions Given by Newton to Bentley Respecting the Books to Be Read before Endeavouring to Read and Understand the *Principia* †

Next after Euclid's Elements the Elements of the Conic sections are to be understood. And for this end you may read either the first part of the *Elementa Curvarum* of John De Witt, or De la Hire's late treatise of the conick sections, or Dr Barrow's epitome of Apollonius.

For Algebra read first Bartholin's introduction and then peruse such Problems as you will find scattered up and down in the Commentaries on Cartes's Geometry and other Alegraical [*sic*] writings of Francis Schooten. I do not mean that you should read over all those Commentaries, but only the solutions of such Problems as you will here and there meet with. You may meet with De Witt's *Elementa curvarum* and Bartholin's introduction bound up together with Carte's Geometry and Schooten's commentaries.

For Astronomy read first the short account of the Copernican System in the end of Gassendus's Astronomy and then so much of Mercator's Astronomy as concerns the same system and the new discoveries made in the heavens by Telescopes in the Appendix.

These are sufficient for understanding my book: but if you can procure Hugenius's *Horologium oscillatorium*, the perusal of that will make you much more ready.

At the first perusal of my Book it's enough if you understand the Propositions with some of the Demonstrations which are easier then the rest. For when you understand the easier they will afterwards give you light into the harder. When you have read the first 60 pages, pass on to

† *The Correspondence of Isaac Newton*, eds. H. W. Turnbull, J. F. Scott, A. Rupert Hall, and Laura Tilling, 7 vols. (Cambridge: Cambridge University Press, 1959–77), vol. 3, pp. 155–56. Reprinted with the permission of Cambridge University Press. Richard Bentley, an aspiring young cleric who would go on to establish himself as England's greatest classical scholar, set out to master the *Principia* in 1691. He applied to Newton for assistance and received Newton's suggestion of helpful reading probably about July of that year.

the 3d Book and when you see the design of that you may turn back to such Propositions as you shall have a desire to know, or peruse the whole in order if you think fit.

Definitions †

Definition 1

The quantity of matter is the measure of the same, arising from its density and bulk conjointly.

Thus air of a double density, in a double space, is quadruple in quantity; in a triple space, sextuple in quantity. The same thing is to be understood of snow, and fine dust or powders, that are condensed by compression or liquefaction, and of all bodies that are by any causes whatever differently condensed. I have no regard in this place to a medium, if any such there is, that freely pervades the interstices between the parts of bodies. It is this quantity that I mean hereafter everywhere under the name of body or mass. And the same is known by the weight of each body, for it is proportional to the weight, as I have found by experiments on pendulums, very accurately made, which shall be shown hereafter.

Definition 2

The quantity of motion is the measure of the same, arising from the velocity and quantity of matter conjointly.

The motion of the whole is the sum of the motions of all the parts; and therefore in a body double in quantity, with equal velocity, the motion is double; with twice the velocity, it is quadruple.

Definition 3

The vis insita, or innate force of matter, is a power of resisting, by which every body, as much as in it lies, continues in its present state, whether it be of rest, or of moving uniformly forwards in a right line.

This force is always proportional to the body whose force it is and differs nothing from the inactivity of the mass, but in our manner of conceiving it. A body, from the inert nature of matter, is not without difficulty put out of its state of rest or motion. Upon which account, this

† Isaac Newton, *Mathematical Principles of Natural Philosophy* and *System of the World*, translated by Andrew Motte, revised by Florian Cajori (Berkeley and Los Angeles: University of California Press, 1934 and later printings), pp. 1–8. Copyright © 1934 and 1962 Regents of the University of California. Reprinted by permission. The *Principia* opens with the set of definitions of fundamental concepts that have formed the foundations of the science of mechanics and of modern science as a whole ever since. The scholium that follows the Definitions was a statement of personal conviction. See note on the Cajori translation on p. 116.

vis insita may, by a most significant name, be called inertia *(vis inertiæ)* or force of inactivity. But a body only exerts this force when another force, impressed upon it, endeavors to change its condition; and the exercise of this force may be considered as both resistance and impulse; it is resistance so far as the body, for maintaining its present state, opposes the force impressed; it is impulse so far as the body, by not easily giving way to the impressed force of another, endeavors to change the state of that other. Resistance is usually ascribed to bodies at rest, and impulse to those in motion; but motion and rest, as commonly conceived, are only relatively distinguished; nor are those bodies always truly at rest, which commonly are taken to be so.

Definition 4

An impressed force is an action exerted upon a body, in order to change its state, either of rest, or of uniform motion in a right line.

This force consists in the action only, and remains no longer in the body when the action is over. For a body maintains every new state it acquires, by its inertia only. But impressed forces are of different origins, as from percussion, from pressure, from centripetal force.

Definition 5

A centripetal force is that by which bodies are drawn or impelled, or any way tend, towards a point as to a centre.

Of this sort is gravity, by which bodies tend to the centre of the earth; magnetism, by which iron tends to the loadstone; and that force, whatever it is, by which the planets are continually drawn aside from the rectilinear motions, which otherwise they would pursue, and made to revolve in curvilinear orbits. A stone, whirled about in a sling, endeavors to recede from the hand that turns it; and by that endeavor, distends the sling, and that with so much the greater force, as it is revolved with the greater velocity, and as soon as it is let go, flies away. That force which opposes itself to this endeavor, and by which the sling continually draws back the stone towards the hand, and retains it in its orbit, because it is directed to the hand as the centre of the orbit, I call the centripetal force. And the same thing is to be understood of all bodies, revolved in any orbits. They all endeavor to recede from the centres of their orbits; and were it not for the opposition of a contrary force which restrains them to, and detains them in their orbits, which I therefore call centripetal, would fly off in right lines, with an uniform motion. A projectile, if it was not for the force of gravity, would not deviate towards the earth, but would go off from it in a right line, and that with an uniform motion, if the resistance of the air was taken away. It is by its gravity that it is drawn aside continually from its rectilinear course, and made to deviate towards the earth, more or less, according to the force of its gravity, and the velocity of its motion. The less its gravity is, or the quantity of its matter, or the greater the velocity with which it is projected, the less will it deviate from a rectilinear course, and the farther it will go. If a leaden ball, projected from the top of a mountain by the force of gunpowder, with a given velocity, and in a direction parallel to the horizon, is carried in a curved line to the distance of two miles before it falls to the ground; the same, if the resistance of the air were taken away, with a double or decuple velocity, would fly twice or ten times as far. And by increasing the velocity, we may at pleasure increase the distance to which it might be projected, and diminish the curvature of the line which it might describe, till at last it should fall at the distance of 10, 30, or 90 degrees, or even might go quite round the whole earth before it falls; or lastly, so that it might never fall to the earth, but go forwards into the celestial spaces, and proceed in its motion *in infinitum*. And after the same manner that a projectile, by the force of gravity, may be made to revolve in an orbit, and go round the whole earth, the moon also, either by the force of gravity, if it is endued with gravity, or by any other force, that impels it towards the earth, may be continually drawn aside towards the earth, out of the rectilinear way which by its innate force it would pursue; and would be made to revolve in the orbit which it now describes; nor could the moon without some such force be retained in its orbit. If this force was too small, it would not sufficiently turn the moon out of a rectilinear course; if it was too great, it would turn it too much, and draw down the moon from its orbit towards the earth. It is necessary that the force be of a just quantity, and it belongs to the mathematicians to find the force that may serve exactly to retain a body in a given orbit with a given velocity; and *vice versa*, to determine the curvilinear way into which a body projected from a given place, with a given velocity, may be made to deviate from its natural rectilinear way, by means of a given force.

The quantity of any centripetal force may be considered as of three kinds: absolute, accelerative, and motive.

Definition 6

The absolute quantity of a centripetal force is the measure of the same, proportional to the efficacy of the cause that propagates it from the centre, through the spaces round about.

Thus the magnetic force is greater in one loadstone and less in another, according to their sizes and strength of intensity.

Definition 7

The accelerative quantity of a centripetal force is the measure of the same, proportional to the velocity which it generates in a given time.

Thus the force of the same loadstone is greater at a less distance, and less at a greater: also the force of gravity is greater in valleys, less on tops of exceeding high mountains; and yet less (as shall hereafter be shown), at greater distances from the body of the earth; but at equal distances, it is the same everywhere; because (taking away, or allowing for, the resistance of the air), it equally accelerates all falling bodies, whether heavy or light, great or small.

Definition 8

The motive quantity of a centripetal force is the measure of the same, proportional to the motion which it generates in a given time.

Thus the weight is greater in a greater body, less in a less body; and, in the same body, it is greater near to the earth, and less at remoter distances. This sort of quantity is the centripetency, or propension of the whole body towards the centre, or, as I may say, its weight; and it is always known by the quantity of an equal and contrary force just sufficient to hinder the descent of the body.

These quantities of forces, we may, for the sake of brevity, call by the names of motive, accelerative, and absolute forces; and, for the sake of distinction, consider them with respect to the bodies that tend to the centre, to the places of those bodies, and to the centre of force towards which they tend; that is to say, I refer the motive force to the body as an endeavor and propensity of the whole towards a centre, arising from the propensities of the several parts taken together; the accelerative force to the place of the body, as a certain power diffused from the centre to all places around to move the bodies that are in them; and the absolute force to the centre, as endued with some cause, without which those motive forces would not be propagated through the spaces round about; whether that cause be some central body (such as is the magnet in the centre of the magnetic force, or the earth in the centre of the gravitating force), or anything else that does not yet appear. For I here design only to give a mathematical notion of those forces, without considering their physical causes and seats.

Wherefore the accelerative force will stand in the same relation to the motive, as celerity does to motion. For the quantity of motion arises from the celerity multiplied by the quantity of matter; and the motive force arises from the accelerative force multiplied by the same quantity of matter. For the sum of the actions of the accelerative force, upon the several particles of the body, is the motive force of the whole. Hence it is, that near the surface of the earth, where the accelerative gravity, or force productive of gravity, in all bodies is the same, the motive gravity or the weight is as the body; but if we should ascend to higher regions, where the accelerative gravity is less, the weight would be equally diminished, and would always be as the product of the body, by the accelerative gravity. So in those regions, where the accelerative gravity is diminished into one-half, the weight of a body two or three times less, will be four or six times less.

I likewise call attractions and impulses, in the same sense, accelerative, and motive; and use the words attraction, impulse, or propensity of any sort towards a centre, promiscuously, and indifferently, one for another; considering those forces not physically, but mathematically: wherefore the reader is not to imagine that by those words I anywhere take upon me to define the kind, or the manner of any action, the causes or the physical reason thereof, or that I attribute forces, in a true and physical sense, to certain centres (which are only mathematical points); when at any time I happen to speak of centres as attracting, or as endued with attractive powers.

Scholium

Hitherto I have laid down the definitions of such words as are less known, and explained the sense in which I would have them to be understood in the following discourse. I do not define time, space, place, and motion, as being well known to all. Only I must observe, that the common people conceive those quantities under no other notions but from the relation they bear to sensible objects. And thence arise certain prejudices, for the removing of which it will be convenient to distinguish them into absolute and relative, true and apparent, mathematical and common.

1. Absolute, true, and mathematical time, of itself, and from its own nature, flows equably without relation to anything external, and by another name is called duration: relative, apparent, and common time, is some sensible and external (whether accurate or unequable) measure of duration by the means of motion, which is commonly used instead of true time; such as an hour, a day, a month, a year.

2. Absolute space, in its own nature, without relation to anything external, remains always similar and immovable. Relative space is some movable dimension or measure of the absolute spaces; which our senses determine by its position to bodies; and which is commonly taken for immovable space; such is the dimension of a subterraneous, an aerial, or celestial space, determined by its position in respect of the earth. Absolute and relative space are the same in figure and magnitude; but they do not remain always numerically the same. For if the earth, for instance, moves, a space of our air, which relatively and in respect of the earth remains always the same, will at one time be one part of the absolute space into which the air passes; at another time it will be another part of the same, and so, absolutely understood, it will be continually changed.

3. Place is a part of space which a body takes up, and is according to

the space, either absolute or relative. I say, a part of space; not the situation, nor the external surface of the body. For the places of equal solids are always equal; but their surfaces, by reason of their dissimilar figures, are often unequal. Positions properly have no quantity, nor are they so much the places themselves, as the properties of places. The motion of the whole is the same with the sum of the motions of the parts; that is, the translation of the whole, out of its place, is the same thing with the sum of the translations of the parts out of their places; and therefore the place of the whole is the same as the sum of the places of the parts, and for that reason, it is internal, and in the whole body.

4. Absolute motion is the translation of a body from one absolute place into another; and relative motion, the translation from one relative place into another. Thus in a ship under sail, the relative place of a body is that part of the ship which the body possesses; or that part of the cavity which the body fills, and which therefore moves together with the ship: and relative rest is the continuance of the body in the same part of the ship, or of its cavity. But real, absolute rest, is the continuance of the body in the same part of that immovable space, in which the ship itself, its cavity, and all that it contains, is moved. Wherefore, if the earth is really at rest, the body, which relatively rests in the ship, will really and absolutely move with the same velocity which the ship has on the earth. But if the earth also moves, the true and absolute motion of the body will arise, partly from the true motion of the earth, in immovable space, partly from the relative motion of the ship on the earth; and if the body moves also relatively in the ship, its true motion will arise, partly from the true motion of the earth, in immovable space, and partly from the relative motions as well of the ship on the earth, as of the body in the ship; and from these relative motions will arise the relative motion of the body on the earth. As if that part of the earth, where the ship is, was truly moved towards the east, with a velocity of 10010 parts; while the ship itself, with a fresh gale, and full sails, is carried towards the west, with a velocity expressed by 10 of those parts; but a sailor walks in the ship towards the east, with 1 part of the said velocity; then the sailor will be moved truly in immovable space towards the east, with a velocity of 10001 parts, and relatively on the earth towards the west, with a velocity of 9 of those parts.

Absolute time, in astronomy, is distinguished from relative, by the equation or correction of the apparent time. For the natural days are truly unequal, though they are commonly considered as equal, and used for a measure of time; astronomers correct this inequality that they may measure the celestial motions by a more accurate time. It may be, that there is no such thing as an equable motion, whereby time may be accurately measured. All motions may be accelerated and retarded, but the flowing of absolute time is not liable to any change. The duration or perseverance of the existence of things remains the same, whether the motions are swift or slow, or none at all: and therefore this duration ought to be distinguished from what are only sensible measures thereof; and from which we deduce it, by means of the astronomical equation. The necessity of this equation, for determining the times of a phenomenon, is evinced as well from the experiments of the pendulum clock, as by eclipses of the satellites of Jupiter.

As the order of the parts of time is immutable, so also is the order of the parts of space. Suppose those parts to be moved out of their places, and they will be moved (if the expression may be allowed) out of themselves. For times and spaces are, as it were, the places as well of themselves as of all other things. All things are placed in time as to order of succession; and in space as to order of situation. It is from their essence or nature that they are places; and that the primary places of things should be movable, is absurd. These are therefore the absolute places; and translations out of those places, are the only absolute motions.

But because the parts of space cannot be seen, or distinguished from one another by our senses, therefore in their stead we use sensible measures of them. For from the positions and distances of things from any body considered as immovable, we define all places; and then with respect to such places, we estimate all motions, considering bodies as transferred from some of those places into others. And so, instead of absolute places and motions, we use relative ones; and that without any inconvenience in common affairs; but in philosophical disquisitions, we ought to abstract from our senses, and consider things themselves, distinct from what are only sensible measures of them. For it may be that there is no body really at rest, to which the places and motions of others may be referred.

* * *

Laws of Motion †

Law 1

Every body continues in its state of rest, or of uniform motion in a right line, unless it is compelled to change that state by forces impressed upon it.

Projectiles continue in their motions, so far as they are not retarded by the resistance of the air, or impelled downwards by the force of grav-

† Isaac Newton, *Mathematical Principles of Natural Philosophy* and *System of the World*, translated by Andrew Motte, revised by Florian Cajori (Berkeley and Los Angeles: University of California Press, 1934 and later printings), pp. 13–21. With the laws of motion, Newton established a quantitative science of dynamics. Newton's Latin text of the first law says that every body "perseveres" in "its state," rather than "continues." The three laws continue to be taught today at the beginning of nearly every course in elementary physics. See note on the Cajori translation on p. 116.

ity. A top, whose parts by their cohesion are continually drawn aside from rectilinear motions, does not cease its rotation, otherwise than as it is retarded by the air. The greater bodies of the planets and comets, meeting with less resistance in freer spaces, preserve their motions both progressive and circular for a much longer time.

Law 2

The change of motion is proportional to the motive force impressed; and is made in the direction of the right line in which that force is impressed.

If any force generates a motion, a double force will generate double the motion, a triple force triple the motion, whether that force be impressed altogether and at once, or gradually and successively. And this motion (being always directed the same way with the generating force), if the body moved before, is added to or subtracted from the former motion, according as they directly conspire with or are directly contrary to each other; or obliquely joined, when they are oblique, so as to produce a new motion compounded from the determination of both.

Law 3

To every action there is always opposed an equal reaction: or, the mutual actions of two bodies upon each other are always equal, and directed to contrary parts.

Whatever draws or presses another is as much drawn or pressed by that other. If you press a stone with your finger, the finger is also pressed by the stone. If a horse draws a stone tied to a rope, the horse (if I may so say) will be equally drawn back towards the stone; for the distended rope, by the same endeavor to relax or unbend itself, will draw the horse as much towards the stone as it does the stone towards the horse, and will obstruct the progress of the one as much as it advances that of the other. If a body impinge upon another, and by its force change the motion of the other, that body also (because of the equality of the mutual pressure) will undergo an equal change, in its own motion, towards the contrary part. The changes made by these actions are equal, not in the velocities but in the motions of bodies; that is to say, if the bodies are not hindered by any other impediments. For, because the motions are equally changed, the changes of the velocities made towards contrary parts are inversely proportional to the bodies. This law takes place also in attractions, as will be proved in the next Scholium.

Corollary 1

A body, acted on by two forces simultaneously, will describe the diagonal of a parallelogram in the same time as it would describe the sides by those forces separately.

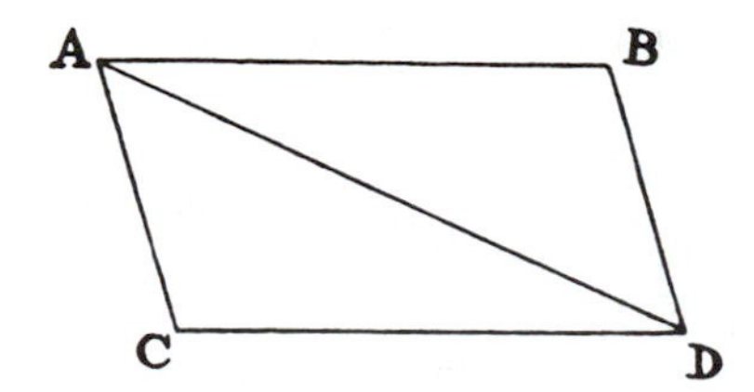

If a body in a given time, by the force M impressed apart in the place A, should with an uniform motion be carried from A to B, and by the force N impressed apart in the same place, should be carried from A to C, let the parallelogram ABCD be completed, and, by both forces acting together, it will in the same time be carried in the diagonal from A to D. For since the force N acts in the direction of the line AC, parallel to BD, this force (by the second Law) will not at all alter the velocity generated by the other force M, by which the body is carried towards the line BD. The body therefore will arrive at the line BD in the same time, whether the force N be impressed or not; and therefore at the end of that time it will be found somewhere in the line BD. By the same argument, at the end of the same time it will be found somewhere in the line CD. Therefore it will be found in the point D, where both lines meet. But it will move in a right line from A to D, by Law 1.

Corollary 2

And hence is explained the composition of any one direct force AD, out of any two oblique forces AC and CD; and, on the contrary, the resolution of any one direct force AD into two oblique forces AC and CD: which composition and resolution are abundantly confirmed from mechanics.

* * *

Corollary 3

The quantity of motion, which is obtained by taking the sum of the motions directed towards the same parts, and the difference of those that are directed to contrary parts, suffers no change from the action of bodies among themselves.

For action and its opposite reaction are equal, by Law 3, and therefore, by Law 2, they produce in the motions equal changes towards opposite parts. Therefore if the motions are directed towards the same parts, whatever is added to the motion of the preceding body will be subtracted from the motion of that which follows; so that the sum will be the same as before. If the bodies meet, with contrary motions, there will be an equal deduction from the motions of both; and therefore the difference of the motions directed towards opposite parts will remain the same.

Thus, if a spherical body A is 3 times greater than the spherical body B, and has a velocity=2, and B follows in the same direction with a velocity=10, then the motion of A : motion of B=6 : 10. Suppose, then, their motions to be of 6 parts and of 10 parts, and the sum will be 16 parts. Therefore, upon the meeting of the bodies, if A acquire 3, 4, or 5 parts of motion, B will lose as many; and therefore after reflection A will proceed with 9, 10, or 11 parts, and B with 7, 6, or 5 parts; the sum remaining always of 16 parts as before.

* * *

Corollary 4

The common centre of gravity of two or more bodies does not alter its state of motion or rest by the actions of the bodies among themselves; and therefore the common centre of gravity of all bodies acting upon each other (excluding external actions and impediments) is either at rest, or moves uniformly in a right line.

For if two points proceed with an uniform motion in right lines, and their distance be divided in a given ratio, the dividing point will be either at rest, or proceed uniformly in a right line. This is demonstrated hereafter in Lem. 23 and Corollary, when the points are moved in the same plane; and by a like way of arguing, it may be demonstrated when the points are not moved in the same plane. Therefore if any number of bodies move uniformly in right lines, the common centre of gravity of any two of them is either at rest, or proceeds uniformly in a right line; because the line which connects the centres of those two bodies so moving is divided at that common centre in a given ratio. In like manner the common centre of those two and that of a third body will be either at rest or moving uniformly in a right line; because at that centre the distance between the common centre of the two bodies, and the centre of this last, is divided in a given ratio. In like manner the common centre of these three, and of a fourth body, is either at rest, or moves uniformly in a right line; because the distance between the common centre of the three bodies, and the centre of the fourth, is there also divided in a given ratio, and so on *in infinitum*. Therefore, in a system of bodies where there is neither any mutual action among themselves, nor any foreign force impressed upon them from without, and which consequently move uniformly in right lines, the common centre of gravity of them all is either at rest or moves uniformly forwards in a right line.

Moreover, in a system of two bodies acting upon each other, since the distances between their centres and the common centre of gravity of both are reciprocally as the bodies, the relative motions of those bodies, whether of approaching to or of receding from that centre, will be equal among themselves. Therefore since the changes which happen to motions are equal and directed to contrary parts, the common centre of those bodies, by their mutual action between themselves, is neither accelerated nor retarded, nor suffers any change as to its state of motion or rest. But in a system of several bodies, because the common centre of gravity of any two acting upon each other suffers no change in its state by that action; and much less the common centre of gravity of the others with which that action does not intervene; but the distance between those two centres is divided by the common centre of gravity of all the bodies into parts inversely proportional to the total sums of those bodies whose centres they are; and therefore while those two centres retain their state of motion or rest, the common centre of all does also retain its state: it is manifest that the common centre of all never suffers any change in the state of its motion or rest from the actions of any two bodies between themselves. But in such a system all the actions of the bodies among themselves either happen between two bodies, or are composed of actions interchanged between some two bodies; and therefore they do never produce any alteration in the common centre of all as to its state of motion or rest. Wherefore since that centre, when the bodies do not act one upon another, either is at rest or moves uniformly forwards in some right line, it will, notwithstanding the mutual actions of the bodies among themselves, always continue in its state, either of rest, or of proceeding uniformly in a right line, unless it is forced out of this state by the action of some power impressed from without upon the whole system. And therefore the same law takes place in a system consisting of many bodies as in one single body, with regard to their persevering in their state of motion or of rest. For the progressive motion, whether of one single body, or of a whole system of bodies, is always to be estimated from the motion of the centre of gravity.

Corollary 5

The motions of bodies included in a given space are the same among themselves, whether that space is at rest, or moves uniformly forwards in a right line without any circular motion.

For the differences of the motions tending towards the same parts, and the sums of those that tend towards contrary parts, are, at first (by supposition), in both cases the same; and it is from those sums and differences that the collisions and impulses do arise with which the bodies impinge one upon another. Wherefore (by Law 2), the effects of those collisions will be equal in both cases; and therefore the mutual motions of the bodies among themselves in the one case will remain equal to the motions of the bodies among themselves in the other. A clear proof of this we have from the experiment of a ship; where all motions happen after the same manner, whether the ship is at rest, or is carried uniformly forwards in a right line.

Corollary 6

If bodies, moved in any manner among themselves, are urged in the direction of parallel lines by equal accelerative forces, they will all continue to move among themselves, after the same manner as if they had not been urged by those forces.

For these forces acting equally (with respect to the quantities of the bodies to be moved), and in the direction of parallel lines, will (by Law 2) move all the bodies equally (as to velocity), and therefore will never produce any change in the positions or motions of the bodies among themselves.

* * *

Selected Propositions from the *Principia*, Book 1 †

Proposition 1

The areas which revolving bodies describe by radii drawn to an immovable centre of force do lie in the same immovable planes, and are proportional to the times in which they are described.

For suppose the time to be divided into equal parts, and in the first part of that time let the body by its innate force describe the right line AB. In the second part of that time, the same would (by Law 1), if not hindered, proceed directly to *c*, along the line B*c* equal to AB; so that by the radii AS, BS, *c*S, drawn to the centre, the equal areas ASB, BS*c*, would be described. But when the body is arrived at B, suppose that a centripetal force acts at once with a great impulse, and, turning aside the body from the right line B*c*, compels it afterwards to continue its motion along the right line BC. Draw *c*C parallel to BS, meeting BC in C; and at the end of the second part of the time, the body (by Cor. 1 of the Laws) will be found in C, in the same plane with the triangle ASB. Join SC, and, because SB and C*c* are parallel, the triangle SBC will be equal to the triangle SB*c*, and therefore also to the triangle SAB. By the like argument, if the centripetal force acts successively in C, D, E, etc.,

† Isaac Newton, *Mathematical Principles of Natural Philosophy* and *System of the World*, translated by Andrew Motte, revised by Florian Cajori (Berkeley and Los Angeles: University of California Press, 1934 and later printings), pp. 40–193. Copyright © 1934 and 1962 Regents of the University of California. Reprinted by permission. We have included the demonstrations only of three critical Propositions: 1, 6, and 11. Beyond them we have included the statements of a number of other Propositions to indicate the general structure of Newton's science of mechanics. In introduction and in conclusion to Section 11, in which he considered the motions of a system of bodies that attract each other, Newton made important statements about forces that we also reproduce. See note on the Cajori translation on p. 116.

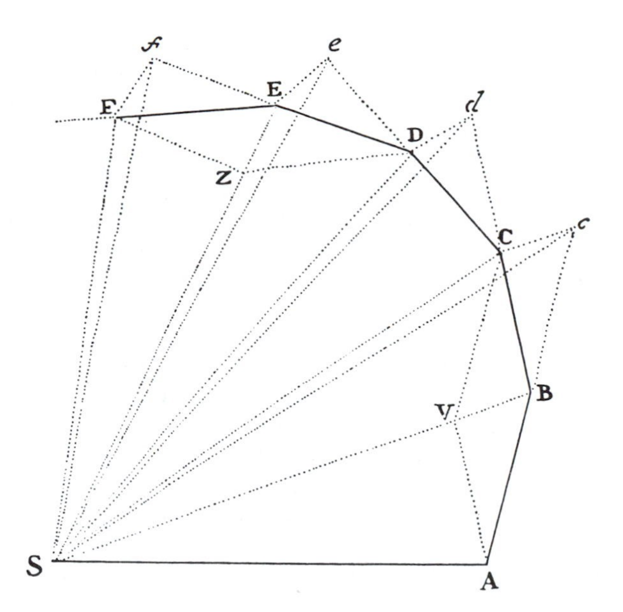

and makes the body, in each single particle of time, to describe the right lines CD, DE, EF, etc., they will all lie in the same plane; and the triangle SCD will be equal to the triangle SBC, and SDE to SCD, and SEF to SDE. And therefore, in equal times, equal areas are described in one immovable plane: and, by composition, any sums SADS, SAFS, of those areas, are to each other as the times in which they are described. Now let the number of those triangles be augmented, and their breadth diminished *in infinitum*; and (by Cor. 4, Lem. 3) their ultimate perimeter ADF will be a curved line: and therefore the centripetal force, by which the body is continually drawn back from the tangent of this curve, will act continually; and any described areas SADS, SAFS, which are always proportional to the times of description, will, in this case also, be proportional to those times. Q.E.D.

Cor. 1. The velocity of a body attracted towards an immovable centre, in spaces void of resistance, is inversely as the perpendicular let fall from that centre on the right line that touches the orbit. For the velocities in those places A, B, C, D, E, are as the bases AB, BC, CD, DE, EF, of equal triangles; and these bases are inversely as the perpendiculars let fall upon them.

Cor. 2. If the chords AB, BC of two arcs, successively described in equal times by the same body, in spaces void of resistance, are completed into a parallelogram, ABCV, and the diagonal BV of this parallelogram, in the position which it ultimately acquires when those arcs are diminished *in infinitum*, is produced both ways, it will pass through the centre of force.

Cor. 3. If the chords AB, BC, and DE, EF, of arcs described in equal times, in spaces void of resistance, are completed into the parallelograms ABCV, DEFZ, the forces in B and E are one to the other in the ultimate ratio of the diagonals BV, EZ, when those arcs are diminished *in infinitum*. For the motions BC and EF of the body (by Cor. 1 of the Laws) are compounded of the motions B*c*, BV, and E*f*, EZ; but BV and EZ, which are equal to C*c* and F*f*, in the demonstration of this Proposition, were generated by the impulses of the centripetal force in B and E, and are therefore proportional to those impulses.

Cor. 4. The forces by which bodies, in spaces void of resistance, are drawn back from rectilinear motions, and turned into curvilinear orbits, are to each other as the versed sines of arcs described in equal times; which versed sines tend to the centre of force, and bisect the chords when those arcs are diminished to infinity. For such versed sines are the halves of the diagonals mentioned in Cor. 3.

Cor. 5. And therefore those forces are to the force of gravity as the said versed sines to the versed sines perpendicular to the horizon of those parabolic arcs which projectiles describe in the same time.

Cor. 6. And the same things do all hold good (by Cor. 5 of the Laws) when the planes in which the bodies are moved, together with the centres of force which are placed in those planes, are not at rest, but move uniformly forwards in right lines.

Proposition 2

Every body that moves in any curved line described in a plane, and by a radius drawn to a point either immovable, or moving forwards with an uniform rectilinear motion, describes about that point areas proportional to the times, is urged by a centripetal force directed to that point.

* * *

Proposition 3

Every body, that by a radius drawn to the centre of another body, howsoever moved, describes areas about that centre proportional to the times, is urged by a force compounded of the centripetal force tending to that other body, and of all the accelerative force by which that other body is impelled.

* * *

Proposition 4

The centripetal forces of bodies, which by equable motions describe different circles, tend to the centres of the same circles; and are to each other as the squares of the arcs described in equal times divided respectively by the radii of the circles.

* * *

Cor. 6. If the periodic times are as the 3/2th powers of the radii, and therefore the velocities inversely as the square roots of the radii, the centripetal forces will be inversely as the squares of the radii; and conversely.

* * *

Scholium

The case of the sixth Corollary obtains in the celestial bodies (as Sir *Christopher Wren*, Dr. *Hooke*, and Dr. *Halley* have severally observed); and therefore in what follows, I intend to treat more at large of those things which relate to centripetal force decreasing as the squares of the distances from the centres.

Moreover, by means of the preceding Proposition and its Corollaries, we may discover the proportion of a centripetal force to any other known force, such as that of gravity. For if a body by means of its gravity revolves in a circle concentric to the earth, this gravity is the centripetal force of that body. But from the descent of heavy bodies, the time of one entire revolution, as well as the arc described in any given time, is given (by Cor. 9 of this Prop.). And by such propositions, Mr. *Huygens*, in his excellent book *De horologio oscillatorio*, has compared the force of gravity with the centrifugal forces of revolving bodies.

The preceding Proposition may be likewise demonstrated after this manner. In any circle suppose a polygon to be inscribed of any number of sides. And if a body, moved with a given velocity along the sides of the polygon, is reflected from the circle at the several angular points, the force, with which at every reflection it strikes the circle, will be as its velocity: and therefore the sum of the forces, in a given time, will be as the product of that velocity and the number of reflections; that is (if the species of the polygon be given), as the length described in that given time, and increased or diminished in the ratio of the same length to the radius of the circle; that is, as the square of that length divided by the radius; and therefore the polygon, by having its sides diminished *in infinitum*, coincides with the circle, as the square of the arc described in a given time divided by the radius. This is the centrifugal force, with which the body impels the circle; and to which the contrary force, wherewith the circle continually repels the body towards the centre, is equal.

* * *

Proposition 6

In a space void of resistance, if a body revolves in any orbit about an immovable centre, and in the least time describes any arc just then nascent; and the versed sine of that arc is supposed to be drawn bisecting the chord, and produced passing through the centre of force: the centripetal force in the middle of the arc will be directly as the versed sine and inversely as the square of the time.

For the versed sine in a given time is as the force (by Cor. 4, Prop. 1); and augmenting the time in any ratio, because the arc will be augmented in the same ratio, the versed sine will be augmented in the square of that ratio (by Cor. 2 and 3, Lem. 11), and therefore is as the force and the square of the time. Divide both sides by the square of the time, and the force will be directly as the versed sine, and inversely as the square of the time. Q.E.D.

And the same thing may also be easily demonstrated by Cor. 4, Lem. 10.

Cor. 1. If a body P revolving about the centre S describes a curved line APQ, which a right line ZPR touches in any point P; and from any other point Q of the curve, QR is drawn parallel to the distance SP, meeting the tangent in R; and QT is drawn perpendicular to the distance SP; the centripetal force will be inversely as the solid $\frac{SP^2 \cdot QT^2}{QR}$, if the solid be taken of that magnitude which it ultimately acquires when the points P and Q coincide. For QR is equal to the versed sine of double the arc QP, whose middle is P: and double the triangle SQP, or SP · QT is proportional to the time in which that double arc is described; and therefore may be used to represent the time.

Cor. 2. By a like reasoning, the centripetal force is inversely as the solid $\frac{SY^2 \cdot QP^2}{QR}$; if SY is a perpendicular from the centre of force on PR, the tangent of the orbit. For the rectangles SY · QP and SP · QT are equal.

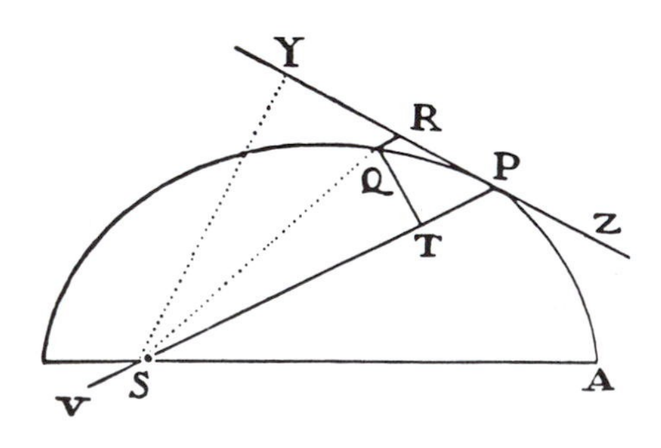

Cor. 3. If the orbit is either a circle, or touches or cuts a circle concentrically, that is, contains with a circle the least angle of contact or section, having the same curvature and the same radius of curvature at the point P; and if PV be a chord of this circle, drawn from the body through the centre of force; the centripetal force will be inversely as the solid $SY^2 \cdot PV$.

$$\text{For PV is } \frac{QP^2}{QR}$$

Cor. 4. The same things being supposed, the centripetal force is as the square of the velocity directly, and that chord inversely. For the velocity is reciprocally as the perpendicular SY, by Cor. 1, Prop. 1.

Cor. 5. Hence if any curvilinear figure APQ is given, and therein a point S is also given, to which a centripetal force is continually directed, that law of centripetal force may be found, by which the body P will be continually drawn back from a rectilinear course, and, being detained in the perimeter of that figure, will describe the same by a continual revolution. That is, we are to find, by computation, either the solid $\frac{SP^2 \cdot QT^2}{QR}$ or the solid $SY^2 \cdot PV$, inversely proportional to this force. Examples of this we shall give in the following Problems.

* * *

Proposition 11

If a body revolves in an ellipse; it is required to find the law of the centripetal force tending to the focus of the ellipse.

Let S be the focus of the ellipse. Draw SP cutting the diameter DK of

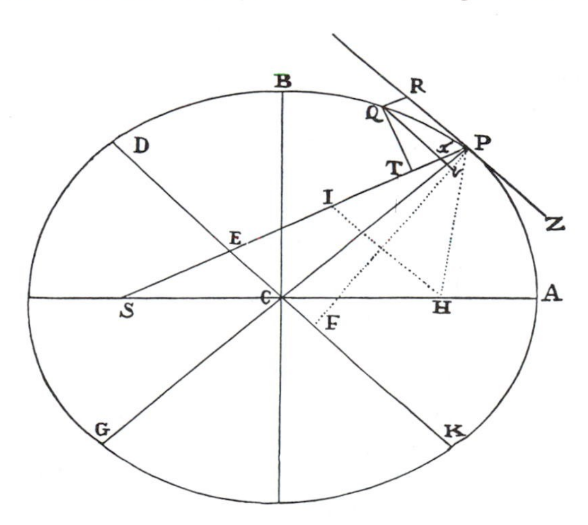

the ellipse in E, and the ordinate Qv in x; and complete the parallelogram $QxPR$. It is evident that EP is equal to the greater semiaxis AC: for drawing HI from the other focus H of the ellipse parallel to EC, because CS, CH are equal, ES, EI will be also equal; so that EP is the half-sum of PS, PI, that is (because of the parallels HI, PR, and the equal angles IPR, HPZ), of PS, PH, which taken together are equal to the whole axis 2AC. Draw QT perpendicular to SP, and putting L for the principal latus rectum of the ellipse (or for $\frac{2BC^2}{AC}$), we shall have

$$L \cdot QR : L \cdot Pv = QR : Pv = PE : PC = AC : PC,$$
$$\text{also, } L \cdot Pv : Gv \cdot Pv = L : Gv, \text{ and, } Gv \cdot Pv : Qv^2 = PC^2 : CD^2.$$

By Cor. 2, Lem. 7, when the points P and Q coincide, $Qv^2 = Qx^2$, and Qx^2 or $Qv^2 : QT^2 = EP^2 : PF^2 = CA^2 : PF^2$, and (by Lem. 12) $= CD^2 : CB^2$. Multiplying together corresponding terms of the four proportions, and simplifying, we shall have

$$L \cdot QR : QT^2 = AC \cdot L \cdot PC^2 \cdot CD^2 : PC \cdot Gv \cdot CD^2 \cdot CB^2 = 2PC : Gv,$$

since $AC \cdot L = 2BC^2$. But the points Q and P coinciding, 2PC and Gv are equal. And therefore the quantities $L \cdot QR$ and QT^2, proportional to these, will be also equal. Let those equals be multiplied by $\frac{SP^2}{QR}$, and $L \cdot SP^2$ will become equal to $\frac{SP^2 \cdot QT^2}{QR}$. And therefore (by Cor. 1 and 5, Prop. 6) the centripetal force is inversely as $L \cdot SP^2$, that is, inversely as the square of the distance SP. Q.E.I.

* * *

Proposition 41

Supposing a centripetal force of any kind, and granting the quadrature [or integration] of curvilinear figures; it is required to find the curves in which bodies will move and the times of their motions in the curves found.

* * *

Introduction, Section 11

The motions of bodies tending to each other with centripetal forces.

I have hitherto been treating of the attractions of bodies towards an immovable centre; though very probably there is no such thing existent in nature. For attractions are made towards bodies, and the actions of the bodies attracted and attracting are always reciprocal and equal, by Law 3; so that if there are two bodies, neither the attracted nor the attracting body is truly at rest, but both (by Cor. 4 of the Laws of Motion), being as it were mutually attracted, revolve about a common centre of gravity. And if there be more bodies, which either are attracted by one body, which is attracted by them again, or which all attract each other mutually, these bodies will be so moved among themselves, that their common centre of gravity will either be at rest, or move uniformly forwards in a right line. I shall therefore at present go on to treat of the motion of bodies attracting each other; considering the centripetal forces as attractions; though perhaps in a physical strictness they may more truly be called impulses. But these Propositions are to be considered as purely mathematical; and therefore, laying aside all physical considerations, I make use of a familiar way of speaking, to make myself the more easily understood by a mathematical reader.

Proposition 57

Two bodies attracting each other mutually describe similar figures about their common centre of gravity, and about each other mutually.

* * *

Proposition 63

To determine the motions of two bodies attracting each other with forces inversely proportional to the squares of their distance, and going off from given places in given directions with given velocities.

* * *

Proposition 66

If three bodies, whose forces decrease as the square of the distances, attract each other; and the accelerative attractions of any two towards the third be between themselves inversely as the squares of the distances; and the two least revolve about the greatest: I say, that the interior of the two revolving bodies will, by radii drawn to the innermost and greatest, describe round that body areas more proportional to the times, and a figure more approaching to that of an ellipse having its focus in the point of intersection of the radii, if that great body be agitated by those attractions, than it would do if that great body were not attracted at all by the lesser, but remained at rest; or than it would do if that great body were very much more or very much less attracted, or very much more or very much less agitated, by the attractions.

* * *

Concluding Scholium to Section 11

These Propositions naturally lead us to the analogy there is between centripetal forces and the central bodies to which those forces are usually directed; for it is reasonable to suppose that forces which are directed to bodies should depend upon the nature and quantity of those bodies, as we see they do in magnetical experiments. And when such cases occur, we are to compute the attractions of the bodies by assigning to each of their particles its proper force, and then finding the sum of them all. I here use the word *attraction* in general for any endeavor whatever, made by bodies to approach to each other, whether that endeavor arise from the action of the bodies themselves, as tending to each other or agitating each other by spirits emitted; or whether it arises from the action of the ether or of the air, or of any medium whatever, whether corporeal or incorporeal, in any manner impelling bodies placed therein towards each other. In the same general sense I use the word *impulse*, not defining in this treatise the species or physical qualities of forces, but investigating the quantities and mathematical proportions of them; as I observed before in the Definitions. In mathematics we are to investigate the quantities of forces with their proportions consequent upon any conditions supposed; then, when we enter upon physics, we compare those proportions with the phenomena of Nature, that we may know what conditions of those forces answer to the several kinds of attractive bodies. And this preparation being made, we argue more safely concerning the physical species, causes, and proportions of the forces. Let us see, then, with what forces spherical bodies consisting of particles endued with attractive powers in the manner above spoken of must act upon one another; and what kind of motions will follow from them.

* * *

Proposition 70

If to every point of a spherical surface there tend equal centripetal forces decreasing as the square of the distances from those points, I say, that a corpuscle placed within that surface will not be attracted by those forces any way.

* * *

Proposition 71

The same things supposed as above, I say, that a corpuscle placed without the spherical surface is attracted towards the centre of the sphere with a force inversely proportional to the square of its distance from that centre.

* * *

Scholium to Section 9, Book 2 of the *Principia* †

Hence it is manifest that the planets are not carried round in corporeal vortices; for, according to the *Copernican* hypothesis, the planets going round the sun revolve in ellipses, having the sun in their common focus; and by radii drawn to the sun describe areas proportional to the times. But the parts of a vortex can never revolve with such a motion. For, let AD, BE, CF represent three orbits described about the sun S, of which let the outmost circle CF be concentric to the sun; let the aphelions of the two innermost be A, B; and their perihelions D, E. Hence a body revolving in the orb CF, describing, by a radius drawn to the sun, areas proportional to the times, will move with an uniform motion. And, according to the laws of astronomy, the body revolving in the orbit BE will move slower in its aphelian B, and swifter in its perihelion E; whereas, according to the laws of mechanics, the matter of the vortex ought to move more swiftly in the narrow space between A and C than in the wide space between D and F; that is, more swiftly in the aphelion than in the perihelion. Now these two conclusions contradict each other. So at the beginning of the sign of Virgo, where the aphelion of Mars is at present, the distance between the orbits of Mars and Venus is to the distance between the same orbits, at the beginning of the sign of Pisces, as about 3 to 2; and therefore the matter of the vortex between those orbits ought to be swifter at the beginning of Pisces than at the

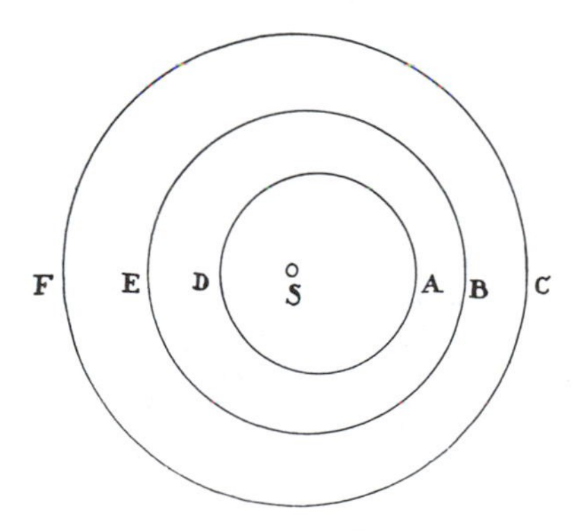

† Isaac Newton, *Mathematical Principles of Natural Philosophy* and *System of the World*, translated by Andrew Motte, revised by Florian Cajori (Berkeley and Los Angeles: University of California Press, 1934 and later printings), pp. 395–96. Copyright © 1934 and 1962 Regents of the University of California. Reprinted by permission. Book 2 of the *Principia* considers motions through material media that resist and the motions of such media. It concludes with an examination of the dynamics of vortical motion. The Scholium to Section 9, which also concludes Book 2, sums up Newton's argument against the Cartesian theory that the solar system is a huge whirlpool, or vortex, of matter. See note on the Cajori translation on p. 116.

beginning of Virgo in the ratio of 3 to 2; for the narrower the space is through which the same quantity of matter passes in the same time of one revolution, the greater will be the velocity with which it passes through it. Therefore if the earth being relatively at rest in this celestial matter should be carried round by it, and revolve together with it about the sun, the velocity of the earth at the beginning of Pisces would be to its velocity at the beginning of Virgo in the ratio of 3 to 2. Therefore the sun's apparent diurnal motion at the beginning of Virgo ought to be above 70 minutes, and at the beginning of Pisces less than 48 minutes; whereas, on the contrary, that apparent motion of the sun is really greater at the beginning of Pisces than at the beginning of Virgo, as experience testifies; and therefore the earth is swifter at the beginning of Virgo than at the beginning of Pisces; so that the hypothesis of vortices is utterly irreconcilable with astronomical phenomena, and rather serves to perplex than explain the heavenly motions. How these motions are performed in free spaces without vortices, may be understood by the first Book; and I shall now more fully treat of it in the following Book.

ALFRED NORTH WHITEHEAD

From *Science and the Modern World* †

* * *

Bacon completely missed the tonality which lay behind the success of seventeenth century science. Science was becoming, and has remained, primarily quantitative. Search for measurable elements among your phenomena, and then search for relations between these measures of physical quantities. Bacon ignores this rule of science. For example, in the quotation given he speaks of action at a distance; but he is thinking qualitatively and not quantitatively. We cannot ask that he should anticipate his younger contemporary Galileo, or his distant successor Newton. But he gives no hint that there should be a search for quantities. Perhaps he was misled by the current logical doctrines which had come down from Aristotle. For, in effect, these doctrines said to the physicist *classify* when they should have said *measure*.

By the end of the century physics had been founded on a satisfactory basis of measurement. The final and adequate exposition was given by Newton. The common measurable element of *mass* was discerned as characterising all bodies in different amounts. Bodies which are appar-

† Alfred North Whitehead, *Science and the Modern World* (Cambridge and New York: Cambridge UP and Macmillan, 1925), pp. 66–69, 70–71. Copyright 1925 by The Macmillan Company, renewed 1953 by Evelyn Whitehead. Reprinted by permission of Macmillan Publishing Company and Cambridge University Press. Whitehead was a prominent English mathematician, philosopher, and logician.

ently identical in substance, shape, and size have very approximately the same mass: the closer the identity, the nearer the equality. The force acting on a body, whether by touch or by action at a distance, was [in effect] defined as being equal to the mass of the body multiplied by the rate of change of the body's velocity, so far as this rate of change is produced by that force. In this way the force is discerned by its effect on the motion of the body. The question now arises whether this conception of the magnitude of a force leads to the discovery of simple quantitative laws involving the alternative determination of forces by circumstances of the configuration of substances and of their physical characters. The Newtonian conception has been brilliantly successful in surviving this test throughout the whole modern period. Its first triumph was the law of gravitation. Its cumulative triumph has been the whole development of dynamical astronomy, of engineering, and of physics.

This subject of the formation of the three laws of motion and of the law of gravitation deserves critical attention. The whole development of thought occupied exactly two generations. It commenced with Galileo and ended with Newton's *Principia*; and Newton was born in the year that Galileo died. Also the lives of Descartes and Huyghens fall within the period occupied by these great terminal figures. The issue of the combined labours of these four men has some right to be considered as the greatest single intellectual success which mankind has achieved. In estimating its size, we must consider the completeness of its range. It constructs for us a vision of the material universe, and it enables us to calculate the minutest detail of a particular occurrence. Galileo took the first step in hitting on the right line of thought. He noted that the critical point to attend to was not the motion of bodies but the changes of their motions. Galileo's discovery is formularised by Newton in his first law of motion:—'Every body continues in its state of rest, or of uniform motion in a straight line, except so far as it may be compelled by force to change that state.'

This formula contains the repudiation of a belief which had blocked the progress of physics for two thousand years. It also deals with a fundamental concept which is essential to scientific theory; I mean, the concept of an ideally isolated system. This conception embodies a fundamental character of things, without which science, or indeed any knowledge on the part of finite intellects, would be impossible. The 'isolated' system is not a solipsist system, apart from which there would be nonentity. It is isolated as within the universe. This means that there are truths respecting this system which require reference only to the remainder of things by way of a uniform systematic scheme of relationships. Thus the conception of an isolated system is not the conception of substantial independence from the remainder of things, but of freedom from casual contingent dependence upon detailed items within the rest of the universe. Further, this freedom from casual dependence is required only in respect to certain abstract characteristics which attach to the isolated system, and not in respect to the system in its full concreteness.

The first law of motion asks what is to be said of a dynamically isolated system so far as concerns its motion as a whole, abstracting from its orientation and its internal arrangement of parts. Aristotle said that you must conceive such a system to be at rest. Galileo added that the state of rest is only a particular case, and that the general statement is 'either in a state of rest, or of uniform motion in a straight line.' Accordingly, an Aristotelean would conceive the forces arising from the reaction of alien bodies as being quantitatively measurable in terms of the velocity they sustain, and as directively determined by the direction of that velocity; while the Galilean would direct attention to the magnitude of the acceleration and to its direction. This difference is illustrated by contrasting Kepler and Newton. They both speculated as to the forces sustaining the planets in their orbits. Kepler looked for tangential forces pushing the planets along, whereas Newton looked for radial forces diverting the directions of the planets' motions.

* * *

Returning to the laws of motion, it is noticeable that no reason was produced in the seventeenth century for the Galilean as distinct from the Aristotelian position. It was an ultimate fact. When in the course of these lectures we come to the modern period, we shall see that the theory of relativity throws complete light on this question; but only by rearranging our whole ideas as to space and time.

It remained for Newton to direct attention to *mass* as a physical quantity inherent in the nature of a material body. Mass remained permanent during all changes of motion. But the proof of the permanence of mass amid chemical transformations had to wait for Lavoisier, a century later. Newton's next task was to find some estimate of the magnitude of the alien force in terms of the mass of the body and of its acceleration. He here had a stroke of luck. For, from the point of view of a mathematician the simplest possible law, namely the product of the two, proved to be the successful one. Again the modern relativity theory modifies this extreme simplicity. But luckily for science the delicate experiments of the physicists of to-day were not then known, or even possible. Accordingly, the world was given the two centuries which it required in order to digest Newton's laws of motion.

* * *

Part 6
SYSTEM OF THE WORLD

Introduction

Historians sometimes speak of the "Newtonian synthesis" in reference to Newton's system of the world in which the two great generalizations of the early seventeenth century, Galileo's kinematics of uniformly accelerated motions and Kepler's three laws of planetary motion, emerged as necessary consequences of a single set of dynamical principles. The Newtonian synthesis also embraced a third major generalization of the early seventeenth century, the conviction that the phenomena of nature must be recognized as products of the mechanical interactions of bodies. In this case, however, Newton radically transformed the earlier generalization. As we saw in Part 5, Rational Mechanics (above), Newton concluded Book 2 of his *Principia* with an argument,drawn from his analysis of vortical motion, that the Cartesian concept of immense cosmic whirlpools of matter in which planets are borne around the sun like twigs floating in water cannot account for the motions that are in fact observed to exist in the heavens. Nevertheless, Newton did not abandon the program of the mechanical philosophy. The whole burden of his *Principia* was to treat celestial motions as problems in mechanics and to show that the same principles of motion that account for phenomena on the surface of the earth also account, equally well, for all the phenomena in the heavens.

In Newton's day, the heavens meant the solar system set in a framework of fixed stars. Newton extended its bounds to include comets, which he proved to be like the planets, orbiting the sun. He thus moved the limits of the solar system to regions beyond the orbit of Saturn. The idea, which dated back to the Greeks, that the universe is finite had already been abandoned, and Newton himself believed that our sun is one among innumerable stars spread through the infinite immensity of space. Although he was quite prepared to speculate about the cosmic order, the infinite number of stars did not enter into his system considered as science. Spread evenly on all sides, as he believed, the stars exercised no net effect on the motions of the system of bodies that move around our sun. The problem to which the *Principia* addressed itself was the mechanical actions that controlled the motions within the solar system.

Newton concluded—it was the most famous generalization of the Scientific Revolution and a central feature of the science that dominated Western thought until the twentieth century—that bodies attract each other and that the phenomena of our system flow directly from the attraction. Not just any attraction, however. Newton was a man of the

In order not to encumber the reader with footnotes we have composed a Biographical Register, in which all the people mentioned in the text are identified, and a Glossary, in which technical terms are briefly explicated and such things as organizations, places, publications, and manuscript collections are identified. Both the Biographical Register and the Glossary are located near the end of the volume.

seventeenth century who was fully imbued with the new ideal of a mathematical science; this is another dimension of the Newtonian synthesis. Newtonian attraction is precisely defined mathematically. It decreases in direct proportion to the square of the distance between two bodies, and its quantity between any two bodies varies directly as the product of their masses. This is the principle of universal gravitation. The word *gravitation* refers to the attraction, of course. The word *universal* asserts that every particle of matter in the universe attracts every other particle with a force precisely defined in the manner just described. Newton was convinced that there are other forces, short range and not necessarily universal, between particles of matter. (See his speculations on the nature of things in Part 1, Natural Philosophy [above].) He was equally convinced that these forces have their own exact mathematical laws, even though he himself had not succeeded in deciphering the laws. The *Principia* meanwhile addressed itself to the one force whose law he had been able to untangle, the cosmic force that controls the motions of the solar system.

Books 1 and 2 of the *Principia* laid the groundwork of the basic principles of motion. Book 3 applied those principles to the solar system and demonstrated first how they implied the existence of a cosmic attraction and then how that attraction could be identified with the cause of heaviness *(gravitas)* on the surface of the earth. In the introduction to Book 3, Newton stated that initially he composed that book in a "popular method," but that he later decided he should present it rather in rigorous mathematical form. After Newton's death, there was printed an English translation of a manuscript work of his in Latin that had been circulated in longhand copies. The printed version was given a catchy title, *A Treatise of the System of the World*, taken from the title Newton had given to Book 3 of the published *Principia*. Almost at once, Newton's heirs, who were anxious to profit from his fame, published this work in the Latin original, giving it the title *De mundi systemate*. It was in fact the first version of Book 3 and not a separate composition. We have chosen to reproduce much of it in this section for the very reason which led Newton to replace it. Its popular method, that is, its prose instead of mathematical propositions, make it more accessible to the general reader, although it retains the logic of the argument.

There are differences between the *System of the World* reproduced here and Book 3 of the published *Principia*. When Newton composed the first version in 1685, he was still deeply immersed in the process of investigation that produced his masterpiece, and he had not yet arrived at his final destination. The essential steps of the argument leading to the principle of universal gravitation were there. He drew on Kepler's third law to show the necessity of an inverse-square force directed toward the sun. The stability of planetary orbits also requires an inverse-square force. Kepler's third law holds for the satellites of Jupiter as well and again requires an inverse-square force toward Jupiter. Some force toward the earth must hold the moon in its orbit. In this case, with a single satellite, Kepler's third law cannot be used, but Newton was able to correlate the acceleration of bodies falling at the surface of the earth with the force that holds the moon in its orbit and to show that the same force, varying inversely as the square of the distance from the center of the earth, governs both motions. Applying then the principle of uniformity (see Rule 2 of his "Rules of Reasoning in Philosophy" in Part 2, Scientific Method [above]), Newton concluded that all the centripetal forces that vary inversely as the square of the distance are one and the same, and to that force he applied the word familiar to philosophers in Western Europe, *gravitas*. In the *System of the World*, Newton went on to indicate that the same force must account for other phenomena not called on in demonstrating its existence. By 1687, when he completed Book 3 in its published form, he did more than nod at the other phenomena; calling on the twenty-two corollaries to Proposition 66 of Book 1 (which were also composed during the intervening months), he subjected the phenomena to the same sort of precise quantitative treatment that lay behind the derivation of the principle of universal gravitation.

Foremost among the phenomena in question were the various anomalies in the motion of the moon. Where he only pointed at them in the early version, Newton inaugurated modern lunar astronomy by showing that the anomalies are perturbations arising from the attraction of the sun on the moon as the moon orbits the earth. There are also tides; the perturbing body, external to the central attracting earth, in this case was the moon, with the sun also contributing. The *Principia* opened a new chapter in mankind's understanding of the tides. The moon (abetted again by the sun) also attracts the bulge of matter around the equator, causing a conical motion of the earth's axis that we perceive as an astronomical phenomenon called precession of the equinoxes. And finally there are comets. In the *System of the World*, Newton expressed his conviction that comets are planet-like bodies orbiting the sun under the control of the same attractive force that holds the planets in their orbits. By 1687, Newton had succeeded in reducing the observed positions of the great comet of 1681–82 to a conical orbit, which he treated as a parabola in 1687 and as a very elongated ellipse in later editions. As we saw, these other phenomena are only alluded to in the *System of the World* reproduced here; if you want to see Newton's mature treatment of them, you must turn to Book 3 of the *Principia* as it was published and later emended.

Newton also inserted another important change in the final form of Book 3. As you will see, in the *System of the World* he stated incautiously that attractions between bodies "arise from the universal nature of matter." By 1687 Newton realized that this was not at all what he wanted to say. He wished rather to insist on the distinction between the mathematical demonstration that some sort of attraction must exist and speculation about the nature of the attraction. The introduction and the Scholium to Section 11 of Book 1 (see Part 5, Rational Mechanics [above]), both making this distinction, were undoubtedly composed between 1685 and 1687, and in the General Scholium (see Part 2, Scientific Method [above], and Part 8, Theology [below]), he expressed the distinction in what became its definitive form: "But hitherto I have not been able to discover the cause of those properties of gravity from phenomena, and I feign no hypotheses," that is, he does not introduce fictional or imagined hypotheses. In fact Newton did imagine more than one hypothesis about the cause of gravity during his life. Early he imagined a universal medium (or aether) that moved bodies toward each other (see the "Hypothesis of Light" in Part 1, Natural Philosophy [above]) and near the end of his life the last queries that he inserted in the *Opticks* returned to a revised form of such an aether (see Part 1 [above]). In between, he appeared to believe that God himself directly causes gravity (see his letters to Bentley in Part 8, Theology [below], and Query 28 in Part 4, Optics [above]). Newton's young followers in the early eighteenth century returned to the assertion of the *System of the World* that universal gravitation arises from the nature of matter. Always, however, Newton maintained the distinction between the mathematical demonstrations in the *Principia*, which proved the existence of the phenomena of attraction, and speculations about the cause of the attraction.

Newton's system of the world was a synthesis of his own life's work as well as a synthesis of the main currents of seventeenth-century scientific thought. It wove the strands of his scientific achievements—in mathematics, natural philosophy, experimental procedure, and mechanics—together into one coherent vision of the universe. Its imposing aspect awed successive generations. The law of universal gravitation became a model that other fields of thought attempted to emulate. Throughout the eighteenth century, students of human affairs pursued the goal of finding its analogues that would bring similar levels of rationality and understanding to political and economic life. Even today, when theoretical physics has moved beyond universal gravitation, the Newtonian system of the world remains one of the most influential elements in the enduring form of Western thought.

The interpretive articles included in Part 1, Natural Philosophy (above), are equally relevant to Newton's system of the world.

Book 3: On the System of the World †

In the preceding books I have laid down the principles of philosophy; principles not philosophical but mathematical: such, namely, as we may build our reasonings upon in philosophical inquiries. These principles are the laws and conditions of certain motions, and powers or forces, which chiefly have respect to philosophy; but, lest they should have appeared of themselves dry and barren, I have illustrated them here and there with some philosophical scholiums, giving an account of such things as are of more general nature, and which philosophy seems chiefly to be founded on; such as the density and the resistance of bodies, spaces void of all bodies, and the motion of light and sounds. It remains that, from the same principles, I now demonstrate the frame of the System of the World. Upon this subject I had, indeed, composed the third Book in a popular method, that it might be read by many; but afterwards, considering that such as had not sufficiently entered into the principles could not easily discern the strength of the consequences, nor lay aside the prejudices to which they had been many years accustomed, therefore, to prevent the disputes which might be raised upon such accounts, I chose to reduce the substance of this Book into the form of Propositions (in the mathematical way), which should be read by those only who had first made themselves masters of the principles established in the preceding Books: not that I would advise anyone to the previous study of every Proposition of those Books; for they abound with such as might cost too much time, even to readers of good mathematical learning. It is enough if one carefully reads the Definitions, the Laws of Motion, and the first three sections of the first Book. He may then pass on to this Book, and consult such of the remaining Propositions of the first two Books, as the references in this, and his occasions, shall require.

From *The System of the World* ‡

[1.] *The matter of the heavens is fluid.*

It was the ancient opinion of not a few, in the earliest ages of philosophy, that the fixed stars stood immovable in the highest parts of the

† Isaac Newton, *Mathematical Principles of Natural Philosophy* and *System of the World*, trans. by Andrew Motte, revised by Florian Cajori (Berkeley and Los Angeles: University of California Press, 1934 and later printings), p. 397. Copyright © 1934 and 1962 Regents of the University of California. Reprinted by permission. After setting forth general principles of dynamics in Books 1 and 2, Newton devoted Book 3 of the *Principia* to their application to the observed phenomena of nature, primarily celestial phenomena. See note on Cajori translation on p. 116.

‡ Isaac Newton, *Mathematical Principles of Natural Philosophy* and *System of the World*, trans.

world; that under the fixed stars the planets were carried about the sun; that the earth, as one of the planets, described an annual course about the sun, while by a diurnal motion it was in the meantime revolved about its own axis; and that the sun, as the common fire which served to warm the whole, was fixed in the centre of the universe.

* * *

It is not to be denied that Anaxagoras, Democritus, and others, did now and then start up, who would have it that the earth possessed the centre of the world, and that the stars were revolved towards the west about the earth quiescent in the centre, some at a swifter, others at a slower rate.

However, it was agreed on both sides that the motions of the celestial bodies were performed in spaces altogether free and void of resistance. The whim of solid orbs was of a later date, introduced by Eudoxus, Calippus, and Aristotle; when the ancient philosophy began to decline, and to give place to the new prevailing fictions of the Greeks.

But, above all things, the phenomena of comets can by no means tolerate the idea of solid orbits. The Chaldeans, the most learned astronomers of their time, looked upon the comets (which of ancient times before had been numbered among the celestial bodies) as a particular sort of planets, which, describing eccentric orbits, presented themselves to view only by turns, once in a revolution, when they descended into the lower parts of their orbits.

And as it was the unavoidable consequence of the hypothesis of solid orbits, while it prevailed, that the comets should be thrust into spaces below the moon; so, when later observations of astronomers restored the comets to their ancient places in the higher heavens, these celestial spaces were necessarily cleared of the incumbrance of solid orbits.

---

by Andrew Motte, revised by Florian Cajori (Berkeley and Los Angeles: University of California Press, 1934 and later printings), pp. 549–615. When Newton first composed a draft of the *Principia*, his intention was to have a work divided into two books. The subject matter of the initial Book 2 (later reworked mathematically to become Book 3 of the *Principia*) spelled out the argument for universal gravitation in what he later called (in the introduction to Book 3 of the *Principia*) a popular method, that is, prose rather than mathematics. After Newton's death, as has been noted, the text of this early draft was published in both an English translation and in the original Latin. It presents the structure of the argument in a manner more accessible to the general reader than does Book 3 of the *Principia*. In the Latin and English printed versions some cross-references to pages or propositions of the *Principia* were introduced, thus making it seem as if Newton had either written or revised this text after, rather than before, composing the *Principia*.

The text reproduced here is taken from Cajori's revision (made in the 1930s) of the translation published anonymously in 1729. We do not know what text was used by the translator, but there is included an oft-quoted paragraph about hypotheses and a "mathematical way" that does not correspond to either of the two manuscript texts among Newton's manuscripts. See note on Cajori translation on p. 116.

[2.] *The principle of circular motion in free spaces.*

After this time, we do not know in what manner the ancients explained the question, how the planets came to be retained within certain bounds in these free spaces, and to be drawn off from the rectilinear courses, which, left to themselves, they should have pursued, into regular revolutions in curvilinear orbits. Probably it was to give some sort of satisfaction to this difficulty that solid orbs had been introduced.

The[1] later philosophers pretend to account for it either by the action of certain vortices, as Kepler and Descartes; or by some other principle of impulse or attraction, as Borelli, Hooke, and others of our nation; for, from the laws of motion, it is most certain that these effects must proceed from the action of some force or other.

But our purpose is only to trace out the quantity and properties of this force from the phenomena, and to apply what we discover in some simple cases as principles, by which, in a mathematical way, we may estimate the effects thereof in more involved cases; for it would be endless and impossible to bring every particular to direct and immediate observation.

We said, *in a mathematical way*, to avoid all questions about the nature or quality of this force, which we would not be understood to determine by any hypothesis; and therefore call it by the general name of a centripetal force, as it is a force which is directed towards some centre; and as it regards more particularly a body in that centre, we call it circumsolar, circumterrestrial, circumjovial; and so in respect of other central bodies.

[3.] *The action of centripetal forces.*

That by means of centripetal forces the planets may be retained in certain orbits, we may easily understand, if we consider the motions of projectiles; for a stone that is projected is by the pressure of its own weight forced out of the rectilinear path, which by the initial projection alone it should have pursued, and made to describe a curved line in the

1. The following two paragraphs have often been cited as an expression of Newton's belief. But, in fact, they do not correspond with the actual words of either Newton's own copy of this text or the copy he prepared for deposit in the University Library, Cambridge. Furthermore, no manuscript copy has ever been found with these two paragraphs.

A literal translation of the corresponding text in Newton's two manuscript copies reads: "Modern [i.e., more recent] philosophers want either vortices to exist, as Kepler and Descartes, or some other principle whether of impulse or attraction, as Borelli, Hooke, and others of our countrymen. From the first law of motion it is most certain that some force is required. Our purpose is to bring out its quantity and properties and to investigate mathematically its effects in moving bodies. Further, in order not to determine the type hypothetically, we have called by the general name 'centripetal' that [force] which tends toward the sun, 'circumterrestrial' [that force] which [tends] toward the earth, 'circumjovial' [that force] which tends toward Jupiter, and so in the others."

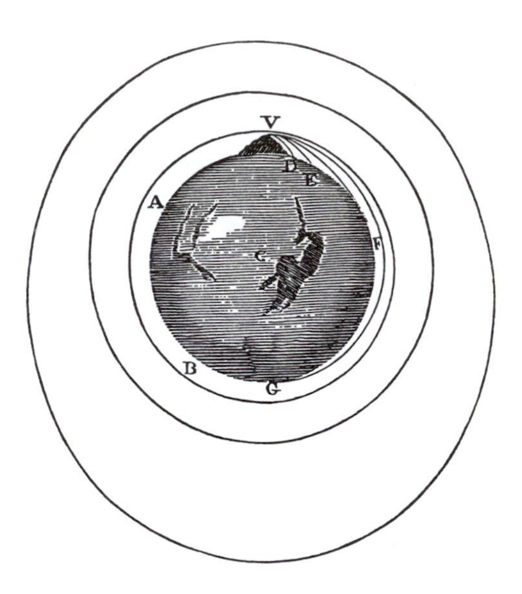

air; and through that crooked way is at last brought down to the ground; and the greater the velocity is with which it is projected, the farther it goes before it falls to the earth. We may therefore suppose the velocity to be so increased, that it would describe an arc of 1, 2, 5, 10, 100, 1000 miles before it arrived at the earth, till at last, exceeding the limits of the earth, it should pass into space without touching it.

Let AFB represent the surface of the earth, C its centre, VD, VE, VF the curved lines which a body would describe, if projected in an horizontal direction from the top of an high mountain successively with more and more velocity; and, because the celestial motions are scarcely retarded by the little or no resistance of the spaces in which they are performed, to keep up the parity of cases, let us suppose either that there is no air about the earth, or at least that it is endowed with little or no power of resisting; and for the same reason that the body projected with a less velocity describes the lesser arc VD, and with a greater velocity the greater arc VE, and, augmenting the velocity, it goes farther and farther to F and G, if the velocity was still more and more augmented, it would reach at last quite beyond the circumference of the earth, and return to the mountain from which it was projected.

And since the areas which by this motion it describes by a radius drawn to the centre of the earth are proportional to the times in which they are described, its velocity, when it returns to the mountain, will be no less than it was at first; and, retaining the same velocity, it will describe the same curve over and over, by the same law.

But if we now imagine bodies to be projected in the directions of lines parallel to the horizon from greater heights, as of 5, 10, 100, 1000, or more miles, or rather as many semidiameters of the earth, those bodies, according to their different velocity, and the different force of gravity in different heights, will describe arcs either concentric with the earth, or variously eccentric, and go on revolving through the heavens in those orbits just as the planets do in their orbits.

[4.] *The certainty of the proof.*

As when a stone is projected obliquely, that is, any way but in the perpendicular direction, the continual deflection thereof towards the earth from the right line in which it was projected is a proof of its gravitation to the earth, no less certain than its direct descent when suffered to fall freely from rest; so the deviation of bodies moving in free spaces from rectilinear paths and continual deflection therefrom towards any place, is a sure indication of the existence of some force which from all quarters impels those bodies towards that place.

And as, from the supposed existence of gravity, it necessarily follows that all bodies about the earth must press downwards, and therefore must either descend directly to the earth, if they are let fall from rest, or at least continually deviate from right lines towards the earth, if they are projected obliquely; so, from the supposed existence of a force directed to any centre, it will follow, by the like necessity, that all bodies upon which this force acts must either descend directly to that centre, or at least deviate continually towards it from right lines, if otherwise they should have moved obliquely in these right lines.

And how from the motions given we may infer the forces, or from the forces given we may determine the motions, is shown in the first two Books of our *Principles of Philosophy*.

If the earth is supposed to stand still, and the fixed stars to be revolved in free spaces in the space of 24 hours, it is certain the forces by which the fixed stars are held in their orbits are not directed to the earth, but to the centres of those orbits, that is, of the several parallel circles, which the fixed stars, declining to one side and the other from the equator, describe daily; also that by radii drawn to the centres of the orbits the fixed stars describe areas exactly proportional to the times of description. Then, because the periodic times are equal, it follows that the centripetal forces are as the radii of the several orbits, and that they will continually revolve in the same orbits. And the like consequences may be drawn from the supposed diurnal motion of the planets.

That forces should be directed to no body on which they physically depend, but to innumerable imaginary points in the axis of the earth, is an hypothesis too incongruous. It is more incongruous still that those forces should increase exactly in proportion of the distances from this axis; for this is an indication of an increase to immensity, or rather to infinity; whereas the forces of natural things commonly decrease in receding from the fountain from which they flow. But, what is yet more absurd, neither are the areas described by the same star proportional to the times, nor are its revolutions performed in the same orbit; for as the star recedes from the neighboring pole, both areas and orbits increase; and from the increase of the area it is demonstrated that the forces are not directed to the axis of the earth. And this difficulty arises from the twofold motion that is observed in the fixed stars, one diurnal round the axis of the earth, the other exceedingly slow round the axis of the ecliptic. And the explication thereof requires a composition of forces so involved and so variable, that it is hardly to be reconciled with any physical theory.

[5.] *Centripetal forces are directed to the individual centres of the planets.*

That there are centripetal forces actually directed to the bodies of the sun, of the earth, and other planets, I thus infer.

The moon revolves about our earth, and by radii drawn to its centre describes areas nearly proportional to the times in which they are described, as is evident from its velocity compared with its apparent diameter; for its motion is slower when its diameter is less (and therefore its distance greater), and its motion is swifter when its diameter is greater.

The revolutions of the satellites of Jupiter about that planet are more regular; for they describe circles concentric with Jupiter by uniform motions, as exactly as our senses can perceive.

And so the satellites of Saturn are revolved about this planet with motions nearly circular and uniform, scarcely disturbed by any eccentricity hitherto observed.

That Venus and Mercury are revolved about the sun, is demonstrable from their moon-like appearances; when they shine with a full face, they are in those parts of their orbits which in respect of the earth lie beyond the sun; when they appear half full, they are in those parts which lie over against the sun; when horned, in those parts which lie between the earth and the sun; and sometimes they pass over the sun's disk, when directly interposed between the earth and the sun.

And Venus, with a motion almost uniform, describes an orbit nearly circular and concentric with the sun.

But Mercury, with a more eccentric motion, makes remarkable approaches to the sun, and goes off again by turns; but it is always swifter as it is near to the sun, and therefore by a radius drawn to the sun still describes areas proportional to the times.

Lastly, that the earth describes about the sun, or the sun about the earth, by a radius from the one to the other, areas exactly proportional to the times, is demonstrable from the apparent diameter of the sun compared with its apparent motion.

These are astronomical experiments; from which it follows, by Prop. 1, 2, 3, in the first Book of our *Principles*, and their Corollaries, that there are centripetal forces actually directed (either accurately or without considerable error) to the centres of the earth, of Jupiter, of Saturn, and of the sun. In Mercury, Venus, Mars, and the lesser planets, where experiments are wanting, the arguments from analogy must be allowed in their place.

[6.] *Centripetal forces decrease inversely as the square of the distances from the centres of the planets.*

* * *

[7.] *The superior planets revolve about the sun, and the radii drawn to the sun describe areas proportional to the times.*

* * *

[8.] *The force which controls the superior planets is not directed to the earth, but to the sun.*

* * *

[9.] *The circumsolar force decreases in all planetary spaces inversely as the square of the distances from the sun.*

The distances of the planets from the sun come out the same, whether, with Tycho, we place the earth in the centre of the system, or the sun with Copernicus: and we have already proved that these distances are true in Jupiter.

Kepler and Boulliau have, with great care, determined the distances of the planets from the sun; and hence it is that their tables agree best with the heavens. And in all the planets, in Jupiter and Mars, in Saturn and the earth, as well as in Venus and Mercury, the cubes of their distances are as the squares of their periodic times; and therefore the centripetal circumsolar force throughout all the planetary regions decreases as the inverse square of the distances from the sun. In examining this proportion, we are to use the mean distances, or the transverse semiaxes of the orbits, and to neglect those little fractions, which, in defining the orbits, may have arisen from the insensible errors of observation, or may be ascribed to other causes which we shall afterwards explain. And thus we shall always find the said proportion to hold exactly; for the distances of Saturn, Jupiter, Mars, the earth, Venus, and Mercury, from the sun, obtained from the observations of astronomers, are, according to the computation of *Kepler*, as the numbers 951000, 519650, 152350, 100000, 72400, 38806; by the computation of Boulliau, as the numbers 954198, 522520, 152350, 100000, 72398, 38585; and from the periodic times they come out 953806, 520116, 152399, 100000, 72333, 38710. Their distances, according to Kepler and Boulliau, scarcely differ by any sensible quantity, and where they differ most the distances calculated from the periodic times fall in between them.

[10.] *The circumterrestrial force decreases inversely as the square of the distances from the earth. This is shown on the hypothesis that the earth is at rest.*

That the circumterrestrial force likewise decreases as the inverse square of the distances, I infer thus.

The mean distance of the moon from the centre of the earth, is, in semidiameters of the earth, according to Ptolemy, Kepler in his Ephemerides, Boulliau, Hewelcke, and Riccioli, 59; according to Flamsteed, 59 1/3; according to Tycho, 56 1/2; to Vendelin, 60; to Copernicus, 60 1/3; to Kircher, 62 1/2.

But Tycho, and all that follow his tables of refraction, making the refractions of the sun and moon (altogether against the nature of light) to exceed those of the fixed stars, and that by about four or five minutes in the horizon, did thereby augment the horizontal parallax of the moon by about the like number of minutes; that is, by about the 12th or 15th part of the whole parallax. Correct this error, and the distance will become 60 or 61 semidiameters of the earth, nearly agreeing with what others have determined.

Let us, then, assume the mean distance of the moon 60 semidiameters of the earth, and its periodic time in respect of the fixed stars 27d. 7h. 43m., as astronomers have determined it. And a body revolved in our air, near the surface of the earth supposed at rest, by means of a centripetal force which should be to the same force at the distance of the moon inversely as the squares of the distances from the centre of the earth, that is, as 3600 to 1, would (excluding the resistance of the air) complete a revolution in 1h. 24m. 27s.

Suppose the circumference of the earth to be 123249600 Paris feet, as has been determined by the late mensuration of the French, then the same body, deprived of its circular motion, and falling by the impulse of the same centripetal force as before, would, in one second of time, describe 15 1/12 Paris feet.

This we infer by a calculus formed upon Prop. 36 of Book 1, and it agrees with what we observe in all bodies about the earth. For by the experiments of pendulums, and a computation based thereon, Huygens hath demonstrated that bodies falling by all that centripetal force with which (of whatever nature it is) they are impelled near the surface of the earth, do, in one second of time, describe 15 1/12 Paris feet.

[11.] *The same proved on the hypothesis that the earth moves.*

* * *

[12.] *The decrease of the forces inversely as the square of the distances from the earth and planets is proved also from the eccentricities of the planets and the very slow motion of the apsides.*

* * *

[18.] *Another analogy between forces and bodies attracted is shown in the heavens.*

Of kin to the analogy we have been describing is another observed between the forces and the bodies attracted. Because the action of the centripetal force upon the planets decreases inversely as the square of the distance, and the periodic time increases as the $^3/_2$th power of the distance, it is evident that the actions of the centripetal force, and therefore the periodic times, would be equal in equal planets at equal distances from the sun; and in equal distances of unequal planets the total actions of the centripetal force would be as the bodies of the planets; for if the actions were not proportional to the bodies to be moved, they could not equally retract these bodies from the tangents of their orbs in equal times: nor could the motions of the satellites of Jupiter be so regular, if it was not that the circumsolar force was equally exerted upon Jupiter and all its satellites in proportion of their several weights. And the same thing is to be said of Saturn in respect of its satellites, and of our earth in respect of the moon. . . . And, therefore, at equal distances, the actions of the centripetal force are equal upon all the planets in proportion to their bodies, or to the quantities of matter in their several bodies; and for the same reason must be the same upon all the particles of the same size of which the planet is composed; for if the action was greater upon some sort of particles than upon others, in proportion to their quantity of matter, it would be also greater or less upon the whole planets, not in proportion to the quantity only, but likewise to the sort of matter more copiously found in one and more sparingly in another.

[19.] *It is found also in terrestrial bodies.*

In such bodies as are found on our earth of very different sorts, I examined this analogy with great care.

If the action of the circumterrestrial force is proportional to the bodies to be moved, it will (by the second Law of Motion) move them with equal velocity in equal times, and will make all bodies, let fall, to descend through equal spaces in equal times, and all bodies, hung by equal threads, to vibrate in equal times. If the action of the force was greater, the times would be less; if that was less, these would be greater.

But it has been long ago observed by others, that (allowance being made for the small resistance of the air) all bodies descend through equal spaces in equal times; and, by the help of pendulums, that equality of times may be observed with great exactness.

I tried the thing in gold, silver, lead, glass, sand, common salt, wood, water, and wheat. I provided two equal wooden boxes. I filled the one with wood, and suspended an equal weight of gold (as exactly as I could) in the centre of oscillation of the other. The boxes, hung by equal threads of 11 feet, made a couple of pendulums perfectly equal in weight and figure, and equally exposed to the resistance of the air: and, placing the one by the other, I observed them to play together forwards and backwards for a long while, with equal vibrations. And therefore the quantity of matter in the gold was to the quantity of matter in the wood as the action of the motive force upon all the gold to the action of the same upon all the wood; that is, as the weight of the one to the weight of the other.

And by these experiments, in bodies of the same weight, one could have discovered a difference of matter less than the thousandth part of the whole.

[20.] *The agreement of those analogies.*

Since the action of the centripetal force upon the bodies attracted is, at equal distances, proportional to the quantities of matter in those bodies, reason requires that it should be also proportional to the quantity of matter in the body attracting.

For all action is mutual, and makes the bodies approach one to the other, and therefore must be the same in both bodies. It is true that we may consider one body as attracting, another as attracted; but this distinction is more mathematical than natural. The attraction resides really in each body towards the other, and is therefore of the same kind in both.

[21.] *Their coincidence.*

And hence it is that the attractive force is found in both. The sun attracts Jupiter and the other planets; Jupiter attracts its satellites; and, for the same reason, the satellites act as well one upon another as upon Jupiter, and all the planets mutually one upon another.

And though the mutual actions of two planets may be distinguished and considered as two, by which each attracts the other, yet, as those actions are between both, they do not make two but one operation between two terms. Two bodies may be attracted each to the other by the contraction of a cord interposed. There is a double cause of action, namely, the disposition of both bodies, as well as a double action so far as the action is considered as upon two bodies; but as between two bodies, it is but one single one. It is not one action by which the sun attracts Jupiter, and another by which Jupiter attracts the sun; but it is one action by which the sun and Jupiter mutually endeavor to approach each the other. By the action with which the sun attracts Jupiter, Jupiter and the sun endeavor to come nearer together; and by the action with which Jupiter attracts the sun. Likewise Jupiter and the sun endeavor to come nearer together. But the sun is not attracted towards Jupiter by a twofold action, nor Jupiter by a twofold action towards the sun; but it is one single intermediate action, by which both approach nearer together.

Thus iron draws the loadstone, as well as the loadstone draws the iron; for all iron in the neighborhood of the loadstone draws other iron. But the action between the loadstone and iron is single, and is considered as single by the philosophers. The action of iron upon the loadstone is, indeed, the action of the loadstone between itself and the iron, by which both endeavor to come nearer together: and so it manifestly appears; for if you remove the loadstone, the whole force of the iron almost ceases.

In this sense it is that we are to conceive one single action to be exerted between two planets arising from the conspiring natures of both; and this action standing in the same relation to both, if it is proportional to the quantity of matter in the one, it will be also proportional to the quantity of matter in the other.

* * *

[23.] *The forces directed towards all terrestrial bodies are proportional to their quantities of matter.*

Let ABCD represent the globe of the earth cut by any plane AC into two parts ACB and ACD. The part ACB bearing upon the part ACD

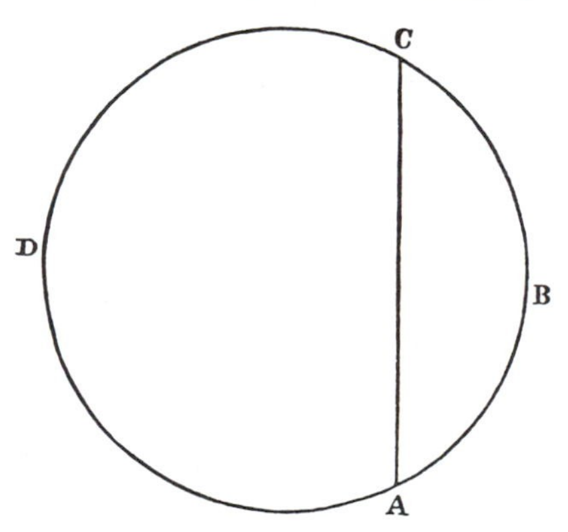

presses it with its whole weight; nor can the part ACD sustain this pressure and continue unmoved, if it is not opposed by an equal contrary pressure. And therefore the parts equally press each other by their weights, that is, equally attract each other, according to the third Law of Motion; and, if separated and let go, would fall towards each other with velocities inversely as the bodies. All this we may try and see in the loadstone, whose attracted part does not propel the part attracting, but is only stopped and sustained thereby.

Suppose now that ACB represents some small body on the earth's surface; then, because the attractions of this particle, and of the remaining part ACD of the earth towards each other, are equal, but the attraction of the particle towards the earth (or its weight) is as the matter of the particle (as we have proved by the experiment on pendulums), the attraction of the earth towards the particle will likewise be as the matter of the particle; and therefore the attractive forces of all terrestrial bodies will be as their several quantities of matter.

[24.] *Shown that the same forces are directed towards celestial bodies.*

The forces, which are as the matter in terrestrial bodies of all forms, and therefore are not mutable with the forms, must be found in all sorts of bodies whatsoever, celestial as well as terrestrial, and be in all proportional to their quantities of matter, because among all there is no difference of substance, but of modes and forms only. But in the celestial bodies the same thing is likewise proved thus. We have shown that the action of the circumsolar force upon all the planets (reduced to equal distances) is as the matter of the planets; that the action of the circumjovial force upon the satellites of Jupiter observes the same law; and the same thing is to be said of the attraction of all the planets towards every planet: but it follows from this that their attractive forces are as their several quantities of matter.

[25.] *The forces decrease from the surfaces of the planets outwardly, inversely as the square of the distances, and inwardly, directly as the distances from the centres.*

As the parts of the earth attract one another so do those of all the planets. If Jupiter and its satellites were brought together, and formed into one globe, without doubt they would continue to attract one another as before. And, on the other hand, if the body of Jupiter was broken into more globes, surely these would no less attract one another than they do the satellites now. From these attractions it is that the bodies of the earth and all the planets assume a spherical figure, and their parts cohere, and are not dispersed through the ether. But we have before proved that these forces arise from the universal nature of matter, and that, therefore, the force of any whole globe is made up of the several forces of all its parts. And from this it follows that the force of every particle decreases inversely as the square of the distance from that particle; and that the force of an entire globe, reckoning from the surface outwards, decreases inversely as the square of the distance, but reckoning inwards, decreases simply as the first power of the distances from the centres, if the matter of the globe be uniform. And when the matter of the globe, reckoning from the centre towards the surface, is not uniform, nevertheless, the decrease from the surface outwards is inversely as the square of the distance, provided that difformity is similar in places round about at equal distances from the centre. And two such globes will attract one the other with a force decreasing inversely as the square of the distance between their centres.

* * *

[27.] *All the planets revolve around the sun.*

From comparing the forces of the planets one with another, we have above seen that the circumsolar does more than a thousand times exceed all the rest; but by the action of a force so great it is unavoidable that all bodies within, nay, and far beyond, the bounds of the planetary system must descend directly to the sun, unless by other motions they are impelled towards other parts: nor is our earth to be excluded from the number of such bodies; for certainly the moon is a body of the same nature with the planets, and subject to the same attractions with the other planets, seeing it is by the circumterrestrial force that it is retained in its orbit. But that the earth and moon are equally attracted towards the sun, we have above proved; we have likewise before proved that all bodies are subject to the said common laws of attraction. Nay, supposing any of those bodies to be deprived of its circular motion about the sun, by having its distance from the sun, we may find in what space of time it would in its descent arrive at the sun; namely, in half that periodic time in which the body might be revolved at one-half of its former distance; or in a space of time that is to the periodic time of the planet as 1 to $4\sqrt{2}$; as that Venus in its descent would arrive at the sun in the space of 40 days, Jupiter in the space of two years and one month, and the earth and moon together in the space of 66 days and 19 hours. But, since no such thing happens, it must needs be, that those bodies are moved towards other parts, nor is every motion sufficient for this purpose. To hinder such a descent, a due proportion of velocity is required. And hence depends the force of the argument drawn from the retardation of the motions of the planets. Unless the circumsolar force decreased as the square of their increasing slowness, the excess thereof would force those bodies to descend to the sun; for instance, if the motion (other things being equal) was retarded by one-half, the planet would be held in its orbit by one-fourth of the former circumsolar force, and by the excess of the other three-fourths would descend to the sun. And therefore the planets (Saturn, Jupiter, Mars, Venus, and Mercury) are not really retarded in their perigees, nor become really stationary, or regressive with slow motions. All these are but apparent, and the absolute motions, by which the planets continue to revolve in their orbits, are always direct, and nearly uniform. But that such motions are performed about the sun, we have already proved; and therefore the sun, as the centre of the absolute motions, is quiescent. For we can by no means allow quiescence to the earth, lest the planets in their perigees should indeed be truly retarded, and become truly stationary and regressive, and so for want of motion should descend to the sun. But further; since the planets (Venus, Mars, Jupiter, and the rest) by radii drawn to the sun describe regular orbits, and areas (as we have shown) nearly and to sense proportional to the times, it follows that the sun is moved with no notable force, unless perhaps with such as all the planets are equally moved with, according to their several quantities of matter, in parallel lines, and so the whole system is transferred in right lines. Reject that translation of the whole system, and the sun will be almost quiescent in the centre thereof. If the sun was revolved about the earth, and carried the other planets round about itself, the earth ought to attract the sun with a great force, but the circumsolar planets with no force producing any sensible effect. . . . Add to this, that if hitherto the earth, because of the gravitation of its parts, has been placed by most authors in the lowermost region of the universe; now, for better reason, the sun possessed of a centripetal force exceeding our terrestrial gravitation a thousand times and more, ought to be depressed into the lowermost place, and to be held for the centre of the system. And thus the true disposition of the whole system will be more fully and more exactly understood.

[28.] *The common centre of gravity of the sun and all the planets is at rest and the sun moves with a very slow motion. Explanation of the solar motion.*

* * *

[29.] *Nevertheless, the planets revolve in ellipses having foci at the centre of the sun; and the radii drawn to the sun describe areas proportional to the times.*

About the sun, thus librated, the other planets are revolved in elliptic orbits, and by radii drawn to the sun, describe areas nearly proportional to the times. . . . If the sun were quiescent, and the other planets did not act mutually one upon another, their orbits would be elliptic, and the areas exactly proportional to the times. But the actions of the planets among themselves, compared with the actions of the sun on the planets, are of no moment, and produce no sensible errors. And those errors are less in revolutions about the sun agitated in the manner but now described than if those revolutions were made about the sun quiescent, especially if the focus of every orbit is placed in the common centre of gravity of all the lower included planets; viz., the focus of the orbit of Mercury in the centre of the sun; the focus of the orbit of Venus in the common centre of gravity of Mercury and the sun; the focus of the orbit of the earth in the common centre of gravity of Venus, Mercury, and the sun; and so of the rest. And by this means the foci of the orbits of all the planets, except Saturn, will not be sensibly removed from the centre of the sun, nor will the focus of the orbit of Saturn recede sensibly from the common centre of gravity of Jupiter and the sun. And therefore astronomers are not far from the truth, when they reckon the sun's centre the common focus of all the planetary orbits. In Saturn itself the error thence arising does not exceed 1′ 45″. And if its orbit, by placing the focus thereof in the common centre of gravity of Jupiter and the sun, shall happen to agree better with the phenomena, from thence all that we have said will be further confirmed.

* * *

[31.] *From the foregoing principles are derived all the lunar motions thus far noted by astronomers.*

* * *

[37.] *The precession of the equinoxes and the libratory motion of the axes of the earth and planets.*

By reason of the diurnal revolutions of the planets, the matter which they contain endeavors to recede from the axis of this motion, and hence the fluid parts rising higher towards the equator than about the poles, would lay the solid parts about the equator under water, if those parts did not rise also; upon this account the planets are somewhat thicker about the equator than about the poles; and their equinoctial points thence become regressive; and their axes, by a motion of nutation, twice in every revolution, librate towards their ecliptics, and twice return again to their former inclination, . . . and hence it is that Jupiter, viewed through very long telescopes, does not appear altogether round, but having its diameter that lies parallel to the ecliptic somewhat longer than that which is drawn from north to south.

[38.] *The ocean must flow twice and ebb twice, each day, and the highest water occurs at the third hour after the approach of the luminaries to the meridian of the place.*

And from the diurnal motion and the attractions of the sun and moon our sea ought twice to rise and twice to fall every day, as well lunar as solar, and the greatest height of the water to happen before the sixth hour of either day and after the twelfth hour preceding. By the slowness of the diurnal motion the flood is retracted to the twelfth hour; and by the force of the motion of reciprocation it is protracted and deferred till a time nearer to the sixth hour. But until that time will be more accurately determined by the phenomena, why should we not choose the middle between those extremes, and conjecture the greatest height of the water to happen at the third hour? In this manner the water will rise all that time in which the force of the luminaries to raise it is greater, and will fall all that time in which their force is less; namely, from the ninth to the third hour when that force is greater, and from the third to the ninth when it is less. The hours I reckon from the approach of each luminary to the meridian of the place, as well under as above the horizon; and by the hours of the lunar day I understand the twenty-fourth parts of that time which the moon spends before it comes about again by its apparent diurnal motion to the meridian of the place which it left the day before.

* * *

[58.] *That comets, when they come into view, are nearer than Jupiter is shown from their parallax in longitude.*

The fixed stars being, therefore, at such vast distances from one another, can neither attract each other perceptibly, nor be attracted by our sun. But the comets must unavoidably be acted on by the circumsolar force; for as the comets were placed by astronomers beyond the moon, because they were found to have no diurnal parallax, so their annual parallax is a convincing proof of their descending into the regions of the planets. For all the comets which move in a direct course, according to the order of the signs, about the end of their appearance become more than ordinarily slow, or retrograde, if the earth is between them and the sun; and more than ordinarily swift if the earth is approaching to a heliocentric opposition with them. Whereas, on the other hand, those comets which move against the order of the signs, towards the end of their appearance, appear swifter than they ought to be, if the earth is between them and the sun; and slower, and perhaps retrograde, if the earth is in the other side of its orbit. This is occasioned by the motion of the earth in different situations. If the earth go the same way with the comet, with a swifter motion, the comet becomes retrograde; if with a slower motion, the comet becomes slower, however; and if the earth move the contrary direction, it becomes swifter; and by ascertaining the differences between the slower and swifter motions, and the sums of the more swift and retrograde motions, and comparing them with the situation and motion of the earth from whence they arise, I found, by means of this parallax, that the distances of the comets at the time they cease to be visible to the naked eye are always less than the distance of Saturn, and generally even less than the distance of Jupiter.

* * *

[72.] *The comets move in conic sections having one focus in the centre of the sun, and by their radii drawn to that centre describe areas proportional to the times.*

And hence it follows that the comets, during the whole time of their appearance unto us, being within the sphere of activity of the circumsolar force, and therefore agitated by the impulse of that force, will be made to move in conic sections that have one focus in the centre of the sun, and, by radii drawn to the sun, to describe areas proportional to the times; for that force is propagated to an immense distance, and will govern the motions of bodies far beyond the orbit of Saturn.

[73.] *These conic sections are near to parabolas. This is inferred from the velocity of the comets.*

There are three hypotheses about comets; for some will have it that they are generated and perish as often as they appear and vanish; others, that they come from the regions of the fixed stars, and are seen by us in their passage through the system of our planets; and, lastly, others will have it, that they are bodies continually revolving about the sun in very eccentric orbits. In the first case, the comets, according to their different velocities, will move in conic sections of all sorts; in the second, they will describe hyperbolas, and in either of the two will frequent indifferently all quarters of the heavens, as well those about the poles as those towards the ecliptic; in the third, their motions will be performed in ellipses very eccentric, and very nearly approaching to parabolas. But (if the law of the planets is observed) their orbits will not much decline from the the plane of the ecliptic; and, so far as I could hitherto observe, the third case obtains; for the comets do, indeed, chiefly frequent the zodiac, and scarcely ever attain to a heliocentric latitude of 40°. And that they move in orbits very nearly parabolic, I infer from their velocity; for the velocity with which a parabola is described is everywhere to the velocity with which a comet or planet may be revolved about the sun in a circle at the same distance in the ratio of $\sqrt{2}$ to 1; and, by my computation, the velocity of comets is found to be much the same. I examined the thing by inferring successively the velocities from the distances, and the distances both from the parallaxes and the phenomena of the tails, and never found the errors of excess or defect in the velocities greater than what might have arisen from the errors in the distances computed after that manner.

* * *

COLIN MACLAURIN

From *An Account of Sir Isaac Newton's Philosophical Discoveries* †

Chap. II.

The moon is a heavy body, and gravitates towards the earth in the same manner as terrestrial bodies.

1. Sir *Isaac Newton* considering that the power of gravity acts equally on all matter on the surface of the earth or near it, that it is not sensibly less on the tops of the highest mountains, that it affects the air and reaches upward to the utmost limits of the atmosphere, and that it cannot be owing to the influence of any sensible terrestrial matter; he could not believe that it broke off abruptly, but was induced, on these grounds, to think it might be a more general principle, and extend to the heavens; so as to affect the moon at least, which is by much the nearest to us of all the bodies in the system. The absurdity of those who had taught that the heavenly bodies were made of some inexplicable substance, essentially different from that of our earth, had sufficiently appeared from modern discoveries: the philosophers no longer made that distinction, which had been founded on superstition and vulgar prejudices only. The earth was allowed to be of the number of the planets, and the planets were considered as like our earth. To complete this resemblance, our author has shewn that they consist of the same heavy gravitating substance of which the earth is formed.

2. The effects of the power of gravity upon terrestrial bodies may be reduced to three classes: *First*, in consequence of it, a body at rest, supported by the ground, or suspended by a string or line of any kind, or that is any way kept from falling, endeavours, however, always to move; and in such cases, its gravity is measured by the pressure of the quiescent body upon the obstacle that hinders its motion. *Secondly*, when a body descends in the vertical or plumb-line, its motion is continually accelerated, in consequence of the power of gravity's acting incessantly upon it;

† Colin Maclaurin, *An Account of Sir Isaac Newton's Philosophical Discoveries, in Four Books* (London: printed for the author's children, 1748, rpt. 1970), chs. 2 and 9. Reprinted by permission of Georg Olms Verlag AG. Maclaurin sets out Newton's argument on the system of the world in an intentionally popular mode.

or if it be projected upwards in the same right line, its motion is continually retarded, in consequence of the same power's acting incessantly upon it with a contrary direction: and, in such cases, the force of gravity is measured by the acceleration or retardation of the motion produced in a given time, by the power continued uniformly for that time: but if the body descend or ascend along an inclined plane, or move in a resisting medium, then, in measuring this power, due regard must be had to the principles of mechanics described in the preceding book. *Thirdly*, when a body is projected in any direction different from the vertical line, the direction of its motion is continually varied, and a curve line is described, in consequence of the incessant action of the power of gravity, which in such cases is measured by the flexure or curvature of the line described by it; for the power is always the greater, *cæteris paribus*, the more it bends the way or course of the body from the tangent or direction in which it was projected. Effects of the power of gravity, of each kind, fall under our constant observation, near the surface of the earth; for the same power which renders bodies heavy while they are at rest, accelerates them when they descend perpendicularly, and bends their motion into a curve line when they are projected in any other direction than that of their gravity. But we have access to judge of the powers that act on the celestial bodies by the effects of the last kind only: we see bodies near the earth falling towards it; but this is a proof of the moon's gravity that cannot be had, till the present state of things comes to its dissolution. When a body is projected in the air, we do not see it fall in the perpendicular towards the earth, but we see it falling every moment from the tangent to the curve, that is, from the direction in which it would have moved if its gravity had not acted for that moment. And this proof we have of the moon's gravity: for tho' we do not see her falling directly towards the earth in a right line, yet we observe her descending every moment towards the earth from the right line which was the direction of her motion at the beginning of that moment; and this is no less evidently a proof of her being acted upon by gravity, or some power like to it, than her rectilineal descent would be was she allowed to fall freely towards the earth.

3. If we had engines of a sufficient force, bodies might be projected from them so as not only to be carried a vast way without falling to the earth, but so as to move over a quarter of a great circle of it, or (abstracting from the effects of the air's resistance) so as to move round the whole earth without touching it, and, after returning to their first place, commence a new revolution with the same force they first received from the engine, and after that a third, and thus revolve as a moon or satellite round the earth for ever. If this could be effected near the earth's surface it might be done higher in the air or even as high as the moon, could the engine, or an equivalent power, be carried up and made to act there. By increasing the force of the power, a body

proportionally larger might be thus projected; and, by a power sufficiently great, a heavy body not inferior to the moon might be put in motion at first; which, being perpetually restrained by it[s] gravity from going off in a right line, might revolve for ever about the earth. Thus Sir *Isaac Newton* saw that the curvilineal motion of the moon in her orbit, and of any projectile at the surface of the earth, were phænomena of the same kind, and might be explained from the same principle extended from the earth so as to reach the moon; and that the moon was only a greater projectile that received its motion, in the beginning of things, from the Almighty Author of the universe.

4. But, to make this perfectly evident, it was necessary to shew that the powers which act on the moon, and on projectiles near the earth, and bend their motions into a curve line, were directed to the same centre, and agreed in the quantity of their force as well as in their direction. All we know of force relates to its direction or quantity, and a constant coincidence and agreement in these two respects is sufficient ground to conclude them to be the same, or similiar, phænomena derived from the same, or from like causes. It was shewn in the last chapter, that the gravity of heavy bodies is directed towards the centre of the earth; and it appears from the observations of astronomers, that the power which acts on the moon, incessantly bending her motion into a curve, is directed towards the same centre: for they find that the moon does not describe an exact circle about the earth; but an *ellipse* or oval; and that she approaches to the earth, and then recedes from it, in every revolution, but so as to have her motion accelerated while she approaches to the centre of the earth, and retarded as she recedes from it; which is an indication that she is acted on by a power directed, accurately or nearly, towards the centre.

* * *

[Maclaurin proceeds, following the lines of Newton's argument, to show that the moon's closed orbit around the earth requires that the earth attract it. Comparing the rate at which the moon's orbit diverges from a tangent with the measured acceleration of gravity on the surface of the earth indicates that the same attraction by the earth, decreasing in intensity as the square of the distance from the center of the earth, causes both phenomena. The observed periods of the planets in their orbits and their distances from the sun require that they be attracted to the sun by a force that also varies inversely as the square of the distance.]

10. But the universality of this law, and the uniformity of nature, still farther appears by comparing the motions of the different planets. The power which acts on a planet that is nearer the sun is manifestly greater than that which acts on a planet more remote; both because it moves with more velocity, and because it moves in a lesser orbit, which has more curvature, and separates farther from its tangent, in arcs of the

same length, than a greater orbit. By comparing the motions of the planets, it is found that the velocity of a nearer planet is greater than the velocity of one more remote, in proportion as the square root of the number which expresses the greater distance to the square root of that which expresses the lesser distance; so that if one planet was four times farther from the sun than another planet, the velocity of the first would be half the velocity of the latter, and the nearer planet would describe an arc in one minute, equal to the arc described by the higher planet in two minutes: and tho' the curvature of the orbits was the same, the nearer planet would fall by its gravity as much in one minute as the other would fall in two, and therefore the nearer planet would describe by it gravity four times as much space as the other would describe in the same time, by the law of motion of falling bodies so often mentioned; the gravity of the nearer planet would therefore appear to be quadruple, from the consideration of its greater velocity only. But besides, as the radius of the lesser orbit is supposed to be four times less than the radius of the other, the lesser orbit must be four times more curved, and the extremity of a small arc of the same length will be four times farther below the tangent drawn at the other extremity in the lesser orbit than in the greater; so that, tho' the velocities were equal, the gravity of the nearer planet would, on this account only, be found to be quadruple. On both these accounts together, the greater velocity of the nearer planet, and the greater curvature of its orbit, its gravity towards the sun must be supposed sixteen times greater, tho' its distance from the sun is only four times less than that of the other; that is, when the distances are as 1 to 4, the gravities are reciprocally as the squares of these numbers or as 16 to 1. In the same manner, by comparing the motions of all the planets, it is found that their gravities decrease as the squares of their distances from the sun increase.

11. Thus, by comparing the motions of any one planet in the different parts of its elliptic orbit, and the motions of the different planets in their different orbits, it appears that there is a power like the gravity of heavy bodies so well known to us on the earth, extending from the sun to all distances, and constantly decreasing as the squares of these distances increase. If any one planet descended to the distance of another, it would be acted on in the same manner, and by the same power, as that other: and as gravity preserves the substance of the earth together, and hinders its looser parts from being dissipated by its various motions; so a like power, acting at the surface of the sun, and within its body, keeps its parts together and preserves its figure, notwithstanding its rotation on its axis.

12. In the same manner as this principle governs the motions of the planets in the great solar system, it governs also the motions of the satellites in the lesser systems of which the greater is composed. There is the same harmony in their motions compared with their distances, as in the

great system: we see *Jupiter*'s satellites bending their way round him, and falling every moment from the lines that are the directions of their motions, or the tangents of their orbits, towards him; each describing equal areas in equal times by a ray drawn to his centre, to which their gravity is therefore directed. The nearer satellites move with greater celerity, in the same proportion as the nearer primary planets move more swiftly round the sun, and their gravity, therefore, varies according to the same law. The same is to be said of *Saturn*'s satellites. There is, therefore, a power that preserves the substance of these planets in their various motions, acts at their surfaces, and is extended around them, decreasing in the same manner as that which is extended from the earth and sun to all distances.

13. These secondary planets must also gravitate towards the sun. It is impossible they should move so regularly round their respective primaries, if they were not acted on by the same powers. If we suppose them to be acted on by the same accelerating power in parallel lines, there will no disorder or perplexity arise from thence; for they will then accompany their primary planets in their motions round the sun, and move about them at the same time, with the same regularity as if their primary planets were at rest. It will be as in a ship, or in any space carried uniformly forward: in which the mutual actions of bodies are the same as if the space was at rest, being no way affected by that motion which is common to all the bodies. As every projectile, while it moves in the air, gravitates towards the sun, and is carried along with the earth about the sun, while its own motion in its curve is as regular as if the earth was at rest; so the moon, which we have shewed to be only a greater projectile, must gravitate toward the sun, and while it is carried along with the earth about the sun, is not hindered by that motion from performing its monthly revolutions round the earth. *Jupiter*'s satellites gravitate toward the sun as every part of *Jupiter*'s body, and *Saturn*'s satellites gravitate toward the sun as if they were parts of *Saturn*. Thus the motions in the great solar system, and in the lesser particular systems of each planet, are consistent with each other, and are carried on with a regular harmony without any confusion, or mutually interfering with one another, but what necessarily arises from small inequalities in the gravities of primary and secondary planets, and the want of exact parallelism in the directions of those gravities; of which we are to treat afterwards.

14. Nor is there any body that comes, tho' rarely and as a stranger, into the lower parts of our system, exempted from this universal gravitation toward the sun. When a *comet* appears, we see the effect of the same power acting on it; since it descends with an accelerated motion as it approaches the sun; and ascends with a retarded motion, bending its way about the sun, and describing equal areas in equal times by a ray drawn from it to his centre. This power that acts on the comets varies

according to the same law as the gravity of the planets, as appears from their describing either *parabolas*, or very eccentric *ellipses* having one of their *foci* in the centre of the sun: our author having demonstrated, that the power which makes a body describe a parabola about its focus, must likewise vary according to the law so often mentioned. If a body was projected from our earth in a line perpendicular to the horizon, with a certain force, (*viz*, that which would carry it over about 420 miles with an uniform motion in a minute), it would rise in that line for ever and return to the earth no more. Its gravity would, indeed, retard its motion continually, but never be able to exhaust it, the force of gravity upon it decreasing as it rises to a greater height. If the body was projected with the same force in any other direction, it would go off in a *parabola* having its *focus* in the centre of the earth, and never return to the earth again. A force a little less would make it move in a very eccentric *ellipsis*, in which it would return after a long period to its first place; if it was not diverted in its course by approaching too near to some celestial body. In the same manner, a planet projected with a certain force would go off for ever in a parabolic curve having the sun in its focus; and if it was projected with a force a little less would revolve in a very eccentric ellipsis having its focus in the sun. All these motions, therefore, proceed from the same principle, acting in a various but most regular manner in different circumstances, and are all analogous to the motions of heavy bodies projected from our earth. Effects so similar are to be resolved into the same cause, and there is hardly more evidence for supposing that it is the same power of gravity that acts upon terrestrial bodies in *Europe* and in *America*, at the equator and at the poles, than that it is the same principle which acts over the whole system, from the centre of the sun to the remote orb of *Saturn*, or to the utmost altitude of the most eccentric comet.

* * *

6. The plain argument for the existence of the Deity, obvious to all and carrying irresistible conviction with it, is from the evident contrivance and fitness of things for one another, which we meet with throughout all parts of the universe. There is no need of nice or subtle reasonings in this matter: a manifest contrivance immediately suggests a contriver. It strikes us like a sensation; and artful reasonings against it may puzzle us, but it is without shaking our belief. No person, for example, that knows the principles of optics and the structure of the eye, can believe that it was formed without skill in that science; or that the ear was formed without the knowledge of sounds; or that the male and female in animals were not formed for each other, and for continuing the species. All our accounts of nature are full of instances of this kind. The admirable and beautiful structure of things for final causes, exalt our idea of the *Contriver*: the unity of design shews him to be *One*. The great

motions in the system, performed with the same facility as the least, suggest his *Almighty Power*, which gave motion to the earth and the celestial bodies, with equal ease as to the minutest particles. The subtility of the motions and actions in the internal parts of bodies, shews that his influence penetrates the inmost recesses of things, and that He is equally *active* and *present* every where. The simplicity of the laws that prevail in the world, the excellent disposition of things, in order to obtain the best ends, and the beauty which adorns the works of nature, far superior to any thing in art, suggest his consummate *Wisdom*. The usefulness of the whole scheme, so well contrived for the intelligent beings that enjoy it, with the internal disposition and moral structure of those beings themselves, shew his unbounded *Goodness*. These are the arguments which are sufficiently open to the views and capacities of the unlearned, while at the same time they acquire new strength and lustre from the discoveries of the learned. The Deity's acting and interposing in the universe, shew that he *governs* it as well as formed it, and the depth of his counsels, even in conducting the material universe, of which a great part surpasses our knowledge, keep up an inward veneration and awe of this great Being, and dispose us to receive what may be otherwise revealed to us concerning him. It has been justly observed, that some of the laws of nature, now known to us, must have escaped us if we had wanted the sense of seeing. It may be in his power to bestow upon us other senses of which we have at present no idea; without which it may be impossible for us to know all his works, or to have more adequate ideas of himself. In our present state, we know enough to be satisfied of our dependency upon him, and of the duty we owe to him the lord and disposer of all things. He is not the object of sense; his essence, and indeed that of all other substances, is beyond the reach of all our discoveries; but his attributes clearly appear in his admirable works. We know that the highest conceptions we are able to form of them are still beneath his real perfections; but his power and dominion over us, and our duty towards him, are manifest.

7. Sir *Isaac Newton* is particularly careful, always to represent him as a free agent; being justly apprehensive of the dangerous consequences of that doctrine which introduces a fatal or absolute necessity presiding over all things. He made the world, not from any necessity determining him, but when he thought fit: matter is not infinite or necessary, but he created as much of it as he thought proper: he placed the systems of the fixed stars at various distances from each other, at his pleasure: in the solar system, he formed the planets of such a number, and disposed them at various distances from the sun, as he pleased: he has made them all move from west to east, tho' it is evident from the motions of the comets that he might have made them move from east to west. In these and other instances, we plainly perceive the vestiges of a wise agent, but acting freely and with perfect liberty.

As caution was a distinguishing part of Sir *Isaac Newton*'s character, but no way derogatory from his penetration and the acuteness and sublimity of his genius; so we have particular reason on this occasion to applaud it, and to own that his philosophy has proved always subservient to the most valuable purposes, without ever tending to hurt them.

* * *

DAVID KUBRIN

Newton and the Cyclical Cosmos: Providence and the Mechanical Philosophy †

The important debate between Newton and Leibniz in 1715 over metaphysical principles served to bring out many fundamental differences in the way the two conceived of physical reality. At the heart of the debate were several basic tenets of Newtonian science which Leibniz objected to, one of which was Newton's 1706 statement of the world's decay. Newton had said that though the system of the sun and planets would continue for "many Ages," over the course of years irregularities arising from the mutual attraction of the planets and the comets ". . . will be apt to increase, till this System wants a Reformation . . ."

Leibniz objected to such a conception of an imperfect system of the world: to him it implied an imperfect Creator, lacking either the foresight or the ability to fashion a cosmic machinery able to last without His constant meddling. A truly perfect Creator, Leibniz insisted, would have fashioned a world which would last forever unless He were to intervene purposely to destroy it. This contrasted with Newton's belief that God would wisely fashion His creation in such a way that ". . . nothing is done without his continual government and inspection . . . ," so that God had to act merely to allow the world to continue. Left by itself, an imperfect system made of mere dead matter, the world would tend over the course of centuries to become so unwound that a new creation—or reformation, as Newton put it—would be necessary.

This aspect of Newton's thought is, of course, well known. But I do not believe its real significance and meaning have been fathomed. In this paper, I would like to show why Newton was led to believe the world was unwinding and to relate this opinion to Newton's cosmogony, a cosmogony which indicated how the world would eventually be corrected or reset by its Creator. I shall treat first the reasons for Newton's believing in the unwinding cosmos, follow this by a brief description of

† *Journal of the History of Ideas* 28 (1967): 325–46. Reprinted by permission of The Johns Hopkins University Press. Kubrin is a contemporary student of seventeenth-century science.

Newton's cosmogony in its mature form, and then give an account of the development of these views. To understand the context of this aspect of Newton's thought, we must consider first the reaction of most English philosophers to the mechanical philosophy which was the world-view of the late scientific revolution. Many Englishmen, while initially seeing in the mechanism offered by Descartes a support both for natural philosophy and for religious orthodoxy, had by the late 1660's severe misgivings that Cartesianism would usher out of the world all notions of Providence. Henry More, the Cambridge Platonist, Robert Boyle, the natural philosopher, and Walter Charleton, the physician, for example, all saw that the mechanical philosophy, to be acceptable, had to make God more than a mere Creator; for a mere Creator, once His task was done, might become a mere absentee deity, and such a view of God was dangerously similar to the teachings of the deists.

To avoid such an implication, many of the English adopted an interpretation of the mechanical philosophy which made God responsible not only for initially creating matter and motion—the two principles responsible for all phenomena according to the mechanical philosophy—but also for preserving motion in bodies. Merely to persist in their movements, bodies needed constant Providential care by God; in this sense, He was the cause of motion. Worried by the dangers inherent in a thoroughly mechanized world, many English philosophers would allow neither their growing knowledge of the laws of motion nor the concept of inertia (claiming that a body in motion will stay in that state unless disturbed) to persuade them that motion could persist without God's care. Among English divines and natural philosophers, there was a further fear: unless it could be shown that God's Providence acted at the *present* time, some would doubt whether it had *ever* been a force in the world. Criticizing the attempt in George Cheyne's *Philosophical Principles of Natural Religion* (1705) to make motion dependent upon God's will, the English mathematician Brook Taylor—illustrating this danger—wrote:

> As we can conceive a portion of Matter, which now is, to continue its being without the operation of a Cause, to all Eternity, (for it seems rather to require a Cause to make it cease to be, than to continue it) so we may as easily conceive it to have been from all Eternity, or to have had no cause of its existence, that is to be Self-Existen[t].

Taylor extended his argument to the motion of the planets, seeing no reason why this could not have gone on from all eternity. Earlier arguments, similar to Taylor's, had led Richard Bentley to attack in his sermons those who "have asserted, that the same quantity of motion is always kept up in the world; which may seem to favour the opinion of its infinite duration. . . ."

This central problem, that of the relation of God's Providence to the mechanisms at the foundation of the new philosophy, thus arose, in part, from a general concern that the banishment of Providence from the present world would lead men to believe that the world had always been without Providence, indeed, had been without Creator or Creation, lasting from all eternity. Bentley, co-editor of the second edition of Newton's *Principia* (1713), changed certain lines in Edmund Halley's Ode to Newton, which had appeared at the beginning of the first edition, because Bentley thought these lines were open to the interpretation that the world had always existed. Although Halley obtained a promise from Newton that the Ode would appear in its original form for the third edition of 1726, the editor of the third edition, Henry Pemberton, again struck out the offending lines and left them in the form of Bentley's innocuous emendation.

Bentley's and Pemberton's concern about the belief in the world's eternity reflected several decades of argument by the English hierarchy against this particular challenge to orthodoxy. These arguments had been implicitly directed against a few atheists and deists who *were*—in conversation, in manuscripts, and even in printed pamphlets—proclaiming the eternity of the world. Two years after his edition of the *Principia*, in which he persisted in emending Halley's Ode to Newton, Pemberton wrote an exposition of Newtonian philosophy in which he made the logical connection between Newton's belief that the world was unwinding and the orthodox position that the world could not be eternal:

> I think it not improper to mention a reflection made by our excellent author [Newton] upon these small inequalities in the planets motions; which contains under it a very strong philosophical argument against the eternity of the world. It is thus, that these inequalities must continually increase by slow degree, till they render at length the present frame of nature unfit for the purposes it now serves. And a more convincing proof cannot be desired against the present constitutions having existed from eternity than this, that a certain number of years will bring it to an end.

Chiding Leibniz for his pretension of knowing "all the omniscient Creator's purposes in making this world . . . ," Pemberton argued that the Leibnizian position cast "a reflection upon the wisdom of the author of nature, for framing a perishable work."

Newton and Samuel Clarke, in their debate with Leibniz, made this same point in a more pointed way:

> by the same reason that a philosopher can represent all things going on from the beginning of the creation, without any government or interposition of providence; a sceptic will easily argue still farther backwards, and suppose that things have from eternity gone on . . .

> without any true creation or author at all, but only what such arguers call all-wise and eternal nature.

In his fifth and last letter to Leibniz, Clarke asked rhetorically,

> [w]hether my inference from this learned author's [Leibniz] affirming that the universe cannot diminish in perfection . . . [that] the world must needs have been . . . eternal, be a just inference or no, I am willing to leave to the learned . . . to judge.

To maintain a rôle for Providence meant providing essential chores for God to perform, so that He did not rule over a universe able to exist without Him:

> And as those men [said Clarke], who pretend that in an earthly government things may go on perfectly well without the king himself ordering or disposing of any thing, may reasonably be suspected that they would like very well to set the king aside . . . ,

so too those who think that the universe does not constantly need "God's actual government" but that the laws of mechanism alone would allow phenomena to continue, "in effect tend to exclude God out of the world."

Now, in order to include God *in* the world, Newton declared, in the 1706 Latin *Opticks*, that the world by itself tended to dissolution, and consequently needed periodic reformation by the Creator. Newton, however, not only felt the need for these periodic acts of reformation, he later hit upon a possible mechanism by which they could be performed. This mechanism, ultimately controlled by the Providential God, used the recently discovered periodicity of comets to accomplish the acts of reformation and, in Newton's view, was part of a complex cosmogony, involving the creation and subsequent development of stars, planets, moons, and comets, a cosmogony to which we now turn.

It is a commonplace that the Newtonian world-picture consisted of a cosmos which since its Creation *ex nihilo*, had remained substantially the same through the course of time, changing, if at all, only insignificantly. It is, however, a commonplace well worth challenging. There is, to be sure, some evidence to support a static interpretation of the Newtonian cosmos. Did not Newton even discourage speculation about the creation, writing in the 31st Query of the *Opticks* that God at the creation set the material universe in order, and that "if he did so, it's unphilosophical to seek for any other Origin of the World, or to pretend that it might arise out of a Chaos by the mere Laws of Nature"? And did not Newton in his letters to Richard Bentley seek to reassure him that "[t]he Hypothesis of deriving the Frame of the World by mechanical Principles from Matter evenly spread through the Heavens . . . [is] inconsistent with my System . . ."? Newton also seemingly discouraged treatments of the development of the planetary system. He explicitly rejected as erroneous and inconsistent with his system "the *Cartesian* Hypothesis of Suns losing their Light, and then turning into Comets, and Comets [turning] into Planets. . . ." And Newton similarly dismissed as absurd the belief in "the Growth of new Systems [of the sun and planets] out of old ones, without the Mediation of a divine Power. . . ."

It is important, however, to note carefully Newton's qualifications in the above admonitions against cosmogonies: what appeared absurd to Newton was the attempt to show how the system of sun and planets could have arisen by mechanical principles "without the Mediation of a divine Power." If accomplished by the will of such a power, either directly or indirectly, such attempts were allowable. Similar treatments of the development of the already created cosmos were also acceptable. When Thomas Burnet in 1680 sent Newton an attempt to show how God could have accomplished the creation of the Earth by mechanical principles, Newton was in general sympathy with the treatise. He suggested to Burnet several alternative mechanisms by which the surface of the Earth could have been put into its present uneven form, with its numerous caverns, mountains, seas, and rivers. He also discussed with Burnet the possibility of mechanisms by which the rotation of the Earth could gradually have been increased during the six days of the Mosaic Creation, so that Creation could have taken longer than what are now six days. In addition, Newton later encouraged his disciple, William Whiston, to write a treatise on the Creation of the Earth.

We must turn elsewhere to find the development of Newton's cosmogony, for he nowhere followed up his early suggestions to Burnet, and he did not enter later into the controversy surrounding the treatises by Burnet and Whiston. We turn to the seemingly unrelated concern which Newton had for the problem of renewing the sources, whatever they were, of heat, motion, and other forms of activity found in nature. At various times Newton suggested that this renewal was accomplished by certain aethereal spirits. At other times, he suggested that it was performed by what he called "active principles," an agency Newton insisted was necessary in order to reintroduce some principle of activity into nature to act on the matter which the Cartesian mechanical philosophy had made dead and passive. Newton first introduced this concept in the Queries to the 1706 Latin *Opticks*, insisting that from the *vis inertiae*, a mere passive principle of bodies, there could be no motion in the world; for both the beginnings and the conservation of motion, some other, active, principles were necessary. Newton saw such active principles in the causes of gravity, fermentation, light, heat, cohesion, and life.

If the amount of motion and activity decreased without being renewed, there would be an eventual cessation of the various phenomena they generated, and all bodies would become cold, life would cease, and "the Planets and Comets would not remain in their Orbs." Newton thus apparently associated the loss of the amount of motion with the increasing irregularities arising from the mutual attractions of the planets. When he later suggested a mechanism by which the planetary orbs could be reformed, that mechanism was also associated with replenishing the motion and activity in the cosmos.

This reformation, however, was to be of more than physical significance; not only would it reform the planetary orbs and replenish the amount of motion in the cosmos, but it was meant to provide, as promised in the Apocalyptic tradition, for the new Earth to arise after the Millennium. As a student at Cambridge in the 1660's, in the concluding part of his earliest surviving notebook, Newton had written of the Earth, "Its conflagration testified 2 Peter 3d [chapter], vers 6, 7, 10, 11, 12. . . . The succession of worlds, probable from Pet 3c. 13v. . . ." But how was this succession to be carried out? Newton wrote to Burnet in 1680 that probably "all the Planets about our Sun were created together, there being in no history any mention of new ones appearing or old ones ceasing." By 1694, Newton had conceived of a possible source for new planets, and he told his disciple David Gregory that "[t]he Satellites of Jupiter and Saturn can take the places of the Earth, Venus, Mars if they are destroyed, and be held in reserve for a new Creation." Some thirty years later, Newton greatly elaborated the suggestion he had made to Gregory. As John Conduitt related, Newton told him at the end of 1724, that

> it was his [Newton's] *conjecture* . . . that there was a sort of revolution in the heavenly bodies . . . that the vapours and light emitted by the sun . . . gathered themselves by degrees, into a body . . . and at last made a secondary planett [that is, a moon] . . . and then by gathering . . . more matter became a primary planet; and then by increasing still became a comet which [eventually] . . . became a matter set to recruit and replenish the Sun. . . .

Such a "revolution in the heavenly bodies" could account for the succession of worlds, and guided by "the direction of the supreme being," the system would undergo a reformation and have its quantity of motion restored.

This was the cosmogony that Newton held in his final years. It is instructive to see the development of these ideas, for the younger Newton had neither perceived this same solution, nor indeed recognized the problems which would engender this solution. Though a skeletal outline of his final ideas had been formulated relatively early, it was not until the second edition of the *Principia* in 1713 that the flesh of these ideas appeared in something approaching their final form. In Newton's hypothesis of an aethereal mechanism to account for gravity—a mechanism tried and then rejected in his private manuscripts and letters, only to be revived by him at last in the 1717 edition of his *Opticks*—this skeletal outline can be found. But when he first proposed this aethereal hypothesis for gravity about 1664, Newton did not believe that the amount of motion in the world tended to decrease. On the contrary, throughout the manuscript *Quaestiones quaedam Philosophiae* in which his aethereal hypothesis first appeared, Newton went so far as to suggest various ways in which one could obtain perpetual motion.

Later in his career, however, as we have seen, Newton came to hold that the amount of motion in the world does tend to decrease. The first clear reference to this appeared only in the Latin *Opticks* of 1706, but some related forms of "decay" in nature had appeared earlier in the 1687 *Principia*. He was led to this concept of decay, at least in part, by his growing realization that a mechanical universe in which the amount of motion remained the same could be used by atheists to argue against the existence of a Deity. Once he had decided that the amount of motion did decrease, Newton turned to his earlier aethereal hypothesis for an indication of a mechanism by which the amount of motion in the world could be renewed. Newton was able to indicate such a mechanism only after the writing of the second edition of the *Principia*. The remainder of this paper will be concerned with the development of Newton's ideas on this renewal of the cosmos; I shall try to show how he became aware of the problems and in what ways he was led to the solutions which make up his cosmogony.

Newton's aethereal hypothesis for gravity, in one of its forms, pictured the Earth like a sponge, drinking up the constant stream of fine aethereal matter falling from the heavens, this stream by its impact on bodies above the Earth causing them to descend. To prevent the Earth from becoming larger and larger as the aether accumulated, Newton suggested that the aether, having fallen on the Earth, changed its form, and then ascended again into the heavens. As Newton suggested in an hypothesis concerning the properties of light which he sent to Henry Oldenburg in 1675, nature seemed to have its origin in the transmutations of certain aethereal spirits into different forms:

> Perhaps the whole frame of Nature [Newton wrote to Oldenburg] may be nothing but various Contextures of some certaine aethereall Spirits or vapours condens'd as it were by praecipitation, much after the manner that vapours are condensed into water or exhalations into grosser Substances . . . ; and after condensation wrought into various formes. . . . Thus perhaps may all things be originated from aether.

Newton indicated how there followed from this the possibility of transformations back and forth between these various states, so that spiritous matter in space would be absorbed by the thirsty Earth, while gross matter in the bowels of the Earth would be changed to an aereal and then to an aethereal form as it rose first into the atmosphere and then into the heavens:

> nature makeing a circulation by the slow ascent of as much matter out of the bowells of the Earth in an aereall forme which for a time constitutes the Atmosphere, but being continually boyed up by the new Air, Exhalations, and Vapours riseing underneath, at length . . . vanishes againe into the aethereall Spaces, and there perhaps in time . . . is attenuated into its first principle. . . .

From the functions given by Newton to the aethereal matter, it is clear that it served, as would later what he came to call "active principles," as the source of motion and activity in the cosmos. This aethereal source of activity was perpetually being circulated.

> For nature is a perpetuall circulatory worker, generating fluids out of solids, and solids out of fluids, fixed things out of volatile, and volatile out of fixed, subtile out of gross, and gross out of subtile, Some things to ascend, and make the upper terrestriall juices, Rivers, and the Atmosphere; and by consequence others to descend for a Requitall to the former. And as the Earth, so perhaps may the Sun imbibe this Spirit copiously to conserve his Shineing, and keep the Planets from recedeing further from him. And they that will, may also suppose, *that this Spirit affords or carryes with it thither the solary fewell and materiall Principle of Light; And that the vast aethereall Spaces between us, and the stars are for a sufficient repository for this food of the Sunn and Planets. [Emphasis mine.]*

The paper to Oldenburg was written in late 1675; by 1687 when he wrote his *Principia*, Newton was evidently less convinced of the existence of aethereal mechanisms in nature, for nothing was said of either the aether or these mechanisms in the *Principia*. Newton, in avoiding this spiritous aether dispersed through space, turned his attention instead to another possible means of achieving a circulation of the sources of motion. This means he found in comets, a new member of the celestial machinery, using them as causal instruments.

As late as the early 1680's, Newton had not been convinced of the periodic nature of comets. In 1680/81 he argued against the astronomer John Flamsteed's contention that the two appearances of comets in that year on either side of the sun were from one and the same body. By the time of his *Principia*, however, Newton believed that comets, like other bodies of the sun's system, moved around the sun in orbits corresponding to the conic sections. Perhaps the most striking aspect of the appearances of the comets was their tails; these were able to grow in the short time that comets were visible from a mere two or three degrees to fifty or sixty degrees in angular length. Indeed, whatever made up these tails must be a rare and subtle form of matter. There is a tendency, Newton noted in the first edition of the *Principia*, for the matter of these tails slowly to dissipate into space, so that it was

> scattered through the whole heavens, and by little and little . . . attracted towards the planets by its gravity, and mixed with their atmosphere; . . . for the conservation of the seas, and fluids of the planets, comets seem to be required, that, from their exhalations and vapors condensed, the wastes of the planetary fluids spent upon vegetation and putrefaction, and converted into dry earth, may be continually supplied and made up; . . . and *hence it is that the bulk of the solid earth is continually increased*; [emphasis mine] and the fluids, if they are not supplied from without, must be in continual decrease, and quite fail at last. I suspect, moreover, that it is chiefly from the comets that spirit comes, which is indeed the smallest but most subtle and useful part of our air, and so much required to sustain the life of all things with us.

Rather than abandon his earlier conjectures to Oldenburg, which were based on the aether, Newton simply altered the conjectures slightly. In the 1675 paper the circulation throughout the heavens of aethereal matter was the mechanism which renewed motion and activity in the cosmos; but in 1687 Newton suggested that the circulation of the tails of comets performed this function.

Two significant changes in Newton's outlook had taken place, however. In his paper to Oldenburg, Newton had suggested a mechanism to recruit new fuel for the sun and stars as well as for the Earth, but no such mechanism was described in the first edition of the *Principia*; only the Earth was replenished. Since the tails of comets, at their longest when near the sun, were always found pointing *away* from the sun, Newton inferred that there was a force overcoming the gravitational attraction of the sun and stars for these rare vapors. Such a force prevented the vapors from replenishing the sun and stars. There was another change in the *Principia* from his 1675 letter, in which the Earth had been pictured as absorbing aether from the heavens and giving up aereal matter to the heavens, "Some things to ascend . . . and by consequence others to descend for a Requitall to the former." But this balance claimed to exist between the matter being lost and that being gained no longer was accepted in the *Principia* of 1687, where Newton now claimed that "the bulk of the solid earth is continually increased. . . ."

By these changes, Newton for the first time suggested that the cosmos was a machine that was unwinding. Nature in 1675 had been a "perpetual worker." In 1687, by implication, nature would have its period: at a certain time the sun and stars, not being replenished, would lose their fuel; at a certain time also the Earth would have so increased in size that she would no longer fit harmoniously in the present system with the sun and moon. It is not certain that Newton noticed these implications of his *Principia* immediately. But by 1694, he realized that the Earth's system would change dynamically in the course of time:

> Halley say'd that Mr. Newton had lately told him, That there was reason to Conclude That the bulk of the Earth did grow and increase . . . by the perpetuall Accession of New particles attracted out of the Ether by its Gravitating power, and he [Halley] Supposed . . . That this Encrese of the Moles of the Earth would occasion an Acceleration of the Moons Motion, she being at this time Attracted by a Stronger Vis Centripeta than in remote Ages.

It was twelve years later, in the 1706 Queries to the Latin *Opticks*, that the various ways in which Newton believed nature to run down were, for the first time, made explicit and developed at length. For the first time Newton emphasized the increasing irregularities in motions of the planets, which he thought would lead to an end of things if not reformed. For the first time also, he mentioned the tendency for the amount of motion in the world to diminish, which he thought would lead to an end of things if not replenished:

> . . . Motion is more apt to be lost than got, and is always upon the Decay. . . . Seeing therefore the variety of Motion which we find in the World is always decreasing, there is a necessity of conserving and recruiting it by active Principles. . . .

To Bentley Newton had written in 1692 that the frame of nature implied God and His Providence. In 1706 he made explicit the ways God and His Providence were indeed essential. Without His Providence, Newton emphasized, the world could not long continue.

But the question still remained how God was to accomplish this renewal of motion and this reformation of the planetary orbits. Was this to be done by a direct *fiat* or was it to be by God's using secondary mechanisms? "Where natural causes are at hand God uses them as instruments in his works, but I doe not think them alone sufficient for the creation . . . ," Newton had written Burnet in 1680. Nor did natural causes alone seem sufficient for the reformation, for that would seemingly defeat the whole purpose of requiring a reformation.

From 1692 to 1706 Newton was uncertain about the extent of God's rôle in natural phenomena. To Bentley he had written

> Gravity must be caused by an Agent acting constantly according to certain Laws; but whether this Agent be material or immaterial, I have left to the Consideration of my Readers.

The attempt by Newton's friend Fatio de Duillier to provide a mechanical explanation for gravity based on the aether met neither with Newton's outright approval nor with his clear disapproval; while interested in the possibilities of such an explanation, he was more attracted to the supposition that gravity was implanted in matter by God. Newton was also ambiguous about the means by which motion was initiated. In 1706, he suggested that all motion in the world arose either through the effects of the active principles or by "the dictates of a will"; the latter in Newton's sense could be either the will of an individual influencing the movements of his own body or the will of the Deity who has power over the world of matter.

In the decade following 1706,Newton changed his mind about God's rôle, and, resolving his ambiguity, began to commit himself to seemingly mechanical means. At the beginning of the 1717 edition of the *Opticks*, Newton wrote that he had added some indications of how gravity might be the result of an aethereal mechanism ". . . to shew that I do not take Gravity for an essential Property of Bodies. . . ." Similarly, he now attributed motion only to the effects of an active principle, now in effect materialized, instead of to a metaphysical active principle, or dictates of a will, as he had in 1706.

Not only were the underlying causes of gravity and motion in general seemingly mechanical in his opinion, but sometime in the same period he similarly conceived a natural mechanism by which God could reform the system of sun and planets and renew the active principles in the cosmos. Whatever the reasons for his change of mind regarding gravity and motion, his discovery of a mechanism to renew and reform the cosmos seems to have arisen from his work in preparing the second edition of the *Principia*. There he extended his theory of the motion of heavenly bodies to show more precisely how comets moved, using, he wrote, "more examples of the calculation of their orbits, done also with greater accuracy." In the first edition of the *Principia*, Newton had indicated a cometary mechanism which served to replenish the vapors and spirits lost by the planets, but the same mechanism could not have worked for the sun or stars. In the new work on comets for the second edition, he was struck by how close some comets came to the sun, and by the possibility that such comets, if disturbed slightly in their orbits, might fall from their regular orbits into the body of the sun. The regularity and permanence of comets' orbits, so recently established, had turned out to be somewhat dubious. To the second edition of the *Principia* Newton added a new paragraph:

> The comet which appeared in the year 1680 was in its perihelion less distant from the sun than by a sixth part of the sun's diameter; and because of its extreme velocity in that proximity . . . and some density of the sun's atmosphere, it must have suffered some resistance and retardation; and therefore, being attracted somewhat nearer to the sun in every revolution, will at last fall down upon the body of the sun. Nay, in its aphelion, where it moves the slowest, it may sometimes happen to be yet further retarded by the attractions of other comets, and in consequence of this retardation descend to the sun. *So fixed stars*, that have been gradually wasted by the light and vapors emitted from them for a long time, *may be recruited by comets that fall upon them*. . . . [my emphasis.]

Such recruiting of the fuel of stars, Newton suggested, might enable the stars to shine suddenly with new brilliance, explaining the puzzling occasional sudden appearances of new stars in the heavens.

With comets now apt to fall occasionally into stars, the stars' and planets' sources of motion and activity might well be replenished. And thus once more, as in his 1675 paper to Oldenburg, there was a continuous circulation of spiritous matter reaching to *all* parts of the cosmos, and nature once more was a "perpetual circulatory worker." Newton went further, working out a complete theory of the cycles of the cosmos. The cycles of his theory turned upside down the Cartesian hypothesis—which Newton had rejected in his letter to Bentley—of suns turning into comets, and comets, in turn, becoming planets. Newton's cosmogony now accounted both for the creation of the cosmos and for the cyclical development of the already created cosmos. He was able to account for both the periodic recruiting of motion and activity for the sun and planets and the "reformations" necessary to reset the system from time to time.

In a conversation with John Conduitt in March 1724/25, some six years after the second edition of the *Principia*, Newton made Conduitt privy to his ideas:

> [Newton repeated] what he had often hinted to me before, viz. that it was his *conjecture* (he would affirm nothing) that there was a sort of revolution in the heavenly bodies that the vapours and light emitted by the sun which had their sediment in water and other matter, had gathered themselves by degrees in to a body and attracted more matter from the planets and at last made a secondary planett (viz one of those that go round another planet) and then by gathering to them and attracting more matter became a primary planet, and then by increasing still became a comet which after certain revolutions by coming nearer and nearer the sun had all its volatile parts condensed and became a matter set to recruit and replenish the Sun . . . and that would probably be the effect of the comet in 1680 sooner or later. . . .

Newton had told David Gregory in 1694 how the satellites of Jupiter and Saturn "can take the places of the Earth, Venus, Mars if they are destroyed, and be held in reserve for a new Creation." Gregory probably later learned from Newton how his cometary mechanism could accomplish this celestial transmigration, for in Gregory's *Elements of Physical and Geometrical Astronomy*, he told how comets could cause such a change of a moon into a planet:

> There may also be another Effect or Use of a Comet. Namely, if a Comet passes near a Planet . . . it will so attract it that its Orbit will be chang'd . . . whence the Planet's Period will also be chang'd. But the Comet may also by its Attraction so disturb the

> Satellite, as to make it leave its Primary Planet and itself become a Primary Planet about the Sun. . . .

In a similar manner, one imagines a planet could be so disturbed in its orbit as to become a comet, as Newton had also indicated to Conduitt. Newton also told Conduitt of the eventual replenishment of the sun by the comet of 1680,

> that he could not say when this comet would drop in to the sun it might perhaps have 5 or 6 revolutions more first, but whenever it did it would so much encrease the heat of the Sun that this earth would be burnt and no animals in *this earth* could live. . . .

Newton added that it was his belief that the new stars seen by Hipparchus, Tycho, and Kepler were really the effects of the increase of light of regular stars occasioned by such a comet.

Such revolutions in the heavens, replenishing stars and providing a cycle among the heavenly bodies, were accomplished by mechanical means, but Newton believed that they were under divine supervision.

> He seemed to doubt [whether?] there were not intelligent beings superior to us who superintended these revolutions of the heavenly bodies by the direction of the supreme being. . . .

Of course, such a complex machinery as Newton was describing could not be without divine guidance. For the comets to pass by the moons or planets only after their size had so increased that they were fit to be changed into another type of body (planet or comet, as the case may be) and for this, in turn, to occur at the times when new creations were needed to take the place of an earth or a Venus destroyed in the Apocalypse—all this would require the utmost attention to coordinate.

Such coordination by the Creator would indeed require that He be, as Newton had described Him in a letter to Bentley, "very well skilled in Mechanicks and Geometry." And we can understand Newton's insistence that comets, moving in orbits quite different from those of planets, have uses quite different from those of planets in the scheme of things. For to Newton, as to his friends Halley and Whiston, comets were instruments of the divine will. For Newton the comets were instruments which God used to reconstitute the cosmos; for Halley, comets were instruments used to bring about the Noachian deluge, and for Whiston, the fundamental basis for the Creation, deluge, and conflagration as well as for the various changes to the Earth which took place after Adam's Fall. Newton believed that such a reconstitution by comets had occurred in the past and was likely to occur in the future.

> He seemed to be very clearly of the opinion that the inhabitants of this earth were of a short date and alledged as one reason for that opinion that all arts as letters . . . printing needle etc were discov-

> ered within the memory of History which could not have happened if the world had been eternal: and that there were visible marks of ruin upon it which could not be effected by a flood only, when I asked him how this earth could have been repeopled if ever it had undergone the same fate it was threatened with hereafter by the Comet of 1680, he answered that required the power of a Creator. . . .

When Conduitt asked Newton why he did not make these ideas public, Newton answered somewhat characteristically that he would not, because, "I do not deal in conjectures. . . ." Conduitt mentioned, however, the passage in the second edition of the *Principia* where, after noting the close approach to the sun by the comet of 1680, Newton had suggested that the fixed stars could be replenished by comets falling into them. Conduitt relates:

> I observing that he [Newton] said there of that comet [of 1680] incident in corpus solis, and in the next paragraph adds stellae fixae refici poss[unt] etc told him I thought he owned there what wee had been talking about—viz. that the Comet would drop into the sun, and that fixed stars were recruited and replenished by Comets when they dropt in to them, and consequently the sun would be recruited too and asked him, why he would not own as freely what he thought of the Sun as well as what he thought of the fixed stars—he said that concerned us more, and laughing added he had said enough for people to know his meaning. . . .

"That concerned us more . . ."—Newton felt free to express his ideas as they applied to a system of stars and planets far removed from us, but felt that to speak openly of the system of *our* sun and planets was not advisable. For Newton's ideas implied the existence of Earths before this one, with the presence of races of man before Adam, and it was probable that the creation of the Earth described in *Genesis* was only one in a series of creations. Carrying the implications even further, an orthodox divine might have seen in Newton's conjectures the belief that the world in one form or another had existed from all eternity.

This, indeed, was the danger in the attempt by Newton—and by certain of his contemporaries—to enforce the belief in God's Providence by showing how, at regular intervals, He must intervene in the mechanisms of the world: such an assertion of intervention, or re-creation from time to time, tended to lead to the inference that a series of Earths have existed from eternity, each one arising out of the ruins of its predecessor. Paradoxically, it had been the fear of this very notion of an eternal Earth which had prompted the English philosophers' concern to demonstrate that God's Providence acted continuously. Such, it seems, was the almost inevitable conflict between natural philosophy and religion in seventeenth- and early eighteenth-century England, a conflict not between reason and revelation so much as between a mechanistic philosophy and a Providential God.

To be sure, each new Earth, according to Newton, arose out of a past Earth only through "the Mediation of a divine Power." But the necessity for that mediation could and would be overlooked by those deists, sceptics, and atheists who wished to use the mechanical means provided by Newton and certain of his contemporaries to show that no other divine means were at all necessary. In fact, some among Newton's friends were thought to have so negated Providence. Edmund Halley, whose lines in the Ode at the beginning of the *Principia* had been changed because they seemed to imply such an eternity of the world, had failed in 1694 to obtain the position of Savilian Professor of Astronomy at Oxford because the ecclesiastical authorities thought Halley "guilty of asserting the eternity of the world." Newton, who had kept his own unorthodox questioning of the divinity of Christ secret in order not to lose his position at Cambridge, would not jeopardize that position by disclosing his unorthodox cosmogony.

Conclusion

Although Newton was unwilling explicitly to indicate his cosmogonic speculations, I think it clear that he did entertain such ideas. He was led to these ideas as a result of his belief that the cosmos declined in its powers and regularity, a belief he shared with many other Englishmen. Thus he hoped to avoid the doctrine of the world's eternity. Once having decided that the cosmos declined, Newton sought a mechanism by which the Creator at times could renew the amount of motion and the regularity of the motions of the heavenly bodies. He found such a mechanism in comets. Having shown how comets could account for the circulation of the sources of motion, he then showed how they could account for changes in the bodies of the sun's system. This vision of the cosmos explained not merely the renewal of the amount of motion but also the continual cyclical re-creation of the system and its subsequent development in time until the moment of the next creation.

This being so, two widespread interpretations of seventeenth-century scientific thought seem open to reconsideration. The first is that given by the late R. F. Jones in his *Ancients and Moderns, A Study of the Rise of the Scientific Movement in Seventeenth-Century England*; here he characterized the scientific revolution as proceeding from the energy released by man's new-found confidence in his powers of reason once the notion of the world's decay had been abandoned. Such an interpretation ignores the fact that in seventeenth-century England the idea of the decline of the world meant not that the world would end in an ignoble dissolution, but rather, that the Millennium and second coming of Christ was at hand. Even at the end of the seventeenth century, millennial thought was still quite widespread in England. The various treatises on world-making written near the end of the century by Burnet, John Ray, and Whiston were all concerned not only with the creation, but also with the future conflagration of the world and the millennium associated with it. In addition to the millennial aspects of his cosmogony, Newton dealt with the future millennium in his theological writings. Those who anticipated the millennium did so with optimism rather than pessimism. This optimistic millennialism is associated, no doubt, with primitivism in seventeenth- and eighteenth-century English thought, a subject which cannot be explored in this paper. A revealing statement by Newton's disciple Whiston, however, reveals the extent to which the notion of decay was associated with a joyous expectation of the dissolution and subsequent reconstitution of the world. Whiston wrote of Newton's discovery of the gravitational principles of the world:

> Which noble discovery proved the happy occasion of the invention of the wonderful Newtonian philosophy: which indeed, I look upon in a higher light than others, and as an eminent prelude and preparation to those happy times of the restitution of all things, which God has spoken of . . . since the world began, Acts iii, 21.

Whiston's point is clear: with the writing of Newton's *Principia*, man had attained such insight that it brought him to a state of near perfection. And this, in turn, made the Millennium all the more imminent.

The second interpretation of the seventeenth century which I think warrants reconsideration is the idea that the world-view of Newton, and by inference that of the century in general, was a static one. If Newton did have ideas regarding cosmogony, then it is wrong to claim that "the formation of the world . . . was seen during the seventeenth and eighteenth centuries as a single creative event, which once accomplished [the world] was eternally enduring and finished for all time."

This is not to say that I think we should look to Newton for ideas which "anticipated" those of the late eighteenth, still more of the nineteenth century, in which the development of animals, societies, Earth, and cosmos alike were widely treated. Rather, Newton and many of his English contemporaries seem, like the Stoics, to view the cosmos as going through successive cycles. The destroyed Earth of one cycle would serve as the chaos out of which the Earth of the next cycle would emerge. Illustrative of this outlook is the frontispiece of Burnet's *Sacred Theory of the Earth* in which the progress of the Earth is pictured as it goes from primitive chaos to mature Earth and on to final dissolution. The Earth after its dissolution does not fade into nothingness or into a permanent oblivion; instead, Burnet portrays the states of the Earth in cyclical series, and the skeleton of the Earth, after its destruction, remains to develop later into a new Earth. Newton, I think, would have agreed.

Part 7
ALCHEMY AND THEORY OF MATTER

Introduction

If chemistry was not among Newton's first readings in natural philosophy, he soon discovered it and began to pursue it. And not long thereafter, he went beyond ordinary chemistry (if indeed the distinction is valid for the seventeenth century) into alchemy. His accounts show that on a visit to London in 1669 he purchased the great six-volume collection of alchemical writings, *Threatrum chemicum.*[1] He also purchased chemicals, glass equipment, and two furnaces. With those purchases, at the latest, Newton launched an extended career in alchemy.

His reading notes in alchemy, like those in other fields of interest, survive, and they indicate that he not only devoured the *Theatrum*, but he went far beyond it into other alchemical literature. Betty Jo Teeter Dobbs, the authority on the alchemist aspect of Newton, asserts that Newton explored "the whole vast literature of the older alchemy as it has never been probed before or since." Nor did he confine himself to the older alchemy. The seventeenth century was one of the most active periods in the history of the Art, from Michael Maier and Michael Sendivogius at its beginning to Alexandre Toussaint de Limojon de Saint Disdier at its end. Newton studied them all intensely. Among the seventeenth-century alchemists, one of the most influential was Eirenaeus Philalethes, the pseudonym, it has been demonstrated, of George Starkey. Starkey, who had been born in the colonies and educated at Harvard before immigrating to England in the middle of the century, was the first American to play a significant role in science. He was the favorite authority of Newton, who consumed everything he wrote and apparently had access to the Philalethes treatises in manuscript before their publication. Newton had access to other sources of alchemical manuscripts as well; a number of treatises, of which no published version is known to exist, survive among Newton's papers, copied out in his hand. A letter he received from an otherwise unidentified Fran. Meheux discussed alchemical experiments by a third man going forward in London while referring to an ongoing correspondence (now lost), and a memorandum that Newton composed records the visit of an unnamed alchemist from London. On the death of Robert Boyle, it transpired that Newton, Boyle, and John Locke had swapped alchemical information and sworn each other to secrecy. The Newtonian papers contain a very large number (there are well over a million words), written in his distinctive hand, that are devoted to alchemy. They date from about 1669 until

In order not to encumber the reader with footnotes we have composed a Biographical Register, in which all the people mentioned in the text are identified, and a Glossary, in which technical terms are briefly explicated and such things as organizations, places, publications, and manuscript collections are identified. There is also a Glossary of Chemical Terms that will be useful for this part. The Biographical Register, Glossary, and Glossary of Chemical Terms are located near the end of the volume.

1. Lazarus Zetzner, ed., *Theatrum chemicum*, 6 vols. (1659–61). Published originally in 1602.

the middle 1690s; something approaching half of them come from the years immediately following the *Principia*.

As he read, Newton did not neglect the apparatus that he had also purchased in London. Up against the wall of the Trinity College chapel, he constructed a laboratory in the garden attached to his chamber. Here, Humphrey Newton, his amanuensis (or secretary) in the years 1683–88, a young man who came from Newton's native Grantham but was not a relative despite the name, found him hard at work,

> especially at the Spring and Fall of the Leaf, at which Times he used to imploy about 6 weeks in his Elaboratory, the Fire scarcely going out either Night or Day, he siting up one Night, as I did another, till he had finished his Chymical experiments, in the Performance of which he was the most accurate, strict, exact: What his Aim might be, I was not able to penetrate into, but his Pains, his Diligence at those sett Times, made me think, he aimed at something beyond the Reach of humane Art and Industry.

Like most of the paper to which he ever set pen, the notes from Newton's chemical experiments survive, dated records that stretch over a period of more than two decades, from the early 1670s until 1696, less than two months before he left Cambridge for London and the mint. The notes are extremely difficult to interpret, but Dobbs has had success in correlating some of the early ones with processes described in the alchemical manuscripts. Some of the later ones are interrupted by exclamations couched in the allegorical language of alchemy, such as, "I understood the Trident," "I saw sophic sal ammoniac," "I made Jupiter fly on his eagle."

The issue of Newton and alchemy is actively debated, frequently with passion, among Newtonian scholars. Most of those who have studied the large volume of alchemical manuscripts at length are convinced that his chemical experimentation needs to be understood as alchemical experimentation and that, in more general terms, alchemy needs to be seen as an important dimension of Newton's intellectual life. Other Newtonian scholars insist, with at least equal vehemence, that the alchemical papers are nothing but reading notes and that the arcane spirit of alchemy was antithetical to the Newtonian enterprise in science. No student of Newton's alchemy has suggested that he was engaged in attempting to "make gold," in the popular image of the Art. On the contrary, those who have pursued this subject argue that Newton saw in alchemy a form of natural philosophy that mitigated the harsh outlines of the mechanistic philosophy he had found in Descartes and Gassendi; part of the attraction of alchemy was a philosophy that asserted the existence of nonmaterial agents in nature and the primacy of spirit over matter in the universe.

We have included three papers in this section. The first consists of two passages from "Of natures obvious laws and processes in vegetation" (as it is known from its first line), a set of reflections written not long after Newton's initial immersion in alchemical literature. It is a very rough manuscript. The original is full of alterations, with words and paragraphs added or deleted, and sometimes what he set down is not in the form of properly spelled words and properly formed sentences. Perhaps you can see in the paper a source of some of the features of the later "Hypothesis of Light"[2] that set that essay off from more orthodox mechanistic philosophies, which undertook to derive all the phenomena of nature from nothing but particles of matter in motion.

Praxis was a late composition, written in 1693 at the earliest, and certainly not much later than that. Like "Of natures obvious laws and processes in vegetation," it contains many alterations and corrections, and there is even an earlier draft. However, unlike the earlier paper, it takes the form of a treatise that has been systematically planned. *Praxis* also suggests a philosophy that saw in nature something different from what orthodox mechanistic philosophies admitted. Even more than Chapter 5 (which has the same title as the treatise as a whole), the first four chapters (not reproduced here) testify, by their numerous citations, to Newton's wide familiarity with the corpus of alchemical literature. If you are interested in learning more about these matters, you can find the two alchemical manuscripts reproduced in their entirety, and several others with them, in the appendix to Dobbs's *The Janus Faces of Genius*.

"De natura acidorum" was also composed in the early 1690s. It devotes itself, not to alchemy, but to a closely related issue, the conception of matter. You may wish to consult as well Query 31 (in Part 1, Natural Philosophy [above]), which is also concerned with the conception of matter.

From "Of Natures Obvious Laws and Processes in Vegetation" †

* * *

That clay which is a great ingredient of this upper crust is nothing but stone poudered. That salts may putrefy and by putrefaction will generate another sort of blackish rotten fat substance the most fertile part of this upper crust and the nearest matter out of which vegetables are extracted and into which after death they returne.[1] And this confirmed in that nothing promotes fermentation and putrefaction more than salts where they are incited to it, they are alone as I may say dead and have noe

2. See Part 1, Natural Philosophy (above).

† Betty Jo Teeter Dobbs, *The Janus Faces of Genius: The Role of Alchemy in Newton's Thought* (Cambridge: Cambridge University Press, 1991), pp. 262–70. Reprinted with the permission of Cambridge University Press. Newton plunged into alchemy, reading all of the classical and seventeenth-century authorities, about 1669. He composed this work early in his study of alchemy.

1. See Glossary, *Alchemy*.

active principle of vegetation in them till they bee incited to it by other substances that are in a live and vegetating state of what they are mixed with all and thence it is that where nature is not powerfull enough to incite them to action they on the contrary retard and hinder her working And thence salted meats are so slow in putrefaction and so hard to digest. But if their latent principle can bee once exerted it shows it selfe more vigorously: Hence ⦶ [niter] seemes the most fertile and inriching of land and lesse powerfull to conserve meats because not so close lockd up and difficult to putrefy. Here note whither the praeparation of salts by putrefaction if it can bee truly attained would not prove a noble way of Physick 2 If ⊖ts [common salts] which are a meane twixt the minerall and other kingdoms will vegetate why may not metalls and that as much more powerfully than ⊖ts as ⊖ts doe than other earth. 3 nay since metalls may putrefy into a black fat rotten stinking substanc why not salts also. And soe much for salts, stones, clay, and fat mold, the cheif ingredients of this upper earth

As for water it is to bee observed how the Alcahest (a minerall spirit of the same root with that which constantly ascends and pervades all things, only prepared by the philosopher etc resolvs all these upper substances into water yea metalline 🜍 [sulfur] it selfe. whence it appears not only that they have one common matter but that the minerall spirit pervading all things may doe the like in som measure to them. Secondly what was dry and grosse may a great part of it by putrefaction relent to water A carcas if distilld before putrefaction will leave a great deale of fixed earth but if it bee laid in the warm son and open air to putrefy it wil resolve and exhale almost of it in tim into fumes And putrefaction resolvs substances not only into water but oyle also as may be seen by their fatnesse and spirit as in the fermentation of beer yea and aire two as is evident from the swelling and bubling

* * *

Now these things thus produced salt stones earth water etc seeme so aleinate from the metalline nature that one would scarce think they took their rise thence, Nay they are at perfect enmity with and if mixed doe hinder or destroy the work. but the reason's manifest. For being changed into these substances not by vegetation but for the most part onely by a gros mechanicall transposition of parts, they are to bee reduced back by the same way, not by vegetation but by the same mechanicall transposition till they bee reduced back to their first order and frame, Since therefore vegetation is the only naturall work of metalls and the reduction of these is besides that work and yet these cannot vegetate as they doe till they bee reduced, they must of necessity hinder their working and so be counted heterogeneous. for what will not comply will disturb the acting.

Yet the reduction of these is possible to bee performed by mechanicall ways unravelling their production. Water by the suns heat and by assention and descention will yeild earth as hath been tryed by distilling it often, Also standing water will putrefy by the suns heat, corrupt and let fall a foeculent earth and that successively without period. Out of these earths may bee extracted a salt. This salt may be brought to putrefy and the minerall spirit thereby set loose from the water with which it was concreted and so returnes to the same state it had at its first ascent out of the earth that is to the nearest metalline matter and (though debilitated by these changes) yet if pervading the earth where other metalls vegetate might enter them receive metallick life and by degrees recover their primitive metalline forme. Air (by which I mean not vapours) but that which cold will not condens to water may be generated 1 Out of water by freezing it. Secondly out of saline or vitriolate spirits by their ebullition when poured together. 3 out of salts and vitriolls in the drawing of their spirits, 4 out of metalls and som other substances by corroding them with acid liquors as aqua fortis. (hence poyson swells a man) 5 by fermentation. Hence ebullition flying of bottle beer etc. swelling after a stroake. In generall by any meanes wher the parts of a body are set a working among themselves. (Which seems to argue an agent in freezing.) that thereby the constringed aire may bee let loos which intimate the earthly substances to be but AEthereall concretions that they so easily approach, towards it again. Of the reduction of aire to a gross body I know but one instance and that in the stone wher during the firs solution much air is generated, enough to burst a weak glas and which yet returns to the stone againe

By minerall dissolutions and fermentations there is constantly a very great quantity of air generated which perpetually ascends with a gentle motion (as is very sensible in mines) being a vehicle to minerall fumes and watry vapors, boying up the clouds and still (protruded by the air ascending under it) riseth higher and hiher till it straggle into the ethereall regions, Carriing also with it many other vapors and exhalations and whole clouds too when they happen to bee so high as to loos their gravity. The quantity of air constantly generated may be aestimated by the quantity of rains that fall of whose ascent we are as insensible as of the airs. But better by the quantity of air compared to its ascent. As if it bee supposed to rise a mile in 3 or 4 days which it may doe with a very gentle and insensible motion: that would amount to 5 foot water in depth round the earth. This constantly crowding for room the AEther will becom prest thereby and so forced continually to descend into the earth from whence the air cam and there tis gradually condensed and interwoven with bodys it meets there and promotes their actions beeing a tender fermet. but in its descent it endeavours to beare along what bodys it passeth through, that is makes them heavy and this action is promoted by the tenacious elastick constituon whereby it takes the greater hold on things in its way; and by its vast swiftness. Soe much AEther ought to descend as air and exhalations ascend, and therefore the AEther being by many degres more thin and rare then air (as air is than wather) it must descend soe much the swifter and consequently have soe much more efficacy to drive bodys downward then air hath to drive them up. And this is very agreeable to natures proceedings to make a circulation of all things. Thus this Earth resembles a great animall or rather inanimate vegetable, draws in aethereall breath for its dayly refreshment and vital ferment and transpires again with gross exhalations. And according to the condition of all other things living ought to have its times of beginning youth old age and perishing This is the subtil spirit which searches the most hiden recesses of all grosser matter which enters their smallest pores and divides them more subtly then any other materiall power what ever. (not after the way of common menstruums by rending them violently assunder etc) this is Natures universall agent, her secret fire, the onely ferment and principle of all vegetation. The material soule of all matter which being constantly inspired from above pervades and concretes with it into one form and then if incited by a gentle heat actuates and enlivens it but so tender and subtile is it withall as to vanish at the least excess and (having once begun to act) to cease acting for ever and congeale in the matter at the defect of heat unless it receive new life from a fresh ferment. And thus perhaps a great part if not all the moles[2] of sensible matter is nothing but AEther congealed and interwoven into various textures whose life depends on that part of it which is in a middl state, not wholy distinct and lose from it like the AEther in which it swims as in a fluid nor wholly joyned and compacted together with it under one forme in som degree condensed united to it yet remaining of a much more rare tender and subtile disposition and so this seems to bee the principle of its acting to resolve the body and bee mutually condensed by it and so mix under one form being of one root and grow together till the compositum attain the same state which the body had before solution. Hence 1 the earth needs a constant fresh supply of aether. 2 Bodys are subtiliated by solution[3]

Note that tis more probable the aether is but a vehicle to some more active spirit. And the bodys may bee concreted of both together, they may imbibe aether as well as air in generation and in that aether the spirit is intangled. This spirit perhaps is the body of light 1 becaus both have a prodigious active principle both are perpetuall workers 2 because all things may bee made to emit light by heat, 3 the same cause (heat) banishes also the vitall principle. 4 Tis suitable with infinite wisdom not to multiply causes without necessity 5 Noe heat is so pleasant and brigh as the suns, 6 light and heat have a mutuall dependance on each other and noe generation without heat. heat is a necessary condition to light and vegetation. heate exites light and light and light exites heat, heat excites the vegetable principle and that increaseth heat. 6 Noe substance soe

2. Mass.
3. Compare with "Hypothesis of Light," Part 1, Natural Philosophy (above).

indifferently, subtily and swiftly pervades all things as light and noe spirit searches bodys so subtily percingly and quickly as the vegetable spirit.

* * *

Nothing can be changed from what it is without putrefaction. no putrefaction can bee without alienating the thing putrefyed from what it was

Nothing can bee generated or nourished (but of putrefyed matter)

All putrefyed matter is capable of having something generated out of it and in motion towards it

All natures opperations are twixt things of differing dispositions. The most powerfall agent acts not upon it selfe

Her first action is to blend and confound mixtures into a putrifyed Chaos

Then are they fitted for new generation or nourishment

All things are corruptible

All things are generable

Nature only works in moyst substances

And with a gentle heat

Art may set nature on work and promote her working in the production of any thing what ever. Thus an oak may stand 100 years without rotting But if it bee scraped thin and kept twixt moyst and dry it may soon by art be brought to dirt and praepared for a new generation. Thus metalls though in a massy body and above grownd where minerall humidity is but weak and thin are in mans memory observed to rot and though they may long persist in the earth without corruption yet duly ordered and mixt with due minerall humidity; may by art soon rot and putrefy Nor is the product less natural then if nature had produced it alone. Is the child artificiall because the mother took physick, or a tree less naturall which is planted in a garden and watered then that which grows alone in the feild. or if a carcass bee put in a glasse and kept warm in B. M. that it may putefy and breed insects are not those insects as naturall as others bred in a ditch without any such artifice.

Natures actions are either vegetable or purely mechanicall (gravity. fluxes. meteors. vulgar Chymistry)

The principles of her vegetable actions are noe other then the seeds or seminall vessels of things those are her onely agents, her fire, her soule, her life,

The seede of things is all that substance in them that is attained to the fullest degree of maturity that is in that thing so that then being nothing more mature to act upon then they acquiesce.

Vegetation is nothing else but the acting of what is most maturated or specificate upon that which is less specificate or mature to make it as mature as it selfe And in that degree of maturity nature ever rests.

The portion fully mature in all things is but very small, and never to bee seene alone, but only as tis inclothed with watry humidity. The whole substance is never maturated but only that part of it which is most disposed The maine bulk being but a watry insipid substance in which rather then upon which the action is performed

Putrefaction is the reduction of a thing from that maturity and specificateness it had attained by generation

1 All vegetables have a disposition to act upon other adventitious substances and alter them to their one temper and nature. And this is to grow in bulk as the alteration of the nourishment may bee called groth in vertue and maturity or specificateness.

2 When the nourishment has attained the same state with the species transmuting the action ceaseth

3 And then is that body thus maturated able in like manner to act upon any new matter and transform it to its owne state and temper. Hence the more to the lesse mature is as agent to patient

4 All these changes thus wrought in the generation of things so far as to sense may appeare to bee nothing but mechanisme or severall dissevering and associating the parts of the matter acted upon and that becaus severall changes to sense may be wrought by such ways without any interceding act of vegetation. Thus acid two pouders mixed each to a third colour, the unctuous parts in milk by a little agitation concret into one mass of butter Nay all the operations in vulgar chemistry (many of which to sense are as strange transmutations as those of nature) are but mechanicall coalitions or separations of particles as may appear in that they returne into their former natures if reconjoned or (when unequally volatile) dissevered, and that without any vegetation.

5 So far therefore as the same changes may bee wrought by the slight mutation of the tinctures of bodys in common chymistry and such like experiments many may judg that such changes made by nature are done the same way that is by the sleighty transpositions of the grosser corpuscles, for upon their disposition onely sensible qualitys depend. But so far as by vegetation such changes are wrought as cannot bee done without it wee must have recourse to som further cause And this difference is vast and fundamentall because nothing could ever yet bee made without vegetation which nature useth to produce by it.

6 There is therefore besides the sensible changes wrough in the textures of the grosser matter a more subtile secret and noble way of working in all vegetation which makes its products distinct from all others and the immeadiate seate of thes operations is not the whole bulk of matter, but rather an exceeding subtile and inimaginably small portion of matter diffused through the masse which if it were seperated there would remain but a dead and inactive earth. And this appeares in that vegetables are deprived of their vegetable vertue, by any small excesse of heat, the tender spirit being either put to flight or at least corrupted thereby (as may appear in an egg) whereas those operations which

depend upon the texture of the grosser matter (as all those in common chemistry do) receive noe dammage by heats far greater. Besides if we consider an egg, noe doubt but when it is first sat upon the whole matter in which the vegetive vertue resides is put into action which if it were the whole substance the rudiments would be spread all over which yet is begun but in a very little space.

7 Tis the office therefore of those grosser substances to bee medium or vehicle in which rather then upon which those vegetable substances perform their actions

8 Yet those grosser substances are very apt to put on various external appearances according to the present state of the invisible inhabitant as to appeare like bones flesh wood fruit etc Namely they consisting of differing particles watry earthy saline aery oyly spirituous etc those parts may bee variously moved one among another according to the acting of the latent vegetable substances and be variously associated and concatenated together by their influence

This vegetable spirit is radically the same in all things and differs but in degre of digestion or maturity from the state of corruption. or as it is applyed to gros matter (viz as metalls differ in both respects)

And it has but but one law of acting that as when two vegetables spirits are mixed of unequall maturity they fall to work, putrefy mix radically and so proceed in perpetuall working till they arrive at the state of the les digested and if nothing hinder they still proced to the state of the more digested where they infallibly stop

Hence it appears how nutrition is made yea by salves outwardly applyed

As metalls in divers states of digestion put on severall forms and unite after divers manners with grosser matter so other vegetable powers

In animals etc the putrefaction is not sensible 1 because it is continuall second quickly finished, thirdly but of a very small portion at once, a greater portion at the same time being in motion to maturity and a far greater portion then that allready mature, by whose contrary dispositions tis allayed as to the production of any eminent sensible qualitys. And that all together seems but one continued action of growing 4 Tis not like the putrefaction of a carcass a confusion of the whole where all opposite qualitys are alike powerfull to destroy each other but much more mild the matter having already been reduced by the putrefactions in vivo[4] and its methodized by the great potency of the body both in quantity and power to convert it to its owne temper. Tis more like the putrefaction or fermentation of wine or bread or mault. 5 its putrefaction or fermentation in turning to blood is insensible yea and that more grosse in the stomak 6 Without such putrefaction how can vermin breed in the body and yet that is in insensible

4. In the living body.

There are exhalations dispersed from every part of the body as well as into the aire and in this sense it may be said to bee totum in toto[5] etc like the foetus in sperm. And these emanations are the fountain of their sperm and perform the same office to the body which sperm doth in the production of an infant, praeparing and distributing nourishment for they being of the same nature with the body (excepting order) they must act after the same maner upon adventitious matter that is prepare it.

Chapter 5 of *Praxis* †

This rod and the male and female serpents joyned in the proportion of 3, 1, 2 compose the three headed Cerberus which keeps the gates of Hell. For being fermented and digested together they resolve and grow dayly more fluid for 15 or 20 days and in 25 or 30 days begin to lack breath and thicken and put on a green colour and in 40 days turn to a rotten black pouder. The green matter may be kept for ferment. Its spirit is the blood of the green Lion. The black pouder is our Pluto, the God of wealth, our Saturn who beholds himself in the looking glass of ♂ [iron], the calcination which they call the first gate, and the sympathetick fire of Snyders, composed of two contrary fires 🜍 [sulfur] and ⦶ [niter] by the mediation of his first fire. This pouder amalgams with ☿ [mercury] and purges out its feces if shaken together in a glass [Epist. N. Fatij].[1] It mixes also with melted metalls and Regulus's and in a little quantity purifies them (as was hinted) but in a greater, burns and calcines them and upon a certain sign, (viz[t] in the beginning of the calcination before the resolved 🜍 of the metal flys away and leaves the Regulus dead like an electrum and relapsed into an hydrophoby) if it be poured out into twice as much ☿ they amalgam and the feces of both are purged out which being well washed of and the matter sublimed with ✳ [sal ammoniac] the Regulus will be found resolved into ☿, that is its 🜍 and ☿ for the salt of the metal will stay below, and may be eliviated.[2] Thus may you make a ☿ of 7, 8, 9 or 10 Eagles with the ✳ [here this symbol means star regulus] of ♂ for the work in common ☉ [gold] and by the ☿ of 1, 2, or 3 eagles resolve ♀ [copper], ♃ [tin] and ♄ [lead] (or the ore of ♄ melted down with ♁) into ☿ and of that ☿ sublimed with the

5. The whole present in the whole—a concept from the Hippocratic doctrine of pangenesis, according to which the sperm, and hence the embryo, is composed of bits from the entire male body.

† Betty Jo Teeter Dobbs, *The Janus Faces of Genius: The Role of Alchemy in Newton's Thought* (Cambridge: Cambridge University Press, 1991), pp. 301–05. Reprinted with the permission of Cambridge University Press. *Praxis* was the most important alchemical treatise that Newton ever composed. It carries no date, but various bits of evidence appear to place it in the summer of 1693, near the end of his active involvement in alchemy.

1. Letter of Nicolas Fatio de Duillier.
2. Elixiviated: thoroughly refined.

salt of Venus [copper] make the cold fire, and then with the black pouder calcine an amalgam of ☉ 1 part and the ☿ of 7 Eagles 2 parts and so soon as it beginns to calcine pour upon it 1 part of the cold fire extracted out of Lead ore with salt of Venus and not yet volatized, and so on till you have poured on eleven parts and all be calcined. For the saturn [lead] will first resolve into water by fusion and then resolve the ☿ies of the bodies into salt. and promote the action of the sympathetic fire that it may in calcination pierce them throughly. And then by sublimation and elixiviation of the residue you will have ten parts of the cold fire or Philosophers ☿ and one of the fixt salt of the ☉ and former ☿, which after purgation are to be decocted together forty days and then the water drawn out till the matter become retentive which must then be decocted again first 5, 6 or seven months to get our 🜍 and then ten more in its sweat to get our tinging stone, and then to be multiplied by the 3 principles. And thus you may understand what the first gate of calcination is and how in the calcination of perfect bodies with the first menstrue nothing unclean enters but the green Lyon and how the King after his resurrection is fed with the blood of this Lyon, and what is the solutio violenta[3] of Sendivoguis under which all other solutions are comprehended, what his humidum radicale metallicum[4] the ashes of the burnt old man; in what sence his aurum is vivum[5] that is by vertue of the sympathetic fire; how he separates the spirit from the water and congeales the water in heat and then adds the spirit to it; how the seed of our saturn purges the matrix of his mother; what is the aqua salis nitri[6] and the menstruum mundi;[7] what his 10 parts of air or water and one of ☉, and how Diana first (that is the Regulus.) and then the King falls into the fountain of milk white water and how Trevisan's Golden book falls in after the King and then he draws out the water with his bucket, till they become retentive that is till two thirds of the water be drawn out (or perhaps more) for the imbibitions and one third remain with the ☉. This is the via sicca[8] and the solution in ☿ per ☿ the other solution and the via humida[9] are as follows.

When the Caduceus with the 2 serpents are set to putrefy and are resolved into water and grown sufficiently liquid which may be in 3 or 4 days or a week; put in the ☿ial precipitate of the net the scepter of ♃ and the ☿ial precipitate of ♃ gradually. Let the scepter be equal to the Caduceus the precipitates to each other. Or better, let a chaos be made of the four Elements ♂, ♃, ♀, ♄ and quintessentia Ψ [bismuth], in

3. Violent solution; that is, dissolution by corrosion in a mineral acid.
4. Radical metallic moisture.
5. His gold is alive.
6. Water of niter, a solution of what chemistry now calls potassium nitrate.
7. Solvent of the world.
8. Dry way.
9. Wet way.

equal proportion and put in first the scepter with as much of the ☿ial precipitate of these. Or else after the two former precipitates are fermented in some competent quantity, put in an amalgam of the Chaos. And note that this Chaos is the hollow oak. But perhaps it must be made with the two Regulus's of ♂ & ♃. When this Chaos is fermented and sufficiently resolved into ☿ which perhaps will be in a few days, wash away the feces and distill it. And sublime it with the salt of saturn. But first impregnate the salt of ♄ with as much volatile salt of ♂ as it will retain for this is the sith[1] with which he must cut of the leggs of ☿ and coagulate him. This is the cold fire, which being fermented with the two dragons in a due proportion as was the rod of ☿ and digested ten or 20 days or till the green colour appear will by distilling give you the blood of the green Lyon. our Venus, our wine, our dry water our Mercurius duplatus.[2] Artephius his third fire, his Vinegar Antimonial saturnine mercurial and of salarmoniac in which there is a double substance of argent vive[3] the one of Antimony the other of ☿ sublimed [with ♄].

In this water 2 digest the Regulus of ♂ 1 the former ☿ 1. for a week till the ♁ be resolved into ☿ (Or if the Regulus of ♂ will not amalgam and resolve without the addition of other metalls, mix it with (♀, ♃, and Ψ, and ana.) or rather with Luna[4] and digest a week.) distill away the ☿, and rectify it, dissolve the rest in Æ [aqua fortis] and you will have our Gold in a black pouder. The same may be got by digesting the ☿ of 7, 8, 9 or 10 Eagles but this way is about. Wash and dry the black pouder. Amalgam it with its rectified ☿ in a due proportion. Wash them well and Dry them and in a digestion of 7 months you will have our tinging 🜍 In the mean time if you putrefy again the mercurial, water till it be like melted pitch and then distill you will have a white and red spirit which are Diana and Apollo, Aqua vitae[5] and vinegre, the virgins milk and blood, and in the bottom will remain a black earth which is Latona our salt of tartar our Gold found in a dunghill, our Toad, our Bacchus. Rectify the spirits 7 times and each time put the feces of the white to the red and those of the red to the black earth. Calcine this earth gently Extract its salt with distilld water amalgam one part of this salt first with 3 parts of the white or red spirit and then with 9 parts of the stone of the same colour and by a short digestion you will have the stone multiplied. Thus you may multiply each stone 4 times and no more for they will then become oyles shining in the dark and fit for magicall uses. You may ferment them with ☉ and ☽ [silver] by keeping the stone and metall in fusion together for a day, and then project upon

1. Scythe.
2. Doubled mercury; that is, the philosophical mercury from which the philosophers' stone is to be made.
3. Quicksilver.
4. Literally, Moon; in alchemy, silver.
5. Literally, water of life; the standard name for brandy.

metalls. This is the multiplication of the stone in vertue. To multiply it in weight ad to it of the first Gold whether philosophic or vulgar. Thus the Sulphur will every multiplication encrease ten times in vertue and if you multiply it with the ☿ of the first or second rotation you may encrease it much more. If you want the Philosophic Gold, you may ad to it Gold vulgar with the fixt salt and multiplying mercuries in the hour of the mercuries nativity that is in the beginning of the Regimen of Luna.

Thus you must do for multiplication. But if you would whiten Latona then distill not the red spirit but cohobate the white spirit upon the black matter with interposed digestions till it bring over all the red spirit with it which you shall know by its the black matter a light dry pouder. Imbibe this pouder first with an eighth part of its weight of the animated spirit then with a seventh then with a sixt then with a fift, and ever after with a fourth, interposing a weeks digestion between every imbibition till the matter be moderately dry and then distilling off the flegm. And when by these imbibitions Latona grows white and fluxible as wax and will ascend, sublime her from the feces, and you shall have the plumbum album sapientum,[6] the white Diana. Imbibe one part of this sublimate with three of the spirit digest for 24 hours distill, imbibe the remainder with thrice its weight of new spirit, digest 24 hours and destill, Imbibe and digest a third and fourth time and all will ascend. Circulate it for eight or nine weeks and you have the Alkahest.

Rectify and dilute with rain water the oyle of good and well purified Hungarian Vitriol. Therein dissolve a clean and unctuous ☿. viz[t] the abovementioned living ☿. Ferment and digest it 30 20 days. Draw of the spirit Ferment and digest again and when the matter is like molten pitch distill and cohobate the spirit to extract the soul and proceed as in the work of ♄ and you shall have the true Alkahest. If you add the said solution of ☿ in oyle of ⊕ [vitriol] unto the cold fire and putrefy them with the two Dragons, you have Snyders his most general ☿ of both a solary and lunary nature, borrowing heat from Venus and coldnes from ♄ and conteining all the vertues of the Univers But to the cold ☿ of ♄ and hot ☿ of Venus, he adds the fixt salt of Terra Adamica[7] to obtein all in all. So Basil Valentine, Set Adam in a water bath, where Venus like her self one hath which the old Dragon hath prepared. This earth he tells us in another place is not likened to any thing that is grown, that is neither to stones nor minerals, Manna[8] saith tis not clay nor mud but a quintessentiall matter or Chaos out of which man and all the world was made and that tis called earth but is not so. So Norton tells us that

6. White lead of the wise.
7. Adamic earth; that is, earth like Adam, original or primitive, the very stuff from which Adam was formed.
8. The name of an alchemical treatise, a manuscript copy of which Newton possessed.

many things help the work but yet there are only two materialls to the white stone, the mother and the child, the female and the male, besides salarmoniack and sulphur gotten out of metalls. The one is fixt in the fire as stones are, but is not a stone in handling nor in sight but a subtil earth broun ruddy and not bright, and yet after some deale white. This is the chief material and he calls it Markasite and after its separation Litharge and saith its of no more value then a lump of clay. The other material is a stone in handling and in sight glorious fair and bright glittering with perspicuity, being of wonderfull diaphanity, colore subalbido[9] like pale urin or like in colour to Orrichine stone, yet glittering with clearness, called Magnesia and being Res aeris in qua latet scientia divina.[1] To all this agrees also that memorable saying, Visita Interiora Terrae Rectificando Invenies Occultum Lapidem Veram Medicinam.[2] Let therefore the waters be compounded with the earth and the compound be fermented by the two Dragons in a due proportion, and in this water decoct ☉ and ☽.

Artefius tells us that his fire dissolves and gives life to stones and Pontanus that their fire is not transmuted with their matter becaus it is not of their matter, but turns it with all its feces into the elixir. Which deserves well to be considered. For this is the best explication of their saying that the stone is made of one only thing.

"De Natura Acidorum" †

The particles of acids are coarser than those of water and therefore less volatile; but they are much finer than those of earth, and therefore much less fixed than they. They are endowed with a great attractive force and in this force their activity consists by which they dissolve bodies and affect and stimulate the organs of the senses. They are of a middle nature between water and [terrestrial] bodies and they attract both. By their attractive force they surround the particles of bodies be they stony or metallic, and they adhere to them very closely on all sides, so that they can scarcely be separated from them by distillation or sublimation. When they are attracted and gathered together on all sides they raise, disjoin and shake the particles of bodies one from another, that is, they dissolve the bodies; and by their force of attraction by which they rush to the [particles of] bodies, they move the fluid and excite heat and

9. Of a whitish color.
1. An aerial thing in which divine knowledge is concealed.
2. The literal translation does not matter. The first letters of the words form the acronym "Vitriolum," or vitriol.
† *The Correspondence of Isaac Newton*, eds. H. W. Turnbull, J. F. Scott, A. Rupert Hall, and Laura Tilling, 7 vols. (Cambridge: Cambridge University Press, 1959–77), vol. 3, pp. 209–10. Reprinted with the permission of The Royal Society. In "De natura acidorum" ("On the nature of acids"), composed about 1692, Newton applied his knowledge of chemical reactions to speculations less obviously alchemical.

shake asunder some particles to such a degree as to turn them into air and generate bubbles: and this is the reason of dissolution and violent fermentation. Acid also, by attracting water and the particles of bodies equally, causes the dissolved particles to mingle readily with water and swim in it after the manner of salts. And as this globe of the Earth by the force of gravity in attracting water more strongly than it does lighter bodies, causes lighter bodies to ascend in the water and to escape from the Earth; so also the particles of salts, by attracting the water, avoid each other and, by receding from one another as far as they can, are diffused throughout the whole water.

The particles of *sal alkali* consist of acid and earthy combined in just this way, but these acid ones prevail with such a strong attractive force that they are not separable from the salt by fire; moreover they precipitate metals dissolved by attracting from them the acid particles by which they were previously dissolved.

If the acid particles are joined with the earthy ones in a lesser proportion they are so closely held by the latter that they are, as it were, suppressed and hidden by them. For they no longer excite the organs of sense, nor do they attract water, but they compose bodies which are sweet and which do not readily mix with water; that is, they compose fatty bodies such as we find in *mercurius dulcis*, ordinary sulphur, *luna cornea* and copper which has been corroded by mercury sublimate. But the attractive force of the acid thus suppressed causes fatty bodies to adhere almost universally to other bodies and to catch fire easily, provided only that the heated acid meets with other particles of bodies in the smoke arising from burning substances which it attracts more strongly than its own. But the acid, suppressed in sulphureous bodies, by attracting the particles of other bodies (for example, earthy ones) more strongly than its own, causes a gentle and natural fermentation and promotes it even to the stage of putrefaction in the compound. This putrefaction arises from this, that the acid particles which have for some time kept up the fermentation do at length insinuate themselves into the minutest interstices, even those which lie between the parts of the first composition, and so, uniting closely with those particles, give rise to a new mixture which may not be done away with or changed back into its earlier form.

Note that what is said by chemists, that everything is made from sulphur and mercury, is true, because by sulphur they mean acid, and by mercury they mean earth.

Note that sea water does not lose its salinity by filtering through sand; but fresh water found on the sea shore comes from river water seeping through the sands, etc.

JOHN MAYNARD KEYNES

From "Newton, the Man" †

In the eighteenth century and since, Newton came to be thought of as the first and greatest of the modern age of scientists, a rationalist, one who taught us to think on the lines of cold and untinctured reason.

I do not see him in this light. I do not think that any one who has pored over the contents of that box which he packed up when he finally left Cambridge in 1696 and which, though partly dispersed, have come down to us, can see him like that. Newton was not the first of the age of reason. He was the last of the magicians, the last of the Babylonians and Sumerians, the last great mind which looked out on the visible and intellectual world with the same eyes as those who began to build our intellectual inheritance rather less than 10,000 years ago. Isaac Newton, a posthumous child born with no father on Christmas Day, 1642, was the last wonder-child to whom the Magi could do sincere and appropriate homage.

Had there been time, I should have liked to read to you the contemporary record of the child Newton. For, though it is well known to his biographers, it has never been published *in extenso*, without comment, just as it stands. Here, indeed, is the makings of a legend of the young magician, a most joyous picture of the opening mind of genius free from the uneasiness, the melancholy and nervous agitation of the young man and student.

For in vulgar modern terms Newton was profoundly neurotic of a not unfamiliar type, but—I should say from the records—a most extreme example. His deepest instincts were occult, esoteric, semantic—with profound shrinking from the world, a paralyzing fear of exposing his thoughts, his beliefs, his discoveries in all nakedness to the inspection and criticism of the world. 'Of the most fearful, cautious and suspicious temper that I ever knew,' said Whiston, his successor in the Lucasian Chair. The too well-known conflicts and ignoble quarrels with Hooke, Flamsteed, Leibnitz are only too clear an evidence of this. Like all his type he was wholly aloof from women. He parted with and published nothing except under the extreme pressure of friends. Until the second phase of his life, he was a wrapt, consecrated solitary, pursuing his stud-

† The Royal Society, *Newton Tercentenary Celebrations, 15–19 July 1946* (Cambridge: Cambridge University Press, 1947), pp. 27–29. Reprinted with the permission of Cambridge University Press. The eminent economist John Maynard Keynes bought heavily at the auction of Newton manuscripts held in 1936. Among other things, he purchased a considerable number of alchemical papers and from them drew his essay on Newton the man, composed for the tercentenary celebration of Newton's birth, postponed by World War II until 1946.

ies by intense introspection with a mental endurance perhaps never equalled.

* * *

Why do I call him a magician? Because he looked on the whole universe and all that is in it *as a riddle*, as a secret which could be read by applying pure thought to certain evidence, certain mystic clues which God had laid about the world to allow a sort of philosopher's treasure hunt to the esoteric brotherhood. He believed that these clues were to be found partly in the evidence of the heavens and in the constitution of elements (and that is what gives the false suggestion of his being an experimental natural philosopher), but also partly in certain papers and traditions handed down by the brethren in an unbroken chain back to the original cryptic revelation in Babylonia. He regarded the universe as a cryptogram set by the Almighty—just as he himself wrapt the discovery of the calculus in a cryptogram when he communicated with Leibnitz. By pure thought, by concentration of mind, the riddle, he believed, would be revealed to the initiate.

He *did* read the riddle of the heavens. And he believed that by the same powers of his introspective imagination he would read the riddle of the Godhead, the riddle of past and future events divinely fore-ordained, the riddle of the elements and their constitution from an original undifferentiated first matter, the riddle of health and of immortality. All would be revealed to him if only he could persevere to the end, uninterrupted, by himself, no one coming into the room, reading, copying, testing—all by himself, no interruption for God's sake, no disclosure, no discordant breakings in or criticism, with fear and shrinking as he assailed these half-ordained, half-forbidden things, creeping back into the bosom of the Godhead as into his mother's womb. 'Voyaging through strange seas of thought *alone*,' not as Charles Lamb 'a fellow who believed nothing unless it was as clear as the three sides of a triangle.'

* * *

BETTY JO TEETER DOBBS

From "Newton's Alchemy and His Theory of Matter" †

* * *

Sometime during his student years Newton became an eclectic corpuscularian, choosing elements of matter theory from Descartes, Gas-

† *Isis* 73 (1982): 512–28. Reprinted with the permission of the University of Chicago Press. Betty Jo Teeter Dobbs made the study of Newton's alchemical manuscripts the focus of her scholarly activity.

sendi (via Charleton), Boyle, Hobbes, Digby, and More and leaving us a record of his thoughts in the *Quaestiones quaedem philosophicae*[1] of his student notebook. The nature "Of the first mater" had him somewhat bemused. It was clearly not composed of mathematical points and parts, nor of a "simple entity before division indistinct," nor was it infinitely divisible. For a short period he concluded with Henry More in favor of *minima naturalia*,[2] but a subsequent cancellation of that passage in the notebook presumably shows that he reopened the question.

At first Newton was a plenist. By postulating a subtle aether, a medium imperceptible to the senses but capable of transmitting effects by pressure and impact, mechanical philosophers had devised a convention that rid natural philosophy of incomprehensible occult influences acting at a distance (e.g., magnetic attraction and lunar effects). For Newton just such a mechanical aether, prevading the whole world and making it a plenum, became an unquestioned assumption. By it he explained gravity and, to a certain extent, the cohesion of particles of matter.

The question of cohesion had always plagued theories of discrete particles, atomism having been criticized even in antiquity on this point. The cohesion of living forms seems intuitively to be qualitatively different from anything that the random, mechanical motion of small particles of matter might produce. Nor does atomism explain even mechanical cohesion in inert materials very well, for it requires the elaboration of *ad hoc*, unverifiable hypotheses about the geometric configurations of the atoms or else speculation about their quiescence under certain circumstances. In the various forms in which corpuscularianism was revived in the seventeenth century, the problems remained and variants of ancient answers were redeployed. Descartes, for example, held that an external pressure from surrounding subtle matter just balanced the internal pressure of the coarser particles that constituted the cohesive body. Thus no special explanation for cohesion was required: the parts cohered simply because they were at rest close to each other in an equilibrated system. Gassendi's atoms, on the other hand, stuck together through the interlacing of antlers or hooks and claws, much as the atoms of Lucretius had before them. Charleton found not only hooks and claws but also the pressure of neighboring atoms and the absence of disturbing atoms necessary to account for cohesion. Francis Bacon introduced certain spirits or "pneumaticals" into his speculations. In a system reminiscent of the Stoics, those ancient critics of atomism, Bacon concluded that gross matter must be associated with active, shaping, material spirits, the spirits being responsible for the forms and qualities of tangible bodies, producing organized shapes, effecting digestion, assimilation, and so forth. For Newton during his student years, with

1. See selections from the "Quaestiones" in Part 1, Natural Philosophy (above). [Editor]
2. Natural minima; that is, the smallest parts into which bodies could be divided. [Editor]

his mechanical aether ready at hand, a pressure mechanism seemed sufficient to explain cohesion; he rejected quiescence but affirmed that "the close crouding of all the matter in the world" might account for it. Yet he also examined a geometric approach ("Whither hard bodys stick together by branchy particles foulded together"), and he even then suggested that "it may be some other power by which matter is kept close together."

It was to be a long, circuitous, even tortuous journey that carried Newton away from these rather indefinite reflections on matter in his student *Quaestiones*. Within a very short time, perhaps five years at the most, he had begun to modify his mechanical philosophy with an alchemical one, and about 1669 he prepared a short paper containing a series of alchemical propositions.

Gold, silver, iron, copper, tin, lead, mercury, and "magnesia" are all the species of the art, he said, and all of them are from one root. If Newton had been concerned with the unity of matter during his brief years of strict mechanism, no evidence from his early papers has yet appeared. Investigators (myself included) have often tacitly assumed that Newton accepted the unity of matter from contemporary mechanical philosophy. Certainly talk among the mechanical philosophers of the particles of one catholic and universal matter did nothing to undermine ancient doctrines of prime matter, even though among Presocratics, Aristotelians, and alchemists *materia prima*[3] was not considered particulate. Yet here we find Newton's lucid expression for the unity of matter in an alchemical context—"all species are from one root." Whether he had first absorbed the notion in a mechanical or other philosophical context or not, his early alchemical work evidently secured him in a conviction from which he never seriously wavered, and the doctrine of the unity of matter and its transmutability became a part of the published record of his views. The first edition of the *Principia* (1687) carried the most explicit statement: "Any body can be transformed into another, of whatever kind, and all the intermediate degrees of qualities can be induced in it." There is a passage in all editions of the *Principia* in which Newton speculates that matter falling to earth from the tails of comets might be condensed into all types of earthly substances. In his later years Newton stated the doctrine a number of times: in his small tract *On the Nature of Acids*, in the *Opticks*, and to David Gregory, who duly recorded it among his memoranda. Although that most uncompromising statement from the *Principia* of 1687 disappeared in subsequent editions, and although the later *Opticks* passages demonstrate some possible ambiguities, the consensus of recent studies is that Newton maintained to the end his belief in the inertial homogeneity and transformability of matter.

3. First or basic matter. [Editor]

Although alchemy and mechanism do share the doctrine of the ultimate unity of matter, it seems impossible to find a mechanical counterpart for the active, vitalistic alchemical agent Newton introduced into his "Propositions" around 1669. There he called the agent by its code name "magnesia," a term that evoked for the alchemists all the mysterious properties of the magnet and expressed their understanding that certain substances had the capacity to draw into themselves the active vivifying celestial principle necessary for life. Newton aligned "magnesia" with the metals in being from "one root," but he added that magnesia is the only species that revivifies. Newton had become preoccupied with a process of disorganization and reorganization by which developed species of matter might be radically reduced, revivified, and led to generate new forms. The alchemical agent responsible for these changes is vitalistic and universal in its actions; it is a "fermental virtue" or "vegetable spirit" and is eventually to become the force of fermentation of the *Opticks*. In the "Propositions" it is the agent that confounds into chaos and then aggregates anew the particles of matter.

> This and only this is the vital agent diffused through all things that exist in the world.
>
> And it is the mercurial spirit, most subtle and wholly volatile, dispersed through all places.
>
> This agent has the same general method of operating in all things, namely, excited to action by a moderate heat, it is put to flight by a great one, and once an aggregate has been formed, the agent's first action is to putrefy the aggregate and confound it into chaos. Then it proceeds to generation.

From what sources has Newton derived his ideas on the universal vital agent that he here busily attaches to seventeenth-century mechanism? Quite possibly from alchemical sources only, at this early stage in his development, though his vitalistic ideas were soon reinforced by other sources.

Vitalism seems to belong to the very origins of alchemy. In the early Christian centuries metals had not been well characterized as distinct species, but were thought of instead as rather like modern alloys, with variable properties, but even more as like a mix of dough, into which the introduction of a leaven might produce desired changes by a process of fermentation, or even like a material matrix of unformed matter, into which the injection of an active male sperm or seed might lead to a process of generation. By analogy alchemists referred to this critical phase of the alchemical process as fermentation or generation, and the search for the vital ferment or seed became a fundamental part of their quest. Similar ideas occur in Aristotle and are commonplace in Newton's time.

Inspired by his interest in a vital agent, Newton had begun to grope his way toward mending the deficiencies of ancient atomism and contemporary corpuscularianism. He had concerned himself with life and cohesion. He now sought the source of all the apparently spontaneous processes of fermentation, putrefaction, generation, and vegetation (that is, everything associated with normal life and growth, such as digestion and assimilation, vegetation being originally from the Latin *vegetare*, to animate, enliven). These processes produced the endless variety of living forms and could not be relegated to the mechanical actions of gross corpuscles, a point he had made explicit by the mid-1670s. Mechanical action could never account for the process of assimilation, in which food stuffs were turned into the bodies of animals, vegetables, and minerals. Nor could it account for the sheer variety of forms in the world, all of which had somehow sprung from the common matter. As Newton was finally to say in the General Scholium to the *Principia*,[4] "Blind metaphysical necessity [i.e., mechanical action], which is certainly the same always and everywhere, could produce no variety of things." Ultimately, it was God who was responsible, God, who in his wisdom and with his dominion, his providence, and the final causes known only to himself, produced "all that diversity of natural things which we find suited to different times and places." But God was the ultimate cause, and what Newton desired to locate in the natural world was the more proximate cause of the phenomena of life that was God's agent in these matters.

The most comprehensive answer to such problems in antiquity had been given by the Stoics. The Stoics postulated a continuous material medium, the tension and activity of which molded the cosmos into a living whole and the various parts of the cosmic animal into coherent bodies as well. Compounded of air and a creative fire, the Stoic *pneuma* was related to the concept of the "breath of life" that escapes from a living body at the time of death and allows the formerly coherent body in which it had resided to disintegrate into its disparate parts. Although always material, the *pneuma* becomes finer and more active as one ascends the scale of being, and the (more corporeal) air decreases as the (less corporeal) fire increases. Thus the Deity, literally omnipresent in the universe, is the hottest, most tense and creative form of the cosmic *pneuma* or aether, pure fire or nearly so. The cosmos permeated and shaped by the *pneuma* is not only living, it is rational and orderly and under the benevolent, providential care of the Deity. Though the Stoics were determinists, their deity was immanent and active in the cosmos, and one of their most telling arguments against the atomists was that the order, beauty, symmetry, and purpose to be seen in the world could never have come from random, mechanical action. Only a providential God could produce and maintain such lovely, meaningful forms. The universe, as a living body, was born when the creative fire generated the

4. See Part 8, Theology (below). [Editor]

four elements; it lived out its lifespan, permeated by vital heat and breath, cycling back to final conflagration in the divine active principle, and ever regenerated itself.

The original writings of the Stoics were mostly lost, but not before ideas of *pneuma* and *spiritus* came to pervade medical doctrine, alchemical theory, and indeed the general culture with form-giving spirits, souls, and vital principles. Spiritualized forms of the *pneuma* entered early Christian theology in discussions of the immanence and transcendence of God and of the Holy Ghost, just as the Stoic arguments that order and beauty demonstrate the existence of God and of providence entered Christianity as the "argument from design." The creative emanations of Stoic fire melded with the creative emanations of light in Neoplatonism. In addition to this broad spectrum of at least vaguely Stoic ideas, excellent, though not always sympathetic, summaries of philosophical Stoicism were available in Cicero, Seneca, Plutarch, Diogenes Laertius, and Sextus Empiricus.

By the seventeenth century ideas compatible with Stoicism were very widely diffused, and latter-day Stoics, Pythagoreans, Platonists, and Peripatetics all vied with each other in celebrating the occult virtues of a cosmic aether that was the vehicle of a pure, hidden creative fire. Nonetheless, such a vital aether was to be found in its most developed form in philosophical Stoicism. It is possible, as Newton's concern for the processes of life and cohesion grew apace in the early 1670s, that he amplified his mechanical philosophy further by a close reading of the material available to him from classical Rome: Cicero, Diogenes Laertius, Plutarch, Seneca, and Sextus Empiricus were in his library. Such reading would have affected his alchemy only in reinforcing certain critical ideas, for most of his early alchemical sources were distinctively Neoplatonic in tone, and in them the universal spirit or soul of the world already permeated the cosmos with its fermental virtue. But Stoic ideas would have affected his views on the mechanical aether of his student years. We must conclude that if Newton had not read the Stoics, then he must independently have reached answers similar to theirs when confronted with similar problems, for by about 1674 the original mechanical aether of his *Quaestiones* had assumed a strongly Stoic cast.

The new vital aether is described in a long alchemical treatise left untitled by Newton but usually known by its initial phrase, "Of nature's obvious laws and processes in vegetation." The earth is "a great animal," he says, "or rather an inanimate vegetable [that] draws in aethereal breath for its daily refreshment and vital ferment and transpires again with gross exhalations." He goes on to describe this aethereal breath as a "subtle spirit," "nature's universal agent, her secret fire," and the "material soul of all matter." The similarity between this particular Newtonian aether and the Stoic *pneuma* is unmistakable: they are both material and both somehow inspire the forms of bodies and give to bodies the continuity and coherence of form that is associated with life. Newton expands upon that theme, saying that the earth, "according to the condition of all other things living, ought to have its times of beginning, youth, old age, and perishing," and that the subtle aethereal agent is the "only ferment and principle of all vegetation." One may trace the vivid imagery of the earth-animal back through Stoic and Neoplatonic commentators on Plato, as one may trace the "perishing" of the earth to which Newton alludes here forward to his later convictions regarding a final cosmic conflagration.

In this treatise Newton makes a sharp distinction between vegetation and mechanism. "Nature's actions," he says, "are either vegetable or purely mechanical," and as mechanical he lists, among other things, "vulgar chemistry." Vulgar chemistry may readily be identified with the kind of chemistry he discussed in the *Opticks*, the operations of which take place only among the "grosser" particles of matter. As he says here in 1674, "all the operations in vulgar chemistry (many of which to sense are as strange transmutations as those of nature) are but mechanical coalitions or separations of particles . . . and that without any vegetation." Newton admits that to many it may seem that all the "changes made by nature" may be done the same way, "that is by the sleighty transpositions of the grosser corpuscles, for, upon their disposition only, sensible qualities depend." But he argues that such is far from being the case. There is a "vast and fundamental" difference between vulgar chemistry and vegetation, which requires that we have recourse to some further cause.

He continues with a development of themes from his earlier "Propositions" on the subtle nature of the vital agent, on its sensitivity to heat, and on its universality—emphasizing all the while the great differences between vulgar and vegetable chemistry.

> 6 There is, therefore, besides the sensible changes wrought in the textures of grosser matter, a more subtle, secret, and noble way of working in all vegetables which makes its products distinct from all others; and the immediate seat of these operations is not the whole bulk of the matter, but rather an exceeding subtle and unimaginably small portion of matter diffused through the mass, which, if it were separated, there would remain but a dead and inactive earth. And this appears in that vegetables are deprived of their vegetable virtue by any small excess of heat, the tender spirit being either put to flight or at least corrupted thereby (as may appear in an egg), whereas those operations which depend upon the texture of the grosser matter (as all those in common chemistry do) receive no damage by heats far greater. . . .
>
> 7 'Tis the office therefore of those grosser substances to be medium or vehicle in which rather than upon which those vegetable substances perform their actions.

> 8 Yet those grosser substances are very apt to put on various external appearances according to the present state of the invisible inhabitant, as to appear bones, flesh, wood, fruit, etc. Namely, they consisting of differing particles, watery, earthy, saline, airy, oily, spiritous, etc., those parts may be variously moved one among another according to the acting of the latent vegetable substances and be variously associated and concatenated together by their influence.

In these distinctions between mechanical and vegetable chemistry Newton is working toward his famous hierarchical system of parts and pores arranged in three-dimensional netlike patterns. Let us take his statement about the "grosser corpuscles" from 1674: "upon their disposition only, sensible qualities depend." It is identical in meaning with one from the *Opticks* in which Newton describes the building up of the hierarchies of matter "until the Progression end in the biggest Particles on which the Operations in Chymistry, and the Colours of natural Bodies depend, and which by cohering compose Bodies of a sensible Magnitude."

Or let us take another statement from 1674: grosser substances "consisting of differing particles, watery, earthy, saline, airy, oily, spiritous, etc., these parts may be . . . variously associated and concatenated together. . . ." These smaller units of watery, saline, and the like particles form subunits of the largest ones, and their characteristics are drawn from contemporary chemical systems of (usually) five or six chemical elements or principles derived from sixteenth- and seventeenth-century combinations of Aristotelian matter theory (four elements: earth, air, fire, water) with Paracelsian (three principles: salt, sulfur, mercury). Similar intermediate particles appear in both the *Opticks* and in *On the Nature of Acids*.

Furthermore, when Newton discusses putrefaction in 1674, he not only expands upon the view expressed in the "Propositions" a few years earlier but also adumbrates the final section of *On the Nature of Acids*:

> Nothing can be changed from what it is without putrefaction. . . .
> No putrefaction can be without alienating the thing putrefied from what it was.
> Nothing can be generated or nourished (but of putrefied matter).
>
> * * *
>
> Her [Nature's] first action is to blind and confound mixtures into a putrefied chaos.
> Then they are fitted for new generation or nourishment.

It is putrefaction that reduces matter to its ultimate state of disorganization, where the particles of matter are all alike and hence can be remodeled in any form whatsoever. Although the later notion of pores is missing in the 1674 tract on vegetation, in other respects this version of Newton's matter theory closely resembles *On the Nature of Acids*. There, if a menstruum could adequately penetrate the pores of gold, or if gold could "ferment," it could be reduced to its most primordial particles. Then "it could be transformed into any other substance. And so of tin, or any other bodies, as common nourishment is turned into the bodies of animals and vegetables."

Although Newton's early alchemical papers contain both the doctrine of the ultimate unity of matter and the rudiments of a hierarchical system of parts, they do not exhibit all aspects of his final theory of matter. Missing are the pores devoid of matter which later become an essential feature of his structured hierarchies. Missing also is any mention of forces, although the addition of forces to matter theory proved to be his most significant modification of corpuscularianism. Consideration of these further developments perforce leads us into some of Newton's theological concerns, and into a brief excursion on work preliminary to the *Principia*, as well as into more of his alchemical labor.

* * *

Conclusion

The relationship between Newton's alchemy and his published theory of matter has been a persistent problem in Newtonian scholarship for two and a half centuries. The last half century, however, has yielded some intensive investigations of other aspects of Newton's work which provide an intellectual matrix for the resolution of the problem. Especially when considering Newton's theological concerns, one can now understand his intense interest in the alchemical process, for he saw it as the epitome of God's providential, nonmechanical action in the world.

In addition, new evidence from Newton's alchemical papers, especially from the 1674 treatise on vegetation, in which Newton makes explicit the relationships between vegetable and mechanical chemistry, makes it possible to trace an evolutionary process in which alchemy and corpuscularianism interact to produce his published theory of matter. We have shown that his doctrine of the unity of matter and its transformability appear very early in an alchemical context; that his final notion of structured particulate hierarchies was formulated in the 1670s, when he differentiated between common chemistry and vegetable action; and that the active principles that operate between and among the small particles of matter in the *Opticks* are identical with those that so operate in the alchemical papers. Whether they be called forces, virtues, media, principles, or spirits, and whether they operate by corporeal or incorporeal means—all that is in the end only of secondary importance, for activity requires divinity, and nonmechanical action indicates the presence of the divine in the natural order. Universal gravity demonstrates the omnipresence of God the Father; vegetable actions in micromatter indicate continuing supervision of the world by God's viceroy, the Christ. But now perhaps Newton has finally said enough for us to grasp his meaning, and we may conclude with that final triumphant cry by which he summed up his life's work, both for himself and for his public: "And thus much concerning God; to discourse of whom from the appearances of things does certainly belong to Natural Philosophy."

Part 8
THEOLOGY

Introduction

As a son of the seventeenth century, Newton was undoubtedly deeply concerned with religious matters, but his papers do not reveal any sustained study of the subject during his student days, including the two years following his graduation as a bachelor of arts that led up to his master of arts degree and his fellowship in Trinity College. Theology did not constitute a further dimension of the *annus mirabilis*. The fellowship itself, however, may have changed this state of affairs. The statutes of the college prescribed that all fellows be ordained to the Anglican clergy[1] within seven years of receiving the master's degree or face ejection, and Newton was never one to take an obligation lightly. In any event, his papers reveal that he turned to serious reading of theology some time late in the 1660s, not long after he received the master's degree and with it became a senior fellow of the college.

Theology quickly drove physics and mathematics out of Newton's active concern, and together with the other new study to which he turned at about the same time, alchemy, it largely dominated his consciousness for well over a decade. With the mid-1680s, the *Principia* broke the ascendancy of theology over Newton's mind, and during the following two decades, he devoted much less attention to it. He returned to theology in the early eighteenth century, and it furnished the principal staple of his intellectual life during his old age. The religious studies that began shortly after Newton's student days, then, continued unbroken, though with a period of sharply reduced intensity, for the remaining sixty years of his life.

Short passages on theology, one of which (the General Scholium at the end of the *Principia*) we reproduce in this part, made their way into Newton's published works. Query 28 (in Part 4, Optics [above]) closes with a consideration of the same theme, and the set of four letters that Newton wrote to the theologian Richard Bentley in the winter of 1692–93 contain his most extended discussion of the argument from design. In some respects these passages are typical of a religious genre that was widely pursued by scientists of the age: natural theology. Robert Boyle, the greatest chemist of the time, John Ray, the leading naturalist, and others too numerous to mention here called on the latest discoveries of science to demonstrate the existence of God. Newton did the same, drawing of course on the branches of science that he knew best. The conception of God as pantocrator, arbitrary dictator of the cosmos, was

In order not to encumber the reader with footnotes we have composed a Biographical Register, in which all the people mentioned in the text are identified, and a Glossary, in which technical terms are briefly explicated and such things as organizations, places, publications, and manuscript collections are identified. Both the Biographical Register and the Glossary are located near the end of the volume.

1. That is, clergy of the established Church of England, or Anglican Church.

not typical, however. On the contrary, in this form it was unique to Newton and constitutes one of his characteristic doctrines.

The great bulk of Newton's writings on religion, an immense volume of papers running to several million words, remain unpublished to this day. Some of them are notes from his reading. He started with the Bible; twenty-five years later, John Locke would confess that he had never met anyone with a deeper knowledge of the Scriptures. From the Bible, Newton proceeded on to the early Fathers of the Christian church. Again he was nothing if not thorough; he read extensively in the works of such men as Origen, Athanasius, Gregory Nazianzen, Justin Martyr, and Augustine. If we can be guided by the notes he left, Newton became as exhaustively familiar with patristic literature as he was with Scripture.

Mere passive reading did not long quench his curiosity. The program of study to prepare him for ordination made ordination impossible, for an early product of it was the conviction that the doctrine of the trinity was untrue. It was more than untrue. It was a monstrous perversion and corruption of pristine Christianity, which had not known any such teaching. In a later composition sent to John Locke, Newton, who was one of the founders of the critical study of the text of Scripture, demonstrated that the two crucial passages in the Bible on which trinitarians had relied (1 John 5.7 and 1 Timothy 3.16) appeared there for the first time in the fourth century. Newton identified with Arius, a Father of the fourth century for whom Christ was the created intermediary between God and mankind and therefore not an eternal part of the Godhead, and sometime near 1670, Newton began to compose Arian statements about the nature of Christ, one of which we reproduce.

His theological education nearly cost Newton his academic career. Arian opinions would have led to his immediate expulsion from the university had they been known. Newton took considerable pains to be sure that they were not. The necessity for ordination remained, however, and Newton would not perjure himself in ordination. As 1675 dawned, he was preparing to lay down his fellowship in Trinity College. At that time, Newton had been the Lucasian Professor of Mathematics for more than five years, and he could perhaps have continued on in the university without a fellowship. The statues of the Lucasian chair also demanded conformity to the Anglican religion, however, and Newton might have found it difficult to conceal his reasons for laying down a lucrative fellowship. At the last moment, the clouds lifted. Probably through the intervention of Isaac Barrow, master of Trinity College, a royal dispensation, not to Newton but to the Lucasian professor in perpetuity, excused him from any statutory requirement for ordination. Newton continued to hold the theological position taken near 1670 until the end of his life, always under compulsion not to broadcast his views under pain of ejection, initially from the university and then after 1696 from his position at the mint. We include two brief statements of his theological stance, "A short schem of the true Religion" and an untitled set of twelve articles, composed toward the end of his life, in which his Arian views find a somewhat different expression.

Almost from the beginning of his theological study, the interpretion of the prophecies furnished one of its dimensions. This was the one aspect of Newton's religious studies that became known, for shortly after his death his heirs published *Observations upon the Prophecies of Daniel and the Apocalypse of St. John*. The manuscript they published was a product of Newton's old age, and in his continuing concern to conceal his heterodox opinions, he thoroughly sanitized a work that had started in the very period of his Arian studies and revealed their pervasive influence. The selection we include, an introduction to his interpretation of the Apocalypse of St. John, dates from the early period. Nothing in it refers explicitly to Arius; all of it expresses his sense of possessing an important but dangerous truth.

From a Memorandum by David Gregory †

. . . His Doubt was whether he should put the last Quære thus. *What the space that is empty of body is filled with*. The plain truth is, that he believes God to be omnipresent in the literal sense; And that as we are sensible of Objects when their Images are brought home within the brain,[1] so God must be sensible of every thing, being intimately present with every thing: for he supposes that as God is present in space where there is no body, he is present in space where a body is also present. But if this way of proposing this his notion be too bold, he thinks of doing it thus. *What Cause did the Ancients assign of Gravity*. He believes that they reckoned God the Cause of it, nothing els, that is no body being the cause; since every body is heavy.

* * *

† Walter George Hiscock, ed. *David Gregory, Isaac Newton, and Their Circle* (Oxford: Printed for the Editor, 1937), p. 30. David Gregory, a Scottish mathematician and natural philosopher a generation younger than Newton, frequently visited him and kept extensive notes of their conversations. He dated this memorandum December 21, 1705.

1. See Glossary, *Sensorium*.

Four Letters to Richard Bentley †

Newton to Bentley, December 10, 1692

Sir

When I wrote my treatise about our Systeme[1] I had an eye upon such Principles as might work with considering men for the belief of a Deity and nothing can rejoyce me more than to find it usefull for that purpose. But if I have done the publick any service this way 'tis due to nothing but industry and patient thought.

As to your first Query, it seems to me, that if the matter of our Sun and Planets and all the matter in the Universe was eavenly scattered throughout all the heavens, and every particle had an innate gravity towards all the rest and the whole space throughout which this matter was scattered was but finite: the matter on the outside of this space would by its gravity tend towards all the matter on the inside and by consequence fall down to the middle of the whole space and there compose one great spherical mass. But if the matter was eavenly diffused through an infinite space, it would never convene into one mass but some of it convene into one mass and some into another so as to make an infinite number of great masses scattered at great distances from one to another throughout all that infinite space. And thus might the Sun and Fixt stars be formed supposing the matter were of a lucid nature. But how the matter should divide it self into two sorts and that part of it which is fit to compose a shining body should fall down into one mass and make a Sun and the rest which is fit to compose an opake body should coalesce not into one great body like the shining matter but into many little ones: or if the Sun was at first an opake body like the Planets, or the Planets lucid bodies like the Sun, how he alone should be changed into a shining body whilst all they continue opake or all they be changed into opake ones whilst he remains unchanged, I do not think explicable by mere natural causes but am forced to ascribe it to the counsel and contrivance of a voluntary Agent. The same power, whether natural or supernatural, which placed the Sun in the center of the Orbs of the six primary Planets, placed Saturn in the center of the orbs of his five secondary Planets and Jupiter in the center of the orbs of his four secondary ones and the earth in the center of the Moons orb; and therefore had this cause been

† *The Correspondence of Isaac Newton*, eds. H. W. Turnbull, J. F. Scott, A. Rupert Hall, and Laura Tilling, 7 vols. (Cambridge: Cambridge University Press, 1959–77), vol. 3, pp. 233–56. Reprinted with the permission of The Royal Society. In his will, Robert Boyle, who died on December 30, 1691, endowed a series of lectures to defend religion from atheism. The young theologian Richard Bentley, who drew heavily on the *Principia* for the content of the first Boyle Lectures, applied to Newton for help on a number of points as he prepared his lectures for publication in late 1692. In all, Newton addressed four letters on God and natural philosophy to Bentley during the following weeks.

1. The *Principia*.

a blind one without contrivance and designe the Sun would have been a body of the same kind with Saturn Jupiter and the earth, that is without light and heat. Why there is one body in our Systeme qualified to give light and heat to all the rest I know no reason but because the author of the Systeme thought it convenient, and why there is but one body of this kind I know no reason but because one was sufficient to warm and enlighten all the rest. For the Cartesian Hypothesis of Sun's loosing their light and then turning into Comets and Comets into Planets can have no place in my systeme and is plainly erroneous because its certain that Comets as often as they appear to us descend into the system of our Planets lower then the orb of Jupiter and sometimes lower then the orbs of Venus and Mercury, and yet never stay here but always return from the Sun with the same degrees of motion by which they approached him.

To your second Query I answer that the motions which the Planets now have could not spring from any naturall cause alone but were imprest by an intelligent Agent. For since Comets descend into the region of our Planets and here move all manner of ways going sometimes the same way with the Planets sometimes the contrary way and sometimes in cross ways in planes inclined to the plane of the Ecliptick at all kinds of angles: its plaine that there is no naturall cause which could determine all the Planets both primary and secondary to move the same way and in the same plane without any considerable variation. This must have been the effect of Counsel. Nor is there any natural cause which could give the Planets those just degrees of velocity in proportion to their distances from the Sun and other central bodies about which they move and to the quantity of matter conteined in those bodies, which were requisite to make them move in concentrick orbs about those bodies. Had the Planets been as swift as Comets in proportion to their distances from the Sun (as they would have been, had their motions been caused by their gravity, whereby the matter at the first formation of the Planets might fall from the remotest regions towards the Sun) they would not move in concentric orbs but in such excentric ones as the Comets move in. Were all the Planets as swift as Mercury or as slow as Saturn or his Satellites, or were their several velocities otherwise much greater or less then they are (as they might have been had they arose from any other cause then their gravity) or had their distances from the centers about which they move been greater or less then they are with the same velocities; or had the quantity of matter in the Sun or in Saturn, Jupiter and the earth and by consequence their gravitating power been greater or less then it is: the primary Planets could not have revolved about the Sun nor the secondary ones about Saturn, Jupiter and the earth in concentrick circles as they do, but would have moved in Hyperbolas or Parabolas or in Ellipses very excentric. To make this systeme therefore with all its motions, required a

Cause which understood and compared together the quantities of matter in the several bodies of the Sun and Planets and the gravitating powers resulting from thence, the several distances of the primary Planets from the Sun and secondary ones from Saturn Jupiter and the earth, and the velocities with which these Planets could revolve at those distances about those quantities of matter in the central bodies. And to compare and adjust all these things together in so great a variety of bodies argues that cause to be not blind and fortuitous, but very well skilled in Mechanicks and Geometry.

To your third Query I answer that it may be represented that the Sun may by heating those Planets most which are nearest to him cause them to be better concocted and more condensed by concoction. But when I consider that our earth is much more heated in its bowells below the upper crust by subterraneous fermentations of mineral bodies[2] then by the Sun, I see not why the interior parts of Jupiter and Saturn might not be as much heated concocted and coagulated by those fermentations as our earth is, and therefore this various density should have some other cause then the various distances of the Planets from the Sun: and I am confirmed in this opinion by considering that the Planets of Jupiter and Saturn as they are rarer then the rest so they are vastly greater and contein a far greater quantity of matter and have many Satellites about them: which qualifications surely arose not from their being placed at so great a distance from the Sun but were rather the cause why the creator placed them at that great distance. For by their gravitating powers they disturb one anothers motions very sensibly as I find by some late Observations of Mr Flamsteed, and had they been placed much nearer to the Sun and to one another they would by the same powers have caused a considerable disturbance in the whole Systeme.

To the 4th Query I answer that in the Hypotheses of Vortices the inclination of the axis of the earth might in my opinion be ascribed to the situation of the earth's vortex before it was absorbed by the neighbouring vortices and the earth turned from a Sun to a Comet; but this inclination ought constantly to decrease in compliance with the motion of the earths vortex, whose axis is much less inclined to the Ecliptick as appears by the motion of the Moon carried about therein. If the sun by his rays could carry about the Planets, yet I do not see how he could thereby affect their diurnal motions.

Lastly I see nothing extraordinary in the inclination of the Earth's axis for proving a Deity unless you will urge it as a contrivance for winter and summer and for making the earth habitable towards the poles, and that the diurnal rotations of the Sun and Planets as they could hardly arise from any cause purely mechanical, so by being determined all the same way with the annual and menstrual motions they seem to make

2. See Query 31 in Part 1, Natural Philosophy (above).

up that harmony in the systeme which (as I explained above) was the effect of choice rather then of chance.

There is yet another argument for a Deity which I take to be a very strong one, but till principles on which tis grounded be better received I think it more advisable to let it sleep. I am

Your most humble Servant to command

Is. Newton

Newton to Bentley, January 17, 1692/3

Sir

I agree with you that if matter eavenly diffused through a finite space not spherical, should fall into a solid mass, this mass would affect the figure of the whole space, provided it were not soft like the old Chaos, but so hard and solid from the beginning, that the weight of its protuberant parts could not make it yeild to their pressure. Yet by earthquakes loosing the parts of this solid, the protuberances might sometimes sink a little by their Weight, and thereby the mass might by degrees approach a spherical figure.

The reason why matter eavenly scattered through a finite space would convene in the midst you conceive the same with me: but that there should be a Central particle so accurately placed in the middle as to be always equally attracted on all sides and thereby continue without motion, seems to me a supposition fully as hard as to make the sharpest needle stand upright on its point upon a looking glass. For if the very mathematical center of the central particle be not accurately in the very mathematical center of the attractive power of the whole mass, the particle will not be attracted equally on all sides.

And much harder it is to suppose that all the particles in an infinite space should be so accurately poised one among another as to stand still in a perfect equilibrium. For I reccon this as hard as to make not one needle only but an infinite number of them (so many as there are particles in an infinite space) stand accurately poised upon their points. Yet I grant it possible, at least by a divine power; and if they were once so placed I agree with you that they would continue in that posture without motion for ever, unless put into new motion by the same power. When therefore I said that matter eavenly spread through all spaces would convene by its gravity into one or more great masses, I understand it of matter not resting in an accurate poise.

But you argue in the next paragraph of your letter that every particle of matter in an infinite space has an infinite quantity of matter on all sides and by consequence an infinite attraction every way and therefore must rest *in equilibrio* because all infinites are equal. Yet you suspect a parallogism in this argument, and I conceive the parallogism lies in the position that all infinites are equal. The generality of mankind consider infinites no other ways then definitely, and in this sense they say all infinites are equal, though they would speak more truly if they should say they are neither equal nor unequal nor have any certain difference or proportion one to another. In this sense therefore no conclusions can be drawn from them about the equality, proportions or differences of things, and they that attempt to do it, usually fall into parallogism. So when men argue against the infinite divisibility of magnitude, by saying that if an inch may be divided into an infinite number of parts, the sum of those parts will be an inch, and if a foot may be divided into an infinite number of parts the sum of those parts must be a foot, and therefore since all infinites are equal those summs must be equal, that is an inch equal to a foot. The falsness of the conclusions shews an error in the premisses, and the error lies in the position that all infinites are equal. There is therefore another way of considering infinites used by Mathematicians, and that is under certain definite restrictions and limitations whereby infinites are determined to have certain differences or proportions to one another. Thus Dr Wallis considers them in his *Arithmetica Infinitorum*, where by the various proportions of infinite summs he gathers the various proportions of infinite magnitudes: which way of arguing is generally allowed by Mathematicians and yet would not be good were all infinites equall. According to the same way of Considering infinites, a Mathematician would tell you that though there be an infinite number of infinitely little parts in an inch yet there is twelve times that number of such parts in a foot; that is, the infinite number of those parts in a foot is not equall to, but twelve times bigger then the infinite number of them in an inch. And so a Mathematician will tell you that if a body stood *in equilibrio* between any two equal and contrary attracting infinite forces, and if to either of those forces you add any new finite attracting force: that new force how little so ever will destroy the equilibrium and put the body into the same motion into which it would put it were those two contrary equal forces but finite or even none at all: so that in this case two equal infinites by the addition of a finite to either of them become unequal in our ways of recconning. And after these ways we must reccon if from the consideration of infinites we would always draw true conclusions.

To the last part of your letter I answer first that if the earth (without the moon) were placed any where with its center in the *Orbis magnus*[3] and stood still there without any gravitation or projection and then at once were infused into it both a gravitating energy towards the sun and a transverse impulse of a just quantity moving it directly in a tangent to the *Orbis magnus*: the compound of this attraction and projection would according to my notion cause a circular revolution of the earth about the Sun. But the transverse impulse must be of a just quantity, for if it

3. The great orb or orbit, the orbit of the earth about the sun.

be too big or too little it will cause the earth to move in some other line.

Secondly I do not know any power in nature which could cause this transverse motion without the divine arm. Blondel tells us some where in his book of Bombs that Plato affirms that the motion of the planets is such as if they had all of them been created by God in some region very remote from our Systeme and let fall from thence towards the Sun, and so soon as they arrived at their several orbs their motion of falling turned aside into a transverse one; and this is true supposing the gravitating power of the Sun was doubled at that moment of time in which they all arrive at their several orbs: but then the divine power is here required in a double respect; namely to turn the descending motion of the falling planets into a side motion, and at the same time to double the attractive power of the Sun. So then gravity may put the planets into motion but without the divine power it could never put them into such a Circulating motion as they have about the Sun, and therefore for this as well as other reasons I am compelled to ascribe the frame of this Systeme to an intelligent agent.

You sometimes speak of gravity as essential and inherent to matter: pray do not ascribe that notion to me, for the cause of gravity is what I do not pretend to know, and therefore would take more time to consider of it.[4] I fear what I have said of infinites will seem obscure to you: but it is enough if you understand that infinites when considered absolutely without any restriction or limitation, are neither equal nor unequal nor have any certain proportion to one another, and therefore the principle that all infinites are equal is a precarious one. Sir I am

Your most humble Servant

Is. Newton.

Newton to Bentley, February 11 1692/3

Sir

The Hypothesis of deriving the frame of the world by mechanical principles from matter eavenly spread through the heavens being inconsistent with my systeme, I had considered it very little before your letters put me upon it, and therefore trouble you with a line or two more about it if this come not too late for your use. In my former I represented that the diurnal rotations of the Planets could not be derived from gravity but required a divine power to impress them. And thô gravity might give the Planets a motion of descent towards the sun either directly or with some little obliquity, yet the transverse motions by which they revolve in their several orbs required the divine Arm to impress them according to the tangents of their orbs. I would now add that the Hypothesis of matters being at first eavenly spread through the heavens is, in my opinion,

4. See passage on the cause of gravity from the General Scholium to the *Principia*, in Part 2, Scientific Method (above), and the entire General Scholium later in this part.

inconsistent with the Hypothesis of innate gravity without a supernatural power to reconcile them, and therefore it infers a Deity. For if there be innate gravity its impossible now for the matter of the earth and all the Planets and stars to fly up from them and become eavenly spread throughout all the heavens without a supernatural power, and certainly that which can never be hereafter without a supernatural power could never be heretofore without the same power.

You queried whether matter eavenly spread throughout a finite space of some other figure then spherical, would not in falling down towards a centrall body cause that body to be of the same figure with the whole space, and I answered, Yes. But in my answer it's to be supposed that the matter descnds directly downwards to that body and that that body has no diurnal rotation. This Sir is all that I would add to my former Letters. I am

Your most humble Servant
Is. Newton

Newton to Bentley, February 25, 1692/3

Sir

Because you desire speed I'l answer your letter with what brevity I can. In the six positions you lay down in the beginning of your Letter I agree with you. Your assuming the *Orbis Magnus* 7000 diameters of the earth wide implies the Sun's horizontal Parallax to be half a minute. Flamsteed and Cassini have of late observed it to be but about 10″, and thus the *Orbis magnus* must be 21000 or in a rounder number 20000 diameters of the earth wide. Either assumption will do well and I think it not worth your while to alter your numbers.

In the next part of your letter you lay down four other positions founded upon the six first. The first of these four seems very evident supposing you take attraction so generally as by it to understand any force by which distant bodies endeavour to come together without mechanical impulse.

The second seems not so clear. For it may be said that there might be other systemes of worlds before the present ones and others before those and so on to all past eternity and by consequence that gravity might be coeternal to matter and have that same effect from all eternity as at present: unless you have somewhere proved that old systems cannot gradually wast and pass into new ones or that this system had not it's originall from the exhaling matter of former decaying systems but from a chaos of matter eavenly dispersed throughout all space. For something of this kind I think you say was the subject of your sixt sermon: and the growth of new systems out of old ones without the mediation of a divine power seems to me apparently absurd.

The last clause of your second Position I like very well. Tis unconceivable that inanimate brute matter should (without the mediation of something else which is not material) operate upon and affect other matter without mutual contact; as it must if gravitation in the sense of Epicurus be essential and inherent in it. And this is one reason why I desired you would not ascribe innate gravity to me. That gravity should be innate inherent and essential to matter so that one body may act upon another at a distance through a vacuum without the mediation of any thing else by and through which their action or force may be conveyed from one to another is to me so great an absurdity that I beleive no man who has in philosophical matters any competent faculty of thinking can ever fall into it. Gravity must be caused by an agent acting constantly according to certain laws, but whether this agent be material or immaterial is a question I have left to the consideration of my readers.

Your fourth assertion that the world could not be formed by innate gravity alone you confirm by three arguments. But in your first Argument you seem to make a *petito principij*.[5] For whereas many ancient Philosophers and others as well Theists as Atheists have allowed that there may be worlds and parcels of matter innumerable or infinite, you deny this by representing it as absurd as that there should be positively an infinite arithmetical summ or number which is a contradiction *in terminis*: but you do not prove it as absurd. Neither do you prove that what men mean by an infinite summ or number is a contradiction in nature. For a contradiction *in terminis* argues nothing more then an impropriety of speech. Those things which men understand by improper and contradictious phrases may be sometimes really in nature without any contradiction at all. A silver inkhorn a paper Lanthorn an iron whetstone are absurd phrases and yet the things signified thereby are really in nature. If any man should say that a number and a summ (to speak properly) is that which may be numbered and summed, but things infinite are numberless or (as we usually speak) innumerable and summless or insummable and therefore ought not to be called a number or summ: he will speak properly enough and your argument against him will I fear lose its force. And yet if any man shall take the words number and summ in a larger sense so as to understand thereby things which in the proper way of speaking are numberless and sumless (as you do when you seem to allow an infinite number of points in a line) I could readily allow him the use of the contradictious phrases of an innumerable number or summless summ without inferring from thence any absurdity in the thing he means by those phrases. However if by this or any other argument you have proved the finiteness of the universe it follows that all matter would fall down from the outsides and convene in the middle. Yet the matter in falling might concrete into many round masses like the bodies of the Planets and these by attracting one another might

5. Begging of the question; that is, assuming the answer in the premises of an argument.

acquire an obliquity of descent by means of which they might fall not upon the great central body but on one side of it and fetch a compass about it and then ascend again by the same steps and degrees of motion and velocity with which they descended before, much after the manner that Comets revolve about the Sun. But a circular motion in a concentrick orbs about the Sun they could never acquire by gravity alone.

And tho all the matter were at first divided into several system and every system by a divine power constituted like our's: yet would the outward systemes descend towards the middlemost so that this frame of things could not always subsist without a divine power to conserve it. Which is your second Argument, and to your third I fully assent.

As for the passage of Plato, there is no common place from whence all the Planets being let fall and descending with uniform and equal gravities (as Gallileo[6] supposes) would at their arrival to their several Orbs acquire their several velocities with which they now revolve in them. If we suppose the gravity of all the Planets towards the Sun to be of such a quantity as it really is and that the motions of the Planets are turned upwards, every Planet will ascend to twice its height from the Sun. Saturn will ascend till he be twice as high from the Sun as he is at present and no higher. Jupiter will ascend as high again as at present; that is, at little above the orb of Saturn. Mercury will ascend to twice his present height, that is to the orb of Venus and so of the rest. And then by falling down again from the places to which they ascended they will arrive again at their several orbs with the same velocities they had at first and with which they now revolve.

But if so soon as their motions by which they revolve are turned upwards, the gravitating power of the Sun by which their ascent is perpetualy retarded, will be diminished by one half they will now ascend perpetually and all of them at all equal distances from the sun will be equally swift. Mercury when he arrives at the orb of Venus will be as swift as Venus and he and Venus when they arrive at the orb of the earth will be as swift as the earth and so of the rest. If they begin all of them to ascend at once and ascend in the same line they will constantly in ascending become nearer and nearer together and their motions will constantly approach to an equality and become at length slower then any motion assigneable. Suppose therefore that they ascended till they were almost contiguous and their motions inconsiderably little and that all their motions were at the same moment of time turned back again or (which comes almost to the same thing) that they were only deprived of their motions and let fall at that time: they would all at once arrive at their several orbs each with the velocity it had at first; and if their motions were then turned sideways and at the same time the gravitating power of the Sun doubled that it might be strong enough to retain them

6. The passage in question appears in Galileo's *Dialogue Concerning the Two Chief World Systems* (1632).

in their Orbs, they would revolve in them as before their ascent. But if the gravitating power of the Sun were not doubled, they would go away from their Orbs into the highest heavens in Parabolical lines. These things follow from my Princip. Math. lib. 1.[7] Prop. 33, 34, 36, 37. I thank you very kindly for your designed present and rest

Your most humble Servant to command
Is. Newton

General Scholium †

The hypothesis of vortices is pressed with many difficulties. That every planet by a radius drawn to the sun may describe areas proportional to the times of description, the periodic times of the several parts of the vortices should observe the square of their distances from the sun; but that the periodic times of the planets may obtain the $^{3}/_{2}$th power of their distances from the sun, the periodic times of the parts of the vortex ought to be as the $^{3}/_{2}$th power of their distances. That the smaller vortices may maintain their lesser revolutions about Saturn, Jupiter, and other planets, and swim quietly and undisturbed in the greater vortex of the sun, the periodic times of the parts of the sun's vortex should be equal; but the rotation of the sun and planets about their axes, which ought to correspond with the motions of their vortices, recede far from all these proportions. The motions of the comets are exceedingly regular, are governed by the same laws with the motions of the planets, and can by no means be accounted for by the hypothesis of vortices; for comets are carried with very eccentric motions through all parts of the heavens indifferently, with a freedom that is incompatible with the notion of a vortex.

Bodies projected in our air suffer no resistance but from the air. Withdraw the air, as is done in Mr. *Boyle's* vacuum,[1] and the resistance ceases; for in this void a bit of fine down and a piece of solid gold descend with equal velocity. And the same argument must apply to the celestial spaces above the earth's atmosphere; in these spaces, where there is no air to resist their motions, all bodies will move with the greatest freedom; and the planets and comets will constantly pursue their revolutions in orbits given in kind and position, according to the laws above explained; but though these bodies may, indeed, continue in their orbits by the mere laws of gravity, yet they could by no means have at

7. That is, the *Principia*, Book 1.

† Isaac Newton, *Mathematical Principles of Natural Philosophy* and *System of the World*, trans. by Andrew Motte, revised by Florian Cajori (Berkeley and Los Angeles: University of California Press, 1934 and later printings), pp. 543–47. To the second edition of the *Principia*, published in 1713, Newton added a concluding statement of his conception of natural philosophy, which he called the General Scholium. It contains his most important discussion of the relation of God to the physical universe. See note on the Cajori translation on p. 116.

1. This refers to the vacuum in the receiver of Boyle's air pump.

first derived the regular position of the orbits themselves from those laws.

The six primary planets are revolved about the sun in circles concentric with the sun, and with motions directed towards the same parts, and almost in the same plane. Ten moons are revolved about the earth, Jupiter, and Saturn, in circles concentric with them, with the same direction of motion, and nearly in the planes of the orbits of those planets; but it is not to be conceived that mere mechanical causes could give birth to so many regular motions, since the comets range over all parts of the heavens in very eccentric orbits; for by that kind of motion they pass easily through the orbs of the planets, and with great rapidity; and in their aphelions, where they move the slowest, and are detained the longest, they recede to the greatest distances from each other, and hence suffer the least disturbance from their mutual attractions. This most beautiful system of the sun, planets, and comets, could only proceed from the counsel and dominion of an intelligent and powerful Being. And if the fixed stars are the centres of other like systems, these, being formed by the like wise counsel, must be all subject to the dominion of One; especially since the light of the fixed stars is of the same nature with the light of the sun, and from every system light passes into all the other systems: and lest the systems of the fixed stars should, by their gravity, fall on each other, he hath placed those systems at immense distances from one another.

This Being governs all things, not as the soul of the world, but as Lord over all; and on account of his dominion he is wont to be called *Lord God παντοκράτωρ*, or *Universal Ruler*; for *God* is a relative word, and has a respect to servants; and *Deity* is the dominion of God not over his own body, as those imagine who fancy God to be the soul of the world, but over servants. The Supreme God is a Being eternal, infinite, absolutely perfect; but a being, however perfect, without dominion, cannot be said to be Lord God; for we say, my God, your God, the God of *Israel*, the God of Gods, and Lord of Lords; but we do not say, my Eternal, your Eternal, the Eternal of *Israel*, the Eternal of Gods; we do not say, my Infinite, or my Perfect: these are titles which have no respect to servants. The word God usually signifies *Lord*; but every lord is not a God. It is the dominion of a spiritual being which constitutes a God: a true, supreme, or imaginary dominion makes a true, supreme, or imaginary God. And from his true dominion it follows that the true God is a living, intelligent, and powerful Being; and, from his other perfections, that he is supreme, or most perfect. He is eternal and infinite, omnipotent and omniscient; that is, his duration reaches from eternity to eternity; his presence from infinity to infinity; he governs all things, and knows all things that are or can be done. He is not eternity and infinity, but eternal and infinite; he is not duration or space, but he endures and is present. He endures forever, and is everywhere present; and, by existing always and everywhere, he constitutes duration and space.[2] Since every particle of space is *always*, and every indivisible moment of duration is *everywhere*, certainly the Maker and Lord of all things cannot be *never* and *nowhere*. Every soul that has perception is, though in different times and in different organs of sense and motion, still the same indivisible person. There are given successive parts in duration, coexistent parts in space, but neither the one nor the other in the person of a man, or his thinking principle; and much less can they be found in the thinking substance of God. Every man, so far as he is a thing that has perception, is one and the same man during his whole life, in all and each of his organs of sense. God is the same God, always and everywhere. He is omnipresent not *virtually* only, but also *substantially*; for virtue cannot subsist without substance. In him are all things contained and moved; yet neither affects the other: God suffers nothing from the motion of bodies; bodies find no resistance from the omnipresence of God. It is allowed by all that the Supreme God exists necessarily; and by the same necessity he exists *always* and *everywhere*. Whence also he is all similar, all eye, all ear, all brain, all arm, all power to perceive, to understand, and to act; but in a manner not at all human, in a manner not at all corporeal, in a manner utterly unknown to us. As a blind man has no idea of colors, so have we no idea of the manner by which the all-wise God perceives and understands all things. He is utterly void of all body and bodily figure, and can therefore neither be seen, nor heard, nor touched; nor ought he to be worshiped under the representation of any corporeal thing. We have ideas of his attributes, but what the real substance of anything is we know not. In bodies, we see only their figures and colors, we hear only the sounds, we touch only their outward surfaces, we smell only the smells, and taste the savors; but their inward substances are not to be known either by our senses, or by any reflex act of our minds: much less, then, have we any idea of the substance of God. We know him only by his most wise and excellent contrivances of things, and final causes; we admire him for his perfections; but we reverence and adore him on account of his dominion: for we adore him as his servants; and a god without dominion, providence, and final causes, is nothing else but Fate and Nature. Blind metaphysical necessity, which is certainly the same always and everywhere, could produce no variety of things. All that diversity of natural things which we find suited to different times and places could arise from nothing but the ideas and will of a Being necessarily existing. But, by way of allegory, God is said to see, to speak, to laugh, to love, to hate, to desire, to give, to receive, to rejoice, to be angry, to fight, to frame, to work, to build; for all our

2. See the Scholium to the definitions from the *Principia* in Part 5, Rational Mechanics (above).

notions of God are taken from the ways of mankind by a certain similitude, which, though not perfect, has some likeness, however. And thus much concerning God; to discourse of whom from the appearances of things, does certainly belong to Natural Philosophy.

Hitherto we have explained the phenomena of the heavens and of our sea by the power of gravity, but have not yet assigned the cause of this power. This is certain, that it must proceed from a cause that penetrates to the very centres of the sun and planets, without suffering the least diminution of its force; that operates not according to the quantity of the surfaces of the particles upon which it acts (as mechanical causes used to do), but according to the quantity of the solid matter which they contain, and propagates its virtue on all sides to immense distances, decreasing always as the inverse square of the distances. Gravitation towards the sun is made up out of the gravitations towards the several particles of which the body of the sun is composed; and in receding from the sun decreases accurately as the inverse square of the distances as far as the orbit of Saturn, as evidently appears from the quiescence of the aphelion of the planets; nay, and even to the remotest aphelion of the comets, if those aphelions are also quiescent. But hitherto I have not been able to discover the cause of those properties of gravity from phenomena, and I frame no hypothesis; for whatever is not deduced from the phenomena is to be called an hypothesis; and hypotheses, whether metaphysical or physical, whether of occult qualities or mechanical, have no place in experimental philosophy. In this philosophy particular propositions are inferred from the phenomena, and afterwards rendered general by induction. Thus it was that the impenetrability, the mobility, and the impulsive force of bodies, and the laws of motion and of gravitation, were discovered. And to us it is enough that gravity does really exist, and act according to the laws which we have explained, and abundantly serves to account for all the motions of the celestial bodies, and of our sea.

* * *

An Early Theological Manuscript †

1. The [word] God is no where in the scriptures used to signify more then one of the thre persons at once.
2. The word God put absolutly without particular restriction to the Son or Holy ghost doth always signify the Father from one end of the scriptures to the other.

† Richard S. Westfall, *Never at Rest: A Biography of Isaac Newton* (Cambridge: Cambridge University Press, 1980), pp. 315–16. Reprinted with the permission of Cambridge University Press and The Jewish National and University Library. Newton began serious theological study in the early 1670s. One of the first fruits of that study was a set of twelve points on the nature of Christ apparently composed in the period 1672–75.

3. When ever it is said in the scriptures that there is but one God, it is meant of the Father
4. When, after some heretiques had taken Christ for a meare man and others for the supreme God, St John in his Gospel indeavoured to state his nature so that men might have from thence a right apprehension of him and avoyd those haeresies and to that end calls him the word or *logos*: we must suppose that he intended that terme in the same sence that it was taken in the world before he used it when in like manner applied to an intelligent being. For if the Apostles had not used words as they found them how could they expect to have been rightly understood. Now the term *logos* before St John wrote, was generally used in the sense of the Platonists, when applied to an intelligent being, and the Arrians understood it in the same sence, and therefore theirs is the true sense of St John.
5. The son in several places confesseth his dependance on the will of the father.
6. The son confesseth the father greater then him calls him his God, etc.
7. The Son acknowledgeth the original praescience of all future things to be in the father onely.
8. There is no where made mention of a humane soul in our saviour besides the word, by the mediation of which the word should be incarnate. But the word it self was made flesh and took upon him the form of a servant.
9. It was the son of God which he sent into the world and not a humane soul that suffered for us. If there had been such a human soul in our Saviour, it would have been a thing of too great consequence to have been wholly omitted by the Apostles.
10. It is a proper epithete of the father to be called almighty. For by God almighty we always understand the Father. Yet this is not to limit the power of the Son, For he doth what soever he seeth the Father do; but to acknowledg that all power is originally in the Father and that the son hath no power in him but what he derives from the father for he professes that of himself he can do nothing.
11. The son in all things submits his will to the will of the father. which would be unreasonable if he were equall to the father.
12. The union between him and the father he interprets to be like that of the saints one with another. That is in agreement of will and counsil.

A Short Schem of the True Religion †

Religion is partly fundamental and immutable, partly circumstantial and mutable. The first was the religion of Adam, Enoch, Noah, Abraham, Moses, Christ and all the saints, and consists of two parts, our duty towards God and our duty towards man, or piety and righteousness, which I will here call Godliness and Humanity.

Of Godliness

Godliness consists in the knowledge, love, and worship of God, Humanity in love, righteousness, and good offices towards man. Thou shalt love the Lord they God with all thy heart, and with all thy soul, and with all thy mind: this is the first and great commandment, and the second is like unto it, Thou shalt love they neighbour as thyself. On these two commandments hang all the law and the prophets. Mat. 22 The first is enjoined in the four first commandments of the Decalogue, and the second in the six last.

Of Atheism

Opposite to the first is Atheism in profession and Idolatry in practice. Atheism is so senseless and odious to mankind that it never had many professors. Can it be by accident that all birds, beasts and men have their right side and left side alike shaped (except in their bowels), and just two eyes and no more on either side the face, and just two ears on either side the head, and a nose with two holes and no more between the eyes, and one mouth under the nose, and either two fore-legs or two wings or two arms on the shoulders, and two legs on the hips, one on either side and no more? Whence arises this uniformity in all their outward shapes but from the counsel and contrivance of an Author? Whence is it that all the eyes of all sorts of living creatures are transparent to the very bottom and the only transparent members in the body, having on the outside a hard transparent skin and within transparent juyces with a crystalline lens in the middle and a pupil before the lens, all of them so truly shaped and fitted for vision that no Artist can mend them? Did blind chance know that there was light and what was its refraction, and fit the eyes of all creatures after the most curious manner to make use of it?[1] These and such like considerations always have and ever will prevail with mankind, to believe that there is a being who

† Keynes ms. 7; King's College, Cambridge. Reprinted by permission of the Provost and Fellows, King's College, Cambridge. Theology was Newton's primary intellectual pursuit during the final two decades of his life. He composed "A Short Schem of the True Religion" during this period.

1. See Query 28, in Part 4, Optics (above).

made all things, and has all things in his power, and who is therefore to be feared.

Of Idolatry

Idolatry is a more dangerous crime, because it is apt by the authority of Kings and under very specious pretences to insinuate itself into mankind, kings being apt to enjoyn the honour of their dead ancestors; and it seeming very plausible to honour the souls of Heroes and Saints, and to believe that they can hear us and help us and are mediating between God and man, and reside and act principally in the temples and statues dedicated to their honour and memory. And yet, this being against the principal part of religion, is in scripture condemned and detested above all other crimes. The sin consists first in omitting the service of the true God. For the more time and devotion one spends in the worship of false Gods, the less he is able to spend in that of the true one; secondly, in serving false or feigned Gods, that is, Ghosts or Spirits of dead men or such like beings which you make your Gods, by feigning that they can hear your prayers, do you good or hurt, and praying to them for protection and blessings and trust in them for the same, and which are false Gods because they have not the powers which you ascribe to them, and on which you trust. Whether you call them Dii or Divi, Gods or Saints, or by any other name is not material. If you ascribe such powers to them and put such trust in them as the heathens ascribed to and put in their Gods, you make them such gods as the heathens worshipped, and as are forbidden in the first commandment. St. Paul tells the heathens that the gods which they worshipped were not Gods. He does not mean that they were not infinite, eternal, omnipotent and omniscient beings (for the heathens did not take them to be such), but he means they were not not what the heathens called Gods, they were not such Gods as the heathens took them to be, that is, spirits able to hear and see their worshippers and do them good or hurt. To place such powers in the souls of dead men is that doctrine of Devils or Demons condemned by the Apostle. An Idol is nothing in the world, a vanity, a lie, a fictitious power. The Egyptians and other heathens who propagated Idolatry believed the transmigration of souls, and accordingly taught that the souls of men after death went into several subjects as the Ox, Apis, and other sacred animals of Egypt, into the sun moon and stars, into images consecrated to them etc., and on this opinion grounded their worship of those subjects, supposing that the stars by these intelligences were moved in their orbs and understood and governed human affairs, and that statues by these spirits could hear and help us and sometimes move themselves and give oracles. And these are the Devils or Demons which idolators worshipped (Lev. vii, 7, Deut. xxxii, 17, 2 Chron. xi, 15, Psal. cvi, 37, 1 Cor. x, 20, Rev. ix, 20) and whose worship the prophets upbraid with folly by representing that the idols can neither hear nor see nor walk, that is, that they are not animated by such souls as those by which men hear and see and walk, but are mere inanimate stocks and stones void of all life and power. [So covetous men, by putting that trust in riches which they should put in God become a sort of Idolators. And much more plainly is it idolatrous to trust in charms, ceremonies, dead bodies, consecrated substances, and the like. All this is worshipping the creature instead of the creator.] And thirdly, the sin of Idolatry consists in making and worshipping the images of dead men, or of other things in heaven above or in the earth beneath or in the waters below the earth, that is, of birds, beasts, or fishes (contrary to the second commandment) upon a supposition that, by virtue of the souls of dead men, or of the supreme God or any other Spirits or Demons good or bad inhabiting them, or upon any other account, they can hear and see their worshippers or do them good or hurt. To ascribe such powers to them is to feign them Gods (such Gods as the heathens worshipped) and to love or fear or trust in them, or express such love, fear, or trust by prayers, praises, thanksgivings, sacrifices, adorations, or any other outward action or service is the idolatry of the old heathens, forbidden in the second commandment. Stocks and stones have no such powers; they are not inhabited by the souls of dead men; eyes have they and see not, ears have they and hear not. An Idol is nothing in the world. They are vanities, lies, fictitious powers, and on this account they are called false Gods, and derided as such by all the old Prophets. And of the same kind of folly is it to place any trust in the bodies or bones of dead men, or in things consecrated, or other things without life, or in any ceremonies or charms: for even the trusting in riches is by the Apostle called Idolatry.

We are therefore to acknowledge one God, infinite, eternal, omnipresent, omniscient, omnipotent, the creator of all things, most wise, most just, most good, most holy, and to have no other Gods but him. We must love him, fear him, honour him, trust in him, pray to him, give him thanks, praise him, hallow his name, obey his commandments, and set times apart for his service, as we are directed in the third and fourth commandments. For this is the love of God, that we keep his commandments, and his commandments are not grievous. 1 John v, 3. These things we must do, not to any mediators between him and us, but to him alone, that he may give his angels charge over us, who, being our fellow-servants, are pleased with the worship which we give to their God. And this is the first and principal part of religion. This always was and always will be the religion of all God's people, from the beginning to the end of the world.

Of Humanity

The other part of the true religion is our duty to man. We must love our neighbours as ourselves, we must be charitable to all men, for charity is the greatest of graces, greater than even faith or hope and covers a multitude of sins. We must be righteous, and do to all men as we would they should do to us. In Politics Salus populi suprema lex[2]; in private concerns Quod tibi fieri non vis alteri nec fieri[3] were acknowledged by Heathens and are or ought to be the laws of all mankind. This was the ethics, morality, or good manners taught the first ages by Noah and his sons in some of their seven precepts, the later heathens by Socrates, Cicero, Confucius and other philosophers, the Israelites by Moses and the Prophets, and the Christians more fully by Christ and his Apostles. This is that law which the Apostle tells you was written in the hearts of the Gentiles, and by which they are to be judged in the last day. Rom. ii 12, 14, 15. . . . Thus you see there is but one law for all nations, the law of righteousness and charity dictated to the Christians by Christ, to the Jews by Moses, and to all mankind by the light of reason, and by this law all men are to be judged at the last day. This was the religion of the first ages till they forsook the right worship of the true God and turned aside to the worship of dead men and Idols, and their God gave them over to their lusts and passions for working all manner of unrighteousness. But Moses made a reformation among the Israelites, not from the ancient religion propagated by Noah and his posterity to the nations but from the idolatry and immorality with which the nations had corrupted themselves. For as many of the heathens as were converted from their corruptions to worship only the true God and follow the law of righteousness were admitted by the Jews into their Gates and outward court of the Temple as Proselytes, though they did not receive the law of Moses. The Jews rejected not the Religion of Noah and the first nations, but proselyted the heathens to it as to the true ancient religion, though a religion which they accounted not so perfect as that of Moses. And in like manner we may lawfully proselyte heathens to it (that is, to purity and righteousness) and ought to value and love those who profess and practise it, even though they do not yet believe in Christ. For it is the true religion of Christians as well as heathens, though not all the true Christian religion. Tis so great and necessary a part of the Christian religion that the righteousness of the saints is the white clothing of the Lamb's wife, Apoc. xix, 8, and the righteous go into eternal life, Matt. xxv, 46, and as Christ is righteous so every one that hath righteousness is born of God, 1 John ii, 29. Abel was righteous, (Hebs. xi, 4; Matt. xxiii, 35; 1 John iii, 12) and Noah was a preacher of righteousness, (2 Peter ii, 5) and by his righteousness was

2. The welfare of the people is the highest law.
3. Do not do unto others what you would not wish to be done unto yourself.

saved from the flood (Gen. vii, 1.). Christ is called the righteous (1 John ii, 1) and by his righteousness we are saved, (Rom. iii, 25 and v, 18; 1 Cor. i, 30) and except our righteousness exceed the righteousness of the Scribes and Pharisees we shall not enter into the kingdom of heaven (Matt. v. 20.) Righteousness is the religion of the kingdom of heaven (2 Peter iii, 13; Isaiah lx, 21) and even the property of God himself (Jud. v, 11; 1 Sam. xii, 7; Ezra ix, 15; Nehem. ix, 8; Ps. cxix, 137) towards man. Righteousness and love are inseparable, *for he that loveth another hath fulfilled the law*. . . Romans xiii, 8, 9, 10. He that loveth his brother abideth in the light and there is no occasion of stumbling. 1 John ii, 10. . . .

Twelve Articles †

ARTIC. 1. There is one God the Father everliving, omnipresent, omniscient, almighty, the maker of heaven and earth, and one Mediator between God and Man the Man Christ Jesus.

ARTIC. 2. The father is the invisible God whom no eye hath seen or can see, all other beings are sometimes visible.

ARTIC. 3. The Father hath life in himself and hath given the Son to have life in himself.

ARTIC. 4. The father is omniscient and hath all knowledge originally in his own breast, and communicates knowledge of future things to Jesus Christ and none in heaven or earth or under the earth is worthy to receive knowledge of future things immediately from the father except the Lamb. And therefore the testimony of Jesus is the Spirit of Prophecy and Jesus is the Word or Prophet of God.

ARTIC. 5. The father is immoveable no place being capable of becoming emptier or fuller of him then it is by the eternal necessity of nature: all other being are moveable from place to place.[1]

ARTIC. 6. All the worship (whether of prayer praise or thanks giving which was due to the father before the coming of Christ is still due to him. Christ came not to diminish the worship of his father.

ARTIC. 7. Prayers are most prevalent when directed to the father in the name of the son.

ARTIC. 8. We are to return thanks to the father alone for creating us and giving us food and raiment and other blessings of this life and whatsoever we are to thank him for or desire that he would do for us we ask of him immediately in the name of Christ.

ARTIC. 9. We need not pray to Christ to intercede for us. If we pray the father aright he will intercede.

† Keynes ms. 8; King's College, Cambridge. Reprinted by permission of the Provost and Fellows, King's College, Cambridge. The twelve articles of religion that Newton set down on this paper were also a product of his old age.

1. See the discussions of absolute space in the Scholium to the Definitions in the *Principia*, in Part 5, Rational Mechanics (above), and in the General Scholium to the *Principia* in this part.

ARTIC. 10. It is not necessary to salvation to direct our prayers to any other then the father in the name of the son.

ARTIC. 11. To give the name of God to Angels or Kings is not against the first commandment. To give the worship of the God of the Jews to Angels or Kings is against it. The meaning of the commandment is Thou shalt worship no other Gods but me.

ARTIC. 12. To us there is but one God the father of whom are all things and we of him and one Lord Jesus Christ by whom are all things and we by him. That is, we are to worship the father alone as God Almighty and Jesus alone as the Lord the Messiah the Great King the Lamb of God who was slain and hath redeemed us with his blood and made us kings and Priests.

Introduction to a Treatise on Revelation†

Having searched after knowledge in the prophetique scriptures, I have thought my self bound to communicate it for the benefit of others, remembring the judgment of him who hid his talent in a napkin. For I am perswaded that this will prove of great benefit to those who think it not enough for a sincere Christian to sit down contented with the principles of the doctrin of Christ such as the Apostel accounts the doctrin of Baptisms and of laying on of hands and of the resurrection of the dead and of eternall judgment, but leaving these and the like principles desire to go on unto perfection until they become of full age and by reason of use have their senses exercised to discern both good and evil. Hebr 5.12

I would not have any discouraged by the difficulty and ill success that men have hitherto met with in these attempts. This is nothing but what ought to have been. For it was revealed to Daniel that the prophecies concerning the last times should be closed up and sealed untill the time of the end: but then the wise should understand, and knowledge should be increased. Dan 12. 4, 9, 10. And therefore the longer they have continued in obscurity, the more hopes there is that the time is at hand in which they are to be made manifest. If they are never to be understood, to what end did God reveale them? Certainly he did it for the edification of the church; and if so, then it is as certain that the church shall at length attain to the understanding thereof. I mean not all that call themselves Christians, but a remnant, a few scattered persons which God hath chosen, such as without being led by interest, education, or humane authorities, can set themselves sincerely and earnestly to search after truth. For as Daniel hath said that the wise shall understand, so he hath said also that none of the wicked shall understand.

† Frank Manuel, *The Religion of Isaac Newton* (Oxford: Clarendon Press, 1974), pp. 107–16. Newton began to study the prophecies in the Bible, first the Book of Revelation and then Daniel, about the same time that he began to study theology. His first full-scale interpretation of Revelation, a very long treatise that has never been published except for a few extracts, dated from about 1675.

Let me therefore beg of thee not to trust to the opinion of any man concerning these things, for so it is great odds but thou shalt be deceived. Much less oughtest thou to rely upon the judgment of the multitude, for so thou shalt certainly be deceived. But search the scriptures thy self and that by frequent reading and constant meditation upon what thou readest, and earnest prayer to God to enlighten thine understanding if thou desirest to find the truth. Which if thou shalt at length attain thou wilt value above all other treasures in the world by reason of the assurance and vigour it will add to thy faith, and steddy satisfaction to thy mind which he onely can know how to estimate who shall experience it.

That the benefit which may accrew by understanding the sacred Prophesies and the danger by neglecting them is very great and that the obligation to study them is as great may appear by considering the like case of the Jews at the coming of Christ. For the rules whereby they were to know their Messiah were the prophesies of the old Testament. And these our Saviour recommended to their consideration in the very beginning of his preaching Luke 4.21: And afterward commanded the study of them for that end saying, Search the scriptures for in them ye think ye have eternall life, and these are they which testify of mee: And at another time severely reproved their ignorance herein, saying to them when they required a sign, Ye Hypocrites ye can discern the face of the sky but can ye not discern the signes of the times And after his resurrection he reproved also this ignorance in his disciples, saying unto them, O fools and slow of heart to beleive all that the Prophets have spoken! Ought not Christ to have suffered these things, and to enter into his glory? And beginning at Moses and all the Prophets he expounded unto them in all the scriptures the things concerning himself. Thus also the Apostles and those who in the first ages propagated the gospel urged chiefly these Prophesies and exhorted their hearers to search and see whether all things concerning our Saviour ought not to have been as they fell out. And in a word it was the ignorance of the Jews in these Prophesies which caused them to reject their Messiah and by consequence to be not onely captivated by the Romans but to incur eternall damnation. Luke 19. 42, 44.

If then the Prophesies which concerned the Apostolique age were given for the conversion of the men of that age to the truth and for the establishment of their faith, and if it was their duty to search diligently into those Prophecies: why should we not think that the Prophesies which concern the latter times into which we are fallen were in like manner intended for our use that in the midst of Apostacies we might be able to discern the truth and be established in the faith thereof, and consequently that it is also our duty to search with all diligence into these Prophesies. And if God was so angry with the Jews for not searching more diligently into the Prophesies which he had given them to know Christ by: why should we think he will excuse us for not searching into the Prophesies which he hath given us to know Antichrist by? For certainly it must be as dangerous and as easy an error for Christians to adhere to Antichrist as it was for the Jews to reject Christ. And therefore it is as much our duty to indeavour to be able to know him that we may avoyd him, as it was theirs to know Christ that they might follow him.

Thou seest therefore that this is no idle speculation, no matter of indifferency but a duty of the greatest moment. Wherefore it concerns thee to look about thee narrowly least thou shouldest in so degenerate an age be dangerously seduced and not know it. Antichrist was to seduce the whole Christian world and therefore he may easily seduce thee if thou beest not well prepared to discern him. But if he should not be yet come into the world yet amidst so many religions of which there can be but one true and perhaps none of those that thou art acquainted with it is great odds but thou mayst be deceived and therefore it concerns thee to be very circumspect.

Consider how our Saviour taught the Jews in Parables that in hearing they might hear and not understand and in seeing they might see and not perceive. And as these Parables were spoken to try the Jews so the mysticall scriptures were written to try us. Therefore beware that thou be not found wanting in this tryall. For if thou beest, the obscurity of these scriptures will as little excuse thee as the obscurity of our Saviours Parables excused the Jews.

Consider also the instructions of our Saviour concerning these latter times by the Parable of the Fig-tree. Now learn a parable of the Figtree, saith he: When his branch is yet tender and putteth forth leaves, ye know that Summer is nigh. So likewise ye when ye see these things know that it is near even at the doors.—Watch therefore for ye know not what hower your Lord doth come. Wherefore it is thy duty to learn the signes of the times that thou mayst know how to watch, and be able to discern what times are coming on the earth by the things that are already past. If thou doest watch thou mayst know when it is at the door as a man knows by the leaves of a figtee that Somer is nigh. But if through ignorance of the signes thou shalt say in thine heart My Lord delayeth his coming; And shalt begin to smite thy fellow servants and to eat and drink with the drunken: Thy Lord will come in a day when thou lookest not for him and in an hower that thou art not aware of, and cut these asunder and appoint thy portion with the Hypocrites, and there shall be weeping and gnashing of teeth. Matt 24. If thou doest not watch, how canst thou escape more than other men, For as a snare shall it come on all them that dwell upon the face of the whole earth. Luke 21.

Consider that the same Prophets who foretold our saviours first coming foretold also his second coming; and if it was the main and indispensable duty of the Church before the first coming of Christ to have searched into and understood those prophesies aforehand, why should it not be as much the duty of the church before his second coming to understand the same prophesies aforehand so far as they are yet to be fulfilled? Or how knowest thou that the christian church if they continue to neglect, shall not be punished even in this world as severely as ever were the Jews? Yea will not the Jews rise up in judgment against us? For they had some regard to these prophesies insomuch as to be in generall expectation of our Saviour about that time when he came, onely they were not aware of the manner of his two comings; they understood the description of his second coming, and onely were mistaken in applying that to the time of his first coming. Consider therefore, if the description of his second coming was so much more plain and perspicuous then that of the first, that the Jews who could not so much as perceive any thing of the first could yet understand the second, how shall we escape who understand nothing of the second but have turned the whole description of it into Allegories. And if the Jews were so severely punished for not understanding the more difficult Prophesy, what can we plead who know nothing of the more perspicuous; and yet have this advantage above them that the first which is a key to the second and was hidden from them is made manifest to us, and that we have the second also much further explained in the new Testament.

Again consider how the Apostels instructed the Churches of the first age in the knowledg of these latter times 2 Thes 2.5. And if it was the duty of those Christians to understand them which were not to live in them, shall we think that the knowledg thereof is of no concernment to us.

Consider also the designe of the Apocalypse. Was it not given for the use of the Church to guide and direct her in the right way, And is not this the end of all prophetick Scripture? If there was no need of it, or if it cannot be understood, then why did God give it? Does he trifle? But if it was necessary for the Church then why doest thou neglect it, or how knowest thou that thou art in the right way, and yet doest not understand it? This was the principal caus of the reformations which have hitherto been made from the Roman errors first by Waldenses and Albigenses and then by the Protestants, and therefore we have reason to beleive that God foreseeing how much the Church would want a guide in these latter ages designed this Prophesy for this end and by consequence we may expect that he hath some further counsel to be brought about by the fuller manifestation of it.

Lastly consider the Blessing which is promised to them that read and study and keep the things which are written in this Prophesy. Blessed is he that readeth and they that hear the words of this Prophesy and keep the things which are written therein, for the time is at hand, Rev. 1.3. And again to reinforce the invitation to take these things into consideration, the same Blessing is repeated in Ch 22.7 And does God ever annex his blessings to trifles or things of indifferency? Wherefore be not overwise in thine own conceipt, but as thou desirest to inherit this blessing consider and search into these Scriptures which God hath given to be a guide in these latter times, and be not discouraged by the gainsaying which these things will meet with in the world.

They will call thee it may be a hot-headed fellow, a Bigot, a Fanatique, a Heretique etc: And tell thee of the uncertainty of these interpretations, and vanity of attending to them: Not considering that the prophesies concerning our Saviour's first coming were of more difficult interpretation, and yet God rejected the Jews for not attending better to them. And whither they will beleive it or not, there are greater judgments hang over the Christians for their remissness then ever the Jews yet felt. But the world loves to be deceived, they will not understand, they never consider equally, but are wholly led by prejudice, interest, the prais of men, and authority of the Church they live in: as is plain becaus all parties keep close to the Religion they have been brought up in, and yet in all parties there are wise and learned as well as fools and ignorant. There are but few that seek to understand the religion they profess, and those that study for understanding therein, do it rather for worldly ends, or that they may defend it, then to examin whither it be true with a resolution to choose and profess that religion which in their judgment appears the truest. And as is their faith so is their practise. For where are the men that do never yeild to anger nor seek revenge, nor disobey governours, nor censure and speak evil of them, nor cheat, nor lye, nor swear, nor use God's name idly in their common talk, nor are proud nor ambitious nor covetous, nor unchast, nor drink immoderately? Where are they that live like the primitive Christians, that love God with all their hearts and with all their souls and with all their might, and their neighbour as their selves; and that in what they do well are not rather led by fashions and principles of Gentility then religion, and where those disagree do not account it rudeness to depart from the former? I feare there are but few whose righteousness exceeds the righteousness of the Scribes and Pharisees.

This is the guise of the world, and therefore trust it not, nor value their censures and contempt. But rather consider that it is the wisdom of God that his Church should appear despicable to the world to try the faithfull. For this end he made it a curs under Law to hang upon a tree that the scandal of the Cross might be a tryall to the Jews; and for the like Tryall of the Christians he hath suffered the Apostacy of the latter times, as is declared in calling it the hower of temptation which should come upon all the world to try them that dwell upon the earth Rev. 3.10. Be not therefore scandalised at the reproaches of the world but rather looke upon them as a mark of the true church.

And when thou art convinced be not ashamed to profess the truth. For otherwise thou mayst become a stumbling block to others, and inherit the lot of those Rulers of the Jews who beleived in Christ but yet were afraid to confess him least they should be put out of the Synagogue.

Wherefore when thou art convinced be not ashamed of the truth but profess it openly and indeavour to convince thy Brother also that thou mayst inherit at the resurrection the promis made in Daniel 12.3, that they who turn many to righteousness shall shine as the starrs for ever and ever. And rejoyce if thou art counted worthy to suffer in thy reputation or any other way for the sake of the Gospel, for then great is thy reward.

But yet I would not have thee too forward in becoming a teacher, like those men who catch at a few similitudes and scripture phrases, and for want of further knowledg make use of them to censure and reproach superiours and rail at all things that displeas them. Be not heady like them, but first be throughly instructed thy self and that not only in the prophetique Scriptures but more especially in the plain doctrines delivered therein so as to put them in practice and make them familiar and habituall to thy self. And when thou hast thus pulled out the beam out of thine own eye then shalt thou see clearly to pull out the mote out of thy Brothers eye. Otherwise how wilt thou say to thy Brother, Let me pull out the mote out of thine eye and behold a beam is in thine own eye.

Some I know will be offended that I propound these things so earnestly to all men as if they were fit onely for the contemplation of the learned. But they should consider that God who best knows the capacities of men does hide his mysteries from the wise and prudent of this world and reveal them unto babes. They were not the Scribes and Pharisees but the inferiour people who beleived on Christ and apprehended the true meaning of his Parables and of the Prophesies in the old Testament concerning him. The wise men of the world are often too much prepossest with their own imaginations and too much intangled in designes for this life. One has bought a piece of ground, another has bought five yoke of Oxen, a third has Married a wife, and therefore since they are for the most part otherwise ingaged it was fit that the poor and the maimed and the halt and the blind and those that are in the high ways and hedges should be also invited. God who intended this Prophecy chiefly for their sakes is able to fit their understanding to it. And it is the gift of God and not of human wisdom so to understand it as to beleive it.

Tis true that without a guide it would be very difficult not onely for them but even for the most learned to understand it right But if the interpretation be done to their hands, I know not why by the help of such a guide they may not by attentive and often reading be capable of understanding and judging of it as well as men of greater education. And such a guide I hope this Book will prove: especially if the judgment of the Reader be prepared by considering well the following Rules for inabling him to know when an interpretation is genuine and of two interpretations which is the Best.

It was the judiciously learned and conscientious Mr Mede who first made way into these interpretations, and him I have for the most part followed. For what I found true in him it was not lawful for me to recede from, and I rather wonder that he erred so little then that he erred in some things. His mistakes were chiefly in his Clavis, and had that been perfect, the rest would have fallen in naturally. Whence may be guessed the great uncertainty of others who without any such previous methodising of the Apocalyps have immediately fallen upon giving interpretations. For so by taking the liberty to twist the parts of the Prophesy out of their natural order according to their pleasure without having regard to the internall characters whereby they were first to be connected, it might be no very difficult matter amongst the great variety of things in the world to apply them more ways then one to such as should have some show of an interpretation. And yet all that I have seen besides the labours of Mr Mede have been so botched and framed without any due proportion, that I fear some of these Authors did not so much as beleive their own interpretations, which makes me wish that they had been moved to more caution by considering the curs that is annexed to the end of this Prophesy.

I testify unto every man that heareth the words of the Prophesy of this book; If any man shall add unto these things God shall add unto him the plagues that are written in this book. And if any man shall take away from the words of the book of this Prophesy, God shall take away his part out of the book of life, and out of the holy city and from the things which are written in this book.

For to frame fals interpretations is to prejudice men and divert them from the right understanding of this book. And this is a corruption equipollent to the adding or taking from it, since it equally deprives men of the use and benefit thereof. But yet I hope they did it neither out of the vanity of appearing somebody in the world, nor out of designe to promote the externall splendor and felicity of Churches rather then the internall purity which is of infinitely more value, nor out of any other temporal ends, but with an upright heart that God may not lay it to their charge.

Yet I could wish that those who make all to be long since past, even in the Apostels age, had considered that when according to them this Prophesy should have been usefull to the Church, their interpretations were not so much as thought upon. All sacred Prophecies are given for the use of the Church, and therefore they are all to be understood by the Church in those ages for whose use God intended them. But these prophesies were never understood by the Church in the former ages. They did not so much as pretend to understand them, nor thought that they concerned their times, but with one universall consent delivered down to posterity the famous Tradition of the Antichrist described therein to come in the latter ages. And therefore since they were never yet understood, and God cannot be disappointed, we must acknowledg that they were written and shall prove for the benefit of the present and future ages, and so are not yet fulfilled. Wherefore let men be carefull how they indeavour to divert or hinder the use of these scriptures, least they be found to fight against God.

Considering therefore the great concernment of these scriptures and danger of erring in their interpretation, it concerns us to proceed with all circumspection. And for that end I shall make use of this Method.

First I shall lay down certain general Rules of Interpretation, the consideration of which may prepare the judgment of the Reader and inable him to know when an interpretation is genuine and of two interpretations which is the best.

Secondly, To prepare the Reader also for understanding the Prophetique language I shall lay down a short description thereof, showing how it is borrowed from comparing a kingdom either to the Univers or to a Beast: So that by the resemblance of their parts the signification of the figurative words and expressions in these Prophecies may be apprehended at one view and limited from the grownd thereof. By which means the Language of the Prophets will become certain and the liberty of wresting it to private imaginations be cut of. The heads to which I reduce these words I call Definitions.

Thirdly, These things being premised, I compare the parts of the Apocalyps one with another and digest them into order by those internal characters which the Holy-ghost hath for this end imprest upon them. And this I do by drawing up the substance of the Prophesy into Propositions, and subjoyning the reasons for the truth of every Proposition.

And here I cannot but loudly proclaim the admirable and more then humane wisdom that shines in the contexture of this Prophesy and its accurate consent with all other prophesies of the old and new Testament.

* * *

RICHARD S. WESTFALL

Newton and Christianity †

Living, as we do in the twentieth century, in the shadow of Darwinism, an issue that remains very much with us, we tend automatically to

† Frank T. Birtel, ed. *Religion, Science, and Public Policy* (New York: Crossroads, 1987), pp. 79–94. The principal corpus of Newton's theological manuscripts were not available for study until about two decades ago. The paper "Newton and Christianity" is one of the early ones drawn primarily from his manuscripts instead of from his published statements about religion. Not every student of the manuscripts agrees with this interpretation.

think of the question of science and religion in terms of conflict. The titles of books such as Andrew D. White's *History of the Warfare of Science with Theology* serve powerfully to reinforce our tendency. The seventeenth century, in contrast, saw the matter differently. Even then there were a few who thought in terms of a conflict between science and Christianity; on one hand were men like Thomas Hobbes, and on the other, theological conservatives. To me, at least, such men appear to have stood decidedly on the fringes of opinion, while the majority, especially the majority of scientists, and more especially still the majority of scientists in Britain, saw instead harmony between the two realms of knowledge and activity. The works of God magnify the glory of God. The works they had studied. Glory they had found, and from one end of the century to the other they raised their hymn of praise to its author. Robert Boyle, a most prolific author, sounded the theme in virtually every one of his many books, and toward the end of his life, in case the message had failed to be heard, he formulated his definitive statement of it in *The Christian Virtuoso*,[1] a title that we can translate without serious inaccuracy into more familiar language as *The Christian Scientist*. John Ray, the leading naturalist of the age, stated the same idea in his book, *The Wisdom of God Manifested in the Works of the Creation*.[2] There were so many other versions of a similar outlook that it would be difficult to list all of them.

The theme was prominent also in the works of Isaac Newton. "When I wrote my treatise about our Systeme," he began a letter to the theologian Richard Bentley, "I had an eye upon such Principles as might work with considering men for the beleife of a Deity." From such a point of view, science appeared as the handmaiden of religion. Its purpose was not to manipulate nature for the material benefit of mankind, but to demonstrate the existence of the Creator. The "main Business of natural Philosophy," Newton asserted elsewhere (and let me insist on the significance of the adjective *main*), "is to argue from Phaenomena without feigning Hypotheses, and to deduce Causes from Effects, till we come to the very first Cause, which certainly is not mechanical." Every step along the way brings us closer to the goal "and on that account is to be highly valued." Again I want to insist on the significance of the phrase *on that account*.

Ray the naturalist found God in the multiplicity of nature and the perfect adaptation of every creature to the life it must live. Newton the physicist, in contrast, found him in the structure of the cosmos. Let us assume, he argued in the letter to Bentley quoted above, that in the beginning matter was evenly diffused through the universe. If the universe had been finite, mutual gravitation would have caused all matter to congregate together in a single body. If the universe had been infinite,

1. *The Christian Virtuoso* (1690). [Editor]
2. *Wisdom of God* (1691). [Editor]

matter would have congregated in a number of bodies held in equilibrium by their mutual attractions, and if all matter had been luminous, we could explain the system of the sun and stars by natural causes alone. But all matter is not luminous, and by the operation of natural causes alone we cannot explain the separation of luminous from nonluminous matter. For this we have to call upon an intelligent Creator. Moreover, the sun is at the center of our system. If chance—that is, the blind operation of natural causes—had formed our system, the central body could just as well have been without light and heat; it required a God to understand the necessity that the central body be a sun. Why is there only one sun in our system? God saw that one was sufficient. Moreover, all of the planets move in the same direction in the same plane, an ordered whole as we plainly see when we compare the planetary system with the disorder of comets. "To make this systeme therefore with all its motions, required a Cause which understood and compared together the quantities of matter in the several bodies of the Sun and Planets and the gravitating powers resulting from thence, the several distances of the primary Planets from the Sun and secondary ones from Saturn Jupiter and the earth, and the velocities with which these Planets could revolve at those distances about those quantities of matter in the central bodies. And to compare and adjust all these things together in so great a variety of bodies argues that cause to be not blind and fortuitous, but very well skilled in Mechanicks and Geometry."

In the *Principia*, Newton implicitly presented a similar argument. The first book of the *Principia* consistently examined the operation of two basic force laws, forces that vary inversely as the square of the distance, and forces that vary directly as the distance. Under these two laws, and under these two laws alone, bodies will revolve in conical orbits around central attracting bodies (located at the focus in the case of the inverse square attraction and at the center in the case of the direct distance one). Under these two laws, and, among plausible ones, under these two alone, orbits will remain stable in space with the line of apsides pointing always in the same direction relative to fixed stars. Under these two laws, and under these two laws alone, composite bodies made up of attracting particles will attract according to the same law as their components. The law of variation in proportion to distance is not suitable to an ordered universe, however. In an infinite universe, as Newton believed ours to be, such a law would entail infinite forces, infinite accelerations, and infinite velocities, which are physically absurd. The ultimate demonstration of the wisdom of God lies in the fact that he did in fact employ in the Creation the only law suitable for a rationally ordered universe. God, we might say, had shown himself to be the equal of Newton in his understanding of the laws of mechanics. Or rather, let us say that only a scientist like Newton could fully appreciate the wisdom of God. Like Boyle, Newton was a Christian virtuoso gazing in reverent awe at the glory he perceived in God's creation.

I wish to contend that these arguments represent the traditional element in Newton's religion. It is the most visible part of his religion, and until recently it was virtually the only aspect of it that was known. If we concentrate on these arguments alone, they are apt to mislead us, for two different reasons. In the first place, we may make the mistake of taking the arguments at face value. But Newton did not find God in nature. Quite the contrary, he imposed God upon nature. That is, the arguments did not so much derive from the study of nature as descend from the long tradition of Christianity in western Europe. Consider the letter to Bentley. If God created an ordered universe, whence arose the disorder of the comets, to which Newton himself referred? By what criterion did Newton determine that the order of the planetary system was more typical of the whole than the disorder of the comets? If it was the purpose of God to reveal his wisdom by making the planets move in the same plane, we need to note that he bungled egregiously. The planetary planes are inclined to each other by as much as five degrees. What eighteenth-century artisan, building an orrery, would have tolerated an error that large? That is, Newton's arguments reveal above all a determination to find God in nature. They were the deposit of centuries of Christianity in the West, an inherited piety, that part of Newton's religion not yet disturbed by the rise of modern science. "I don't know what I may seem to the world," he is reported to have said near the end of his life, "but, as to myself, I seem to have been only like a boy playing on the sea shore, and diverting myself in now and then finding a smoother pebble or a prettier shell than ordinary, whilst the great ocean of truth lay all undiscovered before me." A similar figure appeared among the papers of Robert Boyle, who compared the student of nature to a man traveling down a great river. The farther he goes, the more the shores recede on either side until, when he reaches the river's mouth, he finds himself before the boundless sea. The Christian Virtuoso of the seventeenth century was like the boy or man on the shore confronting the ocean of truth. His attitude resembled the conviction of medieval philosophers, an earlier expression of the tradition in which Newton stood, that there are truths that, by their nature, are beyond the capacity of the human mind.

The second reason why Newton's arguments for the existence of God are apt to mislead us is that we may mistake his manifest piety for the whole of his religion. In fact, the story was far more complicated. It was more complicated with all of the English scientists. When we read only one or two of their refutations of atheism, we may find them impressive testimony, but by the time we read the tenth repetition of the same argument, we begin to sense some uneasiness behind it. Boyle offers a prime example. After a lifetime devoted to the refutation of atheism, he left provision in his will to endow a series of public lectures. What were the lectures supposed to do? Refute atheism some more. When during the previous fifteen hundred years had that appeared necessary? Boyle was aware that the ground was shifting under the traditional foundations of Christianity.

Newton was also aware of that fact, but his reaction differed from Boyle's. Instead of trying to shore up the established foundations, Newton attempted to make the central structure secure by abandoning its faulty members. Lest I be misunderstood, let me dispense with the figure of speech and state my proposition in more direct terms. I mean to say that Newton questioned orthodox theology and rejected some of its teachings that he found contrary to reason. In order to discuss this issue satisfactorily, we must make a distinction between religion and theology. Nothing that I may say is meant to question Newton's sincerity in the passages quoted above. There can be no doubt that Newton believed in the existence of God. Merely to state his belief in these terms is grossly to undervalue it. His belief in God was a living faith that suffused his entire life and gave it meaning. Equally he was convinced that science is in harmony with religion. The God demonstrated to exist from his work in the Creation is not, however, necessarily identical to the God of received Christianity. In the case of Newton, he certainly was not.

We cannot effectively explore this aspect of Newton's religion through his published works. Newton was a man who feared controversy. In the matter of religion, he had good cause to fear controversy, for he had much to lose. The views that he came to hold during his stay at Cambridge would have been grounds for his immediate dismissal, and after his move to the Mint in London, those same views made him ineligible, according to the law of the land, to hold a position in the government. Knowing this full well, he took care that his religious beliefs did not become matters of public knowledge. Newton was also a compulsive writer, however, and he left behind a huge collection of private papers. Only recently have the great bulk of his theological manuscripts become available for study, and they have a story to tell that differs from the one we find in his published works. Since the papers remain largely unknown, let me describe their content with an implicit interpretation embedded in the description.

The papers reveal that Newton began the serious study of theology about 1670, when he was approaching the age of thirty. Note that Newton began intensive theological study when he was a young man at the very height of his powers. Contrary to what has sometimes been asserted, such study was not solely the occupation of his old age, though he did devote a great deal of time to it then as well. The papers do not offer any explanation of why he took up theology, but I am willing to hazard the suggestion that the statutes of Trinity College had something to do with it. The statutes ordained that the holders of fifty-eight of the college's sixty fellowships had to be ordained to the clergy of the Anglican church within seven years of incepting M.A. or face ejection. Newton was never one who took an obligation lightly. His seven years would have expired in 1675, and the approaching deadline would have been incentive enough. Whatever his motives may have been, suffice it to say that the papers establish beyond any doubt that he did undertake vigorous theological studies about 1670.

We have every reason to think that he was at that time entirely orthodox. In the recent past he had taken solemn oaths to that effect on three separate occasions. With each of his two degrees, in 1665 and 1668, he had sworn to three articles, one of which affirmed the faith of the Anglican church, and when he had accepted a fellowship in College of the Holy and Undivided Trinity, he had sworn that he would uphold the one true religion, in a context that equated the one true religion with the doctrine of the Anglican church. Although he had not taken an oath with the Lucasian chair, it did embody a similar requirement; its statutes made heretical belief grounds for dismissal. Everything we know about Newton indicates that he would not have sworn falsely. He must have been orthodox at the time.

In accordance with his universal practice when he turned to a new topic of study, Newton began a systematic compilation of his reading notes, which would organize his new knowledge in an effective manner. He purchased a notebook in which he entered a series of headings under which he expected to gather the fruits of his study (Keynes ms 2). The pages under some of the headings—"The Miracles of Christ," for example—remained blank. Such was not the case for "God the Son" and "Concerning the Trinity," which immediately became the focuses of his interest. Initially, the Bible furnished his reading, and the intensive study of the Scriptures at this time furnished the foundation of the detailed knowledge of them that he carried through his life. From the Bible he advanced to the early Fathers of the Church. It is necessary to plunge into the manuscripts themselves in order to appreciate them fully. They reveal a vast program of reading that led Newton through all of the important Fathers of Christianity. They reveal as well a driving passion, which animated the study. What we meet in the manuscripts is not conventional piety assembling arguments designed to defend the tradition. Quite the contrary, what we meet is the passion of a rebel who had convinced himself that the received tradition was mistaken. *Mistaken* is far too mild a word. Newton convinced himself that the received tradition was a fraud perpetrated by evil men in the fourth century who, for their own selfish purposes, had willfully corrupted the entire heritage. Newton's determination to unmask this ancient crime, together with his study of alchemy, absorbed virtually all of his time for the following fifteen years before a visit from Edmond Halley started the investigation that resulted in the *Principia* and altered the tenor of his existence.

To be specific, Newton embraced Arianism, a heresy of the fourth century which had struggled with Trinitarianism (as expounded especially by Athanasius) for the soul of Christianity. Arianism is similar to modern Unitarianism in so far as it rejects the full divinity of Christ. It differs from Unitarianism in its belief that Christ was also not wholly human. The Arian Christ was a created intermediary between God and man. Newton hinted broadly at an Arian Christology in his theological notebook. In later manuscripts he did more than hint. Among them there is, what appears to me as his most explicit statement, a sheet from the period 1672–1675 with twelve propositions on the nature of Christ which are wholly Arian in tone (Yahuda ms 14, f. 25). From the position taken in the early seventies Newton never retreated, though in one manuscript treatise he does appear to have gone further yet. In his old age, he was still composing Arian statements on the nature of Christ.

The position taken in the early 1670s nearly blighted Newton's career. He still faced the necessity of ordination. In an institution which had learned to pay scant attention to its governing statutes, requirements of ordination were one rule that was never broken. One can understand why. The colleges were filled with aspiring young men, and some no longer so young, patiently working—or better, waiting—their way up the ladder of seniority. They had nothing to gain and much to lose by tolerating the presence of anyone higher on the order of seniority who could be forced out for a failing they had no incentive to imitate themselves. By 1675 Newton had to accept ordination or resign his Fellowship. As a result of his Arianism, he could no longer accept ordination.

There was a possible avenue of escape from his dilemma. Two of the sixty fellowships in Trinity were exempted from the requirement. In 1673, one of the two fell vacant, and Newton forthwith sought appointment to it. Robert Uvedale, a fellow one year his senior, also sought it. The rule of seniority was adamant, and the avenue of escape appeared to close. In a letter to Henry Oldenburg, the secretary of the Royal Society, written early in 1675, Newton mentioned that he would soon have to lay down his fellowship. Perhaps Newton could have stayed on in Cambridge as the Lucasian Professor, though I do not know of another professor who was not associated with a college. The problem was not legality; the chair did not require a fellowship. The problem was the questions that would be asked. Why would anyone in his right mind, who intended to stay on at the university, give up a fellowship worth some sixty-five pounds per annum? Since ordination would obviously have been the sticking point, what would Newton's motives have to have been? Questions would have been asked. It would have been difficult indeed to keep his opinions secret, and once they were out, the professorship—and indeed his entire standing in acceptable society—would have been forfeited.

At the last moment, the cloud lifted. A royal dispensation exempted not Isaac Newton, but the holder of the Lucasian chair in perpetuity from any college requirement of ordination. The dispensation raises a number of questions that cannot be answered with assurance. Who arranged it? The most likely agent was Isaac Barrow, the master of Trinity College, a man known to have the king's ear. Why did he arrange it? Barrow was a man of unimpeachable orthodoxy, the author of a published defense of the doctrine of the Trinity. I find it impossible to imagine him listening with sympathy to a plea of Arianism. I do not find it impossible that he could have accepted a plea of no vocation for the clergy. Barrow valued learning, and he understood the full dimensions of Newton's quality. He would have been anxious to have him continue on in the college and the university. Whoever the agent and whatever his reasons, it is recorded fact that a dispensation granted in the spring of 1675 freed Newton from the requirement of ordination and allowed him to stay on in his academic sanctuary. And in continuing silence, he continued to write theology.

Along with theology he early developed an interest in the prophecies. Newton composed his first interpretation of the book of Revelation in the early seventies, and he worked assiduously at expanding and revising it through the rest of the decade and into the early eighties. His interest in the prophecies is well known. After his death, his heirs published his *Observations upon the Prophecies*. A work of surpassing tedium, which all but the tiniest handful have been spared the necessity to read, the *Observations* defy the reader to find a point in their meandering discussion. The published manuscript was a product of Newton's old age deliberately made obscure in order to conceal his point. The reader of his papers has no problem in finding a point in his early interpretation. It embodied an adaptation of the standard puritan interpretation, which hinged on the concept of the Great Apostasy. To Puritan exegetes, the Great Apostasy was Roman Catholicism. To Newton, the Great Apostasy was Trinitarianism. That is, his interpretation of the prophecies offered an alternative statement of his theological position. The plagues and the vials of wrath in the book of Revelation were prophetic forecasts of the barbarian invasions of Europe, God's punishments on a stiff-necked people who had gone whoring after false gods.

The work contained an inner tension. On one hand, it implied a chronology. In Newton's interpretation Revelation contains repeated references under different figures to a period of 1,260 years immediately preceding the sounding of the seventh trumpet, which will announce the Second Coming of Christ and the Final Judgment. Newton was quite explicit in dating the beginning of that period in 607, from which it follows that he placed the Final Judgment nearly two hundred years in the future. Not by any standard would one call that imminent. On the other hand, there is a sense of expectation in the work that is impossible to miss. The meaning of the prophecies is finally being revealed, and the Great Day must correspondingly be at hand. Intense passion accompanied the inner tension. "Idolators, Blasphemers and spiritual fornicators," Newton thundered at the Trinitarians in the silence of his study in Trinity. And, because only Scripture could adequately convey his fury, "Seducers waxing worse and worse, deceiving and being deceived—such as will not endure sound doctrine but after their own lusts heap to themselves teachers, having itching ears and turning away their ears from the truth unto fables." There is no doubt in my mind that Newton considered himself one of the remnant persecuted by the dragon, one of the saints on whom the beast made war, and he appears to have been expecting early release. Once again, the Great Day must be at hand. Against whom was the passion directed? There is also no doubt in my mind that it was directed at flaccid orthodox Cambridge all about him, the Cambridge from which Newton had largely withdrawn as he isolated himself within the fastness of his own study.

The interpretation of the prophecies implied another program of study, indeed two more. In order to grasp their message, Newton needed to assure himself that he had their correct text. To this purpose he collated some twenty-five different Greek versions of the book of Revelation to establish the true text, and he combed the Bible, of which he considered the prophecies to be the central books, to find confirming passages. The interpretation also implied an exact correlation between the prophetic text and the events of history as they later transpired. Although he read and used the works of his contemporary authorities, he had no intention of resting satisfied with anything less than original sources. For example, Revelation speaks of a silence of half an hour before the sounding of the first trumpet. In Newton's scheme, half an hour corresponded to seven and a half years, which ended in this case with the war between Theodosius and Maximus.[3] In order to track the movements of Maximus in the early 380s, Newton called upon the testimony of Zosimus, Pacatus, Sulpitius Alexander (an eye witness quoted by Gregory of Tours), the letters of Jerome and Ambrose, the Annalium Boiorum, and Gothofredus' commentary on the Theodosian Code.[4] One brief passage on the period from Constantine through 380 cited Theodoret, Sozomen, Socrates (the historian), Ammianus, Claudian, Zosimus, Eusebius, Sigonius, Jerome, Eunapius, Libanus, Marcellinus, Victor,

3. Between 383 and 388, Theodosius and Maximus contended for control of the disintegrating Roman Empire. The victory of Theodosius was an important step toward his recognition as emperor. [Editor]

4. Sources from late antiquity, with the exception of Gothofredus, for the historical details Newton cited. [Editor]

Gregory the Presbyter, Pacatus, Symmachus, Idatius, and Cassiodorus, plus the Theodosian Code, the Alexandran Chronicle, and the letters of Ambrose.[5] Do not mistake my meaning. No one, I believe, would confuse Newton's interpretation of the prophecies with great history. The point I wish to assert is that the interpretation did not rest on superficial research.

Repeatedly the interpretation revealed itself as the work of the man who had recently composed *De methodis*, the definitive exposition of his fluxional calculus, and would soon write the *Principia*. His intention, he insisted, was to methodize the study of the prophecies. He set forth fifteen rules of interpretation—consistently rationalizing rules, such as always to assign only one meaning to one figure, and always to prefer the simplest and most literal meaning—followed by a catalogue of seventy figures and a section called the "Proof," which cited the evidence that supported the meanings he assigned to the seventy figures. Newton was convinced that there had been an accepted language of prophecy in the ancient world, which he could decipher. For the "Proof," he combed the entire Bible plus the writings of Achmet, an Arabian authority on prophecies, and Artemidorus, the Hellenistic author on the interpretation of draems, for corroborating instances. His stated goal was to free the interpretation of the prophecies from individual fancy and to reduce it to demonstration. Passages in his early treatise sound remarkably like passages on method in his letters to the Royal Society on optics, which date from the same period, and like the fourth Rule of Reasoning in Philosophy, which he inserted many years later at the head of Book III of the *Principia*.[6] In its original version, he cast the interpretation in Propositions, though he later altered the word to Positions.

In the late seventies, Newton embodied his interpretation of the prophecies in a history of the early church, a history which, inevitably, cast Athanasius in the role of villain. The history of the church, in turn, led into the well-known essay "Paradoxical Questions concerning the morals & actions of Athanasius and his followers," one of the small number of Newton's theological manuscripts that have been available for a long time. In this period he also became interested in the rise of monasticism, which he associated with Athanasius and Trinitarianism, and the frequent stories of early monks about their temptations and unclean thoughts, which he collected at some length, clearly fascinated him. Solemnly, he lectured the monks on how to cope with unchaste thoughts. "For lust by being forcibly restrained and by struggling with it is always inflamed. The way to be chast is not to contend and struggle with unchast thoughts but to decline them keep the mind imployed

5. Sources, predominantly Christian and mostly from late antiquity, for the historical details Newton cited. [Editor]
6. See Part 2, Scientific Method (above). [Editor]

about other things: for he that's always thinking of chastity will be always thinking of weomen and every contest with unchast thoughts will leave such impressions upon the mind as shall make those thoughts apt to return more frequently." Whatever the value of the advice, it came some 1,300 years too late to help the libidinous monks in the Egyptian desert.

The interpretation of the prophecies acquired a new dimension in the early eighties when Newton began to study Judaism. Again, we find a typically Newtonian exercise which saw him plunge into the talmudic scholars, Josephus, Philo, and Maimonides. He concluded that Jewish rites and the details of Jewish worship had furnished prophetic figures, a theme that survived prominently in the published *Observations*. The study of Judaism led him to investigate the plan of the original temple, a question that took on a life of its own as questions frequently did with Newton. He concluded that chapters 40 through 43 of Ezekiel contained the best description of the temple, and he reconstructed the text of those chapters, using the text to draw a plan and using the inherent necessities of the plan to amend the text. The temple, in turn, raised the further question of the exact length of the sacred cubit of the Jews, which Ezekiel used to measure it, and after extensive investigation Newton concluded that it had been more than 25 1/5 and less than 26 1/4 Roman inches.

About this time, that is, in the early eighties, Newton's interpretation began to suppress the passion that marked the early version and to shift toward the colorless chronology of the early church that characterized the version finally published after his death. The Great Apostacy, the concept that offered the key to the whole, became indistinguishable from Roman Catholicism in his exposition. No single word that I have found explains the change, I will offer the speculation that the rising specter of James Stuart[7] and the threat of a Catholic succession led a man who hated Catholicism passionately to seek common ground with English protestantism and to suppress those features of a work, albeit unpublished and unknown, which would have alienated him from other non-Catholics.

In the early eighties Newton also began to compose a new theological work to which, in the least chaotic of its manuscript remains, he gave the name *Theologiae gentilis origines philosophicae*.[8] It was easily the most important theological treatise he ever wrote, or worked on, and traces of its continuing presence in his thought showed up through the rest of his life.

The central concept of the *Origines* asserted that all the ancient peoples had worshipped twelve gods, the same twelve gods, which were associated with the seven planets, the four elements, and the quintes-

7. As James II, he succeeded Charles II as king of England in 1685. [Editor]
8. "The Philosophical Origins of Gentile Theology." [Editor]

sence. A second concept, not fully integrated with the first, claimed that the twelve gods were their deified ancestors, to wit, Noah, his children, and his grandchildren, from which all mankind had descended. The religion of twelve gods was not the earliest religion; Noah and his family themselves had worshipped the one true God, the Creator of the universe. However, there is an innate tendency toward superstitution and idolatry in man which led him to corrupt the true religion. The Egyptians had led the way in this; the other ancient peoples had learned their idolatry from Egypt. Each people had appropriated the religion to their own history, giving to the twelve gods the names their own records assigned to their ancestors, but the perceptive student of their chronicles could discern the common originals. God had made repeated efforts to lead mankind back to the true religion. Despairing of humanity as a whole, he had chosen the Jewish people and had sent Moses and the prophets to reclaim them. Despairing of the Jews, he had sent Jesus Christ to the gentiles. Jesus had come to recall men to the true religion, which rested on two commandments, to love God and to love one's neighbor. He had added nothing to that religion, Newton insisted; he had come only to call mankind back to its original worship.

We must be careful not to misinterpret the *Origines*. We see references to Noah and the biblical account, quaint themes of seventeenth-century scholarship. We smile tolerantly to realize that even the great Newton indulged in such childish notions, and we run the risk of missing the radical thrust that the quaint themes concealed. To Samuel Bochart, the Huguenot scholar on whom Newton drew extensively, Noah was literally Noah. That is, Noah, in the Hebrew original, was the true name of the common forebear of mankind. To Newton, in contrast, Noah was merely the name most familiar to readers in Christian Europe. To Newton, Egypt rather than Israel was basic. Noah's son was more truely Ammon than Ham. Similarly, Newton treated the historical books of the Old Testament as nothing more than the historical records of the Jewish people, records no more authoritative than those of other peoples to which he compared them.

Above all, the *Origines* deflated the role of Christ in human history. Christ came to call mankind back to the one true religion, and to that religion he added nothing. Its two basic commandments, Newton insisted, "always have and always will be the duty of all nations and the coming of Jesus Christ has made no alteration in them." That is, Christ did not signal a new dispensation and a new religion; he merely recalled mankind to an old one. Trinitarianism, when in its turn it corrupted the restored worship once more, repeated the idolatry of earlier ages by worshipping a man as god. Athanasius, the principal author of Trinitarianism, even repeated the original nefarious role of Egypt in the formation of superstition. Along with its deflation of Christ, the *Origines* likewise suggested that the one true religion is known to mankind from the study of nature. Newton found evidence that everywhere the original inhabitants of the earth had worshipped in similar temples, *prytanea* as he called them, similar in plan to the Jewish temple. The Roman temples of Vesta offered perhaps the most familiar version of such temples, which embodied a representation of the universe. "The whole heavens they recconed to be the true and real temple of God and therefore that a Prytanaeum might deserve the name of his Temple they framed it so as in the fittest manner to represent the whole systeme of the heavens. A point of religion then which nothing can be more rational." We might note that the temples, with a fire in the center and representations of the planets around it, offered a heliocentric picture of the universe. The decay of true philosophy had accompanied the decay of true religion. Meanwhile, the *Origines* asserted that by the proper study of nature men could recognize their Creator and their duties toward him. Christ had affirmed no more.

Newton believed in the concept of divine revelation; as with so much, however, the concept carried a new meaning for him. To him the Bible was not the revelation of mysteries beyond reason unto life eternal. As an Arian he did not accept this position. I have indicated that he did not consider the historical books of the Old Testament to have been divinely revealed. Prophecy was the central element of revelation—prophecy, whereby God, through its fulfillment, demonstrated his dominion over history.

The *Origines* meanwhile appears to have gone beyond Arianism. Although it differed in its attitude from the deists' open hostility toward Christianity, its content was remarkably similar to their works, and it must be seen as the first of the deist tracts, even if it remained unknown to any significant number and probably to everyone. The *Origines* continued to appear important to Newton. Shortly after he composed the original manuscripts in which it survives, he turned to the *Principia*; he chose to begin the first version of its final book with a passage from the *Origines*, though it did not survive in the published work. Again he drew upon it for revisions of Book III in the nineties, revisions which he also suppressed. The strange passage about Noah and his children that concludes the Thirty-first Query to the *Opticks* derived from it, and the "General Scholium" which he appended to the second edition of the *Principia* contained two footnotes based on the *Origines*.[9] In his old age, he sanitized it thoroughly, and that manuscript was published after his death as the *Chronology of Ancient Kingdoms Amended*, a work that rivals in tedium the similarly sanitized interpretation of the prophecies.

The *Principia* marked a break in Newton's theological activities. There are a few theological manuscripts from the two following decades,

9. We have omitted both the final paragraph of Query 31 (in Part 1, Natural Philosophy [above]) and the notes to the General Scholium (in this part). You can find them in any edition of the *Opticks* and the *Principia* respectively. [Editor]

but not many. Sometime during the first decade of the eighteenth century he returned to theology again, and he devoted massive amounts of time to it for the rest of his life. The effort was concerned entirely with reshuffling old ideas, however; he added nothing new. Like his career in science, his period of creativity in theology belonged entirely to his younger age.

A survey of Newton's activity in theology raises a number of questions that cannot be avoided. No one disputes the assertion that Newton was a scientist of major, indeed monumental, importance. What influence did his theology have on his science? It is unclear to me that we can speak validly of any influence. I mean specifically his theology, not his religion. The influence of his religion on his science is universally admitted, and I do not challenge that conclusion. His theology, by which I mean explicitly his Arianism and the associated interpretation of the prophecies, is another matter. Perhaps we can find echoes of the Arian God in the Pantocrator of the "General Scholium," but this leaves us still on such a high level of generality that it tells us very little. If we want to descend to the details of Newton's science, as it is found in the *Principia* and the *Opticks*, I am unable to trace any line of influence that has substance.

Rather, I prefer to trace the influence in the other direction. Theology was the activity with the historically established role in European civilization, a role beginning to be challenged, for the first time in more than a millennium, by a newly rising enterprise—modern science. It appears to me that we are far more apt to find the lines of influence running in this direction.

There have been a series of articles during the last couple of decades that have stressed the traditional elements in Newton's religion. One of them, a doctoral dissertation, is particularly critical of the account I gave of Newton in the final chapter of an early book. That account, he argues, makes Newton too much of an eighteenth-century figure.

All of the works I am now discussing, which were based on the published writings of Newton without the advantage of access to the manuscripts this present discourse draws upon, stress the role of the Bible in Newton's religious thought. There is no doubt that Newton considered the Bible to be the Word of God. Nevertheless, what Newton had in mind when he said *Bible* was far from identical to what that word had meant to the previous Christian tradition. All of these discussions of Newton's religion ignore what appears to me to be the central fact—his Arianism. When I recall the role of Arianism in early Christianity and the role of its offspring, Unitarianism, in the modern world, I find it impossible to ignore the influence of science on his religion. What I have in mind when I say *science* is not what I understand as Newtonian science. To me, the concept of Newtonian science is associated indissolubly with the *Principia* and involves the critical notion of attractions.

Newton assumed his characteristic theological position, however, before he had begun so much as to dream of the *Principia*. Therefore, when I speak of the influence of science on his religion, I am thinking of more basic stands associated with the scientific revolution, especially a new criterion of truth and a new locus on intellectual authority—all that Basil Willey[1] had in mind when he spoke of "the touch of cold philosophy." The seventeenth century's touch of cold philosophy had many sources, but none of them appears to me more crucial than the rise of modern science. Like Boyle, Newton was aware that the ground under Christianity was shifting. The central thrust of his lifelong religious quest was the effort to save Christianity by purging it of irrationalities. Is this interpretation equivalent to making Newton too eighteenth-century a figure? I can only answer that on my calendar the late seventeenth century immediately precedes the eighteenth, and I fail to perceive why it is unhistorical to find the roots of the eighteenth century stretching back across what is, after all, a purely arbitrary demarcation. For that matter, Newton was not only a seventeenth-century scientist; he was also an eighteenth-century theologian who was still writing theology when Voltaire visited London.

The story of Newton and Christianity constitutes, in my perception of things, one chapter in the central drama of European civilization: the conversion of an originally Christian civilization into a scientific one. Newton was by no means alone; many others were wrestling with the same problems. Since Newton made every effort to keep his theological views private, his opinions did not enter prominently into the main channel of religious thought; in so far as they did enter, his endeavor to save Christianity by purging it only contributed to the ultimate change, which went far beyond anything he would have welcomed. How little even the greatest of us understand the consequences of our own actions! I greatly admire the achievement that modern science represents; nevertheless, I do not revel in the decline of Christianity. I am myself a practicing Protestant Christian, and as I look about me at the chaos of contemporary civilization, especially in its American manifestation, it is far from evident to me that the change has all been gain. Nevertheless, whether I or anyone else likes it or not, it is fact; it did happen—the greatest alteration that European civilization has undergone. It is not the least product of the scientific revolution, or of Isaac Newton.

1. "The touch of cold philosophy" is Willey's phrase, taken from the seventeenth century, for the impact of the new philosophy on Christian faith. [Editor]

Part 9
MATHEMATICS

Introduction

Newton's first intellectual passion was mathematics. We know Newton's course of study when he arrived in Cambridge from the reading notes he entered into a notebook that still survives. As far as his papers indicate, mathematics did not figure in the prescribed studies at all. Roughly halfway through his undergraduate years, apparently sometime during 1664, however, he discovered a new course of reading for himself, and along with much else, Newton discovered mathematics.

The seventeenth century was the most creative age of mathematics in the West since the flowering of geometry in ancient Greece. There was a widespread belief that the Greeks, who presented their results in synthetic form, had discovered them by means of an analytic method that had been lost. Mathematicians of the seventeenth century set out to rediscover the lost method, drawing in part on the algebra that Europe had recently elaborated on Arabic foundations. They called the product of their endeavors *analysis*; we know it today as analytic geometry. Their work is what Newton came upon.

Several problems were central to the new analysis. One of them was the drawing of tangents to curves, lines that touch curves at a single point. The problem is closely related to what we call differentiation today. Descartes had devised a method of drawing tangents by constructing the normal to a curve at a given point; the tangent is perpendicular to the normal at the point of contact. Another French mathematician, Pierre Fermat, had developed a different method that dispensed with the normal and employed two points infinitesimally separated from each other along the curve. Infinitesimals figured prominently in a second problem, which seventeenth-century mathematicians called quadratures, the determination of the area under a curve, a problem intimately related to what we call integration.

More than half a century later, Newton described his introduction to mathematics to John Conduitt, the husband of his niece. He had come upon a book of astrology at the Sturbridge Fair held annually in Cambridge. Being unable to cast a figure, as astrologers did, he purchased a copy of Euclid, which did not greatly impress him at that time.

> He bought Descartes's Geometry and read it by himself [Conduitt's account continues]. When he was got over 2 or 3 pages, he could understand no farther. Then he began again and got 3 or 4 pages farther till he came to another difficult place. Then he began again and advanced farther and continued so doing till he made himself

In order not to encumber the reader with footnotes we have composed a Biographical Register, in which all the people mentioned in the text are identified, and a Glossary, in which technical terms are briefly explicated and such things as organizations, places, publications, and manuscript collections are identified. Both the Biographical Register and the Glossary are located near the end of the volume.

> Master of the whole without having the least light or instruction from any body.

By his own account, then, Newton was an autodidact in mathematics. The manuscript record of his efforts remains, witness to an incredible period of concentrated effort that dominated his life to the virtual exclusion of everything else for the following year and a half. In the short space of about twelve months, working alone, Newton absorbed the entire prior achievement of seventeenth-century mathematics. Reading notes were gradually transformed into original investigations. The final product of this endeavor, after an interval when he turned to other studies, was the tract of October 1666, which survives among his papers under the heading, "To resolve Problems by Motion these following Propositions are sufficient." What we call the calculus had been born.

The tract of October 1666 rests squarely on the central insight of the new analytic geometry, that an algebraic equation expresses the nature of the curve. This is the meaning of the statement that introduces Proposition 7: "Having an Equation expressing the relation twixt two or more lines x, y, z etc described by two or more moving bodies . . ." Let us confine ourselves to two lines, or variables; x and y represent the ordinate and abscissa of the curve defined by the equation in question. The strategy of the tract is to start from geometrical intuitions and to demonstrate how purely algebraic manipulations of the equation can yield the solution to otherwise intractable geometrical problems.

The paper rests equally on the conceptions that a line is the path of a moving point and that an area is generated by a moving line. The application of considerations of motion to geometry was not original with Newton, but it did become central to his most important advances in mathematics. He would call his method the fluxional method, a name taken from the past participle of the Latin verb *fluere*, "to flow." He considered that time flows uniformly, the background as it were of every phenomenon of motion, which he could use to express the velocities with which x and y are changing.

Concepts of infinitesimals also pervade the paper. Newton was uneasy with infinitesimals, which had dubious geometrical credentials in his opinion, and he tried to eliminate them through the notion of instantaneous velocities. Behind his instantaneous velocity, however, was the idea of the infinitesimal distance moved in a moment of time, expressed here as o. In the tract of October 1666, Newton uses p and q to express the instantaneous velocities of x and y; they are virtually identical to what we would mean by dx/dt and dy/dt. Later on, Newton would introduce a more familiar notation, in which the fluxion of x would be written $\dot{x}$. Note that instead of thinking of the rate at which x varies with respect to y, Newton sought their instantaneous velocities or the rate at which each varies with respect to the uniform flow of time. The ratio of the velocities, q/p, or dx/dt divided by dy/dt, is equivalent to our dy/dx, however, and it is central to the problem of finding the tangent (or slope) of a curve at a given point. In Example 1, for instance, he uses the ratio to determine the position of h, the point where the tangent to the curve at point c cuts the x axis.

In the demonstration of Proposition 7, Newton substitutes $x + po$ (in effect $x + \Delta x$) and $y + qo$ for x and y and obtains a new equation by multiplication. He followed the seventeenth-century habit of writing all the terms with x and y to a given power in vertical columns. The new equation contains the terms of the original one, which can be eliminated because the equation is equal to zero. All of the remaining terms contain o to some power, so that a single power of o can be factored out. Because o is infinitesimally small, he can neglect all of the remaining terms that still contain o, and thus he obtains an equation in which q/p can be expressed in terms of x and y. Note that his instruction to "multiply each term by so many times p/x as x has dimensions [that is, the power of x] in that term" is identical to our algorithm for differentiation.

Newton's method of quadratures, or finding areas under curves, underlies Proposition 8, in which, from an equation in x and q/p we are to find y. Perhaps the decisive step in the discovery of the fluxional method (or the calculus) was his recognition that the method of quadratures (or integration) is the inverse of the method of tangents (or differentiation). Other mathematicians had developed methods to draw tangents to curves, and still others methods to "square" curves, or integrate. It was Newton who first fully recognized the inverse nature of these two procedures—what we call the fundamental theorem of the calculus. We have interrupted Proposition 8 after his statement of the basic algorithm, which is identical to the one we use in the integration of single terms raised to any power. Note that Newton's word *logarithm* means "exponent," and that his algorithm is valid for any exponent, whether whole or fractional. In the tract he goes on to state that each term in a polynomial can be handled in the same way, and he offers his method of binomial expansion by which a term such as x^{-1} or $(a + x)^{1/2}$ is converted into an infinite series that is equal to the term in value, composed of terms in powers of x, which can be "squared" term by term and the value of the series calculated for any value of x, by adding additional terms, to however many decimals one wishes to go. He also offered suggestions for transforming equations into integrable forms.

We have included only two of the examples of drawing tangents. The tract proceeded on to solve a number of difficult problems. Newton found the curvature at any point on a curve, points of maximum and minimum curvature, and points of inflection. He rectified certain curves, that is, determined the length of given segments of them. He located the centers of gravity of figures defined by curves. Newton had received his bachelor's degree less than six months before he composed the tract of October

1666. At that time, no other mathematician was able even to approach this performance, and there had never been one who could.

The reader might note that in the tract Newton usually refers not to a mathematical point in motion, but to a body in motion. Despite the language, the tract was an exercise in pure mathematics, responding to a tradition of problems that had long been established, and not an exercise in the science of mechanics. Nevertheless, the language is suggestive. The calculus Newton developed was in fact capable of dealing with bodies in nonuniform motion in ways impossible with classical geometry. In the *Principia*, Newton did not employ the calculus as he presented it in the tract of October 1666. He did use its patterns of thought, however, its concept of instantaneous rates of change and its approach to areas and the limiting process. There are, furthermore, many expressions which explicitly declare their fluxional or calculus content and Newton refers frequently to the quadrature of curves or the finding of integrals. In proposition after proposition, Newton makes use of the method of limits in such a way and in such a degree that must declare the *Principia* to be a treatise in the new mathematical style rather than the style of the ancient geometers. We have included the mathematical lemmas that appear at the beginning of Book 1 of the *Principia* and express the mathematical concepts that undergird the apparently classical geometry in which Newton's masterpiece expresses itself. We include also Lemma 2 of Book 2, where more complex problems forced Newton to insert an explicit, albeit brief, statement of his fluxional method. Here Newton shows, among other things, how to find the derivative of polynomials. During the eighteenth century, the calculus, employed in the form that Leibniz gave it, became the core of the pattern that the physical sciences have followed in the West until this day.

Although Newton never again devoted himself singlemindedly to mathematics in the same way, the tract of October 1666 was far from the end of his mathematical endeavor. During the next thirty years, he returned intermittently to his method of fluxions, not so much altering it as seeking a different logical foundation for its concept of instantaneous rates of change. Thus Lemma 2 of Book 2 of the *Principia* differs in its presentation and language from the tract of October 1666. Newton made important contributions to mathematics in addition to the calculus. He made significant advances in the theory and use of infinite series, a feature especially noted in his *Principia*. He explored analytic geometry in the classification of cubic curves. He developed a method of interpolation to assist the calculators of mathematics tables. He tried his hand at projective geometry and even standard geometry. By refusing to publish his method, Newton allowed another mathematician, Leibniz, who worked from much the same sources at much the same problems, to develop a similar method, and thus he set the stage for the passionate priority dispute of the early eighteenth century, in which two independent discoverers hurled charges of plagiarism at each other. The Scholium at the end of Lemma 2, which we give in the final form it assumed in the third edition of the *Principia* in 1726, contains one of Newton's assertions of his priority in the discovery of the calculus. Scholars generally agree that the calculus was produced independently by Leibniz and by Newton. They agree furthermore that Newton had the priority of discovery, but that Leibniz was the first to publish the method.

Readers who want to go beyond the tract and the extracts from the *Principia* can find Newton's entire achievement in mathematics in the outstanding edition of his *Mathematical Papers*, edited by D. T. Whiteside, where it fills eight large volumes.

The Tract of October 1666†

October 1666. To resolve Problems by Motion these following Propositions are sufficient.

1. If the body *a* in the Perimeter of the circle or sphere *adce* moves towards its center *b*, its velocity to each point (*d*, *c*, *e*) of that circumference is as the chords (*ad*, *ac*, *ae*) drawn from that body to those points are [Fig. 1].

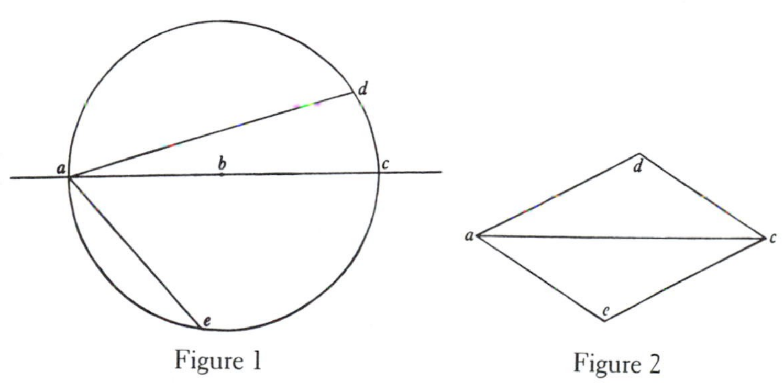

Figure 1 Figure 2

2. If the △s *adc*, *aec*, are alike viz. $ad = ec$ etc. (though in divers plains) and 3 bodies move from the point *a* uniformly and in equall times the first to *d*, the 2d to *e*, the 3d to *c* [Fig. 2]; Then is the thirds motion compounded of the motions of the first and second.

3. All the points of a Body keeping Parallel to it self are in equall velocity.

† A. Rupert Hall and Marie Boas Hall, eds. *Unpublished Scientific Papers of Isaac Newton* (Cambridge: Cambridge University Press, 1962), pp. 15–19, 31–37. Reprinted with the permission of Cambridge University Press. The culmination of Newton's early devotion to mathematics was the tract of October 1666 in which the calculus received its first full statement. A small number of details have been altered in accordance with the editors' reading of the manuscript original.

4. If a body move only $\left\{\begin{matrix}\text{angularly}\\ \text{circularly}\end{matrix}\right\}$ about some axis, the velocity of its points are as their distances from that axis.

5. The motions of all bodies are either parallel or angular, or mixed of them both, after the same manner that the motion towards *c* (Prop 2) is compounded of those towards *d* and *e*. And in mixed motion any line may be taken for the axis (or if a line or superficies move in plano, any point in that plane may be taken for the center) of the angular motion.

6. If the lines *ae*, *ah* being moved do continually intersect; I describe the trapezium *abcd*, and its diagonall *ac*: and say that, the proportion and position of these five lines *ab*, *ad*, *ac*, *cb*, *cd*, being determined by requisite data; shall design the proportion and position of these five motions; viz: of the point *a* fixed in the line *ae* and moving towards *b*, of the point *a* fixed in the line *ah* and moving towards *d*; of the intersection point *a* moving in the plain *abcd* towards *c*, (for those five lines are ever in the same plain, though *ae* and *ah* may chance only to touch that plain in their intersection point *a*); of the intersection point *a* moving in the line *ae* parallely to *cb* and according to the order of the letters *c*, *b*; and of the intersection point *a* moving in the line *ah* parallely to *cd* and according to the order of the letters *c*, *d* [Fig. 3].

Note that one of the lines as *ah* [Figs. 4 and 5] resting, the points *d* and *a* are coincident, and the point *c* shall be in the line *ah* if it be straight [Fig. 4], otherwise in its tangent [Fig. 5].

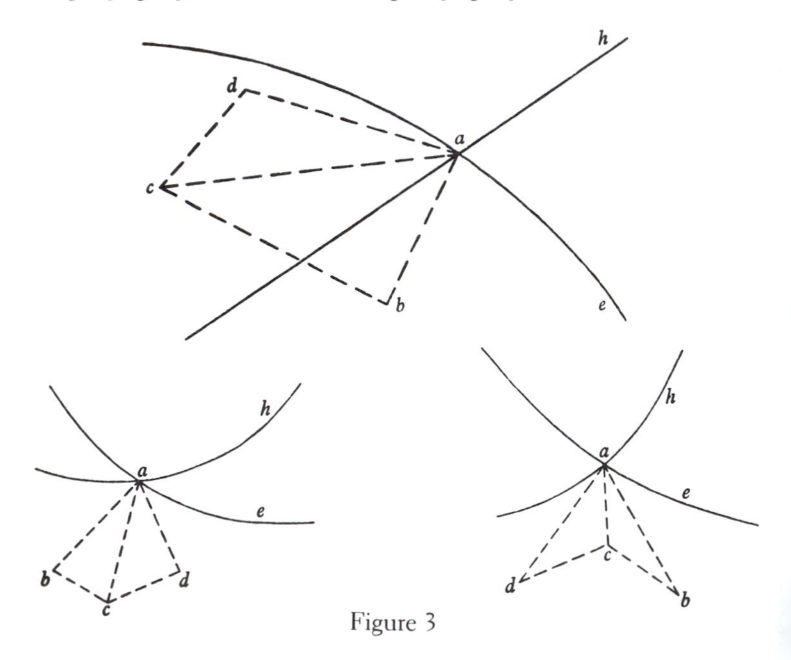

Figure 3

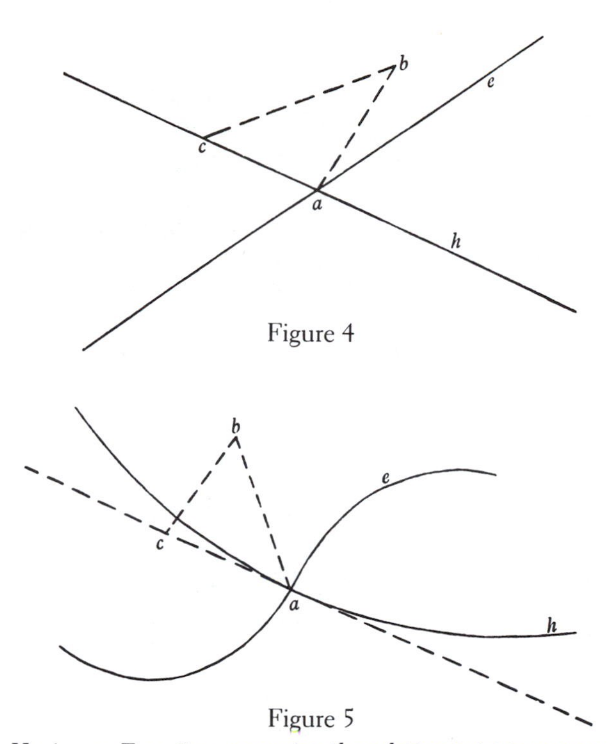

Figure 4

Figure 5

7. Having an Equation expressing the relation twixt two or more lines x, y, z etc. described in the same time by two or more moving bodies A, B, C, etc. [Fig. 6]: the relation of their velocities p, q, r, etc. may be thus found, viz: Set all the terms on one side of the Equation that they become equal to nothing. And first multiply each term by so many times $\frac{p}{x}$ as x has dimensions in that term. Secondly multiply each term by so many times $\frac{q}{y}$ as y has dimensions in it. Thirdly (if there be 3 unknown quantities) multiply each term by so many times $\frac{r}{z}$ as z has dimensions in that term. (and if there be still more unknown quantities do like to every unknown quantity). The sum of all these products shall be equal to nothing. Which Equation gives the relation of the velocities p, q, r, etc.

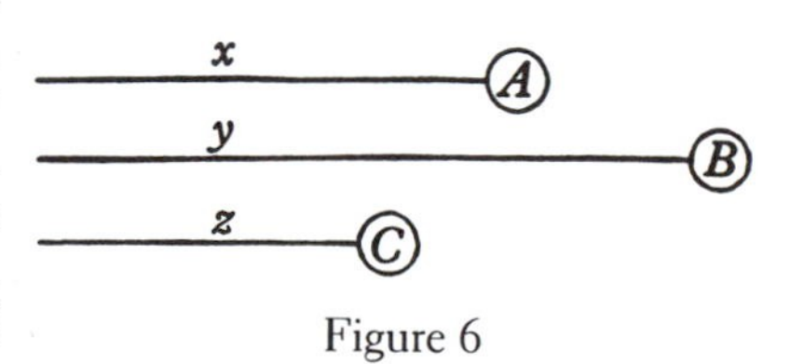

Figure 6

Or thus. Translate all the terms to one side of the equation, and multiply them being ordered according to x by this progression,

$$\text{etc.}\ \frac{3p}{x}\cdot\frac{2p}{x}\cdot\frac{p}{x}\cdot 0\cdot\frac{-p}{x}\cdot\frac{-2p}{x}\cdot\frac{-3p}{x}\cdot\frac{-4p}{x}\cdot\ \text{etc.}$$

and being ordered by the dimensions of y multiply them by this:

$$\text{etc.}\ \cdot\frac{3q}{y}\cdot\frac{2q}{y}\cdot\frac{q}{y}\cdot 0\cdot\frac{-q}{y}\cdot\frac{-2q}{y}\cdot\ \text{etc.}$$

The sum of these products shall be equal to nothing, which equation gives the relation of their velocities p, q, etc.

Or more Generally the Equation may be multiplied by the term of these progressions

$$\frac{ap+4bp}{x}\cdot\frac{ap+3bp}{x}\cdot\frac{ap+2bp}{x}\cdot\frac{ap+bp}{x}\cdot\frac{ap}{x}\cdot\frac{ap-bp}{x}\cdot\frac{ap-2bp}{x}\cdot\ \text{etc,}$$

And $$\frac{aq+2bq}{y}\cdot\frac{aq+bq}{y}\cdot\frac{aq}{y}\cdot\frac{aq-bq}{y}\cdot\ \text{etc.}$$

(a and b signifying any two numbers whither rational or irrational).[1]

8. If two Bodies A and B, by their velocities p and q describe the lines x and y, and an Equation be given expressing the relation twixt one of the lines x, and the ratio $\frac{q}{p}$ of their motions q and p; To find the other line y.

Could this be ever[2] done all problems whatever might be resolved. But by the following rules it may be very often done. (Note that $\pm m$ & $\pm n$ are logarithms or numbers signifying the dimensions of x.)

First get the value of $\frac{q}{p}$. Which if it be rational and its Denominator consist of but one term: Multiply that value by x and divide each terme of it by the logarithm of x in that terme the quotient shall be the value of y. As if

$$ax^{\frac{m}{n}}=\frac{q}{p}$$

Then is $$\frac{na}{m+n}x^{\frac{m+n}{n}}=y.$$

* * *

But the Demonstrations of what has been said must not be wholly omitted.

Proposition 7 Demonstrated

Lemma. If two bodys A, B, move uniformly the $\frac{\text{one}}{\text{other}}$ from $\frac{a}{b}$ to

1. That is, any arithmetic series. This was known as Hudde's rule, after Jan Hudde, who first demonstrated it.
2. That is, always.

$\begin{matrix} c,d,e,f, \\ g,h,k,l, \end{matrix}$ etc. in the same time [Fig. 7]. Then are the lines $\begin{matrix} ac, \\ bg, \end{matrix}$ and $\begin{matrix} cd, \\ gh, \end{matrix}$

Figure 7

and $\begin{matrix} de, \\ hk, \end{matrix}$ and $\begin{matrix} ef, \\ kl, \end{matrix}$ etc. as their velocities $\begin{matrix} p. \\ q. \end{matrix}$ And though they move not uniformly yet are the infinitely little lines which each moment, they describe, as their velocities which they have while they describe them. As if the body A with the velocity p describe the infinitely little line $(cd=)p\times o$ in one moment, in that moment the body B with the velocity q, will describe the line $(gh=)q\times o$. For $p{:}q{::}po{:}qo$. So that if the described lines be $(ac=)x$, and $(bg=)y$, in one moment, they will be $(ad=)x+po$, and $(bh=)y+qo$ in the next.

Demonstration: Now if the equation expressing the relation twixt the lines x and y be $x^3-abx+a^3-dyy=0$. I may substitute $x+po$ and $y+qo$ into the place of x and y; because (by the lemma) they as well as x and y, do signify the lines described by the bodies A and B. By doeing so there results

$$\begin{array}{llll} x^3 & +3poxx & +3ppoox & +p^3o^3-dyy-2dqoy-dqqoo=0. \\ & -abx & -abpo & \\ & & +a^3 & \end{array}$$

But $x^3-abx+a^3-dyy=0$ (by supposition).[3] Therefore there remains only $\begin{array}{l} 3poxx+3ppoox+p^3o^3-2dqoy-dqqoo=0. \\ \qquad\qquad -abpo \end{array}$ Or dividing it by o tis $\begin{array}{l} 3px^2+3ppox+p^3oo-2dqy-dqqo=0. \\ \qquad -abp \end{array}$ Also those terms are infinitely little in which o is. Therefore omitting them there rests $3pxx-abp-2dqy=0$. The like may be done in all other equations.

Hence I observe: First that those terms ever vanish which are not multiplyed by o, they being the propounded equation. Secondly those terms also vanish in which o is of more than one dimension, because they are infinitely less than those in which o is but of one dimension. Thirdly the still remaining terms being divided by o will have that form which, by the 1st rule in Prop 7th, they should have (as may partly appear by the second terms of Mr. Oughtred's latter Analytical table).[4]

After the same manner may this 7th Proposition be demonstrated there being 3 or more unknown quantities x, y, z, etc.

Prop 8th is the Converse of this 7th Prop. and may be therefore Analytically demonstrated by it.

3. It is the equation originally proposed.
4. The table in question appears in Oughtred's *Clavis mathematicae* (1631).

Prop 1st Demonstrated.

If some body A move in the right line *gafc* from *g* towards *c* [Fig. 8]. From any point *d* draw $df \perp ac$ and call, $df = a$, $fg = x$, $dg = y$. Then is $aa + xx - yy = 0$. Now by Prop 7th, may the proportion of (p) the veloc-

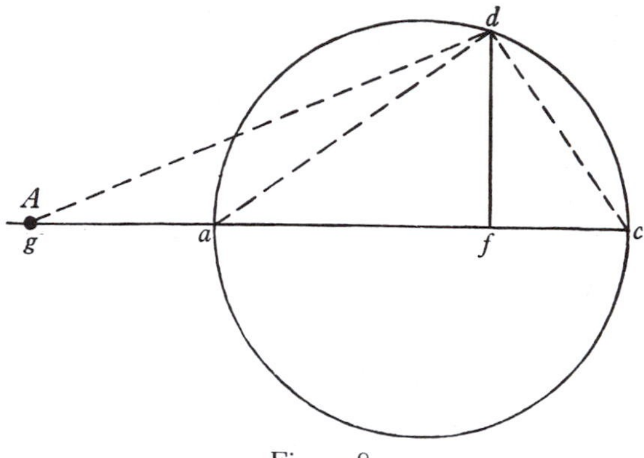

Figure 8

ity of that body towards f; to (q) its velocity towards d be found viz: $2xp - 2yq = 0$. Or $x{:}y :: q{:}p$. That is $gf{:}gd ::$ its velocity to d:its velocity towards f or c. And when the body A is at a, that is when the points g and a are coincident then is $ac{:}ad :: ad{:}af ::$ velocity to c:velocity to d.

Prop. 2d, Demonstrated.

From the points d and e draw $df \perp ac \perp ge$ [Fig. 9]. And let the first body's velocity to d be called ad, the second's to e be ae, and the 3ds toward c be ac. Then shall the first's velocity towards c be af (by Prop 1): and The second's towards c is ag, (prop 1). But $af = gc$ (for $\triangle adc = \triangle aec$, & $\triangle adf = \triangle gec$ by supposition). Therefore $ac = ag + gc = ag + af$. That is the velocity of the third body towards c is equal to the sum of the velocitys of the first and second body towards c.

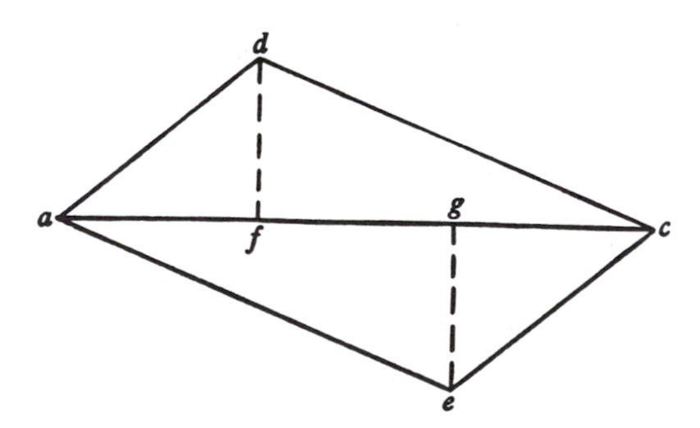

Figure 9

The former Theorems Applied to Resolving of Problems
Problem 1
To draw Tangents to crooked lines.[5]

Seek (by prop 7th; or 3d, 4th and 2d, etc.) the motions of those straight lines to which the crooked line is chiefly referred, and with what velocity they increase or decrease: and they shall give (by prop 6t, or 1st or 2d) the motion of the point describing the crooked line; which motion is in its tangent.

Tangents to Geometricall lines

Example 1 [Fig. 10]. If the crooked line *fac* is described by the intersection of two lines *cb* and *dc* the one moving parallely, viz: $cb \parallel ad$, &

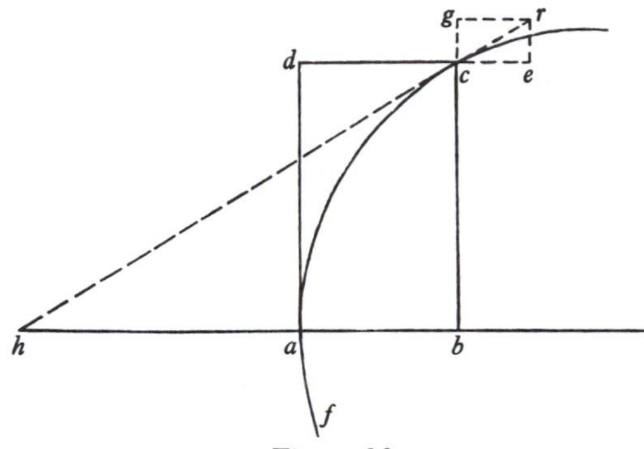

Figure 10

$dc \parallel ab$; so that if $ab = x$, & $bc = y = ad$, Their relation is $x^4 - 3yx^3 + ayxx$
$+10a$
$-2y^3x + a^4 = 0$. To draw the tangent *hcr*; I consider that the point *c* fixed
$-y^4$
in the line *cb* moves towards *e* parallely to *ab* (for so does the line *cb* (by supposition) and consequently all its points): also the point *c* fixed in the line *dc* moves toward *g* parallely to *ad* (by supposition): therefore I draw $ce \parallel ab$ and $cg \parallel ad$, and in such proportion as the motions they designe and so draw $er \parallel cb$, and $gr \parallel dc$, and the diagonal *cr*, (by Prop 6): that is, if the velocity of the line *cb*, (that is the celerity of the increasing of *ab*, or *dc*; or the velocity of the point *c* from *d*) be called *p*, and the velocity of the line *cd* be called *q*; I make

$$ce : gc :: p : q \ (:: ce : er :: hb : cb.)$$

and the point *c* shall move in the diagonal line *cr* (by prop 6) which is therefore the required tangent. Now the relation of *p* and *q* may be found by the foregoing Equation (*p* signifying the increase of *x*, and *q* of *y*) to be

5. That is, as we now say, a curve.

$$4px^3-9pyxx+30paxx+2payx-2py^3-3qx^3+qaxx-6qyyx-4qy^3=0$$

(by Prop 7). And therefore

$$hb=\frac{py}{q}=\frac{3yx^3-ayxx+6y^3x+4y^4}{4x^3-9yxx+30axx+2ayx-2y^3}.$$

which determines the tangent *hc*.

☞ Hence may be observed this General Theorem for drawing Tangents to crooked lines thus referred to straight ones; that is, to such lines in which $y=bc$ is ordinately applied to $x=ab$ at any given angle *abc*. viz:[6] Multiply the termes of the Equation ordered according to the dimensions of y, by any Arithmetical progression which product shall be the Numerator: Again change the signs of the Equation and ordering it according to x, multiply the terms by any Arithmetical progression and the product divided by x shall be the Denominator of the value of *hb*, that is, of x produced from y to the tangent *hc*.

As if $rx-\frac{rxx}{q}=yy$. Then first
$$\begin{array}{cccl} 2. & 1. & 0. & \\ yy & * & +\frac{r}{q}xx=0, & \text{produces } 2yy, \\ & & -rx & \\ 0. & -1. & -2. & \end{array}$$

or $2rx-\frac{2r}{q}xx$. Secondly, $\overset{2.}{-\frac{r}{q}xx}\overset{1.}{+rx}\overset{0.}{-yy}$ produces $rx-\frac{2r}{q}xx$.

Therefore
$$\frac{2yy}{r-\frac{2rx}{q}}=bh.$$

Or else
$$\frac{2rx-\frac{2r}{q}xx}{r-\frac{2r}{q}x}=bh=\frac{2qrx-2rxx}{qr-2rx}.$$

Example 2 [Fig. 11]. If the crooked line *chm* be described by the intersection of two lines *ac*, *bc* circulating about their centers *a* and *b*, so that if $ac=x$, and $bc=y$; their relation is

$$x^3-abx+cyy=0.$$

To draw the tangent *ec* I consider that the point *c* fixed in the line *bc* moves towards *f* in the line $cf\perp bc$ (for the tangent to a circle is perpendicular to its radius). Also the point *c* fixed in the line *ac* moves towards *d* in the line $cd\perp ac$ and from those lines *cd* and *cf* I draw two others $de \parallel cg$ and $ef \parallel bc$ which must be in such proportion one to another as the motions represented by them (prop 6), that is (prop 6) as the motions of

6. That is, y is the ordinate and x the abscissa. Note that the two did not have to be perpendicular as they are in what we now call Cartesian coordinates.

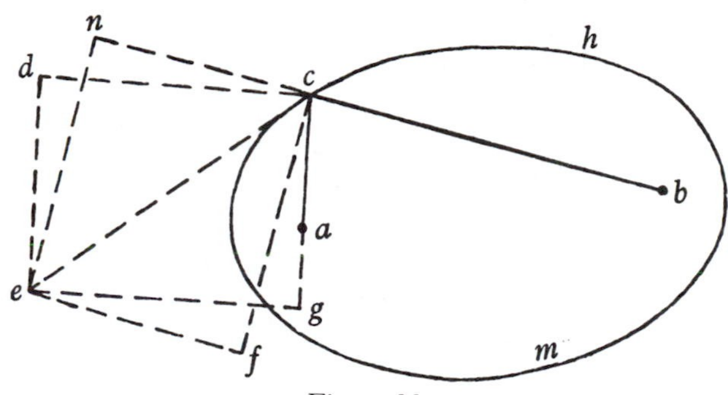

Figure 11

the intersection point c moving in the lines ca and cb to or from the centers a and b; that is, (the celerity of the increase of x being called p, and of y being q), $de{:}ef :: p{:}q$. Then shall the diagonal ce be the required tangent. Or which is the same, (for $\triangle ecg = \triangle ecd$, and $\triangle ecf = \triangle ecn$), I produce ac and bc to g and n, so that $cg{:}cn :: p{:}q$. and then draw $ne \perp bn$, and $ge \perp ag$; and the tangent diagonal ce to their intersection point e. Now the relation of p and q may be found by the given Equation to be, $3pxx - pab + 2qcy = 0$ (by prop 7). Or $2cy{:}ab - 3xx :: p{:}q :: cg{:}cn$, which determines the tangent ce.

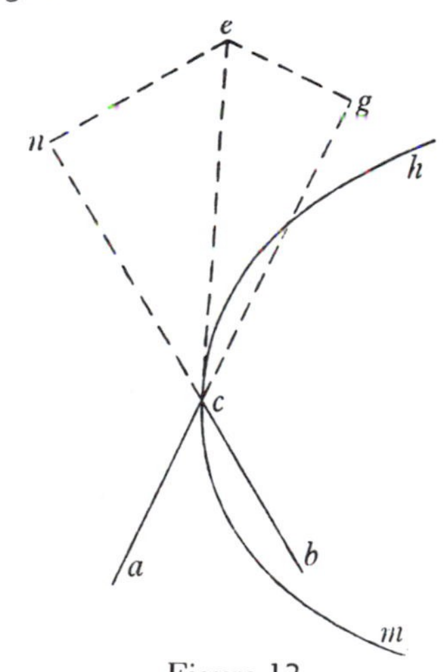

Figure 12

But note that if p, or q be negative, cg or cn must be drawn from c towards a or b; but from a or b if affirmative.

Hence tis easy to pronounce a Theorem for Tangents in such like cases and the like may be done in all other cases however Geometrical lines be referred to straight ones.

* * *

Section 1, Book 1 of the *Principia*†

The method of first and last ratios of quantities, by the help of which we demonstrate the propositions that follow.

Lemma 1

Quantities, and the ratios of quantities, which in any finite time converge continually to equality, and before the end of that time approach nearer to each other than by any given difference, become ultimately equal.

If you deny it, suppose them to be ultimately unequal, and let D be their ultimate difference. Therefore they cannot approach nearer to equality than by that given difference D; which is contrary to the supposition.

Lemma 2

If in any figure AacE, *terminated by the right lines* Aa, AE, *and the curve* acE, *there be inscribed any number of parallelograms* Ab, Bc, Cd, etc., *comprehended under equal bases* AB, BC, CD, etc., *and the sides,* Bb, Cc, Dd, etc., *parallel to one side* Aa *of the figure; and the parallelograms* aKbl, bLcm, cMdn, etc., *are completed: then if the breadth of those parallelograms be supposed to be diminished, and their number to*

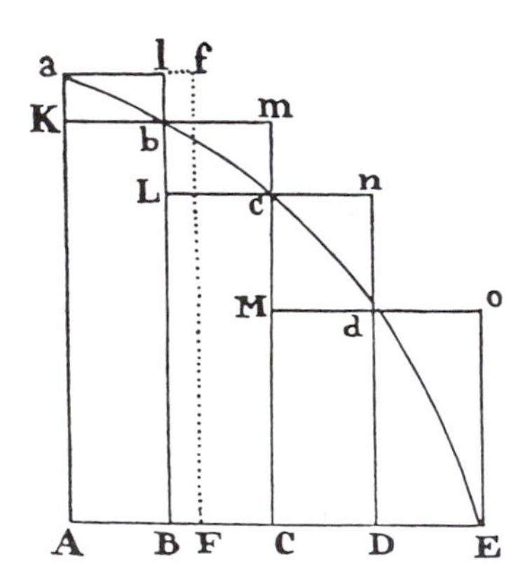

† Isaac Newton, *Mathematical Principles of Natural Philosophy* and *System of the World*, trans. by Andrew Motte, revised by Florian Cajori (Berkeley and Los Angeles: University of California Press, 1934 and later printings), pp. 29–39. Copyright 1934 and 1962 Regents of the University of California. Reprinted by permission. Immediately following the Definitions and the laws of motion, Book 1 of the *Principia* begins with a section that sets forth the method of first and last ratios, or as Newton also called them, nascent and ultimate ratios, in which he composed the work. See note on the Cajori translation on p. 116.

be augmented in infinitum, *I say, that the ultimate ratios which the inscribed figure* AKbLcMdD, *the circumscribed figure* AalbmcndoE, *and curvilinear figure* AabcdE, *will have to one another, are ratios of equality.*

For the difference of the inscribed and circumscribed figures is the sum of the parallelograms K*l*, L*m*, M*n*, D*o*, that is (from the equality of all their bases), the rectangle under one of their bases K*b* and the sum of their altitudes A*a*, that is, the rectangle AB*la*. But this rectangle, because its breadth AB is supposed diminished *in infinitum*, becomes less than any given space. And therefore (by Lem. 1) the figures inscribed and circumscribed become ultimately equal one to the other; and much more will the intermediate curvilinear figure be ultimately equal to either. Q.E.D.

Lemma 3

The same ultimate ratios are also ratios of equality, when the breadths AB, BC, DC, etc., *of the parallelograms are unequal, and are all diminished* in infinitum.

For suppose AF equal to the greatest breadth, and complete the parallelogram FA*af*. This parallelogram will be greater than the difference of the inscribed and circumscribed figures; but, because its breadth AF is diminished *in infinitum*, it will become less than any given rectangle. Q.E.D.

Cor. 1. Hence the ultimate sum of those evanescent parallelograms will in all parts coincide with the curvilinear figure.

Cor. 2. Much more will the rectilinear figure comprehended under the chords of the evanescent arcs *ab*, *bc*, *cd*, etc., ultimately coincide with the curvilinear figure.

Cor. 3. And also the circumscribed rectilinear figure comprehended under the tangents of the same arcs.

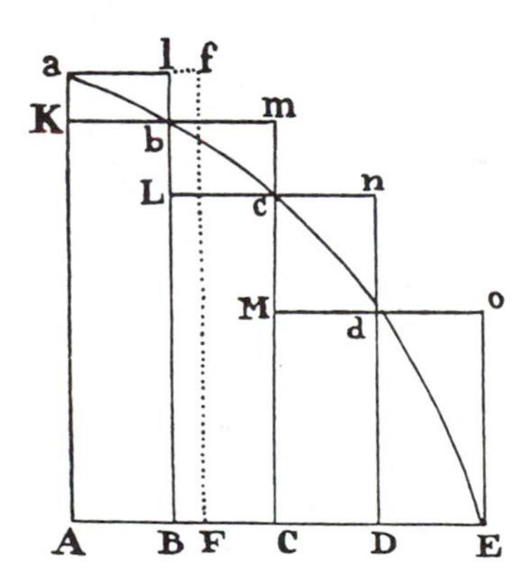

Cor. 4. And therefore these ultimate figures (as to their perimeters *ac*E) are not rectilinear, but curvilinear limits of rectilinear figures.

Lemma 4

If in two figures AacE, PprT, *there are inscribed (as before) two series of parallelograms, an equal number in each series, and, their breadths being diminished* in infinitum, *if the ultimate ratios of the parallelograms in one figure to those in the other, each to each respectively, are the same: I say, that those two figures,* AacE, PprT, *are to each other in that same ratio.*

For as the parallelograms in the one are severally to the parallelograms in the other, so (by composition) is the sum of all in the one to the sum of all in the other; and so is the one figure to the other; because (by Lem. 3) the former figure to the former sum, and the latter figure to the latter sum, are both in the ratio of equality. Q.E.D.

Cor. Hence if two quantities of any kind are divided in any manner into an equal number of parts, and those parts, when their number is augmented, and their magnitude diminished *in infinitum*, have a given ratio to each other, the first to the first, the second to the second, and so on in order, all of them taken together will be to each other in that same given ratio. For if, in the figures of this Lemma, the parallelograms are taken to each other in the ratio of the parts, the sum of the parts will always be as the sum of the parallelograms; and therefore supposing the number of the parallelograms and parts to be augmented, and their magnitudes diminished *in infinitum*, those sums will be in the ultimate ratio of the parallelogram in the one figure to the correspondent parallelogram in the other; that is (by the supposition), in the ultimate ratio of any part of the one quantity to the correspondent part of the other.

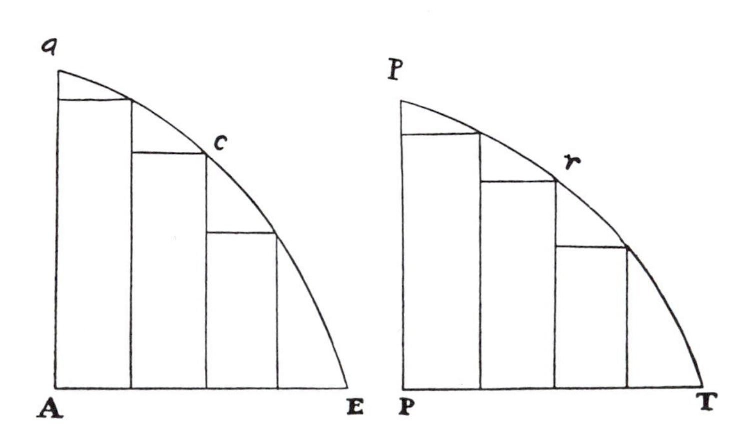

Lemma 5

All homologous sides of similar figures, whether curvilinear or rectilinare, are proportional; and the areas are as the squares of the homologous sides.

Lemma 6

If any arc ACB, *given in position, is subtended by its chord* AB, *and in any point* A, *in the middle of the continued curvature, is touched by a right line* AD, *produced both ways; then if the points* A *and* B *approach one another and meet, I say, the angle* BAD, *contained between the chord and the tangent, will be diminished* in infinitum, *and ultimately will vanish.*

For if that angle does not vanish, the arc ACB will contain with the tangent AD an angle equal to a rectilinear angle; and therefore the curvature at the point A will not be continued, which is against the supposition.

Lemma 7

The same things being supposed, I say that the ultimate ratio of the arc, chord, and tangent, any one to any other, is the ratio of equality.

For while the point B approaches towards the point A, consider always AB and AD as produced to the remote points *b* and *d*; and parallel to the secant BD draw *bd*; and let the arc A*cb* be always similar to the arc ACB. Then, supposing the points A and B to coincide, the angle *d*A*b* will vanish, by the preceding Lemma; and therefore the right lines A*b*, A*d* (which are always finite), and the intermediate arc A*cb*, will coincide, and become equal among themselves. Wherefore, the right lines AB, AD, and the intermediate arc ACB (which are always propor-

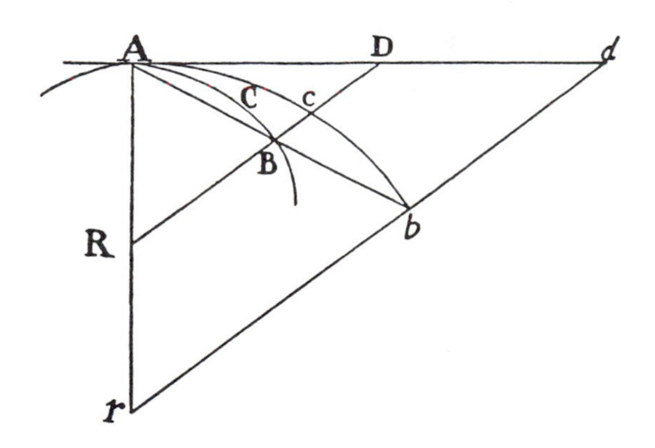

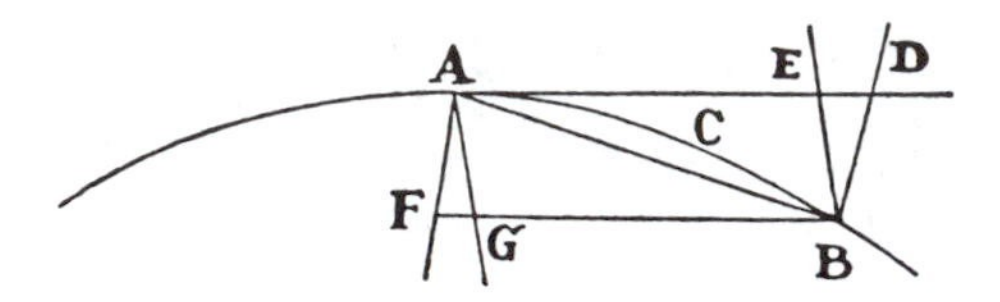

tional to the former), will vanish, and ultimately acquire the ratio of equality. Q.E.D.

Cor. 1. Whence if through B we draw BF parallel to the tangent, always cutting any right line AF passing through A in F, this line BF will be ultimately in the ratio of equality with the evanescent are ACB; because, completing the parallelogram AFBD, it is always in a ratio of equality with AD.

Cor. 2. And if through B and A more right lines are drawn, as BE, BD, AF, AG, cutting the tangent AD and its parallel BF; the ultimate ratio of all the abscissas AD, AE, BF, BG, and of the chord and arc AB, any one to any other, will be the ratio of equality.

Cor. 3. And therefore in all our reasoning about ultimate ratios, we may freely use any one of those lines for any other.

Lemma 8

If the right lines AR, BR, *with the arc* ACB, *the chord* AB, *and the tangent* AD, *constitute three triangles* RAB, RACB, RAD, *and the points* A *and* B *approach and meet: I say, that the ultimate form of these evanescent triangles is that of similitude, and their ultimate ratio that of equality.*

For while the point B approaches towards the point A, consider always AB, AD, AR, as produced to the remote points *b*, *d*, and *r*, and *rbd* as drawn parallel to RD, and let the arc A*cb* be always similar to the arc ACB. Then supposing the points A and B to coincide, the angle *b*A*d* will vanish; and therefore the three triangles *r*A*b*, *r*A*cb*, *r*A*d* which are

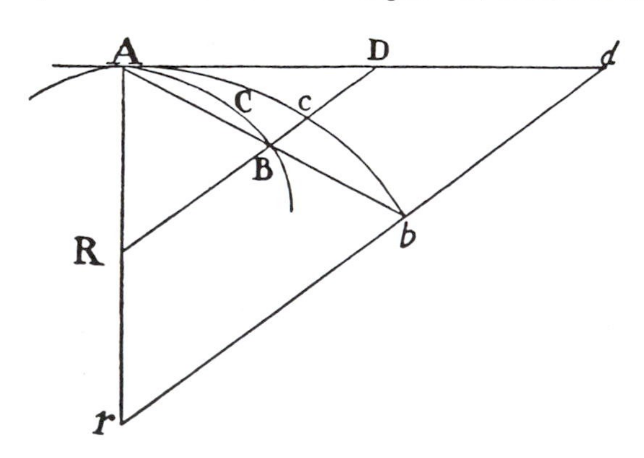

always finite), will coincide, and on that account become both similar and equal. And therefore the triangles *RAB*, *RACB*, *RAD*, which are always similar and proportional to these, will ultimately become both similar and equal among themselves. Q.E.D.

Cor. And hence in all reasonings about ultimate ratios, we may use any one of those triangles for any other.

Lemma 9

If a right line AE, *and a curved line* ABC, *both given by position, cut each other in a given angle,* A; *and to that right line, in another given angle,* BD, CE *are ordinately applied, meeting the curve in* B, C; *and the points* B *and* C *together approach towards and meet in the point* A: I *say, that the areas of the triangles* ABD, ACE, *will ultimately be to each other as the squares of homologous sides.*

For while the points B, C, approach towards the point A, suppose always AD to be produced to the remote points *d* and *e*, so as A*d*, A*e* may be proportional to AD, AE; and the ordinates *db*, *ec*, to be drawn parallel to the ordinates DB and EC, and meeting AB and AC produced in *b* and *c*. Let the curve A*bc* be similar to the curve ABC, and draw the right line A*g* so as to touch both curves in A, and cut the ordinates DB, EC, *db*, *ec*, in F, G, *f*, *g*. Then, supposing the length A*e* to remain the same, let the points B and C meet in the point A; and the angle *c*A*g* vanishing, the curvilinear areas A*bd*, A*ce* will coincide with the rectilinear areas A*fd*, A*ge*; and therefore (by Lem. 5) will be one to the other in the duplicate ratio of the sides A*d*, A*e*. But the areas ABD, ACE are always proportional to these areas; and so the sides AD, AE are to these sides. And therefore the areas ABD, ACE are ultimately to each other as the squares of the sides AD, AE. Q.E.D.

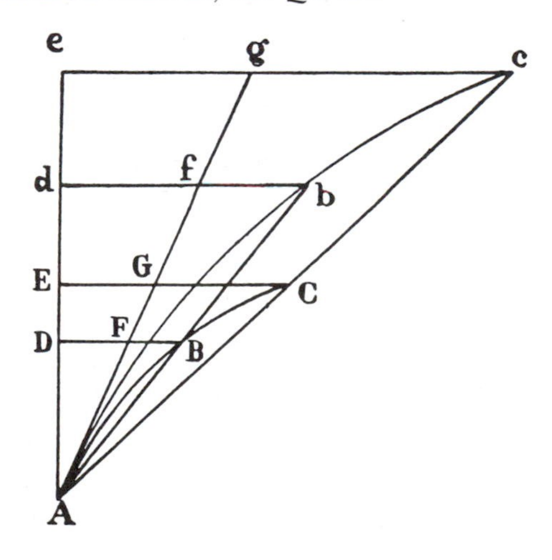

Lemma 10

The spaces which a body describes by any finite force urging it, whether that force is determined and immutable, or is continually augmented or continually diminished, are in the very beginning of the motion to each other as the squares of the times.

Let the times be represented by the lines AD, AE, and the velocities generated in those times by the ordinates DB, EC. the spaces described with these velocities will be as the areas ABD, ACE, described by those ordinates, that is, at the very beginning of the motion (by Lem. 9), in the duplicate ratio of the times AD, AE. Q.E.D.

Cor. 1. And hence one may easily infer, that the errors of bodies describing similar parts of similar figures in proportional times, the errors being generated by any equal forces similarly applied to the bodies, and measured by the distances of the bodies from those places of the similar figures, at which, without the action of those forces, the bodies would have arrived in those proportional times—are nearly as the squares of the times in which they are generated.

Cor. 2. But the errors that are generated by proportional forces, similarly applied to the bodies at similar parts of the similar figures, are as the product of the forces and the squares of the times.

Cor. 3. The same thing is to be understood of any spaces whatsoever described by bodies urged with different forces; all which, in the very beginning of the motion, are as the product of the forces and the squares of the times.

Cor. 4. And therefore the forces are directly as the spaces described in the very beginning of the motion, and inversely as the squares of the times.

Cor. 5. And the squares of the times are directly as the spaces described, and inversely as the forces.

Scholium

If in comparing with each other indeterminate quantities of different sorts, any one is said to be directly or inversely as any other, the meaning is, that the former is augmented or diminished in the same ratio as the latter, or as its reciprocal. And if any one is said to be as any other two or more, directly or inversely, the meaning is, that the first is augmented or diminished in the ratio compounded of the ratios in which the others, or the reciprocals of the others, are augmented or diminished. Thus, if A is said to be as B directly, and C directly, and D inversely, the meaning is, that A is augmented or diminished in the same ratio as $B \cdot C \cdot \frac{1}{D}$, that is to say, that A and $\frac{BC}{D}$ are to each other in a given ratio.

Lemma 11

The evanescent subtense of the angle of contact, in all curves which at the point of contact have a finite curvature, is ultimately as the square of the subtense of the conterminous arc.

Case 1. Let AB be that arc, AD its tangent, BD the subtense of the angle of contact perpendicular on the tangent, AB the subtense of the arc. Draw BG perpendicular to the subtense AB, and AG perpendicular to the tangent AD, meeting in G; then let the points D, B, and G approach to the points *d*, *b*, and *g*, and suppose J to be the ultimate intersection of the lines BG, AG, when the points D, B have come to A. It is evident that the distance GJ may be less than any assignable distance. But (from the nature of the circles passing through the points A, B, and G, and through A, *b*, *g*),

$$\mathrm{AB}^2 = \mathrm{AG} \cdot \mathrm{BD}, \text{ and}$$
$$\mathrm{A}b^2 = \mathrm{A}g \cdot bd.$$

But because GJ may be assumed of less length than any assignable, the ratio of AG to A*g* may be such as to differ from unity by less than any assignable difference; and therefore the ratio of AB^2 to $\mathrm{A}b^2$ may be such as to differ from the ratio of BD to *bd* by less than any assignable difference. Therefore, by Lem. 1, ultimately,

$$\mathrm{AB}^2 : \mathrm{A}b^2 = \mathrm{BD} : bd. \qquad \text{Q.E.D.}$$

Case 2. Now let BD be inclined to AD in any given angle, and the ultimate ratio of BD to *bd* will always be the same as before, and therefore the same with the ratio of AB^2 to $\mathrm{A}b^2$. Q.E.D.

Case 3. And if we suppose the angle D not to be given, but that the

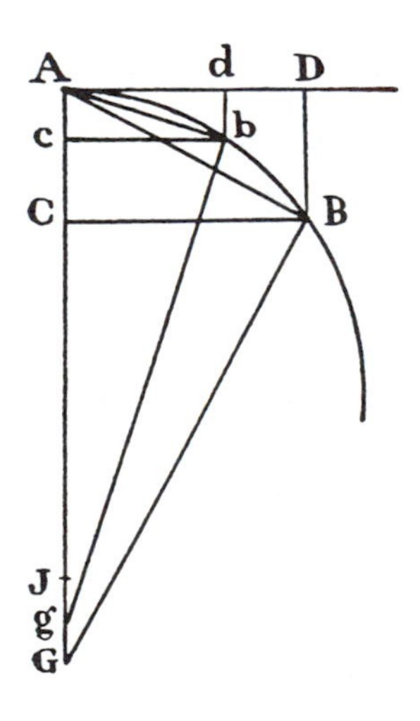

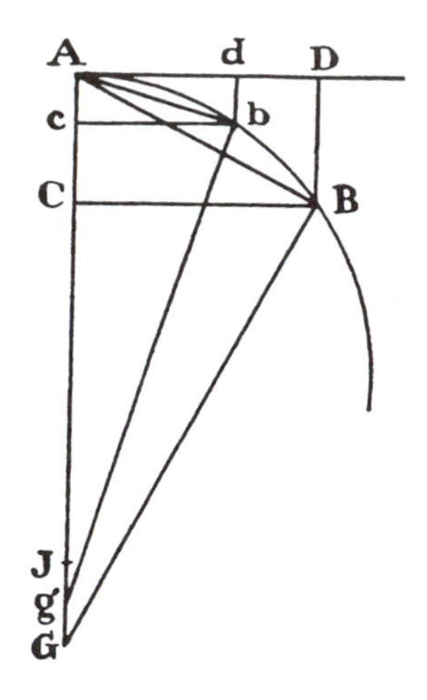

right line BD converges to a given point, or is determined by any other condition whatever; nevertheless the angles D,*d*, being determined by the same law, will always draw nearer to equality, and approach nearer to each other than by any assigned difference, and therefore, by Lem. 1, will at last be equal; and therefore the lines BD, *bd* are in the same ratio to each other as before. Q.E.D.

Cor. 1. Therefore since the tangents AD, A*d*, the arcs AB, A*b*, and their sines, BC, *bc*, become ultimately equal to the chords AB, A*b*, their squares will ultimately become as the subtenses BD, *bd*.

Cor. 2. Their squares are also ultimately as the versed sines of the arcs, bisecting the chords, and converging to a given point. For those versed sines are as the subtenses BD, *bd*.

Cor. 3. And therefore the versed sine is as the square of the time in which a body will describe the arc with a given velocity.

Cor. 4. The ultimate proportion,

$\triangle ADB : \triangle Adb = AD^3 : Ad^3 = DB^{3/2} : db^{3/2}$, is derived from

$\triangle ADB : \triangle Adb = AD \cdot DB : Ad \cdot db$ and from the ultimate proportion

$AD^2 : Ad^2 = DB : db$.

So also is obtained ultimately

$\triangle ABC : \triangle Abc = BC^3 : bc^3$.

Cor. 5. And because DB, *db* are ultimately parallel and as the squares of the lines AD, A*d*, the ultimate curvilinear areas ADB, A*db* will be (by the nature of the parabola) two-thirds of the rectilinear triangles ADB, A*db*, and the segments AB, A*b* will be one-third of the same triangles. And thence those areas and those segments will be as the squares of the tangents AD, A*d*, and also of the chords and arcs AB, A*b*.

Scholium

But we have all along supposed the angle of contact to be neither infinitely greater nor infinitely less than the angles of contact made by circles and their tangents; that is, that the curvature at the point A is neither infinitely small nor infinitely great, and that the interval AJ is of a finite magnitude. For DB may be taken as AD^3: in which case no circle can be drawn through the point A, between the tangent AD and the curve AB, and therefore the angle of contact will be infinitely less than those of circles. And by a like reasoning, if DB be made successfully as AD^4, AD^5, AD^6, AD^7, etc., we shall have a series of angles of contact, proceeding *in infinitum*, wherein every succeeding term is infinitely less than the preceding. And if DB be made successively as AD^2, $AD^{3/2}$, $AD^{4/3}$, $AD^{5/4}$, $AD^{6/5}$, $AD^{7/6}$, etc., we shall have another infinite series of angles of contact, the first of which is of the same sort with those of circles, the second infinitely greater, and every succeeding one infinitely greater than the preceding. But between any two of these angles another series of intermediate angles of contact may be interposed, proceeding both ways *in infinitum*, wherein every succeeding angle shall be infinitely greater or infinitely less than the preceding. As if between the terms AD^2 and AD^3 there were interposed the series $AD^{13/6}$, $AD^{11/5}$, $AD^{9/4}$, $AD^{7/3}$, $AD^{5/2}$, $AD^{8/3}$, $AD^{11/4}$, $AD^{14/5}$, $AD^{17/6}$, etc. And again, between any two angles of this series, a new series of intermediate angles may be interposed, differing from one another by infinite intervals. Nor is Nature confined to any bounds.

Those things which have been demonstrated of curved lines, and the surfaces which they comprehend, may be easily applied to the curved surfaces and contents of solids. These Lemmas are premised to avoid the tediousness of deducing involved demonstrations *ad absurdum*, according to the method of the ancient geometers. For demonstrations are shorter by the method of indivisibles; but because the hypothesis of indivisibles seems somewhat harsh, and therefore that method is reckoned less geometrical, I chose rather to reduce the demonstrations of the following Propositions to the first and last sums and ratios of nascent and evanescent quantities, that is, to the limits of those sums and ratios, and so to premise, as short as I could, the demonstrations of those limits. For hereby the same thing is performed as by the method of indivisibles; and now those principles being demonstrated, we may use them with greater safety. Therefore if hereafter I should happen to consider quantities as made up of particles, or should use little curved lines for right ones, I would not be understood to mean indivisibles, but evanescent divisible quantities; not the sums and ratios of determinate parts, but always the limits of sums and ratios; and that the force of such demonstrations always depends on the method laid down in the foregoing Lemmas.

Perhaps it may be objected, that there is no ultimate proportion of evanescent quantities; because the proportion, before the quantities have vanished, is not the ultimate, and when they are vanished, is none. But by the same argument it may be alleged that a body arriving at a certain place, and there stopping, has no ultimate velocity; because the velocity, before the body comes to the place, is not its ultimate velocity; when it has arrived, there is none. But the answer is easy; for by the ultimate velocity is meant that with which the body is moved, neither before it arrives at its last place and the motion ceases, nor after, but at the very instant it arrives; that is, that velocity with which the body arrives at its last place, and with which the motion ceases. And in like manner, by the ultimate ratio of evanescent quantities is to be understood the ratio of the quantities not before they vanish, nor afterwards, but with which they vanish. In like manner the first ratio of nascent quantities is that with which they begin to be. And the first or last sum is that with which they begin and cease to be (or to be augmented or diminished). There is a limit which the velocity at the end of the motion may attain, but not exceed. This is the ultimate velocity. And there is the like limit in all quantities and proportions that begin and cease to be. And since such limits are certain and definite, to determine the same is a problem strictly geometrical. But whatever is geometrical we may use in determining and demonstrating any other thing that is also geometrical.

It may also be objected, that if the ultimate ratios of evanescent quantities are given, their ultimate magnitudes will be also given: and so all quantities will consist of indivisibles, which is contrary to what *Euclid* has demonstrated concerning incommensurables, in the tenth Book of his *Elements*. But this objection is founded on a false supposition. For those ultimate ratios with which quantities vanish are not truly the ratios of ultimate quantities, but limits towards which the ratios of quantities decreasing without limit do always converge; and to which they approach nearer than by any given difference, but never go beyond, nor in effect attain to, till the quantities are diminished *in infinitum*. This thing will appear more evident in quantities infinitely great. If two quantities, whose difference is given, be augmented *in infinitum*, the ultimate ratio of these quantities will be given, namely, the ratio of equality; but it does not from thence follow, that the ultimate or greatest quantities themselves, whose ratio that is, will be given. Therefore if in what follows, for the sake of being more easily understood, I should happen to mention quantities as le. st, or evanescent, or ultimate, you are not to suppose that quantities of any determinate magnitude are meant, but such as are conceived to be always diminished without end.

Lemma 2, Book 2 of the *Principia* †

The moment of any genitum *is equal to the moments of each of the generating sides multiplied by the indices of the powers of those sides, and by their coefficients continually.*

I call any quantity a *genitum* which is not made by addition or subtraction of divers parts, but is generated or produced in arithmetic by the multiplication, division, or extraction of the root of any terms whatsoever; in geometry by the finding of contents and sides, or of the extremes and means of proportionals. Quantities of this kind are products, quotients, roots, rectangles, squares, cubes, square and cubic sides, and the like. These quantities I here consider as variable and indetermined, and increasing or decreasing, as it were, by a continual motion or flux; and I understand their momentary increments or decrements by the name of moments; so that the increments may be esteemed as added or affirmative moments; and the decrements as subtracted or negative ones. But take care not to look upon finite particles as such. Finite particles are not moments, but the very quantities generated by the moments. We are to conceive them as the just nascent principles of finite magnitudes. Nor do we in this Lemma regard the magnitude of the moments, but their first proportion, as nascent. It will be the same thing, if, instead of moments, we use either the velocities of the increments and decrements (which may also be called the motions, mutations, and fluxions of quantities), or any finite quantities proportional to those velocities. The coefficient of any generating side is the quantity which arises by applying the genitum to that side.

Wherefore the sense of the Lemma is, that if the moments of any quantities A, B, C, etc., increasing or decreasing by a continual flux, or the velocities of the mutations which are proportional to them, be called a, b, c, etc., the moment or mutation of the generated rectangle AB will be aB + bA; the moment of the generated content ABC will be $a\mathrm{BC}+b\mathrm{AC}+c\mathrm{AB}$; and the moments of the generated powers A^2, A^3, A^4, $\mathrm{A}^{1/2}$, $\mathrm{A}^{3/2}$, $\mathrm{A}^{1/3}$, $\mathrm{A}^{2/3}$, A^{-1}, A^{-2} $\mathrm{A}^{-1/2}$ will be $2a\mathrm{A}$, $3a\mathrm{A}^2$, $4a\mathrm{A}^3$, $1/2\, a\mathrm{A}^{-1/2}$, $3/2\, a\mathrm{A}^{1/2}$, $1/3\, a\mathrm{A}^{-2/3}$, $2/3\, a\mathrm{A}^{-1/3}$, $-a\mathrm{A}^{-2}$, $-2a\mathrm{A}^{-3}$, $-1/2\, a\mathrm{A}^{-3/2}$ respectively; and, in general, that the moment of any power $\mathrm{A}^{n/m}$ will be $\frac{n}{m}a\mathrm{A}^{\frac{n-m}{m}}$. Also, that the moment of the generated quantity $\mathrm{A}^2\mathrm{B}$ will be $2a\mathrm{AB}+b\mathrm{A}^2$; the moment of the generated quantity $\mathrm{A}^3\mathrm{B}^4\mathrm{C}^2$ will be $3a\mathrm{A}^2\mathrm{B}^4\mathrm{C}^2+4b\mathrm{A}^3\mathrm{B}^3\mathrm{C}^2+2c\mathrm{A}^3\mathrm{B}^4\mathrm{C}$; and the moment of the generated

† *Isaac Newton: Mathematical Principles of Natural Philosophy* and *System of the World*, trans. by Andrew Motte, revised by Florian Cajori (Berkeley and Los Angeles: University of California Press, 1934 and later printings), pp. 249–52. Newton could not handle some problems in Book 2 of the *Principia* with the method of first and last ratios alone, and he had to introduce explicitly the algorithm for what we now call differentiation. See note on the Cajori translation on p. 116.

quantity $\frac{A^3}{B^2}$ or A^3B^{-2} will be $3aA^2B^{-2} - 2bA^3B^{-3}$; and so on. The Lemma is thus demonstrated.

Case 1. Any rectangle, as AB, augmented by a continual flux, when, as yet, there wanted of the sides A and B half their moments $\frac{1}{2}a$ and $\frac{1}{2}b$, was $A+\frac{1}{2}a$ into $B+\frac{1}{2}b$, or $AB - \frac{1}{2}aB - \frac{1}{2}bA + \frac{1}{4}ab$; but as soon as the sides A and B are augmented by the other half-moments, the rectangle becomes $A + \frac{1}{2}a$ into $B + \frac{1}{2}b$, or $AB + \frac{1}{2}aB + \frac{1}{2}bA + \frac{1}{4}ab$. From this rectangle subtract the former rectangle, and there will remain the excess $aB + bA$. Therefore with the whole increments a and b of the sides, the increment $aB + bA$ of the rectangle is generated. Q.E.D.

Case 2. Suppose AB always equal to G, and then the moment of the content ABC or GC (by Case 1) will be $gC + cG$, that is (putting AB and $aB + bA$ for G and g), $aBC + bAC + cAB$. And the reasoning is the same for contents under ever so many sides. Q.E.D.

Case 3. Suppose the sides A, B, and C, to be always equal among themselves; and the moment $aB + bA$, of A^2, that is, of the rectangle AB, will be $2aA$; and the moment $aBC + bAC + cAB$ of A^3, that is, of the content ABC, will be $3aA^2$. And by the same reasoning the moment of any power A^n is naA^{n-1}. Q.E.D.

Case 4. Therefore since $\frac{1}{A}$ into A is 1, the moment of $\frac{1}{A}$ multiplied by A, together with $\frac{1}{A}$ multiplied by a, will be the moment of 1, that is, nothing. Therefore the moment of $\frac{1}{A}$, or of A^{-1}, is $\frac{-a}{A^2}$. And generally since $\frac{1}{A^n}$ into A^n is 1, the moment of $\frac{1}{A^n}$ multiplied by A^n together with $A\frac{1}{A^n}$ into naA^{n-1} will be nothing. And, therefore, the moment of $\frac{1}{A^n}$ or A^{-n} will be $-\frac{na}{A^{n+1}}$. Q.E.D.

Case 5. And since $A^{1/2}$ into $A^{1/2}$ is A, the moment of $A^{1/2}$ multiplied by $2A^{1/2}$ will be a (by Case 3); and, therefore, the moment of $A^{1/2}$ will be $\frac{a}{2A^{1/2}}$ or $\frac{1}{2}aA^{-1/2}$. And generally, putting $A^{\frac{m}{n}}$ equal to B, then A^m will be equal to B^n, and therefore maA^{m-1} equal to nbB^{n-1}, and maA^{-1} equal to nbB^{-1}, or $nbA^{-\frac{m}{n}}$; and therefore $\frac{m}{n}aA^{\frac{m-n}{n}}$ is equal to b, that is, equal to the moment of $A^{\frac{m}{n}}$. Q.E.D.

Case 6. Therefore the moment of any generated quantity A^mB^n is the moment of A^m multiplied by B^n, together with the moment of B^n multiplied by A^m, that is, $maA^{m-1} B^n + nbB^{n-1} A^m$; and that whether the indices m and n of the powers be whole numbers or fractions, affirmative or negative. And the reasoning is the same for higher powers. Q.E.D.

Cor. 1. Hence in quantities continually proportional, if one term is given, the moments of the rest of the terms will be as the same terms multiplied by the number of intervals between them and the given term. Let A, B, C, D, E, F be continually proportional; then if the term C is given, the moments of the rest of the terms will be among themselves as $-2A$, $-B$, D, 2E, 3F.

Cor. 2. And if in four proportionals the two means are given, the moments of the extremes will be as those extremes. The same is to be understood of the sides of any given rectangle.

Cor. 3. And if the sum or difference of two squares is given, the moments of the sides will be inversely as the sides.

Scholium

In a letter of mine to Mr. *J. Collins*, dated *December* 10, 1672, having described a method of tangents, which I suspected to be the same with *Sluse's* method, which at that time was not made public, I added these words: *This is one particular, or rather a Corollary, of a general method, which extends itself, without any troublesome calculation, not only to the drawing of tangents to any curved lines, whether geometrical or mechanical or in any manner respecting right lines or other curves, but also to the resolving other abstruser kinds of problems about the crookedness, areas, lengths, centres of gravity of curves, etc.; nor is it (as* Hudden's *method* de maximis et minimis) *limited to equations which are free from surd quantities. This method I have interwoven with that other of working in equations, by reducing them to infinite series.* So far that letter. And these last words relate to a treatise I composed on that subject in the year 1671. The foundation of that general method is contained in the preceding Lemma.

Leibniz's Judgment of Newton as a Mathematician †

Leibnitz said that taking Mathematicks from the beginning of the world to the time of Sir I. What he had done was much the better half—

† Richard S. Westfall, *Never at Rest: A Biography of Isaac Newton* (Cambridge: Cambridge University Press, 1980), p. 721. Reprinted with the permission of Cambridge University Press. Newton eventually carried on a ferocious dispute over priority in invention of the calculus with Leibniz. In 1701, before the public dispute began, Leibniz responded in Berlin to a question from the Queen of Prussia about Newton's capacity as a mathematician. No doubt there was a heavy layer of diplomatic politesse in Leibniz's response, but it illustrates what an informed contemporary could say about Newton as a mathematician without appearing ridiculous.

and added that he had consulted all the learned in Europe upon some difficult point without having any satisfaction and that when he wrote to Sir I. he sent him answer by the first post to do so and so and then he would find it out.

Colson's Account of the Method of Fluxions†

39. The *chief principle* upon which the Method of Fluxions is built is this very simple one, taken from the *Rational Mechanics*; which is, that *mathematical quantity*, particularly *extension*, may be conceived as generated by continued *local motion*; and that *all quantities* whatever, (at least by *analogy* and *accommodation*,) may be conceived as generated after a like manner: consequently, there must be *comparative* velocities [or rates] of increase and decrease during such generations; whose *relations* are fixed and determinable, and may therefore (problematically) be proposed to be found.

This problem our author solves by the help of *another principle* not less evident; which supposes that quantity is *infinitely divisible*, or that it may (*mentally* at least) *so far* continually diminish, as at last, before it is *totally* extinguished, to arrive at quantities which may be called *vanishing* quantities, or which are *infinitely little*, and less than any *assignable* quantity: or it supposes that we may form a notion, not indeed of *absolute*, but of *relative* and *comparative infinity*.

It is a very just exception to the Method of *Indivisibles* [of *Cavalerius*], as also to the foreign *Infinitesimal* Method [of *Leibnitz*], that they have recourse at *once* to infinitely little quantities, and infinite orders and graduations of these, not relatively but absolutely such: they assume these quantities *simùl et semèl*,[1] without any ceremony, as quantities that *actually* and *obviously* exist, and make computations with them accordingly; the result of which must needs be as *precarious* as the absolute existence of the quantities they assume.

Absolute infinity, as such, can hardly be the object either of our conceptions or calculations; but *relative* infinity may, under a proper regulation. Our author observes this distinction very strictly, and introduces none but *infinitely little* quantities that are *relatively* so: which he arrives at, by beginning with finite quantities, and proceeding by a gradual and necessary progress of diminution: his computations always commence by *finite* and *intelligible* quantities; and then, at last, he inquires what will be the result, in *certain circumstances*, when such or such quantities are diminished *in infinitum*. This is a constant practice even in *Com-*

† From the preface to John Colson's *The Method of Fluxions and Infinite Series* (London, 1737) as presented in William Hales, *Analysis Fluxionum* (London, 1800). The expressions within square brackets were added by Hales.

1. The phrase *simùl et semèl* (which was used by Newton in his discussion of the second law of motion in the *Principia*) has the sense of "all at once" as opposed to *successive et gradatim* or "successively by degrees."

mon Algebra and *Geometry;* and is no more than descending from a *general proposition* to a *particular case* which is certainly included in it.

40. And from these *easy* principles, managed with a vast deal of skill and sagacity, he deduces his *Method of Fluxions:* which if we consider only *so far* as he himself has carried it, together with the *application* he has made of it, either here, or elsewhere, directly or indirectly, expressly or tacitly to the most curious discoveries in *art* and *nature*, and to the sublimest *theories*, we may deservedly esteem it as the *greatest work of genius*, and as the noblest effort that ever was made by the human mind.

41. Indeed it must be owned, that many useful *improvements* and *new applications* have been *since* made by others, and probably will be *still* made, every day: for it is no mean excellence of this method, that it is doubtless still *capable* of a greater degree of perfection, and will always afford an inexhaustible fund of curious matter, to reward the pains of the ingenious and industrious *analyst*.

42. It should be well considered by these *gentlemen objectors*,[2] that the great number of *examples* they will find here, to which the Method of Fluxions is successfully applied, are so many *vouchers* for the truth of the principles on which that method is founded: for the deductions are *always conformable* to what has been derived from other *uncontroverted* principles; and therefore must be acknowledged as *true*.

This argument should have its due weight even with such as *cannot*, as well as with such as *will not* enter into the proof of the principles themselves. And the *hypothesis* that has been advanced to evade this conclusion—*of one error in reasoning being still corrected by another equal and contrary thereto*—and that, *so regularly, constantly, and frequently*, as it must be supposed to do here;—this hypothesis, I say, ought not to be seriously refuted, because I can hardly think it is seriously proposed. . . .

GEORGE BERKELEY

From *The Analyst* †

* * *

3. The Method of Fluxions is the general key by help whereof the modern mathematicians unlock the secrets of Geometry, and consequently of Nature. And, as it is that which hath enabled them so

2. He refers to George Berkeley; see following selection.

† George Berkeley, *The Analyst* (London: Tonson, 1734), pp. 6–19. Soon after Newton's death, the Anglo-Irish philosopher George Berkeley raised serious problems about the logical foundation of the calculus. The questions continued to plague mathematicians for a century, even while they used and extended the calculus, until the French mathematician Augustin Louis Cauchy put them to rest in the early nineteenth century with a rigorous application of the concept of limits.

remarkably to outgo the ancients in discovering theorems and solving problems, the exercise and application thereof is become the main if not sole employment of all those who in this age pass for profound geometers. But whether this method be clear or obscure, consistent or repugnant, demonstrative or precarious, as I shall inquire with the utmost impartiality, so I submit my inquiry to your own judgment, and that of every candid reader.—Lines are supposed to be generated by the motion of points, planes by the motion of lines, and solids by the motion of planes. And whereas quantities generated in equal times are greater or lesser according to the greater or lesser velocity wherewith they increase and are generated, a method hath been found to determine quantities from the velocities of their generating motions. And such velocities are called fluxions: and the quantities generated are called flowing quantities. These fluxions are said to be nearly as the increments of the flowing quantities, generated in the least equal particles of time; and to be accurately in the first proportion of the nascent, or in the last of the evanescent increments. Sometimes, instead of velocities, the momentaneous increments or decrements of undetermined flowing quantities are considered, under the appellation of moments.

4. By moments we are not to understand finite particles. These are said not to be moments, but quantities generated from moments, which last are only the nascent principles of finite quantities. It is said that the minutest errors are not to be neglected in mathematics: that the fluxions are celerities, not proportional to the finite increments, though ever so small; but only to the moments or nascent increments, whereof the proportion alone, and not the magnitude, is considered. And of the aforesaid fluxions there be other fluxions, which fluxions of fluxions are called second fluxions. And the fluxions of these second fluxions are called third fluxions: and so on, fourth, fifth, sixth, etc. *ad infinitum*. Now, as our Sense is strained and puzzled with the perception of objects extremely minute, even so the Imagination, which faculty derives from sense, is very much strained and puzzled to frame clear ideas of the least particles of time, or the least increments generated therein: and much more so to comprehend the moments, or those increments of the flowing quantities in *statu nascenti*,[1] in their very first origin or beginning to exist, before they become finite particles. And it seems still more difficult to conceive the abstracted velocities of such nascent imperfect entities. But the velocities of the velocities—the second, third, fourth, and fifth velocities, etc.—exceed, if I mistake not, all human understanding. The further the mind analyseth and pursueth these fugitive ideas the more it is lost and bewildered; the objects, at first fleeting and minute, soon vanishing out of sight. Certainly, in any sense, a second or third fluxion seems an obscure Mystery. The incipient celerity of an

1. Literally, in the state of being born; that is, nascent. [Editor]

incipient celerity, the nascent augment of a nascent augment, i.e. of a thing which hath no magnitude—take it in what light you please, the clear conception of it will, if I mistake not, be found impossible; whether it be so or no I appeal to the trial of every thinking reader. And if a second fluxion be inconceivable, what are we to think of third, fourth, fifth fluxions, and so on without end?

5. The foreign mathematicians[2] are supposed by some, even of our own, to proceed in a manner less accurate, perhaps, and geometrical, yet more intelligible. Instead of flowing quantities and their fluxions, they consider the variable finite quantities as increasing or diminishing by the continual addition or subduction of infinitely small quantities. Instead of the velocities wherewith increments are generated, they consider the increments or decrements themselves, which they call differences, and which are supposed to be infinitely small. The difference of a line is an infinitely little line; of a plane an infinitely little plane. They suppose finite quantities to consist of parts infinitely little, and curves to be polygons, whereof the sides are infinitely little, which by the angles they make one with another determine the curvity of the line. Now to conceive a quantity infinitely small—that is, infinitely less than any sensible or imaginable quantity, or any the least finite magnitude—is, I confess, above my capacity. But to conceive a part of such infinitely small quantity that shall be still infinitely less than it, and consequently though multiplied infinitely shall never equal the minutest finite quantity, is, I suspect, an infinite difficulty to any man whatsoever; and will be allowed such by those who candidly say what they think; provided they really think and reflect, and do not take things upon trust.

6. And yet in the *calculus differentialis*, which method serves to all the same intents and ends with that of fluxions, our modern analysts are not content to consider only the differences of finite quantities: they also consider the differences of those differences, and the differences of the differences of the first differences: and so on *ad infinitum*. That is, they consider quantities infinitely less than the least discernible quantity; and others infinitely less than those infinitely small ones; and still others infinitely less than the preceding infinitesimals, and so on without end or limit. Insomuch that we are to admit an infinite succession of infinitesimals, each infinitely less than the foregoing, and infinitely greater than the following. As there are first, second, third, fourth, fifth etc. fluxions, so there are differences, first second, third, fourth, etc. in an infinite progression towards nothing, which you still approach and never arrive at. And (which is most strange) although you should take a million of millions of these infinitesimals, each whereof is supposed infinitely greater than some other real magnitude, and add them to the least given quantity, it shall never be the bigger. For this is one of the modest

2. He refers to Leibniz and his followers and the differential calculus. [Editor]

postulata of our modern mathematicians, and is a corner-stone or ground-work of their speculations.

7. All these points, I say, are supposed and believed by certain rigorous exactors of evidence in religion, men who pretend to believe no further than they can see. That men who have been conversant only about clear points should with difficulty admit obscure ones might not seem altogether unaccountable. But he who can digest a second or third fluxion, a second or third difference, need not, methinks, be squeamish about any point in divinity. There is a natural presumption that men's faculties are made alike. It is on this supposition that they attempt to argue and convince one another. What therefore shall appear evidently impossible and repugnant to one may be presumed the same to another. But with what appearance of reason shall any man presume to say that mysteries may not be objects of faith, at the same time that he himself admits such obscure mysteries to be the object of science?

8. It must indeed be acknowledged the modern mathematicians do not consider these points as mysteries, but as clearly conceived and mastered by their comprehensive minds. They scruple not to say that by the help of these new analytics they can penetrate into infinity itself: that they can even extend their views beyond infinity: that their art comprehends not only infinite, but infinite of infinite (as they express it), or an infinity of infinites. But, notwithstanding all these assertions and pretensions, it may be justly questioned whether, as other men in other inquiries are often deceived by words or terms, so they likewise are not wonderfully deceived and deluded by their own peculiar signs, symbols, or species. Nothing is easier than to devise expressions or notations for fluxions and infinitesimals of the first, second, third, fourth, and subsequent orders, proceeding in the same regular form without end or limit x, $\dot{x}$, $\ddot{x}$, $\dddot{x}$, $\ddddot{x}$ etc., or *dx*, *ddx*, *dddx*, *ddddx*, etc. These expressions, indeed, are clear and distinct, and the mind finds no difficulty in conceiving them to be continued beyond any assignable bounds. But if we remove the veil and look underneath, if, laying aside the expressions, we set ourselves attentively to consider the things themselves which are supposed to be expressed or marked thereby, we shall discover much emptiness, darkness, and confusion; nay, if I mistake not, direct impossibilities and contradictions. Whether this be the case or no, every thinking reader is entreated to examine and judge for himself.

9. Having considered the object, I proceed to consider the principles of this new analysis by momentums, fluxions, or infinitesimals; wherein if it shall appear that your capital points, upon which the rest are supposed to depend, include error and false reasoning; it will then follow that you, who are at a loss to conduct yourselves, cannot with any decency set up for guides to other men. The main point in the method of fluxions is to obtain the fluxion or momentum of the rectangle or product or two intermediate quantities. Inasmuch as from thence are

derived rules for obtaining the fluxions of all other products and powers; be the coefficients or the indexes what they will, integers or fractions, rational or surd. Now, this fundamental point one would think should be very clearly made out, considering how much is built upon it, and that its influence extends throughout the whole analysis. But let the reader judge. This is given for demonstration. Suppose the product or rectangle AB increased by continual motion: and that the momentaneous increments of the sides A and B are a and b. When the sides A and B were deficient, or lesser by one half of their moments, the rectangle was $(A - \frac{1}{2}a) \times (B - \frac{1}{2}b)$, i.e. $AB - \frac{1}{2}aB - \frac{1}{2}bA + \frac{1}{4}ab$. And as soon as the sides A and B are increased by the other two halves of their moments, the rectangle becomes $(A + \frac{1}{2}a) \times (B + \frac{1}{2}b)$ or $AB + \frac{1}{2}aB + \frac{1}{2}bA + \frac{1}{4}ab$. From the latter rectangle subduct the former, and the remaining difference will be $aB + bA$. Therefore the increment of the rectangle generated by the entire increments a and b is $aB + bA$. *Q.E.D.* But it is plain that the direct and true method to obtain the moment or increment of the rectangle AB, is to take the sides as increased by their whole increments, and so multiply them together, $A + a$ by $B + b$, the product whereof $AB + aB + bA + ab$ is the augmented rectangle; whence, if we subduct AB the remainder $aB + bA + ab$ will be the true increment of the rectangle, exceeding that which was obtained by the former illegitimate and indirect method by the quantity ab. And this holds universally by the quantities a and b be what they will, big or little, finite or infinitesimal, increments, moments, or velocities. Nor will it avail to say that ab is a quantity exceeding small; since we are told that *in rebus mathematicis errores quam minimi non sunt contemnendi.*[3]

10. Such reasoning as this for demonstration, nothing but the obscurity of the subject could have encouraged or induced the great author of the fluxionary method to put upon his followers, and nothing but an implicit deference to authority could move them to admit. The case indeed is difficult. There can be nothing done till you have got rid of the quantity ab. In order to this the notion of fluxions is shifted: it is placed in various lights: points which should be clear as first principles are puzzled; and terms which should be steadily used are ambiguous. But, notwithstanding all this address and skill, the point of getting rid of ab cannot be obtained by legitimate reasoning. If a man, by methods not geometrical or demonstrative, shall have satisfied himself of the usefulness of certain rules; which he afterwards shall propose to his disciples for undoubted truths; which he undertakes to demonstrate in a subtle manner, and by the help of nice and intricate notions; it is not hard to conceive that such his disciples may, to save themselves the trouble of thinking, be inclined to confound the usefulness of a rule with the cer-

3. "In mathematics, errors, however small, must not be neglected." [Editor]

tainty of a truth, and accept the one for the other; especially if they are men accustomed rather to compute than to think; earnest rather to go on fast and far, than solicitous to set out warily and see their way distinctly.

11. The points or mere limits of nascent lines are undoubtedly equal, as having no more magnitude one than another, a limit as such being no quantity. If by a momentum you mean more than the very initial limit, it must be either a finite quantity or an infinitesimal. But all finite quantities are expressly excluded from the notion of a momentum. Therefore the momentum must be an infinitesimal. And, indeed, though much artifice hath been employed to escape or avoid the admission of quantities infinitely small, yet it seems ineffectual. For aught I see, you can admit no quantity as a medium between a finite quantity and nothing, without admitting infinitesimals. An increment generated in a finite particle of time is itself a finite particle; and cannot therefore be a momentum. You must therefore take an infinitesimal part of time wherein to generate your momentum. It is said, the magnitude of moments is not considered; and yet these same moments are supposed to be divided into parts. This is not easy to conceive, no more than it is why we should take quantities less than *A* and *B* in order to obtain the increment of *AB*, of which proceeding it must be owned the final cause or motive is obvious; but it is not so obvious or easy to explain a just and legitimate reason for it, or shew it to be geometrical.

* * *

D. T. WHITESIDE

Newton the Mathematician †

A mathematician is born and he is educated. On the genetic origin of Newton's intellectual genius and its putative socio-economic *cum* psychosexual conditioning as he grew up in his Lincolnshire homeland I have very little to say. It seems to me wholly inappropriate to attempt, with C. M. Cox,[1] to assess his intelligence quotient by applying a standard test of so loosely quantifiable an imponderable to the little of his childhood that is known, even through the rosy hue of romanticised hearsay. I do have some slight sympathy for anyone who sees in Isaac a unique vital spark momentarily uniting the earthy Newtons of Woolsthorpe, rising through the generations from the poverty and obscurity of

† Zev Bechler, ed. *Contemporary Newtonian Research* (Dordrecht: Reidel, 1982), pp. 110–16. Copyright © D. T. Whiteside. Reprinted by permission of D. T. Whiteside. D. T. Whiteside, editor of the *Mathematical Papers of Isaac Newton*, is universally acknowledged as the authoritative commentator on Newton's mathematics.

1. Author of a twentieth-century study of the mental traits of geniuses. [Editor]

their yeoman-farmer forbears, and the gentle-born Askews[2] of Market Overton, slowly descending the same social scale from their lordly Tudor heyday. I find emptily extravagant when not totally absurd—forgive me this blindspot—the Eriksonian efforts of one recent biographer[3] to conjoin the scientific achievement of Newton's *annus mirabilis* in the middle 1660's with his conjectured childhood 'longing' for a dead father whom he never knew from beyond the womb and for a well-loved mother equally snatched from him, once born, by quick remarriage to a sexually fertile older man, thence positing 'a relationship between this longing and a later intellectual structure in which a sort of an impulse or attraction is a key term descriptive of a force'. Why not go the whole hog and, with R. W. Meyer,[4] look upon Newtonian attraction as a grand Baroque symbol of a political 'power', emanating from a centre somewhere between Court and Parliament, which maintains the locally sovereign bodies, as they go their several ways, in a perpetual if ever-fluid mutual balance? Or choose your own metaphor from Tolstoy, Marx, Spengler or whomever you prefer of the Messiahs of universal history still living.

In my own simple-minded way I must myself go back to the recorded past, however faintly and distortedly it has endured to the present day. First to the dame schools at nearby Skillington and Stoke which taught Newton his reading and writing, if not the third of his three R's; and then six miles northwards from Woolsthorpe to the small single-roomed King's School at Grantham, under whose headmaster Henry Stokes he was soon intellectually to blossom out. One can—citing Ben Jonson's thin menu of 'small Latine and lesse Greeke' and adding to it a sweetening of Hebrew—all too readily disparage the rote learning which was instilled at such country 'grammar' schools. But in Newton's case at least it was better that that. At Grantham, penned in Stokes' own hand it would seem, there survives a little pocketbook, dated 1654, which is filled with 'Notes for the Mathematicks'. Much is as you would expect of such a compendium of rules for boys destined one day in the main to run their father's farms. We have 'Directions for survaying'—how 'To measure incloses or peeces in comon fields by the chaine only'—and in sequel a worked instance 'To turne primes [tenths of poles] into Acres'. But then come sixty-five pages on 'The measureing of Triangles and Circles'—elementary plane mensurational geometry, we would say—which are of a different order. 'The manner and way to calculate a table of Sines', one reads, 'by finding the Sides of . . . regular bodyes inscribed in a Circle whose Radius is given', together with an 'Example of makeing a septuagon'—understand its periphery and area, given its

2. The family of Newton's mother. [Editor]
3. He refers to Frank Manuel, *A Portrait of Isaac Newton* (1968); Manuel draws on the concepts of the contemporary psychoanalyst Erik Erikson. [Editor]
4. In the book *Leibniz and the Seventeenth-Century Revolution* (1951). [Editor]

diameter, and *vice versa*—with the accompanying prescript that 'Every Circumference is more then triple his Diameter by such a proportion as is more then 10/71 and lesse then 1/7.' Three centuries on, did I at my own North-country grammar school thirty years ago learn how to place a 7-sided equilateral figure within its circumscribing circle? had I heard of Archimedes' lower bound to pi? I think not. And I am impressed that such things were taught at Grantham in the middle 1650's when Newton was his headmaster's prize pupil. Evidence that he himself did imbibe such elements of geometrical drawing may be glimpsed in the interwoven nest of cyclic polygons yet to be seen incised in the plaster of a bedroom window-nook at the Woolsthorpe farmhouse which was, out of termtime, Newton's boyhood home. Years afterwards when he came at Cambridge to study François Viète's mathematical work, his interest was still very much in ruler-and-compasses construction of the regular heptagon and enneagon which are 'trew onely mechanically,' and also in determining the side of a 'square equall to the area of a circle' in ways built upon the 'Pseudomesolabe' (as Viète dubbed it) $\pi = 3/5 \times (3 + \sqrt{5})$. When young Isaac went up to Trinity College in 1661, however else he may have stood in diffident awe at the expanse of scholarly learning suddenly opened up to him, in arithmetic and in mensurational geometry he was no beginner.

To Cambridge in 1661. I need scarcely remind that in that first year of restored monarchy its undergraduate scheme of study held little enough to excite the budding mathematician. The notebook in which Newton set down many of his early reading notes confirms that he was ground through a scholastic mill which had changed little for centuries past: a first entrance to a *trivium* of logic, ethics and rhetoric, followed by a *quadrivium*[5] which gave basic instruction in the tenets of Aristotelian physics along with a little Euclidean geometry, all tested in the verbal thesis and antithesis of formal disputation degenerated to be a near-empty stylistic exercise. One could argue that this brought to Newton its long-term benefits in disciplining him to the orderly and forceful presentation of logical argument which he displayed in his mature reasoning. One might a deal more tentatively surmise that his enforced student grounding in Euclid's *Elements* had an equally lasting effect—that its elegant (sometimes not so elegant) deductions of the properties of triangle, quadrilateral, circle and sphere from a few received axioms and postulates led him easily in later years to frame an extended Euclidean space in which uniform kinematic and enforced dynamical motions are analogously defined. But one should be wary of concluding that the timeless niceties of classical pure geometry were ever his *forte*. You all know the story of Newton being put to 'second posing' at Trinity when tested in his 'quadrivium' year on his knowledge of the *Elements*. As he

5. The trivium (grammar, rhetoric, and logic) and the quadrivium (geometry, arithmetic, music, and astronomy) comprised the seven liberal arts in medieval education. [Editor]

told it to de Moivre in old age, his own account is that when first he met with the *Elements* he 'read only the titles of the propositions, which he found so easy to understand that he wondered how any body would amuse themselves to write any demonstrations of them'; and changed his mind only when he came to the proposition, 1,47, 'that in a right angled Triangle the square of the Hypothenuse is equal to the squares of the two other sides.' A story is only a story. But look at Newton's copy of Barrow's 1655 Latin epitome of the *Elements* which was the prescribed student's text, and you will find that in his reading of its first book he was indeed stopped by this theorem of Pythagoras—and to convince himself of its truth he was put to inserting additional construction lines in its figure. That he should have been halted at this basic metrical theorem for Euclidean space is to me significant: it found no place in the little Grantham book of 'Notes for the Mathematicks'—and, of course, if you deny its truth you are into the treacheries of non-Euclidean realms.

Leaf further through the pages of Newton's copy of Barrow's epitome of the *Elements* and you will see more and more the cast of his youthful mathematical mind. In Book 2 he has taken every care to spell out the algebraic equivalents of its linear and quadratic identities, and its geometrical solution of the general quadratic equation by 'completing the square'. On the pages of the ensuing 'geometrical' Books 3, 4, 6 and 11–13—other than to convert to arithmetical equivalent the expressions for the sides of the regular dodecahedron and icosahedron inscribed in a unit-sphere, which Barrow cites *ex Herigonio*[6] in supplement to the last—he has set not a word of comment or query. In contrast, he has fulsomely annotated the intervening 'arithmetical' Books 5, 7 and 10 where Euclid presents his Pythagorean-*cum*-Eudoxean notions of real and rational number-ratios and of surds. Were I to tax your patience, I could give you instance upon instance in his later writings where Newton betrays a similar disinterest in classical pure geometry. In the early 1680's and again ten years afterwards he was, it is true, to devote much time and effort to resolving such particular problems of the 'ancients' as that of the Euclidean 'locus to 4 lines' and of Apollonius' 3-circles tangency; more widely—founding his restoration, like Viète, Fermat and others before him, upon Pappus' lemmas on the lost works of Euclid and Apollonius on porisms and other species of *τόποι ἀναλυόμενοι*, 'discovering loci'—he worked hard to recover the analysis underlying the post-synthesised arguments in which the Greeks chose to couch their achievements in higher geometry. But each time he was drawn quickly on, to abstract therefrom univeral canons for invariance under projective linear transformation, and to formulate generalised notions of birational point-correspondence. Pardon the fleeting skip into technicalities. Grant me my point that classical Euclidean geometry played only a

6. From Herigone. [Editor]

minor rôle at best in framing the mould and content of Newton's mature mathematical achievement.

What appears to me ever more clearly to be the decisive event guiding the future direction of Newton's mathematical thought and practice was his reading of Descartes' *Geometrie* in the late summer of 1664. To Newton, as *mutatis mutandis*[7] to Christiaan Huygens more than twenty years earlier when he first read Descartes' *Principia*, the work came as a revelation of the endless bounds of the possible. You will perhaps recall Huygens' own remembered reaction to his Cartesian mentor: 'It seemed, when I read this book, that all was going the best in the world, and I believed when I found some difficulty in it, that it was my fault for not properly grasping his thought.' The *Geometrie*—and to some smaller degree Descartes' *Dioptrique* and *Principia*—must have had the same immediate impact upon Newton. In his case, I regret, we have only a clumsy account, third-hand from his lips by way of de Moivre and Conduitt, telling dully of his crawling progress through the book, reading and re-reading its pages 'till by degrees he made himself master of the whole'. But the thick wad of Newton's research papers surviving from the later months of 1664 stand firm witness that it was indeed from the hundred or so pages of the *Geometrie* that his mathematical spirit took fire.

The crucial importance for him of Descartes' short essay lay not so much in its evocation and illustration of the power of coordinate geometry in resolving problems fearsome to treat by classical methods; though the *Geometrie's* reduction of the Euclidean '4-line locus' to the standard Apollonian defining 'symptom' of one or other species of conic section showed him the way how analogously to distinguish the general cubic curve into its numerous component species in a manner which he continued to refine and polish over the next thirty years. Nor did its chief significance for him reside in its other novelties of technique; even though its construction of the subnormal at a point of a curve was the foundation of his own generalised insight into the derivative of a 'smoothly' continuous function, as we would now put it. Above all, I would assert, the *Geometrie* gave him his first true vision of the universalising power of the algebraic free variable, of its capacity to generalise the particular and lay bare its inner structure to outward inspection.

To the bare elements of algebra Newton had, a little while before this late summer of 1664, received a beginner's introduction through William Oughtred's *Clavis Mathematicæ (Key to Mathematics)*. The third book of the *Geometrie* now carried him on to grasp the niceties of reducing cubic and quartic equations to canonical form, and so to standard solutions which the free variable allowed to be encapsulated in one single formula, once for all. But, as Newton came also quickly to understand, equations—unless these be, as we say, identities—confine the

7. Literally, what must be changed having been changed; that is, altering the details that pertain to the individual but keeping the general principle. [Editor]

algebraic expressions which they connect, permitting them only limited possibilities of existence. In contradistinction, a true free variable allows what Newton was soon to call a 'universal arithmetic' of quantities and magnitudes, unimpeded in its capabilities of particular representation. And in geometrical counterpart the way was open—as Descartes let his reader but momentarily glimpse—to a similar universal calculus of all that is spatially definable. If you wish, the geometrical plane which for Newton in his youth had been laboriously marked out by ruler and compasses into measured rectilinear and circular plots was now a communal field in which complexly curving lines could be marked out at will, their intrinsic properties mapped out and hierarchically ordered. Gone were static boundaries and their markers: in their place freely variable points whose traces, 'loci', could be specified generally by defining relationships with respect to base-points and base-lines of whose particular positions they are yet essentially independent. With respect to those 'origins', 'axes' and the co-ordinate line-lengths departing therefrom—any of a whole variety of equivalent systems, generalised Cartesian and polar and combinations of these, which Newton's fertile ingenuity soon contrived—the notion of an arbitrary 'geometrical' curve could now be formulated as one representable by a corresponding algebraic defining relationship between them. The road was open to explore the slope and 'crookednesse' (curvature) of such curves in a general way, to frame procedures for evaluating their areas and arclengths, and for 'analytically' determining the location of their inflexions, nodes and cusps, for ordering them according to the algebraic degrees of their defining equations: an 'obvious' mode of classification which Descartes had not seen point in adopting, but one whose acceptance affords at once the fruitful criterion of invariance of such degree under geometrical transformation, as Newton was quick to seize upon.

And so on, and so on. In the 'magical' twenty-five months from September 1664 which tradition, following his own preference in old age, allows to be Newton's *annus mirabilis* a mathematician was born. Never did seventeenth-century man build up so great a store of mathematical expertise, much of his own discovery, in so short a time. By freeing the upper bounding ordinate of the series of curvilinear areas through whose interpolation Wallis once hoped to attain the exact quadrature of the circle—but had, in lieu, to settle for his infinite product for $4/\pi$—Newton was able straightforwardly to derive the series expansion term by term of its general binomial ordinate, and thereafter analogously to give series quadrature of curves whose ordinate can be approximated by any converging polynomial of 'infinite' degree. From Descartes' mode of constructing the subnormal to a curve he passed to determine a universal rule for finding its tangent-slope; and then; in the steps of Heuraet, to demonstrate that this method of tangents and that of quadrature of curves are inverse operations. Make the base variable in any corpus of algebraic expressions one of uniformly flowing 'time', as Newton was to do in autumn 1665—whether or no he was inspired to do so by attending a contemporary Lucasian lecture of Isaac Barrow's; call the 'speed' of any other fluent quantity with respect to this uniform flow its 'fluxion'; and you have the essence of Newton's analysis by fluents and their fluxional 'moments' of related 'instantaneous' increase or decrement. Add the insight, which he attained by the middle 1680's, that the higher-order fluxions of a fluent quantity are, when divided by the factorials of their order, the successive coefficients of the advancing powers of that fluent in what we call the 'Taylor' expansion of its increment, and the path is wide open to the subtle infinitesimals at which he became so adept in his mature years, and in his *Principia* not least. Descend again to the realm of the numerical, and at once there are waiting to be gathered in offshoot the formulas of finite difference interpolation and of approximate quadrature in whose concoction and employment Newton was without peer in his day. . . .

I am into technicalities again, and to a self-defeating end. Newton's many-faceted mathematical advances are properly to be savoured in their depth only through long hours of private study, with much sucking of one's pen and creasing of the forehead. To their full and just appreciation I know no royal short-cut. The texts of his extant mathematical papers are now to be found collected within the green jackets of eight bulky volumes, upon whose quality and effectiveness it would be narcissistic for me to comment. Well done or no, distorted in their blinkered editorial vision as might be, you may choose—if not, like Dr Johnson when asked his opinion of women preachers, to compare the performance to that of dogs walking upon their hind-legs—at least to murmur your sympathetic wonder that the thing is done at all.

Be that as it may, do let me insist upon what may appear to you a vacuous truism: that a man who makes and goes on making mathematical advances so profound and so far-reaching as Newton did achieve is—whatever else—a mathematician to his toe-tips. From the first, he regarded everything in his view with an outward eye attuned to arithmetical and geometrical niceties, and with an inner vision which sensed the mathematicisable under-structure in all things. General historians of past scientific development rightly concern themselves, even in their most 'internalist' studies, primarily with mathematics in her applied rôle as bonded servant to mechanical, physical and astronomical advance. In their impatience to be hard at the ontologies and methodologies of scientific theories or head down into the concrete workaday realisms of scientific practice, they so often just brush mathematical considerations aside as mere ancillary technicalities wholly secondary to what is important in exploring the unending past quest for the truth underlying observable phenomena, and for its viable codification in predictive rationale. And yet, is it not true that the book of nature which was for Galileo set out in straight lines and circles—and, let me be fair, an occasional parabola—was not penned for him in more complicated form largely because he had no grasp of geometrical curves of higher order? To Newton, who—put his analytical and projective listings together—knew all 78 species of cubic, and also many a curve of higher degree and of transcendental order, the natural world was writ in a correspondingly complex and intricate form.

* * *

POSTSCRIPT

Albert Einstein on Newton's *Opticks* †

Fortunate Newton, happy childhood of science! He who has time and tranquillity can by reading this book live again the wonderful events which the great Newton experienced in his young days. Nature to him was an open book, whose letters he could read without effort. The conceptions which he used to reduce the material of experience to order seemed to flow spontaneously from experience itself, from the beautiful experiments which he ranged in order like playthings and describes with an affectionate wealth of detail. In one person he combined the experimenter, the theorist, the mechanic and, not least, the artist in exposition. He stands before us strong, certain, and alone: his joy in creation and his minute precision are evident in every word and in every figure.

Reflexion, refraction, the formation of images by lenses, the mode of operation of the eye, the spectral decomposition and the recomposition of the different kinds of light, the invention of the reflecting telescope, the first foundations of colour theory, the elementary theory of the rainbow pass by us in procession, and finally come his observations of the colours of thin films as the origin of the next great theoretical advance, which had to await, over a hundred years, the coming of Thomas Young.

Newton's age has long since been passed through the sieve of oblivion, the doubtful striving and suffering of his generation has vanished from our ken; the works of some few great thinkers and artists have remained, to delight and ennoble us and those who come after us. Newton's discoveries have passed into the stock of accepted knowledge: this new edition of his work on optics is nevertheless to be welcomed with warmest thanks, because it alone can afford us the enjoyment of a look at the personal activity of this unique man.

† Isaac Newton, *Opticks*, based on the 4th ed. (New York: Dover Publications, 1952), pp. lix–lx. Reprinted by permission of Dover Publications, Inc.

Biographical Register

Jean Le Rond d'Alembert (1717–83), French mathematician.
Conte Francesco Algarotti (1712–64), Italian literary figure, author of *Newtonianism for the Ladies* (1737).
Anaximander (sixth century BC), early Greek philosopher.
Apelles (fourth century BC), considered to be one of the great artists of ancient Greece, famous for exhibiting his completed works to the public view of passersby.
Apollonius (third century BC), Greek geometer.
Archimedes (c. 287–212 BC), Greek geometer and philosopher.
Aristotle (384–322 BC), philosopher of ancient Greece (see *Aristotelian natural philosophy* in the Glossary).
Arius (d. c. 335), early Christian theologian. The movement espousing his theological views was called Arianism.
Artephius. Two works held in great authority by alchemists carried this name. If there were indeed such a historical person, he was possibly the Arab Al Toghrāi (twelfth century).
Athanasius (c. 295–373), early Christian theologian.
Augustine (354–430), early Christian theologian.
Francis Bacon (1561–1626), English philosopher and statesman, celebrated for writings on scientific method.
Isaac Barrow (1630–77), English mathematician and theologian, Newton's predecessor as Lucasian Professor of Mathematics at Cambridge University.
Erasmus Bartholin (1585–1629), Danish mathematician and crystallographer.
Richard Bentley (1662–1742), English theologian and classical scholar, preached a series of sermons in 1692 that were the first popularizations of the Newtonian system of the world.
Henri Bergson (1859–1941), French philosopher, author of *Creative Evolution* (1907).
Bernard of Trevisan (sometimes given as Bernard of Trier; 1406–1490), Italian (or perhaps German) alchemist.
Johann Bernoulli (1667–1748), Swiss mathematician and natural philosopher.
Nicolas-François Blondel (1618–86), French military engineer; published *L'art de jeter les bombes* (1683).

Samuel Bochart (1599–1667), French Huguenot theologian and scholar.

Roger Joseph Boscovich (1711–87), Jesuit, Croatian natural philosopher, author of *A Theory of Natural Philosophy* (1758).

Robert Boyle (1627–91), English chemist and natural philosopher, improved the air pump and made important experiments on gases.

Gian Domenico Cassini (1625–1712), French astronomer of Italian origin.

Bonaventura Cavalieri (or Cavalerius; c.1598–1647), Italian mathematician, known for theory of "indivisibles," an early version of what developed into the infinitesimal calculus.

Walter Charleton (1620–1707), English natural philosopher.

Marcus Tullius Cicero (106–43 BC), Roman orator, scholar, and statesman.

Alexis-Claude Clairaut (1713–65), French mathematician and astronomer, wrote a commentary on the *Principia* for the French translation by the Marquise du Chastellet (1756).

John Clarke (fl. 1697), translated the Cartesian *Traité de physique* of Jacques Rohault (1620–75) into Latin, the language of university texts, in 1697; in subsequent editions brother Samuel added an increasing number of notes that undercut the Cartesian exposition by introducing "corrections" taken from Newton's *Principia* and *Opticks*. See also **Samuel Clarke.**

Samuel Clarke (1675–1729), English theologian and philosopher, translated Newton's *Opticks* into Latin (London, 1706), defended Newton's natural philosophy in a famous correspondence with Leibniz in 1715–16. See also **John Clarke.**

John Collins (1625–83), English mathematician.

Auguste Comte (1798–1857), French philosopher, author of the philosophy called positivism.

John Conduitt (1688–1737), husband of Newton's niece.

Constantine (c.280–337) effectively became emperor of the western Roman Empire with a military victory in 312; later he consolidated his supremacy over the whole of the empire. His conversion to Christianity in 312 marked the beginning of the conversion of the late empire.

Nicolaus Copernicus (1473–1543), Polish astronomer, proposed in 1543 that the sun rather than the earth is at the center of the universe and that the earth is one among six planets that circle the sun.

Roger Cotes (1682–1716), English mathematician who helped Newton prepare the second edition of his *Principia*.

Ralph Cudworth (1617–88), English philosopher, one of the Cambridge Platonists.

Cylennius, or Silenus, was frequently associated in Greek mythology with Pan, the god of pastures, shepherds, and their flocks.

John Dalton (1766–1844), British chemist, founder of the chemical atomic theory.

Charles Darwin (1809–82), English author of the theory of evolution.

Humphry Davy (1778–1829), British chemist, discovered the chemical element chlorine and other halogens.

Democritus (fifth century BC), Greek philosopher, often considered to be the founder of the atomic theory.

John Theophilus Desaguliers (1683–1744), British experimental physicist of French Huguenot origin.

René Descartes (1596–1650), French philosopher, mathematician, and physicist, considered in Newton's day to be the chief proponent of the mechanical philosophy (for which see the Glossary).

Jan De Witt (1623–72), Dutch mathematician and statesman; his "Elements of Curved Lines" was published in 1661.

Denis Diderot (1713–84), French literary figure and philosopher, editor of the *Encyclopédie* (1751–80).

Kenelm Digby (1603–65), English man of letters and natural philosopher.

Diogenes Laertius (third century), author of a history of Greek philosophy.

Betty Jo Teeter Dobbs (1930–94), a contemporary American historian of science.

Nicolas de Duillier, see **Nicolas Fatio de Duillier.**

Epicurus (341–270 BC), Greek philosopher, endorsed the atomic theory.

Euclid (third century BC), Greek geometer.

Eudoxus (c. 400–c. 347 BC), Greek geometer.

Leonhard Euler (1707–83), Swiss mathematician and physicist, innovator of fluid dynamics and physics of deformable bodies.

Eusebius of Caesarea (c. 260–c. 340), early Christian historian.

Nicolas Fatio de Duillier (1664–1753), Swiss mathematician resident in England.

Pierre de Fermat (1601–65), French mathematician, coinventor with Descartes of analytical geometry.

John Flamsteed (1646–1719), English astronomer.

Galileo Galilei (1564–1642), Italian astronomer, mathematician, and natural philosopher.

Pierre Gassendi (1592–1655), French philosopher, important in revival of atomic theory.

Willem Jacob 'sGravesande (1688–1742), Dutch experimental physicist, author of a major exposition of Newtonian natural philosophy.

Gregory Nazianzen (c. 329–88), early Christian theologian.

David Gregory (1659–1708), Scottish mathematician and natural philosopher, author of an extended commentary on Newton's *Principia*.

Henry Guerlac (1910–85), American historian of science.

Edmond (or Edmund) Halley (c. 1656–1742), English geometer and geophysicist as well as astronomer, discovered that comets move in periodic orbits, the most famous such one being named after him ("Halley's comet," with a period of 75½ years); goaded Newton into writing the *Principia* and saw that work through the press.

Francis Hauksbee (c. 1666–1713), English experimenter employed as a demonstrator by the Royal Society, famous for his experiments on electricity.

Johannes Baptista Van Helmont (1579–1644), a Paracelsian chemist from what is now Belgium.

Heraclides of Pontus (c. 388–c. 315 BC), Greek astronomer, inventor of a system of the universe much like that of Tyche Brahe.

Pierre Herigone (fl. c. 1630–c. 1650), French mathematician.

Hendrik van Heuraet (1633–c. 1660), Dutch mathematician.

Thomas Hobbes (1588–1679), English political and natural philosopher.

Robert Hooke (1635–1702), English natural philosopher who studied light, mechanics, and astronomy, quarreled with Newton over Newton's theory of light and colors and again over priority with respect to universal gravity.

Jan Hudde (1628–1704), Dutch mathematician.

Christiaan Huygens (1629–95), Dutch natural philosopher, mathematician, and astronomer, discovered a satellite of Saturn and was the major advocate of a wave theory of light (see *Iceland spar* in Glossary). He designed the first precision clock. He also discovered that, as long as the mercury remained in contact with the end of the tube, a column as high as seventy inches could be realized in a barometric tube.

Samuel Johnson (1709–84), English man of letters.

Ben Jonson (c. 1573–1637), English dramatist.

Josephus (first century), a major authority in the Jewish tradition.

Justin Martyr (c. 100–c. 165), early Christian theologian.

John Keill (1671–1721), British follower of Newton who wrote a popularized account of his science.

Johannes Kepler (1571–1630), German astronomer, demonstrated in 1609 that the planetary orbits are ellipses rather than circles.

Alexandre Koyré (1892–1964), historian of science and philosophy who stressed the development of scientific ideas in their intellectual context of philosophical and religious thought; made important contributions to our understanding of Galileo, Kepler, and especially Newton.

Joseph-Louis Lagrange (1736–1813), French mathematician, author of *Analytic Mechanics* (1788).

Philippe de La Hire (1649–1718), French geometer, author of

"New Elements of Conic Sections" (1679) and "Conic Sections" (1685).

Charles Lamb (1775–1834), English essayist.

Pierre Simon Marquis de LaPlace (1749–1827), French mathematical physicist, transformed Newton's "rational mechanics" into "celestial mechanics," the title he gave to his book of 1799.

Antoine-Laurent Lavoisier (1734–94), French chemist considered to be the father of modern chemistry.

Gottfried Wilhelm Leibniz (1646–1716), German mathematician and philosopher, generally acknowledged today as an independent co-discoverer with Newton of the calculus; accused by Newton and his followers of plagiarism in the discovery of the calculus; argued that Newton's concept of universal gravity was a return to *occult qualities* (for which see Glossary).

Leucippus (fifth century BC), Greek philosopher often held to be the originator of atomism.

John Locke (1632–1704), English philosopher.

Anthony Lucas (1633–93), English Jesuit who wrote against Newton's theory of colors.

Lucretius (first century BC), Roman poet, expounded the atomic philosophy in his long poem *De rerum natura (On Nature)*.

Ernst Mach (1838–1916), German physicist, positivist philosopher of science, and historian of science.

Colin Maclaurin (1698–1746), Scottish mathematician, author of a popularization of Newton's natural philosophy, *An Account of Sir Isaac Newton's Philosophical Discoveries* (1748).

Pierre Joseph Macquer (1718–1784), French chemist.

Macrobius (fl. c.400), Latin grammarian and philosopher.

Michael Maier (c.1568–1622), German alchemist.

Moses Maimonides (1135–1204), an important authority in the Jewish tradition.

Pierre Louis Moreau de Maupertuis (1698–1759), French scientist, measured a degree along an arc of the meridian in Lapland to prove Newton's theory of the oblate shape of the earth.

John Mayow (1641–79), English chemist and natural philosopher.

Joseph Mede (1586–1638), English biblical scholar, author of *Clavis apocalyptica* (the English version translated this as *The Key of the Revelation*) (1627).

Nicolaus Mercator (or Kauffman; c.1619–87), Danish or German mathematician and astronomer, author of a much used astronomy textbook published in London in 1676.

Abraham de Moivre (1667–1754), English mathematician of French Huguenot origin.

John de Monte-Snyder, (fl. c.1650–c.1700), Dutch or German alchemist.

Henry More (1614–87), English philosopher, one of the Cambridge Platonists.

Louis Bernard Guyton de Morveau (1737–1816), French chemist.

Petrus van Musschenbroek (1692–1761), Dutch experimental physicist, one of the discoverers of the Leyden jar, the first capacitor.

William Neile (1637–70), English mathematician.

Thomas Norton (b. late fourteenth century), English alchemist.

Henry Oldenburg (1618–77), born in Germany but spent most of his adult life in England; became one of the first secretaries of the Royal Society of London; founder and editor of the Royal Society's journal, *Philosophical Transactions*.

Origen (c.185–c.254), early Christian theologian.

Orpheus, a legendary hero of ancient Greece and patron of a religious movement dependent on sacred writings supposed to be his compositions.

Andreas Osiander (1498–1552), saw Copernicus' book, *De revolutionibus orbium coelestium* (1543), through the press. He included an unsigned preface saying that the Copernican system was only a mathematical hypothesis that did not claim to represent physical reality.

William Oughtred (1575–1660), English mathematician.

Pappus (fourth century), Greek geometer whose *Collection* is a major source of information about Greek geometry.

Paracelsus (Theophrastus Bombastus von Hohenheim; 1493–1541), German chemist, founded a new school of chemistry and of medicine based on chemistry.

Ignace Gaston Pardies (1636–73), French Jesuit natural philosopher who made investigations of optics, statics, and kinematics.

Blaise Pascal (1623–62), French mathematician, philosopher, and physicist.

Henry Pemberton (1694–1771), British doctor and amateur mathematician who edited the third edition of the *Principia* under Newton's direction; author of a popularization of Newtonian natural philosophy, *A View of Sir Isaac Newton's Philosophy* (1728).

Philo (c.30 BC–c.AD 45), an authority in the Jewish tradition.

Plato (427–348 or 347 BC), philosopher of ancient Greece.

Pliny the Elder (23–79), famous for his compendium of knowledge titled *Natural History*.

Plutarch (c.46–c.120), Greek biographer and essayist.

Joannes Pontanus (probably Johann Brückner, d. 1572), German alchemist.

Alexander Pope (1688–1744), English poet, author of a famous couplet about Newton and "Nature's laws."

Karl Popper (b. 1902), contemporary Austro-British philosopher of science.

Porphyry (234–c. 305), Neoplatonic philosopher.

Joseph Priestley (1733–1804), British Unitarian theologian, chemist, and natural philosopher, spent his last years in America.

Proclus (410–85), late Greek Neoplatonic philosopher.

Pythagoras (sixth century BC), an early Greek philosopher, resident in the Greek colony in southern Italy, developed a school of number mysticism.

John Ray (1627–1705), English naturalist.

Gilles Personne de Roberval (1602–75), French mathematician and natural philosopher.

Ole Roemer (1644–1710), a Danish astronomer, made the first measurement of the velocity of light from astronomical phenomena.

Jacques Rohault, see **John Clarke.**

Léon Rosenfeld (1904–74), Belgian physicist and historian of science, author of (among other things) "Newton and the Law of Gravitation" (1965).

Alexandre Toussaint de Limojon de Saint Disdier (c. 1630–89), French literary figure and alchemist.

Michael Sendivogius (1566–1636), Polish alchemist.

Lucius Annaeus Seneca (c. 4 BC–AD 65), Roman statesman and philosopher.

Sextus Empiricus (second or third century), Roman author of a work about the skeptical tradition in Greek philosophy.

Silenus, see **Cylennius.**

Simplicius (sixth century), commentator on Aristotle.

René-François de Sluse (1622–85), mathematician from the area that is now Belgium.

Adam Smith (1723–90), Scottish father of economics, author of *The Wealth of Nations* (1776).

Willebrord Snel (or Snel van Royen; 1580–1626), Dutch physicist, discoverer of Snel's law of refraction.

Snyders, see **John de Monte-Snyder.**

Baruch Spinoza (1632–77), Dutch-Jewish philosopher.

George Ernst Stahl (1659–1734), German chemist famous for the concept of phlogiston.

George Starkey (1628–65), Anglo-American alchemist born in Bermuda and educated at Harvard, wrote under the pseudonym of Eirenaeus Philalethes.

Dugald Stewart (1753–1828), Scottish philosopher.

Strabo (63 BC–c. AD 23), Greek geographer and historian.

James Stuart (1633–1701). As James II, he succeeded Charles II as king of England in 1685.

Thales (sixth century BC), the first known Greek philosopher, hence the fountainhead of the Greek philosophic tradition. A resident of one of the Greek cities on the Ionian coast of what is now Turkey.

Evangelista Torricelli (1608–47), Italian mathematician and natural philosopher, constructed the first barometer in 1644. Torricelli's vacuum refers to the space above the mercury in the barometer.

Trevisan, see **Bernard of Trevisan.**

Basil Valentine. A number of alchemical works circulated under this name. There may well not have been such a historical person, but possibly he was a German monk of the fifteenth century.

François Viète (1540–1603), French mathematician who codified algebra.

Virgil (70–19 BC), Roman poet.

Voltaire (Francois-Marie Arouet; 1694–1778), French literary figure and philosopher, author of, among many works, *Letters on the English; or Philosophical Letters* (1734) and a much read *Introduction to the Philosophy of Mr. Newton* (1737).

John Wallis (1616–1703), English mathematician, worked in algebra and developed a method to "integrate" by means of infinitesimals in *Arithmetica infinitorum* (1656).

Richard Watson (1737–1816), British chemist, author of *Chemical Essays* (1781–87).

William Whiston (1667–1752), English natural philosopher.

Andrew D. White (1832–1918), American scholar, author of *History of the Warfare of Science with Theology in Christendom* (1896).

Alfred North Whitehead (1861–1947), English mathematician, philosopher, and logician; in the last part of his life he taught at Harvard.

Derek Thomas Whiteside (b. 1932), editor of the eight-volume set of Newton's *Mathematical Papers*, the world's leading scholar in the area of Newton's mathematics.

Basil Willey (1891–1978), English literary scholar.

Christopher Wren (1632–1723), greatest of English architects, also a geometer and natural philosopher.

Thomas Young (1773–1829), British natural philosopher, revived the wave theory of light.

Glossary

active agent: see **alchemy**.

aether: a kind of material substance that was thought to fill all space, impinging on other bodies and affecting their motion. It was considered to be invisible, imponderable, and not detectable by any of our senses. It could permeate the pores of ordinary bodies and was thought to be the cause of such diverse phenomena as gravitational, magnetic, electrical, and optical effects. See **mechanical philosophy**.

alchemy: although associated in the twentieth-century mind exclusively with the attempt to transmute base metals into gold, alchemy also embodied a conception of nature and its phenomena radically different in most respects from the mechanical philosophy that came to prevail by the end of the seventeenth century. Alchemists saw nature in organic terms and spoke of generation, death, and putrefaction, all of which figured prominently in their descriptions of chemical phenomena; metals, they claimed, also underwent these basic transformations. Alchemists believed that all things, including metals, are generated from male and female principles. Frequently the two principles were identified as sulfur and mercury, although alchemists did not mean common sulfur and mercury. Metals were thought literally to grow, in the earth and in the laboratory, where the process can be accelerated by the alchemist. One common matter was believed to compose all the substances in nature; gold is the most perfect form that it can attain—it is the result of the natural process that generates metals reaching maturity. Alchemists attempted to facilitate this process. An active agent, the source of the transformation of substances, was supposed to lie hidden in all things. Alchemical literature was full of references to this agent under a wild proliferation of metaphors, such as Prometheus, the Green Lion, and the Mercury of Seven Eagles, that suggested activity and power. This agent is also what alchemists called the Philosophers' Stone. The active agent was believed to be encumbered by the base matter in which it was plunged, and many of the alchemical processes were concerned with purging and purifying in order to liberate the active agent, which would then be able to act.

analysis and synthesis: the methods of resolution and composition. According to Newton (*Opticks*, Query 31), analysis "consists in making Experiments and Observations, and in drawing general conclusions from them by Induction," whereas the method of synthesis "consists in assuming the Causes discovered, and established as Principles, and by them explaining the Phaenomena proceeding from them." In mathematics, analysis means the use of algebraic methods, synthesis the use of geometric ones.

aphelion: that point in the orbit of a planet or comet that is farthest from the sun.

Aristotelian natural philosophy: From the revival of higher learning in the thirteenth century until the early seventeenth century, the prevailing natural philosophy in Europe was based on Aristotle. It was utterly unlike the natural philosophy with which the West has been familiar since the seventeenth century. Aristotelian philosophy approached nature primarily in taxonomic terms, seeking to locate each existent being in the hierarchy of natural order more than to uncover laws that govern phenomena. It held that the nature of every existing thing is defined by its specific form and that the form finds existence only as it is embodied in matter. Aristotelian philosophy was organic and applied the categories of living things to the whole natural order. It was also qualitative; that is, in contrast to later philosophy, it asserted that such qualities as color and heat are not merely appearances but existent realities.

Babylonia and Sumer: the sites of two early civilizations in the Near East.

Boyle's law of gases: a law discovered by Robert Boyle, which states that the pressure of an enclosed gas is inversely proportional to the volume.

Cartesian natural philosophy: the new philosophy in Newton's youth, based on the teachings of René Descartes, sometimes known as the mechanical philosophy (see **mechanical philosophy**). Descartes held that the physical world consists of nothing but matter, the nature of which is extension in three dimensions. Thus, he asserted that nature is a plenum of unlimited extent, and he denied the possibility of a vacuum. Matter is divided into particles (which are not atoms, because they can be altered), and all the phenomena of nature are produced by particles of matter in motion. There is a constant quantity of motion in the universe. Because nature is a plenum, motion can only take place in closed orbits. The heavens consist of an infinity of vortices, huge whirlpools with lucid bodies (that is, bodies composed of extremely tiny particles in extremely rapid motion) at their centers, in which other opaque bodies (planets) are carried around. Descartes called the finest matter the first element. It not only composes suns, but it is present throughout nature, filling all the spaces between larger particles. He invoked this matter (see also **aether**) as the cause of numerous natural phenomena. Suns can decay (that is, crust over), at which point they are sucked into other vortices as planets or are flung from vortex to vortex as comets. In the Cartesian philosophy, comets (which had not been reduced to mathematical treatment in Descartes' time) do not follow regular orbits around one sun; he treated the tails of comets as purely optical phenomena, a pecular refraction. Bodies constrained to move in a circular path continually endeavor to recede from the center. Hence, in every vortex there is a constant outward pressure. This was Descartes' conception of light—a pressure transmitted instantaneously through a material medium. The turning of the vortex generates tiny screw-shaped particles, of both left-hand and right-hand threads, by which Descartes explained magnetic phenomena with their two polarities. He explained tides by the pressure of the moon on the matter in the vortex around the earth.

Cartesians: followers of Descartes, who believed in his principles of philosophy and science.

comets: see **Cartesian natural philosophy.**

Commercium Epistolicum: or "Epistolary Exchange"; the title given to a volume published in 1712 by a committee of the Royal Society that investigated the respective claims of Newton and Leibniz to the invention of the calculus; Newton actually wrote the draft of the committee's report.

common matter: see **alchemy.**

conception of light: see **Cartesian natural philosophy.**

constant quantity of motion: see **Cartesian natural philosophy.**

crucial experiment: an experiment especially designed to decide between alternative theories or between alternative suppositions.

death: see **alchemy.**

degree of refrangibility: as light passes from one medium (say, air) into another (say, glass or water), it is refracted (or the ray is bent); for any such combination of mediums (say, air and water), each color has a different degree of refrangibility or is bent by a different amount; see **refraction.**

diffraction: sometimes called inflection in the seventeenth century; a class of optical phenomena, essentially the bending of light rays into the shadow.

double refraction: a phenomenon, discovered by the seventeenth-century Danish physicist Erasmus Bartholin and studied by Huygens and by Newton, whereby (in Iceland crystal or Iceland spar, i.e., calcite), a single incident ray of light emerges as two separate rays that are polarized with respect to each other.

effluvia, electric and magnetic: see **mechanical philosophy.**

endeavor to recede: see **Cartesian natural philosophy.**

experimental philosophy: a name given to the new physical sciences of the seventeenth century, meaning a science based on both experience and what we would recognize as experiment; see **natural philosophy.**

first element: see **Cartesian natural philosophy.**

flexibility: see **diffraction.**

furlong: an eighth of a mile.

generation: see **alchemy.**

gravity (matter causing gravity): see **mechanical philosophy.**

Iceland crystal or Iceland spar: see **double refraction.**

infinitesimals: see **vanishing infinitesimals.**

inflection (or inflexion): see **diffraction.**

intention and remission: technical terms originating in late medieval science to indicate a quantitative increase or decrease in any quality.

Keynes manuscripts: a collection of Newtonian papers in King's College, Cambridge.

law of refraction: see **refraction.**

Leibnizians: followers of the philosopher Leibniz, who adhered to the principles of the mechanical philosophy set forth by Descartes.

locus problem: finding a curve or other geometric figure that satisfies a given set of conditions.

male and female principles: see **alchemy.**

mechanical causes: explanations of natural phenomena in terms of "matter and motion," primarily the impact of one body on another; see **mechanical philosophy.**

mechanical philosophy: a philosophy of nature according to which all explanations of natural phenomena were to be made in terms of matter and motion. Cartesian natural philosophy was one form of mechanical philosophy but not the only one that appeared in the seventeenth century. The ancient atomic philosophy was also revived, and many variations on the theme of particles of matter in motion were possible. All mechanical philosophies called on some form of matter (frequently called aether) that was not directly perceptible to explain phenomena not obviously the result of particles impinging on one another. They posited invisible electrical and magnetic effluvia, for example, to explain attractions and repulsions and a gravitational aether streaming down toward the earth and carrying bodies down with it.

mercury: see **alchemy.**

Micrographia: a book by Robert Hooke, published in 1665, dealing with the use of the microscope, but also containing observations on light and other topics in physics; introduced the expression *experimentum crucis* ("crucial experiment"); see **crucial experiment.**

natural philosophy (or philosophy): a category that, in Newton's day, encompassed the physical sciences and sometimes included aspects of the life and earth sciences as well.

occult qualities: literally, hidden qualities, invoked by Aristotelian philosophers to explain certain phenomena or properties. Such qualities as redness and heat were not occult; they could be perceived directly. The quality by which, for example, the drug scamony purged was occult; the quality itself could not be perceived, although the effect it produced certainly could. Opponents of Newton on the continent accused him of reviving occult qualities, which the mechanical philosophy had banished, with his concept of universal gravitation.

opaque (or totally opaque): see **total internal reflection.**

orbs: see **solid orbs.**

parallax: the parallax of the sun is the angle that would be subtended by the earth's radius if it were seen from the sun. Since the length of the earth's radius is known, the parallax of the sun determines its distance from the earth.

perfect substance: see **alchemy.**

perihelion: that point on the orbit of a planet or comet that is nearest to the sun.

peripatetic: synonymous with Aristotelian; see **Aristotelian natural philosophy.**

Philosophical Transactions: the journal published by the Royal Society of London, one of the oldest such scientific publications; the issues contained reports of research, statements of new theories, book reviews, notes, and letters on scientific subjects from correspondents.

pineal gland: a gland in the brain in which Descartes was convinced the sensorium was located; see **sensorium.**

plenum: see **Cartesian natural philosophy.**

Portsmouth collection: A collection of Newtonian manuscripts in the Cambridge University Library.

presocratics: the Greek philosophers before Socrates (c. 470–399 BC).

Ptolemaic system: the system, devised by Greek astronomers and put into its enduring form by the Alexandrian astronomer Ptolemy in the second century AD, according to which the earth is at rest in the center of the universe and the astronomical phenomena arise from a double motion: a daily rotation of the universe and a motion compounded of circles (deferents and epicycles) for each planet.

purging: see **alchemy.**

purification: see **alchemy.**

putrefaction: see **alchemy.**

qualitative conception of nature: see Aristotelian natural philosophy.

refraction: the phenomenon of change in direction of a ray of light as it passes from one transparent medium into another. This phenomenon—studied by Ptolemy—was reduced to law by the seventeenth-century Dutch scientist Willebrord Snel and by René Descartes; the law of refraction is sometimes known as the law of sines or the sine law; see **Snel's law of refraction.**

refrangibility, see **degree of refrangibility.**

remission, see **intention and remission.**

Royal Society: an organization dedicated to natural philosophy founded in London in 1660. It still exists, the most prestigious body in British and perhaps world science.

screw-shaped particles: see **Cartesian natural philosophy.**

sensorium: the location where, according to seventeenth-century conceptions, information from the senses was brought together and perceived by the immaterial soul. See also **pineal gland.**

sine of incidence: the sine of the angle between an incoming ray of light and the line perpendicular to a surface that the ray strikes.

sine of refraction: the sine of the angle between a ray of light that has been refracted at a surface between two media (say, air and water) and the line perpendicular to the surface.

Snel's law of refraction: the law of refraction of light, or the law of sines, discovered in the seventeenth century by Willebrord Snel; see **refraction.**

solid orbs: in the older (pre-sixteenth-century) astronomy, it was thought that the planets (including the sun and moon) were imbedded in huge crystalline spheres, whose rotation carried the planets around.

specific form: see Aristotelian natural philosophy.

stoics: a school of philosophy in ancient Greece.

sulfur: see **alchemy.**

suns decaying: see **Cartesian natural philosophy.**

synthesis: see **analysis and synthesis.**

tides: see **Cartesian natural philosophy.**

total internal reflection: when light in a transparent medium denser than air (such as glass or water) is incident on a surface at an angle greater than a critical angle, it does not pass through the surface into the air but is reflected back into the medium. The surface is effectively opaque.

vanishing infinitesimals: refers to minimally small increments of variables, in the limit as they tend toward zero; part of mathematics treated today in terms of differentials.

virtuoso: a natural philosopher; frequently the word carried the connotation of a gentlemen amateur who dabbled in natural philosophy.

vortex: see **Cartesian natural philosophy.**

Woolsthorpe: the hamlet in Lincolnshire where Newton was born.

Yahuda Papers: a collection containing the majority of Newton's theological manuscripts in the Jewish National and University Library, Jerusalem.

Glossary of Chemical Terms

AF: aqua fortis; probably what chemistry now calls nitric acid.
alcahest: a term popularized by Helmont to signify the universal solvent or agent.
alchemy (and terms related to alchemy): see Glossary.
allum (or alum): probably what chemistry now calls potassium aluminum sulfate.
ana: in equal quantities.
antimony: what the seventeenth century called antimony was the mineral stibnite, antimony sulfide. What they called regulus of antimony was metallic antimony refined from the mineral.
aqua fortis: probably what chemistry now calls nitric acid.
aqua regia: a mixture of nitric acid and hydrochloric acid.
aqua vitae: literally water of life; the standard name for brandy.
B.M. (Balneum Mariae): literally Mary's bath, a warm water bath.
balsam of sulfur: probably sulfur dissolved in oil or turpentine.
calx: what chemistry now calls an oxide.
cinnabar: a mineral, what chemistry now calls mercuric sulfide.
cuticle: a thin film.
drachm: one eighth of an ounce.
lapis calaminaris: an ore of zinc, zinc carbonate.
litharge: a mineral, probably what chemistry now calls lead monoxide.
luna: literally, moon; in alchemy, silver.
luna cornea: literally hornlike silver: what chemistry now calls the naturally occurring chloride of silver fused.
markasites: a mineral; what chemistry now considers a class of sulfides including iron, copper, and arsenic pyrite.
mercurius dulcis: literally dulcified mercury: calomel, which chemistry now calls mercurious chloride.
mercury sublimate: what chemistry now calls mercuric oxide.
niter (or nitre): saltpeter, what chemistry now calls potassium nitrate.
oil of sulfur per campanam: a concentrated form of what chemistry now calls sulfuric acid, prepared by burning sulfur and condensing the fumes under a bell-like container.
oil of vitriol: what chemistry now calls concentrated sulfuric acid.
orrichine stone: orichalcum (or auricalchum), a yellow ore or alloy of copper.
regulus of antimony: see **antimony.**
run per deliquium: to deliquesce, to dissolve in moisture absorbed from the air.

sal alkali: probably what chemistry now calls potassium carbonate.
sal ammoniac (or sal armoniac): probably what chemistry now calls ammonium chloride.
salt of tartar: probably what chemistry now calls potassium carbonate.
saltpeter: what chemistry now calls potassium nitrate.
spirit of salt: what chemistry now calls hydrochloric acid.
spirit of soot: a product containing ammonium salts obtained by distilling soot.
spirit of urine: an impure aqueous ammonia containing what chemistry now calls ammonium carbonate.
spirit of wine: what chemistry now calls alcohol.
vitriol: what chemistry now calls a sulfate, probably of iron or copper.

Isaac Newton: A Chronology

Early Oct. 1642	Newton's father, Isaac Newton, Sr., dies in Woolsthorpe, Lincolnshire.
Dec. 25, 1642	Newton born in Woolsthorpe, Lincolnshire.
Early 1646	Remarriage of Newton's mother to the Rev. Barnabas Smith. Newton left at Woolsthorpe with grandparents.
Aug. 1653	Death of Newton's stepfather. Newton's mother returned to Woolsthorpe.
Spring 1655	Enrolled in grammar school in Grantham, Lincolnshire.
Dec. 1659	Returned home to manage estate.
Sept. 1660	Returned to grammar school in Grantham.
Spring 1661	Completed grammar school.
June 5, 1661	Admitted to Trinity College, Cambridge.
July 8, 1661	Matriculated in Cambridge University.
Apr. 28, 1664	Elected a Scholar of Trinity College.
1664	Discovered the works of the new mathematics and the new natural philosophy.
Jan. 1665	First serious study of science of mechanics.
Spring 1665	Bachelor of Arts.
Before Aug. 7, 1665	Driven from Cambridge by the plague, returned to Woolsthorpe.
Jan. 1666	Began seriously to elaborate theory of colors.
Mar. 20, 1666	Returned to Cambridge.
June 1666	Driven away by plague a second time.
Oct. 1666	Composed tract of October 1666, setting forth fluxional calculus.
1666	Found inverse-square relation in orbits of planets; compared orbit of moon

	with acceleration of gravity on surface of the earth "and found them answer pretty nearly."
Apr. 1667	Returned again to Cambridge.
Oct. 2, 1667	Fellow of Trinity College.
Early 1669	Built first reflecting telescope.
Aug. 1669	Purchased chemical equipment and *Theatrum chemicum*, a collection of alchemical treatises.
Summer 1669	*De analysi (On Analysis by Infinite Series)* sent to John Collins.
Oct. 29, 1669	Lucasian Professor of Mathematics.
1670–72	Lectures on optics.
1670s–1684	Study of and experimentation on alchemy.
Dec. 1671	Sent reflecting telescope to Royal Society.
Jan. 11, 1672	Fellow of the Royal Society.
Feb. 6, 1672	Sent paper on colors to Royal Society.
About 1672	Began serious study of theology and the prophecies; embraced Arianism.
1672–84	Intensive study of theology and the prophecies.
Apr. 27, 1675	Royal dispensation exempted Lucasian Professor from college requirement of ordination.
Dec. 7, 1675	Sent "Hypothesis of Light" and "Discourse of Observations" (on Newton's rings) to Royal Society.
Summer and autumn 1676	Correspondence with Leibniz on mathematics.
Late 1676	Broke off most correspondence and largely isolated himself in Cambridge.
Feb. 28, 1679	Letter on natural philosophy to Robert Boyle.
Early June 1679	Death of mother.
Nov. 24, 1679–Jan. 17, 1680	Correspondence with Hooke on path of fall on a rotating earth.
Dec. 15, 1680–Apr. 16, 1681	Correspondence with Flamsteed on comet of 1680–81.
Aug. 1684	Visit of Halley posing problem of orbits in inverse-square field of attraction.
Autumn 1684–spring 1687	Composition of *Principia*.
Apr. 21–May 12 1687	Member of university delegation

	appearing before Court of Ecclesiastical Commission.
July 5, 1687	Publication of *Principia*.
Nov.-Dec. 1688	Glorious Revolution.
Jan. 15, 1689	Elected by Cambridge University as delegate to Convention Parliament.
Jan. 22, 1689–Jan. 17, 1690	Member of Convention Parliament.
1689	Beginning of friendship with John Locke and Nicolas Fatio de Duillier.
Summer 1691	Beginning of friendship with David Gregory.
Spring and summer 1693	Composition of *Praxis*, his most important alchemical treatise.
Late summer 1693	Emotional breakdown.
1696–98	Recoinage in England.
Mar. 19, 1696	Appointed Warden of the Mint.
Jan. 29, 1697	Solved challenge problem in mathematics set by Bernoulli.
Dec. 25, 1699	Appointed Master of the Mint.
Dec. 10, 1701	Resigned Lucasian chair.
Dec. 1701	Resigned fellowship in Trinity College.
Dec. 1701	Elected by Cambridge University to Parliament.
Dec. 20, 1701–May 1702	Member of Parliament.
Nov. 30, 1703	Elected president of the Royal Society.
Feb. 1704	Publication of *Opticks*.
Apr. 16, 1705	Knighted by Queen Anne.
May 1705	Defeated in parliamentary election.
1706	Latin edition of *Opticks*.
1707	Publication of *Arithmetica universalis*.
Mar. 1711	Inauguration of priority dispute with Leibniz's complaint to the Royal Society about Keill's suggestion of plagiarism.
Jan. 1713	Publication by the Royal Society of *Commercium Epistolicum*, formally condemning Leibniz for plagiarism.
June 30, 1713	Second edition of *Principia*.
Summer 1714	Appointed to Board of Longitude.
Jan.-Feb. 1715	Anonymous publication of Newton's "Account of the Book entituled *Commercium Epistolicum*" in the *Philosophical Transactions*.

Nov. 1715–Dec. 1716	Correspondence of Leibniz and Clarke on theological issues implied by Newton's natural philosophy.
1716	Composition of "Abstract" of chronology for Princess Caroline.
1717	Second English edition of *Opticks*.
1719	Second Latin edition of *Opticks*.
1720	French edition of *Opticks*.
1721	Third English edition of *Opticks*.
Late 1725	Publication of French translation of the "Abstract" of chronology.
Mar. 25, 1726	Third edition of *Principia*.
Mar. 20, 1727	Death of Newton.
1728	Publication of *Chronology of Ancient Kingdoms Amended*.
1728	Publication of *De mundi systemate* (first draft of Book III of the *Principia*).
1733	Publication of *Observations upon the Prophecies*.

Selected Bibliography

We have confined this bibliography to titles in English. Anyone desiring a more extensive guide to the literature on Newton can find it in Richard S. Westfall, *Never at Rest* (New York, 1980).

Many biographies of Newton have been written. For many years, the best of them was David Brewster, *Memoirs of the Life, Writings, and Discoveries of Sir Isaac Newton*, 2 vols. (Edinburgh, 1855), and it continues to repay attention. Brewster worshiped Newton as a hero. To correct this bias, Augustus De Morgan published a number of critical pieces, three of which were collected together and edited by Philip E. B. Jourdain in *Essays on the Life and Work of Newton* (Chicago, 1914). Louis Trenchard More's *Isaac Newton: A Biography* (New York, 1934) did not wholly succeed in supplanting Brewster as the leading biography. J. W. N. Sullivan's *Isaac Newton, 1642–1727* (London, 1938) is a shorter work with some interesting general interpretive ideas. Westfall's *Never at Rest* is the most recent full-scale biography, based on an extensive study of manuscript sources, presenting both the details of Newton's life and the history and significance of his ideas. Among the large number of popular biographies, unquestionably the best are E. N. da C. Andrade's *Isaac Newton* (London, 1950; and a slightly different version, *Sir Isaac Newton* [London, 1954]) and the longer, more detailed work by Gale E. Christianson, *In the Presence of the Creator: Isaac Newton and His Times* (New York, 1984). No survey of biographies of Newton can omit Frank E. Manuel's *Portrait of Isaac Newton* (Cambridge, MA, 1968), which interprets Newton's character while drawing his portrait but does not deal with his science. The most recent biography, conveniently presented by topics, is A. Rupert Hall, *Isaac Newton: Adventurer in Thought* (Oxford, 1992).

Every aspect of Newton's work and thought has been the subject of numerous studies. E. A. Burtt's *The Metaphysical Foundations of Modern Physical Science* (New York, 1925), a book that helped to create the modern discipline of the history of science, concludes with a long discussion of Newton. I. Bernard Cohen effectively began the Newtonian aspect of his career with *Franklin and Newton: An Inquiry into Speculative Newtonian Experimental Science and Franklin's Work in Electricity as an Example Thereof* (Philadelphia, 1956). As the title indicates, the primary focus of Cohen's work falls beyond Newton; nevertheless, it begins with a long discussion of him as the basis for subsequent work. Note as well Cohen's *The Birth of a New Physics* (Garden City, NY, 1960) and *The Newtonian Revolution with Illustrations of the Transformation of Scientific Ideas* (Cambridge, 1980). In his late years, Alexandre Koyré, who did so much to shape the modern discipline of the history of science, turned his attention to Newton. In this volume, we have included "The Significance of the Newtonian Synthesis," found in Koyré's collection, *Newtonian Studies* (Cambridge, MA, 1965). See as well the parts devoted to Newton in Koyré's book *From the Closed World to the Infinite Universe* (Baltimore, 1965). Henry Guerlac also turned to Newton during the later part of his career. Among a number of articles by Guerlac is "Newton's Optical Aether," *Notes and Records of the Royal Society* 22 (1967): 45–57. In addition to A. Rupert Hall and Marie Boas Hall's "Newton's Theory of Matter," *Isis* 51 (1960): 131–44 (included in this volume), see their introductions in *Unpublished Scientific Papers of Isaac Newton* (Cambridge, 1962). B. J. T. Dobbs's *The Janus Faces of Genius* (New York, 1992), appearing just as we compose this bibliography, will undoubtedly be recognized as a major interpretation of Newton.

Recent studies of Newton have drawn on the extensive manuscripts that he left behind, and in doing so have enriched our understanding of him. John Maynard Keynes, who became a collector of Newton papers, helped to inaugurate the new chapter in Newtonian studies with the article in this volume and in doing so shattered the established pattern of treating Newton as a plaster saint. J. E. McGuire has utilized the manuscript sources in a number of articles, including the one written with P. M. Rattansi, "Newton and the 'Pipes of Pan,' " that you find, somewhat condensed, in this volume. Like McGuire, Ernan McMullin, in *Matter and Activity in Newton* (Notre Dame, IN, 1977), uses Newton's manuscripts to examine philosophical questions in his science. We have also included another general article in this volume: David Kubrin's "Newton and the Cyclical Cosmos: Providence and the Mechanical Philosophy," *Journal of the History of Ideas* 28 (1967): 325–46.

D. T. Whiteside is the authority on Newton's mathematics. The introductory essays and editorial apparatus of his edition of the *Mathematical Papers* and the introduction to a reprint edition of the six mathematical papers published during Newton's life or shortly thereafter (*The Mathematical Works of Isaac Newton*, 2 vols. [New York, 1964]) are not easy reading but reward those who want to know what Newton achieved in mathematics. Whiteside has published a number of articles as well, including "Isaac Newton: Birth of a Mathematician," *Notes and Records of the Royal Society* 19 (1964): 53–62, and the essay in this volume. Carl B. Boyer's *The Concepts of the Calculus: A Critical and Historical Discussion of the Derivative and the Integral* (New York, 1939) also contains a fine discussion of Newton. A. Rupert Hall's *Philosophers at War: The Quarrel between Newton and Leibniz* (Cambridge, 1980) is the best narrative of the priority dispute with Leibniz.

A. Rupert Hall helped to inaugurate the utilization of the Newtonian manuscripts with his article on optics, "Sir Isaac Newton's Note-book, 1661–65," *Cambridge Historical Journal* 9 (1948): 239–50, followed by "Further Optical Experiments of Isaac Newton," *Annals of Science* 11 (1955): 27–43. A. I. Sabra's *Theories of Light from Descartes to Newton* (London, 1967) contains an extensive discussion of Newton. Thomas S. Kuhn's introductory essay to "Newton's Optical Papers," in I. Bernard Cohen's volume of *Papers and Letters* is excellent. The first of three projected volumes of *The Optical Papers of Isaac Newton*, Alan E. Shapiro, ed. (Cambridge, 1984), is in print. In addition to the introductory essays and notes, the editor, the recognized authority on this subject, is the author of numerous articles, including "The Evolving Structure of Newton's Theory of White Light and Color: 1670–1704," *Isis* 71 (1980): 211–35, and the one in this volume. His latest book, *Fits, Passions, and Paroxysms: Physics, Method, and Chemistry and Newton's Theories of Colored Bodies and Fits of Easy Reflection* (Cambridge, 1993), appeared just as we were completing this volume.

I. Bernard Cohen has made the *Principia* his special province. Among his many works is *Introduction to Newton's* Principia (Cambridge, 1971), an invaluable history of the book itself. John Herivel is the leading student of the early development of Newton's mechanics. The essays included in *The Background to Newton's* Principia (Oxford, 1965), which also publishes all of the documents on Newton's mechanics before the *Principia*, sum up a number of articles. Richard S. Westfall's *Force in Newton's Physics* (London, 1971) presents the development of Newton's concepts of dynamics. An admirable presentation of Newton's celestial dynamics is given in Curtis Wilson's "The Newtonian Achievement in Astronomy," in R. Taton and C. Wilson, eds., *Planetary Astronomy from the Renaissance to the Rise of Astrophysics* (Cambridge, 1989), pp. 233–74.

Until recently, Newton's chemistry (and alchemy) were hardly studied. B. J. T. Dobbs, in *The Foundations of Newton's Alchemy: The Hunting of the Greene Lyon* (Cambridge, 1975), ended that state of affairs and began to offer real guidance into the comprehension of the extensive alchemical papers Newton left behind.

Newton's theological manuscripts were not available until the great bulk of them were deposited as the Yahuda Papers in the Jewish National and University Library in Jerusalem. Frank E. Manuel's *The Religion of Isaac Newton* (Oxford, 1974) was the first work, among what remains a small number, to explore them. Manuel's *Isaac Newton, Historian* (Cambridge, MA, 1963) is the only significant study of Newton's chronology, a topic intimately allied with his theology. Margaret Jacob's *The Newtonians and the English Revolution, 1689–1720* (Ithaca, NY, 1976), which sums up a number of earlier articles, examines the interrelation of Newtonian natural philosophy, the practical theology of the Latitudinarians, and the political situation in England at the time of the Glorious Revolution.

In addition to the publications of Newtonian papers of various sorts that we have mentioned above, you should note the following: *The Correspondence of Isaac Newton*, ed. H. W. Turnbull et al., 7 vols. (Cambridge, 1959–77); *Isaac Newton's* Philosophiae naturalis principia mathematica, eds. Alexandre Koyré and I. Bernard Cohen, 3rd ed. with variant readings, 2 vols. (Cambridge, 1972); several alchemical papers in the appendices to Dobbs, *The Janus Faces of Genius*; and *Sir Isaac Newton: A Catalogue of Manuscripts and Papers Collected and Published on Microfilm by Chadwyck-Healey*, ed. Peter Jones (Cambridge, 1991). John Harrison's *The Library of Isaac Newton* (Cambridge, 1978) is a guide to the books studied or read by Newton.

NORTON CRITICAL EDITIONS

ANDERSON *Winesburg, Ohio* edited by Charles E. Modlin and Ray Lewis White
AQUINAS *St. Thomas Aquinas on Politics and Ethics* translated and edited by Paul E. Sigmund
AUSTEN *Emma* edited by Stephen M. Parrish *Third Edition*
AUSTEN *Mansfield Park* edited by Claudia L. Johnson
AUSTEN *Persuasion* edited by Patricia Meyer Spacks
AUSTEN *Pride and Prejudice* edited by Donald Gray *Second Edition*
BALZAC *Père Goriot* translated by Burton Raffel, edited by Peter Brooks
BEHN *Oroonoko* edited by Joanna Lipking
Beowulf (the Donaldson translation) edited by Joseph F. Tuso
BLAKE *Blake's Poetry and Designs* selected and edited by Mary Lynn Johnson and John E. Grant
BOCCACCIO *The Decameron* selected, translated, and edited by Mark Musa and Peter E. Bondanella
BRONTË, CHARLOTTE *Jane Eyre* edited by Richard J. Dunn *Second Edition*
BRONTË, EMILY *Wuthering Heights* edited by William M. Sale, Jr., and Richard Dunn *Third Edition*
BROWNING, ELIZABETH BARRETT *Aurora Leigh* edited by Margaret Reynolds
BROWNING, ROBERT *Browning's Poetry* selected and edited by James F. Loucks
BURNEY *Evelina* edited by Stewart J. Cooke
BYRON *Byron's Poetry* selected and edited by Frank D. McConnell
CARROLL *Alice in Wonderland* edited by Donald J. Gray *Second Edition*
CERVANTES *Don Quijote* translated by Burton Raffel, edited by Diana de Armas Wilson
CHAUCER *The Canterbury Tales: Nine Tales and the General Prologue* edited by V. A. Kolve and Glending Olson
CHEKHOV *Anton Chekhov's Plays* translated and edited by Eugene K. Bristow
CHEKHOV *Anton Chekhov's Short Stories* selected and edited by Ralph E. Matlaw
CHOPIN *The Awakening* edited by Margo Culley *Second Edition*
The Classic Fairy Tales edited by Maria Tatar
CONRAD *Heart of Darkness* edited by Robert Kimbrough *Third Edition*
CONRAD *Lord Jim* edited by Thomas C. Moser *Second Edition*
CONRAD *The Nigger of the "Narcissus"* edited by Robert Kimbrough
CRANE *Maggie: A Girl of the Streets* edited by Thomas A. Gullason
CRANE *The Red Badge of Courage* edited by Donald Pizer *Third Edition*
DARWIN *Darwin* selected and edited by Philip Appleman *Second Edition*
DEFOE *A Journal of the Plague Year* edited by Paula R. Backscheider
DEFOE *Moll Flanders* edited by Edward Kelly
DEFOE *Robinson Crusoe* edited by Michael Shinagel *Second Edition*
DE PIZAN *The Selected Writings of Christine de Pizan* translated by Renate Blumenfeld-Kosinski and Kevin Brownlee, edited by Renate Blumenfeld-Kosinski
DICKENS *Bleak House* edited by George Ford and Sylvère Monod
DICKENS *David Copperfield* edited by Jerome H. Buckley
DICKENS *Great Expectations* edited by Edgar Rosenberg
DICKENS *Hard Times* edited by George Ford and Sylvère Monod *Second Edition*
DICKENS *Oliver Twist* edited by Fred Kaplan
DONNE *John Donne's Poetry* selected and edited by Arthur L. Clements *Second Edition*
DOSTOEVSKY *The Brothers Karamazov* (the Garnett translation) edited by Ralph E. Matlaw
DOSTOEVSKY *Crime and Punishment* (the Coulson translation) edited by George Gibian *Third Edition*
DOSTOEVSKY *Notes from Underground* translated and edited by Michael R. Katz

DOUGLASS *Narrative of the Life of Frederick Douglass, an American Slave, Written by Himse*
edited by William L. Andrews and William S. McFeely
DREISER *Sister Carrie* edited by Donald Pizer *Second Edition*
Eight Modern Plays edited by Anthony Caputi
DU BOIS *The Souls of Black Folk* edited by Henry Louis Gates, Jr., and Terri Oliver
ELIOT *Middlemarch* edited by Bert G. Hornback
ELIOT *The Mill on the Floss* edited by Carol T. Christ
ERASMUS *The Praise of Folly and Other Writings* translated and edited by Robert M. Adams
FAULKNER *The Sound and the Fury* edited by David Minter *Second Edition*
FIELDING *Joseph Andrews with Shamela and Related Writings* edited by Homer Goldberg
FIELDING *Tom Jones* edited by Sheridan Baker *Second Edition*
FLAUBERT *Madame Bovary* edited with a substantially new translation by Paul de Man
FORD *The Good Soldier* edited by Martin Stannard
FORSTER *Howards End* edited by Paul B. Armstrong
FRANKLIN *Benjamin Franklin's Autobiography* edited by J. A. Leo Lemay and P. M. Zall
FULLER *Woman in the Nineteenth Century* edited by Larry J. Reynolds
GOETHE *Faust* translated by Walter Arndt, edited by Cyrus Hamlin
GOGOL *Dead Souls* (the Reavey translation) edited by George Gibian
HARDY *Far from the Madding Crowd* edited by Robert C. Schweik
HARDY *Jude the Obscure* edited by Norman Page *Second Edition*
HARDY *The Mayor of Casterbridge* edited by James K. Robinson
HARDY *The Return of the Native* edited by James Gindin
HARDY *Tess of the d'Urbervilles* edited by Scott Elledge *Third Edition*
HAWTHORNE *The Blithedale Romance* edited by Seymour Gross and Rosalie Murphy
HAWTHORNE *The House of the Seven Gables* edited by Seymour Gross
HAWTHORNE *Nathaniel Hawthorne's Tales* edited by James McIntosh
HAWTHORNE *The Scarlet Letter* edited by Seymour Gross, Sculley Bradley,
Richmond Croom Beatty, and E. Hudson Long *Third Edition*
HERBERT *George Herbert and the Seventeenth-Century Religious Poets* selected and edited b
Mario A. DiCesare
HERODOTUS *The Histories* translated and selected by Walter E. Blanco, edited by
Walter E. Blanco and Jennifer Roberts
HOBBES *Leviathan* edited by Richard E. Flathman and David Johnston
HOMER *The Odyssey* translated and edited by Albert Cook *Second Edition*
HOWELLS *The Rise of Silas Lapham* edited by Don L. Cook
IBSEN *The Wild Duck* translated and edited by Dounia B. Christiani
JAMES *The Ambassadors* edited by S. P. Rosenbaum *Second Edition*
JAMES *The American* edited by James W. Tuttleton
JAMES *The Portrait of a Lady* edited by Robert D. Bamberg *Second Edition*
JAMES *Tales of Henry James* edited by Christof Wegelin
JAMES *The Turn of the Screw* edited by Deborah Esch and Jonathan Warren *Second Edition*
JAMES *The Wings of the Dove* edited by J. Donald Crowley and Richard A. Hocks
JONSON *Ben Jonson and the Cavalier Poets* selected and edited by Hugh Maclean
JONSON *Ben Jonson's Plays and Masques* selected and edited by Robert M. Adams
KAFKA *The Metamorphosis* translated and edited by Stanley Corngold
LAFAYETTE *The Princess of Clèves* edited and with a revised translation by John D. Lyons
MACHIAVELLI *The Prince* translated and edited by Robert M. Adams *Second Edition*
MALTHUS *An Essay on the Principle of Population* edited by Philip Appleman
MANN *Death in Venice* translated and edited by Clayton Koelb
MARX *The Communist Manifesto* edited by Frederic L. Bender
MELVILLE *The Confidence-Man* edited by Hershel Parker
MELVILLE *Moby-Dick* edited by Harrison Hayford and Hershel Parker
MEREDITH *The Egoist* edited by Robert M. Adams
Middle English Lyrics selected and edited by Maxwell S. Luria and Richard L. Hoffman
Middle English Romances selected and edited by Stephen H. A. Shepherd
MILL *Mill: The Spirit of the Age, On Liberty, The Subjection of Women*
selected and edited by Alan Ryan

MILTON *Paradise Lost* edited by Scott Elledge *Second Edition*
Modern Irish Drama edited by John P. Harrington
MORE *Utopia* translated and edited by Robert M. Adams *Second Edition*
NEWMAN *Apologia Pro Vita Sua* edited by David J. DeLaura
NEWTON *Newton* edited by I. Bernard Cohen and Richard S. Westfall
NORRIS *McTeague* edited by Donald Pizer *Second Edition*
Restoration and Eighteenth-Century Comedy edited by Scott McMillin *Second Edition*
RHYS *Wide Sargasso Sea* edited by Judith L. Raiskin
RICH *Adrienne Rich's Poetry and Prose* edited by Barbara Charlesworth Gelpi and Albert Gelpi
ROUSSEAU *Rousseau's Political Writings* edited by Alan Ritter, translated by Julia Conaway Bondanella
ST. PAUL *The Writings of St. Paul* edited by Wayne A. Meeks
SHAKESPEARE *Hamlet* edited by Cyrus Hoy *Second Edition*
SHAKESPEARE *Henry IV, Part I* edited by James L. Sanderson *Second Edition*
SHAW *Bernard Shaw's Plays* edited by Warren Sylvester Smith
SHELLEY, MARY *Frankenstein* edited by J. Paul Hunter
SHELLEY, PERCY BYSSHE *Shelley's Poetry and Prose* selected and edited by Donald H. Reiman and Sharon B. Powers
SMOLLETT *Humphry Clinker* edited by James L. Thorson
SOPHOCLES *Oedipus Tyrannus* translated and edited by Luci Berkowitz and Theodore F. Brunner
SPENSER *Edmund Spenser's Poetry* selected and edited by Hugh Maclean and Anne Lake Prescott *Third Edition*
STENDHAL *Red and Black* translated and edited by Robert M. Adams
STERNE *Tristram Shandy* edited by Howard Anderson
STOKER *Dracula* edited by Nina Auerbach and David Skal
STOWE *Uncle Tom's Cabin* edited by Elizabeth Ammons
SWIFT *Gulliver's Travels* edited by Robert A. Greenberg *Second Edition*
SWIFT *The Writings of Jonathan Swift* edited by Robert A. Greenberg and William B. Piper
TENNYSON *In Memoriam* edited by Robert H. Ross
TENNYSON *Tennyson's Poetry* selected and edited by Robert W. Hill, Jr. *Second Edition*
THACKERAY *Vanity Fair* edited by Peter Shillingsburg
THOREAU *Walden and Resistance to Civil Government* edited by William Rossi *Second Edition*
THUCYDIDES *The Peloponnesian War* translated by Walter Blanco, edited by Walter Blanco and Jennifer Tolbert Roberts
TOLSTOY *Anna Karenina* edited and with a revised translation by George Gibian *Second Edition*
TOLSTOY *Tolstoy's Short Fiction* edited and with revised translations by Michael R. Katz
TOLSTOY *War and Peace* (the Maude translation) edited by George Gibian *Second Edition*
TOOMER *Cane* edited by Darwin T. Turner
TURGENEV *Fathers and Sons* translated and edited by Michael R. Katz
TWAIN *Adventures of Huckleberry Finn* edited by Thomas Cooley *Third Edition*
TWAIN *A Connecticut Yankee in King Arthur's Court* edited by Allison R. Ensor
TWAIN *Pudd'nhead Wilson and Those Extraordinary Twins* edited by Sidney E. Berger
VOLTAIRE *Candide* translated and edited by Robert M. Adams *Second Edition*
WASHINGTON *Up From Slavery* edited by William L. Andrews
WATSON *The Double Helix: A Personal Account of the Discovery of the Structure of DNA* edited by Gunther S. Stent
WHARTON *Ethan Frome* edited by Kristin O. Lauer and Cynthia Griffin Wolff
WHARTON *The House of Mirth* edited by Elizabeth Ammons
WHITMAN *Leaves of Grass* edited by Sculley Bradley and Harold W. Blodgett
WILDE *The Picture of Dorian Gray* edited by Donald L. Lawler
WOLLSTONECRAFT *A Vindication of the Rights of Woman* edited by Carol H. Poston *Second Edition*
WORDSWORTH *The Prelude: 1799, 1805, 1850* edited by Jonathan Wordsworth, M. H. Abrams, and Stephen Gill